Becoming a Public Relations Writer

Fourth Edition

Becoming a Public Relations Writer is a comprehensive guide to the writing process for public relations practice. Using straightforward, no-nonsense language, realistic examples, easy-to-follow steps, and practical exercises, this text introduces the various formats and styles of writing you will encounter as a public relations practitioner. A focus on ethical and legal issues is woven throughout, with examples and exercises addressing public relations as practiced by corporations, non-profit agencies, and other types of organizations both large and small. In addition, the book offers the most comprehensive list of public relations writing formats to be found anywhere—from the standard news release to electronic mail and other opportunities using a variety of technologies and media.

The fourth edition has been updated to reflect significant developments in the public relations field, including:

- A new chapter on multimedia and social media releases
- A new chapter on websites, blogs, and wikis
- Expansion of the chapter on direct mail and online appeals
- Updated examples of actual pieces of public relations writing
- A companion website with resources for instructors and students, including a glossary, flashcards, exercises, and appendices on ethical standards, careers in public relations, and professional organizations.

Through its comprehensive and accessible approach, *Becoming a Public Relations Writer* is an invaluable resource for future and current public relations practitioners.

Ronald D. Smith is Professor of Public Communication and former Chair of the Communication Department at Buffalo State (SUNY). He currently serves as interim Associate Dean of the School of Arts and Humanities. He is an accredited member of the Public Relations Society of America.

Becoming a Public Relations Writer

A Writing Workbook for Emerging and Established Media

Fourth Edition

Ronald D. Smith

NEW YORK AND LONDON

Please visit the companion website at www.routledge.com/cw/smith

Fourth edition published 2012
by Routledge
711 Third Avenue, New York, NY 10017

Simultaneously published in the UK
by Routledge
2 Park Square, Milton Park, Abingdon, Oxon OX14 4RN

Routledge is an imprint of the Taylor & Francis Group, an informa business

First edition published by HarperCollins 1995
Third edition published by Routledge 2008

Library of Congress Cataloging in Publication Data
Smith, Ronald D., 1948–
Becoming a public relations writer : a writing workbook for emerging and established media/Ronald D. Smith.—4th ed.
p. cm.
Includes bibliographical references and index.
1. Public relations. 2. Public relations—Authorship. 3. Publicity. I. Title.
HM1221.S768 2012
659.2—dc23 2011027445

ISBN: 978–0–415–89342–8 (hbk)
ISBN: 978–0–415–88802–8 (pbk)
ISBN: 978–0–203–18275–8 (ebk)

Typeset in Abode Caslon and Times New Roman
by Florence Production Ltd, Stoodleigh, Devon

Printed and bound by CPI Group (UK) Ltd, Croydon, CR0 4YY

Brief Contents

Contents

Preface

Note to the Student

The one skill that employers consistently say they seek among candidates for public relations positions is an ability to write well. Other skills are important; good writing is crucial. If you develop your writing abilities now, you can look confidently toward a bright professional future.

Becoming a Public Relations Writer can help you develop that writing skill. As a student in a public relations class, your progress toward becoming an effective professional writer rests on four pillars: yourself, your classmates, your instructor, and this book.

Your Role

As the student, you are expected to put forth your best efforts in this class. Work hard and open yourself to advice and constructive criticism. You will need to face head-on the challenges that this program of study will offer you.

Your Classmates

No student is alone in this learning process. You are part of a team, and your classmates will be learning along with you. They also will share their ideas about writing in general and about your writing in particular. They will expect you to share your honest thoughts and advice about their writing as well.

Your Instructor

Every team needs a coach, and that is the major role your instructor will play. Your instructor will get you started and give you feedback and correction. You will get help when you need it and receive praise when it is due. Don't expect your instructor to have all the answers. For some questions there may be no single, right answer. Rather, look to your instructor as someone who has traveled this road before you, someone who can share the benefit of personal experience as a writer and who can help you draw on your own experience and insight as you seek to develop as a professional writer.

This Book

Becoming a Public Relations Writer has been written to help guide you through the writing process. It will lead you through the various steps and stages of writing and will help you explore many formats and styles necessary to public relations writers. Because this book grows out of the author's professional and teaching experience, it is limited to the insight of one person. Your own experiences and those of your instructor and colleagues are likely to add to the conclusions and the advice offered here.

There may be times when your instructor will disagree with something in this book. So, too, there probably will be times when future employers and colleagues also disagree with this book, and with each other, with your instructor, and probably with you. Celebrate this intellectual diversity and divergent professional perspectives. Revel in the flexibility that is part of the art of public relations. Your chosen profession is rich with nuance and alive to various interpretations.

Note to the Instructor

Becoming a Public Relations Writer is based on a process approach to writing, which builds into the class a significant interaction between the student and the instructor as well as among the students. With this in mind, the book presumes and encourages an interactive environment, and it has been written to make use of several course-related activities. The following activities are likely to be part of your experience as you use this book.

In-Class Writing

Because information necessary for students has been included in the book, the instructor can focus a majority of in-class time on practice writing rather than lecturing about writing. Each chapter has exercises designed to provide a basis for these in-class activities. On some occasions, students may write in the presence of the instructor, who provides direction and feedback. At other times, students may use class time for rewriting, an integral part of the writing process. In-class writing is meant to be critiqued but not necessarily graded.

Out-of-Class Writing

Each chapter includes exercises that provide the basis for out-of-class writing assignments. When they receive homework assignments, students should leave the classroom knowing what needs to be done, perhaps having discussed in general terms how they will approach the assignment. An effective learning situation is to invite students, upon turning in these assignments at a subsequent class meeting, to discuss their experiences with the assignment. It is especially helpful to focus on what worked and what didn't work. It has been my experience that this provides an opportunity to reinforce and/or clarify the concepts important to the assignment. Throughout the interactive classroom environment, students should be encouraged to share problems, successes, and insights with their instructor and their classmates.

Discussion Topics

Many exercises in this book are designed for an interactive learning approach built on discussion among students who help each other develop their writing skills. Each chapter has certain exercises that call for students to gather their thoughts in freewriting and then to discuss particular topics. Such procedures are designed to encourage participation, foster shared learning, and build levels of trust that will support student writing groups. I have found that this is time well spent in the learning process.

Writing Models

This book provides models and samples of various kinds of public relations writing so students can see in them patterns and guides. These models are not meant to be copied but rather to stimulate ideas for students' own writing. Some of these models use either actual or hypothetical scenarios developed by the author; others are provided by public relations practitioners using examples of their professional writing. Students also are encouraged to share with each other samples of their writing. Instructors may find it useful to share some of their own writing with students. Regardless of the source, these models should be considered helpful samples rather than perfect examples.

Writing Conferences

Ideally, this course will include one-on-one writing conferences between the student and the instructor. Such conferences can provide an opportunity for students to evaluate their own progress and to discuss their writing strengths and areas in which they need to improve. Conferences also offer an occasion for seeking and giving advice about making the writing process easier and better.

Writing Groups

As students move from the introductory materials into writing projects based on various formats used in public relations writing, they are encouraged to participate in out-of-class writing groups with other students in the class. Such groups provide opportunities for students to share advice, learn from each other, and sharpen their editing and critiquing skills. They also provide a valuable support to each student moving through the coursework.

Changes in This Fourth Edition

Textbooks go through revisions so that they can be kept current and can feature new topics and themes. This fourth edition of *Becoming a Public Relations Writer* is no exception.

I have been pleased with the acceptance of the previous three editions since the book was first introduced in 1995. To date, at least 138 colleges and universities in the United States and Canada have adopted this text for public relations writing classes. More than 550 academic libraries in the U.S., Canada, Asia, Africa, Australia, Latin America, the Middle East, and both Western and Eastern Europe have acquired it for their collections.

As the author, I am humbled by the confidence that instructors have placed in this book, and I am aware of my responsibility to students to provide the best teaching tool that I can.

This newest edition maintains the process approach to writing, with some new topics for discussion and interaction among students and with their instructors. This edition has updated examples of actual pieces of public relations writing.

This edition features most of the topics that were part of the previous editions, particularly the sections on writing in general, writing through journalistic media, and writing through organizational and promotional media.

Instructors, reviewers, and public relations writers themselves who are familiar with the previous version will find a major (and I hope, positive) shift in the content of this edition.

The new subtitle for this text—*A Writing Workbook for Emerging and Established Media*—emphasizes the obvious technological developments in the Internet and social media that have occurred since the earlier editions of the book. The mushrooming public relations opportunities of these technologies offer many benefits for our profession.

This fourth edition of *Becoming a Public Relations Writer* maintains instruction on the established print and broadcast media venues that traditionally have been associated with the practice of public relations.

In addition, this edition has several new chapters devoted to these emerging media: Chapter 10 on Multimedia and Social Media Release; Chapter 14 on Website, Blog, and Wiki; and a major expansion in Chapter 16 on Direct Mail and Online Appeal. Woven throughout all of the chapters are examples and guidelines dealing with websites, blogs, social media networking sites, e-mail, digital audio and video, and related aspects of contemporary practice in public relations.

Acknowledgments

John Donne got it right: No one is an island. Neither does an author write alone. Rather, we writers reflect in some way the insight of others in the field who write, teach, study, and engage in the practice.

Becoming a Public Relations Writer enjoys the input of many people. As the author of this textbook, I take personal responsibility for any errors or omissions, but I'm confident that these are fewer because of the advice and assistance of many knowledgable people who helped with this book.

Collectively, my students have been major contributors to this book. It is in the classroom that I have tested and refined the ideas contained herein. My students have prodded me to articulate my ideas and to bolster them with plenty of real-world examples.

My academic colleagues at Buffalo State emphasize practical, applied communication, and I have benefited from ongoing professional conversations with them, as well as my interaction with friends at other colleges and universities. My colleagues within the Public Relations Society of America have consistently helped me with their insight and constructive criticism.

My publishing team at Routledge/Taylor & Francis has been helpful and supportive through the progress of this fourth edition. In particular my editor, Linda Bathgate, has piloted this craft through the publishing waters.

Authors appreciate the comments and criticism of their peers, and I am particularly grateful to the faculty across the country who have taken time from their busy teaching schedules to offer comments and suggestions. Likewise, I have appreciated the comments and suggestions I have received not only from the PRSA but also from people associated with the Canadian Public Relations Society and even from international groups, such as the Public Relations Society of Azerbaijan, which requested permission to translate and circulate material from this text. This book also is enriched because of conversations initiated by public relations educators in places such as Russia, Turkey, and China.

I also appreciate the comments of students who use this book. You are the ultimate experts on whether this is an effective aid to your professional education.

Personal Dedication

Like the entirety of my life, this book is dedicated to my family. Though they don't realize it, my three sons have been an inspiration as I worked on this book. We would sometimes sit across the desk from each other, me working at my computer, one of them at theirs.

As he progressed through college in Buffalo and eventually earned a doctorate at Osaka University, my son Josh has challenged me to explain public relations every time I suggested that he consider the insights of the discipline on his own work as a sociologist studying and participating in Japanese culture and ethnomusicology.

My son Aaron graduated with a degree in public relations, having had the dubious experience of having me as instructor for two of his courses. After starting his own career in the field of public relations and marketing, Aaron took his communication and strategic planning talents to the Army, where he has proudly (and safely) served in Qatar.

My youngest son Matt is pursuing a career dealing with business in horticulture and an active avocation in music. I am confident that his writing talent and artistic sensitivity will serve him well wherever these studies take him.

Whether by their presence or Skype-facilitated association with me, my daughters-in-law Satomi and Jen and my two wonderful granddaughters Miana and Mariella provide me with the love and encouragement any writer needs to be successful, and baby grandson Kazutaka (aka "Hawk") provides a wonderful reason to step away from my writing from time to time.

My greatest appreciation goes to my wife, Dawn Minier Smith. During the evolution of this book from conception to this fourth edition, Dawn has been my sounding-board. A writing teacher herself, she has lent her ear as I tested ideas, tried out new ways to present lessons, and attempted to make sense of theories, cases, and observations. Since she doesn't see any domestic value in a wife fawning over her husband, Dawn's constructive criticism has been always trustworthy and thus most valuable. I always take her suggestions seriously. Sometimes I've even had the good sense to follow them.

An Invitation

This book is the result of much dialogue with others, particularly feedback from my students. But reader reaction is inevitably useful. I invite all readers—students, teachers, and practitioners—to share your thoughts with me. Send your comments and suggestions for future editions. Share your success stories and your frustrations with this book. You can contact me via e-mail at smithrd@buffalostate.edu.

I also invite you to use my website, where I have included an expanding number of pages and links related to public relations and other aspects of strategic communication: faculty.buffalostate.edu/smithrd "Professional Information."

Likewise, I invite you to the publisher's companion website for this book at www.routledge.com/cw/smith.

About the Author

Ronald D. Smith, APR, is Professor of Public Communication at Buffalo State College, the largest college within the State University of New York. He has taught courses in public relations planning, research, writing, and related areas to undergraduate and graduate students.

He has worked as a consultant in public relations and strategic communications, assisting businesses and nonprofit organizations with planning, research, communication management, and media training. He has also served as a consultant with other educational institutions in creating and assessing programs to teach public relations.

For seven years, Ron served as Chair of the 700-student Communication Department at Buffalo State. Under his leadership, the college became the only public institution in New York State with degree programs recognized by the Accrediting Council for Education and Journalism and Mass Communication.

In 2010, he was appointed interim Associate Dean of the School of Arts and Humanities at Buffalo State.

In this book, Ron draws on considerable professional experience in print, broadcast, and digital media. In addition to more than 20 years as an educator, he worked for 10 years as public relations director and eight years as a newspaper reporter and editor. He also served as a Navy journalist in Vietnam.

Ron holds a bachelor's degree in English education from Lock Haven University and a master's degree in public relations from Syracuse University. He has presented numerous professional workshops and seminars and has published research on public relations and persuasive communication. He is the author of *Strategic Planning for Public Relations* (4th edition, in press, Routledge) and co-author of *MediaWriting* (4th edition, 2012, Routledge). He is also author of "Campaign Design and Management" in Eadie's *SAGE 21st Century Reference Series: Communication* (2009, Sage).

Ron is also Director of his college's American Indian Policy and Media Initiative, which focuses on the intersection of Native American issues, public policy, and media. He is co-editor of *Shoot the Indian: Media, Misperception and Native Truth* (2007, AIPMI) and has conducted and published research on topics such as the media coverage of the Cherokee citizenship vote and media coverage in New York State on Indian treaty, sovereignty, and taxation issues. He has assisted in strategic planning with the Smithsonian's National Museum of the American Indian and the National Congress of American Indians and has worked with research and strategic planning with several individual tribes. He has presented original research on Native Americans and media at the Association for Education in Journalism and Mass Communications.

Ron is an accredited member of the Public Relations Society of America and has served as President of PRSA's Buffalo/Niagara chapter and Chair of the Northeast District. He has been named "Practitioner of the Year" by his local chapter, which has also given him several special service and project awards. He also received a Distinguished Service medal for his work in helping prepare candidates for accreditation.

Part One

PRINCIPLES OF EFFECTIVE WRITING

You already are a writer! You wouldn't have made it this far, wouldn't have been allowed to register for a college writing course if you aren't already a writer with sufficient skill. The issue before you now is: Do you want to become a public relations writer? Do you want to build skills to help you succeed in your career in public relations? With this book and a fair amount of work, you can succeed. Repeat that thought: *You can become a public relations writer!* You'll probably even find yourself carried to a higher level of enjoyment with your writing.

As Desiderius Erasmus, the Dutch Renaissance-era scholar, observed: "The desire to write grows with writing." So sharpen your writing talent and begin what can be a pleasurable journey toward becoming a public relations writer.

Part One of this book deals with the basics of writing in professional contexts. It begins with an exploration of your attitudes toward writing and follows with a brief refresher on writing principles. It also features an overview of communication theory and a methodical look at some practices basic to all kinds of public relations writing, both as it is associated with established print and broadcast media and with newer emerging digital media.

Because it deals with the basics of writing, this section of *Becoming a Public Relations Writer* also should give you a footing for yet-undeveloped media opportunities that undoubtedly will come in the future. Work progresses on phones, computer tablets, and related technologies that will offer quicker, more mobile, and more efficient multimedia opportunities. Engineers are developing technology that is much less expensive and less reliant on digital infrastructures, so that one day computers may be in the hands of virtually everyone in the world, regardless of their socio-economic status. Software offering reliable and high-quality instant translations, both written and oral, may help us communicate with people across today's political, cultural, and language barriers. Let your imagination soar as you dream of the possibilities that the future may bring.

Yet amid all these visions of what may take place next, the need also will remain for clear, effective, persuasive, and ethical writing. That is the basis of Part One of this book, which includes four chapters and a concluding section:

- Chapter 1: Writing . . . and What It Means to You
- Chapter 2: Effective Writing
- Chapter 3: Persuasive and Ethical Communication
- Chapter 4: The Writing Process
- Wrap-Up for Part One.

1 Writing . . . and What It Means to You

Writing. It is the most important professional skill for public relations practitioners. Employers complain that job candidates can't write adequately. Teachers fret that today's students don't write as well as their predecessors. And in moments of candor, most students admit they are unsure about their writing skill.

Throughout your academic career, you have been faced with many ideas about writing. Perhaps you have become aware of some mixed messages. If you have, that's to be expected, because there certainly are a lot of different thoughts about writing—what it is, how we learn to write well, how we can use writing personally and professionally, and whether we are any good at it.

This chapter will help you begin to sort through what you have learned about writing and what you have experienced through writing. It will help you identify your own relationship with writing. We'll start with freewriting, then look at the creative and functional aspects of writing, and end with a discussion of how to become a better writer and your personal commitment to this outcome.

Eventually, these writing basics will lead you to apply your writing skills to the many and varied opportunities available to public relations writers. Some of these will be associated with traditional print and broadcast media. Others are associated with new and emerging media.

Here are your learning objectives for this chapter:

- To use the technique of freewriting
- To understand the relationship between creative and functional writing
- To explain the concept of writing to influence
- To develop a process of drafting and revising.

Freewriting

Before we proceed, you need to learn a writing technique that you will be using a lot in this program—freewriting. As prescriptions for better writing go, this one is pretty painless when taken in moderation. **Freewriting** is a kind of stream-of-consciousness writing without stopping and without self-editing for a period of time. Its purpose is to get your initial thoughts on paper. Freewriting is a simple and effective procedure that can help you in several ways:

- Getting started when you're not quite sure where you're going
- Organizing your thoughts
- Preparing to write more formally or to go public with your writing
- Overcoming writer's block.

How do you freewrite? Take pen in hand or hand to keyboard. Simply start writing. Keep writing for a certain period of time; five minutes is a good length. Much longer, and freewriting becomes drafting, and then you're not freewriting anymore.

The method is simple: Force yourself to keep writing throughout the five minutes. Don't pause to ponder. Don't edit. Don't correct spelling or grammatical errors. Freewriting is very informal, and it's usually not meant for anyone else to read. Rather, it can serve as the basis for a very rough first draft. Here is one of the author's freewrites that helped set the stage for this chapter:

> Begin by talking about the fun of writing, and the fear. I can do it. That's what the reader should take home. How to get to that point? Probably by talking about ideas like why to write, how to get in the mood, what writing can accomplish. Things like purpose. Motivation. Fun. Challenge. Motivation is a major goal of the opening chapter. Too often we think we can't when really we could if only we know how. Just a matter of learning something new, or a better way of doing it. I want my students to begin this course with the thought, belief, that they can become better writers. Through it all, a course like this should be fun. Challenging, but fun too.

So what do you think about writing? Like so much about the art of writing, this question has no right or wrong answers. Merely by considering the question you can begin to arrive at your own conclusions. Or perhaps you can simply become more comfortable in your ambiguity. But, as you consider your own perspectives on writing, you are already in the process of becoming a better writer.

The 12th-century Chinese philosopher, Xi Zhi, urged his students to practice self-examination every day: "If you find faults, correct them. When you find none, try even harder." Good advice! As you seek to become a better writer, take time to poke around the wrinkles of your mind. Probe your attitudes about writing. Consider your comfort level as a wordsmith.

Think about what you think about writing, especially your own. Have you been told, for example, that you are a good writer? If so, has the affirmation come from somebody who knows what he or she is talking about (that is, from a good writer, or a competent editor)? Or was it your grandmother who praised your Valentine poem? Praise from family and friends is important, but you can't necessarily build on it.

On the other hand, do you think of yourself as an inadequate writer? It's unlikely that strangers on the street or little children in the park have pointed this out to you, so where did you get the negative notion? What have you done to dismiss it as perhaps the exaggeration of your overly self-conscious ego, or perhaps to embrace it as a worthy opponent to be bested? The point is, the more self-aware you are of yourself as a writer, the better writer you can become.

Exercise 1.1

Freewriting on Writing

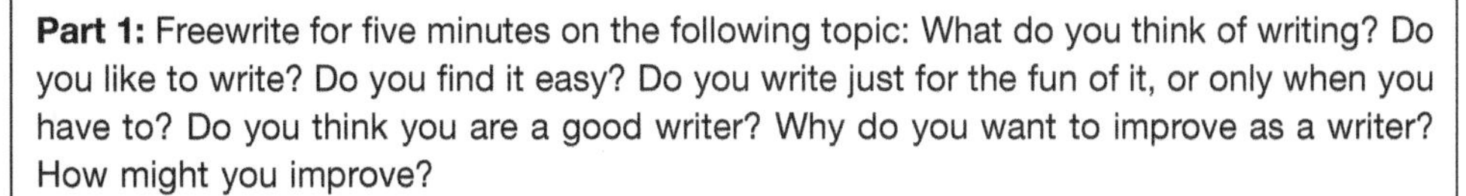

Part 1: Freewrite for five minutes on the following topic: What do you think of writing? Do you like to write? Do you find it easy? Do you write just for the fun of it, or only when you have to? Do you think you are a good writer? Why do you want to improve as a writer? How might you improve?

Part 2: Take a few minutes to review what you wrote in Part 1. Go back and underline what you think is the most important or most insightful sentence or phrase. Discuss this with your instructor or with other students in your class.

Writing: Creative or Functional

Self-examination is the first step toward excellence. You have already begun to become a better writer just by completing the first exercise. Now let's tighten the margins a bit and look at two relationships within writing that are important to us as public relations writers: creative writing and functional writing.

Sometimes, students in public relations writing classes have said they like creative writing but are unsure of themselves with the functional writing they expect to find in public relations. That's understandable. The formats we use for various public relations purposes—news releases, organizational reports and proposals, persuasive appeals, and so on—often have a number of "rules" to follow. It can feel like a paint-by-numbers approach to writing. Where's the creativity? Where's the fun? At what point does skill become talent?

Exercise 1.2

Creative and Functional Writing

Part 1: Look up the following words in your dictionary and note their similarities and differences: creative, artistic, artful, imaginative, innovative, and aesthetic. Now do the same with another set of words: Purpose, intention, function, rationale, and objective.

Part 2: Freewrite for five minutes on the following topic: How do creative and functional writing compare? How do these definitions come together to describe writing? Discuss this with your classmates.

Creative Writing

All writing is creative and artistic. **Creative writing** emphasizes imaginative, artistic, and sometimes innovative style. It is the result of one mind creating an idea and sharing it with someone else. The idea may take various forms—a science fiction adventure, a carefully researched historical novel, lyrical poetry, a corporate report, an informative news release, a compelling sales letter, and so on. Writing is creative when we use it to shape a thought—molding it, wrapping it in a particular writing format, and ultimately sharing it with another person.

Creative writing is not solely a product of the imagination, although it may begin there. But it could just as well begin in an interview or through painstaking research. What fills writing with creativity is the insight and ownership a writer brings to the ideas and facts. A public relations writer will adopt the task at hand and, however fleetingly, will possess the ideas and thoughts surrounding the writing project. A good writer will caress a thought, coupling facts and ideas, giving birth to vignettes and parables, gaining insight and making observations.

All this to promote a supermarket opening? Ah, but that's where the art takes shape, as the writer weaves words and phrases, facts and ideas, putting them before the reader in a way that serves the original purpose. We write creatively when we take a thought, wherever it originated, and artfully share it with others.

Functional Writing

Functional writing is an approach to writing that emphasizes purpose, format, and objective. It is writing on a mission. Think about this. We always write for some reason. We hope to accomplish something through our words, so we write with purpose—more often, with several purposes.

Recall the last writing assignment you completed for a class. What was your purpose in writing it? To show your professor that you understood the subject matter? To get a good grade? To make your professor happy? To simply have something, anything, to turn in so you wouldn't get scolded? These are all reasons for writing (some, obviously, better reasons than others). Now consider: What was the purpose behind the last business letter you wrote? How about the last job application? The last e-mail home? Or your most recent blog entry? You wrote each for a reason, too.

Think about what you already know about the following purposes of any type of writing:

- To describe someone or something
- To explain or justify
- To provide information
- To express an opinion
- To persuade toward some feeling or action
- To entertain
- To inspire or motivate
- To express our inner thoughts.

The novelist F. Scott Fitzgerald reminded us about such purposeful writing: "You don't write because you want to say something, you write because you have something to say." The thought pre-exists, giving rise to the act of writing.

A novel may be written to entertain or to present a point of view. Or maybe it's simply written to sell a lot of copies and make a bundle of money for the author. Consider poetry. Its purpose may be to enlighten the mind of the reader, enrage one to action, inspire the soul. Maybe it's simply a means for self-expression, or part of an elaborate seduction scheme aimed at your new boyfriend or girlfriend. Maybe it's just a way to kill a gloomy afternoon when your friends aren't around.

Likewise there is purpose and reason behind every kind of writing—short story, rap lyric, parable, love letter, Web page, greeting card, prayer, essay, feature story, research report . . .

and public relations writing. The purpose may be profound or practical, but it's your reason for writing.

In the profession of public relations, we find use for virtually every writing purpose except, perhaps, self-expression. We write news releases to inform external audiences and newsletters to share information with internal ones. We write brochures to explain our products and services. We write letters and guest editorials to express opinions, and public service advertisements to persuade. We prepare scripts for speeches and television programs that we hope will influence our audiences, and we create Web pages to educate and motivate. These are just some of the purposes and some of the formats a public relations writer will use to communicate effectively.

Creativity and Functionality

In Exercise 1.2, you were asked to consider the relationship between creative and functional writing. Reconsider what you wrote there in light of this observation: Creativity and functionality *can* co-exist in your writing.

You may not have considered this idea before. Instead of either/or, think of both/and. You don't have to put writing into boxes—one marked "creative writing," the other marked "functional writing." Your writing actually can be both. It is more like a see-saw, one side balancing toward functional writing, the other pointing more toward creative writing. Both aspects of writing complement each other. It is a matter of looking at the balance between the two. Let's combine creativity and functionality in writing under the heading "Writing to Influence." That's what public relations writing is all about.

Writing to Influence

Because there are so many different formats for public relations writing, it can be useful to categorize them into different types. A common division is to group public relations writing as being either informational or persuasive. Each of these segments is said to have certain formats. For example, news releases and brochures usually are seen as formats for informational writing, whereas speeches and public service advertising are said to be formats for persuasive writing.

That's a neat distinction in some ways. It helps us understand that there are various writing formats and that their differences influence how and when they can be used. But there is a problem with such a distinction because it is an oversimplification. All public relations writing attempts to influence people in some way. If you aren't trying to make an impact on your readers, why write? Without intending to affect readers in some way, you're just wasting time.

So let's look for a more unified perspective. As a writer, you have a particular effect in mind when you write. You want to increase your public's knowledge and understanding about something, you want people to feel a certain way about this information, and you probably want them to respond to that information in a particular way.

In some journalism-oriented formats such as news releases, information is presented in an objective manner. But the writer still can attempt to persuade, using techniques such as persuasive message sources and appeals. On the other hand, some public relations writing is meant to enhance relationships and to communicate between an organization and its publics in a quest for mutual benefits. Here too, however, the writer is trying to influence readers, seeking at least to motivate and empower them in their efforts to strengthen the relationship.

Exercise 1.3

Defining Public Relations

Background: Many people are confused about the meaning of public relations, and no uniform definition exists even among public relations practitioners. Meanwhile, some people are critical of what they presume public relations to be about. Nevertheless, some commonly held characteristics of public relations include two-way communication, research and strategic planning, accuracy and honesty, effective and ethical behavior, and mutual benefits for both an organization and its public.

Scenario: A relative whom you respect is trying to dissuade you from entering public relations. This person says that public relations practitioners are manipulators who rely on half-truths and hype on behalf of unworthy clients.

Part 1: Write a short letter to this relative, telling him or her what public relations means to you. Address this person's concerns about your likely profession.

Part 2: After writing this letter, review your freewrite from Exercise 1.2 about creative and functional writing. Then, with this in mind, freewrite on the following topic: How is my letter an attempt to provide information, and how is it an attempt to persuade the reader? Discuss this with your classmates.

Becoming a Better Writer

Some college students have no problem with self-confidence. They often think they are better writers than they really are: "But I always got good grades for my writing." If you are such a student, you may be troubled when your public relations instructor requires you to conform to higher writing standards than you are used to. You may find it difficult to make a transition from an anything-goes freewriting style into the type of logical, focused writing needed in most forms of public relations writing.

On the other hand, too many students express discomfort and lack of confidence with their writing abilities, often because they don't know if their writing is good or not. As a student, two factors work against your feeling good about yourself as a writer. For one thing, in your educational career you have been in class for thousands of days, tens of thousands of hours. You may have had someone telling you that your writing needs to be corrected . . . and here's how. After a while, the message comes through: Your writing always needs to be improved, and you can't do it by yourself.

In either scenario, the fact may be simply that you aren't an accomplished writer—yet. But in this course, by using this book and following your teacher's advice, you can try to change that. How?

- By having plenty of opportunities to break bad writing habits and build better ones (translation: homework and writing assignments)
- By learning and applying the elements of good public relations writing

- By gaining some criteria for evaluating your own writing. Then you won't have to guess if it is good writing or not. You'll know when it is. And you'll know when it isn't, so you can fix it.

An Acquired Talent

Speaking is natural communication. Writing isn't! People are born with a natural ability and inclination to speak, but no one is born with a special ability to write well. Writing is a learned skill. In our society, we begin learning to write early in life and continue to develop as writers throughout our lifetimes.

Learning to write is a lot like learning to play the saxophone, cultivating a strong backhand for tennis, or becoming a good dancer. A dancer, for example, must have an element of natural talent, but that talent improves with practice. Not just casual or occasional practice, but intensive, conscious, and passionate practice. That's why prima ballerinas go to class every morning to fine-tune their skills. Similarly, that's why world-class athletes spend hours every day in exercise, muscle training, and nutritional eating. Excellence doesn't come cheaply, and quality is built not on dreams but on persistent effort. Writing practice, in fact, has real longevity. Long after the athlete's arm is shot and the ballerina's flexibility is but a memory, a writer's talent improves with age.

When you learn to write, you need the ingredients: a bit of ability, a good teacher and writing coach, a sense of order and beauty, respect for precision and innovation, confidence, and another dose of confidence. Then you need the recipe for writing: practice, practice, and a bit more practice.

Encouragement for such consistency came from Publilius Syrus, a writer, philosopher, and slave in classical Rome: "Practice is the best of all instructors." Twenty centuries later, Thomas Wolfe suggested: "Write every day." One student in a public relations writing class observed: "The more I write, the better my writing becomes." Yay! She gets it!

A Developing Talent

When you read, do you ever stop and think, "Wow! I like the way the writer said that"? If you really want to become a better writer, train yourself to be a more critical observer of other people's writing. Take note of how a writer has used the language, how words and phrases have been woven together.

But remember that effective writing is a continuing process of writing and rewriting. As a reader who wants to write, you may have a significant disadvantage. Your entire background in reading has exposed you mainly to the finished work of other writers. From the stories of J.K. Rowling to Henry David Thoreau and Mark Twain, from the Bill of Rights to *Sports Illustrated*—you have seen completed pieces of writing. Too bad, because you've been missing a lot of good stuff.

The acclaimed novelist Ernest Hemingway was characteristically blunt: "The first draft of anything is shit." Supreme Court Justice Louis Brandeis had said it a bit more elegantly: "There is no great writing, only great rewriting." Novelist James Michener echoed that thought: "I'm not a very good writer, but I'm an excellent rewriter."

When we see only the final writing, we focus on the talent of the authors. We use words like "gifted" and "genius" to describe them. But finished products don't allow us to see the so-called great writers as wordsmiths—technicians who have fashioned their works of art, one word at a time. The playwright and novelist Oscar Wilde gave this wonderful anecdote into the attention that writers give to their use of language: "I was working on the proof of one of my poems all morning, and took out a comma. In the afternoon I put it back again."

Distinguished literature and powerful rhetoric seldom come by inspiration, delivered as a finished package. Rather, the great writers craft their words with care, often with patience and fortitude.

What might you find if you compared the various drafts of the Gettysburg Address with its final version? You would find, for example, that the first version had one sentence of 82 words, with several grammatical errors. Abraham Lincoln revised his text through six versions. He changed some phrases. "It is rather for us, the living, to stand here" evolved into "It is for us the living, rather, to be dedicated here to the unfinished work which they who fought here have thus far so nobly advanced." Far more eloquent phrasing. Lincoln also added some phrases, most notably "under God" in his draft phrase "that this nation under God shall have a new birth of freedom."

Do you think you could learn something about Ernest Hemingway by seeing what he added or deleted as he completed the final manuscript for *A Farewell to Arms*? Would it be interesting to compare the script revisions of your favorite *Family Guy* reruns or episodes of *The Vampire Diaries*? You might take comfort in knowing that some successful writers have been less than proficient about the mechanics of writing. Presidents have speechwriters; corporate officers have assistants who help shape their writing.

Even respected literary figures get help sometimes. Theodore Dreiser, who is ranked among the best American novelists, reportedly had several rewriters who polished and smoothed out his prose. F. Scott Fitzgerald is said to have been such a dreadful speller that his writing bordered on illiteracy. But he had supportive editors, and Fitzgerald has come to be regarded as one of the great novelists of the Jazz Age of American literature.

In public relations, plan on producing several drafts of any piece of writing. You will find that each version gets better. Each becomes more effective for your purposes, until eventually you are satisfied that you have produced the best piece of writing you can (within limitations of time and resources, of course). This book will help you develop your written communication skills, strengthening what works and perhaps finding something that can work even better.

Throughout this book, you will find many opportunities to develop your writing talents. Sometimes you will be given samples of writing at various stages of development. You may share preliminary versions with classmates, and you may make suggestions on how other students might improve their writing. You might also ask to see examples of how your instructor writes in various versions. You can gain confidence and competence in seeing how other writers work over the words to create a more perfect piece of writing.

Do you think you can convince anyone that writing is an art to be learned? A skill to be cultivated? Even more important, are you convinced yourself? Your answer is crucial to your success in this course. You've got to be convinced, beyond a reasonable doubt, of two things. One, that writing can be learned. Two, that *you* can learn to be a better writer. Give some thought to this as you work on the following exercise.

Exercise 1.4

Committing to Becoming a Better Writer

Type a letter of commitment to your instructor. In this letter, express your goals for this course and affirm your confidence that you can make progress toward becoming a better writer. This letter should be about a page long.

An Ongoing Commitment

To become more effective in your writing, you must be in it for the long haul. Good writing requires consistent effort. The following two exercises are continuing projects that will last through the entire semester or academic term. Both are designed to help you build a stronger habit of frequent writing. Select one as an extended assignment.

Exercise 1.5

Creating a Writing Journal

Too many people don't write unless they have to for school or work, and that lack of involvement with writing shows. This exercise gives you a lot of freedom, so have fun with your writing. Develop it as a leisure-time activity and become a better writer in the process.

Turn in to your instructor two pages each week on any topic and in any writing format that interests you. Or write a weekly entry in your blog. Your writing does not have to be related to the formats explored in this class. Rather, use this assignment to expand your writing horizons by picking topics and formats unrelated to any class you are taking this term. Here are some ideas for writing topics:

- Write a letter to a cousin you haven't seen in a while, or to your grandfather
- Write a poem or song lyrics
- Set out your thoughts on politics, religion, or the state of affairs in the world
- Write a new ending for an episode of your favorite television show
- Review a book you recently read, or a concert you attended
- Reminisce about a place you once visited, or speculate about a place you would like to visit
- Write about a sports figure, entertainer, or politician you admire (or dislike)
- Discuss your hopes and dreams for the future or your problems of the present
- Meditate on the eternal agony in the fires of hell, which await the girl or guy who dumped you
- Write limericks if you want to . . . just write!

Exercise 1.6

Developing a Journal of Professional Observations

In this exercise, you will learn to develop a critical eye into your intended profession. Test your insights in new areas; let your curiosity lead you to poke around previously unexplored nooks and crannies. Have fun with this assignment as you ponder the public relations aspects of all that you encounter. You'll be surprised how useful public relations is in making sense out of life around you. You'll also be surprised how the habit of keeping a professional journal can enhance your writing skills as well as your professional insights.

Write two pages each week about your observations of public relations activities in everyday life. Situations full of public relations possibilities are all around you—a government official handling criticism, a charity raising money, a company fighting a corporate takeover, a Little League team seeking a sponsor, a sorority dealing with pledges, your boss handling new employees, a military spokesperson fielding press inquiries, a Tupperware hostess holding a party.

Your observations may come from books or periodicals, news media, events with which you are familiar, or situations in which you are personally involved. Your writing will be evaluated on the basis of insight into public relations thought and practice, cohesive and logical organization, creative thinking and problem solving, and of course, effective writing.

2 Effective Writing

Too often, people write under the false belief that fancy words and long sentences are impressive. In reality, this doesn't impress most people. It's harder to read and less likely to be understood and remembered. Rather than trying to impress readers with fancy writing, public relations practitioners should attempt to make an impression on readers with the quality of their writing and the importance of their message.

Aim for simple sentences, but remember that simple sentences shouldn't be simplistic. Even the most lofty and complex ideas can be expressed using simple, everyday language. The goal is to make your writing accessible to your readers. This chapter should remind you of rules and guidelines you already know about making your writing more effective. These suggestions and guidelines provide a foundation for all kinds of writing: organizational publications, releases for print and broadcast media, blog entries, scripts for speeches, and text for websites, e-mail, and other communication vehicles.

This chapter is subdivided into four sections dealing with standard usage, simple language, meaningful language, and inclusive language. Here are your learning objectives for Chapter 2:

- To effectively use standard conventions of the English language
- To construct simple and understandable messages
- To enhance the meaning your words convey
- To use language ethically
- To avoid biased language.

Standard Usage

The aim of public relations writing is to communicate clearly with your target publics. A basic ingredient in clear communication is correct use of language. This section outlines some of the standard approaches to **syntax**—the part of grammar that deals with the orderly arrangement of words into sentences. Syntax is what makes a sentence make sense.

Exercise 2.1

Knowing the Rules of Standard English

Freewrite on the following topic: *What does it matter if I follow the "rules" of standard English?* Discuss this with your classmates.

Usage Tip 1: Rules and Guidelines

The ultimate rule of public relations writing is to write so the reader can understand. How can you do this? By following the standard and ordinary guidelines of language use, including the basic rules of good grammar, word choice, and common spelling. Using proper English doesn't mean making your writing stilted or stale. Occasionally, writers are tempted to bend a rule of grammar in order to maintain the higher rule of understanding. A lofty goal, perhaps, but such bending should be done only with understanding and careful consideration, never out of ignorance of the rules. It is better simply to revise the offending passage so that it is both understandable and correct.

As a student, begin now to enhance your writing resources. First, get an up-to-date dictionary (the Associated Press recommends two that are commonly used by reporters: *Webster's New World College Dictionary* and, for more complete information, Webster's Third New International Dictionary of the English Language). Buy The New Roget's Thesaurus and Merriam-Webster's Dictionary of Synonyms, and adopt a good contemporary grammar reference book such as the *Prentice-Hall Handbook for Writers*, Stunk and White's *The Elements of Style*, or Kessler and McDonald's *When Words Collide*. Also, have access to a current edition of *The World Almanac and Book of Facts*. Once you have accumulated this mini library, use these resources often.

Correct English requires accurate spelling. There really is little choice here. Poor spelling signals a writer who isn't careful, and that will throw suspicion on the accuracy of everything you write. William Shakespeare sometimes used different spellings for the same word. He even spelled his own name three different ways. But times have changed, and anyhow—you're not Shakespeare. Stick with the appropriate spelling. That's where a **stylebook** and a dictionary can help. If the dictionary lists two acceptable spellings, check the stylebook; one of the alternatives is likely preferred.

Another important practical detail of effective writing is consistency. The news media have adopted certain standards of language usage to provide consistency of style, particularly for writing. Public relations writers should be familiar with these stylebooks. It is helpful to adopt one and incorporate it into all of your writing. The Associated Press Stylebook is by far the most commonly used guide in the United States. Reuters Stylebook is often used in Canada and other English-speaking nations. Individual newspapers and magazines often have their own, usually based on the AP Stylebook.

Appendix A of this book, "Common Sense Stylebook for Public Relations Writers," provides the basics of writing style generally consistent with the Associated Press. It is useful with external materials such as news releases and other writing for newspapers, magazines, and the electronic media. This stylebook also provides some variations for a house style that can be appropriate for organizational media such as websites, newsletters, and other publications, as well as style adjustments for broadcast media.

Usage Tip 2: Grammatical Myths

Myths and legends about the proper use of English abound. *Shall* or *will*? *Who* or *whom*? *That* or *which*? Certainly you need to pay attention to rules, and there is no place in public relations for sloppy writing. But be aware that some rules are changing. Some rules weren't really rules at all, just denizens of a grammatical netherworld. Here are some of the most common language misconceptions:

- Sentence fragments have a purpose and a right to exist. Sometimes. Especially in speeches, broadcast scripts, blogs, and advertising copy.
- *Shall* is close to being listed as an archaic future form of the verb *to be*, as its older brother *shalt* already is. Not many people use the word precisely. Besides, for some people the word carries negative connotations from grade school, writing "I shall not bite the teacher" (100 times). And don't even think of using its negative contraction, *shan't*.
- Sometimes infinitives (the word *to* plus a verb) can be split. Occasionally they need to be. It would be difficult to improve on Star Trek's "to boldly go" where no one had gone before. For 600 years English writers have been putting adverbs within an infinitive, precisely to call particular attention to the adverb. So split away, as long as you want to intentionally emphasize the adverb.
- Not all sentences need a stated subject before the verb. Understood? Of course.
- Some purisms such as *agendum*, *stadia*, and *referenda* are falling into disuse. Others such as *datum* cause confusion and occasional fights. Your public relations writing is no place to show off arcane linguistic knowledge.
- Sentences can end in a preposition. Occasionally, it's something we have to put up with.
- A double negative may not work well in mathematics. But in language we call this a **litotes** ((LY-tuh-teez)), which is a negation of the contrary. We use it for understatement. *I'm not unhappy* is a perfectly fine sentence. It is a negative statement with attitude, and it doesn't mean quite the same as *I'm happy*. But use this form sparingly, and only when it clearly enhances your writing.

Usage Tip 3: Levels of Formality

Effective public relations writers are fluent in **operational English** (also known as **standard English**, or **network standard** because it is commonly used by television reporters). This is the version of English most appropriate for professional interaction, such as in business or education. It is the type of writing you learned in school, and the type you will most likely be expected to use in your career.

Good writers also know how and when to use some of the many other varieties of English, a language rich in diversity. English has a formal style, informal versions, and many geographic and cultural variations. Together, these provide much of the beauty and power of the English language. This variety can be very useful to public relations writers. Position statements and news releases, for example, generally call for the use of formal and objective language. Appeal letters and blog entries lend themselves to more informal and personal language.

Some writing is meant to be heard rather than read, and this sometimes calls for a particular language form. Language drawn from a particular cultural variation like Cajun or urban hip-hop may be appropriate for the script of a public service message. For some writers, Creole, Pennsylvania Dutch, or other flavorful regional variations or dialects may be a useful writing tool. The key is to use the style most appropriate to the particular writing project and the target public and to carefully pretest to make sure the writing is not offensive or condescending to your readers.

Usage Tip 4: Bulky Sentences

Strive for simplicity. A good sentence should carry only one thought, and its phrases and clauses should support that thought rather than introduce extraneous information. This is particularly true when you are preparing a speech or writing a script or release for the broadcast media, because the audiences will not be able to reread an awkward sentence. Keep the subject and verb close together, making it easier for the hearer to understand the sentence.

Usage Tip 5: Evolving Usage and Rules

The essayist E.B. White once wrote in *The New Yorker* magazine that "the living language is like a cowpath; it is the creation of the cows themselves who, having created it, follow it or depart from it according to their whim and their needs. From daily use, the path undergoes change." Great allusion!

English is indeed a living and changing language. Words come, words go. Some move in and out of common usage, while others find that their meanings have changed. Something can be so bad that it's good, and so cool that it's hot. The dictionary says that *gay* means lively and happy, but if you proclaim yourself to be in a gay mood, people probably won't think you are referring to your current disposition. Similarly, the word *propaganda* used to be an accepted synonym for promotion or publicity, but the word has since taken on a negative tone associated with deception and misleading information.

Usage Tip 6: Noun–Pronoun Agreement

A **singular noun** is the usual type of noun. It takes a singular pronoun. The same logic applies to **plural nouns**, which take plural pronouns. That's why we write, *The girl reads her book. The girls read their books.*

But not all nouns are singular or plural. A **collective noun** is a singular word with a plural meaning. These words represent individuals working together as a unit, and they sometimes can be confusing for writers.

Collective nouns, generally groups of people acting as one entity, are singular in construction, even though they imply something in the plural: *The board will hold its annual meeting.* We don't write *their annual meeting*, because the board is a singular noun. It may be a group of people, but when they become a board they act singularly, as one body. In public relations writing, most references to organizations involve singular pronouns. Company, management, corporation, committee, council . . . all of these call for *it* rather than *they*.

Usage Tip 7: Subject–Verb Agreement

Trust your ear, but first train it not to deceive you. If the subject is singular, use a singular verb. If the subject is plural, use a plural verb. What could be simpler? *The boy was happy* (singular noun, singular verb). *The boys were happy* (plural noun, plural verb). You wouldn't say *The boys was happy* because your ear tells you it is wrong. The best way to train your ear for good language usage is to read many writers: news and current affairs, novels, poetry, histories and biographies, textbooks. Learn to listen critically so your ear will be comfortable with correct phrasing, such as *the media are* . . . and *ethics is* . . . Be aware of some problem situations that can cloud the issue of subject–verb agreement:

- Collective nouns are singular: *The class wants to postpone the exam. The agency is pitching a new account.*
- When a phrase or clause comes between the subject and the verb, use the verb that goes with the subject: *Several editions of the company newsletter were illustrated by Bibi Johenger (editions were). The news release published in 15 daily newspapers was considered a success (release was).*
- Some pronouns take singular verbs: *Anyone, anybody, each, either, everyone, everybody, neither, no one, nobody, someone, somebody.* Examples of this usage: *Everyone is in her automobile. Nobody is taking his walk.*
- Some pronouns take plural verbs: *Both, few, many, several, some.* Examples: *Many are the problems. Several were available for comment.*
- Still other pronouns can take singular or plural verbs, depending on the context (usually forecast by the associated noun): *All, any, most, none, some.* Examples: *Some of the candy was gone. Some of the people were happy to see her.*
- Compound subjects joined by *and* always take a plural verb: *Edward Bernays and Ivy Lee are important figures in the development of public relations as a profession.*
- Singular compound subjects joined by *or* or *nor* take singular verbs: *Either Carl Jung or Sigmund Freud was Edward Bernays' uncle; I can't remember which.*
- Compound subjects involving both a singular noun and a plural noun joined by *or* or *nor* agree with the subject closest to the verb. Examples: *Either the editor or the copy editors were very observant. Neither the copy editors nor the editor was observant.*
- Some singular nouns end with the letter *s*, but that doesn't make them plural. *Public relations is an interesting career choice.* Don't rely too much on computer spell checks, which often fail to recognize that terms such as *ethics* or *public relations* really are singular nouns, despite their endings.
- Plural nouns with irregular endings still take plural verbs, even though they don't end in an *s*: *The media are important to public relations practitioners. The alumni were supportive.*

Usage Tip 8: Simple Punctuation

In general, use simple punctuation: commas, periods, question marks, and quotation marks. Be wary of semicolons and exclamation points. A problem that sometimes plagues student writers involves punctuation for **appositives** (a word or grouping of words that defines, describes, or renames the preceding noun). *John Wortman, the company's new vice president, will visit the plant next Wednesday.* You can remove the appositive phrase *the company's new vice president* and still have a decent sentence: *John Wortman will visit the plant next Wednesday.* Use commas at both the beginning and the end of such descriptive phrases.

Usage Tip 9: Proper Word Placement

Make sure the words you use fit appropriately into the sentence. Consider the different meanings that result from the placement of the modifier *only* in the following sentences:

> *Only the producer for the video complained about her salary.* (Not the writer or director)
>
> *The only producer for the video complained about her salary.* (Just one producer)
>
> *The producer for the only video complained about her salary.* (Just one video)
>
> *The producer for the video only complained about her salary.* (Complained, not threatened or whined)
>
> *The producer for the video complained only about her salary.* (Just a salary complaint, not about equipment or facilities)

The placement of modifying phrases also can affect the meaning of a sentence. Using common syntax, the noun or pronoun following a modifying phrase is the subject of the action. *Going to class, Bella met her former roommate.* (Bella was going to class.) Violations of this order sometimes are instantly recognized because they evoke comical images in our minds. Consider these two sentences, confusing because of the modifying phrase:

> *While running laps, my grandmother waited for practice to end.* (Grandma running laps?) A clearer way to say it might be, *While I ran laps, my grandma waited for practice to end.*
>
> *As an artist, I need your opinion about how to illustrate this article.* (Who is the artist, you or I? This sentence says that I am.) How about writing this sentence with greater clarity? *I need your artistic opinion about how to illustrate this article.*

In these examples, the modifier may be misplaced. It certainly is in the example about grandma. A misplaced modifier can cause a **non sequitur** (a Latin phrase meaning "it does not follow") because the main point of the sentence does not follow logically from the introductory phrase.

Here is an example of a non sequitur caused by awkward word placement: *The newsletter will include a story about your promotion next month.* The problem is with *next month.* Is it next month's promotion or next month's newsletter?

Here are a few other examples: *The device emits a noise that annoys rodents up to 100 feet.* Those are big rodents! Who would even consider annoying the critters mentioned in this sentence from an actual newspaper advertisement? The problem is with the phrase *up to 100 feet*; the simple addition of the word *away* at the end of the sentence would clear things up nicely.

The Associated Press reported that fighting in South Africa "has left 100 persons dead a week." Then what, they came back as zombies?

A Colorado newspaper had this gem: "Wearing a bad haircut with a blue rhinestone collar, a woman reported her missing poodle."

Or *House Beautiful* magazine: "Designed in 1792 for $500 by James Hoban, an Irish architect, John Adams became the first U.S. president to reside at 1600 Pennsylvania Avenue."

The way to fix such problems is simple: Listen to what you write. Read it out loud, and you'll probably hear the mistakes.

Usage Tip 10: Parallel Structure

Parallel structure means repeating a grammatical pattern for elements that are part of a series or compound construction, such as a series of nouns, verb phrases, infinitives, clauses, and so on. Balance a noun with a noun, an adjective with an adjective, a gerund phrase (-ing verb) with a gerund phrase, and so on.

Make sure items presented in a series are used in parallel fashion. Good writing doesn't mix elements in a series or switch voice. For example, you wouldn't write *Since my last visit, the baby has learned to crawl, roll over, and eating with two hands* because the final element is not parallel with the first two (a gerund following two infinitives, with the *to* implied with the second infinitive). Rather, you would write *The baby has learned to crawl, roll over, and eat with two hands* (all infinitives). Or perhaps, *The baby has learned the skills of crawling, rolling over, and eating with two hands* (all gerund phrases).

Sometimes, writers signal that a parallel structure is coming. For example, they use words such as *either, neither, both,* and *not only*. The reader knows that two things are being introduced by these signals, and the writer knows to present them in parallel fashion: *We've decided that we are either seeing a movie or going to the mall* (two gerund phrases). *Both where to go and what to do there were decisions left to their dates* (two noun clauses). *Not only functionality but also creativity is part of public relations writing* (two nouns).

Another way writers signal parallel elements is by introducing a sequence or signaling an upcoming series. Here's a verb series: *First, mix in the egg whites and milk; second, knead the dough; third, bake for one hour.* Here's a gerund series: *This recipe has three steps: mixing the egg whites and the milk, kneading the dough, and baking for one hour.*

Often, parallel structure is accomplished by using what writers call the **rule of threes**:

- *I came; I saw; I conquered*
- *. . . government of the people, by the people, for the people*
- *Location. Location. Location*
- *Lies, damned lies, and statistics*
- *Stop, drop, and roll.*

Such parallelism carries with it a rhythm that can inspire the reader. We use it so naturally that we often don't think much about it.

Another structure for parallelism with a similar impact is the **turnaround statement**. Half a century later, people are still inspired by the invitation that President John F. Kennedy gave in his inaugural address: "And so, my fellow Americans: ask not what your country can do for you—ask what you can do for your country."

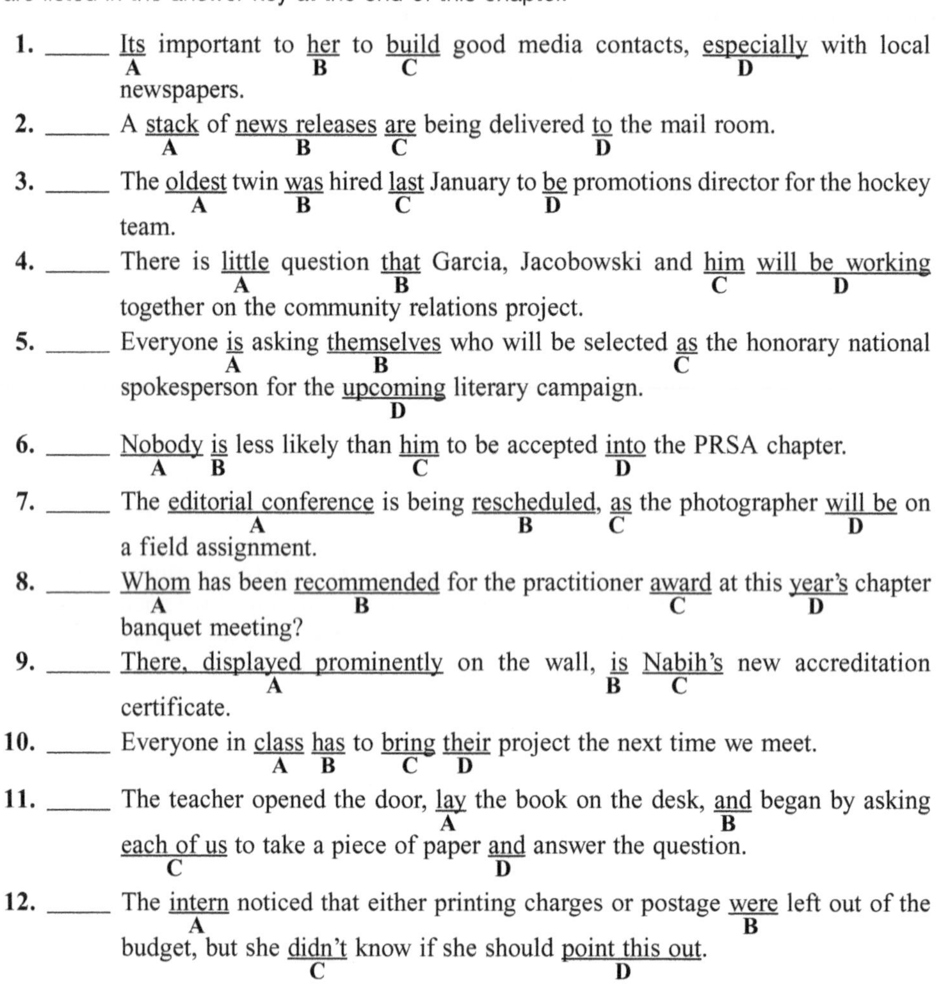

Exercise 2.2

Correcting Standard Usage Problems

Read each sentence and decide if there is an error in usage in any of the underlined parts of the sentence. If you find an error, note the letter printed under the wrong word or phrase and write the letter in the blank space. You do not need to write the correct word. If you do not find an error, write the letter "E." No sentence has more than one error. Answers are listed in the answer key at the end of this chapter.

1. _____ Its (A) important to her (B) to build (C) good media contacts, especially (D) with local newspapers.
2. _____ A stack (A) of news releases (B) are (C) being delivered to (D) the mail room.
3. _____ The oldest (A) twin was (B) hired last (C) January to be (D) promotions director for the hockey team.
4. _____ There is little (A) question that (B) Garcia, Jacobowski and him (C) will be working (D) together on the community relations project.
5. _____ Everyone is (A) asking themselves (B) who will be selected as (C) the honorary national spokesperson for the upcoming (D) literary campaign.
6. _____ Nobody (A) is (B) less likely than him (C) to be accepted into (D) the PRSA chapter.
7. _____ The editorial conference (A) is being rescheduled, (B) as (C) the photographer will be (D) on a field assignment.
8. _____ Whom (A) has been recommended (B) for the practitioner award (C) at this year's (D) chapter banquet meeting?
9. _____ There, displayed prominently (A) on the wall, is (B) Nabih's (C) new accreditation certificate.
10. _____ Everyone in class (A) has (B) to bring (C) their (D) project the next time we meet.
11. _____ The teacher opened the door, lay (A) the book on the desk, and (B) began by asking each of us (C) to take a piece of paper and (D) answer the question.
12. _____ The intern (A) noticed that either printing charges or postage were (B) left out of the budget, but she didn't (C) know if she should point this out (D).

Simple Language

The novelist Ernest Hemingway said it well: "The first and most important thing of all, at least for writers today, is to strip language clean, to lay it bare down to the bone."

What was true in 1952 for Hemingway is equally important for us today. The public relations writer should keep one central idea in mind: People are doing you a favor by reading what you write. Don't make them work too hard. They won't read your messages if your writing is difficult or uninteresting.

Language Tip 1: Writing Naturally

In general, write the way you talk. Sometimes people try too hard to effect a writing style that isn't natural for them or their audience. Your goal should be to write in a way that sounds real and genuine rather than artificial or strained. At the same time, writing for a print release often requires greater attention to grammatical detail than writing that will be presented orally.

As you are trying to master the art of writing naturally, try reading your words aloud. A well-written piece will work not only on paper but also on the ear. A poorly written piece will sound bad, which should prod you to work on it some more.

As you read, listen for the cadence of your words—the rise and fall of the voice, the tempo and meter of the words, the rhythmical pattern of the sentence. In particular, listen for any **rhyme** (words ending with the same sound) or **alliteration** (words beginning with the same letter or sound). Make sure your writing sounds natural and that it doesn't unwittingly usher in a rhyming or sing-song effect. Use rhyme or other techniques if you wish, but don't fall into them accidentally.

Language Tip 2: Wordy Phrases

Treat your writing as a butcher treats meat: Trim the fat. Empty phrases take up unnecessary space. Instead of writing *Will the committee make a recommendation to increase the price?* why not ask simply *Will the committee recommend a price increase?* It's cleaner, shorter, and easier to understand. Writers continually have to make decisions on when to write simply and when to use decorative words and elaborate phrases.

Exercise 2.3

Trimming Wordy Phrases

Rewrite the following sentences by trimming away the unnecessary wordiness. Examples are listed at the end of this chapter.

1. It is necessary to remember to proofread carefully.
2. It has been learned that the university will extend library hours due to the fact that finals are next week.
3. At this point in time, our client is ready to begin the research project.
4. There are five students who have outstanding records.
5. It is an accepted fact that the building was purchased in 1923.
6. The reason for the team's loss is because there were several key players who were sick.
7. The program will be beginning next month.

Language Tip 3: Simple Words

Abjure sesquipedalian obfuscatory terminology. If you understand this advice, follow it. If you don't know what it means, you're probably better off; you won't be tempted to use unnecessarily fancy words. (Translation: Swear off big, confusing words.) *Keep it Simple* could be a motto for the effective public relations writer.

Readability research shows that simpler, more common words make it easier for readers to understand a text. Messages averaging 1½ syllables a word have been found to be easiest to read. Some states have adopted the 1½-syllable formula as a standard for consumer-oriented legal documents for warranties, loans, and contracts. The U.S. Army requires its training manuals to be written at a 6th-grade level so every enlisted person can easily understand them.

Some of the world's most profound ideas have been presented in easy-to-read sentences accessible to virtually any audience. The Gettysburg Address, written by President Abraham Lincoln, for example, averages 1.3 syllables a word. Of 271 words, 202 have only one syllable. Yet it has many powerful and memorable phrases: "Four score and seven years ago our fathers brought forth on this continent, a new nation, conceived in Liberty, and dedicated to the proposition that all men are created equal." Indeed, the message Lincoln expressed 150 years ago is still considered one of the most eloquent in the entire American experience.

Fifty years after Lincoln delivered his dedication speech at the battlefield cemetery at Gettysburg, Lord George Curzon, a British statesman and orator, judged the address one of the three greatest speeches in the English language, calling it "a marvelous piece of English composition . . . a pure well of English undefiled. The more closely the address is analyzed, the more one must confess astonishment at his choice of words, the precision of its thought, its simplicity, directness, and effectiveness." FYI, the other two speeches topping Lord Curzon's list were Lincoln's second inaugural address ("with malice toward none, with charity for all") and William Pitt's victory toast after the English defeated Napoleon at the Battle of Trafalgar ("England has saved herself by her exertions, and will, I trust, save Europe by her example").

Obviously there are times when the writer needs to use complex terms and phrases. But ask yourself these questions: What works best in this particular writing situation? Can I eliminate the technical words and still convey the meaning using examples or analogies? If I need the technical words, can I describe them in simple terms? Are there appropriate synonyms I should consider? Can I use one word instead of two? Can I use two or three simple words instead of one complicated word?

Language Tip 4: Short Sentences

"In art, economy is always beauty." So said novelist and literary critic Henry James. That's particularly true concerning the economy of writing.

Strive for simplicity in your writing, but avoid monotony. Not every sentence needs to begin with a subject. Phrases and clauses can introduce variety and enhance readability. Compound and complex sentences are also useful writing tools.

Studies on readability show that shorter sentences are easier to understand. These studies suggest that general audiences have the best comprehension with sentences of about 16 words.

That's an average. Some will be longer. Some shorter. As the writer, you will want to give variety and a rhythm to your text.

The **Gunning Readability Formula**, also known as the **Fog Index**, is a good tool for the public relations writer. This is a simple way to measure the level of reading ease or difficulty for any piece of writing. To calculate the Fog Index, paste your writing (or a portion of it) in one of the calculators available through an Internet search for "Fog Index calculator" or "readability calculator." The index does not determine if the writing is too basic or too advanced for the audience. It simply reflects the grade-level equivalent needed to understand the writing easily. As the writer, you decide what is appropriate for your readers.

Another readability tool is the **Flesch–Kincaid grade-level scale**. Some computer word-processing programs automatically calculate this, providing some guidance for writers in revising their work.

For example, the Fog Index calculates the previous two paragraphs as 12 or 13, indicating that a high school senior or college freshman should easily be able to understand it. The Flesch–Kincaid scale calculates it at 11 or 12. (Different online calculators may arrive at slightly different readings.) Regardless of the variance, the calculation seems quite reasonable for a textbook typically used by college sophomores or juniors. The passage has an average sentence length of 17 words, also appropriate for the audience for this textbook.

Readers can understand writing that measures lower than their educational achievement. Newspapers are written at a language level that can serve both their readers who may be highly educated professionals, as well as people who did not complete high school. Writing can be simple without being simplistic.

Remember that people always can understand writing that is less than their educational achievement without necessarily feeling that the writing is beneath them. Indeed, it's easier for us to read at less-than-challenging levels.

General-interest newspapers, for example, are written at about an 8th-grade level; Associated Press wire copy is written at the level of an 11th-grade reader. The news media deal with some very sophisticated and complicated subjects in a style that makes their writing accessible to most adults.

Language Tip 5: Redundancies

Redundancies are phrases in which one or more of the words add no meaning to the sentence. Like weeds in a garden, redundancies take up space without adding anything useful. They compete for the reader's attention but offer nothing in return.

For instance, what does *puppy dog* tell you that the single word *puppy* doesn't? Eliminate from your writing phrases such as *bare naked*, *evil villain*, and *hot water heater*. Avoid writing about the *affluent rich* who have their own *jet planes* and who keep their *sailing yachts* at the *boat marina*. Be particularly careful about redundancies that are accidents of translation, such as *Rio Grande River* or *Sierra Nevada Mountains*.

Redundancies usually are adjectives, but don't dismiss all adjectives as being redundant. The problem with redundancies is that, as adjectives, they provide superfluous descriptions and tell us what we already know.

Remember, however, that the repetition of words and phrases can be a useful tool in writing. What is to be avoided is not repetition for effect and comprehension but rather the redundant use of words that add no new meaning to the text.

Exercise 2.4

Eliminating Redundancies

Underline the redundant words that can be eliminated from the following sentences without losing any meaning. Examples are at the end of this chapter.

1. In the final outcome, we expect to see that important foreign imports will continue to maintain a positive current trend.
2. Local residents of this quiet little village will join together to do some advance planning for their annual family picnic on Easter Sunday, just as they have done previously each year.
3. Whether or not we are absolutely sure about Thelma's skill as an ice skater, we are convinced that she is a very unique personality who will be a positive asset to our team.
4. The study committee will refer back to its minutes to learn more about the past history of this important project to improve tourism for the city of Philadelphia.
5. The general consensus of opinion is that, at this point in time, the high school students should not protest against a school-night curfew.
6. The university recently produced two different versions of the report, giving close scrutiny to new techniques for growing crops in rice paddies and cornfields.
7. The Jewish rabbi met with the Episcopal priest and the Muslim imam.

Language Tip 6: Active Voice

Voice is the grammatical term that refers to the relationship between the subject and predicate of a sentence. **Active voice** means the subject is doing the action. **Passive voice** means the action is being done to the subject. Look at the following examples:

- Active voice: *The president asked the community affairs director to coordinate an open house* (12 words). Passive voice: *It was requested by the president that an open house be coordinated by the community affairs director* (17 words).
- Active: *The director will study the report* (6 words). Passive: *The report will be studied by the director* (8 words).
- Active: *The editor accomplished little good when she attempted to revise the newsletter without conducting a reader-interest survey* (17 words). Passive: *Little good was accomplished when the editor attempted to revise the newsletter without conducting a reader-interest survey* (17 words).
- Active: *The company reported a 50 percent increase in its first-quarter profits* (11 words). Passive: *It was reported that the company had a 50 percent increase in its first-quarter profits* (15 words).
- Active: *After the wheel fell off the airplane, it hit the ground and bounced over the house* (16 words). Passive: *The house was bounced over by the wheel after it fell off the airplane and hit the ground* (18 words).
- Active: *All of the participants ran a fast race* (8 words). Passive: *A fast race was run by all of the participants* (10 words).

Both active and passive voice offer something useful to the writer, whose job it is to decide which is more appropriate for each sentence. Here are some of the benefits of active voice:

- Eliminates unnecessary words. Active voice almost always is shorter. In the first set of the sentences above, note that the active version is 12 words to the passive version's 17, a saving of 30 percent.
- Gets to the point quickly. For example, in the second set of sentences above, the active version is quite straightforward. Readers learn quickly what the director will do.
- Increases readability. The Gunning Readability Formula and other similar tools are based on research showing that shorter sentences are easier to understand than longer ones.
- Provides more specific information. For example, in the sentences in the third set above, the active sentence informs the reader that the editor is a woman. In the fourth set, the reader learns that the company made the report. The passive versions lack that information.

Likewise, passive voice also has several benefits for writers:

- Emphasizes the receiver: *Miriam Yosaka has been given the Platinum Excalibur Award for excellence in public relations by the local chapter of PRSA*. This is a form often used in leads for news releases and newsletter articles because the news focus should be on the recipient of a promotion or award and not on the giver.
- Diverts attention from the doer: *Spaghetti sauce was spilled on the guest of honor*. The active alternative would be to call attention to the person who performed the action, such as *Donna spilled spaghetti sauce on the guest of honor*.
- Is useful when the doer is unknown or unimportant: *The banquet hall was repainted 15 years ago*.

Language Tip 7: Adjectives and Adverbs

A principle of effective public relations writing is to be judicious with adjectives and adverbs. Both can be helpful in explaining and qualifying, but they also can be overused. In his novel *Pudd'nhead Wilson*, Mark Twain had some excellent advice for writers: "As to the adjective: When in doubt, strike it out." Another American author, Kip Fadiman, made this observation: "The adjective is the bananna peel of the parts of speech." Be careful not to slip!

An **adjective** modifies a noun or a word acting as a noun. **Limiting adjectives** qualify or limit meanings to a particular type or quantity. *The veteran firefighter ran through the side doorway carrying the year-old infant* (the limiting adjectives are *veteran*, *side*, and *year-old*). Writers who want to write with objectivity use limiting adjectives, because these can add rich detail to the story.

Another type of adjective, the **descriptive adjective**, describes a quality of the object. *The exhausted firefighter ran through the fiery doorway carrying the frightened infant* (the descriptive adjectives are *exhausted*, *fiery*, and *frightened*). While descriptive adjectives can enliven basic information, public relations writers try to limit their use of descriptive adjectives because they often ask the reader to trust the observations and conclusions of the writer. For example, it is an objective fact to report that a building is *40 storeys high*, a limiting adjective. But using a descriptive adjective such as calling it a *tall building* asks the reader to accept the writer's interpretation of tall. For a reader in Manhattan, 40 storeys isn't particularly tall; from the perspective of someone in Flagstaff, Ariz., it is quite tall. Let readers interpret objective information for themselves.

As adjectives modify nouns, **adverbs** do the same thing for verbs. They provide nuance and detail. For example, *The writer approached the task happily.* Or *fearfully.* Or *half-heartedly.* Adverbs should be used even more sparingly than adjectives, because so often they result from what the writer observed. Remember that good writers try not to ask a reader to accept their conclusions; rather, they provide details to allow readers to draw their own conclusions.

Meaningful Language

> "When I use a word," Humpty Dumpty said, in rather a scornful tone, "it means just what I choose it to mean—neither more nor less."
>
> "The question is," said Alice, "whether you can make words mean so many different things."

In *Through the Looking-Glass*, Lewis Carroll gives us that exchange. Humpty Dumpty can claim what he likes, but Alice's question is right on. Can writers expect a word to mean simply what they want? Or should we use words the way our readers will best understand them?

A public relations writer's greatest strength is the ability to share meaning and communicate accurate understandings between organizations and their publics. It's a matter of **diction**, the literary term associated with word choice, particularly the careful selection of words and phrases to best carry the meaning that the writer has in mind.

Read the following note that Mark Twain sent to a 12-year-old boy who had written to him—and pretend he was writing to you:

> I notice that you use plain, simple language, short words and brief sentences. That is the way to write English—it is the modern way and the best way. Stick to it; don't let fluff and flowers and verbosity creep in. When you catch an adjective, kill it. No, I don't mean utterly, but kill most of them—then the rest will be valuable. They weaken when they are close together. They give strength when they are wide apart. An adjective habit, or a wordy, diffuse, flowery habit, once fastened upon a person, is as hard to get rid of as any other vice.

Here are some tips to help you write with more meaningful use of language.

Diction Tip 1: Word Pictures

A good writer is one who has learned how to weave such a richness into language that the reader not only grasps the meaning but also feels an experience of the story. Here are several techniques for creating word pictures that can inspire the reader.

Description. Show, don't tell. That's common advice for public relations writers. Writing is most powerful when it demonstrates a fact and invites the reader to draw a conclusion, rather than when it interprets the situation for the reader. Russian short-story writer Anton Chekhov had it right: "Don't tell me the moon is shining; show me the glint of light on broken glass."

Effective writers provide information so their readers can properly interpret a situation for themselves. In the sentence *The little girl was happy to see her grandfather*, the reader must trust that the writer witnessed, understood, and accurately represented some interchange between grandparent and child. More specific is *The little girl smiled, ran to her grandfather, and hugged him.* Now readers can "see" the happiness and draw their own conclusion rather than rely on the writer's interpretation.

Detail. An effective writer gives details. Instead of asking the reader to trust the writer's judgment and skill in observation, the writer simply presents the reader with evidence. Rather than reporting *The company lost a lot of money last year*, we provide much more meaning by stating *The company lost $1.5 million last year*. Likewise, try to use words that provide specific information rather than generalities. Here's an example of vague wording: *As soon as possible, we should complete this contract.* When is as soon as possible? And what does *complete* mean in this context? To write the contract? To reach agreement on the terms? To sign it? To fulfill the work required?

Comparison. Analogies, metaphors, and similes are types of figurative language that allow the writer to make lucid comparisons for the reader. An **analogy** is an effective way to show something in a way that readers can understand. Analogies are comparisons that explain unfamiliar concepts by using familiar terms and imagery. For example, one student in a public relations writing class described cholesterol by creating a verbal image of gridlock on a busy city street where the flow of traffic was slowed by a truck that is double-parked. That is an analogy of how clogged arteries constrict the blood flow. It takes something readers already understand (traffic) and uses this image to explain something they may not understand (the effects of cholesterol). Effective public relations writers develop the ability to find common, everyday parallels for complex situations.

Using analogies requires systematic reasoning. As a student, you may have been exposed to such reasoning on standardized tests: Puppy is to dog as (a) tabby is to cat, (b) sparrow is to bird, (c) flock is to duck, (d) fawn is to deer. Think logically about the relationships. You know that a puppy is a young dog. Consider the choices. Is a tabby a young cat? Is a sparrow a young bird? Is a flock a young duck? Is a fawn a young deer? Through this reasoning, it's clear that (d) is the correct answer.

Two other useful literary techniques are related to each other. The **simile** ((SIH-muh-lee)) is a direct comparison between two dissimilar concepts. Similes use the word *like* or *as* to make the comparison. For example, *The music of the orchestra was like the sound of birds chirping at daybreak.* Meanwhile the **metaphor** also makes an indirect comparison and does not use the word *like* or *as*. For example, *The soccer team steamrolled over the competition.* Because of the poetic imagery used in metaphors, writers don't often use them in public relations writing.

Diction Tip 2: Precise Language

Mark Twain pointed out that the difference between the correct word and the almost correct word is the difference between lightning and a lightning bug. Good advice.

Some words seem alike but have significantly different meanings. Good writers don't necessarily avoid words with nuanced meanings, but they certainly make sure they use the correct word. *Disinterested* isn't the same as *uninterested. Comprise* is different from *include.* Likewise with *farther* and *further*, *imply* and *infer*, *less* and *fewer*. If you aren't sure of the differences among these sets of words, look them up in your dictionary and in the AP Stylebook.

Also use the right combination of words. *Try to* is preferable to *try and*. *Different from* makes more sense than *different than*. *Neither* requires a *nor*, and *not only* must be followed by *but also*.

Sometimes meanings built into words makes them inappropriate for linking with certain other words, because doing so would lead to a contradiction. The term for this is **oxymoron** (from the Greek, "acutely foolish"). A writer may consciously use an oxymoron for creative effect, such as describing an audience reaction as *thunderous silence* or a committee's recommendation as a *definite maybe*. Occasionally, however, an unintended and unfortunate oxymoron creeps into a sentence, such as reference to an *uncrowned king*, *genuine imitation*, or *paid volunteer*.

Diction Tip 3: Strong Words

The way to avoid ambiguity is to use strong words, especially verbs. We noted earlier some of the problems associated with descriptive adjectives and adverbs. Amateur writers sometimes try to "dress up" their writing with too many flowery descriptions.

There is a better way to improve your writing. Professional writers rely on the power of the verbs. For example, verbs based on *be*, *have*, *go*, and *make* provide basic information, but they don't communicate a rich meaning. Consider the difference between *The committee had meetings* and *The committee sponsored meetings* or *conducted meetings*. Compare the power of verbs in *The union had a vote* with *The union wanted a vote* or *called for*, *demanded*, or *threatened*.

Weak *is* and *go* verbs can be strengthened with more precise and meaningful verbs. *She has a new house* becomes stronger and more specific as *She lives in a new house* (or *leases* or *owns*). *He went to school yesterday* becomes much more meaningful if the reader learns *He ran to school yesterday*. Or *drove*. Or *walked*. Or *dashed*. Or *moseyed*.

"I love you," he said. Aw, that's nice! But notice how the meaning of this sentence becomes richer with a more precise verb. *"I love you," he sobbed*. Or *muttered*. Or *shouted*. Or *snickered*. Or *announced*. Or *panted*.

Effective writers choose specific verbs based on the writing context, the norms and conventions associated with each particular writing format. For example, in a news release, the writer probably would stick with the word *said* because it is a neutral verb. Some of the more interpretive and descriptive verbs might be used in feature releases, appeal letters, and other formats.

Diction Tip 4: Clichés and Journalese

Familiarity breeds contempt, or at least boredom. A **cliché** ((klee-SHAY)) is a familiar expression overused to the point where it has become weary and stale. Clichés tell your reader where you are going before you get there. Avoid them.

Replace clichés with your own fresh expressions, and challenge common phrases that carry little information. For example, how long is it *until the cows come home*? And just where is *Square One*? And is it really any sweeter to be *last but not least*?

Another note of caution: Avoid **journalese**. That's the kind of wording, especially for verbs, sometimes found in newspaper headlines. In the language of journalese, costs *skyrocket* and temperatures *soar*. Fires *rage* and rivers *rampage*. Projects are *kicked off*. Opponents *weigh in*. In journalese, people get a *go-ahead* and projects get a *green light*. While this might be appropriate for headlines, such writing can quickly become trite and overdone.

Exercise 2.5

Eliminating Clichés

Revise each of the following sentences by using original language in place of the cliché.

1. Let's run this idea up the flagpole and see who salutes.
2. After 9 p.m., taxis are few and far between.
3. It's time for journalists and public relations practitioners to bury the hatchet.
4. Get a ballpark estimate of how much it will cost to print the brochure.
5. It's time to bite the bullet and announce the layoffs.
6. John was green with envy when Lee was given the Oxford account.

Diction Tip 5: Loaded Words

Would you rather be called *fat* or *amply proportioned*? How about *corpulent*? *husky*? *pudgy*? *stout*? *big-boned*? It makes a difference, which is why dressmakers have XL–Petite sizes and advertisers promote queen-size panty hose.

If you want to see the power of language—and the importance of avoiding loaded words—consider this: Will you get the same response if you tell your mother that she is *nagging* you than if you say she's being too *persistent*? Is calling someone *a colored person* the same as referring to *a person of color*? What's the difference among *indulgent*, *permissive*, and *tolerant* parents? These can be loaded words, and you should use them very carefully.

The English language has many different, sometimes opposing, ways of expressing some ideas. Public relations writers take great care in choosing words with the appropriate denotation and connotation.

- **Denotation** is the basic dictionary definition of a word, its direct and explicit meaning.
- **Connotation** is the deeper meaning, the implicit suggestion or nuance that goes beyond the explicit meaning.

Often it is a matter of personal interpretation, giving rise to emotional associations. For example, *chat*, *chatter*, *prattle*, and *babble* all denote the same thing—a loose and ready flow of inconsequential talk. But each connotes a different meaning—a light and friendly chat, aimless and rapid chatter, childish prattle, and unintelligible babble.

Diction Tip 6: Jargon

One of the biggest contributions a good public relations writer can make to an organization is to translate its bureaucratic language into words and phrases that are meaningful to people new to or outside of the organization.

Jargon (also known as **technical language**) refers to words and phrases familiar within a particular group (such as an organization, industry, profession, hobby, and so on) but unfamiliar to people outside the group. Faced with technical language, or language that is unintelligible for a lay audience, you have several choices: translate it into more accessible English, explain it in simple terms, use it in obvious context, or delete the jargon altogether.

Faced with jargon, a writer may paraphrase. But don't simply put quotation marks around jargon. This merely calls attention to the technical language but does little to interpret it for readers.

Jargon is sometimes appropriate. You can use technical and "in" words freely, as long as your audiences are likely to understand them. Jargon might well be appropriate in pieces such as articles in industry newsletters, news releases to specific interest magazines, or speeches before professional groups.

The use of jargon can raise ethical questions when it is meant to obscure the meaning for uninformed or uninitiated readers.

Exercise 2.6

Working with Technical Language

Part 1: Each of the following passages offers a medical explanation related to a type of cancer. Select either one of the medical explanations. Rewrite this explanation in lay terms so it is complete yet understandable to a first-year college student without a medical background.

Part 2: Add one or two paragraphs of additional information that you believe would be particularly relevant to readers as a way of encouraging them to adopt the habit of using the self-examination techniques that are associated with each disease. This might include information you find about people who have survived the disease and/or information about how the disease and detection techniques are particularly relevant to a college-age audience.

Resources: Use information you can find in general and medical encyclopedias, books, magazines and journals, interviews with medical professionals, and so on. You'll find accurate information from organizations such as the American Cancer Society or the National Institutes of Health. Use a search engine to find authoritative websites dealing with breast cancer or testicular cancer.

Breast Cancer. Highly treatable, carcinoma of the breast is most often curable when detected in early stages. Staging of breast cancer indicates the risk of metastasis; thus the need for early detection and treatment. Simultaneous bilateral breast cancer is uncommon; however, there is a progressive risk of recurrence.

Many breast cancers are initially discovered as lumps detected by the patient herself, with 80 percent of these being noncarcinomatous cysts or benign tumors. Physicians verify the suspicion of carcinoma through a series of examination procedures and imaging techniques, including palpation, aspiration, ultrasonography, thermography, and diaphanography. Mammography is the most important screening modality for the early detection of breast cancer.

Clinical diagnosis of breast cancer is accomplished via biopsy. The most common primary treatment is surgery (including lumpectomy, segmented mastectomy, simple mastectomy, modified radical mastectomy, and radical mastectomy).

continued . . .

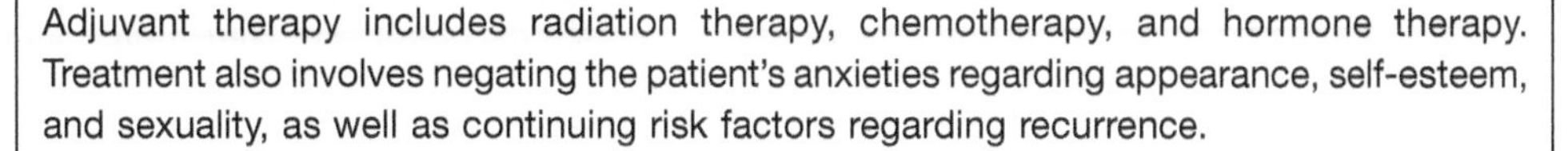
Exercise 2.6 . . . continued

Adjuvant therapy includes radiation therapy, chemotherapy, and hormone therapy. Treatment also involves negating the patient's anxieties regarding appearance, self-esteem, and sexuality, as well as continuing risk factors regarding recurrence.

Lifelong follow-up is required to detect recurrences, which can occur as late as 30 years after the initial diagnosis. The risk of a primary cancer in the contralateral breast is significant, approximately 1 percent per year cumulatively. Therefore, patients should be instructed in breast self-examination and should have periodic examinations aimed at early detection, including routine mammograms after age 40.

Testicular Cancer. Highly treatable and curable at a more than 90 percent rate depending on type, carcinoma of the testicle usually develops in men from post-pubescence through early middle-age (ages 15 to 34) and is the most prevalent carcinomatic variety for that age group. Testicular cancer can metastasize at a rapid rate; thus the need for early detection and treatment. Testicular cancer is seldom bilateral, and it carries only a slight rate of recurrence.

Most testicular cancers are initially discovered by the patient himself. Physicians verify the suspicion of carcinoma through a series of physical and radiologic examinations and testing procedures.

Diagnostic evaluation via imaging techniques includes computed tomography, intravenous pyelography, lymphangiography, and ultrasonography. Primary treatment of a testicular mass is accomplished via radical inguinal orchiectomy and microscopic examination. Adjuvant therapy includes radiation therapy or chemotherapy. Treatment also involves negating the patient's anxieties regarding sterility, impotency, and ejaculatory ability which are seldom the result of orchiectomy but which may be temporarily present due to therapeutic treatment.

Patients who have been cured of testicular cancer have a 5 percent cumulative risk of developing a cancer in the opposite testicle over the 25 years after initial diagnosis, though disease-free survival of three years is considered tantamount to a cure. Patients should be instructed in testicular self-examination and should have periodic examinations aimed at early detection.

Diction Tip 7: New Words

Business and academic writers sometimes have to create new words, such as when dealing with an emerging field within science or high technology, for example. But writers who create new words are often simply seeking a short cut, which can confuse or alienate readers.

Two particular problem areas involve the use of the suffixes *-ify* and *-ize* to create a noun-verb hybrid. Some hybrids have crept into common usage, and we talk about *computerizing a classroom.*

But there are limits. Don't take a perfectly good noun, add a suffix, and expect people to appreciate a silly verblike structure, such as *Martin wants to Mac-ify the office.* Sometimes parallel construction is not possible. We can *Latinize* a culture, but can we also *Paraguayanize* it or *Kenyanize* it? Should we even try?

Meanwhile, adding *-ation* to the end of verbs can also lead to awkwardness, as in these unfortunate words that have been used in print: *conscienticization, Frenchification*, and *teacherization*.

Diction Tip 8: Foreign Words

Public relations writers generally try to avoid using non-English words and phrases that have not been adopted into the language. This is not about legitimate English words rooted in other languages—alcohol, alleluia, bona fide, restaurant, sushi, and tobacco, for example.

Beware of truly foreign words and phrases: *ex post facto, a priori, poco a poco, mano a mano*. Don't use such terms with general audiences, who probably won't know that you are using a Latin phrase for "after the fact" and "prior to" and Spanish phrases for "little by little" and "hand to hand."

However, you might use such terms within specialized groups that understand the meaning. For example, classically trained musicians may appreciate subtle put-down in a theater review noting that *The applause began adagio and built to andante* (adagio is slow; andante isn't much faster) or *The audience left the theater prestissimo* (prestissimo means as fast as possible).

When you must use foreign words for a general audience, make sure you use them correctly. That B-minus you got in Spanish II may not be the best foundation for your writing. Use quotation marks around foreign words, and provide a translation: *The nursing supervisor noted with pride that Mercy Women's Health Center has been committed to the treatment of women "ab initio" (a Latin phrase meaning "from the beginning"), pointing out that the clinic was founded in 1842 as Sisters of Mercy Hospital for Women.*

Diction Tip 9: Pretentious Language

Pretentious language involves the use of words inflated to sound more impressive than they warrant. The car dealership advertises *experienced vehicles*. A government report refers to cows, pigs, and chickens collectively as *grain-consuming animal units*.

Often this is harmless, sometimes even silly. Bald people are called *follically impaired*, short people are *vertically challenged*, and senior citizens are *chronologically experienced*. Midriff bulge is called *personal insulation*. Cute! But senseless or nonsensical, pretentious language slows down the reader and sometimes is unclear in its meaning. Avoid it.

Diction Tip 10: Honest Language

Codes of ethics of the Public Relations Society of America, the Canadian Public Relations Society, the International Association of Business Communicators, and other professional organizations commit public relations writers to honesty and integrity, refraining from misleading information and correcting inaccuracies and misunderstandings.

The car dealership noted above sells *experienced vehicles*, the local thrift shop advertises *pre-worn jeans*, and a carpet store has *semi-antique rugs*. Interesting use of language and nobody gets hurt, so why fuss? Because sometimes people do get hurt. When pretentious language crosses the line, it loses its innocence and becomes dishonest. For example, when a marketer advertises rhinestones as *genuine artificial diamonds*, who gets hurt? Perhaps the new immigrant unfamiliar with the wiles of the marketplace. Maybe it's just the 10-year-old looking for a present for Mother's Day, who ends up disappointed because he spent his paper-route money on junk.

The term **doublespeak** refers to language that intentionally obscures the real meaning behind the words. The use of doublespeak raises serious ethical questions for writers. It's a serious matter of misleading the public when the military reports the killing of civilian men, women, and children as *collateral damage*, a term deliberately chosen to obscure reality and minimize opposition. The Army used the term frequently during the Vietnam War, with little public disapproval. But there was an outcry over that same military term when American terrorist Timothy McVeigh used it in reference to the children and adults killed when he bombed the Federal Building in Oklahoma City. It returned in Afghanistan, Iraq, and Lebanon, but by then audiences had begun to understand it to mean civilian casualties; the phrase doesn't mask reality as much as it once did.

Similarly, it's outright deception when an annual report calls budget cuts *advanced downward adjustments* or when the Air Force says that civilians have been put on *nonduty, nonpay status*. (As in fired?) Ethical writers know they should not use language that others will probably misunderstand.

A practical problem with doublespeak is that it often harms the reputation of the person or organization that engages in it. For example, after several months of clean-up following the 1989 Alaskan oil spill, Exxon officials said Prince William Sound was becoming "environmentally stabilized." But an Alaskan state official called this "an Exxon term . . . As far as we're concerned, it's meaningless." Much the same with some of BP's utterances during the oil disaster in the Gulf of Mexico.

The National Council of Teachers of English, through its Doublespeak Award, has gone to battle with individuals and groups who do violence to the concept of meaningful language. The council has criticized corporations for using doublespeak such as *initiate operations improvement*, *employee repositioning*, and *proactive downsizing* when they lay off employees. It has identified deforestation projects that strip every tree and bush from hundreds of acres of forest, calling them instead *temporary meadows*. It has criticized government reports that call death *failure to thrive* and medical reports that a patient *failed to fulfill his wellness potential* when he died.

The committee's outlook is global. It criticized a Russian report that a driver wasn't drunk, just in a *non-sober condition*. It likewise criticized French police who said they don't kill but *neutralize* terrorists, and the Bosnian army officer who announced that *the only way to negotiate is to fight*.

Each year the committee presents its Doublespeak Award "to public speakers who have perpetuated language that is deceptive, evasive, euphemistic, confusing & self-centered." Since 1974, it has recognized individuals such as Palestinian leader Yasser Arafat (for saying that "it is precisely because we have been advocating coexistence that we have shed so much blood"), Army officer Oliver North (for his claim that he was *cleaning up the historical record* when, the committee said, he had "lied, destroyed official government documents, and created false documents"), and the first President Bush (for vetoing the Parental and Medical Leave bill amid assurances "that women do not have to worry about getting their jobs back after having a child or caring for a child during a serious illness"). The committee also has cited groups like the Department of Defense (for referring to a bombing mission as *visiting a site*, and for calling human beings *soft targets* of such visits); the State Department (for referring to killing as *unlawful or arbitrary deprivation of life*); and the nuclear power industry (for inventing euphemisms around the Three Mile Island accident that referred to an explosion as *energetic disassembly*, fire as *rapid oxidation*, and an accident as an *event*, an *abnormal evolution*, and a *normal aberration*).

During the second Bush administration, the president received the dubious award three different times, and three other times it went to members of his administration. The committee said George W. Bush "has set a high standard for his team by the inspired creation of the phrase 'weapons of mass destruction-related program activities' to describe what has yet to be seen." The committee also called former Defense Secretary Donald Rumsfeld's dismissive description of the Abu Ghraib prison torture "brilliantly mind-befuddling." It also noted that the notorious *body bags* that carried dead soldiers home from the Vietnam War became *human remains pouches* during the Gulf War of Bush 1 and then morphed into *transfer tubes* during the Iraq and Afghanistan wars of Bush 2. The recent award went to Fox TV celebrity Glenn Beck.

What are the practical consequences of doublespeak? Companies have faced personal injury lawsuits because their written instructions were considered jumbled and unclear. In Connecticut a few years ago, a judge said one company's contract wording was so murky it must have been made so on purpose, and the company had to pay a hefty fine. Try your hand at a situation ripe for doublespeak in "What Would You Do? *Avoiding Doublespeak*."

What Would You Do? *Avoiding Doublespeak*

You are a public relations writer for City College. The academic dean wants you to write a news release because CC has recently been recertified by the National Council for Accreditation of Teacher Education. (NCATE certification is hard to come by, and makes a big difference when it comes to recruiting and fundraising.) The dean wants you to write that CC is the only college with NCATE certification in the state, which is true, although four *universities* in the state also have the same certification. What would you do? How would you justify your decision?

Exercise 2.7

Freewriting on Language Ethics

Freewrite for five minutes on the following topic: *What is the difference between using language that misleads the reader and emphasizing the positive side of a situation?* Discuss this with your classmates.

Inclusive Language

Effective public relations writers are careful to use **inclusive language**—words and phrases that apply to all readers, without unnecessary exclusiveness. For example, *student* is an inclusive term for a kindergarten-through-graduate school audience; *schoolchildren* is more exclusive, suggesting people in the lower grades.

Why avoid bias in your writing? Not because it is the "nice" thing to do, and certainly not because it's "politically correct." For the public relations writer, the reason to avoid biased language is more self-serving: Using inclusive language makes you a more effective writer. If even one member of your audience feels excluded from what you are writing, you have created a barrier to communication. Notice the use of the word *feels*. It matters little if you meant to exclude. If any reader feels excluded, you are failing to communicate effectively. The fault is yours, however unintentional; the solution must also be yours.

Sometimes you may find people who don't find biased words offensive. Some women are comfortable with terms like *mankind*, and some women's organizations refer to their leaders as *chairmen*. Sometimes members of a minority group may use terms among themselves that would be offensive coming from someone outside the group.

It doesn't really matter what *most* people would feel is appropriate; public relations is not determined by majority rule. Each individual in your audience decides if your writing is non-biased; each reader has a veto. You must care not only about the majority who may think *fireman* is OK but also about the perhaps minority of women firefighters who don't see themselves or their colleagues reflected in that term. Use words that include the man in a wheelchair who refuses to identify himself as handicapped because the term does not mirror his capabilities.

The problem with biased language of any kind is that it presumes one group sets the standard for the other. It buys into the idea that the majority sets the rules for the minority. That presumption is wrong, sometimes the result of arrogance, ignorance, or insensitivity. Writers cannot afford such indiscretions. We must do everything in our power to make our publics and our audiences feel included in what we are writing about.

Let's look at some of the ways to eliminate bias based on gender, physical characteristics, and ethnicity, culture or lifestyle.

Bias Tip 1: Gender

Gender bias, sometimes called **sexist language**, results when the writer or speaker uses words that make someone feel left out because the reference seems to be only to the other gender. Almost always, the presumption is that men and masculine things are the norm; women and feminine things are seen in contrast to that norm. And that's bias. Here are a few ways of writing around such bias.

Avoid Masculine Pronouns. Avoid using masculine pronouns as the default when you refer to groups that can include both men and women. In the past, the pronoun *he* was used to refer to both sexes, but this is no longer accepted in many situations. Consider this sentence: *The professional artist should take great care of his brushes*. Here are several alternatives, each with a slightly difference nuance, giving the public relations writer many possibilities for avoiding pronoun bias:

- Use the plural form: *Professional artists should take great care of their brushes*. This may be the easiest way to handle the problem of exclusive language.
- Eliminate the possessive pronoun altogether: *The professional artist should take great care of brushes*.
- Use first or second person to make the reference more general: *As professional artists, we should take great care of our brushes*. Or, *As a professional artist, you should take great care of your brushes*.

- Use passive voice to eliminate the focus on the doer of the action: *For the professional artist, great care should be taken with brushes.*
- Use double pronouns: *The professional artist should take great care of his or her brushes*. Do this sparingly because it draws attention to its inclusiveness. Artificial forms such as *he/she* and *s/he* may be appropriate for business or internal writing formats but not for external publics.
- Use the word *one* for the pronoun, though this may sound stilted: *One should take great care of one's brushes*. Use it sparingly.

Avoid Masculine Nouns. Avoid using masculine words rooted in a generic sense. It is also important to avoid using feminine words generically, but this is seldom a problem. Find an alternative to *man* in the sense of *all people*.

Avoid Gender Stereotypes. Avoid using words that portray a gender stereotype. When possible, use words that are not gender specific to refer to both sexes. In a generic sense that does not identify particular individuals; words like *doctor*, *lawyer*, *actor*, and *senator* include both women and men. Be careful not to create or perpetuate false stereotypes based on gender. Words commonly but falsely associated only with women—*secretary*, *nurse*, *kindergarten teacher*—refer to both sexes. On the other hand, some words are inherently associated with only one gender—*nun*, *ballerina*, *husband*.

Exercise 2.8

Eliminating Gender Bias

List generic alternatives for each of the following gender-specific words. Examples are listed at the end of this chapter.

Bellboy	Housewife
Clergyman	Public relations man
Congressman	Seaman
Deliveryman	Spokesman
Forefathers	Statesman
Foreman	Stewardess
Garbage man	Watchman

Use Inclusive Terms. Avoid words with feminine and masculine forms when an inclusive form can be used more effectively. Whenever possible, use the same word to refer to male and female members of the same group. In generic references, use terms like *business executive* rather than *businessman* or *businesswoman*, or *police officer* rather than *policeman* or *policewoman*. Of course, gender-specific terms such as *chairwoman* or *fireman* are appropriate when you are referring to a particular woman or man.

Avoid archaic or dated feminine forms as well, such as *poetess*, *Jewess*, *aviatrix*, and *priestess*. Even *actress* seems to be losing favor as the preferred term for many women television or movie performers, particularly those who seek out serious roles. Meanwhile, be careful with the Latin-based variants of *alumnus* (one man), *alumna* (one woman), *alumni* (several men, or a mixed group), and *alumnae* (several women) when referring to graduates of a college or university. Or simply call them *graduates*. Note also that, despite what some alumni offices mistakenly think, *alum* is not an acceptable short form. Outside the field of chemistry, it's not even a word.

Paraphrase Direct Quotations. In direct quotations, it may be necessary to paraphrase in order to avoid using exclusive language. Or, in your role as public relations adviser, you may ask the person you are quoting to reconsider a particular word or phrase.

Use Parallel Treatment. Treat women and men the same in similar situations. Don't use deferential, polite, or honorary terms differently for men and women in the same reference. *The movie starred Clooney, Diesel, and Miss Lohan.*

Avoid Gender References. Avoid inappropriate references to the gender of a person involved in activities stereotypically associated with the other gender. It may be legitimate news that a woman has been elected president of the rod-and-gun club or that a man has received the hospital's Nurse of the Year award. Each case may represent the first occasion that someone of that gender has received the position or the award, and an insightful public relations writer will recognize the news value in such a first-of-a-kind situation and report it accordingly.

But not every situation deserves to have the spotlight shine on gender issues. Be smooth. Just because you think "Wow, that's a strange thing for a woman to be doing," you don't need to call inappropriate attention to it. Find an appropriate way of identifying a person or mentioning gender without calling undue attention. For example, instead of the sentence *The woman judge explained the charges to the jury, telling them not to discuss the case with anyone else*, you might write *When the judge explained the charges to the jury, she told them not to discuss the case with anyone else*. In both versions, it is clear to the reader that the judge is a woman, but the second version is smoother and more subtle.

Omit Unnecessary Personal Characteristics. Avoid unnecessary references to marital status, dress, and other irrelevant personal characteristics. The key is significance. Writers always have more information than they use, and one of their responsibilities is to sort out the germane information from that which is immaterial.

When you are wondering about using a particular piece of information, the other-foot test might be helpful. Ask yourself: If the shoe were on the other foot, would I still want to write this? If you can honestly say that in your writing you would mention the occupation of the wife of one political candidate, then it's probably OK to write similarly about the husband of another. If you would mention what the male politician wore to the rally, then in fairness you can mention what the woman politician wore. But when you apply the other-foot test, often you realize that the information is really inappropriate and unnecessary.

If the fact that a person is single or divorced, married or partnered is significant to the story, then report it. But if it is superfluous information, don't use it.

Bias Tip 2: Physical Characteristics

In your writing, use discretion when you describe physical and other personal characteristics. If physical condition, age, or other personal descriptions are relevant, provide the information in a nonbiased way. However, don't use such personal information without good reason. In the past, newspapers routinely described people by using their age, occupation, and addresses. Amid growing concerns about personal privacy, however, people in public communications need to question the relevance of such information. Does it matter that the new principal is 39?

Age bias can focus on words identified with youth or age. Avoid using phrases such as *old man* and referring to women who work in an office as *the girls*.

Use appropriate terms to indicate physical conditions. Terms such as *dumb* or *crippled* no longer carry neutral connotations; instead, we might say someone is *unable to speak* or *uses a wheelchair to get around* (a better phrasing, by the way, than *confined to a wheelchair*). It's often a matter of putting the focus on the person rather than on the problem, such as writing about *people with handicaps* rather than *handicapped people* or a *man living with AIDS* rather than an *AIDS victim*. Likewise, consider the connotations for designations of mental or emotional conditions.

Don't confuse the distinction among diseases, injuries, and physical conditions. For example, don't portray pregnancy, menopause, or advanced age as illnesses or afflictions. These are physical conditions, but not necessarily negative ones.

Bias Tip 3: Race and Ethnicity

Avoid stereotypes based on supposed characteristics associated with race, ethnicity, and national background.

Avoid offensive, outdated, and otherwise inappropriate terms. Obvious racial slurs seldom find their way into respectable media, unless a report is citing inappropriate language spouted by a celebrity or politician. But writers' sensitivities sometimes aren't fine-tuned about terms that are considered disrespectful by some groups. Words such as *mick*, *squaw*, and *Canuck* carry negative connotations that make them inappropriate in many writing situations.

Don't betray a Eurocentric bias, such as a survey that lists demographic categories as English, Irish, German, French, Italian, Spanish, Asian, Black, and other.

It should be a basic principle of public relations writing that people deserve to be called by the names they prefer for themselves. Use those terms. For example, avoid using outdated terms such as *colored* or *Afro-American*. Today more accepted terms are *person of color* or *African-American*. Undoubtedly, new terms will emerge as English continues to evolve.

Bias Tip 4: Culture and Lifestyle

Avoid language that calls undue attention to culture, religion, lifestyle, sexual orientation, and other personal characteristics of a person.

Use inclusive references. Consider this sentence: *The mayor met with representatives of various churches in the city*. This includes people who worship in churches, but it's not inclusive if the mayor also met with leaders of people who worship at the synagogue, temple, mosque, kiva, or longhouse. The sentence might be more accurate if it reported: *The mayor met with representatives of various religious groups in the city*.

Be attentive to people in alternative lifestyles and nontraditional families. Many gay and lesbian couples consider themselves to be just as committed as legal spouses, and other people find that their identity as families is not bound by legal contracts and religious rituals. Whether you personally agree with such lifestyles is not the point. Rather, be aware in your professional writing that not everyone lives stereotypical lives.

Revisit the advice in the tip about not mentioning unnecessary gender information. Just as it's probably inappropriate to note that a surgeon is a woman or that the kindergarten teacher is a man, it's probably even less appropriate to write that he or she is gay, Hispanic, a Republican, Catholic, or any number of other descriptors that, while accurate, are irrelevant. If the information is part of the story, then by all means use it in context. But don't go out of your way to point out something that you personally may find odd or interesting unless it adds to the telling of the story.

Exercise 2.9

Eliminating Language Bias

Rewrite the following sentences as needed to eliminate any biased language. Answers are listed at the end of this chapter.

1. The medical report dealt with the birth process for monkeys, gorillas, and man.
2. "Do something about your son," her neighbor's wife screamed out the back door.
3. According to union rules, policemen must be in proper uniform when they appear in public.
4. The highway gas station is manned at all times of the day and night for the convenience of travelers.
5. Mrs. Ramadera was elected chairman of the League of Women Voters.
6. Early immigrants to the country included Frenchmen, Germans, Swedes, and Scotsmen.
7. The new chief of surgery is a woman doctor from Pittsburgh.
8. Five students in the class—three girls and two men—wrote the winning essays on malnutrition.

Answers to Chapter Exercises

Exercise 2.2

1-A, 2-C, 3-A, 4-C, 5-B, 6-C, 7-C, 8-A, 9-E, 10-D, 11-A, 12-B

Exercise 2.3

1. Remember to proofread carefully.
2. The university will extend library hours because finals are next week.
3. Now our client is ready to begin the research project.
4. Five students have outstanding records.
5. The building was purchased in 1923.
6. The team lost because several key players were sick.
7. The program will begin next month.

Exercise 2.4

1. In the final outcome, we expect to see that important foreign imports will continue to maintain a positive current trend.
2. Local residents of this quiet little village will join together to do some advance planning for their annual family picnic on Easter Sunday, just as they have done previously each year.
3. Whether or not we are absolutely sure about Thelma's skill as an ice skater, we are convinced that she is a very unique personality who will be a positive asset to our team.
4. The study committee will refer back to its minutes to learn more about the past history of this important project to improve tourism for the city of Philadelphia.
5. The general consensus of opinion is that, at this point in time, the high school students should not protest against a school-night curfew.
6. The university recently produced two different versions of the report, giving close scrutiny to new techniques for growing crops in rice paddies and cornfields.
7. The Jewish rabbi met with the Episcopal priest and the Muslim imam.

Exercise 2.8

Bellboy = bellhop, luggage attendant
Clergyman = rabbi, imam, roshi, priest, minister
Congressman = Representative
Deliveryman = driver
Forefathers = ancestors
Foreman = supervisor
Garbage man = garbage collector
Housewife = homemaker
Public relations man = public relations practitioner
Seaman = sailor
Spokesman = spokesperson, company representative
Statesman = diplomat
Stewardess = flight attendant
Watchman = guard

Exercise 2.9

1. . . . birth process for monkeys, gorillas, and humans.
2. . . . her neighbor screamed . . .
3. . . . police officers must be in proper uniform . . .
4. . . . is staffed at all times . . .
5. . . . elected to chair the League . . . (or elected head of the League).
6. . . . included people from France, Germany, Sweden, and Scotland.
7. . . . is a doctor from Pittsburgh. (Indicate her gender in subsequent reference.)
8. . . . three girls and two boys . . . (or three women and two men, but don't indicate gender at all unless it is relevant to the story).

3 Persuasive and Ethical Communication

In this chapter you will review the art and science of communication—what it is and what it isn't. It's a false notion that research is tedious and theory is impractical. Research can be both interesting and illuminating, and theory can be a functional tool. For public relations writers, both are helpful approaches that provide guidelines and suggestions for creating messages that are meaningful. They offer many guidelines and practical suggestions about how to be influential and effective in using message sources and message content.

The chapter also looks at the social environment for public relations communication. While encouraging a strong ethical base to the professional, the chapter also provides an overview of propaganda, an unethical aspect of persuasive communication. Here are your learning objectives for Chapter 3:

- To understand various theories about communication
- To explain the role of persuasion in public relations writing
- To apply lessons from persuasion theory in your writing
- To explain the difference between persuasion and propaganda.

Theories of Public Communication

Researchers and theorists from many backgrounds have offered insights into the nature of **public communication**—the range of communication that extends beyond the purely personal interaction between people or small groups. The relevant research can be divided into three areas: the process of communication, the object of communication, and the effects of communication. Understanding each of these areas helps the public relations writer be more effective, because theory offers guidance and insight into what works, why it works, and how it might work under different circumstances.

Process of Communication

Sociologist Harold Lasswell gave a classic definition of communication: who says what in which channel to whom, with what effect. That was in 1948. More than half a century later, the question of what public communication is remains important to public relations writers.

Claude Shannon and Warren Weaver's **mathematical theory of communication**, better known as **information theory**, grew out of the field of telecommunications. Shannon and

Weaver observe that an information source produces a message that is converted by a transmitter and sent via some channel to a receiver that reconstructs the message for the destination person. The clarity of this message may be reduced by **noise**, defined as something added to the signal not intended by the source. Noise can take many forms, including the linguistic clutter that the writing reminders in the previous chapter would help you avoid. One way to offset message disintegration caused by noise is to introduce redundancy, the deliberate repetition of the message. What this means is that the more that noise causes the message to become distorted and misunderstood, the greater the need for repetition of the message. This is why public relations practitioners are seldom content to present a one-time-only message, but rather are continually seeking ways to repeat and reinforce the message.

The concept of **feedback** was drawn from **systems theory**, particularly Norbert Wiener's 1954 treatise on **cybernetics**, a field of study that deals with sensors and control mechanisms. With a better understanding of the role of feedback in the communication process, public relations writers try to create opportunities for organizations to talk with their publics rather than talking at them. Wilbur Schramm observed this instrumental approach to communication and outlined what has become a classic model. The message begins with the sender, who encodes it in some way and transmits it through a signal to a destination where it is decoded by the receiver.

Object of Communication

It's perhaps the most famous koan of the Western world: If a tree falls in the forest and no one is nearby, does it make a sound? Let's give the question a communication twist: If you give a speech that no one hears, are you communicating? If you write a news release that doesn't get published, are you communicating?

A concept useful for public relations writing is that communication is a **receiver phenomenon**. Communication is not controlled by the sender but rather by the receiver. The speaker may be gifted, even eloquent, but if the speech is in Swahili and the audience does not understand Swahili, no real communication takes place. If the message is presented in sign language, Arabic script, Morse code, Japanese katakana, or any other system of language presentation that the audience does not understand, communication is thwarted.

The communication process can be blocked in many ways. As public relations writers, we should understand that our audiences will always be in control of the communication process. They will choose whether to pay attention to a message. Their interests and abilities will determine if they understand the message, and eventually it will be their choice whether to act on it in any way.

For the public relations writer, meaning is a rich concept with many opportunities, some pitfalls, and much room for effective creativity. Sven Windahl and Benno Signitzer, two contemporary European communication scholars, offer a model showing how meaning can take on different shapes during the communication process. They trace the evolution of the message as it was intended, sent, structured, received, and perceived. If public relations writers are to communicate clearly, we should take into account factors such as interpretation, control, intermediaries, connotation, and denotation.

One of the earliest theories to focus on the receiver in the communication process was the **uses-and-gratifications theory** associated with researchers Elihu Katz and Jay Blumler. This theory suggests that people make choices in selecting media for particular purposes. Among those reasons are information, entertainment, value reassurance, social interaction, and emotional release. Technologies such as interactive cable and information-on-demand rely on the validity of the uses-and-gratifications theory.

Martin Fishbein helped lay the groundwork for the related **expectancy-value theory**, which observes that people make media choices based on what they want, what they expect from the media, and how they evaluate the ability of the media to meet those expectations. Sandra Ball-Rokeach and Melvin DeFleur, meanwhile, developed the **dependency theory** that audiences, the media, and society in general are in a three-way relationship.

Audiences use the media to the extent that the media provide information important to society and people's role in it. The more relevant that information is, the more influential the media become.

Effect of Communication

Throughout the latter half of the 20th century and into the 21st, social scientists have been researching the roles that media play in impacting on people's interests and attitudes, opinions and behaviors. The decades have seen the pendulum swing in both directions.

Powerful Effects. Theories from the first third of the 20th century presumed a **powerful effects model** for the mass media, in which researchers concluded that the media exert a direct, strong, and predictable influence over people's attitudes, opinions, and behavior. Terms such as **bullet theory** and **hypodermic needle theory** are associated with this cause-and-effect relationship between message and response. This model drew on **stimulus-response theory** or **conditioned reflex theory**, a simple approach typified by famous experiments by Ivan Pavlov, who conditioned dogs to anticipate food when they heard a particular sound. Closely associated with this approach is the **operant conditioning theory** of B.F. Skinner focusing on the role of reinforcement of behavior in creating attitude change.

The conditioning orientation of such theories does not translate well to public communication, however, because publics can be very complex. These learning-based theories suggest that certain information presented in a particular way causes people to arrive at a specific conclusion. Sometimes this works, especially when audiences have little personal interest in the issue at hand. But the more personally audiences are involved in an issue, the less useful these cognitive theories are to public relations writers.

Limited Effects. Around the middle of the previous century, the powerful effects model gave way to a **limited effects model** that saw communication as being a weak influence over people. Educators Joseph Klapper and Hope Lunin Klapper argued that public communication ordinarily does not cause significant audience effects and has minimal consequence.

Closely associated with this model is the **two-step flow of communication theory**. Two social science researchers, Paul Lazarsfeld and Elihu Katz, studied communication and voting, identifying a predictable communication pattern. Instead of directly changing attitudes, they found, the media may influence opinion leaders, who then influence others through interpersonal means. Lazarsfeld eventually extended this idea into a **multistep flow of communication theory** which identifies several layers in the process.

Moderate-to-Powerful Effects. During the past several decades, the pendulum has swung back toward where it was a century ago. This stage of research is leading to a **moderate-to-powerful effects model**. Several researchers have shown that public media have strong, long-term effects on audiences and on public opinion, though these do not occur easily or predictably.

George Gerbner's **cultivation theory** reasons that exposure to public media cultivates a person's perceptions and expectations, with a major difference between heavy and light TV viewers. One primary cultivation effect Gerbner reports is that heavy viewers have a perception of a "mean world," with exaggerated fear, distrust, and pessimism. Meanwhile, Elisabeth Noelle-Neumann's **spiral of silence theory** suggests that one media effect may actually be to hinder the communication process by giving people an exaggerated sense of isolation and a reluctance to express their opinions if they learn that their opinion seems not to be shared by others. Psychologist Albert Bandura's **social learning theory** suggests that the media provide examples, or modeling, that become part of a personal reality to which audiences respond. Newer studies in the media's long-term effects on issues such as violence, sexuality, and citizenship tend to boost the return to the powerful effects model.

In 1922, journalist Walter Lippmann identified an imagined pseudoenvironment constructed by the media that impacts public opinion. In 1972, journalism professors Donald Shaw and Maxwell McCombs extended this to the **agenda-setting theory** of the media, in which the media direct not what people think but rather what they think about. This observation has important implications for public relations practitioners, who try both to link organizational issues with those on the media agenda and to interest the media in issues important to the organization.

Associated with the agenda-setting theory are the related concepts of **priming**, how a news topic reminds media audiences of previous information, and **framing**, the way the news media treat a particular topic. If agenda setting deals with what people think about, priming reminds them what they already know about the topic, and framing deals with how they think about the topic. Here is an example of framing. Many U.S. states are concerned with the issue of taxation or lack of taxation on Indian lands. Research from the American Indian Policy and Media Initiative at Buffalo State College points out that most mainstream news media unquestioningly adopt the framing language of state government, which often talks about "losing" money because of untaxed sales on Indian lands. Seldom do reporters frame the story from a Native perspective: that because Indian lands are controlled by federal treaty and are not subject to state government, the states have no legal claim in the first place to the money they lament losing. Because framing offers a perspective on the news and presents a lens through which to make sense of the world, public relations writers often are quite concerned about how their message is framed by the media.

Exercise 3.1

Freewriting on Communication Theory

Freewrite for five minutes on the following topic: *How are theories about communication useful to a public writer?* Discuss this with your classmates.

Communication and Persuasion

In Chapter 1 you were asked to view communication not as an either-or (either informational or promotional) but rather to understand that all public relations writing seeks to influence people in some way. Both-and is the operative metaphor. You may present information both in the neutral style of journalistic writing, and you may weave it into promotional formats. But whatever the format, you will use information to foster various effects. These are the objectives discussed in the previous section.

What is **persuasive communication**? The term means different things to people. A lot of conflicting connotations revolve around the notion of persuasion, with subtle differences in how people interpret it.

Persuasion

Various perspectives about persuasion exist, but for our purposes as public relations writers, let's claim the following understanding: **Persuasion** is a process of communication that intends to influence people using ethical means that enhance a democratic society. Let's look more closely at each part of this definition.

Persuasion is a process of communication. Public relations writers focus on communication, so the role of messages and feedback is important to us. Further, understanding communication as a process helps us look at persuasion as an ongoing series of messages and responses, part of the cycle of interaction between an organization and its many publics.

Persuasion intends to influence people. If we are to profit by a deeper understanding of persuasion, we need to see it as being linked with people, our target publics. In public relations, we are trying to provide information that will influence our publics in some way or enhance our relationship with them.

Persuasion uses ethical means. For the public relations writer, any attempt at persuasion must be based on solid professional standards. If communication becomes misleading, deceptive, or manipulative—by intention or through negligence—it has moved beyond the legitimate boundaries of persuasion. For some people, persuasion has a tarnished image because subversive communication techniques have occasionally been used to manipulate unknowing or gullible publics. For the public relations writer, however, persuasion is a noble concept because, by definition, it is not debased into misinformation or propaganda.

Persuasion enhances a democratic society. Philosophically and legally, organizations may try to persuade. In a democratic society, individuals and organizations enjoy the right of free speech that allows them to espouse a point of view, share it in the marketplace of ideas, and attempt to influence others to adopt that point of view. One of the basic roles of public relations people is to help organizations exercise this right. But people who receive an organization's messages must be seen as having the freedom not to be persuaded. Public relations practitioners must uphold a person's right to ignore or reject our messages.

Communication that doesn't meet these criteria should not be called persuasion. If communication makes no attempt to influence, by definition it is not trying to persuade. If communication is unethical or immoral, it instead should be called propaganda, not persuasive communication. And if the goal of communication is not to enhance relationships within an open society, then it is self-serving, nonresponsive, and involved in something other than persuasion.

Historical Roots

The art of persuasion is an ancient one, deeply rooted in classical civilization. More than 4,000 years ago, the philosopher Ptah-Hotep advised court speakers in Egypt to link their messages to the concern of the audiences. In the 5th century B.C.E. in the northern Mediterranean, the rhetorician Corax of Syracuse wrote a book about persuasive speaking.

Meanwhile in Greece, Socrates of Athens and his student, Plato, studied and practiced **rhetoric**, the art of persuasive communication. Plato's student, Aristotle, later wrote "Rhetoric," a treatise discussing persuasion as the art of proving something to be true or false. In Rome, Marcus Tullius Cicero developed this rhetorical method for presenting persuasive arguments in public, and Marcus Fabius Quintilianus taught about the ethical content of persuasion.

Religion played a role in applying and handing on the rhetorical tradition. The early Christian Church preserved and enhanced the concepts of Greek and Roman rhetoric. In Roman Africa in the 4th and 5th centuries, Augustine of Hippo developed the art of preaching, insisting that truth is the ultimate goal of such public speaking. Later, in northern Europe during the 8th century, the Saxon theologian Alcuin reinterpreted Roman rhetorical teachings for the Emperor Charlemagne.

For a time after the fall of Roman civilization, Aristotle was lost to much of the Western world. Muslim scholars, Christian Arabs, and Arabic-speaking Jews introduced Aristotle's teaching on rhetoric to the Islamic world during the 9th century. In the centuries that followed, Aristotle was reintroduced to the West, mainly via translations through Arabic and by the writings of both Arab and Jewish scholars. In the 14th century, the Christian philosopher-monk Thomas Aquinas revisited Aristotle to study the persuasive nature of religious communication.

Throughout the centuries, the various branches of the Christian Church developed the area of **apologetics**, the systematic attempt to assert the reasonableness of faith and to refute opposing arguments. Modern-day preachers and evangelists continue this tradition in persuasive communication for religious purposes. Following in their footsteps are the secular advocates of self-fulfillment who figure prominently in television infomercials that promote everything from financial independence to physical attractiveness or emotional fulfillment.

Persuasive communication has been at the heart of much of Western social and political development. It is a fundamental element of democracy that played a major role in the American Revolution, with examples such as Thomas Paine and Samuel Adams. The American movements for abolition, women's suffrage, civil rights, and gay rights all have drawn heavily on the concepts and applications of persuasive communication, as has most war rhetoric in recent decades.

Just as persuasion is an ancient art, it also is becoming a contemporary science. This is true nowhere more than in the political arena. Recent political campaigns have become sophisticated strategic experiments with in-depth research, nuanced crafting of messages, careful and costly implementation, and ongoing evaluation. Meanwhile, throughout much of the 20th century, social scientists dealing with psychology, sociology, and communication have given increasing scholarly attention to persuasive communication.

Attention to persuasive communication is primarily a product of Western, European-based civilization. Asian, African, Semitic, and Native American traditions generally have put a lesser premium on influencing others. The philosophers and linguists of these cultures more often have focused on storytelling, the graceful use of language, the development of consensus, even the communicative value of silence. Don't interpret this observation as suggesting that persuasive communication is not a universal aspect of human interaction, or that certain cultures are incapable of being persuasive. It simply points out the priority in Western culture for a social assertiveness and a preference for the more functional aspects of language.

Research on Persuasion

Many theories about persuasive communication draw heavily on the field of social and personal psychology, since persuasion is seen as a personal phenomenon rather than simply an issue about the techniques and process of communication. Other theories deal more specifically with personality.

Social Psychology Research

One set of theories about persuasion revolves around the observation that people seek consistency between attitudes and information about those attitudes. The message source is an important factor in these consistency theories. The **balance theory** or **consonance theory** associated with Fritz Heider and the **symmetry theory** proposed by Theodore Newcomb suggest that people seek an attitude similar to that of their communication partners. They will agree or disagree with a person not only because of what that person says but also because of their relationship with the other person.

The implications of these consistency-based theories for public relations writers is that we can foster persuasion by building on good relationships between a source and our publics.

The **congruity theory** developed by psychologists Charles Osgood and Percy Tannenbaum suggests that people experience confusion when two attitudes are in conflict. Usually, this is resolved by the adoption of the easier attitude or by a blend of opposing attitudes. Similarly, the **cognitive dissonance theory** articulated by Leon Festinger focuses on the confusion that arises when information is out of step with a person's attitude. People will try to reduce the confusion, perhaps by changing the attitude but more likely by avoiding or ignoring the negative information, by seeking positive information to replace it, or simply by distorting or reinterpreting it to fit their attitudes.

Cognitive dissonance theory helps explain why public relations writers are sometimes frustrated because our publics don't seem to act on information in the way we think they should. Closely related to cognitive dissonance are several concepts dealing with selectivity.

Through **selective exposure** and **selective avoidance**, people expose themselves to messages they think they will like and avoid what they expect not to like. These choices apparently are made because of personal interest rather than a deliberate avoidance of opposing viewpoints. Using **selective attention**, people pay attention to information that supports their attitudes and ignore information opposed to their attitudes. With both selective exposure and selective attention, we pay attention to what interests us. **Selective perception** leads people to interpret information based on how it fits their attitudes; we see what we want to see and what we expect to see. Similarly, using **selection retention** people remember information that is of interest and forget information that seems not to be relevant to them. Finally, via **selective recall**, people are more likely to remember information that supports their attitudes and conveniently forget conflicting information; we remember primarily what supports our beliefs.

Researchers Muzafer Sherif and Carl Hovland offered the **social judgment theory** which states that attitude change is more a change in a person's perception rather than a change in belief. From this theory, the writer may find it more useful to focus on presenting a new image about a client or organization rather than trying to change the beliefs and values of members of a target public.

Another area of theory into the process of persuasive communication returns to the threefold classical Greek emphasis articulated by Aristotle: **ethos** (source credibility), **pathos** (appeals to emotion or sentiment), and **logos** (appeals to logic or reason).

Personality Research

Two personality-based approaches are **psychological type theory**, stemming from Carl Jung and modified by Isabel Myers and Catherine Briggs, and **temperament theory**, a modification of the Myers–Briggs approach by David Keirsey and Marilyn Bates.

These related theories suggest that innate personality factors give each person a predisposition toward certain types of persuasive techniques. Some people are naturally more attracted to facts, figures, and cause-and-effect examples. Others are persuaded more by nuance, a touching story, a poignant example, or personal application. These theories offer much potential when public relations writers are able to match appropriate message styles with the personalities of their publics.

An outgrowth of personality theory is the field of **psychographics**, the study of consumer lifestyles. One model is VALS (Value and Lifestyles), a consumer segmentation system developed in 1978 by Arnold Mitchell and the Stanford Research Institute of Menlo Park, Calif. It was revised in 1989 as VALS2, incorporating newer lifestyle trends and providing greater application to strategic communication in areas such as marketing, advertising, promotions, and public relations. VALS identifies categories of people such as actualizers, fulfillers, believers, achievers, strivers, experiencers, makers, and strugglers, based on the resources at their disposal and on their orientation inwardly or outwardly. Such studies into psychographics can help persuaders better understand the motivation of various publics.

Another system with application to persuasive communication is **geodemographics**, which combines sociology, geography, and demography to segment the country into neighborhood or residential types. This is based on the presumption that such segmentation identifies categories of people with similar lifestyles, values, attitudes, and consumer patterns. With this model, public relations practitioners can target messages to publics on the basis of where they can be reached and the types of people associated with particular environments. A prime application of geodemographics is the PRIZM classification developed by the Claritas Corporation of Alexandria, Va., which links ZIP codes with sociographic and psychographic characteristics of residents. Other applications are GeoVALS, a blending of the traditional VALS segmentation with geodemographic data, and Strategic Mapping's ClusterPLUS, developed for marketing and customer-relationship purposes.

Exercise 3.2

Freewriting on Persuasion and Public Relations

Part 1: Look up each of the following words in your dictionary and write a brief definition: advocate, convince, entice, induce, influence, manipulate, persuade.

Part 2: Freewrite for five minutes on the following topic: *How does persuasion fit into the activities of a public relations writer?* Then discuss this with your classmates.

Lessons from Research

So far, this chapter has dealt with many of the theories related to communication and persuasion. The value of a theory is its ability to help us develop guidelines and make predictions. So let's put these theories to work.

The following guidelines are drawn from various researchers who have studied communication and persuasion over many years. Some guidelines are the result of several concurring studies; others are less conclusive, even speculative. They are offered here not as a list of dos and don'ts but rather as a series of tips and idea generators.

Message Source

The source of a message, both the organization and the spokesperson, is important to any consideration of public relations writing. Some sources are better than others because they are more likely to be believed by a particular public. Carl Hovland was one of the first researchers to study the issue of **source credibility**, and his work still offers much insight into source effectiveness.

An effective communicator is a person or organization perceived by an audience as having the Three Cs—credibility, charisma, and control. In each category, note that the focus is on how the audience perceives a source, warranted or not. Let's look at the Three Cs of an effective communicator.

Credibility. A communicator with **credibility** is one who has expertise to speak about a particular subject, a recognized status or prestige, and a competence to communicate effectively, as well as apparent honesty, sincerity, and lack of bias.

Credibility is particularly enhanced by **expertise**. The source of a message that has expert knowledge or experience regarding the subject is more credible; people are more likely to believe those who seem to know what they are talking about. The public relations writer can increase a communicator's credibility by emphasizing his or her education or personal experience. Likewise, audiences tend to put their faith in message sources with **status**, that is, with recognized social or organizational standing—also something the public relations writer can draw attention to. Credibility is also enhanced by a message source with **communication competence**, a speaker who is composed, articulate, and, if not eloquent, at least proficient in oral communication. In addition, credibility is enhanced by **sincerity**, the character of trustworthiness. People are likely to believe someone who is reliable and honorable. Sources are especially credible when they appear to be unbiased. This is apparent when message sources speak apart from their expected positions, particularly when they speak against their own apparent self-interests or when they speak on behalf of organizations or causes other than their own.

Charisma. A communicator with **charisma** is one who is likable and who may be familiar to the audience, similar to the audience, and/or physically attractive.

Athletes and entertainers are sought after to endorse products and speak for causes because audiences tend to believe sources they admire and respect. This **likability** is an ambiguous characteristic that often differs even among various members of the same target public. Closely related is **familiarity**, the characteristic of being known by the audience. These two characteristics account for the frequent use of celebrity spokespeople, who audiences know (or think they know) and like.

Meanwhile, a source who shares characteristics with the audience may be more effective in persuasion than someone without those similarities. This **similarity** has many dimensions such as age, gender, race, ethnicity, occupation, and affiliations. Shared attitudes are even stronger than demographic similarities. Audiences sometimes are more easily persuaded by

attractiveness, that is, by someone whom the audience considers to be physically appealing, handsome, beautiful, or sexy. This, however, is the least effective attribute of a persuasive source. And in some cases, physical attractiveness can work against a source's persuasive power by diminishing other, more important characteristics such as credibility.

Control. A communicator who exhibits the characteristic of **control** is one who has power or authority over the audience or who is in a position to examine and pass judgment over the audience. Audiences are more likely to be persuaded by someone in a position of **power** or **authority**. That is why employers, teachers, and particularly parents are effective persuaders. Another aspect of control is **scrutiny**, the ability of a message source to investigate members of the audience, hold them accountable in some way, and pass judgment on them.

Research dealing with sources of persuasive communication suggests the following applications for public relations writers.

- Highly credible sources are more likely to be perceived as being fair and their conclusions viewed as justified. Some studies have reported attitude change 3½ times more often when the source is highly credible.
- A positive message from a stranger has more impact than the same message from a friend, probably because praise from a stranger seems more sincere than when it comes from a friend. Similarly, a negative message from a friend has more impact than criticism from a stranger, probably because it is seen as more sincere.
- The credibility of an original source is enhanced when the message is reiterated by an opinion leader.
- Likable sources are perceived as more credible only when the audience has little personal involvement in the issue. With issues of higher personal involvement, likability is not a significant factor.
- Sources that are very attractive physically risk distracting audiences, who sometimes remember the source but not the message.
- Highly credible sources are especially effective in persuading audiences to change attitudes immediately after their presentation of the message. This effectiveness decreases over time.
- Attitude change produced by a noncredible source increases over time. This so-called **sleeper effect** suggests that at first people may consciously reject a message from a source they dislike or distrust, but that over time their memory of the source may fade while they remember the message. Some researchers argue that such a sleeper effect does not exist.

Public relations writers should remember that message sources are not only persons. Organizations are also seen as sources. Writers should consider that the way an organization is perceived, especially its visibility and reputation, has an impact on its effectiveness as a source in persuasive communication.

For example, reputations for quality and responsibility helped both Johnson & Johnson's Tylenol survive the cyanide emergency and Pepsi-Cola deal with the syringe hoax. But obvious self-interest has rendered the tobacco industry unable to convince the public to disbelieve links between smoking and ill health. And Philip Morris tobacco company received a lot of criticism when it created a costly TV advertising campaign to congratulate itself on making a modest charitable contribution. The reputation of focusing on profits above the public interest led to major and lingering problems for Big Business, particularly companies such as BP,

Exxon, Texaco, and other players in the "Big Oil" arena who have been embroiled for years over various industrial and consumer problems.

Many organizations enjoy a favorable perception or reputation with the public, but even this is very changeable. Polls show that big institutions—medicine, law, religion, higher education, and the media—have lost some credibility. They have to work harder in their persuasive communication to remain effective communicators. Other institutions including government, politics, and business traditionally have been viewed with significant skepticism, causing special difficulties for their public relations writers. "Tips for Better Writing—Effective Message Sources" contains all the elements that should be taken into consideration when choosing a message source.

Tips for Better Writing *Effective Message Sources*

Use this checklist to make sure you have included each of the major elements of an effective message source.

- Credibility, based on one or more of the following elements:
  - Expertise, experience
  - Status, prestige
  - Communication competence
  - Honesty, sincerity, lack of bias.
- Charisma, based on one or more of the following elements:
  - Likability
  - Familiarity to the audience
  - Similarity to the audience
  - Physical attractiveness.
- Control, based on one or more of the following elements:
  - Power over the audience
  - Control over the audience
  - Ability to scrutinize or pass judgment on the audience.

Exercise 3.3

Effective Message Sources

You are a public relations writer for the local sheriff's department, assigned to develop a public service video aimed at high school students. The message is: Don't drink and drive on prom night. The sheriff has asked for your recommendations for a spokesperson for the video, which will be disseminated via television and over the Internet. Prepare the following information.

Part 1: Because the sheriff likes to have choices, identify three possible spokespersons to present your message. Analyze each as to their likely effectiveness as the source of persuasive communication, based on the Three Cs of an effective communicator, as noted above.

Part 2: Indicate your recommendation of the spokesperson you think would be most effective in persuading your target public. Justify this choice by discussing the particular elements of persuasive message sources that are evident in your choice.

Message Structure

Various research studies have found that the structure of a message can significantly affect the persuasion process. Specifically, researchers have looked at three elements of structure—the order of presentation, the value of drawing conclusions or making recommendations, and repetition within the message itself. Following are some of the lessons that can be drawn from this research.

- No significant difference exists between presenting arguments in order of least-to-most important or vice versa.
- Though research findings are not conclusive, many practitioners have found that it is usually best to sandwich the arguments. Present your own argument first, refute opposing arguments, then restate your own argument.
- The final word is the one most likely to be remembered by the audience, especially with less educated audiences or ones less personally involved in the issue.
- Presenting two sides of an argument is more effective than giving only one side, especially with sophisticated or educated audiences. This is especially important when the audience eventually will be exposed to a contrary message.
- Presentation of only one side of an argument may cause temporary attitudinal change, but this can be wiped out when the audience later hears opposing arguments. Presentation of both sides of an argument results in an even larger attitude change than presentation of only one side, and this change is likely to remain high even if the audience later hears opposing arguments.
- Drawing a conclusion or making a recommendation is usually more persuasive than leaving it to the audience to draw the conclusion.
- Some evidence suggests that if an audience draws its own conclusion, it is more likely to resist changing that attitude in the future.
- Messages, especially those presented through the public media, are quickly forgotten if they are not at least moderately reinforced by repetition.
- Repetition is useful for keeping issues on the public agenda. It has also been shown to be helpful in increasing actions such as voter turnout.
- Too much repetition can cause the audience to tire of the message to the point of disagreeing with it.

Message Content

Research has looked at the content of messages, especially the relationship between emotion and logic, **fear appeals** or appeals to guilt, the use of humor and sex appeal. Here are some observations based on that research:

- A combination of factual and emotional appeals is more effective than either approach alone. By some criteria, two-thirds of the American population prefers factual presentations.
- Messages that are directed to the self-interests of the audience are more likely to gain audience awareness and interest.
- Appeals to fear, guilt, and other negative emotions, as well as the presentations of threats to the audience, can cause the audience to avoid or distort the message.
- With moderate interest levels, low-to-moderate fear appeals can be more effective than strong fear appeals in producing attitude change.

- If the audience has a high interest level, strong fear appeals may be more effective in changing attitudes than weaker appeals. Fear appeals are also more persuasive when presented by sources with high credibility.
- Fear appeals are more effective when coupled with reassurances and specific recommendations for corrective action to reduce fears.
- A mix of advocacy and entertainment is more acceptable than advocacy alone.
- Fear appeals can affect acceptance and behavioral intentions without having subsequent impact on action. Specific instructions with fear appeals can affect action first without affecting either attitude or opinion.
- Three aspects make fear appeals persuasive: the degree of harm, the likelihood of harm, and the likelihood of an effective solution to eliminate the harm.
- Humor is more effective in increasing awareness and generating interest than in producing changes in attitude or action.
- Humor sometimes can generate a liking for the message source, but this can backfire if the audience thinks the use of humor is a manipulative device. The determining factor may be if the humor seems natural or contrived and whether it's appropriate to the subject.
- Humor sometimes causes audiences to evaluate a message not on its persuasive content but merely as an entertainment vehicle.
- Appeals based on humor quickly lose their persuasive effect with repetition.
- Appeals based on sex appeal, such as the use of alluring models, can enhance the awareness and interest of audiences, especially younger ones.

Exercise 3.4

Effective Message Content

Part 1: Using the persuasive communicator you identified in Exercise 3.3, write a brief message (150–200 words) for a radio spot aimed at high school students. The purpose is to persuade them not to drink and drive as they celebrate their prom and graduation.

Part 2: Annotate this message by writing margin notes or footnotes to identify the persuasive tactics you use related to message structure and message content.

Media Factors

Research has looked at the media in relation to persuasion in an attempt to learn if some channels of communication are more effective in the persuasion process than other channels. Here are some of the insights stemming from this research.

- Face-to-face communication is more effective in changing attitudes than messages presented through any type of media.
- Speech produces less comprehension than a written message, but more acceptance.
- Little difference exists between intense oral exhortations and more subdued speaking. Both types of speech are more persuasive than written messages.

- Personal communication is more likely to be persuasive in all three categories of effects: awareness, acceptance and action.
- Public media are better at reinforcing existing attitudes than in changing attitudes.
- Public media may produce modification or minor attitude change but rarely can they convert audiences to the opposite point of view.
- Public media have more effect on weak or new attitudes than on established ones. The implication for public relations writers may be to use news and advertising media to reach neutrals and to seek early adoption of attitudes in new situations.
- A combination of public media and personal communication is more effective in changing attitudes than either type of communication alone.
- Print media produce greater attention and voluntary re-exposure than electronic media.
- Print media produce more comprehension, especially with complex issues, than broadcast media.
- Broadcast media produce more attention than print media.
- There is little difference in the persuasive effectiveness of mediated communication. In one study, a message was equally effective in written, audiotaped, and videotaped formats.
- Televised or videotaped presentations heighten the impact of source factors.

Audience Factors

Much research also has been conducted with a focus on the audience receiving the persuasive message, leading to the following applications.

- Unsubstantiated messages produce more attitude change in people with low self-esteem than in people with higher self-esteem.
- People with high self-esteem are more likely to be persuaded by complex and well-substantiated messages. Those with low self-esteem are more likely to be persuaded by fear appeals.
- Audiences that make a commitment or personal decision are likely to resist subsequent pressures to change attitudes and opinions.
- The more involved the audience is in the persuasive situation, the more likely the persuasion will be effective. For example, low-involvement communication situations such as television viewing are less persuasive than high-involvement situations such as face-to-face communication.
- Audiences that participate actively in making decisions, such as role playing or assessing alternative solutions, retain attitude change over longer periods of time.
- A few studies have suggested that women may be more easily persuaded than men. But the conclusion here is weak and inconsistent.
- Some studies have shown that men are more persuasive as message sources than women are, regardless of the gender of the receiver. Other studies suggest that societal changes are eliminating any gender differences in persuasion.

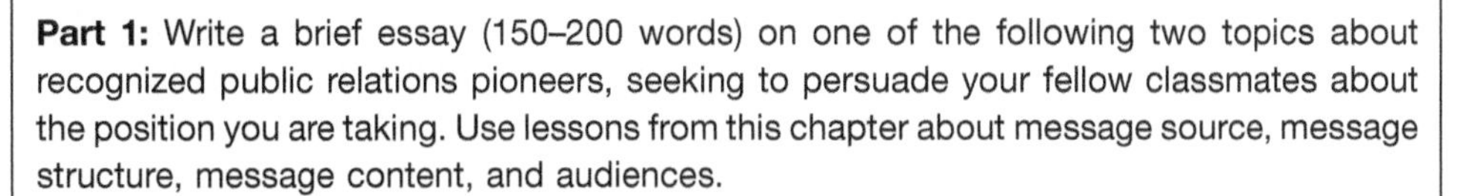

Exercise 3.5

Persuasive Messages

Part 1: Write a brief essay (150–200 words) on one of the following two topics about recognized public relations pioneers, seeking to persuade your fellow classmates about the position you are taking. Use lessons from this chapter about message source, message structure, message content, and audiences.

- Ivy Lee manipulated information and misled the public in his campaign to rehabilitate the image of John D. Rockefeller. Therefore, he should not be considered a model of ethical public relations because . . . *OR* Nevertheless, he can be considered a model of ethical public relations because . . .
- Edward Bernays exploited people and risked their health by encouraging women to smoke cigarettes in public. Therefore, he should not be considered a model of ethical public relations because . . . *OR* Nevertheless, he can be considered a model of ethical public relations because . . .

Part 2: After you have written this essay, write margin notes or footnotes to indicate the lessons in this section you used to design your persuasive message.

Propaganda

Earlier in this chapter, we defined persuasion as a process of communication that intends to influence using ethical means which enhance a democratic society. Persuasion plays many important and useful roles in society. For example, organizations attempt to persuade people to drive defensively, avoid unhealthy diets, and reduce the risk of disease. Advertisers try to convince consumers to use a company's products or services. Charities solicit contributions from donors to achieve a social good. Groups lobby government officials or advocate in public forums to generate support for their causes or programs.

Each of these examples of persuasive communication seeks voluntary change. Each involves the skillful presentation of an argument in an attempt to convince someone about the rightness of a cause, the value of a service, or the merit of an idea—all ethical and respectable goals. But a darker side to persuasive communication can be seen in activities such as false advertising, information campaigns that withhold important facts, and deliberate misrepresentations by public officials. This type of persuasion is **propaganda**—persuasive communication gone bad.

Propaganda did not always have a bad reputation. The word itself is related to *propagate*, meaning "to grow" or "to publicize." As a synonym for persuasive communication, it grew out of the name of the Catholic Church's 17th-century missionary activity, the Congregatio de Propaganda Fide (Congregation for the Propagation of the Faith). Until the early 1900s, the term was commonly used to mean information, promotion, and persuasion. Even the founders of the public relations profession, such as Edward Bernays, used *propaganda* as a synonym for promotion and publicity.

Gradually though, in the popular mind, the word came to be associated with deceptive communication efforts, stemming largely from the Nazi propaganda bureau of the 1930s, and more recently with disinformation campaigns of the 1950s and 1960s Cold War and even more recent governmental and political operations that have used news and information as a weapon to discredit and deceive.

The problem with propaganda, as the term now is understood, is not that it promotes ideological causes but that it does so dishonestly. Propaganda sneaks its message into an unsuspecting audience and indoctrinates people without their realizing what is happening. It is communication that conceals the identity of the source or the purpose of the message, and in doing so tries to manipulate rather than persuade.

In 1925, when public relations was in its infancy, Ivy Lee warned of the dangers of propaganda and helped set an ethical tone for the emerging profession. Addressing the American Association of Teachers of Journalism, he explained that the "essential evil of propaganda is failure to disclose the source of information." Lee took a consumer approach. He advised editors to use good judgment when information reached their desks, and he urged the public to "exercise your right to demand knowledge as to the source of the information."

Persuasion versus Propaganda

Observers of society and how persuasion has been attempted have identified several categories of propaganda. Some are persuasive tactics that can be used ethically in some circumstances; others have little if any ethical applications and rightly fall under the designation of propaganda tactics.

Public relations writers should be careful with all of the following writing techniques, which can easily degenerate into oversimplification and deception. Here is a common listing for persuasive tactics that can also become tools of propaganda. Each tactic raises ethical issues for public relations writers.

The first five tactics—plain folks, testimonial, bandwagon, transfer, and repetition—are sometimes used by public relations writers.

The technique of **plain folk appeal** tries to convince the audience that the message source is unsophisticated, average, just like you and me. It has been used by everybody from Abraham Lincoln to Adolf Hitler. The ethical public relations writer will be satisfied that the impression is accurate before using such an appeal.

Testimonials involve the supportive words or images of a well-known and supposed expert. Social causes use celebrities such as Daniel Radcliffe for a crisis support program for gay and bisexual young people, Sandra Bullock and Dave Matthews for restoring the Gulf of Mexico after the oil spill, and Chris Rock on global warming. Corporations also feature celebrity testimonials. For example, Nike uses many athletes including LeBron James, Alex Rodriguez, Derek Jeter, Ronaldinho, Roger Federer, Michael Jordan, even Tiger Woods after his scandalous fall from grace. The ethical public relations writer will ask several questions: Does the so-called expert really have a particular knowledge of the subject? Has the expert actually used the product or supported the cause? Is the testimony paid for? Is the testimony legitimate?

Parades are led by **bandwagons** that get the ambivalent crowds revved up and raring to go. As a communication technique, it presents the suggestion that "Everyone else is doing it, so why not you? Don't be the last kid on the block to buy this, wear that, smoke this, drink that." The ethical public relations writer will ask if the momentum is beneficial and warranted.

The **transfer** technique associates a respected symbol for something else. We wrap the nation's flag around an idea and then appeal to the public's patriotism, or we try to identify our cause with symbols of godliness or goodness, purity or political correctness. Conversely, we accuse political opponents of being unpatriotic or immoral. The ethical public relations writer will avoid associations that are questionable exaggerations.

Repetition is the presentation of the same information or official line over and over again. When it lacks an ethical base, it becomes "the big lie," an outrageous falsehood that some hearers accept when it is repeated often enough. Ethical public relations writers will not use the technique of repetition to provide a foundation for untruths.

The remaining techniques—name calling, card stacking, glittering generalities, and stereotypes—are less frequently used for legitimate public relations purposes, because they carry with them ethical problems in most situations. Public relations writers often find they must expend energy and resources fighting against those techniques that have been turned against their organizations.

The technique of **name calling** is the opposite of the transfer technique. It involves creating scapegoats by associating opponents with unsavory people or ideas, rendering them equally reprehensible. The ethical public relations writer will let the facts speak for themselves without unfairly demeaning people on the other side of the argument.

Card stacking involves giving only one side of the story or deliberately misrepresenting the other side. The ethical public relations writer will try to make the case while admitting that the issue is a complex one with other legitimate points of view.

Glittering generalities are attempts to hide behind vague concepts that nobody could oppose. Politicians picture themselves as patriotic, clergy as godly, doctors as caring. Everyone is for peace, happiness, and freedom. But often such generalities take the place of specifics. The ethical public relations writer will provide specific examples and details on which publics can make informed decisions.

Stereotypes are images people have about members of a particular social group. These highly simplified notions provide a convenient shorthand and often come into play in promotional writing, but an ethical public relations writer will avoid negative stereotypes that denigrate people.

Exercise 3.6

Writing Ethical Messages

You are a public relations writer for an organization seeking to interest college freshmen in one of the following:

- Fitness and exercise
- Gay and lesbian rights
- A local political issue.

Write four persuasive ethical messages of about 25 words each for your organization. The first version of the message should use the plain folks technique; the second version should use the testimonial technique; the third, bandwagon; and the fourth, transfer.

Codes of Ethics

In each of the persuasive/propaganda techniques described above, adherence to ethical standards can offer guidance and direction to help the writer use these persuasive devices properly.

For example, the Member Code of Ethics of the Public Relations Society of America is clear. It advises the practitioner to:

- Serve the public interest
- Exemplify high standards of honesty and integrity
- Build mutual understanding and credibility
- Adhere to the highest standards of accuracy and truth
- Deal fairly with clients and employers, as well as with competitors and the media
- Respect all opinions and promote free expression and the free exchange of unprejudiced communication.

Meanwhile, the Canadian Public Relations Society highlights ethical conduct in its Declaration of Principles and its Code of Professional Standards:

- Obligations of a public trust are inherent in the practice of public relations
- Maintain high standards . . . so as to ensure that public relations shall be esteemed as an honourable profession
- The highest standards of honesty, accuracy, and truth.

Similarly but more simply, the Code of Standards of the International Association of Business Communicators commits members to "the practice of honest, candid and timely communication." The Code of Ethics of the International Public Relations Association calls upon professionals to "establish communications patterns and channels which [foster] the free flow of essential information" and to refrain from "circulating information which is not based on established and ascertainable facts" or "taking part in any venture or undertaking which is unethical or dishonest or capable of impairing human dignity and integrity."

See the online resource, "Ethical Standards," for the complete text of codes of professional ethics (available at: www.routledge.com/cw/smith).

What Would You Do? *Accuracy*

You are a public relations writer for your college or university. Yesterday you sent a news release quoting the treasurer of your school that the operating budget will be short this year by $1,200,000. Today you learn that the figure was inflated; it did not include $400,000 already saved by energy improvements. What is your ethical judgment about how you should act? What do the professional codes advise?

You are preparing a newsletter for a friend who is one of several candidates for a local town council. The major opponent is a married man and father who has built a campaign championing family values. From two different sources, you have heard a rumor about this opponent: that he has a mistress. In addition, a friend of yours who is a police officer has told you confidentially that police once were called for apparent abuse of this woman, though she declined to press charges. What is your ethical judgment about how to act? What do the professional codes advise?

You are a public relations writer for a company that makes plumbing supplies. You are seeking a media placement in the trade press, a monthly magazine read by independent plumbing contractors. You know that buying an advertisement increases the likelihood of news coverage and positive editorial commentary. Such editorial and advertising packages seem to be common within this publication. You have a budget for advertising, to be used at your discretion. What is your ethical judgment about how to act? What do the professional codes advise?

4 The Writing Process

Like other writing genres, public relations writing involves making decisions about various important questions. Who are my publics? What do they know about my organization or client? What do they think about this? What information will be interesting and useful to them? How can I best reach them? How can I inform and persuade them? This chapter will help you with these considerations as you make the decisions that lead to effective writing.

Another ingredient in good writing is a focus on the process of writing itself. Quality writing doesn't take shape instantly. It emerges slowly, one draft after another. Effective public relations writers have learned how to take time with their writing—building and shaping the words, molding, refining, and caressing them.

This chapter will help you identify and analyze your publics, set your objectives, and develop a planning sheet for each writing task. It will introduce you to communication research techniques and will present a nine-step writing process. Here are your learning objectives for Chapter 4:

- To organize a writing project using a planning sheet
- To conduct research for public relations writing
- To use the nine-step process to prepare a publishable piece of writing.

Strategic Planning

Any public relations program or campaign begins with a strong strategic plan, and it is likely that any particular writing task you may undertake will be part of your implementation of such a plan. Since this textbook focuses on public relations writing, it is not the intention here to provide a comprehensive approach to writing goals and objectives or developing strategies. You can find some information on that at the companion website: www.routledge.com/cw/smith.

However, objectives and other aspects of strategic planning are part of developing a public relations campaign. When a specific task comes to a public relations writer, it most likely is part of a broader campaign or program, at least it should be. Thus the objectives and wider strategy will already be known, and the writer will work from within that framework.

The heart of public relations planning is to focus on your **publics**, the people who are the focus of the communication you are planning. Publics are the groups of people who share a common bond or relationship with an organization. They are the groups of people who can affect your organization and be affected by it. Public relations focuses on groups rather than on isolated individuals. Note that there is no such thing as a "general public." Define your publics as specifically as possible. For example, think not merely of "students" as a public for your college or university but the more specific variations: graduate students, entering students, minority students, honor students, commuters, and so on.

Elsewhere in your public relations education you will learn to identify and analyze publics. One method for this is to conduct a **public relations audit**, listing all of the possible publics important to your organization, then prioritizing each and identifying one or a few key publics you want to communicate with for this particular writing project. Note that *Becoming a Public Relations Writer* uses the term **key publics** to identify those specific publics that you identify as being most important to your writing activity. Other books sometimes use the term **target public**, though this seems to suggest that the public is more a bullseye for the organization's darts than part of a reciprocal relationship.

Analysis of Key Publics

For the purposes of this book, we will presume that you already know the key publics, which ideally have been identified in the strategic planning for the campaign or program in which this writing is part. We will pick up on the specific task of the writer: To analyze the key publics so you can understand and empathize with them, and thus be more effective in your writing.

In this analysis, get up close and personal. Delve into the gut-level motivations of your publics. What would interest them? What do they like and dislike? What do they need or think they need? Keep the focus on the needs of your publics, not on what information you want to provide them. Think of WIN (wants, interests, and needs): You will win your publics' support by addressing *their* wants, interests, and needs rather than your own.

Three approaches from the social sciences can help the public relations writer identify the wants, interests, and needs of the key public. One approach comes from sociologist Harold Lasswell, who described eight motivations for people: power, wealth, respect, well-being, affection, skill, rectitude (moral correctness), and enlightenment. He called these **value categories** that he said motivate most people.

Another approach comes from Vance Packard, who used consumer research to identify what he called **hidden persuaders** of marketing: eight compelling but veiled needs of consumers. These are emotional security, reassurance of self-worth, ego gratification, creative outlets, love objects, sense of power, sense of roots, and immortality. Packard's book, called *The Hidden Persuaders*, questions the ethics of using these elements, particularly in the advertising industry.

The third convenient starting point is the **hierarchy of needs** presented by psychologist Abraham Maslow. His typology, generally visualized as a pyramid, presents five levels of basic human needs operating in sequence, separated into lower and higher sections. Here are the four levels at the lower section of Maslow's pyramid:

1. *Survival*: Physiological needs must come first. These include such things as food, water, shelter, and other aspects of self-preservation.
2. *Security*: After survival needs are met, a person can focus on safety concerns such as protection, freedom, financial welfare, structured environment, and future well-being.

3. *Belonging*: Social needs include acceptance, friendship, companionship, peer approval, interpersonal relationships, and group identity, as well as giving and receiving love and intimacy.
4. *Esteem*: When the first three levels of needs are met, a person can address needs such as self-esteem, confidence, appreciation, social accomplishment, and respect.
5. Maslow crowned his pyramid image with a fifth level of needs separated into a category all its own. He noted that an element missing from the first four levels creates tension or a sense of yearning for an individual, while elements in the top level offer people opportunities to explore and add to their sense of accomplishment.
6. *Fulfillment*: When all the other needs are met, a person is free to pursue self-actualization by addressing concerns such as beauty, meaning, creativity, and spiritual insight; and by seeking knowledge, achieving potential, developing talent, and having a sense of purpose.

Though the visual metaphor image is often oversimplified into a single pyramid, the image of the two-part pyramid in Exhibit 4.1 actually is a better reflection of Maslow's theory, showing that the fifth level of needs is significantly different from—and elevated above—the others.

Maslow observed that each level of needs must be satisfied before people are able to pay much attention to the next level. He called this the principal of **prepotency**. For example, a person underwater gasping for breath doesn't worry about living in a safe neighborhood,

Exhibit 4.1—MASLOW'S HIERARCHY OF NEEDS

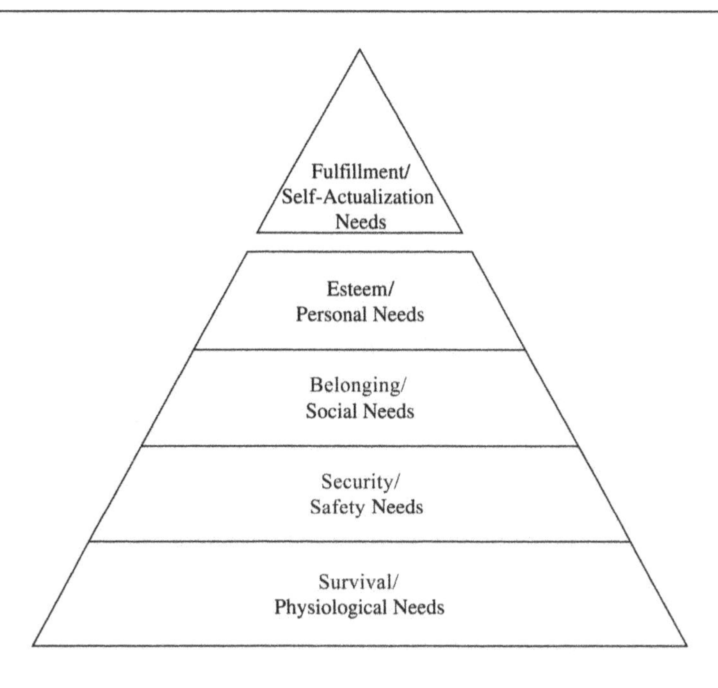

someone out of work with no job prospects isn't likely to think much about public fame, and a person preoccupied with loneliness probably won't be interested in taking art lessons (unless you can position art lessons as a way to overcome loneliness).

Beyond the contributions of Lasswell, Packard, and Maslow, another approach to human needs and interests can be useful for the public relations writer. Another important category of human need, particularly useful for public relations practitioners working in volunteerism, philanthropy, and related areas, is **altruism**. This is the very real human need to help others. Much of human history has been shaped by the phenomenon of people helping each other. Charity, mercy, and compassion are not only a basis of religious and moral codes; they also are fundamental elements of human nature. The task of the public relations writer preparing organizational appeals may be to give readers an opportunity both to help others and to exercise their own altruistic needs.

In analyzing key publics, public relations writers should consider both positive and negative perspectives. We are interested not only in what members of the key publics want; we also should be aware of what they don't want. Giving thought to apprehension and resistance within the key publics can help us avoid messages that are likely to be resisted by our publics.

As part of your analysis of the publics, include a listing and analysis of the demographic and sociographic barriers to communication. Deal with matters such as ethnic differences between the organization and its publics, and the implied differences in language, culture, values, lifestyle, and so on.

Another useful point of analysis for each public is drawn from Grunig's **situational theory** of publics, which identifies three factors in the evolution of publics: (1) the extent to which they are aware that a problem exists, thus knowing that they need information, (2) the extent to which they see themselves as either limited or free to act on the situation, and (3) the extent to which they recognize that they are involved in or affected by the situation.

Planning Sheet

Good writing progresses logically. It emerges from the mind of the writer, based on careful and clear consideration of both the purpose for writing and the strategy for achieving this purpose. Good writing evolves from a plan. Planning takes time, but it is time well spent.

A **planning sheet** is an outline of what you should think about to make your writing planning more effective. As you explore various elements of a planning sheet, keep this thought in mind: The planning sheet is meant to guide you toward an effective piece of writing. It is not for public consumption, so don't worry about crafting an eloquent statement. It is simply an outline of things to come. It is like an artist's sketchbook or an architect's preliminary drawing of the floor plans.

Note that the planning sheet is not the same as a public relations plan or a campaign book. The larger plan would deal with goals, objectives, and other aspects of strategy, with a variety of tactics, and with various administrative details such as budgets and timelines. The planning sheet, on the other hand, is an approach to a particular written tactic such as a news release, Facebook entry, brochure, appeal letter, etc. It may pull elements such as key publics and objectives from the overall public relations plan, but it is part of the implementation of the tactics identified in such a plan.

Elements of a Planning Sheet

The planning sheet consists of eight parts: public relations situation, key publics, news pitch, benefit statement, tone of message, intended outcomes, action statement, and readability range. Here is an example of a completed planning sheet for Exhibits 4.2–4.5.

Planning Sheet

Public Relations Situation: Promotional campaign to attract more customers for Teeny Tykes Day Care Center.

Analysis of Key Publics

1. Families with no at-home parent(s):
   - Quality day care
   - Safety for child
   - Stimulating environment
   - Comfort of knowing that work schedule not detrimental to child's development.
2. Families with at-home parent(s):
   - Occasional time away from child
   - Opportunity for child to socialize with other children.

News Pitch: Teeny Tykes invites parents to day care open house to see how children thrive in a safe environment fostering social skills and emotional growth.

Benefit Statement: Teeny Tykes can assure members of the key public that it can provide quality day care for their children, with emphasis on safety, socialization, and emotional and intellectual development. Teeny Tykes can provide parents with certification reports and testimonials from other parents.

Tone of Message: Communication with potential new client families should be positive, encouraging. It should be child centered, demonstrating that although the parent will pay the bill, the center considers the child to be the primary customer.

Intended Outcomes

- To increase parents' understanding of the range of programs and services available
- To instill confidence that Teeny Tykes would be a good environment for their child
- To encourage and facilitate enrollment in Teeny Tykes.

Action Statement: Inviting parents to open house and driving traffic to Teeny Tykes website.

Readability Range: A grade level of 9–11 would make this information accessible to the key publics.

Public Relations Situation. Begin the planning sheet with a brief note on the general scope of this particular writing activity. In its brevity it will start you off on the right foot. Here are some examples:

- Membership in Hidden Valley Riding Club
- Promotion for a new website
- CEO's banquet for retired employees
- Search for a new vice principal
- Fundraising campaign for a new scholarship program
- Public education about a company's opposition to a highway-tax proposal.

Key Publics. List one or a few key publics that you will address in this piece of writing—probably no more than three publics. More than that, and you should consider preparing separate pieces for each. Then write a brief analysis of each of these publics; identify their major characteristics and note their wants, interests, and needs.

News Pitch. You've heard of the **elevator pitch**, the one-minute speech in which a person should be able to pitch an idea. One minute to convince someone to publish your book, vote for this candidate, buy that product, ask your roommate to go on a blind date with my cousin. The *news pitch* is similar. It's a brief statement that sums up the main newsworthy message that you are preparing to write about. Keep this brief. In fact, try to keep it to Twitter's 140-character limit. This will come in handy later on when we write a social media news release.

Benefit Statement. Prepare a concise **benefit statement** for your readers. What one thing do you want them to remember? Be clear in your own mind about what value your organization offers the key publics. Ideally, this will be the flip side of the previous analysis of the key publics, providing a clear statement of how the organization can satisfy the public's wants, interests, and needs.

Tone of Message. How do you want your message to feel? Consider if humor or fear appeals are appropriate. Weigh the pros and cons of a dispassionate and objective presentation, or the relative merits of emotions and logical approaches.

Intended Outcomes. In other classes and other textbooks, you learn how to develop comprehensive objectives for public relations campaigns and programs. For individual writing projects, you would draw on those objectives. In this planning sheet, note in simple terms the outcomes that you intend with your writing.

Action Statement. Good public relations writing provides specific ways to facilitate the next step that you intend for your readers. It is an implementation of the simple objectives that you noted in the previous section. Indicate here what you will do to invite readers for follow-up action.

Readability Range. Indicate the grade-level range of members of your key public. This estimate will be useful later when you apply a readability rating such as the Fog Index or the Flesch–Kincaid Scale to your writing (review Chapter 2 for details about readability ratings).

Exercise 4.1

Preparing a Planning Sheet

You have been hired as a public relations writer to draft the copy for a brochure or a direct-mail letter. Prepare a planning sheet for one of the following:

- MacFarland Driving School, promoting a program to help senior citizens improve their driving skills
- Statewide Insurance Company, promoting renters' insurance for college roommates in off-campus apartments
- Upstate United, an advocacy group organizing a protest against plans to dam a local creek as a non-recreational reservoir
- Another organization identified by your instructor.

Researching the Topic

Before you start to write, you may have to learn more about your topic. In other words, you might need to do **research**, which is simply a systematic way of gathering information about your topic. Good writers always know more about the topic than they actually write. You must gather enough information to make some reasonable judgments: what to put in and what to leave out, what to quote and what to paraphrase, what to attribute and what to let stand as common knowledge, what to stress and what to present with less emphasis.

Public relations writers don't always have the luxury of time. Research may need to be accomplished in a very short time, and the effective public relations writer is the one who can both research and write under deadline pressure.

Research is divided into three types: casual, secondary, and primary. No hierarchy of importance is implied here. In some instances, it makes sense to begin with casual research, then proceed to secondary research. In other situations, secondary research is often the logical first step before an interview. Primary research is seldom necessary for a specific piece of writing, but it is often part of a wider public relations campaign. Let's take a look at each type.

Casual Research

Casual research is an informal process of finding out what already is known by the writer or the writer's organization or client. Think about the situation. Ask around. Whatever you are writing about, somebody someplace can give you needed information.

- *Informal Interviewing*: This is the art of asking what people know about the topic. Adopt an attitude of being open to advice, and take every opportunity to find out what people are thinking. Pick the brains of your client and co-workers. Talk with people with experience and expertise.
- *Formal Interviewing*: This takes the information-gathering process to a higher level. It is more planned and methodical, more strategic. **Intensive interviews** are those that use the same structure and ask the same questions to several different people.

Interviews remain one of the most important tools for a public relations writer. Interviews may be conducted in person or by phone, mail, e-mail, or video teleconferencing. In-person interviews generally are the most fruitful, because you can "read" body language and obtain some insights into the person being interviewed.

Effective public relations writers are sensitive to the comfort level of the person being interviewed. Some people are nervous about doing interviews, perhaps because they have been misquoted in the past. Remind them that you are on their side. Unlike a journalist who is sent out to obtain information for a particular story, you are collaborating with the interview subject. Let that person know you recognize him or her as an expert who shares with you a common idea, cause, or concern. You both want to present the information in its best light, in ways that will make it most easily understood, and in a manner that will support your organization's mission.

Unlike a journalist, a public relations writer will generally invite the subject of an interview to review the writing before it is released. Even if such approval isn't required, it is a good idea to invite the interviewee to review technical or sensitive matters.

The value of interviews often depends on who is being interviewed. The best advice: Get as close to the source as possible. For example, interviewing members of the sales department may be more productive than interviewing the CEO if you're working on a piece of product literature. The sales staff probably knows more about the competition, sales points to emphasize, possible objections, and so on.

During the interview, take good notes. If the interview is done in person or by telephone, it's good practice to record the conversation, always with the knowledge and consent of the person you are interviewing. But even if you record the interview, taking some notes makes it easier to ask follow-up questions and saves you much embarrassment if the recorder doesn't work. Here are some other suggestions for effective interviewing:

- *Write out your questions before the interview.* Begin with these questions, but remain flexible to follow the interviewee into areas you did not anticipate if it is relevant.
- *Establish rapport.* Show an interest in the person being interviewed and in the topic under discussion.
- *Explain the purpose of the interview.* Indicate how it can be an advantage for the interviewee to share information on an important topic.
- *Discuss the background research* you did in preparing for the interview. This will signal that you are prepared and will allow the interviewee to use this research as the basis for updating what you already know.
- *Distinguish between fact questions and opinion questions.* You need both kinds of information, so don't concentrate solely on obtaining simply factual information. Ask questions like: What does this mean? Why is this important? How will this help somebody? Enlist the interviewee's help in framing this information within the interests of your intended audience.
- *Conclude by inviting the interviewee to add anything else* that seems to be relevant to the topic or important for the key public to understand.
- *Rely more on open-ended questions* rather than simple yes/no questions.

Exercise 4.2

Preparing for an Interview

Prepare for an interview based on this scenario: Another student in your class has been chosen to participate in a three-week study tour to Moscow, Russia; Kiev, Ukraine; Warsaw, Poland; and Riga, Latvia. The International Public Relations Education Committee sponsors the tour. This student was selected in part because of faculty recommendations and in part because of his/her essay about the role of public relations in the development of democracy in Eastern Europe.

Part 1: Develop a series of questions that you would ask the student if you were preparing a news release for IPREC.

Part 2: Using these questions, play the role of a public relations writer and interview another student, who will answer your questions without volunteering more information than the question seeks.

Part 3: Then collaborate with your fellow student interviewee to analyze the interview and evaluate each question's effectiveness. Suggest other questions that might have been useful.

Secondary Research

Secondary research is research conducted to find out what information is already available through existing sources. Writers have many possible sources of information about their topics. Your decision on how deeply to research the topic will be made on the basis of time and resources available, as well as on the importance of the writing project and your need for detailed information. Following is a look at some of these potential sources.

Organizational Files. The files held within an organization can provide a wealth of information, and many public relations practitioners develop files that may span decades of their organization's life. Develop the habit of clipping, scanning and saving pieces of information relevant to your organization or client.

Archives. Official archives are an organization's formal collection of documents, records, photographs, letters, and sometimes memorabilia related to the organization. Nonprofit organizations often make their archives available to outside researchers whose purpose serves the interests of the organization.

Libraries. Public and academic libraries have many resource materials in both published form and electronic files. Some organizations such as hospitals, professional associations, and religious organizations often have specialized libraries with potential opportunities for public relations researchers. Consider comprehensive ones like Encyclopaedia Britannica and World Book Encyclopedia, as well as the many specialized publications that are available. Publications such as yearbooks, almanacs and fact books also are useful. Consider the credibility of the publisher, and particularly avoid online encyclopedias that rely on contributions from volunteer writers rather than on verified staff entries.

Government Materials. At every level of government, information is available that offers another important secondary information source for the public relations writer. Many public records are available in government offices or through libraries. Yearbooks, census and data books, policy indexes, and government reports can be useful research sources. The federal government generates much information, most of it available online through the various agencies. Special indexes, yearbooks, and directories also can assist in searching for federal information, and some agencies have telephone and online research assistance.

Online Resources. The Internet provides a great resource for public relations writers. Articles in academic and professional journals are available online, sometimes through a library database. Most news media have searchable archives. Rummage around the Internet with your favorite search engine to identify sites with authoritative information about your subject. "Authoritative" is the key. Anybody can put up a website, so be wary of information posted by individuals without professional credentials. Seek out sites with known and trustworthy sources, and be wary of wikis in which any user can edit the online text.

Professional Materials. Many national organizations offer information useful for public relations writers. Additionally, many local associations as well as businesses and agencies have professional libraries that may be used by researchers and writers. Hospitals, law offices, corporations, and religious and human service organizations may be willing to provide specialized information to public relations writers, especially when the writing project serves their organizational purposes.

Primary Research

Sometimes it may be necessary to conduct **primary research**—research that generates new data collected specifically for a particular project. Also known as **formal research**, this includes surveys, content analyses, and focus groups. Usually, these will be part of a broad public relations campaign rather than an individual writing project.

Formal research associated with public relations often involves methodologies such as surveys, focus groups, and content analyses. As important as formal research is, it is beyond the scope of this book. See the Bibliography for a listing of some books on formal research methodologies useful to public relations practitioners.

Media Directories

In addition to topical research, the public relations writer should develop a familiarity with another set of information resources, **media directories**. These include collections of data related to newspapers and magazines, radio and television, blogs and social media, telecommunications, advertising, and other media-related areas. They are essential tools in helping writers identify media contacts, develop story ideas, and effectively disseminate information about a client or employer. Hundreds of media directories are published throughout North America in print or online.

Nine Steps to Effective Writing

Like any good process, writing progresses along a clearly marked path. The following approach is drawn from the experiences of many different writers. Use it for the remainder of this writing course. Adopt it as your own system for producing effective writing for any public relations purpose. Here is an outline of nine steps:

1. Plan what you want to write.
2. Research the needed information.
3. Organize your writing.
4. Write and print the first draft.
5. Review your planning sheet and revise the first draft.
6. Polish the language in the second draft and print this.
7. Proofread this draft for language mechanics.
8. Get the necessary approvals.
9. Publish your writing in its final form.

Step 1: Plan. The purpose of the planning stage is to get ready to present your message. The writing process begins as you prepare a planning sheet, focusing your attention on the task at hand. The decisions you make now will help you to carry on to the other steps in the writing process.

Step 2: Research. At the research stage, gather the necessary information so you can write your message. Gather information you want to communicate to your key publics. Identify issues and questions to be addressed. Check documents such as files and books to obtain this information. Interview people familiar with the topic. Conduct formal research if necessary. After you have gathered all the information you need, organize it into appropriate themes and segments.

Step 3: Organize. The goal of the organizing stage is to develop a flexible outline for your writing. It's not necessary to use a formal outline with categories and subcategories marked with capital letters, Arabic and Roman numerals. You might find it easier to sort out your thoughts is by using a **graphic organizer**. This is a visual tool that offers more flexibility than traditional outlines. Graphic organizers such as the ones shown in Exhibit 4.2 can include charts, graphs, and diagrams that represent ideas and information. They can help writers organize their thoughts and visualize the relationship between different concepts.

Step 4: Draft. The drafting stage is a starting point for your writing. Write the draft of your message. Let the words flow freely, and focus on the logical unfolding of your message rather than on the format or mechanics of your writing.

Occasionally, you may have **writer's block**, a situation in which a writer simply cannot think of how to start. If this happens, go back to the first step and review your ideas. Freewriting about the topic and your difficulties with it also can be a good way to unblock the mind. Usually, the planning sheet will help you overcome any confusion about how to approach the writing.

You don't need to start at the beginning as you write this first draft. It may be easier to begin simply by writing a quote, an example, or an easy-to-write explanation of some point. Then add detail, eventually returning to the beginning to write an introduction or lead.

Step 5: Review and Revise. The purpose of the revision stage is to make sure you are on target with what you planned earlier. The nature of computers, with transient words on the screen, enhances this part of the writing process by inviting you to work with your words.

First, review your analysis of the key publics in your planning sheet, particularly their wants, interests, and needs. Then review your intended outcome. Read your first draft to see if you addressed the interests of each public. Make sure you wrote to your objectives. If you left out any important information, add it now. Delete anything that might distract readers from your stated purpose. Reposition sentences and paragraphs so information is presented in a logical order.

In the revision stage, seek input from others. As a student, incorporate the suggestions of your instructor and fellow students; in the field, consider the input of colleagues and co-workers. Collaboration and teamwork are important in the practice of public relations, and it is not uncommon for writing projects to reflect the work of several different writers and editors.

Step 6: Polish. The goal of the polishing stage is to smooth out your writing so it becomes more understandable and interesting. This is a good time to take a break. Put some distance between you and your writing; if possible, set it aside and return to it the next day. This incubation time will make you fresh and ready to approach your writing objectively. At the least, give yourself a half-hour or so to step away from your writing. Even in a deadline situation, a brief respite to get a drink, make some phone calls, or walk around the block can do wonders for your writing.

Read the second draft out loud. Hearing your words will help you notice mistakes and correct a variety of writing problems. Tune your ear for obstacles to good writing, such as poor or missing transitions, lack of sentence variety, and awkward phrases or sentences.

Finally, apply a readability check to this draft, and decide if it needs to be rewritten at a level more appropriate for your readers.

Step 7: Proofread. The goal of the proofreading stage is to assure correctness in the mechanics of writing. By applying the previous steps, you have already produced a version that includes appropriate information, meets your objectives, and uses language smoothly. Now turn your attention to the details of style, especially punctuation, spelling, and grammar. Edit your writing for these mechanical details. If any of these give you particular difficulty, read your draft one time through with only this problem in mind. For example, if you know that you often have errors with commas, read your draft once again and focus all of your concentration on the proper placement of commas. Make sure your writing conforms to appropriate stylebook standards. Here are some tips and a word of caution about the proofreading stage:

- Tip 1: A trick of book editors and newspaper copy editors is to read backwards—right to left, bottom to top. That way each word becomes the object of your attention, and you are likely to spot errors.
- Tip 2: Just as computers can be your friend, they also can deceive you. It is much easier to spot mistakes when you are looking at a piece of paper rather than at a computer monitor. Print a hard copy of what you have written, and proofread from this.
- Tip 3: Develop a list of your personal devils. Make a list of your personal writing weaknesses and keep it next to your computer as a quality control before you let anything go. For instance, maybe you often overlook *pubic* for *public* or consistently use *they* when you mean *it*. Fast typing can make your fingers trip over *research* as *resaerch* or to end words with *-ting* instead of *-tion*.
- And a word of caution: Like all tools, spelling and grammar checkers on computers are only as good as the person using them. Don't let yourself rely on these so much that you fail to copy read your writing. Compound nouns such as ethics and public relations confuse some computers. Meanwhile, *its* and *it's*; *read* and *reed*; *right*, *write*, *rite*, and *wright* are all words the computer will accept as being spelled correctly, but it may not distinguish their grammatical usage.

Here's a little poem, "Spellbound" (author unknown). It reminds us that it takes a human being to know which word is appropriate for the writing context:

> I have a spelling checker, it came with my PC
>
> It plainly marks four my review mistakes I cannot sea.
>
> I've run this poem threw it, I'm sure your please to no,
>
> Its letter perfect in it's weigh, my checker tolled me sew.

Step 8: Get Approvals. The goal of the approval stage is to obtain permission necessary to present the piece publicly. Public relations writers need approvals or sign-offs before they can publish or disseminate their writing. Junior staffers must submit their writing to their managers. Department managers themselves may find that either organizational policy or professional discretion causes them to route their writing to executives or to other interested departments (such as the legal staff) for approval. Experienced practitioners who have built a level of trust often find that such approvals are not necessary.

Agency writers always submit the writing to clients, who themselves may have an elaborate pecking order of approvals before the piece of writing is deemed appropriate for publication or distribution. It is not unusual for this approval process to add days, even weeks, to the production schedule, so writers should know the procedure and develop a schedule that allows for delays. Often, the approval process will throw the writer back to Step 5, revising the piece based on the input of the reviewers.

Step 9: Publish. The goal of this final stage is to present your writing in its most professional version. Prepare the "publishable" version that you will share with members of your publics: the news release to be sent to editors, the draft of the speech to be given, the brochure to be handed out, the appeal letter to be mailed, the Web page to be uploaded. Make this your writing at its finest and most complete.

Going through the Process

Following is an example of how a piece of writing developed from the idea stage represented by the planning sheet through the final version. The writing project is based on the planning sheet presented earlier in this chapter, part of a promotional campaign for a day care center. In the research step, the writer addressed the following questions: What does the program offer? How can parents use the service? What costs are involved? How can a parent sign up?

Exhibit 4.2—GRAPHIC ORGANIZER

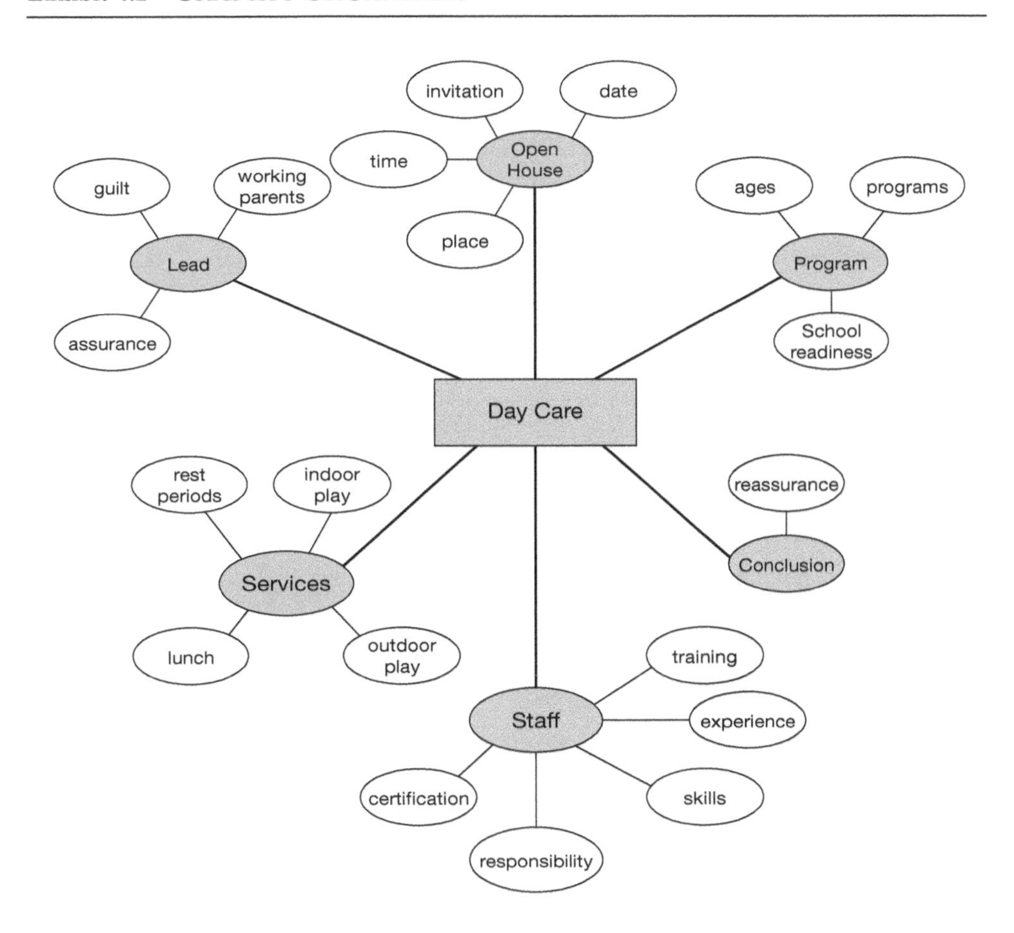

Exhibit 4.2 depicts a graphic organizer based on the information to be presented to the key public. Exhibit 4.3 shows the first draft of the writing project. Note that this is a very rough version. Marked on this draft is a major revision in which the writer has reviewed the objectives, added some information not included in the first draft, and deleted other information that is less important. Exhibit 4.4 is the revised second text. The writer has polished the draft by smoothing out the language; note the attention to transitions and sentence structure. The writer has also edited the piece, correcting spelling and punctuation. Exhibit 4.5 is the final publishable presentation. The draft has been thoroughly revised, edited, and finally prepared for public use.

Exhibit 4.3—EDITED FIRST DRAFT

It is tough enough being a parent *today* ~~in these troubled times~~ without ~~having to~~ feel*ing* guilty about leaving your child when you go ~~off~~ to work. The staff and management of Teeny Tykes ~~want to eaze your burden~~ *offer you a re-assuring choice*.

You ~~may be interested in attending~~ *are invited to* an Open House on Monday, July 13 ~~This Open House is free for parents and children. It is located~~ *at the Teeny Tykes Day Care Center* at 15 Kinderhausen Lane in Northfield. *Bring your family and see what Teeny Tykes can offer your child.*

Teeny Tykes is a full service day care center for children 2-5 years. ~~For the younger children~~ we provide supervised games, crafts *and* stories ~~and naptime~~. We also worked with the Northfield School District to provide a school-readyness program to help prepare our children for higher education after they graduate from Teeny Tykes. We ~~also~~ have nutritious lunches, *quiet rest periods,* ~~and snacks~~ and ~~a closed in~~ *supervised play in our* outdoor playground.

~~All~~ our staff have training in early childhood education and *first aid.* ~~emergency medical care~~. *All of us are certified by the state. Most importantly,* we really care about children entrusted to us, and we take seriously our responsibility to you and your child. ~~At~~ *Come see how* Teeny Tykes ~~we~~ *can give you peace of mind and* make your job ~~as parents~~ *of parenting* a little bit easier.

Exhibit 4.4—REVISED DRAFT

It's tough being a parent today without feeling guilty about leaving your child when you go to work. The staff and management of Teeny Tykes offer you a re-assuring choice.

What You Need to Know

You are invited to an Open House on Monday, July 13, at the Teeny Tykes Day Care Center at 15 Kinderhausen Lane in Northfield. Bring your family and see what Teeny Tykes can offer your child.

About Day Care

Teeny Tykes is a full service day care center for children aged 2 to 6 ~~2-5 years~~. We provide ~~supervized~~ games, crafts and stories. We have nutritious lunches, quiet rest periods, and supervized play in our outdoor playground. We ~~also~~ worked with the Northfield School District to develop ~~provide~~ a school-readyness program to help prepare our children for higher education after they graduate from Teeny Tykes.

For Your Child

Our staff members have training in early childhood education and first aid. All ~~of us~~ are certifyed by the state. Even more ~~Most~~ importantly, we really care about the children you entrust~~ed~~ to us~~, and we take seriously our responsibility to you and your child.~~ Come see how Teen Tykes can give you peace of mind and make your job of parenting a little bit easier.

Teeny Tykes
Putting the CARE in Day Care

Bodoni Bold Italic 36 pt
20 pt

Exhibit 4.5—FINAL PRESENTATION

It's tough being a parent today without feeling guilty about leaving your child when you go to work. The staff and management of Teen Tykes offer you a reassuring choice.

What You Need to Know

You are invited to an Open House on Monday, July 13, at the Teeny Tykes Day Care Center at 15 Kinderhausen Lane in Northfield. Bring your family. See what Teeny Tykes can offer your child.

About Day Care

Teeny Tykes is a full-service day care center for children aged 2 to 5. We provide games, crafts and stories. We have nutritious lunches, quiet rest periods, and supervised play in our outdoor playground. We worked with the Northfield School District to develop a school-readiness program to help prepare our children for "higher education" after they graduate from Teen Tykes.

For Your Child

All our staff members have training in early childhood education and first aid. All are certified by the state. Even more important, we really care about the children you entrust to us. Come see how Teen Tykes can give you peace of mind and make your job of parenting a little easier.

Teeny Tykes

Putting the CARE in Day Care

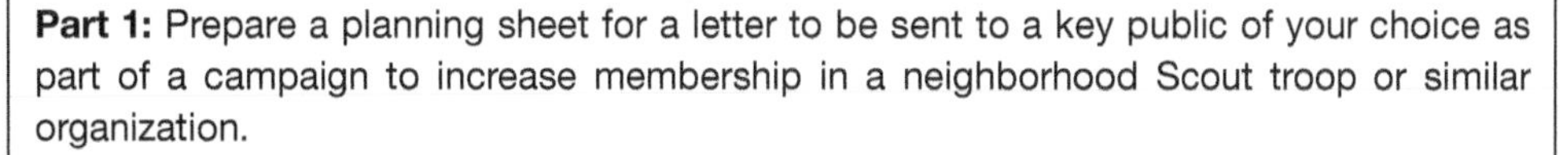

Exercise 4.3

Practicing the Writing Process

Part 1: Prepare a planning sheet for a letter to be sent to a key public of your choice as part of a campaign to increase membership in a neighborhood Scout troop or similar organization.

Part 2: Do whatever research is necessary to obtain information for this writing project. Perhaps your instructor or another student will play the role of the information source to provide you with needed information. Then develop a graphic organizer to outline the various elements or sections you want to include in your writing.

Part 3: Type a draft of this letter. Aim for about 200 words. Then review your objectives and reconsider what you wrote in the first draft. Pay particular attention to your earlier analysis of the key public and the organization's objectives. Based on your review of the planning sheet, handwrite your revisions on your first draft. Read this draft aloud, and pay close attention to polishing the language. Handwrite your revisions for polishing the language. Then transfer the handwritten changes onto your computer and print out a second draft.

Part 4: Mark copy editing changes on this draft as you edit it for details such as spelling, punctuation, grammar, and AP Style. Then make the handwritten polishing and editing changes on your computer or word processor and print out a final version.

Reminder: You will turn in five pages for this assignment: a planning sheet, a graphic organizer, a first draft with handwritten revisions, and a second draft with handwritten polishing and copy editing, and the final version.

Wrap-Up for Part One

In this introductory section to *Becoming a Public Relations Writer*, you have focused on foundation skills needed for all public relations writing projects. Review the learning objectives for each chapter. If you read carefully and did most of the exercises, you should be able . . .

- To use the technique of freewriting
- To understand the relationship between creative and functional writing
- To explain the concept of writing to influence
- To develop a process of drafting and revising
- To effectively use standard conventions of the English language
- To construct simple and understandable messages
- To enhance the meaning your words convey
- To use language ethically
- To avoid biased language
- To understand various theories about communication
- To explain the role of persuasion in public relations writing
- To apply lessons from persuasion theory in your writing
- To explain the difference between persuasion and propaganda
- To organize a writing project using a planning sheet
- To conduct research for public relations writing
- To use the nine-step process to prepare a publishable piece of writing.

That's an impressive list of information you have learned so far through this book. It's difficult to synthesize so much information. However, the underlying message of Part One is for you to focus on three approaches to your writing: (1) to write professionally, by mastering and observing the basic conventions of good writing; (2) to write strategically, with planning and purpose, for a specific organization and for a particular audience; and (3) to write ethically, always aware of your responsibility to yourself and to society to value accuracy, appreciate honesty, safeguard your own integrity, and respect your publics and media audiences.

So where do we go from here? The next two sections of *Becoming a Public Relations Writer* will introduce you to two broad areas of writing. One deals with journalistic venues, which offer many opportunities for organizations to present their message, extend their visibility, and promote their ideas and ideals. The other deals with media internal to organizations or controlled by them, through which public relations writers can present their messages.

Both media environments are important. You'll find some overlap in these two broad categories of writing venues. Taken together, they offer many opportunities for writers skilled in the basics of public relations and knowledgable about the nuanced standards associated with the various media tools.

Both subsequent sections of this book will deal with many writing venues. Some are associated with established print and broadcast media, others with emerging digital media. Since most organizations blend the two, students who use *Becoming a Public Relations Writer* to hone their writing skills will find themselves well prepared for the job market after graduation.

Part Two

PUBLIC RELATIONS WRITING FOR JOURNALISTIC MEDIA

In the popular mind, public relations is closely linked with the news media. Indeed, media relations is the only aspect of public relations that many people outside the profession know about. The ranks of journalism have supplied more public relations practitioners than any other training ground, and many organizations have developed their public relations efforts along the lines of the public information model. This approach to public relations is based in the notion of news—a somewhat intangible quality that helps information take hold in the public imagination. Any writer interested in succeeding in public relations must appreciate the concept of news. It really is a concept based on respect for an organization's publics.

Public relations writers are not magicians. No sleight of hand can make insignificant information look like news. Rather, effective public relations practitioners are like farmers and gardeners who plant seeds, nurture crops, and sometimes graft different stocks to produce more vibrant offspring. So, too, with public relations writers who help create, nurture, and eventually harvest the newsworthy activities of their organizations.

The specialty of media relations provides the public relations writer with a window through which to expose the organization to its publics. This is an important component within an organization's comprehensive communication program. News releases are the most commonly used tools for media relations, but the field provides many other options for the innovative writer.

Readers of this book are urged to adopt an up-to-date understanding of journalistic media. Don't think only about newspapers. Consider radio and television. Also understand that journalism has become an online phenomenon. Newspapers have online versions; some are published only online. Bloggers increasingly are being seen as online journalists, and public relations practitioners need to see them as potential conduits for organizational information. Public relations itself offers some express ways to take organizations directly to its publics. In Part Two, discussion of public relations communication through the journalistic media includes various venues: print, broadcast, and online.

Part Two of *Becoming a Public Relations Writer* deals with opportunities public relations writers have to maximize the newsworthy aspects of their organizations and to communicate with their various publics through the opportunities provided by newspapers, radio and television, blogs, and social media. It also focuses on the nuance of writing for these various forms of journalistic media.

Part Two deals with journalism-based writing in many varieties. It focuses on venues associated with established media, such as print and broadcast journalism. It also includes venues identified with emerging media, such as those linked with online journalism.

Along with this introduction, Part Two includes eight chapters and a brief concluding section:

- Chapter 5: News and Public Relations
- Chapter 6: Fact Sheet and Advisory
- Chapter 7: News Writing Style
- Chapter 8: Print News Release
- Chapter 9: Broadcast News Release
- Chapter 10: Multimedia and Social Media Release
- Chapter 11: Organizational Feature
- Chapter 12: Advocacy and Opinion
- Wrap-Up for Part Two.

5 News and Public Relations

News is often considered the prerogative of editors and reporters, but public relations practitioners also need to be oriented toward news. We must recognize news and respect it. Successful practitioners appreciate the power of news and the energy it brings to our organizations and clients.

This chapter will introduce you to various aspects of news: what news is, how to recognize and generate it, what makes events newsworthy, and how to enhance the news value of an organization's activities. It also will address legal concepts that affect public relations writing, particularly defamation and privacy. Here are your objectives for Chapter 5:

- To develop an understanding of the elements of news
- To identify and generate newsworthy information about an organization.

Defining News

News is an elusive concept. Professional communicators analyze it, and everybody else talks about it knowingly. Veteran journalists and public relations people seem to just "know" what is newsworthy or how to make something more newsworthy. News is also a matter of preference—like politics, art, religion, and computer platforms.

Dictionaries tell us what we already know: News is new information, something reported, something newsworthy. How wonderfully vague! Journalists and public relations practitioners, past and present, have tried to define news, because having a definition helps us understand how it works. Later in this chapter we'll take a stab at developing our own definition for news.

Public relations writers continually try to anticipate what the gatekeeper will consider to be news. A **gatekeeper** is a person who controls the flow of information. A gatekeeper may be the editor of a newspaper or newsletter, a radio or television news director, a webmaster, a Facebook or MySpace manager, or an individual columnist or blogger. Gatekeepers consider information available to them, then evaluate it in light of the needs and policies of their particular medium and the presumed interests of their audience. They decide whether the information has enough news value to be offered to the audience.

In the end, it all boils down to this: News is what the gatekeeper says is news. The media call the shots. It doesn't matter if you and your boss or client think the information is important. If the media gatekeeper doesn't think it's news, it's not news. No appeals process.

This relationship between media and newsworthiness is important in understanding the relationship of another set of terms: audiences and publics. An **audience** is a group of people who use a particular medium such as newspaper, website, or television station. A **public** is the group of people with a common bond or relationship with an organization who are important to the organization's mission and success. Audiences are important to public relations writers only to the extent that they include members of an organization's publics.

The Venn diagram in Exhibit 5.1 graphically shows that news is the information in overlapping circles of interest for the media gatekeeper and public relations practitioners. Let's look at each of the components.

- **Circle A** indicates information about the organization and issues important to it. This deals with the organization's mission and strategic goals. This circle is of interest to the public relations practitioner. Frankly, the media gatekeeper doesn't care much about this information when it remains in Circle A.

Exhibit 5.1—MODEL OF OVERLAPPING NEWS INTERESTS These overlapping circles graphically indicate the interrelationships among information about an organization, information that is of interest to news media, and information that is of interest to key publics.

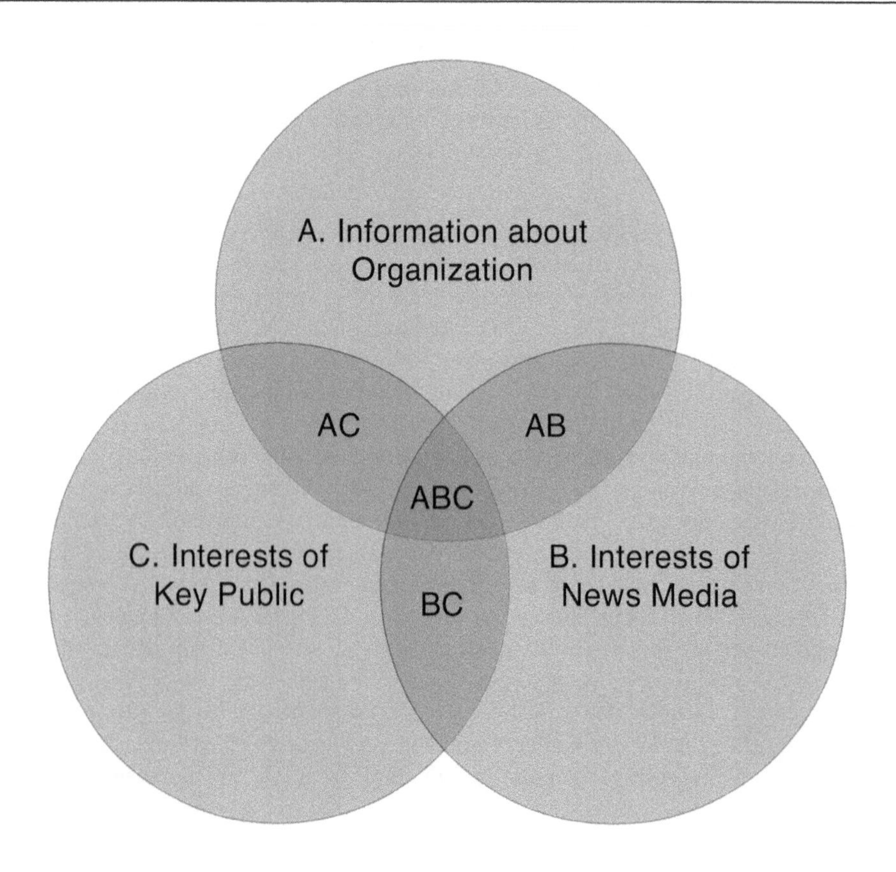

- **Circle B** represents the interests of the news media. It is what the media consider to be newsworthy. This is what the media wish to report on for two reasons: They see it as intrinsically newsworthy (based on their specific definition of news, which can vary from one medium to another) and their presumption about audience interests (which also can vary among media).
- **Circle C** signifies the interests of the organization's key public. This deals with what the public considers important. Whether from a positive or negative perspective, it is something that coincides with their wants, interests, and needs.

Each of these three components exists independent of the others. For example, the organization has many bits of information, much of which the media do not consider newsworthy, much of which also doesn't interest each public. But in certain situations, information in the circles will overlap to varying degrees, providing an environment for public relations to get into the action.

- **Area AB** depicts news. It denotes newsworthy information about the organization that the media might be interested in reporting. The media gatekeeper is focused on the people who read the newspaper or the blog, listen to the radio newscast, or view the television broadcast. Your job, as public relations person, is to find out where Circle A overlaps Circle B, then call this to the attention of the media gatekeeper. Remember that all of this is defined by the individual media. Circle B is much different for an employee newsletter than for a daily newspaper, different for a television station than for a special-interest radio station.
- **Area AC** shows what we can call **direct news**. This is information that, though the news media may not care about it, nevertheless is of interest to the key public. When public relations writers note that information exists in the AC area, they are at a decision-action point. One option is to reshape the information or enhance it to make it of more interest to the news media. (We'll look later in this chapter at ways to create or enhance news value.) The alternative is to look for ways to present this information directly to the key public without going through the news. New technologies, particularly those involving the Internet and social media, increasingly make the latter a viable option.
- **Area BC** seems not to be of interest to the public relations writer, because it deals with news that, while of interest to a key public, does not involve the organization. On the surface, it's about some other organization. The first inclination may simply be: hands off. But public relations practitioners might want to look carefully at these agendas for opportunities to insert their organizations into the news of the day.
- **Area ABC** represents **strategic news**, which is information involving your organization that is of interest not only to the news media but also to your key public. Because it is seen as news, it serves the interests of the news media to report. And because it is seen to hold some benefit or consequence to your key public, it is likely to attract their attention. Public relations writers can have a very good day when they deal with strategic news (or a very bad day if the news is negative toward their organization or client).

You can see that having a good understanding of news and its relationship to your organization can be of immense value as you try to work through the news media. However, we are in the midst of a monumental change in media technology and use, and public relations practitioners must deal with media evolution. Technology is reducing the influence of the gatekeepers, and increasingly the definition of news is being determined by the end user, our publics. The information-on-demand phenomenon is driving this change, giving our publics greater access to information they consider newsworthy and useful. The mushrooming readership of Web-based news releases and news blogs, the growth of news distribution via e-mail and texting, the proliferation of specialized cable TV channels, and the success of social media sites all attest to this.

Over the next decade or so, the media landscape will look much different than it does today. Students in the classroom are sitting at the threshold of an era when direct-to-consumer news is becoming the norm.

Exercise 5.1

Part 1: Look up the following words in your dictionary: information, facts, knowledge, news, data, truth, announcement.

Part 2: Freewrite for five minutes on the following topic: *What is news?* Then discuss this with your classmates.

News Interest

News varies with each medium. Definitions of what is newsworthy are different between local and national newspapers, different still with blogs, television news, and social media sites. Even within a specific type of medium, definitions can vary. For example, one local television news station may be interested in high school sports, while a competing station will focus only on playoff and tournament games.

Even a particular medium may have different standards of newsworthiness for different purposes. For example, the regular print version of a newspaper may require a higher level of newsworthiness than the online version of that same publication. Likewise, television stations often post stories on their websites that are not deemed important enough to be shown on air.

Your job as a public relations writer is to know the mind of the gatekeeper; that is, to understand media and anticipate audience interests. To accomplish this, you need a good working definition of news. The best method of approaching a definition of news is to look at the criteria for news or interest value that the gatekeepers use to determine the news value of information. News has certain observable characteristics, particular elements that, when present, transform information into news.

Journalists have identified the following elements of news, also known as **news value**: action, adventure, change, conflict, consequence, contest, controversy, drama, effect, fame, importance, interest, personality, popularity, prominence, and proximity. This long list of descriptors offers clues about what editors and news directors are looking for when they judge the news value of any story. But it isn't an easy definition to carry around in your head.

For the public relations writer, we might look at a simpler listing. Four characteristics are especially important for the public relations writer: significance, localness, balance, and timeliness. Adding these together provides us with a good working definition: **News** is information about matters of *significant* and *local* interest, presented in a *balanced* and *timely* manner. These elements are basic to virtually all news presentations that are used by the media. Two other elements of news value, *unusualness* and *fame*, are not crucial, but they can enhance the likelihood that information will be considered newsworthy. An easy way to remember these elements of news interest is to memorize the acronym **SiLoBaTi + UnFa**, made up from the first two letters of each of the elements. Let's look at each characteristic.

Significance. News interest involves information of significance. It has meaning for many people. If you were not a part of a particular organization and read its news release or posting on its news blog, would you ask, "So what?" If so, it probably is not news. For example, plans to add a dike along Water Street might be broadly significant to an entire community:

> The State University Center for Flood Control is reviewing proposals for an extension of the dike along Water Street. The plan calls for adding a 14-inch cap to hold back water during heavy flood stages to protect the city's downtown business section.

Or, something might be significant if it affects even only a few people but in a major way:

> The State University Center for Flood Control is warning residents of the dozen homes along Canal Street that they risk flood waters in their living rooms if Red Creek is relocated as proposed by the County Highway Administration.

Editors and news directors look for information that makes people talk. They look for the Wow! factor. News is something readers didn't know yesterday but want or need to know today. News is information of consequence to people who know it, something that helps them make informed decisions on topics of significance. A public relations writer should test every story idea against this standard: How much will the reader/viewer/listener care about this information?

Local. News interest involves information about a local community, whatever that means to the particular medium. Newspaper editors say the lack of a local angle is the most common reason why they turn down news releases. Television news directors say the same thing about video news releases. Consider the following examples of the same event—in this case, a college graduation—prepared for two different media. The first version is intended for a metropolitan daily newspaper covering the area in which the college is located, serving the generalized interests of the newspaper and its readers.

> Sen. Nancy Newcomer will receive an honorary degree during graduation ceremonies Friday in Apache Center at Oakwood College. The state senator, who chairs the Joint Legislative Education Task Force, will address the 830 graduates of the suburban college.
>
> During the ceremony, about 125 students will receive awards . . .

A second version is meant for distribution to a small-town weekly newspaper serving a single community located in another county, miles away from the college. Let's call it Hillsvale. The editor there would find the first version to be of little local interest, but this second version would have much relevance to readers:

> Two Hillsvale residents are among the 125 honors graduates who will receive awards at commencement ceremonies Friday at Oakwood College in Martin City. State Senator Nancy Newcomer will address the 830 graduates.
>
> The local graduates are alumni of Hillsvale Junior-Senior High School, where both were varsity athletes.
>
> Jonathan Berman will receive the top academic award for chemistry majors. A former co-captain of the school soccer team, he is the son of Malcolm and Bertha Berman of Main Street.
>
> Sylvie Batherton, a dance major, will receive general academic honors. She is the daughter of Marian Armstrong of Hillsvale R.D. 3. She was a member of the Hillsdale all-district gymnastics team.

The concept of localness is not only defined geographically. It also can be approached from the perspective of what interests a particular public.

For example, the public relations writer might prepare a special version of the news release for *El Tiempo*, a newspaper serving the area's Hispanic community. In it, the writer might list those students who have identified themselves as part of the Hispanic community, or perhaps those graduates who are members of Adalante Estudiantes Latinos, the student organization focusing on Hispanic issues and interests.

Here's another version that might be used for the blog of the Oakwood College Communication Department, which is read mainly by department alumni and by current students and their families:

> Twenty-seven of the 125 honor grads at this year's Commencement are Communication majors. Comm has produced more honor grads over the past five years than any other department at Oakfield. The following Comm honor grads received special recognition at the department's senior reception the evening before college commencement: . . .

Balance. News interest involves information presented in a balanced way. Just as good reporters strive to present all sides of an issue, good public relations writers also should write in a balanced manner. Obviously, as advocates for organizations and clients, we have an obligation to consider their interests, and we want them to be seen in the best possible light. But sometimes light reveals flaws and wrinkles. A good public relations person will acknowledge problems, perhaps even use them to the organization's advantage. Writing in a way that allows us to put our best foot forward generally means considering long-term interests, which are furthered when we earn respect for candor and honesty.

Consider this scenario. Simon Joyce is a candidate for city council in Haven Crest (population 75,000). You are a public relations writer helping his campaign. You are helping Joyce prepare a statement for tonight's electoral debate, which will be televised by the local cable station. You know that one of the topics likely to be addressed during the debate is the proposal for a new state environmental project that involves creating a reservoir for both industrial and recreational use. Joyce is on record as supporting the project. In counseling the candidate for the debate, you must decide how much information to provide. You think the following paragraph seems complete:

> I like the outdoors and I think kids need more recreation opportunities, so of course I think the reservoir is a good idea. A very good idea! As a state project, this will not raise local taxes. But it will bring new jobs to our community, and we will have a better supply of water for our industries. We'll also have a nice picnic area for everybody to enjoy. How could anybody be against the project?

Based on this statement, you hope that debate viewers and readers of tomorrow's news reports will find Joyce portrayed as a community-minded candidate. You've done a good job.

But perhaps there is something else to consider. In your concern about the long-term effect of information, you suggest that the candidate hit head-on one of the issues that may (or may not) arise. Because it's potentially embarrassing information, you counsel your client to add the following to his statement:

> I should tell you that my cousin owns some of the land to be flooded by the project. Vinnie Joyce is going to make some money when the state buys this land. But I don't want anyone thinking I'm getting any financial benefit out of this. First off, everybody knows Vinnie is a tightwad who wouldn't share his profits with anybody, family or not. Second, right here and now I am asking Vinnie and all the folks who own land in the redevelopment area to contribute to a new fund. I'll make the first pledge of $1500 myself. If we get this reservoir, I'd like to see the city buy some small sailboats so families can have some fun.

Imagine the effect of the first statement, unbalanced and incomplete. After an initial favorable news report, there could be embarrassing stories when the cousin's connection becomes known (as it inevitably would). Maybe the criticism would even come out during the debate itself. But by telling the full story, you have helped the candidate avoid embarrassment and turn a potentially negative situation to his advantage.

Timeliness. News interest involves information that is timely. Facts are enhanced when they are connected with a current issue of public interest. Information today is better than yesterday. Information about tomorrow is even better. As a writer, you will determine what to release and when to release it. Consider the differences in the apparent news value of the following three leads:

> CENTERVILLE, Oct. 12—The Jordan Shoe Company appointed Malcolm Tweedly to succeed Aston Dickerson as general manager. The election took place at a stockholders' meeting last week.
>
> CENTERVILLE, Oct. 5—The Jordan Shoe Company today is installing Malcolm Tweedly as the company's general manager, succeeding Aston Dickerson. The decision was made yesterday at the company's annual stockholders' meeting.
>
> CENTERVILLE, Oct. 4—Malcolm Tweedly will become general manager of the Jordan Shoe Company tomorrow afternoon in ceremonies in the plant cafeteria. The promotion was announced today at the company's annual stockholders' meeting. He will succeed Aston Dickerson, who announced his retirement last month.

The first version is clearly dated. The other two take advance planning and quick turnaround on the part of the public relations staff, but the news value is enhanced. Version 2 is a responsible way of dealing with information, but Version 3 is an even more newsworthy way to make the announcement.

Be careful about what you try to announce ahead of time. Organizations trying to use advance news releases to generate early registrations often are thwarted by the timeliness factor. It simply isn't very newsworthy that your organization is planning an appreciation dinner in two months. Certainly you need advance registrations to determine how many dinners to order, but a news release isn't the way to go. Nonpublic media such as websites and e-mail, coupled perhaps with print advertising, can generate advance response.

Unusual. News interest is enhanced when information deals with unusual incidents. Some people call it human interest; others see it as novelty. **Human interest** is like beauty—difficult to define but obvious when you see it. Human interest involves presenting information about people and their experiences, problems, challenges, and achievements, in a way that engages readers and viewers by arousing not only their attention but also their empathy or sympathy.

The concept may be best understood through examples. Human interest is a report about the smallest surviving infant born in your hospital, the graduate of your continuing education program who has overcome major medical or social challenges, the one-millionth unit manufactured at your suburban plant, the piano recital with "The Minute Waltz" played backward. Well, the latter is just bizarre, but if you are working with a music school, it just might attract some interest in your recital.

Fame. News interest is magnified when information deals with famous people. "Names make news" isn't just idle chatter. Information has greater news value when it involves well-known or important people. It is part of human nature to be interested in something that involves people we know or know about. Maybe we respect them; maybe we despise them; or maybe we're just nosey. But people who are well known or in positions of prominence attract public attention, and that means news. Consider the news value in each of the following leads:

> The Chamber of Commerce will dedicate the new Downtown Sports Arena Wednesday afternoon. Area Little league teams have been invited to the ceremony.

The dedication you are promoting as public relations director of the Middleton Chamber of Commerce may be just another event that generates only a modest interest by the media. But let's say you get a celebrity to participate. If the governor were to participate, you've got a news story on your hands.

> Gov. Jesse Glastenhoeven will speak to Little League players Wednesday afternoon as the Chamber of Commerce dedicates the new Downtown Sports Arena.

Maybe the governor isn't coming after all, but good public relations planning can still help you play the fame game.

> One lucky Little League player participating in Wednesday's dedication of the new Downtown Sports Arena will take home a 1986 baseball card that Gov. Jesse Glastenhoeven donated from his personal collection. The card features José Canseco as Rookie of the Year when he was with the Oakland A's.

Exercise 5.2

Noticing News

Using the online archives of a daily newspaper of your choice, find four news stories from the metro or local section and copy each article into your report.

For each article, indicate the characteristics of news interest that you think are the major ingredients in your story idea: significance, localness, balance, timeliness, unusualness, and fame. If you may find that stories have more than one ingredient, indicate all that are relevant but also note which one seems to be the strongest reason that the story was printed in the paper.

Categories of News

All news isn't the same, and journalists see variety within the concept of news. Consider the following categories of news: hard news, breaking news, soft news, and specialized news.

- **Hard news** is information with an edge to it. It deals with momentous events: accidents, crime, death, disaster, scandals, and activities with immediate results such as elections and trials. This often isn't news generated by public relations people, though we may well give organizational responses and background information as journalists cover hard news. Frequently, this deals with the negative news that public relations practitioners hope their organizations can avoid or quickly put behind them.
- **Breaking news** is hard news that is happening even as the media are covering it. This presents a special problem for public relations writers, who may lack the time and facts to prepare a complete report. Instead, they often work with an ongoing series of updates on the basic facts. Breaking news may involve situations in which the outcome is as yet unknown, such as sporting competitions or elections. Breaking news also may take public relations people into the area of crisis communication.
- **Soft news** is lighter information. It deals with routine activities and programs, leisure, entertainment, events of human interest, developments without major consequences, and activities and trends with more distant results. Public relations writers often find that their accounts of upcoming events, new projects and programs, or personnel developments fall into this category of news.
- **Specialized news** deals with information of importance to particular publics and particular segments of the media. This includes news about interest areas such as business, religion, sports, the arts, agriculture, technology, science, health, family, and home. This is an area of news that can be successfully mined by enterprising public relations writers. Successful practitioners are those who have learned to see beyond the general story to exploit information that may interest a particular public or media audience. They then craft focused versions of the story for each of these specialized media.

FYI *What's In a Name?*

Note that the term being used in this textbook is **news release** rather than **press release**. This is for two reasons:

First, a radio or television reporter is not, strictly speaking, a member of the press. The same is true for a digital journalist. Broadcast and online journalism deserves to be considered as something other than an electronic extension of newspapers. The public relations practitioner who understands the unique and complementary roles of broadcast, print, and digital journalism will be more effective.

Second, don't think of yourself as a press agent simply out to attract publicity. News releases report newsworthy activities. Public relations professionals focus on news, and they don't waste reporters' time or risk their own credibility by trying to disguise uninteresting information as news.

Finally, never slip by using the term **handout** when you are referring to a news release. That is a derogatory and demeaning term, certainly inappropriate for what you are producing to carry the strategic information of your company or organization.

Finding News

Part of your responsibility as a public relations writer will be to take the initiative in finding newsworthy activities within your organization. Look carefully to see what is newsworthy. Some organizations have events that are routine occurrences within the organization but that may be of significance and interest to outsiders. Don't overlook this as a possible news activity.

There are two ways to consider the newsworthiness of a story or activity: the systems approach and the functional approach. Let's take a look at each.

Systems Approach. Let's return to the concept of publics, particularly at ways to identify key publics. One way is to apply a **systems approach**, based on the concept of **linkages** associated with systems theory. We might identify four types of publics: consumers, producers, enablers, and limiters. From this perspective, we can probe for news related to each of these significant categories of publics. As a case in point, consider a systems approach to identifying news for a private school:

- Consumer publics include students. Is there something to report about honors lists? Science fairs? Student organizations? Essay contests? Scholarship winners? Parents also comprise a consumer public. Is anything happening with parent associations? Whole-family education?
- Producer publics include teachers. What might you report about new faculty? In-service training? Advanced studies?
- Enabling publics include the school board. Is newsworthy information coming from meetings? Elections? Enabling publics also include the state education department. Is anything happening regarding accreditation? Curricular regulations? New standards?
- Limiting publics might be other schools that are in competition with our school. What might be happening in your school that would be of interest to private academies? School districts? Teacher unions, educational accreditation units, and governmental agencies also can be limiting publics.

Functional Approach. Sometimes public relations writers can benefit from a functional approach to finding news, in which we identify major activities of an organization and view each with an eye toward potential news stories. In this approach, we look at five categories: events, issues and trends, policies and governance, personnel, and relationships. The functional approach applied to a private high school might identify the following potential news categories:

- Events: Assemblies, open houses, graduation, special observances
- Issues/Trends: Standardized test results, enrollment trends, curriculum changes
- Policies/Governance: Drug/Alcohol intervention, athletic eligibility, graduation requirements, progress reports to taxpayers
- Personnel: New administrators, the accomplishments of faculty and staff members
- Relationships: Neighborhood projects, service activities, lobbying efforts on behalf of educational standards, taxpayer bond campaigns.

Exercise 5.3

Identifying Newsworthy Activities

You are a public relations writer for one of the following organizations (try to select an organization with which you are personally familiar):

- A student organization such as club, team, or sorority/fraternity
- A church, synagogue, mosque, or other local religious congregation
- A community league for soccer, basketball, or some other team sport.

Consider both the systems approach and the functional approach as ways to investigate your organization for newsworthy activities. Then identify at least 10 areas of potentially newsworthy activities for your organization.

Finally, indicate if you found either the systems approach or the functional approach more useful in identifying the newsworthy activities of the organization.

Generating News

As a public relations writer, you are not a magician who can just make news appear, like pulling a rabbit out of a top hat. You can't create something from nothing. But you can orchestrate situations so they can become newsworthy. In fact, part of your usefulness to employers and clients, as well as much of your benefit to the media, lies in your ability to develop and orchestrate newsworthy activities.

Consider these four crucial points to effectively generating news for your organization:

- First, know the media, their news formats, and the elements of newsworthiness that they consider important.
- Second, know your organization or client, especially its mission and goals. This information provides the framework for creating news opportunities that serve the needs of the media, the purposes of the organization, and the interests of the publics.
- Third, know your publics and ask yourself what is happening within the organization that interests your publics.
- Finally, pay attention to what is happening both in your community and around the world.

A key to generating news is to link your organization to a topic already on the public and/or media agenda. This is called creating a **news peg**. Think of the peg in a closet on which you can hang your jeans. It's there; you just need to use it. The same is true with a news peg. It already exists as a topic of interest to the news media; you simply need to hang your organization's message on it. Where do you find a news peg? Read the newspapers. Follow television and radio news. Read the blogs and follow social media on themes paralleling your organization's issues. Check out online news related to your organization or client.

Here are 10 general activities that public relations practitioners can use to generate news for their clients and their organizations.

1. Awards. Organizations can draw attention to their values and important issues by giving an award to a person or group that exemplifies these standards. The monetary value of the award is less important than the prestige it seems to carry with both the organization giving it and the publics important to the recipient. For example, Citizens for a Clean Environment may give an award to a local auto-repair garage that allows customers to drop off used tires, which the garage then delivers to a recycling center. In fact, CCE might initiate this by encouraging the garage to offer the service in the first place.

2. Contests. Everybody likes a good contest. Just as with giving awards, the news value is enhanced through a logical relationship between the sponsoring organization and the focus of the contest. A patriotic organization probably could hold a jump-rope contest, but when it sponsors a contest for students to create videos or public-service television spots supporting the Bill of Rights, it is both increasing its level of news interest and advancing its own mission.

3. Personnel. Organizations seem to have no difficulty using this method to generate publicity. All organizations elect officers or hire managers, and these personnel selections are generally of interest to some media. Like the above examples, careful pairing between organizational objectives and these news pegs can be useful. For example, a school district concerned with truancy may announce the appointment of the vice principal to chair a special task force on school attendance. It may be of interest to the local newspaper, definitely to the editor of the school's Facebook page and parent blog.

4. Local Needs. Organizations with something to promote often find local examples of that cause to address. The news value is enhanced when you have something to say about the issue. For example, let's say stray dogs have been scaring children at the neighborhood park and stray cats have been using the sand pile as a litter box. As complaints mount at City Hall, the local Animal Protection League might step in with a timely reminder that it will take in animals that owners no longer can care for, or it might use the occasion to invite new volunteers to help its cause.

5. Reports. This is a complement to addressing a local need. When an organization wants to highlight an issue that is not yet on the public agenda, it can gather information and then issue a report. For example, the Sheriff's Department is concerned because many drivers do not use seat belts. The sheriff assigns a deputy on limited duty recovering from a gunshot wound to search the last year's files for information on traffic accidents, injury, and seat-belt use. After a few days of digging, the deputy has the basis for a new Sheriff's Report on Seat-Belt Use.

You can also take a lesson in what works for other organizations. Because of the inherent news value of the State of the Nation and State of the State addresses by governmental leaders, other organizations are adopting a similar approach to draw attention to their annual progress. You may be able to generate interest among the media by using a State of the Corporation speech, State of the County presentation, State of the School District report, State of the Diocese address, or State of the University summary. Look at the annual State of the Society statement at www.prsa.org (about PRSA).

6. Localized Reports. Along a similar line, most organizations are connected to some extent with larger groups. Whenever the larger body issues a report, the local organization may be able to recast it in local terms and general local news interest. For example, if the state's Small Business Administration reports that 75 percent of the small businesses hired additional employees last year, the local Chamber of Commerce may do a spot check to quickly survey local businesses to see if that pattern is represented locally, then report its findings.

Good relationships with the largest organization often make it possible for the local group to receive an early draft of the report before it is released. This allows the group to prepare its localized version of the report.

7. Campaigns. When an organization launches a campaign, it's almost always newsworthy. But make the campaign appropriate to your organizational objectives. Let's revisit the Sheriff's Department and its concern about the use of seat belts. Let's say the department has observed that pregnant women often do not wear seat belts because they find them uncomfortable and they fear the belts may cause complications for their pregnancy. But the department knows that these are unfounded fears compared to the greater threat of being in a traffic accident while not wearing a seat belt. So the department announces a new program to have its deputies contact each obstetrician, midwife, and childbirth educator in the county and each area hospital and birthing center, urging them to encourage their pregnant patients to wear seat belts. The news reports surrounding the announcement of the new program may reach many pregnant drivers even before the campaign begins.

8. Speeches. People in organizations often give speeches, which the public relations writer can use as the basis for news releases, Web archives, letters to the editor, newsletter articles, blogs, and other communication vehicles. It is potentially newsworthy when your CEO travels to the state capital to speak to a lawmaker about corporate taxation. There also may be news interest when your executive director addresses a local civic organization about the spirit of volunteerism in your community.

9. Celebrities. Names make news, and celebrities can draw attention to organizations and causes. For example, ask someone famous to give a speech to your organization. If you are working with a hunting-and-fishing organization, invite a like-minded member of the state legislature to address your members about the state's program for animal conservation. Or name a local community figure as honorary host for a charity event. Or write a letter of protest to the governor, and then give a copy to the local news media.

10. Public Issues. Good public relations practitioners will know the mission and goals of the organizations they serve, and they will take the initiative to tie into current issues and events in ways that can support that mission and further those goals. Here's an example. In a Northeastern city a few years ago, the local newspaper reported some strong anti-Catholic statements made by a traveling nondenominational preacher. The local Jewish Federation used this as a news peg, issuing a public statement that in essence said, "We know what prejudice feels like, and we abhor this." Religious tolerance was on the federation's agenda. Then some Protestant clergy issued similar statements, because their denominational agendas support inter-religious cooperation. The various religious groups involved themselves because it served their own self-interests to oppose religious intolerance and to maintain good relations among the local religious groups.

Another way of tying into external issues is to be aware of the many special events that may be taking place. *Chases' Annual Events*, a reference guide published each fall and available online as well, is an excellent source of ideas for tie-in stories that can be connected to events, festivals, religious observances, presidential proclamations, civic holidays, anniversaries, and other observances.

But don't just issue a comment; do something newsworthy. For example, if you are public relations director for an agency concerned with alcoholism, you might generate activity around the first weekend in April, observed as Alcohol-Free Weekend at the beginning of Alcohol Awareness Month. You might co-sponsor an alcohol-free dance with an area college, prepare a booklet about how to host alcohol-free social events, and try to interest the news media into reporting on the weekend and your agency's role in promoting it.

Sometimes this approach to generating news involves tragedy. An agency dealing with substance abuse unfortunately may have plenty of opportunities to link to public issues: when a drug-plagued celebrity commits suicide, when an employment report documents the negative relationship between drugs and worker productivity, when police report a local drug-related murder, when a politician admits to a drug problem and goes into treatment. Each of these offers a news peg for the organization to re-present its message.

What Would You Do? *Making News*

Consider some of these ethical questions surrounding news making:

- What is the difference between legitimate news activities taking place within an organization and a publicity stunt?
- Do you find it ethical to create a publicity stunt to get attention for your organization?
- Does it matter if the action that gets attention is newsworthy or not?
- How strong must the news elements be to justify a publicity stunt?
- Are there any limits on the kinds of stunts you might arrange for the organization?

Exercise 5.4

Creating Newsworthy Activities

You are the public relations director for one of the following organizations:

- Maurice Manufacturing Inc., a company that makes small kitchen appliances
- The Bertrand Center, a nonprofit agency advocating for people with physical disabilities
- The Pachysandra Alliance, an inner-city program offering free art classes to children, teens, and young adults.

Using the list of 10 ways to generate news, develop a brief, specific story idea (two to three sentences) for each category.

6 Fact Sheet and Advisory

Public relations writers use many different formats to present news about their organizations. Some of these formats are rooted in journalistic protocols and in fact draw on the same writing practices that journalists use in news reporting. Other formats are simpler. This chapter will begin with those—basic writing formats such as fact sheets and event listings. The more sophisticated news release format will be discussed in detail in the next chapter. Here are your objectives for this chapter:

- To write in the simple news format of a fact sheet
- To write effective media advisories
- To pitch story ideas to reporters and other media writers.

News Fact Sheet

Fact sheets provide information stripped down to the bare facts, making them the easiest and quickest way to disseminate information to the news media. Essentially, they are bits of strategic and newsworthy information that public relations writers give to reporters to provide a basis for stories the reporters will write.

Fact sheets are focused on news or events. To communicate clearly with reporters, they should more properly be called **news fact sheets** (as distinguished from background fact sheets, which will be addressed in the following section of this chapter). News fact sheets answer the standard journalistic questions: Who, what, when, where, why, and how? They might also provide background information, benefit statements, quotes, and other information that the public relations writer thinks would be useful to the reporters.

These fact sheets offer bullet points and quick facts that stand out visually and help busy journalists use the organization's information. Fact sheets can be posted at the organization's website media page, included in a media kit along with a news release, or disseminated to reporters in place of a release. They also can be used beyond media relations, such as vehicles for providing information to employees or consumers.

For an organization with its public relations staff at the central headquarters and a number of outlying sites without public relations staffs, fact sheets can be especially useful. A school district, for example, may have a publicity contact at each school site prepare fact sheets for routine information to be distributed directly to the media or circulated "in house" among the various school buildings and administrative offices. These might provide information on things such as PTA meetings, scheduled athletic events, parent conferences, and open houses.

The structure of a fact sheet is simple:

- *Organization ID*: Include the business name, address, phone number, websites and e-mail contact, probably at the top of the sheet.
- *Contact Info*: Include the name and both phone and e-mail contact for a person who can provide clarification or additional information.
- *Format Label*: Clearly identify this as a fact sheet.
- *Topic*: Highlight the subject of topic of the fact sheet.
- *Content Headings*: List several section headings, following by phrases or sentences with detailed information. These content headings can vary depending on the topic. A fact sheet for the opening of a manufacturing plant might follow a basic journalistic formula of who, what, when, etc., along with perhaps a quote and background on the company. A fact sheet for a new fitness center might instead use subject labels: location, facilities, instructor, physical benefits, health benefits, cost, awards. Another way to provide content is to adopt the FAQ model, posing frequently asked questions about the topic and providing short answers for each.

Note that a defining characteristic of fact sheets, as the term is used here, is that they are event based, dealing with a specific activity. Event-based fact sheets are easy to prepare. They require only minimum writing standards and little experience in writing for the news media, though they include essentially the same information that would be included in a more complex news format such as a news release.

Fact sheets are free-standing; that is, they provide self-contained information and do not generally refer to information that could be found in other documents. If you are providing an online fact sheet, however, you can imbed hyperlinks to offer related information from other sources.

Exercise 6.1

Writing a News Fact Sheet

Presume you were public relations director for one of the historic events listed below. Do a bit of research on the person and the invention or accomplishment, then prepare a fact sheet that could be given to reporters about the event in the scenario you select.

- You were public relations director for the Pharaoh Khufu (aka Cheops), announcing plans to build the Great Pyramid
- You were public relations account executive for a client, Vladimir Zworykin, announcing the invention of the television
- You were public relations consultant for Bartolomeo Christoforo, announcing his invention of the piano
- You were public relations director for God, announcing the creation of the world for the Angel Daily News.

In some business environments, fact sheets are preferred to news releases. Dentsu Public Relations, Japan's largest agency, notes that—for media relations in Japan—a news release that reads like a finished press story is viewed with annoyance and distrust. Japanese reporters "see their job to be that of putting the story together, and the best that the news release can do is to provide them with all the factual information they might need—and the phone number of someone they can contact in order to check further," according to Dentsu's guidebook for doing public relations in Japan. A fact sheet is probably the appropriate vehicle for that.

Here is an example of an event-based fact sheet:

Med-Plast, Limited (A Division of Ogawa Industries)

Fact Sheet: New Textile Plant – Jan. 23, 2011

Who

Med-Plast, Limited (a division of Ogawa Industries)
John DeGarmo, president and CEO

What

Opening new plant
Manufacturing plastic materials for hospitals, pharmaceutical companies, drug stores
Hiring 150 production workers

Where

Rachmaninoff (Mathewson County), small town with 57 percent unemployment

When

Staggered hiring schedule
Renovation of former Central Rails plant begins April 15
Training and production begins Sept. 15

Why

Textiles Limited wishes to expand production
Seeks new plant in area with a plentiful work force
Prefers community that could benefit from this expansion

Benefits

New jobs for currently unemployed workers
Boost to ailing small-town economy

Quote

DeGarmo: "I'm happy about the prospect of coming to Rachmaninoff. The town has had some tough times, but the people here are hard-working and friendly. They are the kind of employees any company would be proud to have."

Background on Textiles Limited

Based in Centerville
The state's third-largest producer of medical plastics
DeGarmo chairs the Manufacturer's Task Force on Depressed Communities

Background on Ogawa Industries
Based in San Diego
Nationwide company

As noted above, fact sheets are pretty simple to write. The decisions are not about how to write but about what information to include. If you are unsure about what to put in the fact sheet, consider using **graphic organizer**. This is an easy-to-use tool that can help you sort out the appropriate information. Exhibit 6.1 shows the graphic organizer used to outline the Med-Plast fact sheet.

Exhibit 6.1—GRAPHIC ORGANIZER FOR A FACT SHEET This model graphically displays the various elements for a news-based fact sheet.

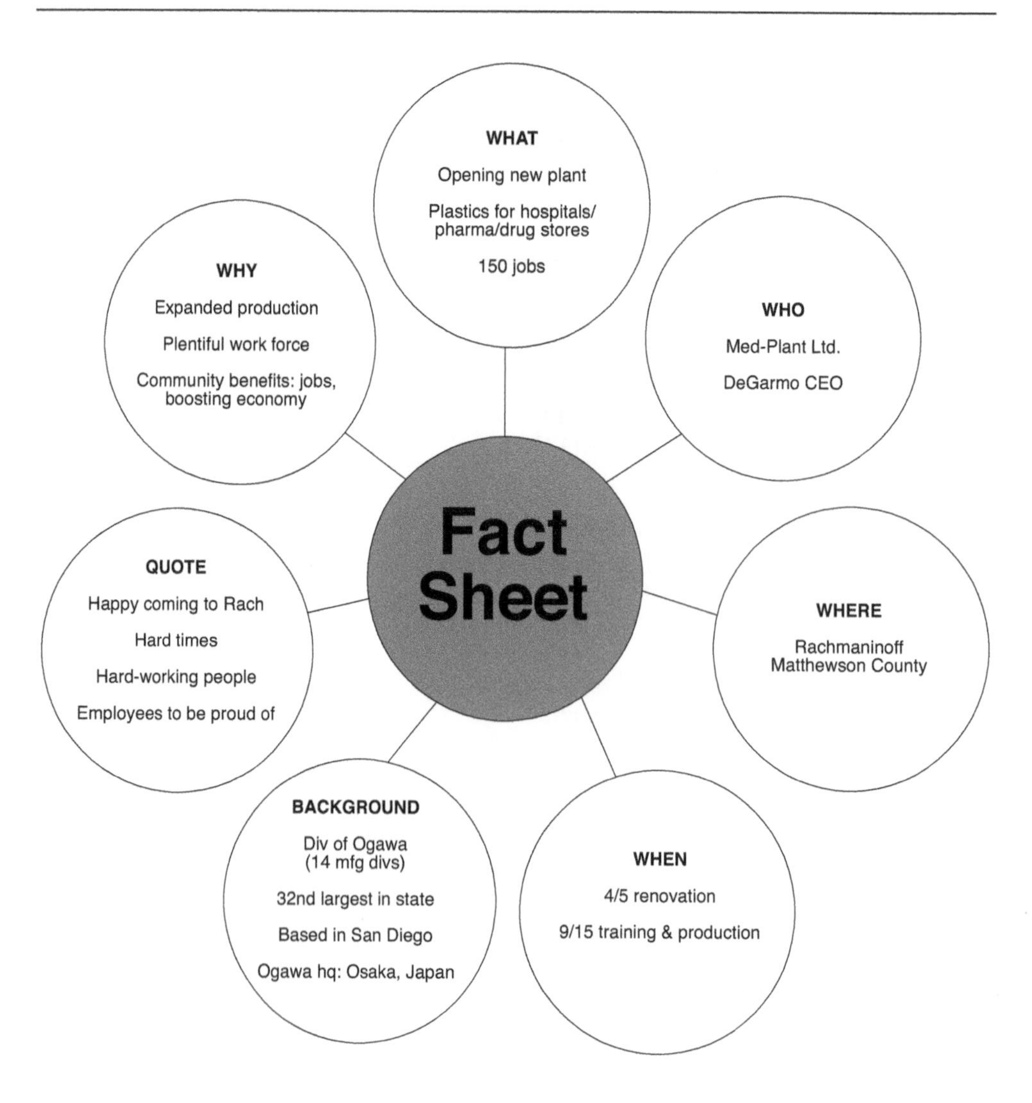

Background Fact Sheet

In addition to event-based fact sheets that serve as substitute news releases, a related communication tool can provide background on issues, programs, or products. This **background fact sheet** is a brief bit of information about an organization and/or the programs or issues it deals with. Sometimes called a **factoid** or a **breaker box**, this is a simple presentation meant to simplify complex information, thus helping reporters and editorial writers—as well as other readers—become familiar with topics of concern to an organization.

(Note that this book uses the term background fact sheet to designate a different type of public relations writing than a backgrounder. The latter is a longer narrative piece, written in news or feature style, that profiles a person, outlines the history of a company, or provides useful information about an issue, project, or product. You will deal with such backgrounders in Chapter 11.)

News fact sheets and background fact sheets are similar in that both include a series of brief notes, often bulleted. But whereas news fact sheets deal with events, background fact sheets deal with issues. For example, a hospital preparing for a high-profile type of experimental heart surgery may prepare a background fact sheet to explain to reporters the various surgical terms, techniques, and equipment involved. A background fact sheet also may provide an overview of the history of an organization or a program, or it may identify milestones in its development. Such materials can be useful not only to reporters but also to many other publics.

News fact sheets and background fact sheets can be complementary. A public relations writer may provide both to reporters—a news fact sheet, for example, to provide information about the opening of a new treatment program for people found to have abused prescription medications, and a background fact sheet to explain the novel treatment methods associated with the program.

Exercise 6.2

Writing a Background Fact Sheet

You are a public relations writer with one of the following organizations. Do some Internet research for appropriate information. Identify appropriate categories of information. Then write a one-page background fact sheet that provides background that can help reporters writing articles for special-interest magazines.

- A network of health care providers promoting self-examination for early detection of breast cancer or testicular cancer
- A travel agency promoting a particular type of vacation such as cruises, wilderness excursions, language immersion, or theater and museum tours
- An organization dealing with some other technical or specialized topic with which you are familiar.

Event Listings

Virtually all print, broadcast, and digital media provide opportunities for organizations to list **event listings**—brief announcements of upcoming activities in various types of community calendars or community bulletin boards.

Don't look at this as an assignment in dull formula writing. Yes, the writing is formulaic, depending on how the particular medium uses the information. But these listings offer an opportunity for the public relations writer to strategically publicize the organization's message, and they deserve thoughtful preparation and attention to detail.

Begin with a plan that identifies your key publics and the media they pay attention to. No use listing an event for young professionals on a radio station with an audience primarily of senior citizens. Write a brief announcement consistent with examples from the relevant publication or broadcast media, then make sure you send the announcement to the proper person. On many newspapers, the city desk does not handle the community events listings. If you send your announcement there, it may end up in the trash. Instead, send it to the calendar editor, events coordinator, or perhaps the public service director; check a media directory or the newspaper website, or telephone the newspaper switchboard to find out where to send your announcement. While it is usually unwise to send duplicate copies of a news release to various sections of a newspaper, a different rule applies to events listings. Most publications will use calendar listings, even if they supplement a news release used in a different section of the publication. Consider how the following media offer such opportunities:

- **Newspaper.** Daily and weekly newspapers have special listings (perhaps even special sections) with calendars that announce events in the arts, sports, business, education, religion, and so on. These listings carry over to the newspaper's website.
- **Magazine.** Sometimes, specialized magazines and other periodicals have sections that list events and activities of interest to their readership.
- **Cable Television.** Cable TV offers opportunities for organizations to use community bulletin boards that list everything from poetry readings to pancake breakfasts. Cable TV may also offer crawls, those messages that scroll across the bottom of the screen in which community organizations can promote their events.
- **Broadcast Television.** Television stations, especially smaller ones, sometimes list local events, both on-air and at their websites.
- **Radio.** Some radio stations may provide listings of major events. Some stations that have community calendars accept written notices or phone-in messages that are recorded for on-air playback. These listings are repeated at the station's website.
- **Wire Service.** For significant events with a high news value, wire services such as the Associated Press or PR Newswire offer an outlet for event listings.
- **Social Media.** Many organizations sponsor various types of social media, such as blogs or Facebook sites, that allow users to post notices of events relevant to the theme of the site.
- **Media Websites.** Most local news media, whether print or broadcast, complement their main venues with websites that often include event listings of potential interest to their audiences.

Media Memo

Public relations writers find that business communiqués to editors, reporters, news directors, bloggers, assignment editors, and other media gatekeepers can generate coverage of their organizations. The most common types of communication are media advisories, public advisories, story idea memos, and pitch letters.

Media Advisory

Public relations writers occasionally find it useful to communicate directly with editors and news directors. A **media advisory**, also called a **media alert** or a **press advisory**, is a straightforward memo notifying the media about an upcoming newsworthy activity related to the organization. Whereas a news release provides information about an event, a media advisory merely informs the media that something newsworthy will occur. For example, you may offer reporters advance access to a visiting celebrity who will be available for an interview. Or you may notify photographers about a photo opportunity that emphasizes the visual aspects of an upcoming activity.

Some media advisories announce "good news" events. For example, if hockey legend Wayne Gretzky is coming to your college or university to present $1,000 scholarships to 30 boys and girls to attend summer hockey camp, your advisory would note this, along with information about place and time. But be careful with more significant news. If you are sending a media advisory to invite reporters to a news conference on a newsworthy topic, be very careful not to provide too much information about the content of the news conference. Just note the topic, for example: *Announcement of the results of a six-month investigation into allegations of financial mismanagement in City Hall.* Save the details for the news conference itself, or you'll read about the findings of your report in the morning newspaper on the day of the news conference.

The writing in media advisories is straightforward, allowing the information to speak for itself. Advisories generally are not full of hype with particularly promotional styles of writing.

Formats for media advisories can vary. Here are two examples of advisories issues by federal agencies. The first is from the U.S. Department of Education announcing a speaking event. The department routinely uses a format that includes an introductory paragraph followed by a bulleted who/what/when outline:

U.S. DEPARTMENT OF EDUCATION ASSISTANT SECRETARY TO SPEAK AT INAUGURAL CONFERENCE OF THE ALLIANCE FOR MULTILINGUAL MULTICULTURAL EDUCATION IN ALBUQUERQUE, NM

U.S. Department of Education Assistant Secretary Thelma Meléndez de Santa Ana will discuss the reauthorization of the Elementary and Secondary Education Act (ESEA) at the inaugural conference of the Alliance for Multilingual Multicultural Education in Albuquerque, New Mexico on Friday, May 21, 2010. Dr. Meléndez de Santa Ana will focus on the importance of language education for linguistically and culturally diverse students.

Who: Assistant Secretary Thelma Meléndez de Santa Ana, U.S. Department of Education, Office of Elementary and Secondary Education

What: Deliver remarks at the inaugural conference of the Alliance for Multilingual Multicultural Education

Where: Albuquerque Convention Center, Ballroom A, 401 2nd Street NW, Albuquerque, NM 87102

When: Friday, May 21, at 8:30 a.m. MT

Dr. Meléndez will speak at 9 a.m.

The second example is from the Pentagon, announcing an upcoming meeting. The advisory format used by the Department of Defense is more narrative in form, imbedding the information in a few paragraphs. Note that the narrative is directed to reporters and is not meant for publication prior to the event.

DOD to Host International Military Sports Council Ceremony

The Department of Defense will host the International Military Sports Council (CISM) Board of Directors meeting March 29. The opening ceremony and press conference will begin at 10 a.m. EDT in the Tuskegee Ball Room at the Bolling Air Force Base club.

With more than 130 countries participating in competitive sports events, CISM is the largest military organization in the world. Its goal is to contribute to world peace by uniting armed forces through sports. Board directors from 17 countries will attend the ceremony.

The opening ceremony will include remarks by Maj. Gen. Gianni Gola, Italy CISM president. Maj. Gen. Darren McDew, U.S. CISM chief of delegation, will also provide remarks. A press conference will immediately follow the ceremony.

Media should arrive at the Bolling Air Force Base South Gate no later than 9:30 a.m. with proof of affiliation and two forms of photo identification. Please e-mail april.cunningham@osd.mil no later than March 26 if you plan to attend. Information about CISM can be found at http://www.armedforcessports.com.

Public Advisory

In emergency situations, organizations may wish to use news channels to communicate with journalists on matters of public interest. They also may take the information directly to the public through websites and various social media. For example, a law-enforcement agency may report a scam artist preying on elderly homeowners, or a hospital may issue a warning about an outbreak of hepatitis. On these occasions, a **public advisory** is issued. This is a direct announcement in which an organization matter-of-factly warns media audiences of potential or imminent harm. Public advisories are brief, factual statements, often listing a follow-up contact.

Here's an example of a public advisory issued by a state health department to warn residents of a potential public health threat. It was posted at the department's website, and it was sent to various media, some of which reported the warning.

Boil Water Advisory Issued for Prudence Island Water District

The Rhode Island Department of Health (HEALTH) has issued a boil water advisory for customers of the Prudence Island Water District (PIWD). HEALTH recommends that water used for bathing of infants, drinking, making ice, brushing teeth or cooking be boiled for one minute and allowed to cool before using. Boiling kills bacteria and other organisms in the water. Bottled water may also be used.

Water system tests confirmed the presence of E. Coli in the public water supply. PIWD is working closely with HEALTH to correct the problem as soon as possible.

The presence of E. Coli bacteria indicates that the water may be contaminated with human or animal wastes. These bacteria can cause diarrhea, cramps, nausea or headaches. Infants, young children, the elderly and anyone with a weakened immune system are at an increased risk for developing more severe symptoms. Consumers who experience any of these symptoms, even if tap water has been avoided, should call their healthcare provider.

This boil water advisory is in effect until further notice from HEALTH. Customers of the Prudence Island Water District are asked to contact neighbors who may not be aware of this advisory.

For information, contact the Prudence Island Water District at 401-835-0475. For general information about drinking water, contact HEALTH's Information Line at 401-222-5960, Monday–Friday, 8:30 a.m.–4:30 p.m. For information on guidelines for food establishments during and after a boil water advisory, visit http://www.health.ri.gov/environment/dwq/boiladvisory.php.

Story Idea Memo

Most news publications are reluctant to use feature stories written by public relations people (community newspapers and trade publications sometimes being the exception). Editors prefer instead to assign their own reporters to write features. Public relations writers can use a **story idea memo** (also called a **tip sheet**) to invite editors and news directors to develop features about interesting people associated with their organization. Often the focus is on the interviewee's activities outside the organization. This kind of story idea memo lets journalists know that you are aware of them and their audiences, even if those stories you suggest have little direct involvement with your organization except for the possibility of being associated with interesting people.

Some public relations practitioners try to provide the media with these ideas on a regular basis. In doing so, they strengthen their own relationship with reporters and keep their organization's name before its publics. Here are examples of potential interviews that might find their way into a story idea memo:

- The society matron who has spent 15 years volunteering at your soup kitchen
- The teacher at your school who each summer takes groups of children from single-parent families on backpacking trips
- The new guy in marketing who is training for the Olympics as a speed skater
- The graduate of your college who just won an Emmy for her work as a television writer.

Here's an example of a story idea memo. Note that it doesn't provide as much information as a new release because it is intended merely to pique the editor's interest in sending a report to do an interview. Note also that the focus is on the potential feature story rather than on the company sending the memo:

When Paul Walbrewster was playing center for his high school basketball team, his focus was to win regardless of the effort involved. The competitive spirit kept him going, and he would spend long hours training and practicing. This determination carried him and the East Bay Oysters to the state championships.

Today Paul is in a wheelchair, the legacy of an automobile accident. But don't call Paul a victim. "It's more like—I'm a survivor," he says. "I don't have time to feel victimized."

This 35-year-old maintains an active training schedule at O'Malley's Gym. He coaches a basketball team for boys and girls with physical handicaps at the East Side Community Center. And he is adjusting to his new promotion as senior sales representative for ComCor Electronics.

If you wish to interview Paul, you may contact him through the ComCor Communications Office at (123) 456–7890.

Pitch Letter

Related to story idea memos, a **pitch letter** is directed to media gatekeepers to entice them to do a story or interview on some aspect of an organization. The previously mentioned story idea memos are understated; they let the information content engage an editor. But there is nothing subtle about a pitch letter. It is unmistakably a sales letter, an attempt to attract the attention of an editor or news director.

An effective pitch letter tries to entice the editor, not with wild exaggerations but rather with enthusiasm and confidence about your program or product. It addresses the benefits to the media if they do the story rather than the advantage to the organization. And it provides a wrap-up, usually with a promise to follow the letter with a telephone call to see if the media have any interest in the issue. Here is an example of a pitch letter designed to get your client on a television talk show. With slight changes, it could easily be used to invite an interview or to ask for photo coverage of a speech.

> Senator Veronica Collingsward is known as one of the "toughest cookies" in the State Senate. Admirers call her "tenacious" and "resourceful." What opponents call her can't be spoken on local television.
>
> Sen. Collingsward has investigated dozens of cases of fraud against nursing home residents. Once, she went undercover, posing as an Alzheimer's patient. The information she gathered helped her colleagues in the Senate pass the Collingsward-O'Halleran bill to establish minimum standards for employees and volunteers at adult day-care facilities.
>
> Without doubt, viewers of your "Morning with Marmaduke" program would be very interested in seeing Sen. Collingsward. Given the right promotion, her guest appearance could be one of your highest-watched segments.
>
> I will contact you this week about arranging an appearance by Sen. Collingsward on "Morning with Marmaduke."

7 News Writing Style

Writing news is different from writing a narrative about something you observe. Let's say you witnessed a car accident. How would you tell about what you saw?

You might start at the beginning: You are walking to the convenience story to get some food for dinner when a car skids around the corner. You recognize the driver as someone from your neighborhood. Butch is his name. He flunked out of college last year and lately has been living on welfare. You've heard that he's been selling drugs as well. You never liked Butch, in part because he is a maniac when he gets behind the wheel. You remember when he nearly hit a woman pushing a baby stroller in the parking lot of your apartment building.

Anyhow, you observe that Butch skids around the corner and hits a parked pick-up truck that belongs to the guy who owns the insurance agency on the corner. Several folks you recognize from the neighborhood also see the accident, but Butch drives away without even stopping. The truck's alarm goes off; the owner comes out of his office and immediately calls 911 on his cell phone, which you notice is one of those new devices with all the features. The insurance business must be doing OK these days.

The cops arrive quickly, which is a surprise, because in the past they haven't had a great track record in responding to police reports from your neighborhood. The insurance guy must have good connections! So when they arrive, several people tell them that Butch was the driver. Later in the day, you hear from a neighbor that the police picked up Butch over in the park. They not only arrested him for the hit-and-run, but it seems they caught him while he was selling weed to some woman. One person in your building says he thinks she works in a new day-care center near the park. Aren't you glad you don't have a kid in that school?

There you have the facts in chronological order, along with some speculation and rumor, irrelevant details, and unsubstantiated claims. That's the way you might tell it to your friend that night, or how you might post it on your Facebook page.

But that's not how you would present the information in a news format. This chapter will give you some guidelines on writing for news purposes. It will focus on structural issues such as short sentences, on stylistic practices associated with identifying people and attributing quotes, and on conceptual approaches such as writing with objectivity. Here are your objectives for this chapter:

- To write in appropriate news style and format
- To explain the legal concept of defamation and privacy.

News Style

Chapter 2 focused on standard writing conventions for all types of writing—things like subject–verb agreement, parallel structure, active voice, and inclusive language. All of these tips and guidelines should carry over into news style. However, news-based reports written by a public relations person generally are rooted in journalistic practice and thus adopt some of the particular conventions of journalistic writing.

Let's review some of these writing protocols. They are based on the need to be both objective and accessible to audiences. Most of what follows will be reminders, since you probably learned these in previous classes. Remember that the same news values and quality writing that make a good news story are needed to make a good news release. You should be a regular reader of the newspapers, magazines, blogs, and other venues where you plan to send your releases.

Short Sentences

All public relations writing should strive for simplicity of style, but news writing especially cries out for this quality. Use short, simple words. Readability studies suggest using words averaging 1½ syllables. Sentences should be brief, with an average of 16 words when the writing is for general audiences.

Paragraphs also should be short. For visual appeal and readability, paragraphs are best kept to about six lines maximum. When text is transferred into newspaper columns, a single typewritten line on 8½-by-11-inch paper will yield about 2½ or three lines of newspaper text. Thus six typed lines of news release type would yield about 15 lines in a newspaper—more than two inches of unbroken type. To ensure easier reading, newspapers need more frequent paragraph breaks.

Exercise 7.1

Simplifying Lengthy Sentences

Rewrite the following lengthy sentences in a shorter version that retains the same information as the original. Your revision probably will be longer than the original because it will include more than one sentence, but no individual sentence should be longer than 20 words.

1. Mitchell Aruba, vice president of research at Mountain Electronics, Ltd., has received the Medal of Distinction given by the Alumni Association of Southeastern University in recognition of his breakthrough invention of the robotic neonatal vascular pump that has become a frequently used tool in cardiac surgery on infants, tripling their chances of survival.
2. Explaining the Potawamiah County Bar Association's opposition to the bill proposed in the County Legislature by Commissioner Carl Frankelberger of

continued . . .

Exercise 7.1 . . . *continued*

Jasonville, association president Bertha Orczynski said the bill would limit the freedom of choice among senior citizens in selecting attorneys of their own choice in civil lawsuits.

3. The Metropolitan Academy for the Arts—a professional training ground for many local musicians and artists—has announced that its new director will be Octavio Diaz, currently managing producer of the Provincial Music Institute and a former professor of arts management at the University of Palos Verdes in your hometown.
4. Milton Redfox will lead a delegation of tribal leaders to the state capital this week, ready to confront state lawmakers over their attempt to collect taxes on goods sold on Indian lands, which Redfox and his supporters note violates their rights to self-governance as a recognized sovereign nation separate from the state, based on the guarantee of several treaties, some of them older than the United States government itself.
5. The Health Advocacy Network of Apple County (HANAC) is creating a county-wide community task force of professionals drawn from the areas of health care, social work, education, religion, government, law enforcement, and business to focus on the growing problem of elder neglect and elder abuse, which HANAC claims is increasing at an alarming 25 percent a year, with the first meeting of the task force scheduled for next Monday at 7 p.m. in the County Building on Macintosh Road.

Simple Language

News releases have a few language idiosyncrasies that should be respected. Here are some of the most common writing conventions for news releases:

- Use past tense *said* to report information that already has been provided or uttered.
- Use the basic word *said* rather than striving for more subjective variations such as *exclaimed*, *proclaimed*, *declared*, *related*, *asserted*, and *remarked*.
- Make careful use of objective varieties such as *noted*, *added*, *pointed out*, *replied*, and *declined to comment*.
- Avoid subjective superlatives such as *best*, *most useful*, and *greatest*.
- Use great care with objective superlatives such as *biggest*, *first*, *unique*, and *only*.
- Avoid hard-sell advertising-based terms such as *breakthrough* and *revolutionary*.
- Use simple verb tenses such as *will begin* rather than the progressive forms such as *will be beginning* that indicate an ongoing action.
- Prefer future forms of verbs such as *will attend* rather than *is planning to attend*.

- Use past perfect forms of verbs for past action of indeterminate timing: *The company has appointed a new director.*
- Use past tense only with specific times, and only when the time is relevant: *The company appointed a new director last week.*

Exercise 7.2

Using Simple Language

Circle the number of the correct answer in each set. Answers are listed at the end of this chapter.

1A. The plan will lead to 200 new jobs, promised the president.
1B. The plan will lead to 200 new jobs, noted the president.
1C. The plan will lead to 200 new jobs, said the president.

2A. The company will market a revolutionary new carpet.
2B. The company will market a carpet with many new features.
2C. The company will market a totally new kind of carpet.

3A. The captain said the ship usually is full.
3B. The captain says the ship usually is full.
3C. The captain says the ship is full more often than not.

4A. InterCity Bank will merge with State Bank.
4B. InterCity Bank has a plan to merge with State Bank.
4C. InterCity Bank announced plans to merge with State Bank.

"Advice from a Pro: David Eisenstadt on News-Style Writing" provides some well-to-heed advice on how to prepare news releases and other media information. He advocates simple and accessible writing, particularly for information about high-tech organizations and clients.

Advice from a Pro *David Eisenstadt on News-Style Writing*

"Market opportunities are missed when the high-technology news release fails to convey the real impact of the new product," says David Eisenstadt, president of The Communications Group Inc., a public relations agency in Toronto. He is a fellow of both the **Public Relations Society of America** and the Canadian Public Relations Association.

The way to ensure news release success is to look at it with the eye of an editor. "It must sell itself to the non-technical decision maker who will decide if it's worth investigating," he says. Eisenstadt offers the following suggestions for public relations writers preparing releases about high-tech products:

continued . . .

Advice from a Pro ***David Eisenstadt . . . continued***

1. Avoid clichés such as "state of the art," "system," and "leading edge of technology."
2. Eliminate jargon. Instead of DBMS use database manager system and explain that term, unless you are sure the audience will understand the term.
3. Don't restructure the English language by toying with capitalization and normal spelling conventions that only confuse readers.
4. Make your "firsts" believable. High-tech industries are full of firsts that quickly become standard operating procedure. If your first solves a problem, deal with it in those terms and don't be overly boastful.
5. Pay attention to physical presentation. A fuzzy gray news release about a high-speed printer somehow rings off-key. Make sure the editor is evaluating your news and not a clumsy presentation of it.
6. Leave out the sales pitch. Business is intensely competitive, but editors have little sympathy for quotes from the marketing manager about how well this little number will sell. Write about what readers want to know, and leave out the bell-ringing prose.
7. Leave out company histories. If it's newsworthy, include a separate brief company history. But don't waste the limited space in a new product release touting what is really irrelevant to the matter at hand.
8. Sell the sizzle, not the steak. Describe equipment in output terms. Readers care less about how the equipment came to be and more about what it can do for them.
9. Give the editor a place to call. Sometimes your new product fits an editorial package you haven't anticipated. Sometimes you've assumed knowledge the editor doesn't have. Always clearly indicate where more information is available.

Titles of People

Public relations writers often find themselves writing about people in their relationship to organizations. We identify people by their occupations, job titles, and functions. How we structure the words to identify people depends upon the person, the title, and the format in which we are writing.

- Formal titles denote authority, professional activity, or academic achievement, such as President, Queen, Gen., Ensign, Dr., and Bishop. These usually precede the name capitalized and with no commas. Follow stylebook rules for abbreviation.
- Short functional and occupational titles may precede the name with no commas and without capitalization. *The book was written by historian John Martin.*
- Longer functional titles may either precede or follow the name, set off by commas, without capitalization. *The book was written by John Martin, professor of history at Jamestown University.*

For a more complete review, see Appendix A in this book, "Common Sense Stylebook for Public Relations Writers," or consult a grammar and usage book or a media stylebook. Look at information dealing with appositives, titles, and commas.

Exercise 7.3

Identifying People by Title

Look at the following examples of titles. Circle the number of the correct choice(s) in each set of sentences. Answers are listed at the end of this chapter.

1A. President Martin Adamson will visit next Tuesday.
1B. Martin Adamson the president will visit next Tuesday.
1C. President Martin Adamson, will visit next Tuesday.

2A. The general manager Heidi Copeland will visit next Tuesday.
2B. The general manager, Heidi Copeland, will visit next Tuesday.
2C. The general manager Heidi Copeland, will visit next Tuesday.

3A. Prime Minister Claude Philippe Dubec, arrived.
3B. Prime Minister Claude Philippe Dubec arrived.
3C. Claude Philippe Dubec, prime minister, arrived.

4A. Hieronymus Kastenzakas the new ambassador, arrived from Greece.
4B. Hieronymus Kastenzakas, the new ambassador arrived from Greece.
4C. Hieronymus Kastenzakas, the new ambassador, arrived from Greece.

Attribution of Quotes

Public relations writers often wish to present information and opinions that come from someone they have interviewed. Such statements may emerge from printed materials, or perhaps the public relations writer wants to suggest an appropriate comment by an organizational spokesperson.

In whatever context, statements made by people need to be attributed to them. The most common attribution involves the past-tense form of the verb *say*, such as *she said* or *they said*. This attribution, also called a **speech tag**, is used not only with direct quotes but also with paraphrases. Conventional news-style writing has a few guidelines on how to use **quotations**, informally called **quotes**, within the format of a news release:

- A full-sentence quote (or the first sentence of a multisentence quote) should begin as a new paragraph.
- Attribution should follow (not precede) a brief full-sentence quote.
- Attribution may interrupt a longer full-sentence or multisentence quote, with the speech tag placed at a logical pause in the sentence such as following a phrase or clause.
- Attribution generally comes before partial quotes.
- Partial quotes cannot lead into a full-sentence quote.
- Paraphrases are appropriate substitutes for cumbersome or unimpressive quotes.
- When attributing quotes directly, use *said*. Natural word order in speaking probably would be the name of the speaker, then the verb, then the quote or paraphrase. *John*

said "Well, that stinks!" But news writing inverts the sentence to begin it with the quote. Use quote-*said*-speaker when the speaker is identified by a full name or long title. *"I am not seeking re-election," said the assistant attorney general.* But use quote-speaker-*said* when the speaker is identified by only a pronoun or a short last name or reference. *"I am not seeking re-election," she said.*
- Attribution should be to people, not to organizations.

Exercise 7.4

Using Speech Tags Properly

Consider each of the following speech tags that sometimes can replace *said*. If you are not sure of the exact meaning of any of the words, look them up in a dictionary. Then briefly note how each word differs from the simple *said*.

1. Admitted
2. Advised
3. Alleged
4. Announced
5. Argued
6. Commented
7. Conceded
8. Contended
9. Declared
10. Disclosed
11. Explained
12. Maintained
13. Mentioned
14. Noted
15. Observed
16. Pointed out
17. Proclaimed
18. Promised
19. Remarked
20. Replied
21. Reported
22. Revealed
23. Stated
24. Vowed
25. Wrote.

As a matter of strategy, public relations writers should observe five criteria in dealing with quotes. First, every quote requires the knowledge and permission of the person being quoted. Second, every quote should be strategic, furthering the organization's public relations objectives. Third, every quote should sound natural; read it out loud as a check to ensure that it does not sound contrived. Fourth, every quote should be strong, with language that will evoke a response from the reader or that will remain in the reader's memory. Finally, the speech tag should be appropriate to how the speaker made the statement or gave the information.

Remember that the quotation marks visually attract a reader's attention. Make sure that the information included within quotation marks is the most strategically effective language you can use. For example, in a newspaper story about prostitution and other vice crimes moving beyond the inner city, a police detective was quoted: "People have their heads in the sand about the suburbs. They still think it's Andy and Barney on patrol, peaceful and quiet. Well, it's not." That's the kind of quote that not only makes the point but stays with the reader for some time.

Exercise 7.5

Attributing Quotes Correctly

Review your skills with the following examples of giving attribution. Circle the number of the correct choice(s) in each set of sentences. Answers are listed at the end of this chapter.

1A. Commissioner Frank Lee Jones said: "This can become a huge asset to our community."

1B. "This can become a huge asset to our community," said Commissioner Frank Lee Jones.

1C. "This can become a huge asset to our community," Commissioner Frank Lee Jones said.

2A. "We expect to see an increase in the number of applicants over the next six months," said the admissions director.

2B. The admissions director said: "We expect to see an increase in the number of applicants over the next six months."

2C. "We expect to see," the admissions director said, "an increase in the number of applicants over the next six months."

3A. Said the federation director: "When you consider the source of this funding and its exceptionally high standards—standards that can be met with only the greatest of difficulty by many organizations—we are especially pleased and honored to have been chosen to receive this prestigious award."

3B. "When you consider," said the federation director, "the source of this funding and its exceptionally high standards—standards that can be met with only the greatest of difficulty by many organizations—we are especially pleased and honored to have been chosen to receive this prestigious award."

3C. The director said she is especially pleased because the federation met the high standards of the foundation.

4A. "When TriChem renovated its plant, we hoped to see some environmental improvements. But we never expected to eliminate the pollution so quickly," said Dayananda.

4B. "When TriChem renovated its plant, we hoped to see some environmental improvements," said Dayananda. "But we never expected to eliminate the pollution so quickly."

4C. "When TriChem renovated," said Dayananda, "its plant, we hoped to see some environmental improvements. But we never expected to eliminate the pollution so quickly."

Objectivity

In news writing, readers should know they are obtaining facts, not the opinion, speculation, rants, or editorial comments of the writer. As a public relations writer preparing news copy, you will need to observe this practice by writing objectively. To do that, avoid commercial plugs, shun condescending or condemnatory rhetoric, and eliminate flowery language and fawning reports.

Does this mean that a news piece includes no opinion? Absolutely not! A news release or any similar news-based writing can have plenty of opinion and comment. But the opinion must be presented with attribution; in other words, it should present the fact that so-and-so expressed an opinion. For example, it may be the writer's opinion that the annual fundraising effort is for a worthy cause, but the writer cannot include that as a matter of fact. However, the writer may report the fact that the mayor called the cause very worthy. The writer also may assemble evidence and include information about the positive community benefits provided through past fundraising efforts, allowing readers to conclude for themselves that the program is worthwhile.

As a public relations writer, you should report facts, attribute opinion, and make clear the difference between the two. Report facts because they provide information that is a matter of record or verification. Attribute opinions and document comments so they become factual records of what someone said, rather than the inappropriate opinions of the writer.

Exercise 7.6

Writing with Objectivity

With the following sets of sentences and paragraphs, circle the number of the preferred choice(s). Answers are listed at the end of this chapter.

1A. Some scientists say that a meteor hitting the earth caused the disappearance of the dinosaur.

1B. Scientists say that a meteor hitting the earth probably caused the disappearance of the dinosaur.

1C. The dinosaur disappeared because a meteor hit the earth.

2A. The ComText Corp. is pleased to announce that its Employee of the Year award will be presented to Manuella Cardamone of Charleston.

2B. The ComText Corp. announced that its Employee of the Year award will be presented to Manuella Cardamone of Charleston.

2C. The ComText Corp. will present its Employee of the Year award to Manuella Cardamone of Charleston.

3A. The Road King Tire Co., which manufactures the safest automobile tires on the road today, will build a quality control center in Moreno County. The new facility, which will employ 234 local workers, will inspect Road King tires before they are shipped to distribution centers throughout North America.

3B. The Road King Tire Co. will build a quality control center in Moreno County. The center will hire 234 local workers to inspect what *Consumer's World* magazine rates as the safest American-made automobile tire.

3C. The manufacturer of popular automobile tires, Road King Tire Co., is pleased to be opening a quality control center in Moreno County. At the new center, 234 local workers will guarantee the safety of the world's best automobile tires on the road today.

continued . . .

Exercise 7.6 . . . *continued*

4A. Critics say Satomi's musical repertoire ranges from jazz to classical.
4B. Satomi's musical repertoire ranges from jazz to classical.
4C. An outstanding musician, Satomi has an amazingly broad repertoire, which easily ranges from jazz to classical.

Neutrality

A well-written piece of public relations writing will always be directed to a particular public. But if it takes a news format, the writer cannot appear to be writing personally to readers. Avoid *you* and *your* statements. Avoid telling readers what to do. Instead, write as if members of your key public were absent. Provide information but not directions. Don't tell readers to go to the organization's website for more information. Instead, report that additional information is available at the website. It's a subtle distinction, but it's one that separates news from promotion, thus making it more likely that the media gatekeepers will see your piece as a legitimate source of the news they seek to present to their listeners, viewers, and/or readers.

Exercise 7.7

Writing with Neutrality

Circle the correct answer in each set. Answers are listed at the end of this chapter.

1A. If you are interested in attending the concert, you may obtain tickets by calling the box office at 123–4567.
1B. Tickets are available through the box office at 123–4567.
1C. Call the box office at 123–4567 for tickets.

2A. Interested students should register for the workshop before Jan. 15.
2B. The registration deadline is Jan. 15.
2C. You can register for the workshop before Jan. 15.

3A. Membership information is available at the museum office at 55 Greenfern Circle.
3B. Don't miss out on this opportunity. Sign up today for membership. Stop by at the museum office at 55 Greenfern Circle.
3C. The membership office at 55 Greenfern Circle will be happy to give out membership information.

Accuracy

Precision is crucial in public relations writing. Check and double-check all facts. Review your writing for spelling, punctuation, and correct use of the stylebook. One way of checking for accuracy is to read your writing out loud. This will help you slow down and will prevent you from overlooking mistakes.

Pay particular attention to names and titles, and make sure there is a full first reference. Information can get lost as a result of rearranging, adding, and deleting information as part of the revision process. Be careful that a stray surname or an unidentified person doesn't pop up within the story.

Newsworthy Information

News writing should not tell us what we already know or what we can easily conclude on our own. For example, don't write that *The CEO is proud of the company's success.* Of course she is, but it's not news. Instead, cite reasons why the CEO is proud—because third-quarter profits were the highest ever or because this was the most accident-free year on record.

Neither is it news that *The employee said she is happy about her promotion* or *When the director asked the committee to meet, the committee chair said a meeting would be scheduled.* Faced with non-news statements such as these, you have two choices: eliminate the statement, which is probably what you'd do about the happy employee, or expand upon the statement, such as by noting more about the rescheduled meeting time and place. If you don't make such changes, the journalist receiving the news release will make the changes for you, or simply toss the whole thing in the garbage.

Legal Issues

Two areas of law can have a significant impact on the work of a public relations writer. These are defamation and privacy. Let's look at each.

Defamation

Anyone who wants to become a public relations writer should be familiar with the legal concept of defamation. Based on English common law with legal roots extending back to classical Rome, the concept has been consistently applied in the American legal system.

Defamation is communication that reasonable and average people in the community believe impugns "the honesty, virtue, or reputation" of a person, who is thereby exposed "to public hatred, contempt, and ridicule." It is negative and harmful language that identifies a person and is published or communicated to a third party, with some degree of fault by the person or organization making the statement in the first place. Defamation takes two forms: **slander** (oral defamation) and **libel** (written or broadcast defamation).

Simply using language that can harm a person's reputation does not make a writer guilty of defamation. Laws vary among states and between states and the federal government, but in general here are the elements that are involved in the legal understanding of defamation:

- **Defamatory Content.** Language is defamatory when it holds someone up to public hatred, contempt, or ridicule, reflecting negatively on a person's morality or integrity or discrediting a person professionally. Courts have ruled that some words are libelous *per se* (Latin for "by itself"). These have been called **odious labels**—words such as *adulterer, blackmail, corrupt, crook, deadbeat, drug addict, drunk, liar, pervert, poor credit risk, prostitute, racist, retarded, terrorist*, and *suicide*. Qualifying words such as *allegedly* or *reportedly* won't save a writer from charges of defamation. Note that the law considers photos and drawings as extensions of words and thus potentially defamatory.

- **Falsity.** Even if a statement holds someone to public ridicule, it must be proven false in order for the courts to rule it as defamation.
- **Identification.** Defamation identifies the person, though this doesn't have to be by name; innuendo and clues sufficient to identify a person may constitute defamation. Mistaken identification, whether from carelessness or through honest error, does not protect a writer from blame.
- **Publication.** Defamation is information published or communicated to a third party. "Publication" is interpreted broadly, and it includes dissemination of information through news releases, newsletters, memos, e-mail notices, blog postings, social media pages, and so on. Broadcast scripts and video presentations are considered parallel to other written forms of communication. It is not usually necessary to prove that a writer even knew that a third party had access to the information, only that it was disseminated.
- **Fault.** Defamation involves fault by the writer, based on some measure of carelessness or malice. Standards vary, depending on the status of the person claiming to have been harmed. A private citizen generally has only to show that the person preparing the message was negligent, but public officials and public figures need to show that the writer was malicious.
- **Harm.** Compensation for defamation is based on personal harm. The five previous criteria can constitute defamation, but legal cases generally are reconciled on the basis of harm. Juries determine if defamation occurred and, if so, the extent of the harm, such as by causing the defamed person to become a social outcast, lose business revenues, or experience emotional problems. That determines the amount of money needed to compensate the victim for the defamation.

There are three common defenses against defamation. One is truth—more specifically, **substantial truth** that can be proven in court. A second defense is that the communication is made in the public interest as a matter of **privilege**, such as a defamatory statement made during official or judicial proceedings or public meetings, or in news reports of such incidents. The third defense against defamation is **fair comment and criticism**, based on the right to critique and criticize in matters of public interest.

Three technical defenses also exist: that the statute of limitations for filing a lawsuit has expired, that the person gave consent or invited the defamatory statement, and that the statement was made as part of a broadcast by political candidates.

Additionally there are a few grey areas in which various courts have inconsistently applied certain concepts, such as the defense that a statement was made in *good faith*, such as passing along information that a person reads in a newspaper. Some jurisdictions exempt statements of opinion from being defamatory, on the premise that opinion is by definition not a statement of fact. A similarly uncertain defense is that the person claiming to be defamed has such a bad reputation as to be incapable of further defamation.

Individual living persons can sue for defamation, but courts have been reluctant to uphold claims of defamation against groups. Companies can claim defamation only if they can prove that the language damaged the company itself, rather than individuals in it. Nonprofit organizations can claim defamation for language that hurts their ability to raise funds, and associations can sue over language that prevents them from attracting members or support.

But the courts have not allowed defamation claims against social, political, religious, and other types of groups. The larger the group, the more difficult it is to show that it was injured through defamation.

Defamation cases usually involve the news media, but public relations practitioners are not immune. Several libel cases revolve around charges contained in news releases. A Fort Lauderdale pharmaceutical company sued a Denver company that issued a news release claiming the Florida company had stolen its computer software. A computer software company sued a competitor for $1 billion, claiming its stock dropped because of false allegations in the competitor's news release. And a New Jersey humane association sued 15 former volunteers over their news release accusing the association of animal cruelty and false advertising.

A 1976 case is a classic in the field of libel and public relations. The research director at a state mental hospital in Michigan sued for libel because Sen. William Proxmire sent out news releases and published in a newsletter that the researcher was wasting public funds. The Supreme Court ruled that the researcher was not a public figure and was entitled to protection as a private citizen. The court said that while the senator was privileged in making defamatory comments in Congress, he lost that privilege when he made those same comments in a news release and a constituent newsletter. The case eventually was settled out of court when Proxmire gave the researcher $10,000 and a public apology.

In another classic case, Marie Luisi filed a $20 million libel suit against the J. Walter Thompson advertising agency, which had fired her. The woman claimed she was libeled because an agency news release said she had been dismissed because of "improper activities" in the finances of her department. The state Supreme Court dismissed the case only because the woman failed to produce enough evidence to substantiate her claim that JWT had acted in a "grossly irresponsible" manner. The court did not dispute the role of the news release as the central and official corporate statement.

In Canada, meanwhile, a former Security Intelligence Service officer sued a member of parliament over her news release claiming he was a Soviet spy, and he received a formal apology from the legislator.

Privacy

Privacy involves the right to be left alone, and invasion of privacy is another legal area that affects the public relations profession. Unlike laws against defamation that hinge on the accuracy of a claim, privacy laws focus on whether a person was singled out for attention without his or her consent, regardless of the accuracy of reports or statements.

Public relations writers generally deal with positive aspects of people's professional lives: promotions, awards, retirements, and so on. But three aspects of law can affect the public relations writer: private facts, intrusion, and misappropriation.

The legal concept of **private facts** refers to personal information that is intimate, offensive, and not of legitimate public concern. Revealing private information about a person's finances, sexuality, or health might be an invasion of privacy unless the information is clearly newsworthy or unless it has been presented with the person's knowledge and consent. A person fired after his arrest for public exposure couldn't sue his former employer for invasion of privacy, even if the employer had issued a public explanation for the firing, because the report was based on a police report.

Intrusion involves gathering information secretly, such as by taping a private face-to-face or telephone conversation or interview without permission. It is permissible to tape public events and meetings without getting permission.

The area of privacy most frequently a problem for public relations people is **misappropriation**. This involves the use of a person's name or image for commercial purposes without permission, such as using someone's picture for promotional or advertising purposes. This includes the use of look-alikes and sound-alikes.

Though state laws vary, in general they are designed to protect people from being exposed unwillingly to the glare of publicity. Recall that truth is the ultimate defense against defamation. In privacy matters, the main legal protection comes through permission. You can write whatever you think is appropriate, as long as you have approval from the person you are writing about. Public relations practitioners can protect themselves and their employers against lawsuits by making sure that the people mentioned in news releases, blogs, and other venues have given their consent, either implicitly or explicitly.

Explicit permission means that the person gives a written statement such as an individual consent release to allow the publication or other use of a photograph or video image. Another form of explicit permission is a blanket consent release, such as a signed statement, often part of an employee file or an employment policy release, which allows an organization to use information or photos for publicity or nonpaid promotional purposes.

Public relations writers sometimes find themselves dealing with **implicit permission**. This is based on the notion that any reasonable observer would see that the person is willingly participating in a situation. A person implies permission by participating in a news interview, a television program, or a posed photograph. It generally is safe to consider implied consent for publicity about an employee in routine situations such as hiring, promotions, and awards.

There may be times when the public relations practitioner is restricted—by law or by organizational policy—to providing only the most basic information about a person. For example, information about current or former employees may be limited to verifying their employment and job title. One public relations manager found her hands tied when a former employee of her company became a whistleblower, telling both the government and the news media about allegedly illegal activity by the corporation. The public relations manager could not tell the fact that the employee may have been biased against the corporation. Neither could she indicate that this employee had made similar accusations against two previous employers, accusations that had been found to be untrue. All she could do was verify the employment status of the whistleblower and endure the criticism of fellow employees who did not understand the legal constraints on her ability to publicly defend their company.

The case of *Vassiliades v. Garfinckel's* stands as an application of privacy law in the public relations arena. Her surgeon photographed Mary Vassiliades before and after she had plastic surgery. The surgeon later showed the photos at an event promoting skin cream sponsored by Garfinckel's department store. The court said that, while the subject was newsworthy, use of Mrs. Vassiliades' photos without her consent for commercial purposes was a violation of her privacy. Because the store could show that the doctor told the company's public relations director that the patient had given her consent to use the photos, liability was placed on the doctor, not the store.

Exercise 7.8

Avoiding Invasion of Privacy Issues

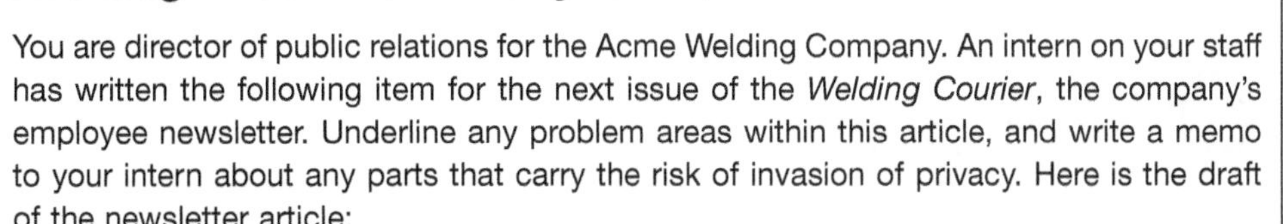

You are director of public relations for the Acme Welding Company. An intern on your staff has written the following item for the next issue of the *Welding Courier*, the company's employee newsletter. Underline any problem areas within this article, and write a memo to your intern about any parts that carry the risk of invasion of privacy. Here is the draft of the newsletter article:

Michael Marakowski, a technician with the computer department, has been named Volunteer of the Year by the Abernathy Preschool Program, where his daughter Amanda is enrolled. Michael's ex-wife is a secretary with the Abernathy Program.

Michael, 35, who works on the night shift, has been with Acme Welding for more than six months. He just received his first performance evaluation and received a "Satisfactory-Plus" rating.

Acme Welding Personnel Director Martha Binetti said she is pleased that community-minded people such as Michael are working for this company.

Michael is also a volunteer peer counselor at the Alternative Men's Health Center in neighboring Indiana County, according to a co-worker. The health center is part of a system of clinics throughout the upstate area that have been active in fighting the spread of AIDS within high-risk populations.

Answers to Chapter Exercises

Exercise 7.2

1C, 2B, 3A, 4A

Exercise 7.3

1A, 2B, 3B, 4C

Exercise 7.5

1B, 2A, 3C, 4B

Exercise 7.6

1A, 2C, 3B, 4B

Exercise 7.7

1B, 2B, 3A

8 Print News Release

Communication historians report that the world's first news release was a graduation announcement issued in 1758 by King's College (now Columbia University). In 1906 Ivy Lee, the man known as the father of modern public relations, developed what apparently was the first corporate news release for his client, the Pennsylvania Railroad. The *New York Times* published the release verbatim, praising the railroad for its openness. Ah, those were the days!

Over the decades, the news release became a mainstay of public relations writing, though that is changing. Today, proportionally fewer people read newspapers than in previous generations; more than one-third of American households do not even subscribe to a newspaper. Television news attracts at most two-thirds of Americans aged 18 to 35. Many people, particularly younger and college-educated Americans, get their news through the Internet, though much of this is from the websites of mainstream newspapers, television networks, and news agencies.

Despite this fragmentation of media, public relations writers still count the news release as one of their most important tools. It is versatile, and it can be used with emerging media. Articles and websites proclaim the death of the news release, but it lives on.

Occasionally, public relations people say they no longer write news releases. But when you observe their output, you'll find an array of e-mails to reporters, postings on their clients' blogs, and information at their organizational websites, all of which function as news releases even if they aren't labeled as such. This is another proof of the versatility and tenacity of news releases.

Organizations in all kinds of situations use news releases to make announcements, encourage support, respond to critics, invite participation, and report progress. Additionally, the same kind of writing associated with news releases is the basis for effective writing for organizational newsletters, websites, e-zines, and internal newspapers. A specialized new form has emerged as the social media release.

For some practitioners, media relations will be the primary focus. For others, it may be less important, but the ability to write with a news approach remains a basic skill needed for professional success. In virtually every career opportunity in public relations, you will be expected to have mastered this type of writing. Job interviews often include an on-the-spot test of your ability to write a news release.

This chapter introduces you to the format and content of news releases. It will explore different types of releases and writing techniques associated with them. You will discover that news releases have many purposes and offer various benefits. They give information to reporters preparing stories for daily newspapers and provide facts to radio and television journalists who will follow up with interviews. They attract photographers to scheduled events and offer wire services information that can be boiled down into briefs and summaries. They serve as prepackaged reports that smaller newspapers and special-interest publications may use as is. Organizations post releases at their websites and social media sites, where they can be read by any interested person and sometimes are picked up by reporters, bloggers, and columnists on news websites to be shared with their audiences. Here are your objectives for this chapter:

- To write different kinds of leads and news briefs
- To write news releases of different types and purposes.

News Release Format

A **news release** is a news story written by a public relations practitioner. It has the look and feel of a journalistic news report because it consciously adopts standard practices of news writing. This format is commonly used by organizations to provide information to the text-based news media such as printed newspapers and their online editions, broadcast media, and purely online news media. The latter include news websites such as the Huffington Post and the Drudge Report, as well as online-only newspapers such as the *Seattle Post-Intelligencer*, the first major U.S. newspaper to drop its print edition and go entirely online.

The news release may be one of the few truly egalitarian elements left in modern society. Whether written by a highly paid public relations practitioner, a college graduate just getting started, or a volunteer at a nonprofit organization, each news release has the same chance of being used by an editor or news director. What determines acceptance or rejection is not where it comes from but how professionally the release is written.

Here are some guidelines about format to help you prepare a standard news release.

- Use standard 8½-by-11-inch paper, preferably white or off-white. Use standard black ink. Avoid decorative borders.
- Justify the left margin and leave the right margin ragged. You want the release to look like a working draft that the editor or news director will mark for publication or air use.
- Set your computer to disallow hyphenation at the end of lines.
- Use a clean, professional-looking type; 12-point Times Roman is the best choice, 11-point if you need to squeeze.
- Make sure you use a quality printer.
- Set margins at least one inch on each side, preferably 1.5 inches. Indent paragraphs the standard five or six spaces, about a half-inch. Use line spacing of 1.5 or 2. Don't use extra spacing between paragraphs.
- Make sure the release is letter perfect in terms of accuracy and neatness.

First impressions are important, and editors often make judgments about the credibility of public relations writing when they first glance at the news release. Several standard components should be part of every news release. Including these components signals that you know your craft. An example of a properly formatted news release is shown in Exhibit 8.1.

Exhibit 8.1—COMPONENTS OF A NEWS RELEASE Here's an example of a properly formatted news release.

NEWS from
Organization's Name

Street Address
City, State, Zip
Website (optional)

Public Relations Contact Person
Office Telephone Number
E-Mail Address

FOR IMMEDIATE RELEASE
Sending Date

HEADLINE, ALL-CAPS AND CENTERED (Optional)
Subhead, caps and lower-case letters (Optional)

DATELINE CITY, State—Begin with the heading information, including the organization's name and address, and perhaps a main telephone number or website. Include the name and contact information for the public relations director or writer.

A news flag is an optional part of the heading. Note both the sending date and the release date, usually indicated by the phrase "For Immediate Release." Keep this heading as small as possible so as not to take up valuable space for the news release.

You may include a headline. If you do, use present tense and type it in all-capital letters and centered over the body of the news release.

Begin the body of the release immediately after the optional dateline, or after the date if you do not use a headline. Allow left and right margins of at least one inch. Type copy in line-spacing intervals of 1.5 or 2 to allow the editor to make up the copy. Also, use an unjustified (ragged) right margin. Do not hyphenate words at the ends of lines.

Keep paragraphs short, usually between two and five typed lines. Remember that one line of typed copy will equal about three lines of type in newspaper columns. Use standard paragraph indents of about one-half-inch, with no extra spacing between paragraphs.

"The news release should look like a manuscript," said Ron Smith, the author of this textbook. "You want the editor to take out a pencil and begin marking up your news release for use in the paper. That's your immediate objective."

Make every effort to keep the release to a single page, and conclude the release with an end mark centered below the last line, said Smith.

If it is necessary to continue the news release to a second page, make the break on a paragraph. Never break in the middle of a paragraph. Include a more line at the bottom of the first page, and include a slug line at the top of the second page.

#####

Following are several elements that public relations writers include in most news releases. Adopt these into your own writing practices.

News Flag. A **news flag** simply is the word *News* printed in large type. This is an optional part of the release heading. Some writers use a news flag to make it absolutely clear to an editor that this is a news release rather than some other type of communication. Other writers feel that the news release format is obvious and does not need the flag.

Organization Identification. This information may be part of the letterhead. It should feature the name and address of the sending organization. Limit your use of extraneous information and corporate tags such as affiliation with a parent company or a nonprofit funding source.

Contact Information. The heading should identify the public relations contact person (usually the same person who prepared the news release). Include the name and telephone numbers, e-mail address, and perhaps a fax number. Include the Web address, particularly if you have developed a Web space for reporters. Try to use as little space as possible.

Distribution Date. News releases usually have two dates. The first is the day the release is mailed, e-mailed, faxed, delivered, or otherwise distributed (implicitly, the date it is written and released). This is presented in the conventional manner for the editor or news director receiving the release: month, day, and year (*June 26, 2011*) for U.S. media; day, month, and year (*26 June 2011*) for releases prepared for media in other parts of the world or for military media.

The amount of time it takes reporters and other media professionals to gather and present their news is called **lead time**. This varies with both the type of medium and the kind of presentation that will be given. The best way to know the lead time required by various media is to ask. Contact the city editor of a newspaper, the news director or assignment editor of a radio or television station, or the acquisitions editor or news editor of a magazine. Or ask an individual reporter or columnist. In general, here are typical lead times needed for various news media tactics:

- *Daily newspapers* may need a week's notice for routine information, a day or several hours for important news, and less than an hour for major on-deadline news.
- *Nondaily newspapers* need more lead time. Plan to provide information at least one publication date before the relevant date of the information. For example, at least a week for a weekly newspaper.
- *Magazines* published on a monthly basis may require a two-month lead. Weekly news magazines have a much shorter lead time, but they seldom take information from public relations sources.
- *Radio stations* should have about a week's notice for routine information and for upcoming events that reporters might cover, with important news being handled up to news time. Breaking news may be covered live. Talk shows and other programs with guests may require several weeks to schedule.
- *Television* news operations should be given up to a week's notice for routine information and for events that reporters might cover, with important news being handled up to news time. Breaking news may be covered live. Talk shows and programs with guests may require several weeks to schedule.

- *Blogs* and *news* websites technically have no lead time, because they can be updated continuously. But contact blog editors and columnists to find out their busy times and learn how long it takes them to work through information they receive and post it for their readers.

Intended Use Date. The second date indicates when the release may actually be used by the news media. Generally, this is handled with the phrase *For Immediate Release*, signifying that the release may be used as soon as the news media wish to use it. This phrase is standard in most parts of North America. Because journalists take it for granted, some public relations practitioners have stopped using the phrase.

An alternative to immediate release is to indicate an **embargo**, in which you ask that the release not be used before a specific time and day, such as *For release after 6 a.m., June 26, 2011.*

In most news situations, an embargo is obsolete. It imposes no obligation on the news media, and it may make you the source of conflict among various media if the embargo is not equally observed by each of them. Second, it seems to tease reporters with advance information they are asked not to use.

However, organizations that deal with magazines and feature writers or with reporters on specialized fields such as medicine and science may find embargoes helpful. Such reporters generally respect embargoes, finding it useful to maintain a practice that gives them extra time to prepare their stories. The Census Bureau, for example, posts embargoed news releases at its website (census.gov) and offers a password to reporters. The bureau explains that the embargo gives reporters time to sift through the information and thus write more accurate stories.

Veteran practitioners caution that writers dealing in international situations should take care, because the concept of embargo carries little or no significance in some media cultures.

Headline. The **headline** signals for the editor or news director the content of the release, and thus may attract attention to its contents. It should be visually prominent, with all-capital letters, underlining, boldface, and/or centering immediately above the text of the release. Headlines are written in the standard newspaper style, generally in the present tense.

Some writers prefer to complement the headline with a **subhead** that fleshes out the theme and serves almost as an abstract or teaser for the release. Others prefer to use a **title** to merely indicate the topic. Still other practitioners skip the heading entirely, preferring instead to have the media gatekeeper evaluate the newsworthiness of the release on the basis of the lead paragraph.

Headlines are particularly useful with electronic archives. An agency, for example, may prepare several news releases in the same month for one of its clients. Let's call the client CompuTrim. Without headlines, all of the company's news releases for June would be archived under the same name. But with headlines, the news releases would be distinguishable in an archive such as LexisNexis. For example, *CompuTrim Names New CEO, CompuTrim Announces Record Third-Quarter Profits, CompuTrim Opens Branch in Seattle.*

Dateline. A **dateline** is an occasional element of a news release, featuring the name of the city or town where the release originates. Despite its name, the dateline does not include a date. The name stems from the early days of American journalism, when it took several days or weeks to publish a story from a distant correspondent. With today's technology, all stories usually can be published the day they are disseminated, so the date has disappeared from the dateline, leaving only the point of origin.

Though the dateline is not always needed, it is not optional. Use a dateline when the release is being sent beyond the local area of the sending organization. Use it to localize the release for the geographic location of one of an organization's branch sites.

Use all-capital letters for the city name, followed by the Associated Press Stylebook abbreviation for the state, province, or country in regular text (both caps and lower case). Some cities are well known nationally or regionally and may stand alone without the state/province/country designation. (Consult the AP Stylebook for a listing of these cities.) For datelines in regional releases, omit the state if it is not needed for clarity. For example: PHILADELPHIA or LARAMIE, Wyo., or ST. PIE, Montreal, Canada. Use a dash to separate the dateline from the beginning text of the release.

End Mark. Place a final **end mark** at the conclusion of the release, centered following the last line. The most common version of this is a series of hatch marks (####). Outside of North America, the more common end mark is ((END)) or ((ENDIT)). The end mark often is set off with double parentheses for greater emphasis.

More Line. Multipage news releases should contain a signal to the editor or news director that the release is running more than one page. This **more line** is typed at the bottom of the first page. Common versions are ((more)) or ((more-more-more)), often in double parentheses. Use this notation only after a complete paragraph.

Slug Line. When text continues on a second page, use a **slug line** (usually in capital letters) at the top of the subsequent page, repeating the first few words of the headline or offering a one- or two-word topic, and indicating the page number. For example, *BANK PROMOTIONS—2*. Because the more line is used only after a full paragraph, the slug line will always be followed by a new paragraph of text.

Editor's Note. An optional feature that may follow the end mark is a message directed to editors and news directors and not meant for publication. Such a note may verify an unusual spelling or give a street address for identification. Sometimes the note will offer special access to photographers, or it may offer interviews or additional information. The note is also a place to draw attention to a trademark or service mark or to provide background identification about the sending organization. The news release in Exhibit 8.5 later in this chapter includes a note to editors.

Basics of News Release Writing

Writing for public relations is not like a paint-by-numbers kit; you cannot simply fill in blanks on a news release template and prepare an effective release. Writing a good release takes talent, experience, and planning. However, guidelines do exist to channel your talent and planning toward conventional news-style writing. What follows is not a formula but rather a pattern found in most effective news releases. Learn this model and adapt it to suit the needs of your various writing projects.

Whether from news blogs or either print or online newspapers, most news releases follow a format similar to the basic news article: the well-known **inverted pyramid style**. This style presents the most important information at the top, with information of lesser importance following.

Exhibit 8.2—ELEMENTS OF A NEWS RELEASE This graphic shows the relationship between the various elements of a news brief and a news release.

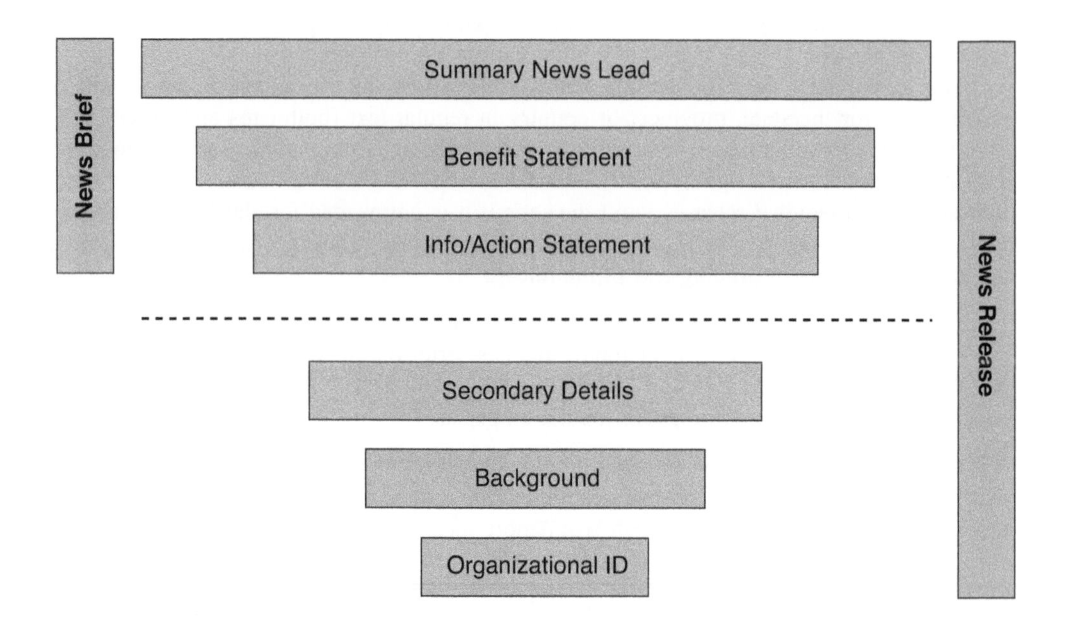

Exhibit 8.2 depicts the elements of a news release following the inverted pyramid style. Note how several of the elements reflect categories from your planning sheet. No formula can dictate how a news release is written. Let this formula be your guide, but temper it with your own news judgment, writing skill, and common sense.

Lead

> "Call me Ishmael."
>
> "Now is the winter of our discontent made glorious summer by this sun of York."
>
> "In the beginning God created the heavens and the earth."
>
> "Yes, Virginia, there is a Santa Claus."
>
> "You already are a writer!"

Beginnings are a big deal in all kinds of writing, and public relations writers take leads seriously. The **lead** (pronounced *leed*) is the first paragraph of a news release. Its purpose is to attract the attention of each member of your key public—first the media gatekeeper who will decide whether to use the release, then the reader, listener or viewer.

Because it serves as the gateway to the entire story, the lead is crucial to the success of a news release. The information in the lead is the basis for gatekeepers' decisions on whether to use the release. First impressions count, and few editors will waste time reading an entire release if the information in the lead does not grab their attention. Likewise, readers will decide whether to spend time with the story on the basis of whether the lead interests them. But a word of caution: A lead is strong not because of fancy writing but because it uses well-crafted writing to present significant information to readers.

The most common type of lead used by public relations writers is the **summary news lead**, which presents the most significant and interesting facts in the first one or two paragraphs. Too little information, and the lead is boring. Too much detail, and the reader becomes confused. As a writer, you strive for an effective middle ground. You can accomplish this by drafting the basic facts, then sifting through additional information and using that which adds to the meaning without creating confusion. Focus on the main newsworthy elements of your story. Remember SiLoBaTi + UnFa from the previous chapter. News involves information that is *significant*, *local*, *balanced*, and *timely*, as well as being *unusual* and associated with *famous* people.

In general, the who/what/when/where/why/how approach is useful for writing leads, but don't try to include each of those elements in a single sentence or even one paragraph. Weigh one element against another, and select the strongest elements for the lead. Save news elements of lesser importance for later in the story.

Exercise 8.1

Focusing the Lead

Look at the following set of facts related to a potential news release to the local newspaper serving the area of your college or university.

- Who: Your Provost or Academic Dean
- What 1: Announcing plans to build a new communication center to house your academic department
- What 2: New center will feature state-of-the-art technology for integrated media re: journalism, public relations, advertising, digital media, and audio/video production and postproduction
- When 1: Planning begins next month
- When 2: Construction should begin a year from now
- When 3: Completion expected 10 months after that
- Where: As the new electrical/heating/cooling plant currently under construction is completed, the old existing plant will be torn down to accommodate the new communication center
- Why 1: Your department is growing in student enrollment and is projecting a 35 percent increase over the next five years
- Why 2: The communication field requires technology and specialized facilities to continue to educate students for communication careers
- How: Alumni and other donors have already contributed $4.5 million. Federal and state higher education grants account for another $2.3 million. $10 million is available through the university's capital fund reserve for new building projects. Approximately $3 remains to be raised, mainly for technology to be used in the new facility.

Consider each of these elements. Then select the two most newsworthy elements that you could build your lead around. Justify your choices that these are the strongest elements in your potential news release.

The most important advice about writing effective leads is to plan carefully, think clearly, and write to the point. Let's look at various aspects of writing effective summary news leads. Also look at the examples in "FYI: Developing a Lead" to see how a lead can be crafted as one bit of information is layered upon another.

FYI *Developing a Lead*

Consider this scenario: Central University has received a $50,000 research grant from the State Council to Combat Drug Abuse. The purpose of this grant is to study persuasive communication, specifically the kinds of messages that are effective in persuading teens and young adults to avoid illegal drug use. First we write the basic information:

> A researcher at Central University has received a grant.

Then we begin to add some details, weaving in some of the information that can make this a newsworthy statement.

> A communication researcher at Central University has received a $50,000 state grant to study drug abuse.

This version gives the reader a bit more to go on, but it's too generic to be considered a good lead. We want to be more specific by narrowing down the subject area, both to more accurately reflect the focus of the grant and to attract reader interest about the project.

> A communication researcher at Central University has received a $50,000 state grant to study ways to persuade college students not to abuse illegal drugs.

Now we have told the reader something about *who*, with more details to come. We've given several bits of information about *what*, and we've mentioned the *why* and the *where*. Certainly these are the major elements of the lead, to be expanded upon later. The *when* element is less important and can be dealt with later in the story. And the *how* will be explained in succeeding paragraphs.

News Element. Lead with the news. Don't begin with a minor detail, such as the attribution. Avoid the too-common mistake of leading with a focus on the organization, or worse, on the head of the organization. In other words, avoid this version:

> Torrance Lakeman, administrator of County Hospital, announced today that a cardiac care unit will be added next year to the hospital's services.

That lead is upside-down. It backs into the news. Instead, present it up front, then follow with the organizational link. In many cases, you can use passive voice because it places the important information (the object of the verb) at the beginning of the sentence.

> County Hospital will expand its services next year by adding a cardiac care unit, superintendent Torrance Lakeman said today.

Context. Where and when can be important elements of some news stories. But news releases sometimes inefficiently begin with a focus on time, location, or some other secondary detail at the expense of the real news. Here are two examples of poorly written leads that focus on the time and circumstance rather than on the news.

At a morning news conference today, Mayor Michael Buckskin criticized the police department for failing to reduce the incidence of drunk driving.

In a speech to her cabinet, district superintendent Dorothy Ernestine Miller said the salary issue will be resolved peacefully.

However, it would be much more effective to begin each news release by focusing on the news rather than on the circumstances in which it occurred.

Mayor Michael Buckskin criticized the police department for failing to reduce the incidence of drunk driving. The reproach was part of the mayor's news conference today.

District superintendent Dorothy Ernestine Miller today assured her cabinet that the salary issue will be resolved peacefully.

Delayed Detail. The lead often gives general information, followed by details. For example, the final version of the lead for the Central University grant in "FYI: Developing a Lead" doesn't identify the professor who received the grant. That would go in the following paragraph. Look at the following example, which delays identification of the key person until the second paragraph.

A Sullivan County pharmacist has been named vice president of the Tri-State Association of Hospital Pharmacists.

Carolyn Teng, staff pharmacist at Sullivan-Memorial Hospital in Lake Point, was elected yesterday at the association's annual meeting in Cordoba.

Names. When should you use a name in a lead, and when should you make only a generic reference to an individual? In general, use the name only if most members of the audience would recognize it. For example, it's safe to identify by name the figure in the following release, because most readers could be expected to be familiar with the name.

Gov. Elena Gutierrez will be the keynote speaker at the annual recognition luncheon on Wednesday sponsored by the League of Community Volunteers.

But suppose the keynote speaker is the president of the local hospital, a person without strong name recognition. In that case, identify the speaker generically at first, then use the name of the president in the following sentence.

The president of Midvale Hospital will be the keynote speaker at the annual recognition luncheon on Wednesday sponsored by League of Community Volunteers.

Dr. Laura Green will discuss the contributions volunteers have made to the quality of life in Midvale.

When the person is well known only in a narrow context, make sure the descriptive reference is dominant. For example, let's say that your college or university is announcing that its commencement speaker will be Peter Diamond, who received the 2010 Nobel Prize for economics. Because Dr. Diamond isn't a household name, you'd need to provide a descriptor.

> A recipient of the Nobel Prize for economics will be the commencement speaker at Summerwood University next Saturday.
>
> Dr. Peter Diamond, economics professor at the Massachusetts Institute of Technology, will address 1,300 graduates at Summerwood's Mercier Auditorium.

Another way to write this release would be to identify the person both by name and by credentials.

> Nobel Prize winner Peter Diamond will be the commencement speaker at Summerwood University next Saturday. The Massachusetts Institute of Technology professor, who received the 2010 prize for economics, will address 1,300 graduates at Summerwood's Mercier Auditorium.

Reference. When providing identification in the paragraph following a generic reference, make sure the link is clear. Don't make the reader guess about whether the name refers to the generic reference. In the first version, the reference is unclear.

> Aethelwulf Public Relations has purchased controlling interest in a small agency begun by two Egbert College graduates.
>
> Baldwin Communications will specialize in public relations research.

In the sentence above, it is unclear that Baldwin Communications is the small agency referred to in the first paragraph. Rewriting can clear up that confusion.

> Aethelwulf Public Relations has purchased controlling interest in a small agency that two Egbert College graduates founded.
>
> The new subsidiary, Baldwin Communications, will specialize in public relations research.

Attribution. While attribution is needed for news releases, it does not have to be placed in the lead sentence. Sentences or paragraphs following the lead sometimes provide attribution for statements made in the lead.

> The Mid-State Turkey Hunters' Club will hold an open house from 6 to 9 p.m. Oct. 15, at the clubhouse on Squawker Road. The open house is part of the club's annual membership campaign, said club president Tony Phillips.

Details such as times, dates, addresses, and fees are best left to follow-up paragraphs. One guideline is to consider if a common noun can be used instead of a proper noun in the lead. While a common noun lacks some of the detail of a proper noun, it also is more likely to provide relevant general information to a reader. Details then follow in subsequent sentences and paragraphs.

Topic. Avoid say-nothing leads that report topics rather than provide information about the topic. For example, the reader learns little if the writer reports the following:

> The Employee Welfare committee met this morning to discuss items of concern to employees.

Rather, the writer might provide information that goes beyond simply identifying the subject matter.

> The Employee Welfare committee endorsed a new employee pension plan when it met this morning.

Historical Context. Avoid leads that begin with the background or historical context of a program or activity. By definition, history is not news. The following lead provides no newsworthy information until later in the story:

> The After-School Child Care program began three years ago at Makowski Elementary School. More than 75 children in kindergarten through 5th grade participate in this program, which currently is beginning a membership drive for the upcoming school year. The program features . . .

Instead, jump right in with the news, then put the program in context.

> Makowski Elementary School is accepting applicants for its After-School Child Care program, which currently includes more than 75 children in kindergarten through 5th grade. The program, which began three years ago, features . . .

Strategic Focus for Lead

Public relations writers often wish to give a particular strategic focus to a news release, particularly the lead. For example, we talk of a *who* lead, a *what* lead, a *where* lead, and so on. The difference is subtle. Does the lead begin with the name of a person or with a reference to an event? Consider the delicate shift in focus for the following leads:

> (Focus on *who/organization*)—Hill College will give an honorary doctor of letters degree to a Hillview physician because of his volunteer work with refugee children.

> (Focus on *who/recipient*)—A Hillview physician will receive an honorary doctor of letters degree from Hill College because of his volunteer work with refugee children.

> (Focus on *what*)—An honorary doctor of letters degree will be given by Hill College to a local physician because of his volunteer work with refugee children.

> (Focus on *when*)—In commencement ceremonies Saturday morning, a Hillview physician will receive an honorary doctor of letters degree from Hill College because of his volunteer work with refugee children.

> (Focus on *where*)—In the Hill College Amphitheater, a Hillview physician will receive an honorary doctor of letters degree from Hill College because of his volunteer work with refugee children.

> (Focus on *why*)—In recognition of his volunteer work with refugee children, a Hillview physician will receive an honorary doctor of letters degree from Hill College.

It's up to the writer to decide which focus is most appropriate for a particular writing situation. Let's consider each of the preceding examples.

The *who/organizational* focus is an approach that some writers would make, with the conscious or unconscious attempt to shine the spotlight on their organization. However, most newspaper editors would rewrite the lead, probably using the *who/recipient* or the *what* focus. They would rewrite the lead because a common newspaper policy is to focus on the recipient of an award or on the award itself rather than the giver. So it becomes important for the public relations writer to make a strategic decision about the lead.

The *when* focus is seldom justified strategically, because the time element generally is not the most important factor.

The *where* focus may be appropriate when the location is of particular relevance. For example, if the award ceremony were to be held in the rotunda of the state capitol, then it might be worth beginning with that fact. But generally, location is not a major factor for most news releases.

As noted above, the *who* and *what* leads may be the most newsworthy from the media's perspective. Both allow the organization to highlight, in this case, the person and/or the award. However, the *why* focus presents a strategic opportunity for the public relations writer to highlight an explanation, sometimes in an attempt to forestall criticism. For example, if the college were concerned that other physicians, perhaps major benefactors, might feel slighted because of the award, the lead with the why focus could minimize some criticism. It also offers a subtle invitation to others to make the kinds of social contributions being honored by the award.

Exercise 8.2

Writing Leads

You are a public relations writer for the Happy Pup Company, which manufactures and distributes dog food. Your company has given Dr. Aaron M. Jones a $300,000 grant to begin a series of support groups for persons who are afraid of animals. Dr. Jones is a psychologist at the college or university where your writing class is being offered. He specializes in human–animal interaction. He has written a best-selling popular book on pets called *Paws for a Moment*. Happy Pup has given the grant as part of a community relations program that seeks to position the company as one that promotes responsible pet ownership for the mutual benefits of both people and animals.

Part 1: Write a *what* summary news lead focusing on your company's grant for the local newspaper.

Part 2: Write a *who* summary news lead focusing on Dr. Jones for the college newspaper.

Part 3: Write a *where* summary news lead focusing on your personal hometown (or another community of your choice) as one of the pilot communities where Dr. Jones will begin the support groups.

Part 4: Write a *why* lead focusing on your company's interest in giving the grant. Write this for the *Happy Pup Times*, an employee online newsletter. As background, you are aware that some employees have been complaining that money spent on community relations programs could instead be used for salary increases.

Exercise 8.3

Simplifying Leads

Each of the following leads has problems. Revise each to make it more appropriate for a news release. Possible revisions are listed at the end of this chapter.

1. The Eastern Cable Company is proud to appoint Euphrasia Gilhoolie as director of Customer Service and Maintenance, where she will direct a staff of 27 repairmen and women dedicated to customer satisfaction.
2. TOBY TYLER'S TOYOTA, known as the Friendliest Car Dealership in Town, happily invites everyone to his open house at the new showroom on James Pike next Monday all day long from 9–9. Free refreshments.
3. On Monday, June 15, at 9 a.m., the Haven High School Hamsters' starting line-up will begin a five-day basketball clinic for kids aged 6–10.
4. Aloysius Terrence O'Malley, president and chief executive officer of O'Malley Enterprises, has appointed as his senior vice president for corporate communications Melinda Hobermeyer.
5. The Department of Social Geography at Oceanview University will host urban planning specialists from Andorra, Liechtenstein, Luxembourg, Monaco, San Marino, and Vatican City who are touring the United States to study examples of effective and innovative space usage by boundary-limited municipalities.
6. ADMIRALTY PARK, Ohio—The Peter Romanov Company, a long-time lock manufacturer located in this upscale community, announces that they have developed a revolutionary new security system for drivers to guarantee the security of their parked cars.

Benefit Statement

The lead in a news release is written from the same principles as the lead in a journalistic news report. But a **benefit statement** is the biggest difference between how a public relations writer prepares a release and how a journalist writes a news story based on the same information. A journalist's purpose is not to point out benefits for readers or viewers. That's your job as a public relations practitioner.

The benefit statement clearly indicates the advantage or opportunity you are offering the key public among the audience for this release. It answers for them "So what?" "Why should I care?", and "What's in it for me?" One of the smoothest ways to highlight the benefit statement is to develop it as a quote or narrative in which you implement your planning sheet ideas for explaining the advantage to your public.

Exercise 8.4

Writing Benefit Statements

Part 1: Using the *what* lead you wrote in Exercise 8.2 above, write a quote from the Happy Pup CEO as a follow-up paragraph that offers a benefit statement to readers.

Part 2: Using the *where* lead from Exercise 8.2, write a narrative or paraphrased follow-up paragraph that offers a benefit statement different from the one you wrote in Part 1.

Info/Action Statement

The **info/action statement** focuses on mobilizing readers and viewers. It gives the key audience how-to instructions on ways to obtain more information. Often, the public relations writer will want to encourage a particular activity for the public: buying concert tickets, visiting the museum, calling for more information, casting the vote, volunteering for the project, making the donation, and so on. One effective focus for an action statement is to direct readers to an organization's website or Facebook page. Try to include some invitation to action or opportunities for follow-up information in every news release.

Exercise 8.5

Writing Info/Action Statements

Using the *who* lead quote in Exercise 8.2, write a one-sentence action statement for a news release that invites the reader to get involved in the same way.

Secondary Detail

Secondary details amplify information in the lead. Look back at each of the elements of the summary news lead: who, what, when, where, and why. This is where you can pick up those elements that you didn't consider important enough to place in the lead. Also review the "So what?" information from the benefit statement. Consider how you might expand upon each of these elements to provide readers with relevant information.

Background Information

Background information provides a context for the report. This information often is an attempt to help address your objectives, perhaps by using quotes. This may include information on the history of a project or its wider setting. For example, when Med-Plast prepared its fact sheet on the new plant (see Chapter 6), it included background information about the parent company. Likewise, if a local hospital were to announce plans for its annual fundraising campaign, readers would want to know the outcome of last year's appeal, both the amount of money raised and how it was used.

Organizational Identification

An optional part of the news release is an **organizational identification**. This is a paragraph with standard wording that routinely is dropped into a news release, usually at the end. For example:

> Apache is the oldest pharmaceutical company in the Southwest. It is a division of Worldwide Medical Products Inc., with offices and research laboratories in North and South America and in Europe.

Many news releases do not include an organizational ID. Such standard information is seldom published. But some writers find IDs useful for providing background on their organization, if not for media audiences, at least for editors and reporters, as well as for non-media readers of releases posted at websites and social media outlets.

Some public relations writers who do use the drop-in paragraphs place them as the closing paragraphs of the release. Others use them as an explanatory note following the text. The final paragraph in the news release in Exhibit 8.4 is an example of an ID paragraph.

Examples of News Releases

This chapter provides several examples of news releases, hypothetical information developed to provide models of the various aspects of releases. Note that each example features a benefit statement and an action statement.

Exhibit 8.3 shows the fabricated example of a news release for local print media by a company we'll call InterGalactic Motors. The release includes the various elements outlined in this chapter. Notice that it begins with a *who/what* lead and offers secondary detail and background information later in the release.

Exhibit 8.4 shows another made-up organization, St. Francis Hospital and Health Center, with this example of a news release for local print media. This one has the essential ingredients in a slightly different order. Note the use of the organizational identification paragraph at the end of the release.

Exhibit 8.5 depicts a new release for the fictitious Capitol Council for the Arts. This news release is recycled from a speech. Because of the nature of this story, there are few secondary details; most of the information presents an expanded benefit statement. This example also shows an editor note.

News Brief

One of the most important elements associated with news releases doesn't even have a well-known name. It is the part of the release that combines the lead and the benefit statement into a statement of interest to both the reader and the organization—part of the overlap areas of the medium's and the organization's circles of interest that we talked about in Chapter 5.

We will call this essential public relations message the **news brief**, with the caution that journalistic writers may think of a news brief as something different from a regular news release rather than the beginning of one. Nevertheless, the concept is a good one to learn.

Think of it this way: A news brief is a capsule of the information in the fuller release; it is clear and concise in serving the interests of the busy reader, who may not read any further. At the same time, a news brief is a well-crafted presentation of the organization's message; it summarizes the information, positioning it in terms that focus on the message's benefit to readers.

Exhibit 8.3—CORPORATE NEWS RELEASE, WITH NEWS BRIEF

Kim Salvatore
Public Relations Director
(123) 456-7809
ksal@intergalactic.com

InterGalactic Motors, Ltd. **Mid-State Division**

123 Harrison Road
Centerville XX 12345

September 25, 2011
FOR IMMEDIATE RELEASE

InterGalactic Motors Sponsoring Safe Driving Clinic

Response to Congressional Request for Auto Makers to Promote Highway Safety

The Mid-State Division of InterGalactic Motors will sponsor a Safe Driving Clinic Saturday, Oct. 13, at its Harrison Road Plant in Lockport. The clinic is free for Marlon County residents.

The clinic will provide both information and hands-on practice in driving safety. Participants also can earn extra points toward reduction of fines for traffic offenses, as well as credits toward discounts for auto insurance.

The Safe Driving Clinic will begin at 9 a.m. at the Employee Cafeteria, located in Building "G" at the plant. Area residents as well as nonresidents attending local colleges may register for the clinic by contacting the InterGalactic Employee Center at 987–6543.

The clinic will be led by InterGalactic Motors training and testing experts and by representatives of the Central Automobile Club of Centerville.

InterGalactic Motors is offering similar clinics at plants throughout the state. The public clinics were scheduled in the wake of testimony before Congress by William Newbauer, InterGalactic Motors president. Newbauer addressed the Joint Committee on Transportation and Safety in Washington last month (Aug.15) on the need for auto manufacturers to take the lead in promoting driving safety.

"We have a responsibility to make safe cars," said Newbauer. "We also want to help train safer drivers, so highways, streets and country roads are as safe as possible."

#####

Exhibit 8.4—NONPROFIT NEWS RELEASE, WITH ORGANIZATIONAL ID

St. Francis Hospital
& Health Center
12345 Main Street
Springfield, Xxx 12345
www.sfhhc.org

Contact: Thomas Tyler
(123) 456-7890
TylerT@sfhhc.org

Banker Re-Elected to Head Local Hospital Foundation

Springfield banker Eli Holcomb has been elected to his second term as president of the board of directors of the St. Francis Hospital Foundation. Holcomb, vice president of the First Springfield Bank and Trust Co., has been a member of the foundation board for seven years.

Other newly elected officers include Marian Demerly, director of the Spring County Library System, as vice president; Rabbi Steven Schneider of Beth Shalom Synagogue, as treasurer; and Sylvia Martain, associate director of the Native American Cultural Center, as secretary.

The hospital board also elected Michael Whitefeather, principle of Mission Academy, to serve a two-year term as a board trustee.

As the fund-raising arm of the hospital, the foundation sponsors the Spring County Medical Appeal. That appeal annually provides more than $12 million for patient services at St. Francis Hospital and its downtown family-care center, St. Claire Clinic.

Details about the foundation, including audited statements of accountability, are available from the foundation office at (123) 456-7890 or at its website: www.sfhhc.org.

St. Francis Hospital and Health Center is a 436-bed facility with full medical services. It features accredited units for cardiac care, oncology, geriatrics, and rehabilitation medicine, as well as emergency care. St. Claire Clinic is an extended-site facilities providing a full range of family health services.

#####

Exhibit 8.5—NEWS RELEASE FROM A SPEECH, WITH EDITOR'S NOTE

capitol council for the ARTS

5432 Charlemagne Boulevard
Capitol City, XX 12345
(1234) 456-7890
www.capitalarts.org

Francesca Brandi, Media Director
Brandi@capitalarts.org

March 23, 2011
FOR IMMEDIATE RELEASE

BUCHANAN TEACHER ASKS FUNDING FOR THE ARTS

Art instructor petitions governor, urges state policy to support arts education

CAPITOL CITY—Education in the arts is just as important as training in math and science, a Buchanan County teacher told Gov. Lucy Halloway this morning.

Joshua Melvert, supervising art instructor at Buchanan City Academy, testified before the state's Select Committee on Education at the invitation of Halloway. The governor was present when Smith argued for greater funding for arts education.

"There is no question that our students need a strong foundation in the sciences and technology so they can compete in the 21st century," Melvert told the committee. "But it is equally clear that culture, as the foundation of our civilization, also deserves to be encouraged in our schools."

The art teacher, an award-winning sculptor, told the committee that schools can give students an appreciation for art, music and other aspects of culture.

Melvert challenged the governor to affirm her campaign platform to make school curriculums more meaningful to students.

"Children are born to be creative and artistic," Melvert said in his testimony. "Even businesses need creative people. State policy should encourage the study of art to build self-esteem and to make young people feel good about themselves. We should help them express their feelings through music and art rather than through violence and drugs."

More-more-more

Exhibit 8.5—NEWS RELEASE FROM A SPEECH, WITH EDITOR'S NOTE . . . *continued*

Capitol Council for the ARTS
Buchanan Teacher … 2

Melvert was one of five teachers from throughout the state invited to address the session with the governor. An art teacher at Buchanan City Academic for 12 years, he was recommended for the testimony by the Capitol Council for the ARTS.

Copies of his testimony to the committee are available from the Capitol Council for the ARTS at (555) 234–5678 or at the council's website: www.capitalarts.org.

#####

Note to Editors and News Directors:
Contact Melvert for interview at Buchanan City Academy, 555–5555

An effective public relations writer will approach every news release as an opportunity to provide such a brief, followed by additional information to add depth and detail.

Most public relations writers do not have the luxury of writing several different versions of each release. By beginning each release with a strategic news brief, the writer serves the needs of newspapers, magazines, wire services, digital media, and broadcast news outlets that can use only a short report. Then, by continuing to build this report into a more in-depth news release, the public relations writer moves on to serve the needs of trade publications, community weeklies, special-interest newspaper sections, and others who can use more than just the brief. The writer thus covers all the bases, producing a piece of writing that is likely to be effective because it has been prepared to satisfy the reader, the news media, and the organization.

Additionally, many organizations find that the news brief makes an excellent summary for a website, with a link to the fuller story for readers who want more information.

Exercise 8.6

Writing a Complete News Release

Prepare a planning sheet and then write a news release for one of the following scenarios. In the release, include the major elements: summary lead, benefit statement, and action statement, along with secondary details and background as needed. Include a quote. Begin with the set of facts provided below. Use your instructor or another student as the information source for your client, and obtain from him or her any additional information you need for the release. Use the proper news release format, including heading information about the sending organization. List yourself as the public relations contact person.

1. Your client is Sforzando Music Company. You are preparing a news release for parents, teachers, and guidance counselors. The focus of this release is a new video about careers in music, such as teaching, performing, management, music therapy, publicity, and journalism. Sforzando is a store with branches throughout two states. It sells music and instruments and provides music lessons.
2. Your client is Vancouver Cruise. You are preparing a news release for travel media. The release will announce a new family-oriented cruise package through the Inside Passage between Vancouver, British Columbia, and Juneau, Alaska. Vancouver Cruise is a shipping line that specializes in Pacific vacation travel.
3. Your client is a senator in your home state. You are preparing a news release about an upcoming public forum sponsored by the senator to obtain testimony about ways your state might assist cities in dealing with an increase in the number of homeless people. The forum will include invited experts, and it will be open to concerned citizens.

Exercise 8.7

Revising a News Release

You are public relations director of Starter Electronics in Albuquerque, N.M. A staff associate newly assigned to your department has given you the following draft of a news release. You realize it has several errors. Instead of returning it for revision, you decide to provide a lesson to your new colleague. Rewrite the following draft. Then explain to your associate why you made the various changes. Notes on this exercise are at the end of this chapter.

* * * * *

Starter Electronics of El Moreno County is proud to announce the appointment of a new superintendent of Starter's Plastics Division. Starter named employee Wesley L. Marlborough to the position. Mr. Marlborough will begin his new assignment at the end of the month.

"I am very happy to have been appointed to this important position," Mr. Marlborough said, barely able to contain his enthusiasm. "I am fortunate to have the opportunity to work for such a wonderful boss as Mrs. Quigley," he said. As superintendent of the Plastic Division, Mr. Marlborough will report to Anastasia Quigly who is in charge of the company's technology divisions.

Mr. Marlborough graduated from East Downhome High School in New Mexico, where he played basketball for the varsity team. After taking two years off to travel the Southwest, he went to college at Upper Pecos College at Fort Sumner. There he studied engineering technology and met his future wife, a dancer named Rita Brown.

He came to work for Starter Electronics six years ago, when he was hired to be a quality control worker. Before coming to Starter he held several odd jobs, and he was an electronics technician in the Navy.

Local News Release

Public relations writers try to focus on the here and now. We've already discussed the time element, why *now* is more newsworthy than *then*. Let's turn our attention to the locality of our news release. Knowing that information about far-away places is less interesting than information from our neighborhood, let's consider ways to maximize the *here* element of our news.

A story should be viewed in terms of what it means for people in various localities who may be affected by or interested in your organization. If your company earned a profit last year, how much was added to the local economy? If your foundation is distributing research grants, how many are going to organizations in a particular area of interest to local media? If your client, an entertainer, has won a national award, when is the next local concert scheduled?

Editors say the No. 1 reason they reject news releases is because there is no apparent or significant local information. This can't be said too strongly: If a story doesn't have a local angle, it's not news. One of your jobs as a public relations writer is to find the local angle, even to create a local angle. Then turn that local concern into the focus of the release.

Special

Localized news releases are sometimes called **specials** because they are written especially for a particular publication (such as *Special to the Sacramento Bee*) or for a particular geographic area (such as *Special to Clinton County Media*). This signals to editors and news directors that the information is of particular interest to their audiences. Consider the example of your college or university sports information office. The writer could prepare a general release to introduce a team's new season, such as the one below:

> BLOOMFIELD, Anystate—The women's basketball team of Mount Bloomfield College will field a starting lineup of two seniors, two juniors, and a freshman, when the Tiger Ladies host the season opener against Carlton College.
>
> Marya Watts, who coached the Tiger Ladies in last year's undefeated season, announced the lineup for next Wednesday's game. The starters include:
>
> - Erica Fisher, sophomore, a graduate of Hill Mall High School.
> - Lasheena Johnson, sophomore, a graduate of City Honors High School in Cinnamon City.
> - Mariella Bradford, senior, a graduate of Mother Teresa Academy in Bradford . . .

However, with this version, an editor would have to dig out information about local residents. To make the release more useful, the writer could have prepared special versions of the same story to highlight the information of local interest. Consider the following examples.

> *Special to the Barry County Gazette*—Erica Fisher, a graduate of Hill Mall High School, has been selected as a starter for the women's varsity basketball team at Mount Bloomfield College.
>
> Fisher, a sophomore center for the Tiger Ladies, will play her first varsity game next Wednesday when Mount Bloomfield hosts Carlton College.
>
> Marya Watts, who coached the Tiger Ladies in last year's undefeated season, called Fisher "an outstanding player with the strength, determination and smarts to be a real winner, on and off the court."
>
> *Special to the Cinnamon City Times*—Lasheena Johnson, a graduate of City Honors High School, has been selected as a starter . . .
>
> *Special to the Bradford Evening News*—Mariella Bradford, a graduate of Mother Teresa Academy, has been selected as a starter . . .

Another way to localize a release is to take a careful look at the bio sheet of a key figure in the release. Let's say you are writing a release to announce that the Sheffield Opera Board of Directors has named Francis Armbruster as its chairman. Armbruster is pastor of Visitation Episcopal Church in Sheffield. You note from the bio sheet that he holds a master of divinity degree from Zion Seminary, he graduated from Harriman Central High School, and he was formerly chaplain at Parkerville Hospital. Armed with this information, you might develop a series of specialized news releases with locally oriented leads for the daily newspapers in Sheffield, Harriman, and Parkerville, and for newsletters and websites of Zion Seminary, Parkerville Hospital, and the local Episcopal diocese.

Think about more than simple geography when you are localizing a news release. Think of other ways to tailor a news release for a particular audience. Consider how to address other demographic and sociographic factors of a particular audience: age, gender, ethnicity, education, economic status, occupation, religion, and so on. For example, if one of the starting basketball players mentioned in the scenario above were Muslim, perhaps a tailored version of the release could be sent to the newspaper and website of the local Islamic association. If another player were Hispanic, you'd consider writing a version for the local Hispanic newspaper.

The merge functions on computer software and data files make it easy to produce several different versions of a news release, allowing you to easily localize information for widespread dissemination.

Exercise 8.8

Writing a Localized News Release

You are a public relations consultant handling publicity for the following educational conference. You decide to use the election of a president to publicize the organization and its mission. Base your release on the following information. If you need additional information, interview another student who will play the role of the new president (or if your instructor allows, make up the needed information, remembering that fabricating information is never a possibility in the real world, only in the hypothesizing world of the classroom). You may suggest an appropriate quote for the new president. (All locations in the following scenario are actual places that can be found by using maps and media directories. The organization is fictitious.)

Part 1: Prepare a news release for general statewide use. Include a planning sheet.

Part 2: Using a media directory, identify four specific locations and print media (including daily and weekly newspapers and organizational newsletters) to receive localized releases focusing on the new president. Write only the leads for three of these four local media.

Part 3: Prepare a planning sheet and a full localized news release for one of these four local areas, using the following information:

- This morning, Marilyn Minsdorf was elected president of the Pennsylvania Association for Teachers of English and Language Arts, formerly the Pennsylvania Association of English Teachers. She will serve a two-year term.
- Minsdorf lives at 125 Elm Street, Jersey Shore, Pa.
- She is a 1982 graduate of Lock Haven State College in Pennsylvania, with a degree in secondary education and certification to teach English. The school's name was changed in 1983 to Lock Haven University.

continued . . .

Exercise 8.8 . . . *continued*

- She teaches 9th-grade Language Arts at Central Mountain High School in Mill Hall, Pa., part of the Keystone Central School District. She has taught there for seven years.
- She used to teach English at Lewisburg (Pa.) Junior High School.
- Her parents are Harvey Grampian and the late Lucinda Shemp Grampian of South Williamsport, Pa.
- She is married to David Minsdorf, president of R&D Construction in Jersey Shore. The couple has four children: Bridget, 15; Clancey, 14; Golda, 10; and Sadie, 3.
- She was the elected representative from PATELA's North Central District for the last two years.
- PATELA has 1,100 members, including high school teachers in public and nonpublic schools and college professors in teacher-education departments.
- The organization is concluding a three-day convention at the Commonwealth Convention Center in Harrisburg. An installation dinner will end the convention this evening.
- PATELA has two primary goals: to improve the status of language teachers, and to encourage quality in language instruction.
- The previous president is Arturo Todd, 10th-grade English teacher at Middletown (Pa.) High School.

Types of News Release

Public relations writers can produce all sorts of news releases, but some are more likely to be used by the media than others. Both announcement and follow-up releases offer the public relations writer a full range of possibilities.

Announcement Release

A news release that provides information about a planned event is called an **announcement release**. This category makes up a large part of the releases most organizations disseminate. Announcement releases cover various subcategories: event releases, personnel releases, progress releases, program releases, product releases, bad-news releases, crisis releases, and financial releases. Let's look briefly at each.

- **Event releases** often have an obvious news value, because they present information about something of interest that will be happening soon. Editors and news directors appreciate this kind of information, especially when it is of significance to large segments of their audiences. Clearly indicate the purpose of the event and the benefit it will provide. Provide logistical details as to time and place, and provide directions for readers on how to obtain additional information.
- **Personnel releases** focusing on promotions and personnel changes often are judged to be newsworthy, especially when they involve management-level positions or people who are well known among the media's audiences. In writing this kind of release, focus on the person and note relevant professional information such as education,

previous jobs, military service, professional accreditation, and awards. Give information on job responsibilities, and note the role the position plays in the organization and perhaps in the community. Attribute the announcement to an official of the organization, and briefly describe the organization's work. Avoid providing personal information unless it is clearly relevant to the position or of newsworthy public interest.

- **Progress releases** focus on developments within an organization. They have a moderate chance of being used by the media, especially when they are amplified by being significant to local audiences. Often these are periodic reports about the organization's progress as it relates to local interests.
- **Program releases** offer organizations, especially nonprofit groups, the opportunity to announce new services of general interest. They may interest specialized media serving small portions of the organization's publics.
- **Product releases** about new or existing products, equipment, capacities, and facilities are the most difficult release to get used by the general media, because they so often suggest self-serving promotion. For corporate public relations writers, announcements of new products may be appropriate for very specialized trade publications, as well as trade or business sections within a general publication. This type of release can be tailored to specific media by focusing on product features or applications of particular interest to the media audience.
- **Bad-news releases** deal with the reality that bad things sometimes happen to good organizations—plant closings, program cutbacks, product recalls, corporate takeovers. Painful as they are to an organization, these activities often warrant news releases, on the strategic notion that bad news is best told by the organization itself than by outside sources. Handled properly, bad-news releases can actually help an organization keep a proper balance amid the scrutiny of reporters and the suspicion of opponents.
- **Crisis releases** are intended to deal directly, swiftly, and accurately with a crisis, which is defined as a major, unfortunate, sudden, and unpredicted event that can seriously disrupt an organization's activity with potentially negative impact on its "bottom line" or mission.
- **Financial releases** differ from other releases in that they often are meant for news venues and audiences with not only an interest in financial matters but also a special knowledge. In addition, financial releases often are bound by special requirements, such as those imposed by government agencies such as the Securities and Exchange Commission. "Advice from a Pro: Financial News Releases" outlines various types within the category.

Advice From a Pro *Financial News Releases*

Laurel O'Brien, APR, is an expert in financial media relations with Lincoln Financial Group in Philadelphia. Writing in *The Public Relations Strategist* (Winter 2001) about the new reality for news releases, O'Brien offers an overview of six categories of news releases written for stockholders, analysts, financial reporters, and other publics of a company's investor relations program.

The *investor release* tries to foster corporate name reputation by generating as many news releases as possible with information for potential investors. People seeking financial information will sift through a company website as they make investment decisions.

The *disclosure release* satisfies the legal requirement to provide material information to their

continued . . .

Advice From a Pro *Financial News Releases*

investors. Many companies provide disclosure even beyond the minimum required by law, as a kind of insurance against any future lawsuit. They then can point to the release as proof that nothing was hidden. Even privately held companies and non-profit organizations can use this approach as a way to foster confidence and forestall criticism.

The *marketing release* focuses on new products and services. Often the information in such releases is aimed at existing customers.

The *crisis release* chronicles a crisis from its own point of view. Though the media undoubtedly will report on a developing crisis situation, the organization can use the crisis release to defend its reputation and shore up the support of its key publics.

The *vendors and alliances release* announces partnerships and vendor relationships, serving the interests of all parties in the alliance and providing potentially useful information to customers or investors. Trade and business publications may be interested in such information, which can be archived at the company website.

The *vanity release* is prepared simply because an executive wants to see his or her pet project on the website. Such releases have a particular use for nonprofit and charitable organizations, as opportunities to thank donors and benefactors in a public environment. They are of little interest to news media.

Exercise 8.9

Writing an Announcement News Release

Write a news release for one of the following four scenarios. Use the set of facts provided. For additional information, interview another student who will play the role of the key figure, or ask your instructor to play that role. Include a planning sheet. Use the proper news release format, including heading information about the sending organization. List yourself as the contact person.

1. *Events/Activities*. The governor of your state will be the keynote speaker at your school's graduation ceremonies on the third Saturday of next May. The governor will also receive an honorary degree from your president. For additional information, "interview" the head of academic affairs or the commencement planning committee.
2. *Personnel activities*. You are public relations director of Canton Electronics located in your hometown. The 15-year-old company manufactures high-tech components for electronics systems in rockets. Most of your work is under contract with NASA. The company has 275 employees. Fill out a hypothetical bio sheet for Florindo Sanvincenzo, who has just been promoted to vice president for research and development, succeeding Milton Williams, who is retiring. Write a news release for Sanvincenzo's hometown newspaper.
3. *Programs/Services*. The Canada County YWCA is beginning a program, "Focus on Finance," to help women plan their personal finances. The focus will be on helping participants develop plans to overcome current financial problems. The program is free to county residents.

continued . . .

Exercise 8.9 . . . *continued*

4. *Products*. Obtain a copy of a consumer-oriented publication or locate a company website that compares features among various brands of the same product. Use the information on the leading brand to prepare a news release introducing that product.

Follow-Up Release

In addition to the previous category of announcement releases, another useful type of news release is the **follow-up release**, which involves responses to an event, an idea, or an earlier report. Following are several types of follow-up releases: new-information releases, comment releases, position releases, public interest tie-in releases, and speech releases. Here's an overview of each.

- **New-information releases** offer an organization the opportunity to provide follow-up information to an earlier reported activity. Examples of this are releases that announce the amount of money raised by a previously announced charity auction or the outcomes of a study or investigation announced in an earlier release. This follow-up may repeat some information from an earlier release, because it is likely that some gatekeepers and many readers may be unfamiliar with the first release.
- **Comment releases** give organizations an opportunity to set the record straight in response to an activity or news report in which they have been involved. For example, a report about mold found on sandwich rolls in an elementary school cafeteria may prompt a response by the bakery that made the rolls, explaining that they were clearly date-marked and that the school should have used them the previous week. The strategy here would be to provide such information without risking its future business with the school district, perhaps by announcing a new service of an e-mail reminder for institutional clients of the expiration dates.
- **Position releases** are those written to present an official opinion on an issue. For example, the media may approach a political candidate on a controversial public issue that relates to the candidate or her constituents. The release would provide accurate background information on the issue and then state the candidate's position on it.
- **Public interest tie-in releases** allow organizations to be heard on current events that may not directly involve them but affect their work or in some other way impact their mission. For example, the City County Council on Drug Abuse may issue a release in response to a series of arrests made by local police agencies, perhaps to applaud a cooperative effort in law enforcement, or to point to a gap in preventative programs.
- **Speech releases** are excellent ways to extend an organization's message by reporting what an official has said about a topic important to the organization and of interest to the media. Because they are reporting something that has recently happened, they are fact-based as news releases should be, but they also offer the opportunity for organizations to present their opinions on subjects of public interest. Exhibit 8.5 on the Capitol Council for the Arts is an example of a speech release.

Exercise 8.10

Writing a Follow-Up News Release

Write a news release for one of the following four scenarios. Use the set of facts provided. For additional information, interview another student who will play the role of the key figure. Include a planning sheet. Use the proper news release format, including heading information about the sending organization. List yourself as the public relations contact person.

1. *New information*. Prepare a follow-up release to the events/activities release in the previous exercise, focused on the YWCA. Quote the director to indicate successful completion of the six-week workshop. Indicate the outcomes of the workshop.
2. *Comment*. Prepare a comment news release focusing on the president of your college or university as a follow-up to your announcement in Exercise 8.9—Events/Activities—responding to the following criticism. The county chairman of the political party opposing the governor has accused your school of "pandering to political opportunism" and "playing to the governor's baseless academic pretense." The critic opposes the granting of the honorary degree because the governor's new budget does not include a 15 percent increase in state scholarship aid for students in both public and private college; the critic was a leading supporter of increased scholarship aid. Just for kicks, let's say the critic is a major supporter of your school and an influential leader in the community; thus another balancing act for the media relations office.
3. *Public issue tie-in*. Prepare a release for the YWCA to tie into a published newspaper report indicating that most area law-enforcement agencies have noted an increase in shoplifting committed by single parents, often accompanied with the excuse that the shoplifting was a desperate attempt to make ends meet. Use the report to call attention to your "Focus on Finance" program, designed to help identify effective and legal means to handle financial difficulties.
4. *Speech*. Do an Internet news search for "speech" or "prepared testimony" within the last three months to obtain the transcript of the verbal communication given recently in your state, provincial or federal capital. Prepare a news release based on this speech. Write as if you are a member of the public relations staff for the person giving the speech or testimony.

Rewriting

Ice cream melts in the summer. Rain falls down, not up. Editors rewrite news releases. It's almost a law of nature. Experienced public relations writers don't think of it as a reflection on their writing ability when their well-crafted news releases are rewritten. With experience, you will get used to this. Sometimes you won't notice any apparent improvement. Sometimes you may conclude that the rewritten version fails to carry over important information from your original. Occasionally, you even may find that the rewrite has introduced ambiguity or error into the report. This, too, is part of reality for a public relations practitioner. Here are some points to consider about why editors rewrite and how to avoid the need for this work.

Poor Writing. Too often, reporters receive poorly written releases, sometimes just plain bad English, other times missing key journalistic basics such as objectivity. Because such releases need major revision for style as well as for content, many editors and news directors habitually rewrite every release. For this reason, journalists respect the work of public relations writers who show that they can produce news-based releases.

Lack of News. Some releases bury the news element in the second paragraph, or in the 22nd. Other releases are more fluff than substance. In either case, non-news releases are likely to be passed over.

Policy. Weekly or community newspapers with small reporting staffs may use a release "as is," but larger daily newspapers seldom do so. Often, this is due to a policy against using "handouts" as they are submitted in order to prevent the embarrassment of using a release identical to one used in another publication.

Starting Point. Reporters often need to expand upon the information provided, using the news release as a starting point (treating it much as they would a fact sheet). An editor or assignment director may have a reporter follow up on the release, contacting the organization and perhaps people on the other side of the issue.

Format. Sometimes releases are rewritten because they do not fit the medium's format. Some newspapers use only short items, so they have to rewrite lengthy releases. Electronic media generally use a release only as an idea-generator, since a radio news director would want some recorded audio and a television reporter may need on-camera interviews and other footage.

Common Errors in News Releases

Too often, the story ideas and news releases of public relations writers end up in the trash. The reason? The journalist is looking for relevant news, but the public relations writer has offered something else. The result is a lot of wasted effort and damage to an organization's reputation as a credible source of news. Following are excerpts from actual news releases sent to a metropolitan daily newspaper. The city editor has indicated the reason why each was rejected. Names and other identifying characteristics have been changed to avoid embarrassing the organization that sent the releases, but each retains its own style (errors and all).

> **Contest**
>
> This summer, the Local Lumberjacks baseball team, in conjunction with WWWW-AM, will participate in the XYZ Paint Company's "Winning Shoot Out Inning" contest.
>
> The contest gives fans the opportunity to win $1,000 cash if the Lumberjacks record three consecutive strike-outs—facing just three batters in a designated inning. If the Lumberjacks simply shut-out their opponent in the designated inning (no runs scored), contestants will win four box seats for an upcoming game. If they fail to shut-out the opposing team, contestants will still win a XYZ painters cap . . .

Editor's Comment: "Too commercial; too promotional." It is also confusing.

Lesson for Public Relations Writers: Find alternatives to public news media for business promotions. Try advertising coupons, in-store promotions, direct mail, and word-of-mouth.

Hospital

The Mammography Imaging Services of Memorial Hospital recently received a three-year accreditation from the American College of Radiology (ACR).

The Memorial Hospital Radiology Department's Mammography Unit was surveyed by the Committee on Mammography Accreditation of the ACR Commission on Standards and Accreditation. The ACR Mammography Accreditation Program offers radiologists the opportunity for peer review and evaluation of their facility's staff qualifications, equipment, quality control and quality assurance programs, image quality, breast dose, and processor quality control.

This voluntary program is directed by the ACR Committee on practice Accreditation of the Commission of Radiologic Practice . . .

Editor's Comment: "Not news." It is not even understandable.

Lesson for Public Relations Writers: Perhaps it could be newsworthy to a general interest newspaper if the writer had dropped the jargon and focused on a short report about what accreditation means to patients.

Library

The Downtown Public Library is sponsoring its yearly summer reading program for children called "Telling Tales, Spinning Yarns." The primary aim of our program is to encourage children to continue to read for enjoyment through the summer months. To achieve this goal, the library provides incentive programming, crafts, games, and prizes for children of all ages, ranging from three year olds through junior high . . .

Editor's Comment: This particular library is two states and 250 miles away. Asks the editor: "Why would anyone mail this to us?"

Lesson for Public Relations Writers: Keep a rein on your mailing list. Don't waste a good local release by distributing it beyond its interest area. Meanwhile, whose program is "our program" and what is "incentive programming"?

Competition

On Wednesday, May 19, from 9 a.m. to 11:30 a.m., students representing 37 high schools from across the State will be in the Convention Center of the State Capitol Plaza to discuss their projects in the annual Student Energy Research Competition. At noon, State Energy Development and Research Authority Chairman and State Energy Commissioner Walter Wattage III will preside at an award ceremony to announce top prize winners . . .

Editor's Comment: "Detail area winners and you'd hook me."

Lesson for Public Relations Writers: An advance release may be too general. Instead, do a follow-up focusing on local news interests.

Training

___ SFI, MTO, MFI, of ___, or ___ County, *[in the original, the blanks were filled in by hand and the appropriate initials circled]* successfully completed the 2010 State Fire Instructors Conference, a part of the new state fire training program offered at the Institute of Fire Science, Falling Rivers.

The Conference included workshops on PRINCIPLES OF CONSTRUCTION, FIRE DEPARTMENT OPERATIONS IN SPRINKLERED BUILDINGS, POSITIVE PRESSURE VENTILATION, AND OSHA TRAINING.

Editor's Comment: Ugh! (Actually, the editor more kindly said this is "not newsworthy.")

Lesson for Public Relations Writers: Fill in the blanks? Don't even think it.

Tree Planting

The Green Suburbs school district as well as several park and recreation areas will be the focal point for the planting of over one hundred trees in the Town of Green. This tree planting effort results from a committee that consists of industry, garden clubs, area government leaders, local schools, and a retirees group. This tree planting committee is responsible for a program called "Rooting For America" . . .

Editor's Comment: "No news. So what? No real hook."

Lesson for Public Relations Writers: There must be a human angle in here someplace—involvement of a biology class from the local high school, students and senior citizens working together, something. A less boring telling of this story would improve it a lot.

Voting Record

Assemblywoman Billie Vohtgetter's (R, McElhatter) voting record on issues that affect the environment recently earned a strong rating from the Environmental Policy Lobby.

"The 2010 legislative session was an environment-oriented session which witnessed the passage of several pieces of legislation that will have lasting impacts on our society," said Vohtgetter, a member of the Legislative Environmental Conservation Committee. "Since many of the bills directly affected every resident of the 234th Legislative District, I always consider their full implications before casting my vote" . . .

Editor's Comment: The editor used a four-letter word for this boorish self-aggrandizement. No, not that word. He said: "PUFF!"

Lesson for Public Relations Writers: Some releases are better reserved for in-house distribution and for friendly gatherings where applause is appropriate. For news releases, stick with news.

Scholarship

Christopher B. Christopher, son of Mr. and Mrs. Clarence Christopher of Lindsey Avenue in South Suburbia, recently began studies as a freshman at Dakota College, a selective liberal arts college located in the Foothills plateau.

Christopher is a graduate of Central Suburbia High School where he was a member of the golf team and a recipient of the Governor's Scholarship and a Presidential Academic Fitness Award.

Dakota College celebrates its 175th anniversary this year . . .

Editor's Comment: This was one of six separate-but-similar releases received in one day from this college, located 200 miles away from the newspaper, in an adjacent state. The editor judged the release as non-news. "We don't use this. Not news. No room. Nobody cares."

Lesson for Public Relations Writers: Even hometown people pleasers must have some news value. If Christopher had made the dean's list, been elected to the student government, or graduated, there might be some interest. The college should have sent the release to the suburban weekly newspaper serving Christopher's neighborhood and to his high school alumni newsletter.

Commentary

Patrick Jones, a political scientist at Mount Martha University and an expert on the economics and politics of security issues in Western Europe, is in Paris next month and is available for commentary and analysis on European unification talks, which will take place Sept. 15.

"The possibility of unification is intriguing," Jones said from his office at the European Unification Research Center at the LaFrance Academy for Social Research, where he is a visiting scholar . . .

Editor's Comment: This college was located 400 miles away from the newspaper. "No local interest; no tie-in." Interestingly, buried deep within the two-page story was information that a university in the newspaper's circulation area had published Jones' book on the subject.

Lesson for Public Relations Writers: Search your information carefully for anything that can be highlighted for local interest. Then prepare a localized version.

Awards (two separate releases)

Mark A. Tree won the Financial Administrator's Institute Competitive Award, it was announced at Jones University's Annual Honors Convocation.

Tree, the son of Mr. and Mrs. Brewster Tree II of Hopachuchu, is a graduate of Hopachuchu Central High School . . .

Lucas G. Tree won the Faculty Award to the Outstanding Student in Finance, the Financial Administrator's Institute Recognition Award, the State Society of Certified Public Accountants Award, the Senior Honor Student Award in the College of Finance, and the Jackson Herkimer Memorial Scholarship, it was announced at Jones University's Annual Honors Convocation.

Tree, the son of Mr. and Mrs. Brewster Tree II of Hopachuchu, is a graduate of Hopachuchu Central High School . . .

Editor's Comment: "Routine," the editor said about each of the two releases that arrived separately on the same day. The editor had missed the apparent relationship between the two releases. Evidently, the public relations writer missed it also.

Lesson for Public Relations Writers: Don't overlook the obvious human interest factor that results from a coincidence of information. In this case, brothers receiving honors in the same field could be newsworthy.

Why So Many Poor Releases?

Two reasons explain the existence of such ineffective news releases: The writers either forgot or didn't understand the needs of their customer—the media.

Sometimes organizational policy gets in the way of good news releases. Here's a real-life example. A public relations intern working at a hospital noticed that the public relations office had an unusual way of preparing news releases. Regardless of news interest, every release prepared by the hospital began the same way: *Memorial Hospital of East Carbon Street in Southtown announces that . . .*

The intern recognized that this was not what she had learned in class about effective ways to begin a release. What should she do? First, her duty as an intern was to follow the organizational policy. Second, she should try to understand the policy. She discovered that the hospital was acting on the recommendation of a fundraising consultant who had observed, correctly, that the small hospital's side-street location meant that many residents did not know where it was located. The consultant had recommended that news releases emphasize the location and the connection with its geographic service area. Thus the policy had a logical basis, though this seems to be a too-rigid application of that logic.

Another student reported a similar problem. The practice at the bank where he interned was to end each news release with two long paragraphs of organizational identification. The first was a six-line paragraph that focused on the bank; the second was four lines that gave background on the holding company that owned the bank—altogether 10 lines, nearly a half page of every news release.

This student's most recent release about a new branch manager featured a one-paragraph lead (four lines) about the appointment, two paragraphs (totaling six lines) about the new officer, and two paragraphs (10 lines) of standard organizational identification. Exactly half of the release was boilerplate info that no self-respecting newspaper would use.

The intern talked with his professor and together they considered his options. He would continue to use the standard paragraphs as his internship supervisor required, but he would also track the releases to learn if the media used the standard paragraphs or any information they included. Then he would try to weave some of the information around more pertinent information in the release. Finally, if the opportunity presented itself, he would ask the supervisor about using a shorter version that had a better chance of being used.

Answers to Chapter Exercises

Exercise 8.3

Following are examples of how the leads could be revised to streamline the language and conform to news-writing style.

1. Euphrasia Gilhoolie has been named director of customer service and maintenance at the Eastern Cable Company. She will direct a staff of 27.
2. Toby Tyler's Toyota will hold an open house at its new showroom on James Place from 9 a.m. to 9 p.m. Monday.
3. The starting players of the Haven High School Hamsters will hold a five-day basketball clinic for children aged 6 to 10 beginning at 9 a.m. Monday, June 15.
4. Melinda Hobermeyer has been named senior vice president for corporate communications at O'Malley Enterprises. Her appointment was announced by Aloysius T. O'Malley, president and CEO.
5. The department of social geography at Oceanview University will host urban planning specialists from six small land-locked countries in Europe. The urban planners are touring the United States to study examples of effective space usage by boundary-limited municipalities. [Later in the story: The planners are from Andorra, Liechtenstein, Luxembourg, Monaco, San Marino, and Vatican City.]

6. The Peter Romanov Company of Admiralty Park has developed a new security system for parked cars.

Exercise 8.7

Major problems with the draft are:

- Focus in the lead on the company rather than the individual.
- Vague time reference for the date.
- First quote is without significance.
- Second quote is self-serving and of no interest to the public.
- Identification of supervisor is anti-climactic; two different spellings for her name.
- Some irrelevant and awkward information with the educational background.
- Vague information about previous work history.
- Missing information about the significance of the position.
- Missing information about the company.

Following is one way to rewrite the news release:

> Wesley L. Marlborough has been appointed superintendent of the plastics division at Starter Electronics, according to Anastasia Quigley, Starter's vice president for production. The appointment will become effective November 30.
>
> Marlborough will direct 30 employees in the division, overseeing production of Starter's line of fiber optics. Starter is a major supplier of fiber-optical materials for the Vegas Cable Television System at Albuquerque.
>
> A native of East Downhome, Marlborough holds a bachelor's degree in engineering technology from Upper Pecos College at Fort Sumner. He was an electronics technician with the Navy before joining Starter in 1989.

9 Broadcast News Release

In most ways, the broadcast news media are interested in the same thing as their print counterparts—news. But radio and television have some particular needs that go beyond what print journalists require. Radio, for example, needs access to interviews, and television seeks stories with strong visual elements. Talk-show hosts seek interesting people to interview.

When public relations writers understand the needs of the broadcast media, they are better able to increase their effectiveness in using radio and television to communicate with their key publics. This chapter expands your repertoire by introducing you to actualities, audio news releases, video news releases, and B-rolls. Here are your objectives for this chapter:

- To write in the style of the broadcast media
- To use pronunciation guides accurately
- To prepare a news release including a radio actuality
- To outline the contents of a video news release.

Broadcast Writing Style

Broadcast media is an umbrella term for radio and television. Cable television is popularly included in this term, though cable is technically not a broadcast medium. The term usually refers to public media and excludes organizational video and audio services.

When public relations writers turn their attention to radio and television, they find both opportunities and challenges. Because of the need for radio and television to present sound and visual action, the written word isn't enough. Unlike releases for the print media, broadcast news releases are not intended to be used verbatim; rather they are idea generators and background resources for reporters.

Some public relations writers have found that it is not always necessary to provide separate releases to the broadcast media. A single news release or a single media kit may serve the purposes of radio and television, as well as newspapers and magazines. Nevertheless, there are times when it is appropriate to do specialized releases for broadcast media. This calls for differences in leads, special stylistic considerations, and a more conversational writing tone.

The overall approach to preparing releases intended for broadcast use can be summed up easily: *Write for the ear*. The style should be conversational but not casual. It should reflect a professional rather than a familiar tone. As with any writing style, read your text aloud as you prepare it. This is the best way to recognize if the writing sounds both natural and appropriate. Here are some general guidelines about preparing broadcast news releases:

- Use short sentences
- Use active voice
- Generally, use present tense of verbs, unless the time factor requires another tense
- Keep the subject and the verb close together
- Use strong verbs
- Limit your use of adverbs and adjectives
- Use contractions
- Avoid relative clauses (those introduced by *who*, *which*, *what*, and *that*) at the beginning of a sentence
- Use generalities rather than specific explanatory details, especially with numbers
- Repeat identifications on second reference
- Use "you" words
- Avoid alliterations and tongue twisters.

News writing shares the basics, whether the writer is preparing information for print or broadcast media. However, broadcast releases present a few special considerations for writers, and some of the usual stylebook guidelines for print media do not apply to writing releases for broadcast media. What follow are examples of some of these broadcast norms.

Names and Titles. Because it is meant for the ear, broadcast style calls for less precision and permits more generalization than would be appropriate with print media.

- Generally, don't use middle initials or middle names, unless the person is known by such use. For example, *Michael J. Fox* or *Sarah Jessica Parker*.
- Use titles before the name rather than after it. For example, write *BioTech president Marguerita Bench will visit* . . . rather than *Marguerita Bench, the president of BioTech, will visit* . . . Alternatively, separate the title from the name, and use the title first, as in *The company president will visit the Bayville plant next month. Marguerita Bench is expected to arrive . . .*
- Simplify job titles. For example, instead of *Colin Kahl served as Deputy Undersecretary of Defense for the Middle East in the Obama Administration*, use *Colin Kahl headed Pentagon Middle East policy for President Obama.*
- Use informal descriptors before the name instead of after. For example, *City Hall spokesman Joe Morrison* or *animal-rights activist Mary Chin.*
- Use an academic or medical title only when the person's credentials are important to the story, such as *Doctor Sanjay Gupta*, but not *Doctor Bill Cosby*. (Note that writing in broadcast style requires that the word "doctor" be spelled out rather than abbreviated.) But don't use the title for holders of honorary doctorates, such as Barack Obama (Notre Dame), Stephen Colbert (Knox College), Dolly Parton (Tennessee), and Kermit the Frog (SUNY Stoneybrook).

Numbers. Numbers are particularly difficult to comprehend by hearing alone. Broadcast style calls for numbers to be used as little as possible. When they are necessary, make them understandable.

- Spell out single-digit numbers (zero to nine) and eleven. Use numerals for numbers between 10 and 999. Use words or a combination of numerals and words for numbers of one thousand or more, such as *12 million*, *14 hundred*, and *three billion*. Notice that no hyphen is used in such cases.

- If possible, use rounded numbers rather than specific numbers. For example, instead of *the $14,946,300 budget* (appropriate for releases to print media), write *the budget of nearly 15 million dollars* for releases to broadcast media. However, specific numbers may be needed for reporting votes, financial reports, and other detailed pieces of information.
- Try to translate numbers into easy-to-understand human terms. For example, instead of *a tax increase of two million dollars for a city of 500,000 residents*, make it more understandable: *a tax increase of four dollars for each city resident.*
- Write out terms associated with numbers, such as *55 dollars* and *78 percent.*
- If age is an important detail, use it before the noun, such as *the 50-year-old company* or *the seven-year-old child.*

Abbreviations. Broadcast copy frequently uses commonly understood abbreviations, in line with the notion of simplifying and making it easier for a listener to understand.

- Use abbreviations for well-known organizations, such as *F-B-I* for the Federal Bureau of Investigation or *U-N* for the United Nations.
- For acronyms of organizational names that are pronounced as words, such as *UNESCO* and *NASA*, write them in all-capital letters without periods.
- For organizational names that are pronounced as individual letters, write acronyms in all-capital letters separated by hyphens, such as *I-A-B-C* or *P-R-S-A*. Some acronyms need special treatment to represent the proper pronunciation, such as *N-C-Double-A* and *Triple A*.
- Use common abbreviations that would be familiar to listeners, but avoid unfamiliar or made-up ones. For example, *U-C-L-A* is an appropriate and understandable abbreviation for the University of California at Los Angeles, but *U-N-D* is not a commonly used abbreviation for the University of Notre Dame.

Punctuation. Writing for broadcast calls for a different use of punctuation than when writing for print. Hyphens are sometimes used in ways not called for by proper spelling, such as to facilitate pronunciation. For example, you would write "recreation" when referring to leisure activities but "re-creation" when referring to a second creation. Hyphens also are used to indicate abbreviations that are pronounced as letters rather than as words (see Abbreviations, above).

Quotations. Quotes pose special problems for writers of broadcast news releases, because the intended audience (the viewer or listener) will not be able to see quotation marks.

- Paraphrase the quotation. This is the easiest and best way to handle quotes. *The senator said the proposal was disrespectful to taxpayers. The report called the recommendation premature.*
- Signal the quotation. Use phrases like: . . . *the proposal was what she called "callous and ineffective,"* . . . *which was, in her words, "unworkable and destined for failure"* or *The secretary's response was: "I'm not going to take the heat for this one."* Other clear indicators that a direct quote is being used: *As she put it* . . ., *To use his words* . . ., *The president's exact words were* . . .. But avoid using the construction *Quote . . . Unquote.*
- Provide an actuality for the reporter covering the story (more on this later in this chapter).

Copy Presentation. Make it as easy as possible for news reporters to understand and read your copy.

- Avoid using abbreviated forms of all words except *Mr.*, *Ms.*, and *Mrs.* Don't abbreviate words that normally would be abbreviated in print releases, such as *street*, *saint*, *doctor*, *company*, and *incorporated.*
- Avoid splitting words from one line to the next. Turn off the hyphen option on your computer, because split words can be confusing for a broadcast reader.
- Capitalize and/or underline the word *not* in crucial situations to draw the attention of the broadcaster. *The mayor said he has decided* not *to seek re-election.*
- To make reading easier, use hyphens for compound words that would not be hyphenated in a release for print media. For example, in broadcast copy include a hyphen in words such as semi-tropical and non-denominational.
- Type broadcast releases using double spacing. Traditionally, broadcast news scripts were typed in all-capital letters. Increasingly, however, broadcast reporters are using regular style (both capitals and lower case letters) because this is easier to read. For broadcast news releases, use caps and lower case.

Exercise 9.1

Writing in Broadcast Style

Rewrite each of the following sentences in a style appropriate for broadcast news copy. Answers are listed at the end of this chapter.

1. The Acme Electronics President and CEO, Mrs. Gail J. Palecki, pointed out that 7 members of her management team will receive a performance bonus because the project was completed ahead of the June 30th schedule.
2. The city's $1,968,957 budget was approved 5–1 with 1 abstention when the City Council met last night. That means a $14.00 average increase in property taxes for every homeowner.
3. The president acknowledged that the new director, 32, is the youngest person ever to serve on the Corporate Leadership Team (CLT).
4. The LPGA contender will give an address before students being honored in the Scholar–Athlete Recognition Luncheon.
5. Only 9% of the funding will come from federal funds, with the remainder coming from state, county, and municipal coffers.
6. Robert L. Jones, Democratic candidate for tax assessor in the Town of Armstrong, has announced the convening of a public forum to receive input from taxpayers.
7. "Comparisons with school districts in other states are inappropriate," said Dr. Janice Harrison, Superintendent of Schools for the Madison County School District.
8. The company promises to return generous dividends to investors, according to information from the Office of the Corporate Treasurer, headed by Treasurer June Dellivan.
9. In the words of Miriam Johansen, kindergarten teacher at Elmwood Elementary: "Kids today are spending entirely too much time with zombie-like mind killers in front of their TVs and video games."

Broadcast Lead

The lead for a broadcast news release often differs from that of a print release because it is slower getting into the actual news. Print releases generally present the news right up front, using the format of a summary news lead. Broadcast copywriters preparing reports of serious events, especially tragedies, sometimes use the same no-nonsense approach: factual, straightforward, crisp.

But not all broadcast stories are major breaking news reports. Many, particularly those stories associated with news releases, often deal with softer news.

Radio listeners and television viewers often rely on the broadcaster to help set the stage before the news is presented. The lead for broadcast releases is where we set the stage. That is especially true for radio audiences, who frequently need to be "rounded up" for a news story because they are paying only partial attention. They are often occupied with the commute to work or household chores, using the media merely as background sound. In these instances, a report that jumps right into the news is likely to be missed. By the time the listener begins paying attention, the important details are past; they hear a report about a serious auto accident, but the detail about where the accident occurred escapes them because they weren't paying attention at the beginning of the news report.

Let's discuss the various types of leads used in broadcast news releases: soft, setup, umbrella, background, question, statement, and punch.

Soft Lead. The summary news lead associated with print releases focuses on the news—the stronger, the better. But for broadcast, a **soft lead** takes a gentler approach. This also has been called a **throw-away lead**, a **tune-in lead**, and a **warm-up lead**. Whatever the name, it is an attention getter, a hook that pulls the casual audience into the story. The following lead might work for a print release:

> Harriet Tubman High School will begin a $4.5 million expansion project featuring a new library and online research center, an expansion of the athletic complex, and 14 new classrooms.

The lead for that same story might be written more softly for a broadcast release:

> A high-tech library, 14 more classrooms, and a bigger sports center highlight the four-and-a-half-million-dollar expansion project at Tubman High.

Setup Lead. Instead of providing even generalized news, some broadcast leads try to set the stage for upcoming news. This is another response to the fact that many members of broadcast audiences, particularly radio listeners, are not giving the medium their full attention. The **setup lead** is a way of pulling them into the story.

With the setup lead, the first sentence doesn't give any news, but it draws the listener into the report. So when the second sentence is given, the reader is now paying attention, ready to obtain more information about pageants. Here are two examples in which the opening sentence exists mainly to gain the attention of casual radio or TV audiences, setting them up for the main news report:

> A local high school is preparing for an extreme makeover. A high-tech library, 14 more classrooms, and a bigger sports center highlight the four-and-a-half-million-dollar expansion project at Tubman High . . .

> Beauty pageants once focused on swimsuits and high heels. Now college grades and volunteer experience also play a role. This morning the National Miss Pageant committee announced new standards for local beauty contests . . .

Umbrella Lead. When a story is a complicated one with several twists and turns, an **umbrella lead** can prepare the listener. Here's an example:

> Two different reactions are greeting the new graduation requirements announced by the state education department. Some parents like higher standards for graduates, but others fear the new policy will increase the drop-out rate.

Background Lead. It's generally not a good idea to begin a news story with a history lesson, but occasionally that's necessary to help the reader understand the context of the news. Here's an example of such a **background lead**:

> Six years ago, Kiowa College was reeling from financial scandal, decreased enrollment, and a nasty strike by faculty members. Today, two years after Louis Eagle became Kiowa president, the campus is calm and peaceful, and well on its way to full enrollment.

Question Lead. Sometimes a **question lead** can focus the listener's attention. Be careful not to overdo question leads, because they often seem to be teasing the audience with guessing games, something good reporters avoid doing. Worse, they can sound like advertisements. Nevertheless, a well-stated question may be the best way to get into a news report. Here is an example:

> How much will it cost your children to attend college? Senator Jon Montoya contacted every college in the state, and his projections are that . . .

Statement Lead. Another type of news opening, the **statement lead**, begins with a compelling fact or opinion in the first sentence, then provides the attribution and context in the second. Here's an example of such a statement lead:

> More college students would volunteer to work with kids and senior citizens, but only if someone asks them personally. That's what public relations students found when they surveyed 400 sophomores at Oakwood University.

Punch Lead. Some leads are short sentences or even sentence fragments. Known as **punch leads**, they are just a bit more conversational than headlines, and they perform the same function. Here is an example:

> Six more weeks of winter, if you believe groundhogs and caterpillars. But forecasters at Weather Watch say the critters are wrong.

Exercise 9.2

Writing Broadcast Leads

Write a broadcast lead for each of the following stories. Ask your instructor or another student to provide details for you to use in your writing.

- *Document discovery*. The head of the history department at your college or university is announcing the discovery of a 200-year-old document that gives Native Americans treaty rights to the land on which the college now stands.
- *Sports signing*. In a release to sports broadcasters, your college or university is announcing the signing of a hot new prospect (use your own name and background) as a starting player for a varsity sport of your choice.
- *Enrollment surge*. The dean of enrollment management at your college or university is explaining why enrollment suddenly surged by 15 percent after several years of steady enrollment. The reason is complicated, based on easier availability of student loans, more scholarship money given by alumni, a marketing "guarantee" that students can graduate in four years, the addition of several new majors dealing with business and computers, and tuition increases in several neighboring colleges.
- *Hate speech*. The dean of students at your college or university is announcing a new policy that will ban so-called hate speech on campus and will guarantee the safety of students living in dorms against harassment or violence based on national background, sexual orientation, and religious identity and practice. The school already has a policy of similar guarantees based on gender and race.
- *Branch campus*. The president of your college or university is making a statement explaining that the school is opening a branch location in a popular suburban mall. This announcement will undoubtedly lead to questions about the watering down of higher education as well as to your school's long-range intention about its present campus location. The branch location will be used for evening programs and professional development seminars.

Pronouncer

One of the important needs of any writing is that it can be read clearly. When you are writing for the ear and are dealing with unfamiliar words, you can make your writing more effective by helping readers pronounce words properly. This is especially important with anything that is meant to be read aloud, such as a broadcast news release or a speech. But even something meant for silent reading can enhance the reader's understanding if you provide assistance in pronouncing difficult words.

The tool for this is the **pronouncer**, also called a **pronunciation guide**. The purpose of this simple phonetic spelling of hard-to-pronounce names, places, and technical terms is to help readers give the proper pronunciation to words that may be unfamiliar to them.

Pronouncers are commonly used in broadcast news releases. Broadcasters' reputations lie, in part, in their ability to be perceived as expert and credible reporters. Mispronunciation hurts that credibility. You will find your reputation as a public relations writer enhanced among broadcast journalists if you can help them avoid the embarrassment of mispronouncing your copy. Pronouncers also enhance speeches and scripts, fact sheets and brochures that include difficult or unusual words.

When using pronouncers, write each syllable separately, using all-caps for accented syllables: California ((kal-ih-FORN-yuh)), Tanzania ((tan-zuh-NEE-uh)). Following are some general phonetic guides:

CONSONANTS:

Use consonants as they are commonly pronounced, with the following exceptions:

S for soft C (city)

K for hard C (canal)

Z for hard S (disease)

G for hard G (grape)

J for soft G (gentle)

SH for soft CH (machine)

CH for hard CH or TCH (channel)

VOWELS:

AY (hate)

A (bat)

AH (father)

AW (awful)

AI (hair)

EE (retreat)

EH (bed)

EYE or Y (file)

IH (pretty)

OH (wrote)

OI (foil)

OO (tool)

OU (ground)

U (foot)

UH (putt)

Generally, pronouncers are written following the word. Enclose them in double parentheses to prevent any confusion for the broadcaster reading your release and mistaking the pronouncer for part of the text. Write each syllable separately, connected by a hyphen. Use all-caps for the accented syllable. Don't use accent marks such as you might find in a dictionary. Likewise, don't underline or boldface the accented syllables.

> The Xiniel ((ZIN-ee-uhl)) Corporation of Java ((JAY-vuh)), New York, will host a Special Olympics competition next Wednesday at its headquarters on Pzrybsko ((PRIB-skoh)) Drive. State Senator Meiko Takako ((MAY-koh tah-KAH-koh)) will present trophies to each participating athlete.

An acceptable alternative to this phonetic guide is to use a common rhyme with a word, such as *James Rwytt ((sounds like "write")).*

The key to writing effective pronouncers is to use such simple and basic spellings that it becomes virtually impossible to mispronounce the word. Public relations writers find that pronunciation guides can be useful in various situations, especially when they are dealing with names of people or places.

Personal Names. Pronouncers are helpful with people's names. Many names have spellings that are not easy to pronounce. This is becoming more common as words from a variety of ethnic heritages are becoming popular and prominent. Careful public relations writers can help broadcast reporters pronounce these names accurately.

Even the print media sometimes use pronouncers, as a metropolitan newspaper did when Edmund Przybyszewski was one of two winners of a $4.5 million state lottery. The paper told its readers that the name was pronounced SHIB-uh-CHEV-skee (probably not the pronunciation most readers would have come up with on their own, though Polish readers may not have been put off by the spelling). Likewise, many readers of newspapers and magazines had trouble when they encountered the name of the president of Iran, Mahmoud Ahmadinejad.

Various print media have different rules for spelling names originally written in a non-Western alphabet. But the pronouncer can make things simpler: ((mah-MOOD ah-mah-dih-nee-ZHAHD)). Similarly, the senior senator from Hawaii, Daniel Inouye ((ee-NOH-way)), Venezuela's President Hugo Chavez ((OO-goh CHAH-vehs)), Ireland's President Mary McAleese ((MAH-ree MACK-uh-lees)).

The website of the government-operated Voice of America radio network has a convenient short list of pronunciations at names.voa.gov.

Place Names. Names of places often need pronunciation guides. In most parts of the United States and Canada, Native American words are frequently used in the names of rivers and lakes, towns and cities. In the Southwest and Southeast, Spanish place names also are common. French names are common in Louisiana, New England, and the northern Great Plains. Some of these names are so well known that they require no pronunciation guide. Public relations writers can presume that broadcasters will be able to properly pronounce Cincinnati, Dakota, Santa Fe, and Massachusetts. But help is appropriate for some of California's offerings: Port Hueneme ((why-NEE-mee)), Marin ((mair-IN)), and Yucaipa ((you-KEYE-puh)). Or some of Pennsylvania's rivers, such as the Monongahela ((muh-NON-guh-HEE-luh)) and Susquehanna ((suhs-kwuh-HAN-uh)).

Some place names have regional pronunciations that are different from what might be expected. For example, the towns and villages of Berlin in a dozen states pronounce their name as BUHR-lin. Or consider Buena Vista; it's pronounced BWAY-nuh Vista in California but BYOO-nuh Vista in Georgia, West Virginia, Colorado, and Iowa.

Pronouncers also are often required for foreign place names. Consider how difficult it is to pronounce the following cities without the help of a pronunciation guide: the capital of North Korea, Pyongyang ((pee-young-YAHNG)); Japan's sacred shrine of Ise ((EE-say)); or the capital of Burkina Faso, Ouagadougou ((WAHG-uh-doo-GOO)).

Exercise 9.3

Writing Pronouncers

Write pronouncers for the following words. If you are uncertain of the proper pronunciation, consult a dictionary, gazetteer, encyclopedia, or pronunciation guidebook. Answers are listed at the end of this chapter.

1. Cairo (Ga.)
2. Coeur d'Alene (Idaho)
3. Ethete (Wyo.)
4. Lodi (Calif.)
5. Louisville (Ky.)
6. Louisville (Ala.)
7. Massillon (Ohio)
8. Ocoee (Fla.)
9. Otsego (Mich.)
10. Penetanguishene (Ontario)
11. Piscataquis River (Maine)
12. Pulaski (Ky.)
13. Pulaski (N.Y.)
14. Raquette Lake (N.Y.)
15. Regina (Saskatchewan)
16. Sacajaewea Peak (Ore.)
17. St. Regis River (N.Y.)
18. Trois Pistoles (Quebec)
19. Willammette River (Ore.)
20. Worcester (Mass.)
21. Worcester (N.Y.)

Broadcast News Release

As technology offers increasing prospects for packaging and transmitting messages, public relations practitioners have been quick to take advantage of the new opportunities in writing a **broadcast news release**, which is the radio/television/digital equivalent to the print news release. Actuality releases, audio and video news releases, B-rolls and new multimedia news releases are among the tools that public relations writers use when they wish to communicate with various publics.

Actuality Release

More sophisticated than the regular news release sent to the broadcast media is an **actuality release**. This is a news release that includes not only printed information but also a brief video- or audio-taped quote for use by the broadcast media. The recorded portion is the **actuality**, commonly called a **sound bite**. Increasingly, public relations writers are sending printed news releases to broadcast stations, in which they invite reporters to obtain recorded actualities from the organization's website or from a special telephone source.

The actuality release begins like any other broadcast release, with an appropriate lead (generally a soft lead). This is followed by one or several paragraphs of additional newsworthy information.

Then the writer uses a **lead-in** to provide the context of the actuality and the sound bite itself, used perhaps to give a benefit statement. This signal is sometimes called a **throw**, because it figuratively throws the report to another voice. The lead-in provides the transition from the reporter to the voice on tape. It also explains the context for the upcoming quote.

One thing a lead-in should not do is steal the thunder from the upcoming quote. Don't create an echo. For example, if you have a quote that starts out "Let me tell you why I'm running for office," don't write a lead-in that says "Brown tells why he's running for office." Instead, write "Brown spoke this morning about the reasons behind his campaign decision." The lead-in must use different words and phrases than the listener will hear in the sound bite. It's best if the lead-in simply provides some background and signals that a taped voice is coming.

There are two types of actualities, in which a person involved in the story presents first-hand information.

- **Factual actualities** offer eyewitness reports or explanations by experts.
- **Opinion actualities** give comments with an organization's viewpoints.

Actualities create a more interesting broadcast report, a plus for journalists and their audiences. They also help organizations by providing a richer message that includes not only the words but also the tone and emotion of the speaker, giving audiences a more realistic experience of the organization's message. A public relations writer preparing an actuality must carefully select a quote that meets two criteria: (1) A sound bite must be newsworthy, warranting its use by the media; and (2) it should be strategic, extending or supporting the organization's message. The first criterion is a condition imposed by the news media; the second is a need based on public relations concerns.

In the release, the actuality should be clearly indicated, and the text of the relevant quote (or audio portion of a video segment) should be included. In typing the release, make the actuality look different from the rest of the release. The most common treatment is to type the actuality text in single spacing, with both right- and left-hand indents. Also indicate the length of the actuality, calculated in seconds.

Public relations writers generally give radio reporters a written news release with actualities available in a digital download file. The technology for producing taped actualities is relatively inexpensive. A high-quality digital recorder and a good unidirectional microphone are all the equipment needed.

In addition to posting sound bites for journalists to download to include in their news reports, public relations practitioners also post selected sound bites as well as perhaps an entire speech or interview so other readers of the websites, blogs, and Facebook pages can download messages directly.

For television reporters, public relations writers often accompany written news releases with a **video B-roll**, an unedited videotaped piece relevant to the story being presented. With technology bringing down the cost of broadcast-quality video cameras, many organizations are able to shoot their own footage. This can be a big advantage to television news teams, which are often short-staffed, especially when the newsworthy situation is in a location that is not easily accessible.

In preparing the actuality, the public relations writer acts as a reporter gathering news—interviewing people and recording presentations. With the tapes edited to feature a couple of brief sound bites, the writer weaves these into a news release. The actualities serve the same purpose as a quote in a news release for print media. Exhibit 9.1 shows how a broadcast release might use an actuality. Note that the sound bite is clearly indicated.

Exhibit 9.1—ACTUALITY RELEASE Note how the actuality is presented in this release for the radio media by Pleasantville Technical Institute. The sound bite is clearly indicated and the note at the end indicates how it can be downloaded for media use.

PLEASANTVILLE TECHNICAL INSTITUTE

One Academy Place
Pleasantville, Any State, 12345

Moira McKinney
Public Information Officer
(123) 456-7890

Local Students Collect Funds for African Orphans

March 23, 2011
FOR IMMEDIATE RELEASE

Because local college students are sharing their lunch money, Rwandan orphans will find a home off the streets.

For about two months, students at both Pleasantville Technical Institute and Tri-County Community College have been giving part of their lunch money to an Orphan's Fund destined for Rwanda. The students collected more than 15 thousand dollars for an African doctor who runs several orphanages in the capital city of Kigali.

Professor Raymond Ramashekhara ((ruh-MAH-shuh-KAH-ruh)) is a native of Rwanda and head of Pleasantville Tech's International Studies program. Last week, he carried the money to Doctor Luke Balyasindu ((BAH-lee-uh-SIN-doo)), who has received the Pan-African Peace Medal for his work with orphans and homeless people.

Doctor Luke tells how he will use the donation.

(SOUND BITE … 15 SECONDS)

We appreciate the generosity of the young people of Pleasantville, America. We will use your gift to provide a home for children who now live in the gutters. Through you, we will reflect the hope that they can grow up to be healthy and hard-working members of the nation of Rwanda, which itself has much hope for the future.

((more-more-more))

Exhibit 9.1—ACTUALITY RELEASE . . . *continued*

LOCAL STUDENTS COLLEGE …..2

Doctor Luke says his new orphanage will house about 150 boys. Because of local custom, orphaned girls usually are cared for by relatives.

This isn't the first time the local colleges have joined to support worthy causes. Previously students at Pleasantville Tech and Tri-County Community raised money for a school in Afghanistan and a medical clinic in Mexico.

Professor Ramashekhara and officials at both schools have praised the generosity of the local students. The professor says the students prove that young Americans do care about the world around them, and he encourages other organizations to tap into the humanitarianism of young people.

Anyone wishing to contact Professor Ramashekhara can reach him at Pleasantville Tech.

#####

Note to News Directors: Dr. Luke's sound bite can be downloaded from the Pleasantville Tech website, media center: www.pleasantville.edu/media

Exercise 9.4

Writing an Actuality Release for Radio

You are a public relations writer for your state chapter of the Association for Cancer Education and Prevention. Prepare a planning sheet and write an actuality release for radio stations. Base your release on the following information:

- ACEP is beginning a cancer-awareness campaign directed to college and university students in your part of the state. It is working with health centers at area schools and with local or regional organizations such as the Medical Society, the Guild of Nurses, and the Association of Health Educators.
- Underlying your release are the specific objectives of this campaign—to increase awareness among the key publics of issues related to breast cancer and testicular cancer, to create positive attitudes in young adults toward treating these diseases seriously, and to have young adults develop the habit of regular self-examination.
- The actuality releases will be distributed to commercial and campus radio stations serving your key publics. Identify the appropriate geographic area for distributing this release. The program will begin in one month, with an information rally at each campus and distribution of printed materials through the health centers. It will also be promoted through relevant courses in personal or public health, biology, and medicine.
- You, as public relations director for ACEP, should provide specific details related to this campaign. Enumerate the number of colleges or universities and the estimated total number of students affected by this regional campaign. Research the topic by obtaining information from general websites such as the American Cancer Society (cancer.org) or the National Cancer Institute (cancer.gov) or from specialized sites such as Testicular Cancer Online (tc-cancer.com), the Testicular Cancer Research Center (tcrc.acor.org), Breast Cancer Online (breastcancer.org), or the Susan G. Komen Breast Cancer Foundation (komen.org).
- Develop a quote appropriate to your key public. Use two or three sentences of this as an actuality, which would be provided as a downloadable link from your website.

Audio News Release

An extension of the actuality release is an **audio news release**, sometimes called a **radio news release**. Instead of a written release accompanied by a taped actuality, the **ANR** is packaged as a finished news segment providing both the announcer and the sound bite.

As ready-for-broadcast pieces, these packages can be dropped into a radio station's broadcast schedule. While this is an appealing resource for short-staffed radio news teams on small stations, ANRs are seldom used by larger radio stations. A study by Medialink, a company that produces and distributes ANRs, found that 84 percent of U.S. radio stations sometimes use ANRs, with most preferring a local angle. Another study by News/Broadcast Network found that 15 percent of radio stations use ANRs provided by satellite feed. The most common format is a 60-second spot aimed at morning drive-time audiences.

VNR-1 Communications of Arlington, Texas (vnr1.com), a company that produces a variety of electronic news releases, calls audio news releases "pound for pound the most cost-effective form of broadcast public relations." The company reports in its study that 83 percent of radio stations use ANRs, with 34 percent saying that printed materials accompanying the broadcast releases are used by radio news departments to localize the story. The company advises clients to have a local or regional tie-in and to use experts who are topical and easily understood. It also advises the time-proven caution: Avoid one-sided self-promotional pieces.

ANRs can be produced by public relations staffs with a modest amount of equipment: broadcast-quality digital recorders, microphones, and a simple audio mixer are the main requirements. Additionally, several companies specialize in the production of audio news releases. Many of these companies not only produce the ANR but also make contact with news directors, sometimes making the news package available as an Internet download or feeding it via telephone to radio stations interested in broadcasting the piece.

Video News Release

Another communication vehicle for the public relations practitioner is the **video news release**, popularly called a **VNR**. This is a packaged public relations release for television. It includes a fully produced segment that can be dropped into a news report, including voice-overs by an announcer. It may also include a partly produced segment that can be dropped into a news report, with a local announcer reading from the script that accompanies the VNR and doing his or her own voice-overs.

When video news releases became popular in the 1980s, they were used mainly for product introductions. This marketing function made them suspect by many news people. Today, however, VNRs have many public relations purposes. Companies use them to deal in crisis situations, such as Pepsi-Cola's distribution of VNRs during its fight against a product-tampering hoax. Nonprofit organizations, meanwhile, use them to explain their work and support their cause, such as those produced by Mothers Against Drunk Driving or the Muscular Dystrophy Association. The United Nations offers a range of VNRs to journalists: news about Darfur, Pakistan flooding, hunger in Niger, and the Haitian earthquake from the World Food Programme, and UNICEF news about Ugandan street children, earthquake aid in China, and youth delegates to a climate-change conference in Africa. The U.S. government, meanwhile, uses VNRs to provide news packages about natural disasters, military recruiting, food safety, and other topics.

Many smaller television stations and some larger ones use VNRs regularly. Nielsen Media Research reported that three out of four television stations use VNRs weekly. The practice is becoming more commonplace as understaffed television news teams find they can rely on VNRs to provide them with accurate and honest video presentations. Additionally, VNRs can help stations fill the expanding news holes created by news segments on morning shows, Internet coverage, and early, midday and late news programming.

Television news operations are looking for new sources of information. The increasing use of VNRs parallels the use of nonlocal news feeds by underfinanced news programs. For example, the Project for Excellence in Journalism reported that material fed from and through television networks nearly doubled between 1998 and 2002, while reports by local correspondents fell from 62 to 43 percent. Many of the largest corporate feeders, such as CNN News and Fox News, pass along VNRs to their local affiliates.

Some broadcasters are concerned about the ethics of using video news releases, particularly when stations fail to let their viewers know that the footage has been provided as a public relations service. See the box "FYI: Ethical Aspects of Public Relations and News."

A study by the Center for Media and Democracy found that 90 percent of VNRs used by local stations did not identify the packages as having been provided by public relations sources. Others are critical of the production quality, lack of local angles, and lack of subtlety with which some VNRs pitch a product or cause. Indeed, the two most common reasons for rejecting footage from public relations sources is that it isn't local or it is too commercial. So when broadcasters complain that some VNRs look like the handiwork of advertisers, public relations writers should listen.

Successful producers identify several criteria for VNRs: a strong news peg, footage otherwise not available to news stations, concise and strategic interviews, and good supporting video.

Organizations extend the life of VNRs by posting them at their websites for non-journalist visitors, where it is accessible not only to people already familiar with the organization but also to information seekers who find the site through a search engine or linked news portal. Sometimes these are posted on video-sharing websites. YouTube is the largest, but reviews consistently list several other top sites (listed alphabetically here): BlipTV, Dailymotion, Facebook, Google Video, Hulu, Metacafe, MySpace, Revver, Yahoo!, and Vimeo.

The difficulty many broadcast journalists have with video news releases is that they cannot be edited. As video packages, they are under the control of the public relations person who has produced them, which is why some journalists hesitate to use them. The most effective way to write a VNR is to provide enough flexibility so reporters can edit the release to fit the needs of the local television station. Often this means providing more than one version or some variation within the package. That is where B-rolls come in handy (we'll discuss these in the next section).

Providing flexibility for the news media to edit VNRs does not mean giving broadcast journalists only bland reports with little value to the organization that produces them. VNRs can be both subtle and persuasive. Your task in writing a VNR is to weave pertinent information about the product, service, or idea in such a way that it doesn't need to be edited out. Save the outright promotion for the advertising team. Let others push the message more aggressively on your website and Facebook page.

What topics are useful for video news releases? Much of the general advice about generating news for an organization works with VNRs. Look for tie-ins with current issues, events, and activities. News directors say VNRs that deal with business, consumer affairs, and the economy get their attention, because those topics are of continuing interest to their audiences. They also give attention to VNRs that deal with new technologies and medical research, as well as pieces strong in human interest.

FYI *Ethical Aspects of Public Relations and News*

Public relations people liken B-rolls, ANRs, and VNRs to print news releases, which provide information in formats that the media can use. They are what is sometimes called ***information subsidies***, newsworthy information packaged in a variety of formats that are provided to the media by public relations practitioners. The media seem to welcome them, and those that are newsworthy and balanced and that serve audience interests sometimes get used.

continued . . .

FYI *Ethical Aspects of Public Relations and News . . . continued*

But some issues surrounding information subsidies have raised important ethical questions.

The Public Relations Society of America identifies three principles: (1) A VNR is the television equivalent of a news release and, as such, should always be truthful and represent the highest in ethical standards. (2) Producers and distributors of VNRs and the organizations they represent should clearly and plainly identify themselves. (3) Television stations airing VNRs should identify sources of the material. The Radio Television Digital News Association similarly calls for stations to inform their audiences when a VNR is used and who produced it.

The government also has something to say about VNRs and related public relations materials. The Food and Drug Administration has special rules that VNRs and B-rolls dealing with medical topics must provide "fair balance." The Federal Communication Commission requires that ANRs and VNRs tell viewers about risks and side effects and provide clear information about limitations of the drugs. The FCC also has told broadcasters to identify the source of political or controversial information they are paid to air. This ruling came after the Government Accountability Office labeled the VNRs illegal government-funded "covert propaganda" when the second Bush White House used them to drum up support to change Medicare.

This is all part of the growing concern about **secured placement** of VNRs and **branded journalism**, both euphemisms for the practice of paying stations to run the pieces. Paid placements, particularly without identification in newscasts, violate the guidelines of both public relations and journalism. Revelations in 2006 that the U.S. Defense Department was covertly paying Iraqi newspaper editors and reporters to print pro-U.S. stories caused a storm of criticism against the Bush administration.

- Should news organizations be able to use information supplied by public relations sources?
- Should audiences be told when such outside-produced footage is being used?
- Should the government require disclosure of the use of VNRs and ANRs?

The answers for this book are "yes," "yes," and "probably not a good idea."

Yes, news departments should be able to use footage and material provided by public relations sources—if they want to.

Yes, the media should disclose when VNRs and ANRs are used, and public relations producers of VNRs should facilitate this. Notice can be given in the lead-in that the footage, actuality, or entire report is provided by such-and-such company, organization, or agency. An on-screen note about the origin of the footage also may be provided.

Finally, it doesn't seem necessary to establish more regulation. Enforcement of existing rules and a stronger sense of accountability to both publics and audiences may be the answer.

Recently, blogs have raised questions about VNRs. The topic also is part of the standard fare for the Center for Media and Democracy, a group critical of most things concerning public relations. According to its prwatch.org website, the center "strengthens participatory democracy by investigating and exposing public relations spin and propaganda." In 2006, it released a study based on a very small sample (less than 1 percent of VNRs used by television stations) and concluded that all video news releases and satellite media tours are propagandistic and "fake news."

Critics sometimes overreach when they see public relations as pernicious propaganda lurking around every corner, but they address the same legitimate questions that responsible public relations professionals are addressing. Embarrassing activities sometimes are done by political and corporate operatives with little connection to the public relations profession. We should be among the first to acknowledge if excesses occur or ethical principles are violated. We call for transparency in the use of public relations messages by the government and the military as well as by corporations and nonprofit groups.

Public relations writers can do several things to increase their chances that broadcasters will decide to use video news releases. Here are several ways to make a VNR more acceptable to reporters.

1. Focus on the news value of the information. The VNR should look and feel like news, because it should really be news. Keep it simple, resembling reports you see on the evening news instead of looking like a Hollywood production with dramatic lighting and special effects.
2. Clearly identify the sponsoring organization, but keep the identification subtle.
3. Highlight the local content of the VNR or help the broadcaster develop a local angle. For example, provide a list of local branches of the organization, area agencies dealing with the issue, or local experts who might be used in interviews.
4. Keep the piece short. Between one and two minutes is best; longer than that, and your chances of having the piece aired are very low. Edit the VNR for several different lengths.
5. Make the piece easy for the station to edit. Keep the natural sound on an audio channel separate from your announcer so the station can edit in its own announcer with ease.
6. Include a written advisory to indicate the news value of the VNR and the unique aspects of the visuals. Include a brief fact sheet about the topic and a short biographical sketch about key people who appear in the VNR, as well as pronunciation guides for names.
7. Include a script and a description of the B-rolls featured in the VNR package. News directors often decide about using VNRs based on what they read in the advisory and script.
8. Provide a point of contact so reporters and editors can obtain additional information.

Exercise 9.5

Writing a Video News Release

You are public relations writer for the national office of RiverGuard, an environmental action group that lobbies federal, state, and local government and advocates with the media and the public for strong laws and enforcement to reduce pollution in lakes, rivers, and streams. Your headquarters are in Chicago. You are preparing a video news release for release in states that are affected by acid rain.

Part 1: Prepare a planning sheet for this release.

Part 2: Using environmental resources, identify states and regions affected by the problem of acid rain. Using media resources, identify the television markets in one of these areas.

Part 3: Identify at least six B-roll segments that could be used with the VNR.

Part 4: Write a basic outline or script for a VNR.

Part 5: Write a cover letter for television news directors in a single television market within one of the areas affected by acid rain. In this letter, highlight the newsworthiness of your VNR to station viewers, indicate that some of the footage is not available elsewhere, and suggest ways television stations might localize the VNR.

B-Roll Package

To accommodate reporters' concern for control over the news segment as it ultimately reaches the audience, public relations practitioners often provide **B-roll packages**. Unlike the ANR or VNR, a B-roll package does not include a written news story. Rather, it provides background information through a series of different pieces of audio clips or video footage. Because it remains unedited, a B-roll package provides a more flexible resource for the broadcast journalist.

The same studies that report television stations using VNRs indicate that most opt for B-roll sound bites. In fact, that was all Pepsi-Cola provided for its announcement of a new policy on freshness dating on cans, which was used in 53 markets and was seen by 34 million viewers. On another occasion when it was fighting a hoax about product tampering, Pepsi produced two B-roll packages. One on the company's bottling process was seen by a reported 182 million viewers; the other showing someone tampering with a Pepsi can was seen by 95 million viewers.

Surveys and interviews with station directors point to a common theme: Broadcast reporters prefer B-rolls, which give the journalists access to information without sacrificing control over how that information is presented to their audiences.

Whereas fully produced VNRs can cost $20,000 or more, B-rolls are much less expensive. Both versions may be distributed to television stations via satellite, but increasingly they are made available on websites so news directors can preview and download them. "Advice from a Pro: Tony Perri on Using B-Roll Packages" offers further tips.

Advice from a Pro *Tony Perri on Using B-Roll Packages*

Executive producer Tony Perri recommends that organizations with newsworthy events present them to the media using B-rolls and natural sound rather than as a prepackaged VNR. Perri recommends including background footage, interviews, and sound bites in the B-rolls.

Tony is president of Perri Productions, a video news service that is part of his Boulder Production Company (tonyperri.com) in Boulder, Colo. He has several other suggestions for increasing the likelihood that television news reporters will use footage supplied by public relations practitioners:

- Focus on lively feature-oriented stories
- Use anecdotes to humanize the story
- Keep the package short, because the stories will be given less than two minutes of air time
- Avoid a strong marketing approach with a heavy emphasis on the organization or especially on its product or service. Remember that the value to reporters is that the footage presents news, not advertising.

As for production matters, Perri recommends not mixing voice-overs and sound bites but instead keeping each on a separate audio channel so local television stations can use their own announcers for voice-overs.

Answers to Chapter Exercises

Exercise 9.1

1. Rewards are in store for some Acme employees who completed the project ahead of schedule. President Gail Palecki ((pah-LEH-kee)) will give a performance bonus to seven members of her management team.
2. City Council approved 5-to-1 a new budget of nearly two million dollars. That means an average 14-dollar increase in property taxes for every homeowner.
3. At age 32, the new director is the youngest person ever to serve on the corporate leadership team.
4. The L-P-G-A contender will be the main speaker at a Scholar-Athlete Recognition Luncheon.
5. Only nine percent of the funding will come from the federal government. Most of the budget will come from the state, county, and local municipalities.
6. A tax-assessor candidate in the Town of Armstrong wants to hear from the voters. Robert Jones, a Democrat, says he will hold a public forum for taxpayer input.
7. Madison County school superintendent Janice Harrison says it's inappropriate to make comparisons with school districts in other states.
8. Corporate treasurer June Dellivan said the company expects investors to earn high dividends.
9. Miriam Johansen is a kindergarten teacher at Elmwood Elementary, where she observes a lot of young children. And she's critical of the amount of time they spend in front of TVs and video games. She called these zombie-like mind killers.

Exercise 9.3

1. Cairo ((KAY-roh))
2. Coeur d'Alene ((KOOR duh-LAYN))
3. Ethete ((EE-thuh-tee))
4. Lodi ((LOH-deye))
5. Louisville (Ky.) ((LOO-ee-vilh))
6. Louisville (Ala.) ((LOO-iss-vihl))
7. Massillon ((MASS-ih-lahn))
8. Ocoee ((oh-KOH-ee))
9. Otsego ((aht-SEE-goh))
10. Penetanguishene ((pehn-uh-tang-guh-SHEEN))
11. Piscataquis River ((pis-KAT-uh-kwis))
12. Pulaski (Ky.) ((puh-LASS-keye))
13. Pulaski (N.Y.) ((puh-LASS-kee))
14. Raquette Lake ((RACK-it))
15. Regina ((ruh-JEYE-nuh))
16. Sacajaewea Peak ((sak-uh-juh-WEE-uh))
17. St. Regis River ((REE-jis))
18. Trois Pistoles (Quebec) ((twah pee-STOHL))
19. Willammette ((wuh-LAM-et))
20. Worcester (Mass.) ((WUH-stuhr))
21. Worcester (N.Y.) ((WOO-stuhr))

10 Multimedia and Social Media Release

Newer communication technology has mushroomed the ways in which public relations practitioners can use the Internet as part of their strategic communication plans. You undoubtedly are familiar with some of the mainstays of such media: Facebook, Twitter, Vimeo, SlideShare. New names are continually being added.

This technology opens public relations practitioners to audiences that reach far beyond traditional journalists, offering opportunities to present more than just text and video. Much of the relevant technology allows for an interactive relationship with our publics and provides a platform for communicating in a multimedia environment.

This chapter will explore some of these newer media opportunities, particularly focusing on how public relations writers can use them. Here are your objectives for this chapter:

- To write an e-mail news release
- To develop a social media release
- To plan for an online newsroom for an organization.

E-Mail Release

News releases written in traditional print format (centered all-cap headlines, double spacing, and so on) are designed for dissemination as **hard copy**, a physical version printed on paper or perhaps sent as a fax which is printed when it is received. It is a permanent reproduction that does not change once it is rendered into its final version.

But dissemination as hard copy may not be the best option for public relations practitioners. Distribution as hard copy is slow, incorporating time needed to print the new release or other material and then to transmit it via postal mail. Fax is a bit quicker.

Printed news releases can be sent as portable document format file attachments, blending the speed of e-mail and Internet with the permanence of hard copy. But PDF attachments cannot easily be edited and sometimes are difficult even to open, so don't send them as the primary information source. Feature the information in the body of the e-mail, with a PDF attachment if you wish, along with links to an online site with the fuller version, as well as photos, backgrounders, and related materials. For attachments, many reporters prefer .txt or .doc (not .docx) files. Many public relations practitioners provide the same attachment in various formats.

E-mail offers a variation on writing and distributing news releases. The **e-mail news release** is written as the text of an e-mail rather than as an attachment. As such, it can be read by any recipient with e-mail capabilities using not only desktop and laptop computers but also smart phones and even smarter devices such as iPads.

E-mail releases generally are shorter than printed releases, often about 350–400 words in about five or six paragraphs, each with two or three sentences. Here are some guidelines for the standard elements of an e-mail release:

- *Start with a news flag.* Clearly indicate in the subject line that this is a news release. Keep this simple. Use the word "News" or the term "News Release."
- *Clearly indicate the subject.* Start with a subject line that incorporates the news flag of the organization and identifies the topic of the release, such as this: "Tyler College News: 8th President to Be Installed."
- *If appropriate, personalize the release.* If circumstances allow, write a brief introductory note to a reporter or editor. "Hi, Jon. When you interviewed our provost last month, you expressed interest in the installation ceremony for our new president, then being planned. Here is the information about that event." You might use a different type font for such a personal note, both to make it stand out for the recipient and to indicate that it is not part of the release itself.
- *Include a release date.* After the subject line, use the phrase "For Immediate Release" to let recipients know that they can use the information as soon as they receive it.
- *Write a strong headline.* Summarize the news being presented and, if possible, the benefit it offers to readers. Avoid using organizational jargon. Type the headline using caps and lower case rather than all caps to ensure easier reading with e-mail fonts and software.
- *Write a summary news lead.* This remains the best way to begin an e-mail release.
- *Simplify secondary information.* Don't include too many details in the body of the release.
- *Consider a strong, strategic quote.* An e-mail release is a perfect place to include a quote from an organizational spokesperson. Follow the same guidelines as outlined in Chapters 7 and 8 about preparing quotes for traditional print releases. Aim for quotes that are strategic and of interest to readers. Avoid quotes that are obsequious or braggadocios or that have the feel of self-serving propaganda. Avoid anything that sounds like advertising promotional copy.
- *End with an ID paragraph.* After presenting the news, conclude with a short identifying paragraph that provides information about the organization. This can include its business history, area of specialization or expertise, and perhaps a list of clients or past projects.
- *Use an end mark.* Conclude with the usual ##### to indicate the end of the news release.
- *Provide contact information.* The reason for e-mailing a news release is to disseminate it quickly, so make sure that the release can accommodate reporters who are working on deadline. Provide a telephone number as well as an e-mail contact for additional information. Also provide a complete link to a relevant website.
- *Write for all computer platforms.* Avoid using color fonts, bold type, and HTML tags, because not all e-mail recipients use the same software. You may imbed links to websites, but also include the full URL for readers whose software does not accept the imbedded links.

Your writing should be at its best. Writers sometimes get a bit sloppy when composing e-mail letters. Remember that this is a news release, not an informal memo. It also is not an advertisement, so avoid being promotional in your writing. Mention the client or sponsoring organization only in a news context. Leave it to your marketing colleagues to use language full of enthusiasm or exuberance.

Send e-mail releases only to editors and reporters you know wish to receive them; otherwise you are sending spam. Most organizations have as part of their media relations plan an ongoing invitation to journalists to opt in to receive news from the organization. This may be by way of **RSS feeds** (which commonly stands for **Really Simple Syndication**, though it was originally called **RDF Site Summary**). Whatever the name, RSS allows journalists and others to subscribe to timely updates of blogs and online news sites that interest them. Alternatively, organizations may contact journalists through e-mail blasts or distribution lists.

Exhibit 10.1 includes an example of an e-mail news release for essentially the same information as presented in Exhibit 8.3 in Chapter 8. Compare both versions of the release.

Exhibit 10.1—E-MAIL NEWS RELEASE Compare this e-mail news release with the print release on the same topic in Exhibit 8.3 in Chapter 8.

Subject: News from InterGalactic Motors: Safe Driving Clinic

FOR IMMEDIATE RELEASE

InterGalactic Motors Sponsoring Safe Driving Clinic;
Response to Congressional Request for Auto Makers to Promote Highway Safety

The Mid-State Division of InterGalactic Motors will sponsor a Safe Driving Clinic Saturday, Oct. 13, at its Harrison Road Plant in Lockport. The clinic is free for Marlon County residents.

CLINIC DETAILS
• The clinic will provide both information and hands-on practice in driving safety.
• Participants can earn extra points toward reduction of fines for traffic offenses, and credits toward discounts for auto insurance.
• Clinic will begin at 9 a.m. at the Employee Cafeteria, Building "G" at the plant.
• Area residents as well as nonresident college students register at 987–6543.
• The clinic will be led by InterGalactic Motors training and testing experts and by representatives of the Central Automobile Club of Centerville.

BACKGROUND
InterGalactic Motors is offering similar clinics at plants throughout the state. The clinics were scheduled in the wake of testimony before Congress by William Newbauer, InterGalactic Motors president. Newbauer addressed the Joint Committee on Transportation and Safety in Washington last month (Aug.15) on the need for auto manufacturers to take the lead in promoting driving safety.

QUOTE
Newbauer: "We have a responsibility to make safe cars. We also want to help train safer drivers, so highways, streets, and country roads are as safe as possible."

#####

Info Contact: Kim Salvatore, Public Relations Director (123) 456-7890, ksal@intergalactic

Exercise 10.1

Writing an E-Mail News Release

Select one of the following for this writing exercise.

1. The scenario you used for Exercise 8.6—Writing a Complete News Release
2. The scenario presented in Exercise 8.8—Writing a Localized News Release
3. The scenario you selected in Exercise 8.9—Writing an Announcement News Release
4. The scenario you chose in Exercise 8.10—Writing a Follow-Up News Release
5. Some other scenario presented by your instructor.

Using the same information you used in that release identified above, as well as any additional information you need, write an e-mail news release. Include the following elements:

- Planning sheet
- Subject line
- Personalized note to one of the reporters receiving the release
- Lead
- Additional and secondary information
- A strategic quote
- Concluding ID paragraph about your organization
- End mark
- Contact information.

Social Media Release

Step into a quick time warp. With continual enhancements in computer technology, the unfolding of the new digital universe is happening at breakneck speed. This technology is taking news releases to new levels.

Less than two decades ago, the **Internet news release (INR)** joined the inventory of tools for public relations writing. INRs began as adaptations of video news releases, taking advantage of improvements in computer and video technology, such as the ability to incorporate streaming video into a website. Imbedded within a written news release, video images and audio bites can be downloaded by readers.

In the mid- to late 1990s, the term then shifted to **multimedia news release (MNR)**, repackaging VNRs, B-rolls, and related productions to feature text, audio, video, and still images. MNRs offer links to websites, video FAQs, and extended or related interviews. The information included in multimedia releases can be customized and sent to key audiences, usually people who are already connected with the organization or who have asked to be kept informed about new developments.

MNRs can be disseminated through organizational websites, via e-mail, or on CD or DVD. They sometimes are distributed through specialized cable networks or through in-house video systems such as are found in hospitals and college dorms. Some find their way into in-flight videos on airplanes.

In 1997, BusinessWire debuted its Smart News Release, an MNR that included digital images. PRNewswire created MultiVu in 2001, featuring an online dashboard that included multimedia elements such as text, video, and audio.

MultiVu hosts many multimedia news release sites that serve various media by packaging information in several different formats. Porsche, for example, used a Web-based multimedia release to announce plans to work on an electric-powered sports car. The release included a print announcement by the CEO, streaming video with options to view three different models of its current top racing cars, downloadable photos, eight imbedded bookmarks, and links to five social media sites. It included an invitation to sign up for Porsche info that could be sent to a mobile device.

The U.S. Mint similarly used a multimedia release for its new Beautiful Quarters program. The website included text, imbedded video, downloadable MPG2 video, downloadable photos, related links and documents, downloadable mobile video, and links to various social media sites.

Growing beyond multimedia features, the field again shifted toward what has become known as a **social media release (SMR)**, which goes one better than the MNR. SMRs include links to social media sites and blogs to engage readers in a conversation by bloggers, citizen journalists, social media junkies, and consumers with the public relations folks within the organization.

A social media release (SMR) differs from a traditional print release in several ways. Traditional releases focus on a single news announcement directed to a key public, whereas SMRs can provide relevant information on various activities and for different publics. They are meant not only for mainstream reporters and editors but also for newer types of journalists such as bloggers and podcasters. As an online presence, they also are seen by (and written for) other audiences, including employees, customers, and competitors.

Unlike print releases, SMRs can include a range of graphic and digital products such as charts, photographs, imbedded movies, audio pieces, links to YouTube videos, and so on. Additionally, they have a longer shelf life; they can reside for months, perhaps years, in online archives.

SMR Writing

The hallmark of a social media release is that it provides for interaction between the organization and its various publics. To write an SMR, begin with the basic print news release outlined in Chapters 7 and 8. Here are some guidelines for writing a social media release.

- *Simplify the text.* Review the text of a written-for-print release to simplify it for online presentation. For example, be freer with bullet paragraphs than might be appropriate for a print release. An example of this might be if you are announcing a presentation that includes three experts on the topic. You could include a bullet paragraph on each person, perhaps with a boldface lead-in with the name and main topic he or she is addressing.
- *Begin with a news pitch.* If you wrote it carefully in your planning sheet, you may be able to use it verbatim. Recall that it was written as a Twitter message of 140 characters. Such writing calls for careful planning, clear thinking, a focused message,

and an enticing idea. It also features short words and tight editing. Focus on what's useful for the reader. If the one-minute elevator pitch is good for delivering a verbal message, the 140-character **Twitter pitch**—we call it a **Twitch**—is good for delivering a succinct message with a hook to social media users.

- *Follow the format previously suggested for e-mail releases.* Begin the text of the release with summary news lead, simplified secondary information and details, strategic quote, and closing organizational ID paragraph. Try to keep the basic SMR to no more than 400 words. This should not be too difficult, since social media releases have so many opportunities for providing links to additional information that does not need to be included within the main text.
- *Imbed links within the text.* Review the body of the release to indicate where you can imbed hyperlinks for additional information, such as a biography of an organizational official quoted in the release or perhaps a LinkedIn profile, history of the organization, past achievements and milestones, technical information about the subject, glossary of terms related to the topic, the text of a speech or report, citations for academic or scientific information, and news archives. Much of this information probably already exists, so it may be as simple as inserting a link for a PDF or text file.
- *Parallel the narrative with a fact sheet.* You want to help journalists gather quick background information for stories they are writing or producing. Consider posting a fact sheet that provides essentially the same information as the news release in bullet form.
- *Add supporting graphics.* After the basic text is ready, consider how to illustrate the message. Prepare and attach appropriate charts, graphs, or maps to visually articulate the key points in your release.
- *Identify photos to illustrate the information.* Think of the various ways to show the product, program, or service. Be wary about using the actual photo within the text. This can make loading slow, discouraging some potential readers from viewing your release. Consider two alternatives instead.

    1. Use only thumbnail photos with the text. Configure this so the reader can hover over the thumbnail with a mouse to expand it to full size, or set it up so the reader can click on the thumbnail to go to a different page with the full-size photo. These methods can be effective with only a few photos.
    2. Attach a photo gallery to post a larger number of photos. As in the option above, this gallery link can include thumbnail photos to give the viewer an idea of what's to be found at the link. It may be appropriate to post the gallery at a photo site such as Flickr.

- *Add audio and/or video components.* In preparing the social media release, you may find that inserting some audio elements can enhance the message. For example, if a speech is a significant aspect of the release, try to include an audio podcast. For a lengthy speech, consider providing a shorter edited version with the most important parts. If an interview is an element of the release, post a similar audio version of the entire interview, perhaps with separate edited highlights. Common audio encoding formats for such components are MP3, WAV, AIFF, and WMA.

- *Add video components.* Likewise, social media releases can have video elements. Following up on the audio example above, an SMR might include a link to a posting of the speech at a video-sharing service such as YouTube, Vimeo, or Google Video. It might also imbed the video in the organization's website using a video format such as MPEG or QuickTime.mov. You might even use a service such as SlideShare or Scribd to post online presentations through PowerPoint or Keynote, perhaps with audio and imbedded links to video-sharing sites. Likewise, if the issue is a new program or a product introduction, provide a video posting that shows viewers what the program features or how the product works.
- *Consider developing a special section for each particular public.* A traditional print or broadcast release generally is focused on a single public. But a social media release can include information for a variety of publics. Provide clear directions for site visitors. For example, a university announcing a new major in sports communication might have a series of special messages directed to various publics: current students, potential students, alumni, journalists, professional sports organizations, and so on. The links could provide relevant information for each individual reader.
- *Identify relevant external links.* You want to provide the reader with useful information, but not all of it needs to come from your organization. Consider authoritative websites such as parent organizations, holding companies or corporate divisions, professional organizations, industry groups, regulatory agencies, think tanks, and relevant academic entities.
- *Add a "share" button.* Engage your readers in disseminating your information. Make it easy for them to send your release along to their friends and colleagues whom they think would be interested. Provide online links to social media sites such as Facebook, LinkedIn, and Twitter.
- *Feature a blog-like space for reader comments.* Some public relations practitioners include this feature because it promotes reader engagement. They are very clear about this: "Tell us what you think." Others avoid it because it could open the organization's official news posting to negative feedback.
- *Include a "Call to Action."* Not all SMR readers are journalists. Many are potential or actual consumers (fans, patients, students, customers, voters) tuned into social media. Let then know what they can do to get more involved, and make it easy for them to act on their interests.
- *Feature a RSS subscription notice.* This allows users to subscribe to your website or blog posts. They sign up, and they receive an e-mail notification when new information is posted. Some organizations have special RSS feeds for journalists.

Many excellent examples of social media news releases are available. You can find many of them at corporate or organizational websites. Check out some automobile manufacturers' websites, such as chevroleteurope.com and pressroom.toyota.com. Browse around multivu.com > "Multimedia News Releases," "Archive," "Examples."

Exercise 10.2

Preparing a Social Media Release

Select one of the following scenarios for this writing exercise:

1. The scenario you used for Exercise 9.4—Writing an Actuality Release for Radio
2. The scenario you used for Exercise 9.5—Writing a Video News Release
3. Some other scenario presented by your instructor.

Using the same information as you used in that release identified above, as well as any additional information you need, write a social media release. Include the following elements:

Part 1: Planning Sheet.

Part 2: News Pitch (maximum 140 characters).

Part 3: Main text of the release (maximum 400 words). Underline five to ten links that you would imbed in the main text.

Part 4: Write a one-sentence explanation of what each link would feature.

Part 5: List at least three graphic elements, including photos, that support the release. Write a one-sentence explanation of each.

Part 6: List at least three audio and/or video elements that support the release, and write a one-sentence explanation of each.

Part 7: Identify at least three relevant external links that support the release, and write a one-sentence explanation of each.

Part 8: List at least three share sites, and write a one-sentence explanation of what elements you would place at each of these sites.

Part 9: List the topics or titles of at least three blogposts that you would include in a blog associated with this release.

Online Newsroom

Social media news releases have paved the way for **social media newsrooms**. These are comprehensive pages within the website of an organization or a public relations host that provides various SMRs. For example, PRNewswire's MultiVu expanded from a focus on multimedia to include social media features such as links to Twitter, Facebook, and other social media sites, as well as share features so readers can easily pass along the info to their friends (real or virtual).

The online newsrooms of some companies can serve as models of effective use of websites for media relations purposes. Take a look at the online newsrooms for IBM (ibm.com/press), Anhauser-Busch (anhauser-busch.com/press), and Pepsi (pepsico.com > "Media").

Similarly, look at the online media sites for some nonprofit organizations such as Mothers Against Drunk Driving (madd.org/media-center), Little League Baseball (little league.org > "Media"), the American Cancer Association (pressroom.cancer.org), and The Leadership Conference, a civil rights coalition (civilrights.org/press).

Many government agencies at the local, state or provincial, and national levels have effective online newsrooms. At whitehouse.gov, look at "Blog," "Photos and Video," and "Briefing Room." The FBI has a comprehensive online newsroom at fbi.gov/news. The Defense Department has an online newsroom at dod.gov/news, as do individual branches of the military, such as navy.mil > "Media Resources."

You'll also find effective online newsrooms operated by international organizations such as the United Nations (un.org/news), the Organization of American States (oas.org > "Media Center"), even the Vatican (vatican.va/news_services).

A survey of journalists on media relations practices, conducted by Bulldog Reporter/TEKGroup International, reported that 97 percent of journalists said they visit online newsrooms as part of their research. The 2009 report found that half the 2,300 responding journalists visit a corporate website or online newsroom at least once every month, and more than half use multimedia information from those sites.

Another survey by PR Newswire asked reporters what they seek in online newsrooms. Their advice: Make content accessible, easy to share, and easy to view. Here are some suggestions for creating effective online newsrooms.

Access. Make it easy to find. The best place for the newsroom is at your home page (second best, from your "about us" page). Keep the newsroom simple; call it something like "Newsroom" or "Press" or "Media." Aim for a simple URL, such as www.news.companyname.com.

Make it easy to access. Don't require a password or other prearrangements for journalists and others to view the site.

Online media pages should include a complete directory of contact information: names, phone numbers, fax numbers, e-mail addresses, as well as mailing information. Reporters working on deadlines don't have time to submit or e-mail questions or requests that someone from the organization contact them.

Content. Feature current news release packages, and news archives categorized so readers can easily find the older material. Make the releases and archives searchable by topic.

Provide organizational information such as executive bios, histories, program/product information, company timelines, annual reports, and corporate backgrounders and fact sheets.

If appropriate, provide a series of organizational advocacy pieces such as white papers and position statements. Try to post transcripts of speeches and interviews as well.

Include an events calendar with upcoming activities that reporters and columnists may find newsworthy. Offer feature and interview opportunities for print, broadcast, and online journalists.

Create an "In the News" section that reprints published articles and social media postings about your organization. Make sure you request permission from the author or publisher before posting it.

Photography. A website can feature high-quality color or black-and-white photographs that can be downloaded by the user. The most common format for online photos is JPEG

(Joint Photographic Experts Group). As a second format, you might also have the same photos available as GIF (Graphics Interchange Format) files.

File photos separately, or use a general thumbnail gallery that loads quickly. Try to include photos in two formats. Print publications need photos that are of high quality, at least 300 dpi. Online media need photos with lower resolution, generally 72 dpi. Try to provide both, ideally with an option to download each thumbnail photo in either format.

Some visually focused organizations, such as museums and art galleries, also use their websites so journalists can order higher-resolution photos for professional publishing.

Finally, include a JPEG of the organizational logo.

Audio or Video Material. Radio and television stations can download audio actualities or video clips and B-rolls, recorded digitally by the organization sponsoring the website. Some organizations use their media pages to provide downloadable video clips of commercial or public service advertisements.

Rather than imbedding the download at the organizational site, some online newsrooms post audio and video at public server sites such as YouTube and include a link to such material.

Some organizations create three-dimensional virtual tours and models that can be downloaded to give reporters and other viewers information about the organization and its products or services.

Many organizations videotape their own news conferences, media interviews, and webcasts, archiving them at their online newsrooms after the initial media reports have been published or broadcast. Some organizations use these archives to set the record straight to correct what they perceive as inaccuracies in media reports.

Readership Aids. Tell journalists how to sign up for RSS feeds and opt-in e-mail notices. Invite them to join the organization's Facebook pages, blog site, and Twitter feeds. If possible, imbed a simple "subscribe" button.

Research your users to learn what key words and search terms they most often use. Try to use these early on the pages, where search engines are more likely to find them. But don't overuse key words or search engines may dismiss them as spam.

Make it easy for journalists to contact public relations personnel by phone and e-mail. Provide contact information not only at the home page of the online newsroom but with each separate release contained at the site.

Navigation. Provide many internal links so readers can navigate around the newsroom from wherever they enter. Not all users will come through the "front door" but instead may enter the newsroom from a search engine link to a particular article or photo.

Site Management. Update your online newsroom as appropriate. Try to build into its structure the ability to update the information from off-site, as this may be necessary in a crisis situation.

Try to anticipate traffic into the online newsroom, particularly in times of crisis or high news interest. Make sure that the servers can handle traffic spikes.

Monitor traffic on your online newsroom. Use analytics software to glean data on exactly what readers are looking for, where they come from, how long they stay, and so on. Be prepared to make adjustments that reflect current usage patterns.

Finally, promote the online newsroom not only within the organization but outside. Feature it in promotional and advertising materials. List it on business cards and brochures.

Consider using a digital distribution company or mass e-mail service occasionally to get your newsroom on the radar of journalists savvy about such online news sources.

Media Page Models

Students often find that they can learn by observing and analyzing examples. Here are a few models of effective online media pages.

Educational Institution. The online press kit of the Culinary Institute of America (ciachef.edu/media) features the following elements:

- Several dozen high-resolution downloadable photos
- Four-year archive of news releases
- Online interactive feature for obtaining interviews with specific individuals, including administrators, chefs, and faculty members
- Online feature for film crews to arrange to shoot video in any of the institute's 40 kitchens, with a list of television shows that have taped at CIA facilities
- Dozens of podcasts by CIA faculty, students, alumni, and administrators, with an RSS subscription feed for journalists
- Information links about the main campus at Hyde Park, N.Y., including its history, academic programs, faculty, facilities, alumni, and accreditation details
- Information links about the satellite campuses at St. Helena, Calif., and San Antonio, Texas
- Listing of media relations contacts at the institute's three campuses
- Link to Culinary Institute Facebook pages
- Link to the CIA blog used by students, faculty, and alumni
- Links to the CIA main pages with academic information, an overview on tourism opportunities for "foodies" interested in visiting the campus, recipes, and a virtual tour of the campuses.

Musical Artist. Many fan-oriented websites and associated blogs function like online media kits. Look at jackjohnsonmusic.com and you'll find information about the recording artist's music and professional career. The site's news section features news releases, published interviews and reviews, and current events. The site includes photos, music videos, press videos, trailers, and a "bonus video" section with items such as a Saturday Night Live skit and video outtakes. Additionally, the website also features links to the musician's Facebook, MySpace, Twitter, YouTube, iTunes, and Ping sites.

Sports Team. Most professional sports teams have comprehensive online media sites. For example, the team sites associated with the National Hockey League (mapleleafs.com, sabersnhl.com, panthers.nhl.com, flyersnhl.com, flamesnhl.com, and so on) offer stats, player bios, news, feature stories, photos, audio and video clips, injury reports, player transaction information, media guides, and RSS feeds—all accessible not only to reporters but also to interested fans. The site also features links to each team's pages on Facebook, YouTube, Twitter, LinkedIn, and other multimedia sites.

Politician. Politicians also develop similar online media centers to support their campaigns and their causes. An Internet search for fan clubs or supporters for some of the candidates currently running for office will reveal many sites—for and against the candidates—with a variety of information on issues, records, testimonials, schedules, and related subtopics. The website of the National Democratic Committee includes a news page with news releases, a blog, press updates, and video clips of President Obama's weekly address. During the Obama administration, the Republican counterpart used its website for fundraising but for several years has not included a media page.

Exercise 10.3

Critiquing an Online Newsroom

Identify an online newsroom for one of the following organizations:

- A pharmaceutical company
- A brand of clothing
- A professional sports team
- Your college or university.

Indicate the site URL and the name of the organization sponsoring the online newsroom. Critique this site by writing a paragraph on each of the following elements. Provide examples and specific references to elements at the site. Base your critique on the categories identified in this section of the textbook.

1. Access to the site
2. Content featured at the site
3. Photography and graphic downloads at the site
4. Audio and/or video material at the site
5. Elements that affect readership through the site
6. Navigation issues of the site
7. Finally, your overall evaluation of this online newsroom.

Optimize Online Presence

An important aspect of creating an effective social media release is to attract as many online visitors as possible. Most Internet users rely on **search engines**, which are programs that look through hundreds of thousands of websites, seeking particular words and phrases indicated by a user. For example, a search for "public relations writing" would identify this text as well as thousands of other entries for other textbooks, workshops, courses, jobs, pages at websites, and companies offering the service.

Google is the largest general search engine, but there are many topic-specific search engines, such as Westlaw for legal information, Bing and Nexis for news, Kayak for travel, OneKey for kid-safe searches, and the self-descriptive GolfSearch, FoodWeb, and MathSearch.

Search engine programs generally include a spider that retrieves websites featuring the key word and an indexer that prioritizes the information according to various criteria. **Search engine optimization (SEO)** refers to the process of increasing the number of visitors to a website or Internet page by placing it high on a list of search engine results.

The higher a website places on a list of search results, the greater the likelihood that searchers will visit the site. Most search results give thousands of results, but rarely do searchers visit more than a few of them, usually sites listed on the first screen. That's the obvious benefit to placing high in search results. Let's say you are public relations director for Oakwood University. It would be nice if your institution placed high on a search engine listing every time someone typed "university" into an online search tool.

How does an organization optimize its placement in Internet searches? SEO looks for **meta tags**, words and phrases imbedded in a Web page that help search engines identify websites relevant to a search. Here are some ways to optimize search placement by focusing on key words, pages, content, interactive features, and site management.

Labels and Key Words. Use clear and descriptive labels for websites and associated pages. Include in page labels and titles indicators of the intended public or market segment.

Write content that includes key words and phrases commonly used in search inquiries. Also write each page at the website with a lead in mind. Search engines often focus on the first 200 or so words, so make sure that your key words, main themes, and identification of publics are used early in each page.

Keep page titles simple and descriptive, because search engines pay particular attention to titles. For example, by using the label "News Release" or simply "News," along with a title or headline, search engines can retrieve your release for searching journalists and bloggers as well as interested publics.

Pages. Increase the number of pages associated with your website. This builds in the potential for search engines to find more relevant information at your site.

Make your own pages distinctive from each other. Search engines get bored and stop looking when many pages within a site repeat the same information.

Create separate pages for each product or topic addressed in your website, rather than including all on a single page. This increases the number of different titles and meta tags for your pages, making it more likely that search engines will find your website through one of its associated pages.

Content. Search engines look for authoritative information, so include in your site credentials of information developers.

Feature information unique to your website. Search engines look for distinctive information, so try not to duplicate content from other, similar sites. Sometimes the jargon associated with the sponsoring organization may be appropriate as key words that search engines can easily find. For example, the Australian Football Association of North America at its website (afana.com) features a "Footy Picture Gallery." "Talking Footy" is its category for various forums. "Footy News" is its release archives. Its online newsletter is "Footy News." In case you haven't figured it out yet, "footy" is the colloquial term for Australian Rules Football, and search engines would easily find the site through this key word.

Frequently update the website content to attract search engines to look more often at your site.

Use text rather than images to display names and other information. Search engines generally cannot read text that may be contained within images. Thus if you use a corporate logo, make sure you also include the corporate name in text form.

Interactive Features. Consider adding a blog to your website, which (if managed properly) builds in an automatic frequent updating process.

Try to increase intrasite links that increase traffic back and forth around the website. Look for opportunities to build new links to and from older material.

Invite other websites to link to yours. This not only increases direct traffic from those sites, but it can encourage search engines to list your site higher in the search results.

Add a site map to your website, making it easier for both human users and search engines to find what's within your site.

Site Management. Repair broken links, because such links to pages that no longer exist can slow down search engines looking over your site.

Use analytics software to track how people use your site. Measure how and how often the website is used. Specifically, look at the **hits** (the number of times a file is requested from an Internet site), **unique visitors** (the number of different users who access the site, providing a good measure of audience size), **page views** (the number of times a particular page is accessed, providing a good reflection of what people find interesting about the site), and **unique page views** (the number of unique visitors who access a particular page). Standard Internet metrics also track new and repeat visitors and the length of time they stay at the site and/or at specific pages.

Some software such as Google Analytics and Yahoo Web Analytics is associated with the search engines. Others are third-party software such as Clicktale, OneStat, Web Trends, and CrazyEgg.

Ethical Issues. Suggestions such as those listed above are known as **white hat SEO** (from the stereotype from old cowboy movies that the good guys wear white hats). These are ethical ways to enhance the visibility of your website and thus attract more traffic to it.

Ethical public relations practitioners avoid **black hat SEO**, sometimes called **spamdexing**. This refers to any number of devious methods to rank a website higher in search engines than is justified by the content. Examples of these methods include adding hidden key words, using key words that have nothing to do with the content of the website, or misdirecting intrasite navigation. Major search engines such as Google and Yahoo have penalized websites using black hat methods, occasionally completely excluding offending sites from being identified by searches.

11 Organizational Feature

Features are a type of journalistic writing that emphasize personalities and human-interest angles rather than hard news.

Feature writing is another form of nonfiction writing related to news writing. Related, but not the same. If news involves the hard-edged reports about fires and floods, trials and political scandals, then features are the reports that go behind the news and beyond it. They focus on the history of the building destroyed by fire, the plight of the families displaced by a flood, the heroism of paramedics. Features outline the development of the legal premise on which a trial revolves, and they call attention to the people whose lives are turned inside-out by a political scandal. Hard news is the who, what, when, and where. Features are the how and why.

News reports and feature articles complement each other. They round out the information and provide audiences with a fuller understanding than either writing style alone might do. At the same time, features provide a growing opportunity for public relations writers, because the mainstream news media are using less and less hard news and more feature material.

Public relations writers have found many opportunities to use features on behalf of their organizations and their clients. This chapter will introduce you to some of these opportunities, namely as they relate to features about people, organizations, and issues. Here are your objectives for this chapter:

- To prepare and write features about people (biographical narratives, profiles, and interviews)
- To prepare and write features about organizations (histories, profiles, and backgrounders)
- To prepare and write features about issues (how-to articles, Q&As, case histories, and information digests)
- To adapt feature article to various opportunities in emerging social media.

Features and Public Relations Writing

As with any type of public relations writing, let your planning lead you to a particular format. Start with a planning sheet. Identify your key publics and analyze their wants, interests, and needs. Determine your objectives as they relate to the key publics. Then, if your planning and research lead you to conclude that a feature article would be an appropriate way to reach your objectives, tackle the project.

Each type of feature has particular strengths as well as some limitations. On the minus side, features are time-consuming to write, and they may not be what an editor is seeking. But when they are appropriate, features offer the organization an opportunity to present its message in more depth, with more soul, and often with a greater level of reader interest than a news release or other tool of media relations. Also, feature articles have a role in other areas of public relations, such as with internal magazines, newsletters, and similar publications, and with websites, blogs, social media sites, and other online opportunities.

Certain writing conventions are associated with features. For example, feature writing is not restricted to the inverted pyramid format. Instead, the writer has more flexibility in choosing a style that fits the particular topic. A biography or an organizational history may be chronological, for example, whereas a service article may present a start-to-finish series of action steps. Because effective features are less time bound in their approach, they often are written to be used next week, next month, or the next time there is a news peg to give it relevance.

Perhaps the defining characteristic of feature writing is its use of what writers and editors call **color**. Color is information that makes the story come alive. It is an apt analogy or a particularly well-phrased metaphor, a revealing quote, or an insightful narration. It is the level of description that helps readers "see" the event for themselves without the writer needing to interpret the event for them. Color goes beyond the basic story. Consider the following two passages about a boy and a dog. The first is a straightforward sentence, the kind that might be used in a news release. The second is a much more colorful version, which might be used in a feature story.

Version 1

The boy called his dog, which came running.

Version 2

"Come," said the oldest boy, a trace of apprehension in his voice. The three children waited in suspense. Then the youngest gave a cry of glee as the Dalmatian turned and bounded across the meadow toward them, leaping the few remaining mounds of late winter snow. For all its inexhaustible enthusiasm, the puppy was learning—finally—the training commands that the boys had practiced so faithfully.

All releases that result in published reports offer a follow-up opportunity, but none so much as the published feature article. **Feature reprints** can extend the life of the article and offer many secondary public relations uses over a considerable length of time. After an article has been printed, public relations practitioners may seek permission from the publication to reprint the article. These reprints are then distributed to important publics—especially consumers, producers, and enablers.

Keep the reprints simple: the publication logo, publication date, and the article, perhaps with a contact address, phone number, and Web address for your organization. Don't dilute the value of the third-party endorsement of the article by repackaging it to look like a promotional piece orchestrated by your organization. Get permission from the publisher if you plan to use reprints beyond a small distribution within the organization.

Of course, whether published or not, feature articles have a place at the website, MySpace page, and other Internet locations that the organization uses.

Exercise 11.1

Freewriting about Features

Freewrite for five minutes on the following topic: *What is the role of feature writing in the practice of public relations?* Then discuss it with your classmates.

Feature Writing Style

Good feature writing follows the standard writing conventions and uses the same consistency style as news writing. However, there are a few stylistic differences when you are writing features.

Feature Lead. Whereas news leads generally provide a summary of the key information, leads for features are more flexible. A feature story may begin with a question or perhaps with a quote from a key person in the story. It may pose a paradox for the reader. Often it is a relevant anecdote that exemplifies the theme of the story. Here are some examples of various types of feature leads:

> **Incident**: [Version 2 in the dog story above is an example of this type of lead].
>
> **Question**: Have you ever wondered what it would take to make it to the Olympics? Maria Willoni knows.
>
> **Direct address**: Sometimes you just want a good night's sleep, but your roommate wants to party.
>
> **Allusion**: Romeo had his Juliet. Tristan had his Isolde. Tony has his Millie and it, too, is a story with a touch of tragedy as in all great love stories. Tony is a beagle mourning the passing of his lifelong companion, Millie the terrier.
>
> **Pun**: Politics lived on the far left. How right it is!
>
> **Description**: It's pretty much your typical dog house: open door for ventilation, flat roof for viewing the neighbors, blue siding to match the garage. But it's the stereo system that sets it apart from other canine casas in the neighborhood.
>
> **Staccato**: Lover boy. Mr. Romance. Hunk. Merlina got all that she wanted in a boyfriend . . . and more. Add Loser. Deadbeat. And, oh yeah, Felon.

Nut Graf. Because feature stories often begin with a few paragraphs designed to build reader interest, writers often need to provide a transition out of the lead into the rest of the story. This is called the **nut graf**, short for **nutshell paragraph** (as in, here's the key point of this story in a nutshell). Essentially the nut graf is the news lead that doesn't begin the story but follows the feature lead. In the example below of the personal profile ("Epiphany Taylor: Her Gentle Obsession"), the third paragraph is a nut graf.

Chip Scanlon, who writes a writing-advice column for the Poynter Institute, says that the nut graph has several purposes:

- It justifies the story by telling readers why they should care.
- It provides a transition from the lead and explains the lead and its connection to the rest of the story.
- It often tells readers why the story is timely.
- It often includes supporting material that helps readers see why the story is important.

See Poynter.org (reporting and writing) for more of Scanlon's advice on writing.

Personal Words. Feature writing calls for less objectivity than new writing. It allows the writer to invite the reader into the story with *you* words, sometimes with *us* and *we* (*me* and *I*, not so much). It invites quotes, often using them to set a mood or reveal a personality.

Kicker. Features are different from news stories in that they have an ending. News articles are written in an inverted pyramid fashion to allow them to be shortened at various points before the end. But features generally cannot be short-circuited. They have an ending called a **kicker**, and it serves to wrap up the piece. The kicker is the punch line. It's the take-away. One way the kicker offers a notable ending for a feature story is that it provides a link back to the lead (as in the final paragraph of the personal profile below). A final quote or a closing scene also can serve as kickers for feature stories.

Writing about People

Much of what we write in the feature style will be about people involved with our organizations: managers and other bosses, guests and dignitaries, award winners, newcomers. Three different kinds of writing approaches lend themselves to writing about people. These are biographical narratives, personal profiles, and personal interviews. Let's look at each type.

Biographical Narrative

Public relations writers often prepare information about people important to an organization, cause or event. The most common way of presenting this information is in a **biographical narrative**. This is a straightforward account of a person's work history, accomplishments, education and so on. Biographical narratives serve the same purpose that file obituaries serve with news agencies and media organizations: They provide information that can be useful as supplements to news releases, advance information for speaking engagements, background for awards presentations and event fliers. Much of the factual basis for written biographies can be found in the bio sheets that most public relations offices keep on file.

A biographical narrative can be especially useful in presenting background information about a person involved in a news-related activity, such as news releases about an upcoming speaker, a person promoted within an organization, or someone selected to lead an important activity or receive a noteworthy honor. These narratives are often brief factual accounts. Some narratives are a chronological presentation of the person's accomplishments; others are sectionalized presentations dealing with significant aspects of the person's life, for example, professional accomplishments, educational achievements, and family background.

Below is an example of a narrative biography. Note that it provides essentially the same kind of information as the personal appointment news release outlined in Chapter 8, minus the news announcement. This is a hypothetical biographical narrative that could be used as a sidebar story, or it could become part of a news release about the subject. It might also be used as a blog entry, part of a series of staff biographies at an organizational website, or a hyperlink from a Web article about the organization and its employees.

Epiphany Taylor—Biographical Sketch

Epiphany Taylor is the author of three award-winning books. *Unrelenting Pain* received the 1999 Elizabeth Gumme Award from the Midwestern Coalition on Domestic Violence. *Lay the Blame Softly* was cited by the Library Association of the Southwest as the 2003 Best Read in the self-help category. *The Secret of the Enchanted Tulip* received the 2010 Alyssa Award for Children's Literature. Taylor currently is editing a book of poetry due to be published next January.

Prior to her career as a novelist, Taylor served as public education director for the Southwestern Alliance Against Domestic Violence. Her work received awards from the National Alliance Against Domestic Violence and the Public Relations Association of the Southwest.

She also worked as a reporter with the *Deansville* (Ariz.) *Bugle*. She received the 1993 award for investigative reporting from the Arizona Journalism Association and a citation from the Southwest Civil Rights League.

Taylor is a 1985 graduate of Oakview University, where she received a bachelor of arts degree in communication arts.

Personal Profile

A **personal profile** goes beyond the biographical narrative and provides information about a person, often someone who is an established figure such as a celebrity or an organizational executive. For such people, interest may lie more in the personality than in particular accomplishments. Whereas biographical narratives often are based on information provided by the person you are writing about, profiles are more likely to focus on what other people say about the subject and on what you observe from your own interviews. Half a dozen personal reminiscences might lay the foundation for a profile.

During the research stage of writing, the writer will identify likely information sources and develop probing questions to ask about the person being profiled. For example, suppose you were assigned to develop a personal profile about a professor at your college or university. Let's call him Gregor Aleksandr, a Russian-language professor who is receiving a President's Award for Distinguished Teaching. This could be a preliminary research program for your profile:

- First, you could interview some of his students: What is Dr. Aleksandr like in the classroom? What can you tell me about how he relates to students? How has he helped you? What do you hear other students saying about Dr. Aleksandr?
- Next, you might interview some of the professor's colleagues: What is it like to teach in the same department as Dr. Aleksandr? What do you recall about the first time you met him? In what way is he the model of an effective professor? What do you hear your students say about Dr. Aleksandr?
- Finally, you might try to interview some of Dr. Aleksandr's former students and members of organizations in which he is active, such as the Council for International Visitors and the Association of Slavic Languages.

From all of these sources, you would weave together a profile, generously sprinkled with quotes and anecdotes from people who know him. The profile would reveal various aspects of Dr. Aleksandr that even people who know him in one context may not have seen before.

Here is a hypothetical biographical profile that provides more insight into its subject than the previous narrative. This might be the kind of profile that the subject's college alumni association would prepare and publish on its website and Facebook page and in its quarterly magazine.

Epiphany Taylor: Her Gentle Obsession

Most people are content to pursue one career. Epiphany Taylor has found success in three.

The 1985 graduate of the Oakview University was a soul in search of expression even as a student majoring in communication arts and working on the college newspaper. "The focal decor in my dorm room was this huge poster that said 'Express Yourself,'" recalls Taylor. "That's been a gentle obsession for me."

When Taylor is in a reflective mood, she sees the poster as a metaphor of her life's work, which has taken her through various roles: journalist, activist, lobbyist, social worker, novelist, poet.

Her first job was as a police reporter with the *Deansville* (Ariz.) *Bugle*. Her triumph there came when she was assigned to cover a local bank robbery. Through a combination of investigative skill and what she readily admits is "a generous serving of luck," the Eppie Taylor byline received national attention when she reported that the bank robber was wanted by police in seven states for bombings against civil rights activists.

A former co-worker recalls that Eppie's clandestine interview reporting that the stolen money was intended to finance more bombings earned for Taylor the 1993 award for investigative reporting from the Arizona Journalism Association. It also brought a citation from the Southwest Civil Rights League. The awards were nice, but Taylor wanted to make a difference to people's lives in a way she could see.

"About that time, I reconnected with an old friend who, I learned, had become a victim of abuse. Her boyfriend beat her, and she felt like she had no choice but to put up with it," recalls Taylor. So she began investigating domestic violence. With what she learned, Taylor was able to help her friend end the abusive relationship. The friend, who prefers not to be identified publicly, still credits Taylor with saving her life.

"It felt really good to help my friend get her life back," says Taylor. "I wanted to do it again for others." So she became public education director with the Southwestern Alliance Against Domestic Violence. For the next five years, she directed an ambitious campaign in six states.

She organized some rallies and successfully lobbied for "Millie's Law," a bill that earned bipartisan support to provide legal anonymity for women taking temporary residence in women's shelters, preventing their boyfriends or husbands from tracking them down.

Adrienne Johnson, director of the Alliance, says that Taylor's campaign is the reason that hundreds of women were able to free themselves from abuse. Once again the awards came, this time from the National Alliance Against Domestic Violence and the Public Relations Association of the Southwest. And once again awards only revealed an unfulfilled need.

"My grandmother had left me a country cottage and a small inheritance, so I decided to become what I had always wanted to be—a writer. Not just a journalist, a writer."

That was more than a dozen years ago. Since then, Taylor has written three novels. Two of them deal with domestic violence. *Unrelenting Pain* received the 1999 Elizabeth Gumme Award from the Midwestern Coalition on Domestic Violence. *Lay the Blame Softly* was cited by the Library Association of the Southwest as the 2003 Best Read in the self-help category. The third novel, *The Secret of the Enchanted Tulip*, received the 2010 Alyssa Award for Children's Literature.

Taylor currently is editing *Voices Beyond the Abyss*, a book of poetry written by victims who have reclaimed their lives after abuse.

"I still have that old dorm poster," said Taylor. "The paper is wrinkled, but the message is still fresh. As long as we're alive, we've all got to find ways to express ourselves. That's why I'm still pursuing my gentle obsession."

Exercise 11.2

Writing Biographical Pieces

Select an adult member of your family. Presume that this person has been named to receive the Mayor's Community Service Medal in (or near) the city or town where he or she resides.

Part 1: Write a biographical narrative of this person (approximately 100–150 words) that could be used as a sidebar to a news release sent out by the mayor's office announcing several award recipients.

Part 2: Expanding on the information in Part 1, write a personal interview (400–500 words) that could be posted at the website of the mayor's Community Service Office. Include quotes by the award recipient. Add an element of a profile with at least one quote from a person who knows him or her.

Personal Interview

Although profiles are useful for writing about who people are and what they have accomplished, interviews often are better tools for writing about what people know. Interviews go right to the source. In a **personal interview**, the writer asks a source to comment on what has, is, or will be happening and to explain what the writer already has discovered in background research. Suppose that you are the writer with a public affairs department of a college or university. You are preparing a feature story about an associate professor in the nutrition department. Let's call her Dr. Mary Catherine Spraeger.

Should you do a profile or an interview? That depends on what you want to accomplish. If your goal is to provide information about Dr. Spraeger because she is being honored as "Science Educator of the Year," then a profile probably is the better vehicle. Her students and colleagues can provide much valuable information. On the other hand, if you wish to do a story about the research Dr. Spraeger has done on traditional ethnic recipes and cholesterol-controlling diets, then an interview would be a better approach. You want information mainly from Dr. Spraeger rather than from her colleagues and students.

In preparing for an interview, begin with the planning sheet. Identify the key publics and their wants, interests and needs. Identify your objectives. Most especially, identify relevant questions to ask your interview subject. Follow this with research into the subject of the interview. Read the person's biography. Review any articles or books written by or about this person.

Using quotes is an important aspect of the interview. Public relations writers have a certain degree of freedom to work with quotes. A disordered series of sentence fragments, interspersed with *ums* and *uhs*, several *y'knows*, and a poorly placed *whatchamacallit* or *thingamajig* may accurately re-create the interview, but it doesn't make for good reading.

Tips for Better Writing *Interview Advice*

Sir David Frost is a veteran television interviewer; some say he's the father of TV news interviews. During his long career, he interviewed six British prime ministers, seven U.S. presidents, the Beatles, Prince Charles, and dozens of other celebrities. His interview with President Richard Nixon was taped for 28¾ hours over 12 days and later became the basis for the stage play and subsequent film adaptation *Frost/Nixon*.

He talked with CNN in 2006 about the elements of a good interview. His advice: Prepare for the interview, listen, create a relationship, and help the interviewee relax.

First, said Frost, "do your homework." He and his team had spent a full year preparing for the Nixon interview.

The second thing is to listen, he said. "Well, of course, you listen, because that's the fun of it, hearing what the person is going to say and following up. That's good fun. But in America, at that time, there were lots of talk-show hosts who had a lot of prepared material that they were more concerned to get to than just doing the questioning and so on."

The third point is "just striking up some relationship with the guest, particularly in a longer interview and so on." Frost said the relationship may not be one of mutual respect; it might be more like mutual awareness. Frost suggested that eye contact with the person you're talking to is the best way to create the relationship.

"And if you relax the person, I mean, that's the other thing," Frost concluded. "Perhaps that's point number four. But if you relax the person, then you get the individual."

Rather than presenting an unedited transcript, an effective writer works with the raw quotes to present the interviewee's ideas in a reasonably faithful-though-edited version. It's sort of like being a speechwriter. Usually, the writer will let the interviewee see the final piece with the revised quotes to make sure the meaning remains intact. Accuracy, honesty, fairness, and other ethical considerations are crucial in this editing/rewriting process.

Interviews can also provide public relations writers with the opportunity to share information and insights of one person with a host of readers. This information can be presented in two ways: as a narrative feature article or as interview notes.

Narrative Feature. A **narrative feature** is a story based on interviews, drawing on the feature-writing skills of the public relations practitioner. Feature writing is an art unto itself. Students interested in developing this art would be well served to take a course or study a good book focused specifically on writing features or magazine articles.

Interview Notes. **Interview notes** are near-verbatim transcripts in a question-and-answer format ("near" in the sense that the transcript should be edited for grammar and for easy flow of language). This style usually begins with either a brief narrative paragraph to set the stage or a biographical sketch of the person being interviewed. These transcripts of in-depth interviews allow reporters to build their stories as they see fit. Sometimes, the interviews are conducted by public relations writers; other times, they are conducted by reporters themselves.

Take a look at the online information resource of the Department of Defense (www.defense.gov/news). CyberJournalist.net called the website "a journalist's gold mine" because the Pentagon archives news releases, briefings, speeches, and interview transcripts, as part of the public record that can be used by other journalists as well as by all interested readers. The site also features audio, video, and photo resources.

Increasingly, magazines, and newspapers also are publishing transcripts of interviews by their own reporters, either in print version or at their websites. Likewise, radio and television news organizations are placing audio and/or video files of full interviews on their websites. These techniques are seen as a way for the news organizations to better serve their audiences.

Sometimes, public relations practitioners tape journalistic interviews and provide online transcripts of them. This can provide interested readers with the whole story, or its purpose may be to set the record straight after a published or aired report that the organization feels may have left an incomplete or misunderstanding of the interview. For example, Denver Archbishop Charles Chaput felt that a *New York Times* reporter had missed some nuanced key points in a published report following an interview with the church leader about the intersection of politics and religious practice. The archdiocese, which had taped the interview, presented online the full transcript of the discussion between the archbishop and the reporter.

Writing about Organizations

Histories, profiles, and backgrounders do for businesses and nonprofit groups what biographies, personal profiles, and interviews do for people. These are the vehicles for writing about organizations. Public relations writers often find it useful to prepare articles that will help the news media understand their organizations and report accurately on their concerns and missions. These organizational stories often are prepared as feature releases. They also may be used for websites and Facebook pages and may be useful for brochures and direct-mail pieces. Let's take a look at each type of organizational feature: history, profile, and backgrounder.

Organizational History

Public relations writers sometimes want to provide information about organizations. A common way to do this is with an **organizational history**, which presents a narrative on the beginnings and development of the organization that is important in explaining what the organization does or stands for. Often, an organization will team a history with a mission statement or vision statement. A **mission statement** indicates the purpose that the organization perceives for itself, while a **vision statement** deals with what the organization hopes to achieve.

Businesses, agencies, schools, associations, and other organizations each have their own unique past and special purpose. There's a story behind the city's first hospital, founded by five nuns as a three-room clinic above a saloon and dance hall (that would be St. Joseph Hospital Health Center in Syracuse, N.Y.). There's also a story flowing from the history of the National Foundation for Infantile Paralysis, founded by President Franklin Roosevelt in 1938 to combat polio. It so successfully supported medical researchers such as Jonas Salk and Albert Sabin, whose vaccines effectively brought polio under control, that the organization effectively achieved its mission. Rather than disband, it renamed itself the March of Dimes and focused on a new mission consistent with its original purposes preventing birth defects and increasing infant mortality.

As a public relations writer, you may want to research your organization's past and put it in a form that is interesting and useful to anyone trying to understand your organization. Such background information can be very helpful in increasing support for the organization today.

Historical articles should have a factual basis that offers names, dates, and other specific pieces of the past. They also should put this into a framework that helps explain the organization's current mission, the contributions and achievements it has made, the problems and opportunities it faces, and perhaps the vision it holds of the future. Like personal biographies, organizational histories may be either chronological narratives or more colorful feature articles.

Remember that brevity is important for organizational histories. Bulleting key points such as milestones and achievements is a useful technique. "What Would You Do? Writing an Organizational History" asks you to consider some ethical issues that might arise in the writing of an organization's history.

What Would You Do? *Writing an Organizational History*

Organizations often have something in their past that they are embarrassed about, or at least that they are reluctant to say much about. Suppose you are public relations director for one such organization, a chapter of the YMCA that was founded during the days of racial segregation. As a consequence, your organization was known for many years as the Black Y.

You know that this was not uncommon years ago. Many communities have a variety of such organizations: a Jewish country club in town founded years ago when Jews weren't admitted to the other country club, a Catholic fraternity at a local university because once no other fraternity would accept Catholic students, a downtown Hispanic religious congregation because Spanish-speaking worshippers didn't feel welcome in another parish, and so on.

What ethical considerations would factor into your decision on how to handle such historical information about your organization, the YMCA?

How would you determine if the issue is relevant today? How would you decide if it would be considered hurtful or divisive today (and whether this would matter in your decision about using such information)?

How would you balance your commitment to your client or boss with your commitment to the truth? And is historical information subject to the same level of commitment to truth as current information?

Organizational Profile

Sometimes, the history is expanded into an organizational profile. In addition to a look back at the organization, these profiles also provide an overview of the organization's mission or purpose, its operating practices and philosophy, and its achievements. **Organizational profiles**, also called **corporate backgrounders**, sometimes are written for readers with technical experience in the field. Others, meant for readers unfamiliar with the field, are written to untangle some of the technical terms and information.

Like other feature formats, profiles allow for flexible writing styles. To find a useful format for your writing, outline the topic. For example, a profile explaining the various departments and organizational components of a large corporation might begin with a section about the executive team, followed by paragraphs on each of the departments. A profile providing information summarizing a human service agency's annual report might begin with a mission statement, operating philosophy, or credo, along with a description of each of the agency's programs, including statistics on costs, and services provided. Below is an organizational history posted at the website of the Public Relations Society of America (prsa.org). It teams with an organizational profile to provide a more complete overview of the professional organization.

> Chartered in 1947, the Public Relations Society of America (PRSA) is the world's largest and foremost organization of public relations professionals. PRSA provides professional development, sets standards of excellence and upholds principles of ethics for its members and, more broadly, the multi-billion-dollar global public relations profession. We also advocate for greater understanding and adoption of public relations services, and act as one of the industry's leading voices on the important business and professional issues of our time.
>
> PRSA is a community of more than 21,000 public relations and communications professionals across the United States, from recent college graduates to the leaders of the world's largest multinational firms. Our members represent nearly every practice area and professional and academic setting within the public relations field. In addition, there are more than 10,000 students who are members of the Public Relations Student Society of America (PRSSA) at colleges and universities here and abroad.

Exercise 11.3

Writing Organizational Profiles

You are public relations writer for the academic department at your college or university that includes the public relations program. You are asked to prepare a backgrounder about the program that can be used for several purposes: to recruit prospective students, to recruit faculty, to raise money from alumni, and to build stronger relationships with public relations professionals around the state. List the section headings for the backgrounder and provide a brief explanation of the content of each section.

Backgrounder

A **backgrounder** is a factual piece that provides a backdrop to a product or service associated with an organization or explains the context of a situation affecting the organization. It also may deal with technical information. In this way, a backgrounder is similar to the background fact sheet introduced in Chapter 6, though generally a backgrounder is more extensive.

As a writer of backgrounders, you will need to research particularly well so you can clearly understand the topic and its significance. You also will need to plan well, having a clear understanding of your key publics and the message to be conveyed to them. Because a backgrounder provides a written source for clear and objective information, it can be used by various people in several different ways:

- By reporters seeking information to help them prepare stories and reports
- By organizational spokespersons preparing to discuss issues with clients, reporters, colleagues, and others
- By public relations writers preparing brochures, news releases, speeches, newsletter articles, Web pages, and other written materials
- By organizational representatives needing to respond to inquiries by colleagues, constituents, reporters, regulators, and consumers
- By writers preparing grant applications and other funding requests.

Writers have much flexibility in choosing a format for backgrounders, as long as it effectively presents the factual information. Some appear as narratives with section subheads, others as chronologies. A graphic organizer can sometimes help make sense of the many different kinds of information that might go into a backgrounder. Many backgrounders are posted on organizational websites. Check out some of the following for examples of backgrounders, fact sheets, policy statements, and related information.

- United Nations: un.org/news/facts
- Democratic National Committee: democrats.org/press.php > "What We Stand for"
- The White House: whitehouse.gov > "Issues"
- U.S. Department of Defense: defense.gov > search "Backgrounder"
- National Council of Churches: ncccusa.org > "NCC Policies"
- U.S. Conference of Catholic Bishops: nccbuscc.org/sdwp > search "Backgrounder"
- American Civil Liberties Union: aclu.org/news > search "Backgrounder."

Exercise 11.4

Writing Backgrounders

You are asked by your college or university to explain the relationship among public relations, advertising, and marketing communication as part of its Web articles about your department. Prepare a backgrounder to be used with potential students and their parents. Include several section headings.

Writing about Issues

Some studies on the use of media releases suggest that articles with a strong consumer approach have the greatest chance of being used by the media. They are full of the key ingredients of SiLoBaTi—information that is significant, local, balanced, and timely. Consumer-interest releases are particularly significant to readers because they examine meaningful problems and suggest practical solutions. Gatekeepers pay attention when we help the media do that for their audiences.

Editors selecting releases for publication are attracted to various kinds of consumer-interest articles in which writers attribute information to their organizations matter-of-factly, without excessive or self-serving promotionalism. This imparts useful information and advice without overt commercialism. Writers achieve the desired tone by focusing on user benefits rather than on the organization providing the goods and services. The following approaches are useful in writing consumer-interest articles:

- Write informally and personally to the reader. Use "you" words freely.
- Be a bit less free with "we" words to avoid sounding preachy or promotional.
- Emphasize what can be accomplished rather than what cannot.
- Consider source credibility. The most persuasive source is a person or organization similar to your key public that has successfully resolved this problem.
- Remember that you are writing for a reader who, though interested, may not have much background in dealing with this problem. Don't overestimate the reader's knowledge about the topic.

Four common approaches to consumer-interest releases are how-to articles, question-and-answer pieces, case studies, and information digests. These can be used as feature releases, or they may be placed on organizational websites or social media. Additionally, they can be printed as brochures or as handouts and direct-mail pieces.

How-To Article

All public relations releases should address the wants, interests, and needs of media audiences. But a **how-to article** (also called a **service article**) is more obvious than other writing formats in addressing such reader interest. It is a consumer-interest release that provides step-by-step instructions in addressing a problem or issue. A how-to article should be timely and significant to local readers. It should also be balanced, objective, and not obviously self-serving to the organization preparing the release.

The how-to article often is overlooked by public relations writers, especially by those involved with corporate organizations. Nonprofit groups, on the other hand, have learned the value of such releases, perhaps because such organizations are program oriented and because their mission is to present information or advocate for a cause. Often, the shoestring budgets of nonprofit organizations have given their public relations writers experience in finding interesting angles that lead to publicity for their organizations. It would be a rare organization—corporate or nonprofit—that does not have some bit of advice to share with members of its publics. Consider the following examples:

- Psychiatric counseling center: Ways to reduce emotional stress during the holiday season
- Waste management firm: How homeowners can dispose of hazardous household garbage
- Private school: How parents can help their children prepare for college entrance exams
- Bank: Ways to encourage financial responsibility among young teens
- Law firm: How to save money when preparing wills
- Mosque, synagogue, or church: How to select appropriate religious gifts for children
- AIDS treatment center: How to show compassion and support for families with a member who has HIV or AIDS
- Fitness center: Ways to exercise at home.

Following are several steps toward developing an effective how-to article, both for use as a feature for newspapers or magazines or for an internal publication or website. The ingredients are the same for both internal and external audiences:

Step 1: Problem. Address a problem of interest to your public. How-to articles grow out of the planning sheet. They are designed to help the reader solve a problem or achieve a desired result, in the process helping the organization achieve its objectives. As such, they begin with a clear statement of the problem. If you have carefully selected your topic, you should be able to identify a problem common to many members of your key public, and readers will easily see their own wants, interests, and needs reflected in the article. This step in writing a service article also introduces the organization that serves as a model for how to address the problem.

Step 2: Cause. Note the cause and background of the problem. Having identified the problem, the writer goes on to explain how it has developed, both in general and with the model organization in particular. What caused it? How has it progressed to date?

Step 3: Significance. Now deal with where the problem is heading and with its significance. How will this affect the model organization or other organizations facing a similar problem? Try to set up a familiar situation with which the audience can identify.

Step 4: Solution. Explain the solution. The heart of the how-to article is a detailed explanation of how to fix the problem. What is the remedy? How did the model organization move toward a solution? How can the reader create that remedy? This part of the service article may unfold step by step as the writer outlines, often with great detail, how to achieve the desired solution. Or the article may list various possible solutions. Either way, try to help readers gain a sufficient understanding so they can re-create the solution for themselves.

Step 5: Conclusion. Wrap up the article for the reader. As a feature story, the how-to article usually has an obvious ending. Often this is a final motivational message or a well-chosen quote summing up the benefit to the model organization and potential imitators among the readers.

The following service article by the Better Business Bureau was posted at its website in 2009. Note how it identifies the problem (increasing unemployment rates), identifies the cause of this issue (increasing numbers of job fairs), notes the significance (fierce competition), and then focuses on various solutions before giving a simple conclusion (obtaining additional information).

How to Stand Out From the Crowd at a Job Fair

With unemployment rates climbing to double digits in some states, job hunters are turning out in record numbers at job fairs hoping to make a good impression and get back into the workforce. Competition for landing a job can be fierce and Better Business Bureau is offering advice on how job hunters can make a strong impression and position themselves as the candidate of choice with potential employers.

In early March, the Georgia Department of Labor organized the largest job fair in the state's history; more than 19,000 attended in order to meet with 100 employers. In California, more than 10,000 people flocked to Dodger Stadium for a job fair. And in Cleveland 7,000 showed up for a job fair vying for 1,000 jobs, causing more than 2,000 job seekers to be turned away by overwhelmed fire marshals.

"Job fairs can be a great way to meet with many potential employers, however, in today's flooded job market, standing out from the crowd and positioning yourself as the best candidate is a tough battle," said Steve Cox, BBB spokesperson. "With a good game plan and some focused preparation, though, job hunters can tip the scales in their favor and greatly increase the probability of making a good impression and securing a new position."

The BBB offers the following advice for job hunters on how to prepare and present themselves at a job fair:

Research companies first. In some cases, only one employer is holding a job fair, which makes research much easier. For larger job fairs bringing in many employers, job hunters should be able to find a list of attending companies at the host's website and begin researching the companies they want to target beforehand. Not only will this help job hunters focus on specific opportunities, but it will also help them develop intelligent, tailored pitches for the employers they want to engage.

Take plenty of résumés. Before walking into a job fair, job hunters should know which businesses are attending, and what positions they are recruiting for. Job hunters should have customized résumés prepared for their target businesses, and should bring plenty of copies of their standard résumé to pass along to other employers. Also, job hunters should take a briefcase or portfolio to organize and hold business cards and other materials.

Perfect an elevator pitch. An elevator pitch is your description of who you are, what your skill set is, and how you can benefit the business. The pitch should be brief, conversational and natural, but should be well-rehearsed. The elevator pitch simply must be memorable and sincere since job hunters may only have a few minutes at the most to make an impression on the potential employer.

Dress and act the part. Putting your best foot forward at a job fair means "looking the part" by wearing professional clothes, such as a suit and removing any unusual piercings and covering tattoos. A job hunter also needs to act like a professional, including not swearing or making inappropriate jokes, or speaking ill of a former employer.

Be confident. While a day at a job fair can be exhausting, it's important to always act confident and enthusiastic. Job hunters should work hard to stay positive and take breaks to get organized and recharge their batteries. In fact, BBB recommends taking a few minutes to review your elevator pitch and materials before approaching each of your target businesses.

Don't become a victim. While instances of scammers setting up shop at a job fair are rare, job hunters should never pay an upfront fee to any potential employer at a job fair, nor should they give any personal information such as bank account or Social Security numbers until they have researched the company fully outside of the fair.

For more advice on finding a job, as well as guidance from BBB on avoiding fraud while on the hunt, go to www.bbb.org.

Exercise 11.5

Writing a How-To Article

In preparation for writing a service article, write a brief step-by-step explanation of how to accomplish one of the following tasks:

1. How to make a favorable and lasting impression on your professor in a class within your major (for an article directed to entering freshmen and transfer students).
2. How to apply for internships in your major (for an article on the department website directed to new majors).
3. How to gain practical work experience in the field of public relations (for an article directed toward first-year students at your college or university).

Question-and-Answer Feature

An often-used writing format among public relations practitioners is the **question-and-answer piece**, informally called a **Q&A**. Writers associated with websites are likely to call this format **frequently asked questions** or **FAQs**. Whatever its name, this format consists of a series of carefully selected questions that address relevant aspects of an issue, followed by short paragraphs responding to the questions.

The key to writing a good Q&A is to understand both the topic and the key public well enough to anticipate all of the important questions. Q&As may be used with internal or external audiences. They may be distributed as information sheets or news releases, or they can be used as the basis for brochures and newsletter articles as well as for Web pages. The process for preparing effective Q&As proceeds logically.

Step 1: Topic. Select a topic of interest. Every organization deals with information that interests someone. The writer for a Q&A should begin with a planning sheet that generates a clearly identified topic interesting members of one of the organization's publics. To qualify for a Q&A, the topic should be sufficiently new or complex to provide readers with useful information.

Step 2: Reader Interest. Every public relations writing activity begins with a planning sheet, and the Q&A is no exception. Focus here on the wants, interests, and needs of the key public. Time spent at this research stage will make the writer more effective in the subsequent steps.

Step 3: Questions. The effectiveness of the finished Q&A rests on the appropriateness of the questions. These should be relevant to the topic and interesting to the key public. They should be presented in a logical order, with each question flowing gently and logically into the next. They also should include the full range of questions that will set the stage for presenting information that meets both the organization's objectives and the reader's interests. Content of the questions should lead both to basic facts as well as to the deeper significance underlying the facts. Readers are most likely to remain interested when the questions are phrased in personal terms: *What can I do? How will I know? What does this mean to me?* An effective way to test your presumptions is to ask a small group of members of your key public if this is the information they want to know.

Step 4: Responses. Having identified the appropriate questions, the writer provides a response to each of them. These answers should be brief. A lengthy answer often indicates that the question is overly complex and perhaps should be divided into several question-and-answer segments. The response is written in a style to complement the question. For example, a series of questions stated in *me* and *I* terms may be answered with a *you* tone. Such a style presents the organization as an expert adviser on the subject.

Step 5: Write. Having done the planning and preparation in the first four steps, write the Q&A feature article. The general format is to begin with an introductory section of a couple of paragraphs in which you state the topic, indicate the significance and benefits, and note the source of the information. It is a good idea to include a quote as part of this introduction. Then provide a series of short questions and concise responses. Q&A pieces often wrap up with a paragraph or two of general information about the organization or the issue.

The main thing to remember when writing a question-and-answer piece for media release is to keep it focused on the audience. A newspaper or magazine is unlikely to use a Q&A that is obviously promoting your organization. Rather, editors are more likely to select a piece that has a strong news peg and that highlights tips and advice for the audience. The same advice holds true for Q&As prepared for brochures or websites. Readers are unlikely to stick with a piece that is highly promotional rather than one that addresses their interests and obviously serves their needs.

Some print and online publications use a variation on the traditional question-answer format: the **short-form Q&A**. This is an article using the traditional question-answer model while tightening up on each. *Newsweek* magazine has a regular feature using this approach. Following is an example of a short-form interview.

Q&A: Alanis Morissette

The raven-haired Canuck is taking a break from music to join the cast of TV's Weeds. *She spoke with Joshua Alston.*

You signed up for seven episodes of *Weeds*, which is a lot.

I'm a huge fan. I used to watch it in the back of my tour bus. We'd come offstage and people would start fading and drifting off to sleep, and I would ensconce myself in the back room and watch six episodes at a time.

What attracts you to acting?

I get to express sides of myself that I would never default to on my own. I'll read a line and think, God, I'd never say that.

How's that different from songwriting?

The acting thing uses a whole different muscle. I consider the songwriting process very feminine, and I think acting requires my masculine self, because it's very applied, willful, and left-brained.

Are you writing music now?

Yes, always. And I'm working on a book.

Is it a novel?

It's kind of nonlinear. It's got some insight and some humor, anecdotes, Q&A, photos, storytelling, dialogues, essays. You could read it from cover to cover, or you could pick it up anywhere.

I know that Fergie sent you a butt-shaped cake after you did a cover of "My Humps." Did you eat it?

I had every intention of eating it, but then I had this party at my house and all my friends were putting their fingers between the cheeks, taking pictures with it. So after everyone had touched it, the butt wasn't very sanitary.

Exercise 11.6

Writing Q&A Features

Your class has been asked by the local Association for Cancer Education and Prevention to prepare a question-and-answer piece about cancer. Some students have been asked to write about breast cancer, others on testicular cancer. The key public for both pieces is students entering area colleges and universities.

Part 1: Prepare a planning sheet to develop an approach for this writing assignment.

Part 2: Write a feature release in question-and-answer style. Include at least eight questions. Quote your instructor as Director of Public Education for the ACEP. For accurate and up-to-date information, check the online resources noted in Exercise 2.6 "Working with Technical Language," or use a search engine to find current and authoritative information about either breast cancer or testicular cancer as these relate to persons of college age.

Case Study

The **case study** (sometimes called a **case history**) is often associated with product publicity, in which the writer provides a narrative of how the product has been used by a representative consumer. But this style of reporting also can be useful for service-oriented businesses and nonprofit organizations. In both instances, the writer profiles actual users of the service. This is source credibility at its best.

This type of consumer-interest feature tells the story of how a program, product, or service has been used by an organization. It shows the program in action. A particular value of the case study is the heightened credibility of third-party endorsements. Instead of the company itself telling about the benefits of its product, the case study allows a real-life customer to explain the benefits to would-be consumers with similar problems.

Writers of case studies should get permission from the organization before they present the story, and they may need to get the customer's approval for the finished article as well. It is not too surprising that some organizations are reluctant to be identified through a case study. They may be embarrassed by having the problem in the first place, or they may not want to share their successful resolution of the problem with competitors. Despite these concerns, however, public relations opportunities abound. Many organizations readily agree to be the focus of a case study, and trade magazines and other specialized publications generally welcome well-written case studies because they serve the interests of their readers.

Planning sheets are especially helpful to a writer preparing a case study. The focus for this type of writing must be clearly on the key public—the reader of the publication that will be asked to publish the case study. With careful writing, this reader will be able to identify with the organization in the case study that serves as an example and a model that has successfully used the product. Case studies generally have four major elements:

Step 1: Problem. Begin by identifying the problem. Based on the planning sheet, the writer begins by clearly indicating the problem being addressed in the study. Focus the article on a particular organization, but make sure the problem is one shared by many organizations.

Step 2: Solution. Explain how the organization solved the problem. Note the decisions and actions that led to a favorable resolution.

Step 3: Benefits. Clearly show the benefits of the solution. The case study article ends with a clear indication of the value of the solution approach to any organization facing a similar problem. Restraint is important. Don't let this conclusion become too commercialized. Hold down the fluff and excessive mention of the product or service.

Step 4: Illustration. If possible, include charts, tables, and photographs to provide visual appeal for the case study. Use illustrations to help the reader identify with the problem and to better understand the proposed solution.

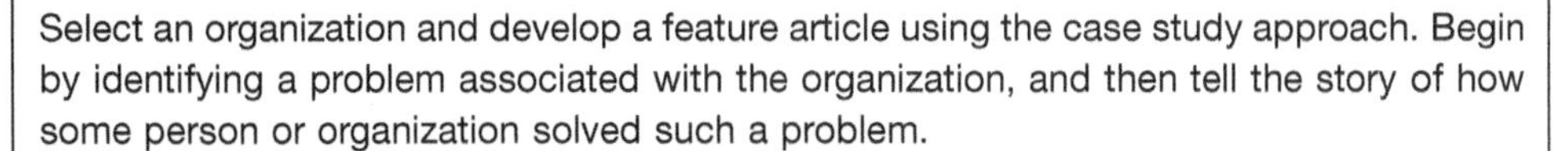

Exercise 11.7

Writing Case Studies

Select an organization and develop a feature article using the case study approach. Begin by identifying a problem associated with the organization, and then tell the story of how some person or organization solved such a problem.

Information Digest

Another vehicle for feature writing is the **information digest**, which takes heavy-duty material such as from research reports or technical accounts and "translates" it into accessible language for the average consumer. This type of writing is a kind of paraphrased reprint of the original material.

Writers need two special abilities to write information digests. First, they must be able to understand complex or technical information. Second, they must then be able to interpret this information for readers who, though interested in the topic, lack the experience, training, or background to grasp the meaning of the original.

At the Great Lakes Environmental Research Laboratory publications website (www.glerl.noaa.gov/pubs) look at some of the information sheets listed as "Non-Scientific Publications." You will find many weighty topics explained in relatively simple, easy-to-understand language.

12 Advocacy and Opinion

Previous chapters have presented writing formats in which blatant advocacy is inappropriate and opinion is suspect. When news rules, writers cannot openly advocate for an organizational point of view. Under the norm of objectivity, writers can present opinion only indirectly and subtly.

But advocacy and opinion are not inappropriate for public relations writers. Sometimes they are just what the writer needs, especially when it is important to clearly state the organization's point of view and attempt to win support for that position. Just as objectivity is important in some writing formats, advocacy calls for transparency. Promotion that is both open and evident is the pillar of several forms of public relations writing.

There are several ways in which a writer can present openly persuasive forms of written communication. The focus of this chapter is how an organization can present opinion to its key publics. Here are your objectives for this chapter:

- To apply concepts of issues management in various writing activities
- To prepare and write advocacy pieces such as position statements, letters to the editor, op-ed commentaries and guest editorials, issue advisories, proclamations, and petitions.

Issues Management

Part of the public relations research process is the monitoring of the environment in which the organization operates. This continual attention to how the organization is affected by social, legal, professional, and economic trends—and the public opinion surrounding them—is known as **issues management**. The public relations practitioner will identify issues that may affect the organization, suggesting ways in which the organization might address these issues. Sometimes these issues emerge slowly; other times they burst on the scene. Foresight can pay off, giving the organization time to prepare a considered response instead of being put on the spot for an unexpected comment.

Identifying Issues

Managing issues important to an organization is an ongoing process of research, analysis, and communication. Writing skills come into play at each step. The public relations writer who is aware of the strategic importance of issues management is a valuable asset to any organization.

Exercise 12.1

Freewriting on Issues Management

Freewrite for five minutes on the following topic: *In what ways do you think a public relations practitioner can help an organization identify and deal with issues affecting its success?* Then discuss this with your classmates.

The public relations practitioner plays two roles in the early stages of managing an issue: (1) identifying pending issues that potentially could affect the organization, and (2) anticipating the likely and eventual emergence of issues. Both identification and prediction are based on the ongoing research conducted by the organization. This systematic analysis of an organization, its communication practices, and its relationship with its publics is called a **public relations audit**.

A public relations audit may include several methods of gathering information, including environmental audits, performance/perception audits, literature reviews, interviews, focus groups, surveys, and content analysis. Following is a look at each of these approaches to conducting a public relations audit.

- **Environmental audits** provide an early-warning system for issues that might affect the organization. Recall that publics can be identified according to their linkages to organizations—consumers, producers, enablers, and limiters. By conducting an environmental audit on a regular basis (at least once a year), you are likely to detect any emerging issues in time to deal with these publics.
- **Performance/perception audits** focus on the organization itself—the quality of its performance in providing products or services, its visibility among key publics, and especially its reputation. Perception is reality. What people think about an organization is just as important as how well it performs. One of your main concerns is to learn if your publics think about you in the same way you think about yourself. You learn that by conducting surveys or interviews, tracking published reports in established media, or monitoring blogs and social media content.
- **Literature reviews** cite references to an issue from newspapers and magazines, academic journals, government documents, authoritative websites, and other information sources, providing a look that can identify trends and emerging issues. Each discipline or industry generates articles, reports, and other literature that offer an excellent insight into current issues within that discipline.
- **Interviews** can be conducted with key people such as top management, managers, community leaders, media leaders, governmental officials, and significant consumers. You also might interview antagonists, outside experts, and others willing to offer constructive criticism and suggestions about your organization.
- **Focus groups** gather a small number of people representing your publics. During a structured group interview, these people can provide informal, anecdotal information about your organization and issues important to it.
- **Surveys** are a more formal research technique that can gather information from larger numbers of respondents. Surveys may focus on internal groups such as employees,

volunteers, and shareholders, or they can deal with external groups such as consumers and community or industry leaders.

- **Content analysis** is research procedure that can identify changing trends in the levels of visibility, criticism, and support. This research measures patterns in attitude and opinion found in texts such as letters to the editor, news reports, blogs and websites, professional publications, and incoming letters.

Analyzing Issues

After you have identified issues and trends that affect your organization, the next step is to assess these issues. This can involve further research to investigate the particular issue. It also involves the continued monitoring of the issue to keep your response current and on track. In the analysis stage, you will look at the issue from two points of view:

- From the organization's perspective, ask these questions: What are the causes of the issue? What is the likely impact, especially the potential for harm? What are the options for dealing with the issue?
- From the public's perspective, ask questions such as these: Is this an issue of interest to people outside the organization? What is its likely impact on them? How does the organization seem to be involved with this issue?

During this stage you will begin writing about the issue. Present the background. Identify the pros and cons. Articulate the impact on both the organization and the various publics that are relevant to this issue. The formal position should grow out of such considerations.

Some public relations writers will find themselves in the interim step of preparing an issues analysis report for the organization's manager. Typically, such an analysis would involve two parts.

The first part is an issue background that outlines the issue, its significance, and its history, current status and projection. The second part presents an overview of the various positions open to the organization, perhaps with a pro-and-con treatment of each possible position. The organization's decision makers would consider these alternatives as they select their official position.

Communicating the Position

Public relations practitioners will define various levels of publics as they plan a communication program for issues management. Certainly, some publics should be notified before others. For example, you might inform stockholders by e-mail of a corporation's formal position at the same time that the financial media are notified, thus communicating directly with stockholders rather than having them read the news in the financial media.

Organizations generally try to present a new position to employees before it is communicated to consumers, especially if the position requires the cooperation of employees to implement. Such formal positions can be communicated through various media, including e-mail, news releases, position statements, letters and other direct-mail pieces, lobbying materials, speeches, and organizational advertising. Most organizations find that a combination of e-mail and Internet-based media provides the best opportunities to communicate with specialized internal audiences quickly and efficiently.

All of this requires a carefully planned timetable to ensure the proper orchestration of the message. Many organizations communicate with internal publics either simultaneous to or just ahead of the release of the information to news media and other public audiences.

Once they are announced, position statements should be posted prominently at the organization's website, corporate blog, and social media sites for public consumption. See how some organizations present their position statements online: American Dietetic Association (eatright.org > "Health Professionals"), International Confederation of Principals (icponline.org > "About ICP"), American Nuclear Society (ans.org > "Public Information"), and Mothers Against Drunk Driving (madd.org > "About Us"). Look back at some of the online sources for backgrounders indicated in the previous chapter. Note the similarity between some backgrounders and position papers.

Position Statement

When organizations want to give their opinion on matters of public or organizational interest, they often issue a **position statement**. This is a presentation of the considered and official position of the organization. Position statements are among the ways that public relations contributes to a democratic society. When written with skill and integrity, they contribute to the unobstructed flow of ideas that is vital in a free society.

A position statement differs from a backgrounder because it includes more. A backgrounder presents facts and explains an issue. A position statement does this, but it also reaches a conclusion of what could and should be done to address the issue. In short, a position statement adds an opinion to the backgrounder and thus becomes a vehicle for advocacy.

Position statements may be given directly to members of external key publics such as legislators, donors, investors, colleagues, community leaders, and so on. They may be distributed to reporters and other media representatives. Additionally, position statements may be distributed to internal publics such as employees, volunteers, and board members to help them understand the actions and policies of the organization.

Position statements sometimes are called **white papers** in contrast to backgrounders that, with less frequency, are called **green papers**. The terms are rooted in 19th-century government practice of a color-coded system for covers of official reports. Agencies of the British Commonwealth issued green papers with background information but no proposals to serve as consultation documents or discussion starters. White papers, on the other hand, were more authoritative and included recommended paths toward addressing the situation. There also were **blue papers**, generally lengthy and tedious reports that sometimes were accompanied by a white paper that served as a kind of executive summary. Now you know.

Position statements vary in depth, intensity, and length.

- A **position paper** may be a lengthy and detailed presentation expressing the opinion of the organization's executives on a major issue of long-term significance. It usually includes a shorter executive summary.
- At the other end of the continuum, a **position paragraph** is a brief statement addressing a transitory or less complex issue.

Content analysis on effective opinion pieces shows that they generally position the issue within a wider context of interest to publics and readers. They summarize the issue and the opinion quickly, with details and follow-up arguments. They use effective analogies and metaphors, as well as literary techniques such as repetition and rhetorical questions.

Flawed opinion pieces share some common weaknesses to be avoided: They pose questions rather than present answers. They oversimplify complex issues or fail to get beyond burdensome details. They present opinions weakly and present facts without drawing logical conclusions. They attack opponents unfairly.

Regardless of their depth, position statements generally follow a similar pattern: background on the issue, justification for the position, and conclusions. Let's look at each part of a position statement.

Part 1: Issue Background

Begin the position statement with a thorough background on the issue. Such a background includes several elements: a clear identification of the issue, an explanation of its significance to the key publics, relevant history, an indication of the current situation, and a projection of likely developments.

Issue Topic. The opening section of every position statement should clearly identify the issue being addressed. Don't side-step controversy or embarrassment, but rather identify and deal with the issue head-on. Failure to address the significant issue can render the statement useless. Worse, it could hurt if it allows for an interpretation that the organization is unclear about the issues or unwilling to deal with them.

Position statements usually deal with matters of public interest that are open to persuasion when persuasion, not force or enforcement, is called for. For example, a school district establishing a new zero-tolerance policy on drug use by athletes probably doesn't need a position paper, because the policy is a matter of regulation. But if the policy needed to be ratified by a vote of parents, then a position statement might be useful for the district to explain reasons for its position and to encourage a supportive vote.

The topic of a position statement generally has more than one side, thus giving it the potential to be controversial. A school district isn't likely to issue a position statement in favor of public education because that issue probably isn't opposed. But consideration of minimum homework or single-sex classes might be multi-sided issues appropriate for a position statement.

Significance. Explain the importance of the issue, carefully indicating how it affects both your organization and its publics. Be clear about the impact on readers. What are the consequences? How will it affect them? Why should they care about the issue?

History. Present background information on the issue being addressed. This section can vary from a few sentences to several pages. For a familiar issue, the background section may be unnecessary. Regardless of the depth to which you present the background information, it should be clear to the audience how the issue has developed to its present point. Present this clearly, simply, and honestly. If you distort the background facts in any way, you are building your case on a weak foundation, and the entire position statement may be rendered useless.

Current Status. Note the current situation and bring the background up to date. A factual analysis—free of bias and advocacy—is needed in this section. Because of the evolving nature of most issues, this section of a position statement may need to be updated frequently.

Projection. It may be appropriate to note the issue's trend, projecting for readers how the issue is likely to develop.

Part 2: Position

After providing the background, give a clear statement of the organization's official position, along with a justification for this position. The justification should include supporting arguments, and it should refute any arguments that opponents are likely to make.

Opinion. This is the heart of the position statement. Here, public relations writers should clearly and explicitly state the organization's point of view. Keep the focus on what the organization feels and why. Beware of allowing this to sound stilted or bureaucratic.

Businesses and nonprofit organizations usually take positions on issues that affect them directly or at least generically. For example, for many years Mobil Oil Corporation engaged in advocacy advertising, publishing a series of position statements on a variety of issues related to business and the economy; the position statements take the form of advertisements in magazines. The American Federation of Teachers publishes position statements on a variety of issues related to public education. Its website now has a prominent section with position statements on issues such as educational reform, school safety, health care, and other topics of interest to the organization and its supporters (aft.org > "Key Issues").

Some advocacy groups regularly take positions on issues that may not affect them directly but affect their constituent publics (or even unrelated groups they consider to be without the ability to advocate for themselves). This is the case, for example, when religious organizations express positions on issues ranging from health care to capital punishment, from abortion to homelessness. Politicians, too, often are expected to have clearly defined position statements on a wide range of issues of interest to their constituents.

Supporting Arguments. Well-stated positions provide a vigorous argument for the stated point of view. A writer preparing a position statement needs to understand the issue well enough to argue for it with credibility and apparent conviction. State reasons that support your opinion. Report facts that bolster your argument, but do so without getting bogged down in detailed statistics that cause readers to lose interest. Recall some of the lessons about persuasive communication, especially those dealing with credible sources, conclusions, and appeals to both logic and sentiment.

Opposing Arguments. Every issue has at least two sides, and it is important for a writer to anticipate opposing viewpoints and alternative solutions. These should be addressed in a position statement. An organization trying to present its opinion and persuade its publics would be foolhardy to ignore opposing sides of the argument on a controversial topic. Research consistently shows that arguments are most effective when they refute rather than ignore opposing claims. Deal honestly and fairly with opposing viewpoints. If you distort opposing claims, you risk being labeled misinformed and illogical—or, worse, dishonest.

Part 3: Conclusion

The position statement ends with recommendations, and sometimes with formal citations that document information included in the statement.

Recommendations. If an organization is going to take a public position on a matter of importance, it owes its publics some reasonable suggestions. End your position statement with recommendations flowing from your stated opinion. Here you may either deal with preferred or possible solutions or you might simply recommend ways in which the reader might get involved.

Citations. Some position statements, particularly those on technical or academic topics, may end with a list of formal citations that identify reports, articles, books, and other sources of the data included in the statement. This allows serious-minded readers to find the explicit documentation and references for the information presented.

Exhibit 12.1—POSITION STATEMENT ON COLLEGE RANKINGS Note how this opinion piece by this hypothetical college has all the elements of an effective position statement.

Finnegan State College Position Paper #17

College Rankings

For several decades, respected directories have published factual and comparable information about colleges and universities that students have found useful as they decide where to advance their education. But in a new commercial twist, some non-academic publishers have begun trying to judge the relative merits of institutions of higher education. Magazines such as *Business Week*, *Kiplinger's*, *Money*, *Time*, and *U.S. News & World Report* publish "best college" rankings that purport to advise students on which colleges offer the highest quality.

Our Observations about "Best College" Rankings ...

Finnegan State notes that "best college" rankings are increasingly being criticized and questioned by educators across the nation. We find these rankings fundamentally flawed because they use criteria inappropriate to the needs of our students and the mission of our College. We further point out that such rankings are of dubious practical value to either students or institutions of higher education.

... increasingly questioned

Even schools that rank high in the listings are criticizing magazine rankings more and more.

- Some colleges have begun refusing to provide data to the magazines. At least 20 independent liberal arts institutions have organized a boycott.
- Other institutions circumvent the rankings by providing their own objective data on websites and other locations accessible to prospective students.
- Student governments at many colleges and universities have asked magazines to stop the numerical rankings. Additionally, students from 40 schools have formed a pressure group to oppose the rankings.
- A new research study points out that rankings based on reputation reflect only past achievements, often underestimating the quality of some schools while overestimating others.

... inappropriate criteria

These rankings feature some criteria biased against institutions such as Finnegan State. More importantly, the criteria are of questionable value to students.

Here are some criteria the rankings use as priority points.

- High faculty salaries
- Low default rate on student loans
- High alumni contributions
- Number of faculty research reports and publications
- Number of faculty, but not the number of teaching assistants
- Number of library books, but not the number of periodicals or electronic resources
- Number of graduates who eventually earn doctorates
- High acceptance standards and low acceptance rates

- - - - -

Position Paper #17
Promulgated January 2011
By Emmanuel Enterline,
President, Finnegan State College
Other position papers available online at www.finnegan.edu

... of dubious value

"Best" rankings earn millions of dollars for magazines. The *U.S. News* rankings issue, for example, is that magazine's annual bestseller. But its value to students is questionable.

- A student survey shows the rankings to have little impact on college choice. Of much more importance are personal sources (other students, college representatives, parents, counselors, and alumni) and materials such as brochures, guidebooks, websites, institutional Facebook pages, and so on.
- In another survey, only six percent of college public information officers found the rankings very helpful to the college-selection process. Most reported the rankings as having only minor impact on recruitment or fundraising.

The Council for Advancement and Support of Education has additional information on college at its website: case.org

Exhibit 12.1—POSITION STATEMENT ON COLLEGE RANKINGS ... *continued*

Our Response ...

Finnegan State does not believe there is a "best college" or a "worse college" – only a college that provides the best choice and the best fit for an individual student.

We believe Finnegan State is the best college choice for many students.

Given the way magazines rank colleges, frankly we don't expect to find Finnegan State at the top of those commercial listings. We don't even want to be there.

Why?

Because Finnegan State values factors the magazines don't emphasize in their criteria, and because we don't particularly stress some of the criteria the magazines do favor.

For example, instead of trying to be exclusive by having low acceptance rates based on unrealistically high entrance requirements, we want to keep Finnegan State's doors open to as many students as possible. We will continue to risk our reputation with the magazines by giving qualified students a chance to succeed, including those promising students who haven't had the same educational opportunities as others.

Or another example: Our professors are exceptionally well qualified, academically and professionally. They teach because they love to teach, and you are more likely to find them in the classroom or an office meeting with students than holed up doing obscure research. An often-heard tribute is that professors at Finnegan State are both accessible and encouraging.

Our Recommendations ...

Instead of worrying about dubious "best college" rankings, we offer the following practical advice for potential students.

Think about what you see in a college. Set your own criteria based on what's important to you.

Use an objective non-ranking directory such as Barron's or Peterson's to identify colleges and universities that meet your individual needs.

Look at majors as well as college-wide generalities. Your college experience will be determined mainly by the courses, teachers, resources, and opportunities associated with your specific major.

Make decisions only after you have visited several colleges and talked with teachers and students there.

And Our Commitment ...

On Reputation ... We believe Finnegan State's solid record of success is the surest foundation for its reputation. We also realize that a reputation grows through good performance and accurate information, and we pledge both to rise to the challenges facing higher education and to keep our students and supporters informed about our progress and plans.

On Student Selectivity ... Finnegan State welcomes top high school students, and we offer challenging courses of study. But we do not close the door after the proven achievers have come in. Finnegan State pledges to remain open to students of average achievement as well. Many of our greatest success stories are students who "just got by" in high school and then blossomed here at Finnegan State, paving the way for high achievements in graduate school and in their careers.

On Teaching ... Finnegan State pledges to remain committed to quality teaching. We aim for small classes and a low student–faculty ratio that encourages student success. We further pledge that all of our classes will continue to be taught by teaching faculty rather than by graduate teaching assistants.

On Student Achievement ... Finnegan State will continue to give students the assistance and encouragement they need to succeed in college. Still, we know that some will opt to leave before they graduate. Recognizing students' right to change their plans, we nevertheless pledge to help every student persevere and graduate in a time that is reasonable for his or her personal, financial, and academic circumstances.

Writing a Position Statement

An effective writer will study the structure and content of position statements from other organizations and the pattern of editorial opinion in various relevant publications, and learn from the examples.

Exhibit 12.2 shows a graphic organizer that serves as a template for a position statement. You might find it helpful to follow this example in your writing, though position statements allow for some flexibility in format. For example, you may find it helpful to begin with the opinion statement, or to deal with the significance of the issue after you have provided its background and current status, or to combine the arguments and refutation of opposing arguments with the section dealing with the background or significance.

Writing a position statement requires careful research. The public relations writer must know the issue and how it affects the organization. The writer also needs to understand how the issue affects the various publics, and whether they are likely to support or oppose the position being taken by the organization. Such understanding can maximize benefits and minimize risks to the organization concerned about maintaining the support of its publics. Recall that public communication is better at reinforcing attitudes than changing them. Regardless of the situation, one of your major concerns should be to maintain the support you already have among sympathetic publics.

Exhibit 12.2—POSITION STATEMENT GRAPHIC ORGANIZER

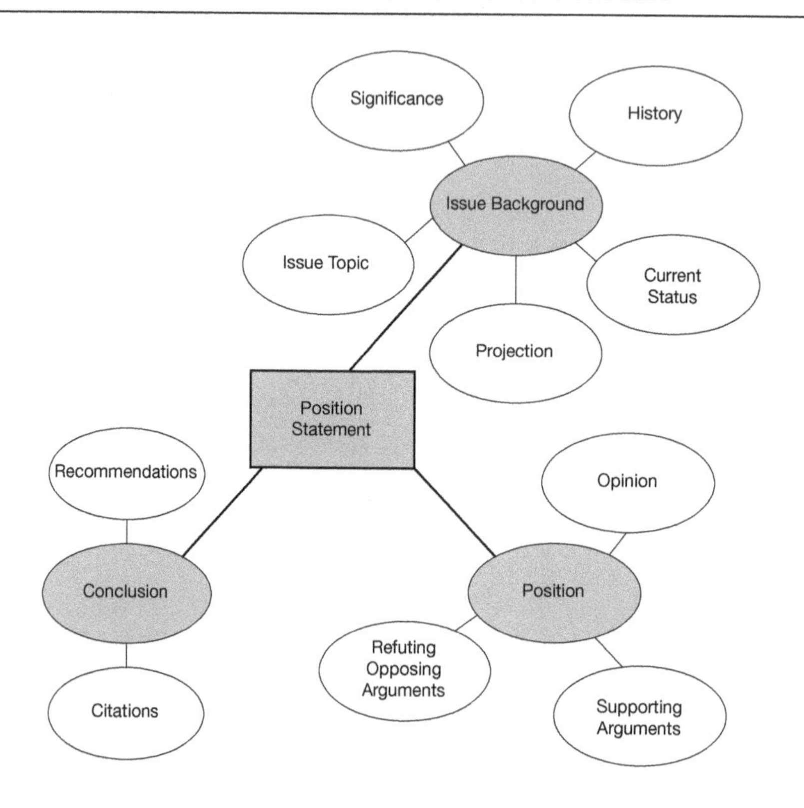

An organization sometimes takes a position contrary to that of some or even most members of key publics. For example, a journalism school might defend the First Amendment rights of an unpopular extremist group, or an inclusive religious organization might support a protest against sectarian prayer in public school assemblies. To do this knowingly can be risky, but perhaps it is necessary on occasion for the integrity of organizational leadership. To do this absentmindedly is a blunder that can be disastrous to the organization.

A good public relations writer will write with both conviction about the topic and respect for opposing points of view. Remember that people may sincerely arrive at different points of view when they consider the same set of facts. Don't be zealous when you deal with opponents, and don't let your own passion for the topic cause you to risk losing the respect or even the attention of people who differ from your organization's position.

Design Elements

Effective position statements feature clear writing that is enhanced by design elements that aid the reader in absorbing the message. An effective technique is to use subheads to clearly identify the various elements of the position statement. Some statements use bold and/or italic type to highlight key elements such as the opinion or the action statement. Virtually any position statement can be made more reader-friendly with such design elements.

Also consider the use of boxes such as summaries, step-by-step instructions, pulled quotes, charts, information graphics, people to contact, and so on. Such design aids contribute much to overall effectiveness in terms of communicating messages.

For practical reasons, position statements should be clearly labeled as such. They also should feature the date when the statement is adopted or endorsed. It sometimes becomes necessary for an organization to change its position. This can be done with little embarrassment when it is clear that the new position is the result of updated information or events that have occurred since the previous position was taken.

Exercise 12.2

Writing Position Statements

Select one of the following scenarios of issues appropriate for a position statement:

- The position of an ethnic, cultural, social, or religious minority on the issue of teaching about that group's history in local schools
- A politician's position on a matter of yet-unsettled public policy of interest to his or her constituents
- A relevant issue of public interest of another organization that interests you. Make sure this issue deals with persuasion; that is, that it is one for which the organization can state an opinion but cannot solve by itself or require others to follow.

Prepare a planning sheet, with careful attention to identifying and analyzing key publics and setting public relations objectives. In preparing your message, consider the impact of the position on the publics and whether they are likely to support or oppose the organization's position. Then research the issue and write the position statement. Use word-processing or publishing software to enhance the design of the final writing.

Organizational Statement

Two other types of writing are related to position statements—official statements and contingency statements. These are examples of position paragraphs.

Official Statement

Official statements are generally brief proclamations by an organization's leadership about timely issues that involve the organization. They are much simpler than formal position statements. Often, official statements are prepared when the organization is facing a controversy. The official statement serves as an opportunity for the organization to speak with one voice on a matter in which it has an interest or on an issue in which its response is being sought. Such statements often are used with external publics such as reporters and consumers. They also can be circulated and published for internal publics within an organization and can be posted at an organization's website and social media sites.

Contingency Statement

Contingency statements, also called **stand-by statements**, may be written to prepare the organization for various potential situations. A contingency statement is a brief position statement written to deal with different pending scenarios facing the organization. Because it is written before the fact, a contingency statement must be held in strict confidence, because the organization could be embarrassed by its premature use.

For example, one resourceful public relations practitioner went to court to hear the verdict of an officer in her organization charged with a financial crime. In her briefcase were two statements. Anticipating that the media would want an official comment from her organization, she was prepared to distribute whichever statement was appropriate following the verdict. One statement expressed regret that the officer had been found guilty and noted the organization's respect for the judicial system. The other expressed pleasure at his acquittal and appreciation for the judicial process. The public relations practitioner was happy to distribute the latter statement.

Exercise 12.3

Writing Contingency Statements

Prepare two contingency statements based on the following scenario: The chief financial officer of your college or university has been on trial for illegally diverting academic scholarship funds for the personal use of varsity athletes.

Write one statement that could be issued if the CFO is found innocent. Write another statement to be used if the CFO is found guilty.

Talk Paper

Some organizations call issue advisories **talk papers** or **talking points**. These are similar to position statements, though generally less interested in providing a balanced background on an issue and instead are written for the purpose of persuasion and advocacy.

The American Legion posts point papers at its website (legion.org > "Legislative Action Center") outlining its stand on military topics (such as defense policy and Don't Ask Don't Tell policy) and relevant civilian issues (flag-protection amendment). Similarly, the Log Cabin Republicans, a gay advocacy group within the GOP, publishes a series of talking points at online.logcabin.org > "Issues" endorsing or opposing proposed legislation dealing with domestic partnerships, definition of marriage, employment non-discrimination, and other issues relevant to the organization's mission.

Letter to the Editor

Many publications—newspapers, magazines, journals, and some newsletters—take seriously their responsibility to provide a forum for their readers. One outlet for this commitment is a **letters to the editor** column in the publication. These columns provide an excellent opportunity for your organization to gain publicity and present a message in its own words.

Newspapers and other publications are not legally required to publish letters from readers, but most do so because the letters column often is one of the most popular features in a publication. Some smaller publications promise to publish all letters that meet stated requirements concerning length, signature, and so on. Larger publications print a sampling of the many letters they receive.

You will increase the chances that your letter is published if you model your writing on effective letters. These are short pieces, generally 200 words or fewer. They feature tight writing, usually addressing only one issue. Despite their brevity, they include or at least allude to all of the elements identified for position statements. For both ethical and practical considerations, public relations practitioners should identify their relationship to the organization on whose behalf they are writing the letter to the editor. Public relations practitioners seldom write letters over their own name. More often, they draft letters to be signed by their clients or bosses.

The key to effectively using a letters column for public relations purposes is to exercise discretion. Don't overuse this avenue. Too much visibility can be a problem in letters columns, as it is in virtually every other media opportunity. Organizations should carefully pace their presence in the media so they do not reduce their credibility with overexposure.

"FYI: Audience Commentary and the Law" discusses the legal requirements for the news media to provide a forum for reader comments and organizational replies.

FYI *Audience Commentary and the Law*

Legal requirements vary concerning whether news media need to provide an outlet for audience opinions. In general, newspapers are under no legal obligation to publish letters to the editor and reader commentaries, while broadcast media have some parallel requirements to provide a forum for the opinions of their audience members.

Newspapers. There is no legal requirement that newspapers or other publications must publish any or all readers' letters. Publications that print letters to the editor do so because they find this to be good journalistic practice, not because the law requires it. Nor is there any requirement for editors to be even-handed in their selection of letters to be published.

In *Miami Herald v. Tornillo*, the Supreme Court ruled in 1974 that the law provides no right of reply to published commentaries, even to persons who feel they have been unfairly criticized by the publication

continued . . .

FYI *Audience Commentary and the Law* *. . . continued*

itself. The court said that the law generally couldn't interfere with a newspaper's content, presumably including news copy or advertising, as well as commentary.

While press responsibility suggests that a newspaper serves its readers best when all sides of an issue are aired, and while journalistic practice generally is to fulfill this responsibility, it is not required by law.

Broadcast Media. Similar opportunities for responsive commentary exist with some radio and television stations that present their own editorial comments. Many stations that present editorials invite public comment. The Federal Communications Commission requires that radio and television stations provide free rebuttal time to persons whose character has been attacked on air, either by the station itself or by other commentators. This requirement, one of the few remaining elements of the Fairness Doctrine that was FCC policy from 1949 to 1987, was endorsed by the Supreme Court in *Red Lion Broadcasting Co. v. FCC* (1969).

However, neither the FCC nor the courts have ruled that broadcasters must provide airtime to individuals or groups who simply want to present their point of view on matters of public interest. In *CBS v. Democratic National Committee*, the Supreme Court ruled in 1973 that broadcasters do not have to sell advertising time. Policies such as these have frustrated some organizations trying to advocate for their positions on various controversial issues. Occasionally, public relations practitioners are faced with broadcast media that arbitrarily refuse to provide them with airtime to present their positions. Generally, stations that refuse to air one side of an issue also refuse to air any point of view on the subject.

Internet and Social Media. Internet law is still evolving, but to date there is little specific to new media. Standard legal issues such as privacy, defamation, copyright, and trademark apply. There is no specific right to respond to criticism or to force a website, blog, or social media site to set the record straight.

Sometimes, Internet entities adopt restrictive rules for users. Wikipedia, for example, bans public relations practitioners from posting anything about their organization. That's not a legal matter but rather a policy internal to the Wikipedia people in which the law has chosen not to interfere.

Writing to Gain Publicity

Organizations sometimes use letters columns to call attention to activities that did not attract the attention of news reporters or did not result in what the organization considers adequate coverage for an event.

These letters usually have a positive tone. Some may take the strategy of offering congratulations for an accomplishment. For example, a company may congratulate its employees for achieving a certain business success, or a school district may applaud its students on reversing an escalating dropout rate. Other such letters may simply present information, without noting that the publication declined to report it in the first place. Rather than criticizing the publication, the public relations writer may simply present the information that the organization feels is of interest to readers.

Sometimes, letters can be written to note that an organization was not included in a publication's prior coverage. An effective response may be to express interest and encouragement in the topic and then to provide the relevant information. For example:

> LMNOP Corporation is pleased to see the Review-Journal taking a lead in reporting on the problem of water pollution in the Caterwallerby River, and we applaud the measures taken by the companies noted in the news report. Though we were not included in the review, we want to note that LMNOP has a major commitment to eliminate pollutants from our water discharges . . .

Writing to Correct Errors

Newspapers and magazines occasionally publish incorrect information. Reporters are human. They can make mistakes. When mistakes happen, organizations sometimes look to the letters column to redress errors in the way a publication reported about the organization. The letters column allows an organization to vindicate itself and set the record straight. But assess this option with great care. Ask yourself: Does the reported error warrant the attention of a letter? Is reopening the issue beneficial to the organization or is it better to simply let it fade away?

If the reported error is of minor consequence, it may be best to overlook it. Perhaps there is another avenue, such as the **corrections column**, which corrects factual misstatements. These generally are written at the discretion of an editor, who often provides merely a sentence correcting a factual error, without context. Here's an example of what a correction statement might look like:

> The provost at Bison State University is Dr. Howard Marion, not Dr. Marion Howard as stated in a recent news article.

It is the lack of context in a corrections column that often moves a public relations practitioner to consider the regular letters-to-the-editor column. When a correction is warranted, writers preparing letters reacting to published error most often prudently decide not to attack the reporter's ethics or ability. For example, the following is not a very good way to begin such a letter:

> The simpleton on your staff obviously can't take accurate notes, so it's no wonder he mistakenly reported that . . .

Rather the effective public relations writer might begin:

> We appreciate the coverage you provided, and we have heard from many people who have told us that they read your report. One point that needs to be clarified is that . . .

The letter might proceed to offer the correction, perhaps under the guise of an information update.

> Readers may be interested to know that the latest figures show . . .

Writers who understand that their effectiveness lies in cultivating long-term relationships with reporters are willing to give the reporter the benefit of the doubt, or at least not to pick a fight in print. Effective public relations writers also know that the publication has the last word, and a corrections letter stands a possibility of being followed by an editorial response that all but negates the letter's value. Be wary about claiming your company was misquoted unless you are certain—a good reason to tape-record every news conference or interview.

As a practical matter, when offering a correction or update to a published article, writers should provide a clear reference—for example, by noting the date, page, and headline of an article that is the basis for a letter to the editor.

Writing to Advocate a Cause

Public relations writers often use letters to the editor to present their opinion on matters of importance to a publication's readers. To be effective, try to link your cause to an issue already on the public agenda. For example, when a man was arrested for killing people while he was drunk, an agency that focuses on alcoholism used the case as an opportunity to present its message. The Research Institute on Addictions, a New York State agency, knew that the drugs-and-violence issue was of interest throughout the state. So when a particularly gruesome and heavily reported incident of drug-induced violence occurred in one community, the institute addressed the news event in the lead of a letter to the editor and then provided information about its findings linking drug or alcohol abuse with violence. Later, when a similar incident occurred in another part of the state, the institute simply rewrote the lead of its letter to focus on the new incident and used the rest of the letter from the earlier version.

Another, more generic lead dealt not with local crime but rather with scientific research that had been reported by the newspaper:

> Does violence have a genetic basis? A recent story in The News described research findings suggesting that abnormal brain chemistry helps to cause aggression. While this research adds an important piece to our understanding of violence, we must also recognize the other factors that contribute to aggression, especially alcohol and drug use.
>
> Studies conducted at the Research Institute on Addictions and elsewhere have shown that . . .

Commentary

In addition to letters, most publications also provide space for longer and more prominent opinion pieces that present the viewpoint of a person or organization not affiliated with the publication on issues of particular interest to readers. This space is known as **op-ed commentary** (so named because of its traditional placement opposite the editorial page). Some publications offer space for **guest editorials**, which are written by invited members of the community instead of members of the editorial board. Others publish bylined commentaries contributed by special-interest organizations. Regardless of how they feature the viewpoints, op-ed commentary gives public relations writers an important vehicle for presenting their organization's position. As with letters, there can be a lot of competition for space. But writers can increase the chances that their editorials will be accepted by carefully preparing their submissions to a publication.

No publication would seriously consider using an op-ed piece on an irrelevant topic. The writer's task is to think like an editor, selecting a topic of interest to the publication and its readers. Use the SiLoBaTi criteria for news (significant, local, balanced, timely) as an indicator of a relevant topic. The guest editorial might not be on a topic that the readers are yet talking about, but it should be on a topic that they will care about when it is presented to them.

The writing itself should be crisp and concise. Before writing the op-ed, review what the publication usually publishes and then write the position statement accordingly. Consider who might be a credible source to carry the organization's message. Seldom does a public relations writer sign a guest editorial. Instead, the public relations person acts as ghostwriter who researches and writes the guest editorial, which is then signed by someone else—usually an organizational leader such as the president, CEO, or executive director. The format for guest editorials generally includes the same elements suggested earlier in this chapter as elements of position papers.

Issue Advisory

A different kind of opinion piece—one that may emerge in a crisis situation—is similar to a position statement. But the **issue advisory** deals with emerging topics of immediate concern to various publics. Often, issue advisories are written for internal publics. Because they focus on an emergency in progress, they allow less preparation time than a position statement. Nevertheless, issue advisories call for some planning if they are to be effective vehicles for public relations communication. The short preparation time does not justify carelessness.

When an organization finds itself in the midst of a public relations crisis, it should adopt the **one-voice principle**. This generally means designating one organizational representative to serve as the public spokesperson. While public relations directors may draft the public statement, they seldom are the spokespersons. That role usually goes to someone else in the organization's leadership, freeing the public relations person to coordinate the response behind the scenes.

The spirit of the one-voice principle is preserved when an organization uses the coordinated voices of more than one spokesperson, which is useful when an organization must communicate simultaneously with different publics. The key in either case is that a consistent message is presented. The one-voice principle is reinforced by communicating with employees, volunteers, board members, and other internal publics—reminding them of the background of the issue, apprising them of the significance of the issue, informing them of the organization's position, and equipping them with information that will reinforce the public position.

Issue advisories have many applications within organizations. If a school district bans the captain of the football team from playing in the homecoming game because of underage drinking, it can explain the policy to its teachers and staff so that they, in turn, can explain it to students and parents.

Consider the following example: A routine blood-screening test at an American Red Cross center inaccurately labeled a donor as being infected with a hepatitis virus. Because of government regulations at the time, the organization was prohibited from notifying the donor. He continued to give blood 28 times over the next 3½ years, and each time the blood had to be thrown out.

When he inadvertently learned of the situation, the donor was confused and angered. He talked with the Red Cross, wrote to local legislators, and finally contacted the newspaper, which published a lengthy report (Sunday edition, Page 1: "Faithful donor learns his effort was all in vain; Red Cross kept drawing blood, then disposing of it").

The community relations department prepared an issue advisory for the many Red Cross employees and volunteers to help them deal with questions from blood donors. The advisory addressed questions people were asking and the organization's response.

> Question: How could you throw the blood away?
> Response: Our mission is to provide the safest possible blood to those in need. The procedures may be cumbersome, but they are designed to ensure the safety of the blood supply.

Question: Why wasn't he notified not to continue donating?
Response: Government regulations at the time prevented us from doing so.

Question: Could this happen again?
Response: No, because new procedures are in place.

Proclamation

Occasionally, public relations writers are asked to prepare a formal statement commemorating an event or issue to be published over the signature of a governmental or other official. Such a statement is called a **proclamation** or a **resolution**. Mayors and county executives often sign proclamations commemorating an event of local significance. Governors and presidents issue proclamations on topics of wider importance. In matters outside the governmental arenas, officials such as union leaders, religious prelates, and organizational executives sometimes issue proclamations. Sometimes, the signers, who ask their public relations people to draft the appropriate proclamations, initiate such resolutions. Others may be initiated by public relations people working in particular organizations or for certain causes, who then will take the proclamation to the appropriate official for its promulgation.

As formal declarations of an organization's opinion, proclamations follow a strict format. The background of the issue is presented by a series of "whereas" paragraphs that build the case, providing a logical base from which to launch toward a conclusion, and a "therefore" or "be it resolved" paragraph that makes the official statement. Alternatively, some proclamations read more like a testimonial letter, with several paragraphs recounting the background of an event or the contributions of an individual or group, followed by a formal declaration: "Now, therefore, I . . . by virtue of the authority vested in me by . . . do hereby proclaim that . . ."

Some organizations use the Internet to promote widespread use of proclamations. The National Women's History Project provides an online template on its website (nwhp.org > "Women's History Month") as a guide for city councils and school districts in issuing similar proclamations.

Following are two proclamations celebrating Cinco de Mayo. One is issued by the mayor of Durango, Colo., the other by the governor of New York. Note how each uses the occasion to highlight the contributions and achievements of constituents of the signer.

PROCLAMATION: CINCO DE MAYO CELEBRATION (Durango, Colo.)

WHEREAS, Hispano-Americans comprise a major portion of the population in the Southern Region of the State of Colorado; and

WHEREAS, the Mexican culture is an integral and essential part of American art and culture; and

WHEREAS, the Hispano/Latino/Chicano population comprises the largest minority in the City of Durango; and

WHEREAS, local landmarks, names, and historical figures signify the Mexican and Spanish influence in the settling of the City of Durango; and

WHEREAS, a part of the celebration of the local Hispano/Latino/Chicano culture is Cinco de Mayo, a proud moment in Mexican history, celebrating the victory of Mexican farmers and villagers over a trained and organized French army on May 5, 1862, in the city of Puebla, Mexico.

NOW, THEREFORE, I, **Michael Rendon**, Mayor of Durango, Colorado do hereby proclaim the week of May 1st through May 8th, 2010, as **Cinco de Mayo Week presented by La Gente de Durango**

And in honor of this festivity urge all citizens to help raise awareness of this cultural event and join the City of Durango in celebrating the richness of our diverse cultural history and strengths.

STATE OF NEW YORK EXECUTIVE CHAMBER: Proclamation

Whereas, New York's greatest strength is its diversity and we appreciate the culture and history of our various communities of people, all of whom add to the greatness of this state, and we are therefore pleased to join with the Mexican American population in celebrating "Cinco de Mayo" which commemorates an event of historical significance and profound meaning to its people, both in the United States and in the homeland of Mexico; and

Whereas, the "Fifth of May" celebration commemorates the defeat of the French army by the Mexicans at the Battle of Puebla in 1862—a conflict that grew out of France's efforts, led by Napoleon III, to invade Mexico and to create a new Mexican empire headed by Maximilian and his wife Carolota in the beleaguered country; and

Whereas, a powerful French army left the port of Veracruz to attack Mexico City, its members mistaken in their belief that the Mexican people would give up without fighting and, under the command of General Zaragoza and Colonel Porfirio Díaz, later to be Mexico's President, the poorly-equipped yet spiritually robust Mexican army met and defeated the overconfident French troops; and

Whereas, this victory came to symbolize the determination of the people of Mexico to remain free and independent and, today, its anniversary provides an opportunity to honor the noteworthy history of the country of Mexico and to recognize the perseverance and strength of its citizenry; and

Whereas, each year, "Cinco de Mayo" recalls the indomitable spirit of the Mexican people who continue to make significant contributions to our state and nation, and also serves to enhance appreciation, among us all, for precious freedom and its value in our daily lives; and

Whereas, this event marked by festivities that illustrate the pride of the Mexican community is a fitting means by which to commemorate a defining moment in Mexican history, and it is furthermore appropriate that New Yorkers of all cultural backgrounds join with our Mexican-American friends in celebrating the two ideals of friendship and liberty which Mexicans and Americans have fought to protect, ever since the Fifth of May, 1862;

Now, Therefore, I David A. Paterson, Governor of the State of New York, do hereby proclaim May 5, 2010 as CINCO DE MAYO in the Empire State.

Petition

Petitions are a hybrid of advocacy letters and proclamations, prepared for many people to sign. The intent of petition writers is to draft a resolute statement—often a request or demand—that will accomplish several purposes: (1) to educate people about a cause and generate interest, (2) to gain the support of people who will sign their name to the petition, and (3) to ultimately be accepted by the person or organization receiving the petition. As a vehicle of advocacy public relations, petitions often are used to exert a degree of public pressure on the recipient and may be accompanied by news releases, news conferences, and other publicity vehicles.

Traditionally, petitions have been circulated person to person, often by volunteers who gather signatures. Many candidates for political offices have used such petitions, as have grassroots movements seeking to impact on government in some way.

Increasingly, petitions are being promoted over the Internet, with invitations being made to potential signers throughout the world. Topics often deal with politics or government as well as civil rights, human rights and consumer rights, as well as advocacy for environmental, religious, and other causes. Online petitions call for the impeachment of the president (in each of the last three administrations) and support for the president. They ask readers to sign on to protect wildlife, free prisoners, and support political candidates.

Some petitions are sponsored by advocates associated with a particular cause, such as Reporters without Borders (rsf.org), Amnesty International (amnesty.org), the civic action group MoveOn.org, and Act for Change (workingforchange.com/activism). The American Civil Liberties Union (aclu.org) sponsored an online petition directed to the Bush White House to allow military chaplains to pray according to their own faith traditions after specifically Christian prayer was banned in public settings. The Internet also provides a forum for individuals with a self-proclaimed cause, such as the animal rights activist who created WhalesRevenge.com to promote a petition calling on the International Whaling Commission to end commercial whaling.

Online petitions also are posted by groups with multiple agenda interests. Project Democracy operates one such online forum for what it calls democratic conversation and deliberative discussions. The organization's website (e-thepeople.org) provides e-mail addresses and connections to thousands of public officials. It also posts a changing series of online petitions and invites signers for reader-generated topics such as religious freedom, rights of military veterans, educational malpractice, and immigration reform.

The effectiveness of online petition drive is seen in cases such as avaaz.org. In one week, the online advocacy organization obtained more than a million signatures on a petition urging China to respect human rights in Tibet.

Following is an example of a petition circulated online by VoteVets, a non-partisan political action committee of more than 100,000 members seeking to elect veterans of the Iraq and Afghanistan wars to public office and to advocate for concerns of men and women in uniform. When the debate over the so-called "Ground Zero Mosque" was flaring, the group asked members and other supports to support its stand in favor of building the community center in Lower Manhattan. The open petition was addressed to Sharif El-Gamal, developer of the community center.

Dear Mr. Gamal,

As veterans of the wars in Iraq and Afghanistan, we are writing to support your right to build a community center on the property you purchased in Lower Manhattan, and urge you to continue on with your project. We encourage you to distribute this letter to all those who may be interested, so they know that veterans like us see this as an important issue of our very Constitution and our national security.

There are two very important reasons we are choosing to speak out. First and foremost, when we signed up for service, we swore to uphold the Constitution. For all the talk these days from some quarters about the importance of protecting the Constitution and allowing the free market to work unfettered, those same people are fighting against your community's right to buy property and worship freely. Our duty to protect the Constitution didn't end when our service did. It's up to us to stand up for the right for all Americans to enjoy the Constitutional freedoms that so many around the world don't have. So, we are standing up for you.

Secondly, allowing the Community Center to move forward will deal a blow to the propaganda of al Qaeda and Islamist extremists, who recruit on the talking point that the United States is in a war against Islam. Of course, we're not. But, if those forces of intolerance win, it will certainly appear that we are in a war against one religion – Islam.

As Matthew Alexander, a former interrogator in Iraq, and VoteVets.org member wrote at the Huffington Post, "Imagine an al Qaeda recruiter attempting to sway a potential charge by citing an imaginary American war against Muslims but having to face the counterargument that Americans built a Muslim community center near the site of the former Twin Towers. The Cordoba House would be a powerful symbol of U.S. tolerance and freedom that will stand in direct contradiction to al Qaeda's narrative that Americans hate Muslims."

That's the point. Defeating al Qaeda will take the use of force. But, it will also take destroying their ability to recruit, and that means winning hearts and minds. As veterans of the wars in Iraq and Afghanistan, we know all too well the importance of having the people on your side.

For our Constitution and for the safety of America and our troops currently in the field, we are writing in full support of your project. As veterans of Iraq and Afghanistan, we believe the construction of your community center isn't "anti-America" at all. In fact, building your community center is about as pro-America as one can get.

Green Dissemination

One final task remains. Planning, researching, and writing news releases and other journalistic pieces remain incomplete until you disseminate them to the appropriate venues that can get them into the hands of your publics.

Once you have written your news release, feature story, or opinion piece, you have to get it into the hands of the most appropriate journalist. The recipient may be the city editor or a section editor at a daily newspaper, the news director of a radio or television news department, or the writer of a topical blog related to your organization.

You can get the names of those people in any good media directory, or call the media outlet and ask. Many newspapers and radio or TV stations also have such information at their websites. When sending information to the media, always try to identify the recipient by name, and update your mailing lists frequently.

It is generally inappropriate to send a news release to more than one reporter at the same publication or station. Editors do not like to be embarrassed by using a release in two different parts of the same publication. However, it may be quite appropriate to send the same release to a reporter and a columnist at the same newspaper, or to a reporter and a talk-show host at the same radio or television station.

Here are three keys to handling multiple releases:

- Establish in advance that more than one person at a media organization wants the release.
- Make certain those involved know that you'll be distributing multiple releases.
- Identify releases accordingly.

How can you get the release from Point A (your hands) to Point B (the hands of the media gatekeeper who will decide its fate)? Ask gatekeepers what they prefer.

To do this most effectively, go green. It's no longer necessary to use up natural resources such as paper and ink to get the job done, nor do you need to add to the carbon footprint by sending releases through the mail. Most everything you have written can be disseminated digitally. This is not only environmentally healthy, it is fast, convenient, and, perhaps most important, preferred by media gatekeepers.

Here are the most common methods of disseminating news releases:

Electronic Mail. **E-mail** is the preferred and most common method for journalists to receive information from public relations practitioners. E-mail saves time for reporters, because the material is ready for editing and typesetting without the need for re-entering it into the publication's computer system. Photos can be attached to the e-mail. With online versions of newspapers, television newsrooms, and increasing numbers of reporter blogs, journalists can receive news 24/7. E-mailed releases allow them to cut and paste quickly.

Online Newsroom Download. Many businesses and nonprofit organizations use their online newsroom to store current and past news releases, annual reports, backgrounders, speeches, photos, and other public documents on a computer network. Frequently these are set up so that the public relations person e-mails reporters to notify them when new information is posted at the media site. Some sites can be accessed through an organization's Facebook page.

Distribution Services. Some companies disseminate news releases and other media information on behalf of organizations with large and frequent mailings. They generally distribute news releases via e-mail or as downloads signaled by RSS feeds or e-mail notices.

Newswires distribute information from corporations, financial institutions, and other organizations with interests that extend over a wide geographic area. Some of the common general-purpose newswires include PR Newswire, PR Web, Canada NewsWire, Vocus, and Press Release Network.

Some distribution services focus on particular topics, such as Environmental News Service, Hip Hop PR Wire, Business Wire, and Travel PR Wire. Other newswires deal with particular ethnic or cultural groups, including Hispanic PR Wire, Black PR Wire, Arab American News Wire, and Catholic PR Wire. Still other services are active on a geographic basis, such as Kyodo News PR Wire for Japanese media and India PRwire.

Fax Distribution. The fax is another way to distribute news releases, a method that some editors prefer over the mailed release. Some states have passed laws limiting mass distribution of unsolicited faxes, a practice known as **bulk faxing** or **broadcast faxing**. Save them for information that is especially timely or for releases that an editor has asked for specifically.

Postal Delivery. Postal delivery is less commonly used, though it still has a place, especially for media kits that reporters are expecting. Mailed releases can be useful when they are combined with a comprehensive media kit with releases, backgrounders, fact sheets, photos, and other materials associated with big events.

Personal Delivery. In many cities, courier delivery services can be useful in getting a number of releases to several competitive media outlets at the same time. Once, public relations people personally delivered their news releases to reporters and editors. But media gatekeepers are too busy these days to accommodate unplanned visits from public relations practitioners, and many newsrooms have policies against visits by outsiders (including public relations people).

Wrap-Up for Part Two

The chapters in Part Two have focused on writing in news style and on the various types of news releases and other journalistic pieces that public relations writers might prepare.

Some of these are associated with established media; others with emerging new media. Taken together, these provide a rich repertoire of writing formats and venues that can help any organization interact with its publics and present its strategic messages.

You have covered a lot of ground in this section of the book. Let's recap what you have learned to do. In these eight chapters, you have learned how . . .

- To develop an understanding of the elements of news
- To identify and generate newsworthy information about an organization
- To write in the simple news format of a fact sheet
- To write effective media advisories
- To pitch story ideas to reporters and other media writers
- To write in appropriate news style and format
- To explain the legal concepts of defamation and privacy
- To write different kinds of leads and news briefs
- To write news releases of different types and purposes
- To write in the style of the broadcast media
- To use pronunciation guides accurately
- To prepare a news release including a radio actuality
- To outline the contents of a video news release
- To write an e-mail news release
- To develop a social media release
- To plan for an online newsroom for an organization
- To prepare and write features about people (biographical narratives, profiles, and interviews)
- To prepare and write features about organizations (histories, profiles, and backgrounders)
- To prepare and write features about issues (how-to articles, Q&As, case histories, and information digests)
- To adapt feature articles to various opportunities in emerging social media

- To apply concepts of issues management in various writing activities
- To prepare and write advocacy pieces such as position statements, letters to the editor, op-ed commentaries and guest editorials, issue advisories, proclamations, and petitions.

Part Three

PUBLIC RELATIONS WRITING FOR ORGANIZATIONAL MEDIA

In today's communications environment, two pivotal changes are taking place in the way public relations writers approach their work. The first change is that both the reach and the impact of the journalistic media are declining. Newspaper readership has been dropping for decades, and the decline has not been offset by any increase in audience size for radio or television news. As a result, newspaper readers and television news viewers are more heavily representative of older age groups.

In addition, newspaper stories are becoming shorter and more feature oriented, and television news is taking on many of the characteristics of entertainment, even of so-called tabloid journalism. Once, an article in the local newspaper and a mention on the 6 o'clock news was a surefire way to reach most of the local audience. Today, media attention alone is not sufficient to measure public relations success.

Meanwhile, polls indicate that news reporters have lessening credibility with audiences in both the print and electronic media. While many Americans devour information on 24/7 cable channels, the credibility of these sources is low. The Pew Research Center for People and the Press reported in 2009 that only 39 percent of people surveyed said the media get the facts straight.

CNN topped the list with 30 percent high credibility (believing all or most of the information reported). This was followed by local TV news at 28 percent and PBS at 27 percent. Three networks—NBC, ABC, and MSNBC—tied at 24 percent. The other two national networks trailed: Fox News at 23 percent and CBS News at 22 percent.

Among print publications, the *Wall Street Journal* led with 25 percent credibility. Following in the Pew survey were *Time* magazine with 21 percent, *U.S. News* at 20 percent, *New York Times* with 18 percent, and tied with 16 percent *Newsweek* magazine, *USA Today* newspaper, and the Associated Press. Again, the category is high credibility, respondents who said they believe all or most of the information these news sources give them.

The Pew study revealed a partisan divide. Democrats rate all the news media significantly more credible than do Republicans. The exception to this was for two specific news outlets, Fox News and the *Wall Street Journal*, which Republicans trust more than Democrats do.

Such findings have been slowly and steadily dropping for the last decade or more. They present two interesting questions for public relations writers: (1) If the news media have such low credibility rates, how useful are they for public relations purposes? (2) Should public relations be looking elsewhere for ways to effectively communicate with their publics?

The second major change in the communications environment is that there are new opportunities for public relations people to circumvent the news media and take their messages directly to their publics. Advances in technologies associated with computers, blogs, social media, video, self-publishing, and electronic mail have made it easier for organizations to develop direct communication links with their publics, without the go-between of reporters and editors. What this means for public relations writers is that renewed attention is warranted for the various kinds of organizational media.

Part Three of *Becoming a Public Relations Writer* focuses on both established and emerging media. Sometimes the communication tool is the same, simply offered through different media venues. In other situations, the emerging media offer not only new venues but even new communication tools.

Often, a close look at the tools of emerging media reveals that they are technological makeovers of long-time staples of traditional media. Blogs, for example, are little more than high-tech newsletters—only better. They reach more people faster and with less expense, and they can be interactive between organizations and their publics.

Blogs and social media, fliers and brochures, newsletters and annual reports, and direct mail and online appeals all have become increasingly important to practitioners. Public relations advertising relies on the public media to carry the message, but unlike journalism-based activities, it allows organizations to manage the content, presentation, and timing of their messages. Likewise, the interpersonal arena of public speaking sometimes involves organizational spokespeople with the news media, but it also provides opportunities in nonjournalistic situations in which the organization manages elements of its message related to content, presentation, and timing.

This shift toward using direct communication under the control of an organization is having a profound impact on the practice of public relations. Whereas past writers were rooted in journalism, successful public relations writers now also need competence with organizational media. Part Three of this book deals with ways in which an organization can manage its communication with its publics by using direct channels of communication. Part Three comprises:

- Chapter 13: Newsletter and Corporate Report
- Chapter 14: Website, Blog, and Wiki
- Chapter 15: Flier and Brochure
- Chapter 16: Direct Mail and Online Appeal
- Chapter 17: Public Relations Advertising
- Chapter 18: Speechwriting
- Wrap-Up for Part Three.

13 Newsletter and Corporate Report

Newsletters are important public relations tools for organizations seeking a communication link with key publics. Many public relations graduates find entry-level public relations positions that involve working on employee newsletters, and many seasoned practitioners find that special-interest newsletters offer lucrative career options. This is a field that will draw on your writing abilities, training in news writing and editing, and skill in organization and planning.

Some organizations expand their print repertoire beyond simple newsletters. They are publishing internal magazines and organizational newspapers, either in print or online. Both businesses and nonprofit organizations also publish various quarterly and annual reports, along with a range of other documents noting progress, outlining major programs, and so on. Each of these is an effort by an organization to communicate with its key publics and to extend its message through all available media. Here are your learning objectives for this chapter:

- To write an effective newsletter article
- To write an effective headline for a newsletter article
- To understand the purpose and importance of corporate reports
- To edit and proofread documents carefully and effectively
- To show an understanding of laws related to copyright and trademark.

Newsletter

Newsletters seem to be everywhere and it's impossible to count how many exist. Print publications decrease in number, but growth has been rapid among online newsletters. But these are just whispers of the total number of newsletters. Local newsletters are innumerable. Many corporate newsletters are not even available to the public. Hundreds of thousands, perhaps millions, of newsletters are published by schools, churches, community singing groups, bridge clubs, sports organizations, fan clubs, and many other such groups.

Newsletters are among the most ancient public relations tools. Herodotus of Thurii, the first recognized Greek historian, is credited with publishing a trade newsletter in 425 B.C.E., and Julius Caesar published a daily handwritten newsletter in Rome during the first century B.C.E. called *Acta Diurna* (Daily Events). The Tang dynasty in 11th-century China circulated a newsletter, as did the financial leaders of many European cities during the Middle Ages and the Renaissance. *Publick Occurrences Both Forreign and Domestick*, the recognized forerunner of American newspapers, was a multipage newsletter published in Massachusetts in 1690; it was intended as a monthly publication but was shut down by the colonial government after its first issue. Many of the other early colonial publications were social and political advocacy newsletters that eventually took up the cause of issues related to American independence from Britain.

Fast-forward to today. Some newsletters have grown into hybrids with names like **magapapers**, **minimags**, and **maganews**. Most printed newsletters have morphed into **e-newsletters** online. Some have grown into **electronic magazines**, more commonly called **e-zines** or **cyberzines**. Essentially, all of these are variations on the same theme, different formats for what traditionally has been considered a **house organ**, that is, a publication with the look and feel of a magazine but the editorial control of a public relations piece. For the writer, all of these publications allow a flexibility of writing styles.

Purpose of Newsletter

What, exactly, is a newsletter? Simply said, a **newsletter** is a printed periodic publication distributed by an organization to a particular information-seeking audience. It is part news, part letter. As a provider of news, a newsletter should focus on information relevant to its audience, which mirrors the key publics of the organization that produces the newsletter. The wants, interests, and needs of the key public should determine the news value of information for newsletters, and the focus of this news value is the reader rather than the organization that publishes the newsletter.

In addition to being news based, the content of newsletters is presented in a writing style that is less formal—more letterlike, more featurish—than is common with many other public relations media. The basic similarity between the publisher and the reader lends itself to the use of jargon and to the presumption of common and often personal interests that are shared by all. Like other practical public relations activities, newsletters are most effective when they build on the mutual interests of both the organization and its publics and when they foster the mutual benefit of both. They serve several different objectives within an organization's public relations plan. Consider the following objectives for an organization publishing a newsletter:

- To maintain a relationship with a public
- To reinforce attitudes and actions beneficial to an organization
- To create and then maintain a dialog between the organization and its publics, or among members of the audience
- To increase or maintain a level of awareness by a public about issues important to an organization
- To increase or maintain a level of interest and/or positive attitudes for an active public about an issue.

Note that these objectives deal with enhancing an organization's relationship with publics that are already interested in the organization's message. A newsletter is not the medium to communicate with disinterested or latent publics; rather, it is published for active information-seeking publics. This is a distinction worth remembering, because you don't want to waste time and money by preparing communication tools that are likely to be inappropriate for your public.

Another consideration is that newsletters need not look like miniature newspapers or little magazines with columns, photos, traditional headlines, and other elements associated with these publications. Some effective newsletters are more like a letter—a string of paragraphs, each with a different topic, sometimes with bold or underlined type to emphasize the topic words and phrases. Online publications have even more flexibility in appearance. The value of newsletters is their frequency, consistency, and easy readability, as well as the authority and currency of the information they provide.

Exercise 13.1

Freewriting on Newsletters

Freewrite for five minutes on the following topic: *How effective have been recent newsletters I have seen?* Then discuss this with your classmates.

Types of Newsletter

Organizations occasionally publish a single newsletter, thinking it will serve their need to communicate with various publics. Usually, they are mistaken, because information that serves one public may be of little value or interest to another. Organizations that communicate effectively have learned that newsletters should be directed to particular audiences. Here are some categories of newsletters focused on various audiences: members, general external publics, special-interest publics, subscribers, consumers, and cause-related readers.

Member Newsletter. Member newsletters are aimed at internal publics—employees, volunteers, retirees, and other groups of people generically classified as members—as well as consumer groups who identify closely with the organization, such as students or alumni. For many organizations, these are the most important publics, and such newsletters often provide the most important communication tool that exists. For examples of member newsletters, download the PDF files from the Flukeprints newsletter archives of the Whale Center of New England in the member news section at whalecenter.org or the Gamofite newsletter archives for members of Gay Mormon Fathers at gamofites.org.

External Newsletter. Not surprisingly, external newsletters are aimed at nonmembers—customers, consumers, electoral constituents, distributors, suppliers, fans, and so on. Like internal newsletters, these external publications are focused on a single organization. Two examples of online community relations newsletters are Scope Monthly (cms.skidmore.edu/community_relations) and Los Angeles Lakers Community (nba.lakers.com/community/newsletter.html). The Navy Band published its Fanfare newsletter at navyband.navy.mil.

Special-Interest Newsletter. Special-interest newsletters deal with a particular profession or industry, or with a particular topic or issue. Professional newsletters for public relations practitioners are examples of this, as are publications directed to owners of a particular class of racing sailboat, people interested in making financial investments, nuns, stamp collectors, or distributors of imported Norwegian lace. In addition to professions and hobbies, special-interest newsletters may also be based on common concerns about politics, economics, religion, hobbies, social issues, lifestyle, and any other issue that provides a common bond among people. The Society of Financial Service Professionals publishes Keeping Current at financialpro.org for financial advisers. The National Coalition of American Nuns' newsletter archives at ncan.us deal with social justice issues in church and society.

Subscription Newsletter. Subscription newsletters provide inside information and expert advice to paying subscribers. They offer a particular challenge to writers because of the high demands by subscribers, who may be paying several hundred dollars a year for valuable information in an easy-to-use format. The most popular topics deal with business, communications, computers, health, investments, and international and legal issues. Because of their high price, subscription newsletters are especially concerned with providing information of interest to readers, who generally are specialists seeking a level of detail not found in mass media coverage. For example, a network news story about congressional debates over health care reform might focus on the legislative battle, scope of reforms, or consequences for the consumers. But a newsletter aimed at insurance agents who market health care policies might give details about specific provisions of the bill relating to licensure of agents, their education requirements, and commission controls. The Kiplinger Letter (kiplinger.com), one of the oldest and most respected subscription newsletters, has a circulation of 135,000 subscribers interested in its insight into government and business. Jack O'Dwyer's Newsletter, with nearly 6,000 subscribers interested in public relations and marketing communication, is available at odwyerpr.com.

Consumer Newsletter. Consumer newsletters provide how-to information for readers interested in a particular topic, such as hydroponic gardening, line dancing, and beekeeping. Many of the consumer publications are produced by government agencies as part of their mission to increase understanding and acceptance.

Advocacy Newsletter. Advocacy newsletters attempt to persuade readers by providing a consistent point of view and supportive information about a particular issue. Organizations that produce advocacy newsletters are likely to be focused on politics, the environment, health and safety, and other topics in which persuasion plays a key role. The U.N. Educational, Scientific and Cultural Organization posts various newsletters and other publications at unesco.org/archives.

Newsletter Writing

The planning process for newsletters involves attention to the wants, interests, and needs of key publics and to the objectives of the organization. This planning often leads organizations to develop a **mission statement** that sets out in writing the philosophy and commitment of the organization that publishes the newsletter. For example, the Gay and Lesbian Alliance Against Defamation presents this simple mission statement:

> The Gay & Lesbian Alliance Against Defamation (GLAAD) amplifies the voice of the LGBT community by empowering real people to share their stories, holding the media accountable for the words and images they present, and helping grassroots organizations communicate effectively. By ensuring that the stories of LGBT people are heard through the media, GLAAD promotes understanding, increases acceptance, and advances equality.

Editorial statements, meanwhile, may be more comprehensive and are focused on practical issues and details. They often include information on acceptance policies, publication criteria, style and tone, reprint guidelines, distribution schedules, and other practical information. Here's the editorial mission statement of *O* magazine:

> *"With this magazine we have an opportunity to make a real mark. To speak and connect to women in a way no other publication ever has. To help women see every experience and challenge as an opportunity to grow and discover their best self. To convince women that the real goal is becoming more of who they really are. To embrace their life."*—Oprah
>
> O's point of view puts a fresh spin on all the elements of a well-lived life—from fashion and beauty, to relationships, food, home design, books, health and fitness, work and finance, technology, self-discovery and caring for others.
>
> It's a banquet of lush images, generous in scale and spirit; a feast of good writing that offers women compelling ideas, good sense, good taste and a good time.
>
> Oprah has made a phenomenal success out of connecting with people where they live. The magazine, like her, conveys integrity, evokes trust, promises pleasure. It's inspiring, sensual, warm, intimate, energetic.
>
> The magazine talks heart-to-heart with the reader, encouraging her to think about her life, what is true for her, what she wants rather than just what is wanted of her.

Just as with news releases, public relations writers working on organizational newsletters need to generate interesting and relevant ideas. Often you will be aided by a close collaboration with the human resources department, as well as with various department heads and other employees.

A good public relations writer needs to access many different resources and to develop a nose for news within the organization so that the articles, especially features, can be of interest to the newsletter's audiences. Review the section on "Generating News" in Chapter 5. And remember that, even though you may be writing for an internal audience, you must satisfy your readers' news interests.

Audience Focus

The interests of the intended audience, defined in terms of key publics, will determine the content and writing style of the newsletter. Internal newsletters, for example, often are informal, while external newsletters may be much more businesslike. Special-interest newsletters show a variety of approaches, each reflecting the nature of a particular readership. Most newsletters take on the tone of the leadership of the organization that publishes them. Newsletters often suggest the personality of an organization: techy, open, issue oriented, growing, familial.

What can you write about in a newsletter? Whatever interests your readers. One way to identify those interests is to ask. Focus groups and readership surveys can be effective ways of learning about reader interests.

The writing process begins with the planning sheet. It is here that the writer carefully considers both the reader's interests and the organization's purpose for writing for this reader. The writing is made much easier when you visualize readers or, better yet, one individual—a typical reader who has the characteristics of your key public. It might be Aunt Bertha or Cousin Arlo, or the brother-in-law of your next-door neighbor. Maybe it's an old friend from high school. Whoever it is, conjure up an image and write to this person.

Newsletter Writing Style

Writing in effective newsletters often displays the following characteristics:

- Informal, but not chatty
- Businesslike language

- Strong verbs
- Few adverbs and adjectives
- Short sentences
- Quotes to personalize and brighten a story.

Newsletter writing generally is concise and crisp. Articles are often packaged in four to six paragraphs, and the average length for articles in most newsletters and organizational newspapers is between 300 and 500 words. Organizational magazines, meanwhile, generally feature much longer articles.

Newsletters generally include free use of jargon appropriate to the audience, but they should avoid clichés. They usually are supportive of the sponsoring organization without being overly promotional. They frequently present a respectful tone toward the sponsoring organization, for example, by using capital initial letters for departments and job titles that would be typed in lower case for external release. Appendix A: "Common Sense Stylebook for Public Relations Writers" notes how the standard Associated Press Stylebook might be modified for organizational newsletters.

Good newsletters also attempt to humanize the message by focusing on people, especially when the message deals with concepts and products. Remember that newsletter readers often share a closer relationship than readers of most other publications. They work for the same company, went to the same university, support the same zoo. They may know each other; they may share many of the same experiences and perspectives.

A good public relations writer should be flexible about various kinds of writing. Sometimes this means news-based writing that is appropriate for news releases. Other times it may involve more of an opinion or feature approach. The newsletter mission statement will determine the appropriate style, the objectives for a particular writing assignment, and the needs of the key

Exercise 13.2

Analyzing Newsletter Articles

Part 1: Obtain a copy of an organizational newsletter, perhaps one produced by your college or university. Check with your college/university relations department or with a specific group such as the alumni association, sports information department, or international exchange program. Identify the category of this newsletter: member, external, special interest, subscription, consumer, or advocacy. Write a brief explanation of why you identified this category.

Part 2: List each article in the newsletter. Identify the apparent key public, and rate each on how interesting you think it is to that public (using a scale of 1 = little or no apparent interest, 2 = some interest, 3 = much interest).

Part 3: Identify at least three other story ideas that you think would be of interest to the readers of this newsletter.

Part 4: Evaluate the overall effectiveness of this newsletter, based on your presumption of the intended key public.

public. Nevertheless, editors of internal newsletters, especially those published by corporations for their employees, are sometimes faced with the task of writing about corporate policies and regulations. This challenges the writer and editor to find an appropriate balance between policy detail and reader interest.

Exercise 13.3

Writing a Newsletter Article

Retrieve a copy of the news leads you prepared in Exercise 8.2 about the Happy Pup Company's grant to Dr. Aaron M. Jones. Select one of the leads, and add to it to prepare a full article for *Bow Wow Bulletin*, the monthly employee newsletter of the Happy Pup Company. Here is some additional information, to which you may add appropriate quotes and other relevant information:

- Company president Charles Emerson is preparing an extensive public relations campaign for next year, in which the company will aggressively seek out new clients. Part of this campaign will be an attempt to encourage people who do not currently have a pet to consider getting one. Thus, he sees the grant as helping to build a larger potential customer base for the company.
- The company public relations director, Tomiko Sagimoto, believes the grant complements the company's mission statement, which pledges Happy Pup to "promote responsible pet ownership that benefits both animals and humans." She has said on several occasions that the company should do more to be seen as an industry leader in enhancing human–animal relationships.
- Major competitors for Happy Pup include other premium-quality dog goods, including Iams and Science Diet, which together control approximately 60 percent of the premium dog food market in North America. HP now accounts for about 18 percent of sales of premium dog food.
- The Happy Pup marketing director, Candace Calloway, reports that the sale of HP dog food has stabilized after moderate decline, from a high three years ago of 22 percent of the market. She attributes the stabilization to a renewed advertising program, which last year cost $1.3 million. By contrast, the public relations budget is about $250,000. Ms. Calloway's current marketing plan calls for a greater use of public relations tactics to increase brand recognition among breeders, veterinarians, and pet owners.
- Happy Pup has 250 employees and distributes its products through pet shows, veterinarians, and grocery stores in every U.S. state and Canadian province.

Include a planning sheet with information that focuses on the key publics and their wants, interests, and needs.

Newsletter Headline

Headlines are both an information component and a design element of newsletters, and the effective writer will consider both of these aspects. As an information component, the headline is meant to summarize the article's contents and/or to attract reader interest. As design elements, headlines play a role in attracting a reader to a particular article and provide a graphical signal to the reader: This is where you should begin. For example, headlines at the top or center of a page, especially those with few words set in large type, will easily attract the reader's eye. Smaller and less imposing headlines, especially those in the bottom half of a page, suggest to the reader that these articles are of lesser importance.

For the writer, headlines pose a particular challenge: How to use just a few words to summarize an entire article or to intrigue a reader. Following are some guidelines for writing headlines, drawn from the disciplines of magazine and newspaper editing.

- Keep headlines short.
- Use short, easy-to-understand words.
- Whenever possible, use active voice.
- Use present or future tense.
- Use nouns and verbs but not complete sentences.
- Use strong words and phrases, each word packed with meaning.
- Do not allow words to break over to a new line.
- Keep prepositional phrases and verb phrases together rather than separating them onto two lines.
- Avoid all-cap headlines, which are difficult to read. Instead, use boldface type to attract reader attention to headlines or italic heads for features or softer news or to provide a visual contrast with other nearby headlines.
- Adopt a capitalization style. **Up style** calls for the capitalization of every word except short conjunctions and prepositions (such as *and, to*, and *of*). The more contemporary **down style** calls for the use of lower-case letters for everything except the first word of a headline and for proper nouns or proper adjectives. A newsletter may use either style, as long as the style is consistently applied.

Newsletters lend themselves to a variety of presentation formats for headlines. Here are some of the most common types of headlines.

Main News Headline. We are most familiar with main news headlines, which capsulize the information in the article. News headlines should include a verb so as not to become a mere label. Notice how the subject, verb, and object in the following example provide a sentencelike summary:

> Faculty senate seeks more evening classes

Standing Head. Another typographic device known as **standing heads** or **column heads** are labels for frequently used columns in newsletters. The best advice is to avoid them, because they can be pretty dull. Rather than writing headlines such as "President's Remarks" or "New Employees," try using these as kickers for a headline that captures the essence of the article.

Title. Some newsletters feature verbless titles rather than headlines. These can be effective particularly with online publications that may use a template with limited space for headlines. Here are some examples from a university online newsletter.

Student Scholarship Winners
AP Award for Internship Reporting
Sports Communication

Feature Head. While news heads summarize the contents of an article, **feature heads** are meant to entice the reader, often with a playful approach to language. Some feature headlines ask a question. Others promise that the reader will learn something new and of interest. Often this is written as a "how to." They often focus on the "selling point" of the article.

Fourteen Ways to Extend Your Gardening Season (*Mother Earth News*)

Yes, you can create your own job (*Public Relations Journal*)

How getting engaged will change your relationship (*Brides*)

How to teach ancient history: A multicultural model (*American Educator*)

Kicker. Typographic devices such as **kickers**, also called **overlines**, are introductory sections set in smaller type above the main news headline. They usually are short labels, though sometimes they can be written as longer explanations. Kickers can set the stage for the main headline or round it out to provide additional information for the reader. Kickers should be independent of the main head and should not read into it.

Dean opposed
Faculty senate seeks more evening classes

Dean calls plan "wasteful, needless"
Faculty senate seeks more evening classes

When Bad Dates Happen to Good People . . .
12 Real-Life Dating Disasters (and How to Avoid Them) (*Seventeen* magazine)

Deckhead. Another design element of many headlines is the use of a **deckhead** or **underline** following the main feature headline. In this style, the feature headline consists of a few powerful words, and the deckhead provides the context and substance of the accompanying article. The following headlines are from magazines, an excellent source of models for headline writers in newsletters.

Olé! Olé!
José María Olazábal of Spain reigned at the Masters to become the sixth European winner in seven years (*Sports Illustrated*)

Mama's WHITE
In two probing personal essays, a Black daughter and her White mother explore their love, their relationship and the sting of America's reaction (*Essence*)

The Family
Canadians see tradition in crisis even as a new poll uncovers enduring strength (*MacLean's*)

The Neighbors from Hell
Their kids are loud and unruly, their dog barks all night and their house is an eyesore. If you complain, it only makes matters worse. But there is hope for this all-too-common problem. (*Ladies' Home Journal*)

Exercise 13.4

Writing Headlines

Write the following types of headlines for one of the newsletter leads you wrote in Exercise 8.2 about the Happy Pup Company's grant:

- Main news headline
- Kicker with main news headline
- Feature headline with deckhead
- Title.

Corporate Report

Federal law requires companies that issue stock to publish **corporate reports** each year to their stockholders that discuss the company's financial activity and overall progress. Australia, Canada, and the European Union also require financial disclosure. Such information is important to investors, financial analysts, and business reporters. Meanwhile, governmental agencies and political groups are required to make public certain information, financial and otherwise. And many nonprofit organizations voluntarily provide their donors, members, and other constituents with information on finance, governance, programs, and other issues.

The purpose of such reporting is to provide for transparency in administrative issues and accountability to key publics.

Annual Report

Annual reports are formal corporate progress reports issued by companies and other organizations. The first corporate report was issued either by the Borden Company in 1854 or (depending on the definition of annual report) by the Vatican in Annuarium Statistum 1600. In 1899, the New York Stock Exchange began requiring companies to make public financial statements. In 1933, Congress required financial disclosure and a year later created the Securities and Exchange Commission and required annual reports.

Annual reports issued by many organizations go far beyond what the government requires. Many corporations develop elaborate magazinelike publications with high-quality graphics and well-written feature stories about the year's successes, new products, industry future, and so on. Annual reports can cost millions of dollars, adding pressure to the maxim: The most expensive annual report is the one not read.

Thus public relations people go to great lengths in designing, writing, and producing top-notch annual reports that grow from the interests and information needs of the intended readers. Some reports take the form of a booklet or a magazine, often with elaborate artwork and photography. Some organizations have experimented with newspaper or video formats. Most made the reports available online. A few are published in different languages, even in Braille.

Meanwhile, many nonprofit organizations voluntarily publish annual reports because they find it to be in their best interests to report to their key publics: employees, volunteers, donors, funding sources, government supporters, and others. Three-quarters of all annual reports are written in-house by company employees, according to a survey by the National Investor Relations Institute.

Though annual reports may differ in style and design, they often include the following elements:

- Distinctive cover and consistent design theme that reflect the organization's character
- Letter from the organization's CEO or chairman of the board
- Listing of directors and officers of the company
- Financial highlights of the previous year, and often a 10-year financial/management history, with plain-English text along with charts and graphs to explain the financial aspects of the company
- Description of the organization's products or services and the markets where they are sold, with an emphasis on new elements during the previous year
- Discussion of the industry or environment within which the organization operates
- Discussion of key issues facing the organization, perhaps with the organization's approach to those issues
- Audited financial statements, especially those required by the Securities and Exchange Commission, prepared by the company's financial staff to report on earnings, income, cash flow, and other financial matters
- An **opinion letter**, the official statement by an outside auditor attesting to the accuracy of the financial information
- Social-responsibility report on corporate philanthropy, environmental progress, and other benefits the organization brought to its community.

Planning the annual report begins like any other public relations tool: Identify and analyze the wants, interests, and needs of the key publics; indicate benefits for the publics; set public relations objectives; make decisions about the tone or the theme of the report; and consider how the effectiveness of the report will be evaluated.

Writing for annual reports calls for accuracy above all else. This means both technical accuracy in reporting numbers as well as an honest telling of the organization's story. Overly enthusiastic predictions and self-congratulation have no place in annual reports. Good narrative writing can personalize the numbers being reported.

Because annual reports are regulated by the SEC, typographical errors that involve statistics or financial projections are not only mistakes, they also are violations of the law requiring a company to be absolutely accurate when communicating officially with its stockholders. Writing and editing the annual report often involves working in close collaboration with the legal department. Financial relations experts tell of the need to have every page read and signed off before the publication can be printed.

Annual reports fit each category of public relations objectives: awareness, acceptance, and action. They mainly have an effect on awareness by providing information that allows key publics to better understand the organization. They also seek to create a favorable impression and foster a positive attitude toward the organization, but effective writers of annual reports make sure that their writing is honest and not simply corporate or organizational propaganda. Ultimately, they seek to have an effect on behavior, whether the purchasing of stock or other demonstrations of support.

Writers interested in working on corporate reports need to have a good understanding of three things: effective writing, public relations strategy, and corporate finance. Professional resources for this specialty include the National Investor Relations Institute at niri.org and a private website by Cato Communications (sidcato.com) that bills itself as the Official Annual Report website.

Effective annual reports also should be readable. Be particularly careful about using company jargon and bureaucratic language. The Fog Index and other readability issues were discussed in Chapter 2. Apply such a readability check to your written draft for annual reports. See "FYI: of Annual Reports" for a recent study.

FYI *Readability of Annual Reports*

Annual reports are difficult to read. That's unnecessary, it's getting worse, and it may be intentional. These are some conclusions that might be drawn from a 2006 study by Professor Feng Li at the University of Michigan.

A Fog Index of 12–14 is considered ideal in writing for annual reports. Higher than 18 is considered unreadable for most audiences.

Li found that annual reports in his study earned a rating of 19.4, meaning they require about 19 years of education (doctoral level) to be easily read and understood.

He also found that, for a few years following the SEC's plain-English requirement in 1998, readership levels of annual reports temporarily improved. But in recent years, it has become even more difficult for readers than before the SEC requirement.

In a more troubling finding, Li reported that annual reports of poorly performing companies are more difficult to read than those of companies that are doing well financially.

A cynic might suggest that this is an attempt on the part of corporate decision makers and their annual report writers to deliberately obscure bad information by burying it in a sea of spin, jargon, vagueness, and excess verbiage. More positively, an optimist would find in this an opportunity to model more ethical writing.

Graphically, annual reports should be reader friendly. Use clear headlines or section titles, with enough subheads to help the reader stay focused. Make sure that all pictures have informative captions. Use charts and graphs to give meaning to financial statistics. Sidebars and boxes also can be helpful for readers.

Quarterly reports and other organizational variations are much less regulated than annual reports. Many organizations use these as a kind of newsletter, brochure, or Web posting to keep their publics, particularly potential clients, informed about their activities.

Copy Editing

Publications require careful editing, because they carry the name of the organization and impact upon its reputation. Sloppy editing suggests either that the organization does not place a high priority on communicating with the reader or that professional standards are low.

An effective newsletter is a well-edited venue that enjoys the support and involvement of the organization's management without heavy-handed control. The newsletter addresses the mutual interest of both the organization and its readers, doing so in a way that is both professional and polished. Good editing is at the heart of such a publication.

Public relations writers pay attention both to copy editing and proofreading.

Copy editing is the process of reviewing the draft of a piece of writing to make it better. It involves fact checking, revising for style, correcting grammar, rewriting for smoother and more easily understandable language, and so on.

Proofreading is a follow-up, often final stage of the editing process. It involves identifying format problems and correcting errors.

Following are some guidelines to follow carefully while copy editing an organizational publication such as a newsletter or an annual report. "Tips for Better Writing: Proverbs for Proofreaders" offers additional suggestions for effective proofreading.

- *Check the facts.* Make sure names, statistics, and other information are accurate. Verify historical references. Be vigilant for information that raises ethical questions or that could lead to lawsuits.
- *Eliminate wordiness and redundancies.* Crisply edited newsletters avoid overwritten prose and wordiness, as well as unnecessary and belabored detail. Strive for clear and readable copy.
- *Use quotes with impact.* Make sure that material set off in quotation marks warrants the attention. Avoid the trap of presenting puff and fluff by scrutinizing every quote. If the information is merely factual data, paraphrase it. If it is overtly promotional or self-congratulatory, edit this out. On the other hand, keep the quotation that provides an insightful understanding or an effective explanation.
- *Use pull quotes to highlight important information.* A typographic and editorial device that originated with magazines, **pull quotes** are highlighted excerpts from an article that are used both as graphic elements to relieve columns of text and as ways to draw the reader's attention to particularly significant quotes. Pull quotes may be actual short quotes drawn from the article, or they may be edited quotes or even careful paraphrases.
- *Follow a stylebook.* Readers may not pay attention to editing details, but they will notice inconsistency of style. Some publications adopt a particular standard, notably the Associated Press Stylebook. Others create their own **house style**, modifying a style to their own editorial taste. Following the accepted stylebook can prevent unnecessary difficulties for editors, such as the embarrassment of capitalizing one person's title but not another's. Appendix A, "Common Sense Stylebook for Public Relations Writers," includes guidelines for house style. While consistent with the Associated Press Stylebook, this guide offers additional writing and editing principles for internal publications such as newsletters as well as for broadcast copy.
- *Use accepted copy-editing symbols.* Because more than one person is involved in the process of preparing copy for publication, writers and editors have developed a standard set of symbols and notations. Anyone involved in editing should use these symbols. Appendix E, "Copy Editing," provides examples of standard copy-editing symbols.

Tips for Better Writing *Proverbs for Proofreading*

1. *Love is nearsighted.* When you are the writer, editor, typist, or typesetter proofreading your own work, you will almost certainly suffer from myopia. You are too close to see all the errors. Get help.
2. *Familiarity breeds content.* When you see the same copy over and over again through the different stages of production and revision, you may well miss new errors. Fresh eyes are needed.
3. *If it's as plain as the nose on your face, everybody can see it but you.* Where is the reader most likely to notice errors? In a headline, in a title, in the first line, first paragraph, or first page of copy; and in the top lines of a new page. These are precisely the places where editors and proofreaders are most likely to miss errors. Take extra care at every beginning.
4. *When you change horses in midstream, you can get wet.* It's easy to overlook an error set in type that is different from the text face you are reading. Watch out when type changes to all caps, italics, boldface, small sizes, and large sizes. Watch out when underscores appear in typewritten copy.
5. *Don't fall off the horse in the home stretch.* Errors often slip by at the ends of tables, chapters, sections, and unusually long lines.
6. *Mistakery loves company.* Errors often cluster. When you find one, look hard for others nearby.
7. *The more, the messier.* Be careful when errors are frequent; the greater the number of errors, the greater the number of opportunities to miss them.
8. *Glass houses invite stones.* Beware of copy that discusses errors. When the subject is typographical quality, the copy must be typographically perfect. When the topic is errors in grammar or spelling, the copy must be error-free. Keep alert for words like *typographical* or *proofreading*.
9. *The footbone conneckit to the kneebone?* Numerical and alphabetical sequences often go awry. Check for omissions and duplications in page numbers, footnote numbers, or notations in outlines and lists. Check any numeration, anything in alphabetical order, and anything sequential (such as the path of arrows in a flowchart).
10. *It takes two to boogie.* An opening parenthesis needs a closing parenthesis. Brackets, quotation marks, and sometimes dashes belong in pairs. Catch the bachelors.
11. *Every yoohoo deserves a yoohoo back.* A footnote reference calls out for its footnote; a first reference to a table or an illustration calls out for the table or the illustration. Be sure a footnote begins on the same page or column as its callout. Be sure a table or illustration follows its callout as soon as possible.
12. *Figures can speak louder than words.* Misprints in figures (numerals) can be catastrophic. Take extraordinary care with dollar figures and dates and with figures in statistics, tables, or technical text. Read all numerals character by character; for example, read "1987" as "one nine eight seven." Be sure any figures in your handwriting are unmistakable.
13. *Two plus two is twenty-two.* The simplest math can go wrong. Do not trust percentages or fractions or the "total" lines in tables. Watch for misplaced decimal points. Use your calculator.
14. *Don't use buckshot when one bullet will do.* Recurring errors may need only one instruction instead of a mark at each instance.
15. *Sweat the small stuff.* A simple transposition turns *marital strife* into *martial strife*, *board room* into *broad room*. One missing character turns *he'll* into *hell*, *public* into *pubic*.
16. *Above all, never assume that all is well.* As the saying goes, "ass-u-me makes an ass out of u and me."

Used with permission. *Mark My Words: Instruction and Practice in Proofreading*, by Peggy Smith, published by EEI, 66 Canal Center Place, Suite 200, Alexandria, VA 22314.

Exercise 13.5

Copy Editing (Student Newsletter)

You are editor of *The Student Writer*, a newsletter aimed at college and university students. Edit the following newsletter article written by one of your staff reporters. Your aim is to make the article stylistically correct. Use the copy-editing symbols in Appendix B, "Copy Editing."

(Note: This exercise is available at the companion website www.routledge.com/cw/smith so you can print the draft and then mark the copy-editing symbols.)

"Trust Your Instincts" is the advice that Dr. Scholastica Penner often gives to her students at Outpost State Univ. "Effective writers are those who have learned when and how to following their intuition," I tell my students.

Dr. Penner believes there are three steps that writers can take in learning to trust rely on their instincts.

First, know yor writing preferences and predispositions in writing. For sample, do you naturally write wordy passages with alot of description and examples, or do you get to the point quick. In per suasive writing, do you typical present facts or do you weave a story to personalize the situation? Analyze your writing to identify your prefferences.

Two, determine what is needed by your audience or your medium. A newsletter, for example, may have only limited space, or raeders of a consumer magazine may expect fact's and comparisons. Third, compare your writing predispositions with this analysis of the audience and the medium. That will tell you if you can trust your instincts or if you need to intentionally write different.

"Either way you can be an effective writer," says Doctor penner. "This really is an example of when insight leads to effectivness."

Exercise 13.6

Copy Editing (Alumni Newsletter)

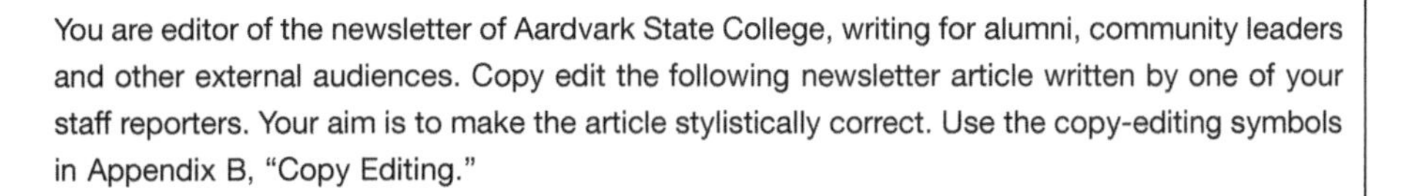

You are editor of the newsletter of Aardvark State College, writing for alumni, community leaders and other external audiences. Copy edit the following newsletter article written by one of your staff reporters. Your aim is to make the article stylistically correct. Use the copy-editing symbols in Appendix B, "Copy Editing."

(Note: This exercise is available at the companion website www.routledge.com/cw/smith so you can print the draft and then mark the copy-editing symbols.)

continued . . .

Exercise 13.6 . . . continued

FOR IMMEDEATE RELEASE

Mar. 15, 2011

AARDVARK STATE NAMES COMMUNICATION DIRECTOR Aardvark N.M.—Aardvark Sate Col. in Aardvark, New Mexico, today (15 March, 2011) announced that they has appointed a former newspaper editor and public relations practicioner, as the colleges new director of communication.

Roger Writesright will begin his new positon on April 1, 2011.

The Aardvark State President, Dr. Mariah Murphy said the new director of communications will oversee the work of the Colleges' advertising, marketing, and media relatiations directors, as well as the publications editor and web editor. He also will be part ofthe presdient's Council to advice on issues managementment, college reputation and crises communications

She proclaimed this new position was created so that the College it can integreat it's various communications activities.

Mr. Writesright said: "The consensus of opinion among large college presidents is that strategic communication plays a very unique role in todays management. I plan to bring my knowlidge of the new media and publec relations to help Aard vark Sate tell its' story more effectivly.

Wrightsright, is a former graduate of AArdvark state with a BS in journalism, 1985, and once was editor at the "Daily Times and Express" in Saint Louis, Mossouri. He also was a managing partner in Writesright and Spellsgood an award winning public relations agency from Seattle.

Intellectual Property Law

As we discussed in Chapter 7, issues of privacy and libel should be matters of concern to all public relations writers. Another area of law is especially significant for people writing for internal publications. This is the issue of **intellectual property**, an umbrella legal term including the concepts of copyright, trademark, and service mark. The term refers to the ownership of ideas.

Copyright

Copyright is the legal designation of ownership for original written and other artistic creations. When material is copyrighted, in most circumstances it may not be used without permission. The U.S. Copyright Act was revised in 1976. Copyright law protects articles, stories and opinion pieces, websites, blogs, newsletters, brochures, videos, public service advertisements, commercial advertisements, advertising copy, software, TV broadcasts, musical works and lyrics, artistic works (such as sculpture, paintings and photographs), and artistic performances (such as choreographs and dances).

Print news releases and other public relations materials aimed at the news media generally are not copyrighted because they are meant to be used without restriction by the media. However, some practitioners and communication attorneys suggest that some time and use restrictions may be appropriate for video news releases.

Copyright protection extends only to the fixed form of artistic works. It does not cover ideas themselves but rather merely the expression that a writer or artist has given to those ideas. Thus copyright law does not protect themes, plots, processes, formulas, or titles of books or plays. Nor does copyright law protect basic information such as calendars, measurement charts, and government documents. Likewise, it does not prohibit another writer from paraphrasing and referencing an original document.

Copyright Claims. The person who creates an artistic work can claim copyright in one of two ways. A **copyright notice** (also called **noticed copyright**) is claimed when the creator uses the word "Copyright," the abbreviation "Copr." and/or the international copyright symbol of the letter C inside a circle (©). Each type of designation also includes the year and the name of the person or organization owning the copyright. Here are some examples of how noticed copyright is referenced:

Copyright, 2011, Smith Communication Counsel

© 2011, Ronald D. Smith

© Copyright 2011, Smith Communication Counsel

The second you create something, it is copyrighted and protected. The Berne Convention for the Protection of Literary and Artistic Works presumes automatic copyright to the creator of artistic works, even if the copyright notice is not displayed. In 1989, the United States became one of the last of the 162 signer countries to adopt the Berne Convention.

Though a copyright notice is not necessary, it is easier to enforce copyright protection if the copyright is registered. In the United States, the copyright owner may register the copyright with the federal government (Copyright Office, Library of Congress, Washington, DC, 20559–6000; loc.gov/copyright). Currently this requires a $35 fee for basic online registration and submission of file copies (two for published works, one for unpublished works).

Fair Use. Copyright generally is meant to prevent others from using the copyrighted material, except with permission. Often, this permission is granted only by payment of a fee or royalty. However, there are certain **fair use** conditions under which copyrighted information may be used without permission:

- One fair use involves nonprofit or noncommercial purposes. For example, teachers and others involved in advancing knowledge or the public interest may use some copyrighted material with classroom students, giving proper credit to the copyright holder. Such fair use also includes news and commentary, satire, parody, and noncommercial research. Courts have extended this use to cover videotaping of television documentaries and news programs. Small numbers of newspaper or magazine reprints for internal use are considered fair use, but large numbers of reprints require permission; note that courts have not definitively established the exact number of reprints allowed. Fair-use provisions generally do not cover using copyrighted material for advertising or entertainment purposes. In 2003, federal courts ruled that fair-use provisions permit thumbnail photos on the Internet.

- Additionally, comment fair use extends to brief reviews or excerpts. Some courts have interpreted this as involving quotations of up to 400 words from a full-length book or up to 50 words for a periodical, though these limits are not defined by law. In working with reviews or excerpts, public relations writers always should give proper credit to the copyright holder.
- Another exemption is given for purposes of research. Generally, library users have been free to make copies of copyrighted material, both for personal use and for professional noncommercial research use. However, in the case of *American Geophysical Union v. Texaco*, a federal district court ruled that the fair-use provision of the copyright law does not allow corporate researchers to copy articles from library journals for use in their work with eventual profit potential.

Newsletter editors and other public relations practitioners need to recognize the distinction the Copyright Act makes between **original works** owned by an individual author or artist and **works for hire** owned by an organization that pays the author or artist, either as a salary or as a commission. The law presumes that an employer owns the copyright to artistic or creative works produced as part of the employee's job performance. This presumption affects people who work in public relations, either for an organization or an agency. However, freelancers are not considered employees unless a contract specifically identifies their creations as "works for hire." Otherwise, it is presumed that freelancers give a publisher only one-time rights and retain copyright ownership in their own name.

Public relations practitioners should give special attention to copyright issues involved in their work with freelance writers, photographers, and similar artists. In a 1989 case (*Community for Creative Non-Violence v. Reid*), the Supreme Court declared that a sculptor who used his own tools and studio, even though on commission to an organization, was not an employee and therefore retained ownership of his artistic creation.

Trademark

A **trademark** is a legal tool offering protection to a distinctive name, logo, word or phrase, symbol, design, and other unique identification of a company and its products. Trademarks are like the cattle brands of the Old West, identifying products as the property of particular companies or organizations. Even today, **brand name** is the common (though nonlegal) term for a trademark or a service mark.

Unlike copyrights that are meant to protect owners of creative works and prevent their use by others, trademarks are intended only to protect the relationship between a product name and the company that makes that product. Others may use the name, as long as it is identified with the company that holds the trademark.

Registered Trademark. The federal government administers trademarks through the U.S. Patent and Trademark Office of the Department of Commerce (uspto.gov). The Canadian Intellectual Property Office (opic.gc.ca) administers both trademarks and copyrights. Filing for U.S. trademarks costs $100 or more, depending on type of registration needed. Additionally, international assistance with trademarks is available from the International Trademark Association (inta.org).

The law makes a distinction between a **common trademark**, indicated by the small capital letters TM set in superscript (™) and a **registered trademark**, designated by a capital R in a circle (®). All trademarks are protected by law, but those registered with the Patent and

Trademark Office and identified by the trademark symbol are provided worldwide protection guaranteed by international treaties, enjoy more publicity, and generally are easier to enforce.

Trademark Protection. Companies go to great lengths to protect their trademarks because if the names slip into generic use, the companies no longer can maintain the link with their product. In effect, the company loses its distinctive name. Zipper, aspirin, mimeograph, escalator, yo-yo, and cellophane once were trademarks that lost their unique association with a particular company's product. Now any company may manufacture products under those names. This is why today, companies like Xerox worry about writers who incorrectly refer to "xeroxing" as a generic verb. Other companies work hard to protect the uniqueness of trademarks such as Coke, Kleenex, Plexiglas, Velcro, Walkman, and Scotch Tape. "FYI: Trademarks: Treat 'Em with Respect" lists some common terms that are protected as trademarks.

FYI *Trademarks: Treat 'Em with Respect*

Below are some common terms that are protected as trademarks. Writers should capitalize these terms when they are used in print. They also may be used with or replaced by their generic equivalents, noted here in parentheses.

- Astroturf (artificial grass)
- Band-Aid (adhesive bandage)
- Chap Stick (lip balm)
- Jell-O (gelatin dessert)
- Jockey (underwear)
- Kleenex (facial tissue)
- Nautilus (exercise machine)
- Novocain (anesthetic)
- NutraSweet (sugar substitute)
- Ping-Pong (table tennis)
- Pyrex (heat-resistant glassware)
- Q-Tip (cotton swab)
- Rolodex (card file)
- Scotch Tape (plastic tape)
- Scrabble (crossword game)
- Stetson (hat)
- Styrofoam (plastic foam)
- Teflon (nonstick coating)
- Vaseline (petroleum jelly)
- Walkman (portable cassette player)
- Weight Watchers (diet program)
- Xerox (photocopier)

Trademarks also protect phrases associated with companies and their products. "Reach Out and Touch Someone" belongs to AT&T. "This Bud's for You" is only for Budweiser. "We bring good things to life" is a claim only General Electric may make, and only Clairol may ask, "Does she or doesn't she?" Burger King is the only restaurant that may claim to be the "Home of the Whopper" and the *New York Times* is the only paper that has "All the News That's Fit to Print."

Corporate lawyers are vigilant in monitoring the use of trademarks, which extend beyond product names and slogans. Creations such as the Disney and the Peanuts characters, Barbie and Ken dolls, Superman, even college and sports mascots also are protected by trademarks. Trademark protection can extend even to faces and voices, and companies have been sued for using look-alike or sound-alike actors. For example, Bette Midler received a $400,000 jury award against an advertising agency that used a sound-alike in a car commercial. Vanna White successfully sued a company for using a Vanna-like robot in an advertisement.

A trademark protects not only Tarzan but also his yell, and *Vogue* magazine was sued for trademark infringement for a fashion feature entitled "Tarzan, Meet Jane."

Designs and packaging also are matters for trademark protection, and some companies have trademarked distinctive typographical treatments of their names, such as the interlocking Xs of Exxon and the backward R of Toys Я Us. Other examples are the McDonald's golden arches and the Apple apple.

Even the classic shape of a Coca-Cola bottle, the front grill of a Rolls Royce, and the goldfish shape of Pepperidge Farm snack crackers are protected as trademarks known as **trade dress**. Color is another element of trade dress. Protection has been extended to Owens-Corning for the use of the pink color of its insulation and the black-and-yellow packaging of Kodak film. Trade dress often carries the same legal protections as unregistered trademarks.

Companies and nonprofit organizations take great care to protect their trademarked items. Look at information from the Cooperative Forest Fire Prevention Program at 2004_Smokey_Bear_Guidelines.doc. You'll find a 17-page guide on how to properly and legally use the Smokey Bear mascot in advertising, art, educational materials, and personal appearances. The guide includes detailed color formulas for various parts of the iconic bear (hat, eyes, face, muzzle, pants, belt, buckle, and so on). It also details how Smokey may be used (never endorsing a product; not with other characters; always presenting a message on wildfire prevention).

Corporate attorneys and public relations practitioners sometimes turn their attention to other legal issues surrounding trademarks. For example, trademarks are not permitted for names that are deceptive or immoral. On the latter point, morality groups in both England and North America challenged the right of UK-based clothing company French Connection to trademark its acronym, fcuk™, saying it was a thinly veiled allusion to an obscenity, especially when used with its products such as its "fcuk him™" and "fcuk her™" fragrances and T-shirts with "fcuk me™" and "fcuk football™." The company had to go to court to retain the right to use its acronym as a trademark.

Although companies are vigilant in protecting their trademarks, courts have been reluctant to require journalists and other writers to likewise protect companies. Ted Davis, a specialist in intellectual property law, said courts put the pressure on people who use a company's trademark as if it were their own. But there's not much legal action against writers. Writing in *Editor and Publisher* (December 3, 2001), Davis said there isn't much a company can do other than send an intimidating letter to a writer who has used a trademarked name generically.

Writing about Trademarks. At the very least, public relations writers should capitalize trademarked names in print. Trademarked names also may be followed by the word "brand" and/or by an appropriate generic noun, such as Kleenex tissues or Jell-O brand gelatin. For internal publications such as newsletters on organizations and websites, and in their blogs and Tweets, public relations writers often treat trademarked words distinctively, perhaps printing them in all-capital letters, using boldface or italic type, setting them in quotation marks, even printing them in color. Internal publications often feature the trademark symbol as well.

In line with journalistic stylebooks, writers generally do not do this for news releases but rather would capitalize the first letter of the trademarked word and perhaps follow it with the trademark symbol and the word "brand." Often they include a reminder, frequently as a final paragraph of a news release or note to editors, pointing out that a particular term is a registered trademark that must not be used generically.

When public relations writers refer to the trademarked product of companies other than their own, they may determine that the actual trademarked name is not essential to meaning. If this is the case, the trademarked name can be eliminated completely, leaving only a generic reference, for example, to tissues or gelatin.

Service Mark

A **service mark** is similar to a trademark, except that it protects symbols and words associated with services and programs rather than product names. Service marks enjoy the same legal protections as trademarks and also are protected by the U.S. Patent and Trademark Office. Examples of service marks are names such as Maid Brigade for the cleaning service and the Hugo Award of the World Science Fiction Society. Both the Better Business Bureau name and the torch logo are service marks of the Council of Better Business Bureaus, Inc. Only Huntington Beach, Calif. can claim to be Surf City USA^{SM}, and only the U.S. Army Reserve can legally use the slogan “Be All That You Can Be.”

When organizations wish to point out that their phrase is a service mark, they may follow it with small capital letters SM set in superscript (^{SM}). The letters are in a circle if the service mark is registered with the Patent Office.

14 Website, Blog, and Wiki

It's almost inconceivable to think of any self-respecting organization that would not have a website these days. Websites provide so much online interaction between an organization and its publics that we have to wonder just how organizations did business in the days (not so long ago) before the Internet. The technology offers many opportunities to enhance the public relations mission of any organization.

The strategic presentation of information in websites and blogs is much the same as for other types of public relations writing. This means knowing the organization's objectives, understanding who the publics are and what benefits-based messages might be addressed to them, identifying persuasive sources and effective message strategies, and having a plan to evaluate the communication.

Online writing itself tends to be crisper in style and usually shorter in length than writing for either print or broadcast. Public relations writers have found that writing for websites and blogs calls for them to be concise, to write with an objective tone rather than a promotional one, and perhaps to be somewhat informal in their writing. All this within a structure that is scannable (more on that later in this chapter).

This chapter will consider writing for websites and blogs, as well as standards for evaluating their effectiveness. It also will deal with wikis and the role they can play in an organization's public relations program. Here are your learning objectives for this chapter:

- To analyze a website for effective presentation of information
- To plan a blog to support an organization's public relations plan
- To write effective blog posts for public relations purposes.

Website

The Internet is an amazing tool for public relations communication and one of the most commonly used media. In a few short years, the Internet has changed the way organizations communicate with their publics. It's difficult to understand how we communicated efficiently before the Internet.

Virtually all organizations have an Internet presence via a website, often with interactive features. Hotels provide online booking of rooms. Churches and mosques use websites to promote religious services and provide religious education. Theaters stream movie trailers online. TV stations use the Internet to post stories they didn't have time for on air. Political candidates and elected officials use their websites to raise money, advocate their positions, and interact with their constituents.

As a public relations writer, you should be aware of the relationship among the major elements of a website: structure, graphics, organization, and writing.

Effective Web managers also pay careful attention to how information flows, specifically the ease and efficiency with which readers can navigate through all the information at the site. Web pages often are designed with elegant and catchy graphics; this is what wins awards and grabs the attention of clients and readers alike. As important as information flow and graphics are, writing is even more important. Too often, not enough attention is given to writing at websites.

It's important to understand how readers use the Internet. The Web is not a linear medium, with users moving from Point A to Point B. Rather, it is an interactive and interlinking medium. Online readers are used to finding their own way through the information, and effective public relations writing should make their journey easy and efficient.

Web designers sometimes simply drop in existing text and focus most of their attention on the look and flow of the site. It's called **shovelware**, carrying text from one storage medium to another without adapting it to the destination medium. So we find websites that simply repeat the text of a brochure. That misses the point completely. Readers will return to a website only when the written information gives them solid reason to return.

Web writers must be translators of the written word, transposing it into an online format. That's why, earlier in this textbook, we presented information on how to tailor text-based news releases for multimedia purposes instead of merely posting the print version online. It's the same reason that newspapers develop Internet-oriented news articles instead of merely posting the story as it was published in the morning edition.

How can you accomplish this? Like any good public relations writing, Web writing begins with a planning sheet. Be clear with yourself about your key publics—who they are, what they are interested in, and what they need to know. Also be clear about what they *don't* need to know. Remember that with the Internet, an organization can address several different publics through the same online site.

Additionally, the planning sheet should articulate your organization's objectives in developing the website. Particularly important in planning a website is to consider the reading level of your key publics, as well as their fluency and familiarity with the Internet.

Jakob Nielsen, a leading researcher on writing for the Internet, recommends that online writing should be concise, scannable, and objective. Each of these elements is described in the following sections. "Tips for Better Writing: Measuring the Effects of Web Writing" describes one of Nielsen's research projects. As you look through various websites, pay attention to how the points discussed below are exhibited in these pages.

Nielsen's recent studies have looked at how different groups of Web users read online material. He has noted that low-literacy readers are less likely to scan text. Instead they often focus on each word with a narrow field of vision, ignoring objects outside the main flow of the text. Alternatively, when things become complicated, they skip over whole chunks of text. In addition, they easily lose their place when they have to scroll down pages.

Spelling deficiencies of low-literacy readers, meanwhile, often diminish the usefulness of a website's internal search features. Similar difficulties have been studied involving people with disabilities as well as with teenagers, who often have both low reading abilities and little patience for dealing with texts that are not user-friendly.

All of these issues can cause problems for a Web writer, but the difficulties can be minimized with a few writing practices: Write to a 6th-grade reading level, prioritize information, avoid animated text, streamline page design, and simplify navigation.

You can make online writing more effective by ensuring that it is concise, scannable, objective, and interactive. Let's look at each of these.

Concise Web Writing

The same rules and recommendations that guide other types of public relations writing are important in online writing. Effective writing is short, active, and clear. It also should be accurate and stylistically consistent.

Presume that Web readers will scan and peruse online pages rather than read the content word for word. An obvious exception to this is the presentation of the full text of a piece of writing, such as magazine articles and teaching materials. Your readers will follow such text using scrolling pages.

Try to make the full text an option for the reader rather than the only choice. Further, assist readers by making it easy for them to download longer documents to disk and print full texts for easier reading on paper.

Following is a look at each of the various characteristics of effective online writing.

- *Keep Web writing short.* Computer screens are harder on the eye than printed pages in magazines or newspapers. A survey by Sun Microsystems found that 70 percent of people who visit websites scan the material rather than read it word for word.
- *Write for a single screen.* Studies also have found that most readers do not scroll; they read the information available on the opening screen and then generally move on. Try to limit your online information to a single screen, two at the most.
- *Use active voice.* Just as with other media, Web writers should use active voice because it is clear, more direct, and more powerful.
- *Write clearly.* Studies show that generous use of subheads helps the reader flow through the text. Make sure subheads are meaningful rather than cute. Headlines should be self-explanatory, and their context should be self-evident. Web pages are not a good place for feature or teaser heads; stick with the conventional summary news headlines or with plain titles.
- *Emphasize accuracy.* Correct grammar and spelling are important in any medium, but errors seem to leap from a video monitor. Proofread carefully. Use the spell check and grammar check, but don't rely solely on your computer to make everything right. The ultimate responsibility for accurate writing lies with the writer, ideally with the assistance of an editor.
- *Adopt a style guide.* As with any other writing medium, online writing calls for consistency. Some organizations adopt a standard style guide—such as the widely used Associated Press Style or the more literary Chicago Style or MLA (Modern Language Association) Style. Others modify these or develop their own online style guide. The Common Sense Stylebook in Appendix A gives you a start with this. Style guides often include not only assistance in writing, spelling, capitalization, and usage, but also standards for the type font and size, bullets, colors, and templates. As an example, look at the online style guide adopted by the Environmental Protection Agency (epa.gov/productreview/guide/app3.html) and another by National Geographic

(nationalgeographic.com > "The Magazine" > "NG Style Manual"). Style guides also often identify specific dictionaries and other printed or online reference works as the final word; they also may identify how the organization uses its own trademark and other references to patents or copyrighted information. The Web Style Guide (webstyleguide.com) developed by writer Patrick Lynch and technology specialist Sarah Horton is a helpful resource for online writers.

Scannable Web Writing

Effective online writing should be **scannable**. That is, it should feature information that is chunked into segments, making it easy for the reader to move through it. Physiologically, it is more difficult to read from a computer monitor than it is from a printed sheet of paper.

Remember the nature of online reading when you are developing your site. In particular, pay attention to how the text is displayed. Present information according to the inverted pyramid model, and use user-friendly writing elements such as summaries and tables of contents. Additionally, use simple background designs, make sure the page loads quickly, and don't use high-resolution photographs and other demanding graphics unless they are necessary.

Chunked Text. Avoid long paragraphs and lengthy passages of unrelieved text, which are more difficult to read on a monitor. If lengthy passages are necessary, break them down into several shorter sections that are easier to comprehend.

Links and Navigation Tools. The ease of using websites is increased when the site has well-placed links to help users navigate around the site. Links need to be clear so the user is not left wondering where to go next for wanted information. Check your outlinks often to make sure they are still active. Likewise, good websites have clear navigation tools, forward and back arrows, returns to home pages, and other aids to help users find their way around the site.

Display. Accent the text with a variety of visual elements to emphasize key words or concepts. Consider typographical devices such as bullets, indents, italics, boldface, underlines, and colored text. But don't overdo these to the point of distraction. Be generous in your use of headlines, titles, and subheads.

Table of Contents. Consider adding a table of contents to your Web pages so the reader can easily navigate throughout your site. When providing a table of contents, make it easy for a reader to find a particular page. For example, it may be easy for a public relations office to arrange news releases in an archive by release date, but that doesn't necessarily help a reader find a particular release. Consider arranging them topically rather than chronologically. Another helpful feature is a site map that presents an outline of how your site is put together.

Inverted Pyramid. The standard journalistic format is a good one to use in online writing. Begin with the conclusion or summary, then follow with supporting information, and finally incorporate background information.

Summary. Many Web users read only the first sentence of a paragraph, and effective Web pages often include carefully crafted topic sentences for each paragraph. Some sites providing news-based information have found it useful to begin with a summary paragraph set apart from a following news article. A good way to accommodate readers is to provide a summary and a hypertext link to the longer story or the full text. That way, readers can read or print only the summary without wasting time on the longer text if it isn't relevant. This is a good place for the Twitter-like summary from the planning sheet.

Legible Text. Use a simple type font, preferably a serif font, with both capital and lowercase letters for easiest reading. Use black lettering on a white or light background. Less effective is reverse type, dark-colored text that contrasts with a light background (less effective because studies show that most people find it more difficult to read). Use text large enough for your readers. In general, avoid text that is moving, blinking, or zooming. Remember also that color-blindness is fairly common. An estimated 8 percent of Caucasian males—nearly one in 12—are unable to distinguish between reds and greens. The rate is less than half that for men of African origin and 3 percent for men of Asian background. Color-blindness is very rare among women; only about 0.5 percent have the deficiency.

Simple Background. Don't overload your pages with fancy designs or graphics. A simple background color is preferable to a background pattern, which not only can get in the way of reading but also can make printing difficult and loading times long. If you choose to use photos or graphics, make certain they are relevant to the text. Don't include graphics just for show. When they are integral to your story or report, consider including them as hypertext links rather than fixing them within the text. That will make it easier for users to read and print the text only, the graphic only, or both, depending on the reader's interest. Also, when using photos, always include a caption.

Objective Web Writing

Nielsen's research shows that unexaggerated, nonpromotional Web writing is measurably more effective than hype, or **marketese**, because the latter is often associated with advertising and other marketing communication (see "Tips for Better Writing: Measuring the Effects of Web Writing"). As such, it is important that Web writing be journalistic and balanced in nature and should include links to other sites.

Tips for Better Writing *Measuring the Effects of Web Writing*

Jakob Nielsen, a prolific researcher and recognized expert on Web usability, advises that Web users detest promotional writing with boastful subjective claims. He and research partner John Morkes tested five different versions of the same message about Nebraska tourism, using four performance measures (time, errors, memory, and site structure). Here are the test messages and their results.

Promotional writing using "marketese," which the researchers calculated with a base of 0 percent of reading effectiveness:

> Nebraska is filled with internationally recognized attractions that draw large crowds of people every year, without fail. Some of the most popular places were Fort Robinson State Park (355,000 visitors a year), Scotts Bluff National Monument (132,166), Arbor Lodge State Historical Park & Museum (100,000), Carhenge (86,598), Stuhr Museum of the Prairie Pioneer (60,002), and Buffalo Bill Ranch State Historical Park (28,446).

Concise (nonpromotional) text, calculated as 58 percent better writing:

> In 1996, six of the best attended attractions in Nebraska were Fort Robinson State Park, Scotts Bluff National Monument, Arbor Lodge State Historical

continued . . .

Tips for Better Writing *Measuring the Effects of Web Writing . . . continued*

Park & Museum, Carhenge, Stuhr Museum of the Prairie Pioneer, and Buffalo Bill Ranch State Historical Park.

Scannable layout, 47 percent better writing:

Nebraska is filled with internationally recognized attractions that draw large crowds of people every year, without fail. In 1996, some of the most popular places were:

- Fort Robinson State Park (355,000 visitors)
- Scotts Bluff National Monument (132,166)
- Arbor Lodge State Historical Park & Museum (100,000)
- Carhenge (86,598)
- Stuhr Museum of the Prairie Pioneer (60,002)
- Buffalo Bill Ranch State Historical Park (28,446).

Objective language, 27 percent better writing:

Nebraska has several attractions. In 1996, some of the most visited places were Fort Robinson State Park (355,000 visitors), Scotts Bluff National Monument (132,166), Arbor Lodge State Historical Park & Museum (100,000), Carhenge (86,598), Stuhr Museum of the Prairie Pioneer (60,002), and Buffalo Bill Ranch State Historical Park (28,446).

Combined improved version (concise, scannable and objective), calculated as 124 percent better writing:

In 1996, six of the most visited places in Nebraska were:

- Fort Robinson State Park
- Scotts Bluff National Monument
- Arbor Lodge State Historical Park & Museum
- Carhenge
- Stuhr Museum of the Prairie Pioneer
- Buffalo Bill Ranch State Historical Park.

In reporting his test, Nielsen said he expected the performance outcome to be similar for promotional and objective writing. Instead, he found that the more objective the writing, the more usable and preferable it was for the readers.

Why? Nielsen suggested that the finding could be explained by his observation that promotional language imposes a **cognitive burden** on users, who must expend mental energy to filter out the hype from the facts, which in turn slows them down and distracts them from gaining usable, memorable information.

Nielsen's Web research and advice are available at his website: useit.com

Journalistic. Avoid promotional writing associated with advertising and other aspects of marketing. Web writing needs to be more journalistic—objective, neutral, professional, and unexaggerated. Let the information stand on its own.

Balance. It often is difficult to find just the right balance between the public relations and marketing needs of an organizational website. Remember, however, that research on reader usability is on the side of unexaggerated, nonpromotional writing.

Outbound Links. Inviting your reader to visit other sites is good business. It enhances your credibility much the same as citations enhance an academic report. In both cases, the author is helping readers compare information and ideas with those of other sources. Make sure to check these often, and purge or update any dead links pointing to nonexistent sites.

Interactive Website

An advantage of websites is that they can be made interactive, with opportunities for readers to communicate with the organization and vice versa. This provides a great benefit to public relations practitioners trying to connect their organizations and publics in meaningful ways. Following is an overview of some of the ways in which an organization's website can engage users.

E-Mail Link. Among the simplest ways to accomplish this is to include a "mailto" hot link back to the organization or to a menu of key staff within the organization. This lets the user click on the appropriate icon and be offered the opportunity to write, edit, and send an e-mail message to the organization. It is good to supplement this with a listing of traditional contacts, such as telephone numbers, fax numbers, and postal addresses.

Electronic Forms. E-mail responses can be structured so the user provides asked-for information that can be edited and then submitted to the host website. Such information can deal with online scheduling, applications, order forms, surveys, and a range of other uses.

Search Feature. A feature that can greatly enhance the interactive aspect of a website is an internal search function, such as a pull-down menu that allows the user to click onto various pages or to link to a certain topic. Other search tools allow users to type in a word or phrase and link to the appropriate online page. A study on Internet usability by Jakob Nielsen found that half of all Web users depend on a site's search function rather than do their own navigating.

Audio Options. New technology makes it easier to include in a website options for voice, music, audio news clips, and sound effects. Because of the unevenness of user capabilities, it is best to offer these as on-demand options rather than trying to imbed them in a basic website.

Video Options. Web designers can use video for purposes similar to audio, and it can be useful in product or service demonstrations, news clips, artistic performances, and so on. For audiences used to television, computer-based video options can provide valuable information in an agreeable format. But remember that standard production values should be maintained. Dull, corporate talking heads are no more exciting on the computer screen than they are on the television screen. Technological developments offer new ways to deliver video over a website, such as streaming video or downloads.

Animation. Technology also offers possibilities for including animation, such as three-dimensional views of models and graphics, virtual tours, transitions, and so on. Keep animation to a minimum, because many users find it more annoying than helpful. Also make sure it is appropriate to the organization. Use it with a strategic purpose rather than simply for effect.

Cookie Technology. Another aspect of interactivity is the ability of Internet technology to help the organization anticipate the interest of individual visitors to the website. **Cookies** are information that becomes active whenever the user connects to a particular website. They enable the site to "remember" information about the user—name, previous connections, stated interests, and so on. Thus the organization can deliver messages of particular interest to the user. A website that is designed by an organization committed to ethical communication will tell visitors about its use of cookies, offer users the opportunity to disengage the technology, and explain how the cookie-gathered information will be used or shared.

E-Commerce. Nonprofit and political fundraising organizations can use e-commerce technology to receive online contributions from donors. In addition to online payment systems, common e-commerce features include online applications, order forms, order tracking, and requests for information.

Pop-Up Window. Using Java programming, websites can feature **pop-up windows** (also called **interstitials**) that can enhance user interaction. This feature could provide users with a variety of public relations messages or opportunities to contact the organization or obtain information on demand. Sometimes, pop-up windows can include streaming audio or streaming video, which immediately engages the visitor. To aid readers, consider allowing users to skip such windows. Repeat visitors will greatly appreciate this.

Website Evaluation

Websites can provide top-quality information or plain old garbage, and it's important to be able to determine the difference. Remember that anybody with Internet access and minimal computer skills can put together a Web page. If you are developing a site for your organization, keep in mind some of the objective criteria for evaluating online information, so you can build into your site the necessary ingredients that will identify your site as one of excellence. The following sections describe some objective criteria for evaluating websites.

Tips for Better Writing *Evaluating Websites*

Here is a checklist of things to look for in evaluating any website, your own or someone else's.

- Concise writing
- Pages viewable on one or two screens
- Chunked text
- Easy-to-follow navigation links
- Legible text
- Simple background
- Objective, journalistic writing style
- Recognized sponsor
- Verifiable and documented information
- Authoritative information
- Objective information
- Up-to-date information, with appropriate updates
- Comprehensive information
- Outbound links
- Ease of navigation within site
- Logical flow of pages
- Quick loading
- Appropriately interactive
- Appropriately accessible, accountability for language use and disability
- Cultural sensitivity.

Recognized Sponsor. A quality website is one that is hosted by a legitimate and recognized organization or individual. The domain name of most websites reflects the name of the sponsoring organization. For example, the domain name of most college or university websites will feature some variation of the institution's name, followed by .edu. A university name followed by .com might indicate a rogue site set up by someone wishing to embarrass the institution or to mislead online visitors. The user should readily be able to determine the difference. Sometimes, spyware and other intruders hijack legitimate websites and divert visitors to rival, commercial, or even fake sites.

Verifiable Information. Quality websites provide documentation about the source of their information. The source could be an individual, an organization, or a document such as a research report, but the user should be able to easily identify where the information originally came from. An e-mail contact should be provided for the author or webmaster.

Authoritative Information. Information at websites should be attributed to an expert authority, such as the site host or another expert. The site should include information about the qualifications and credentials of the author of the page or site. It should be clear whether information reflects the official organizational information or the opinion of one person.

Objective Information. It should be clear to the user whether a website is advocating a cause, selling a product or service, soliciting support, or offering objective information.

Up-to-Date Information. Websites should be kept current. Quality sites will note revision dates not only for the home page but also for substantive inside pages. Pay particular attention to sites that provide information based on annual statistics; these should be no more than a year old.

Comprehensive Information. The best websites provide a range of information about topics relevant to the sponsoring organization and potential users.

Audio-Visual Elements. Features such as photos, animations, and audio or video clips can be useful enhancements for a website. These elements should explain, clarify, and supplement the written information.

Quick-Loading Features. Downloads for Web pages should be quick. Studies show that users often abort downloads that take too long to load. Images, charts, and unnecessary coding and META tags can slow download time. Make sure the text loads before the graphics. If you wish to use a photo, keep it small, perhaps with a link to a larger version at a separate page. Remember that while the site may load easily on *your* computer, some people may not have access to state-of-the-art hardware or software. Make sure your site is accessible to average users. Consider offering a flexible menu of download options, such as both a flash version and a simpler loading format.

User-Friendly. Websites should be well designed, with the user in mind. It should be easy for users to locate information. Site maps, menus, and internal search tools can be particularly helpful to a visitor who may be unfamiliar with the structure of the website or the organization sponsoring it. Easy-to-navigate sites also feature both quick-loading pages and single-screen pages, as well as "Back," "Next," and "Menu" buttons.

Accessibility. Websites should be accessible to anyone who might be counted as the audience. For sites with an international focus, this may mean that they should offer multilingual sites or translations into various languages.

An Internet marketing firm, Internet World Stats, reported in 2010 that Asians account for 42 percent of all Internet users, followed by 24 percent for Europeans, 14 percent for North Americans, 10 percent for people in Latin America and the Caribbean, 6 percent for Africans, 3 percent for people in the Middle East, and 1 percent for residents of Oceania and Australia. The highest growth rate is found in Africa, the Middle East, and Latin America.

The report also focused on Internet penetration—the percentage of a population with access to the Internet. Worldwide, the penetration is only 29 percent, but this is steadily growing (nearly doubling in the past three years). Top-ranked countries include Iceland (where

97 percent of the population has access to the Internet), Norway (94 percent), Sweden (92 percent), and Greenland (90 percent). Other countries with high penetration include South Korea (81 percent), Japan (78 percent), and the United States and Canada (both 77 percent).

English is the most common Internet language (27 percent), followed by Chinese (23 percent), Spanish (8 percent), Japanese (5 percent), and Portuguese (4 percent). Together these five languages account for two-thirds of all online languages.

All in all, this is a lot of statistics—but they point to the advisability for public relations writers to be aware of this diversity and perhaps to be accessible to a wide variety of potential online visitors.

Websites also might need to be made accessible to persons with visual, hearing, or motor handicaps. Some organizations are required to make their websites conform to guidelines of the Americans with Disabilities Act or to similar laws and regulations in other countries.

Cultural Consideration. In addition to the above general criteria, some websites call for special consideration, often based on cultural factors. For example, in evaluating a website dealing with American Indian issues, here are some additional questions to ask about the site: Is it authentic? Is a specific tribal affiliation noted (a common practice among most Native peoples)? Is the tribal name accurate (for example, the Native term Lenape instead of the English-colonial equivalent, Delaware)? If the site claims to present a tribal view, does the tribal government authorize it, and does it include the presence of the president, chairman, or chief? Does the site feature images that are contemporary and respectful? Is cultural and historic information authoritative and verified?

Exercise 14.1

Analyzing Websites

Select two websites for similar organizations (such as two universities, two auto dealerships, two sports teams, etc.) or use two sites identified by your instructor.

Part 1: Do a side-by-side comparison on each of the following points as outlined above:

- Sponsor (including reliability, credentials)
- Verifiable information (including author contact info)
- Authoritative information (including both the quality of info presented and the written presentation itself in terms of spelling and punctuation)
- Objective information (including journalistic versus marketing language)
- Up-to-date information
- Comprehensive information
- Audio-visual elements
- Quick loading features
- User-friendliness (including search features)
- Accessibility
- Cultural consideration

Part 2: Write an overall assessment of each site. Note whether the purposes seems to be to provide information or advocacy. As a visitor to the site, evaluate how effective you find it to be.

Blog

A **blog** is a type of website built around a series of **posts** (also called **entries**). These are separate (usually short) articles, each with a title and body. Usually each post includes a section for reader comments. Blogs generally are posted with the most recent entries first. Posts can be coded so readers can reorganize them by category (as it was designated by the blogger) and by publishing date (usually by the month).

Different from a blog post is a **blog page**, which contains information that doesn't change. A blog might have pages dedicated to specific topics, such as an "About Us" (or "About Me") section, audio or video posts, a photo gallery, or editorial policy.

Blogs also include external links, such as an organization might provide to lead readers to its website, Facebook or MySpace page, YouTube site, and other organizational sites online.

Most early blogs were written by individuals, often as a kind of online diary to express their opinion or post personal rants. Gradually, public relations writers adopted blogs as a tool for their organizations and clients to communicate with their publics. This type of blog often has several contributing editors. Entries generally indicate the name of the author of each post.

Blogs allow an individual or an organization to serve as a type of online newspaper. In the past, public relations people had to get through the media gatekeepers (editors, reporters, news directors, and so on) to have their information presented as news to media audiences. With blogs, public relations writers can publish their news online without the gatekeeper intermediary.

This brings both advantages and disadvantages. The obvious advantage is that an organization can be its own reporter, editor, and publisher, posting information directly for readers. A disadvantage is that readers have learned that, despite occasional flaws and missteps, newspapers and TV news stations try to be objective as they sift through information, presenting for their audiences only information that is accurate and complete. As a result, audiences often place higher credibility in news organizations and in information posted directly by an organization at its blog or website.

Blog versus Website

What's the difference between a blog and a website? A blog is designed for easy updates and interaction between the organization and readers. That's an advantage for blogs. A website may include such features, but not necessarily. Websites went through guest books and discussion boards, but it was the innovation of the blog (literally **web log**) that made it easy for organizations to engage their readers.

On a blog, every article can invite and display reader comments, allowing readers to interact not only with the organization but also with each other. The comments function much like a letters-to-the-editor column in a newspaper or magazine. Generally the reader comments are not visible to blog readers, who must click on the "Comments" section to link to entries there. These generally also are presented in reverse chronological order. Blog editors generally can disable specific comments if they feel the reader has posted something contrary to the editorial policy of the blog.

An advantage that websites have over blogs is that they can provide much more information and can allow readers to drill down through various layers of information. The downside of this is that, too often, organizations use websites for static information, as a sort of online brochure.

Whereas websites can offer readers navigation around the site, a blog pretty much lays it all out in a single view, with time-stamped articles presented in chronological fashion (newest to oldest). Most blogs feature archives to organize and store older posts.

In practical terms, the differences between websites and blogs are disappearing, as technology makes websites easier to create and manage, particularly by easy posting of information and by engaging readers. Likewise, digital technology is allowing blogs to become more multidimensional so they can move beyond primarily being a series of chronological postings.

Many blogs exist primarily as newsletters. Others feature newsletters as a major ingredient. Blog newsletters offer several benefits for an organization's public relations program. Here are a few:

- Blog newsletters develop a long-term relationship between the organization and its publics, creating loyalty and a reason for people to keep coming back to the organization's online site.
- Blog newsletters also can invite subscribers who sign up to receive e-mail notices when a new blog is posted, creating more traffic for the site.
- Because most blogs feature a comments section, newsletter blogs serve as a focus for interaction and engagement between the organization and blog readers.

Additionally, some organizations have found ways to use blogs as part of their media relations program. Some participate in general reporter blogs such as Help a Reporter Out (helpareporter.com), a free site with separate sections for reporters and for sources, and PitchEngine (pitchengine.com), a tool linking journalists and public relations professionals.

Attracting Readers

Audiences for blogs vary, though it is more or less an adult activity that fits well with the key publics of many organizations. A 2010 report by the Pew Research Center found that blogs are being read less often by teens and young adults, who instead pay more attention to social media sites.

In planning your blog, go back to the planning sheet that you have developed for most of your other writing tasks. Make this planning sheet about the entire blog, rather than a specific entry. Run through the process: Who are your publics, how are they connected with your organization, and what do they need or want? What benefit can you offer them? What tone is appropriate for your writing? What are your intended outcomes, and what do you expect to achieve through this blog? What is the readability level of your potential readers?

Make your blog writing about your readers' interests rather than your own. You may want to promote your clothing store, but you can't turn all your blogs into sales pitches without losing readers. You can, however, offer tips on how to select clothing that is versatile, trendy, or durable. You can explain differences in fabrics or provide information on this season's color trends. In other words, you can help your readers solve their problems or gain information that is useful to them, and in the process subtly promote your store.

Think also about how people arrive at your blog site. In general, there are three ways in which people reach a new blog:

1. A search engine directs them to your blog site.
2. They come to your site through a link from another blog.
3. They subscribe to your RSS feed or bookmark your site.

No. 3 would be nice, and eventually it may be that many of you develop a group of repeat readers and loyal followers of your blog. But that's not where they start. Probably No. 1 is where you'll get your first readers, so make your site name and the titles and key words associated with your posts as descriptive as possible.

If you do a good job with your blog, you may find other bloggers linking to your site. You can nurture this by asking them if you might link to their site. Technically you can do this without their permission, but by contacting them you make yourself known to them and encourage them to reciprocate by linking to your blog site.

Blog Name

In attracting readers to a blog, consider the blog's title. An effective name is like a book title: It should be descriptive, memorable, and readable. It also should be original.

One naming approach is to make the title specific and descriptive. There is no ambiguity about the topic of these blogs: "Sports Law Blog," "Jewish Music Blog," and "Greenhouse Catalog Blog."

If you don't want to use the word "blog," consider alternative labels such as "thoughts," "news," "musings," "journal," or "advice."

Some blog titles use jargon for readers already familiar with the topic. The National Basketball Association features the "Hang Time Blog" at its nba.com website. "Footy Blog" focuses on soccer. The Philadelphia Flyers hockey team calls its blog "On the Fly!" "In One Breath" is a blog for enthusiasts of the shakuhachi, the Japanese bamboo flute.

This naming approach also is used by some business blogs. For example, "Media Relations Blog," "The Reputation Doctor," and "Fast Pitch Blog" are titles used by various public relations companies.

Good blog titles also can be unique, catchy, and fun. "MenWithPens" is a blog for a copywriting/web design company. "WriteMyFire" is a blog on writing and publishing fiction.

Some blog titles even feature invented words, which can work as long as they are understandable. For instance, there is no question about the subject of the "Baseballistic" blog.

Another approach is to use a name that promises something. Some colleges host "How to Succeed in College" or "How to Study" blogs. "The Learn Spanish Rapidly Blog" is not only a descriptive name, but it also implies a promise that other language blogs might not offer.

Blog Content

As with other websites, blogs should feature writing that is scannable. Some analysts estimate that the average blog visitor will spend about five seconds in determining whether to stay or leave. They suggest writing for **diagonal readers**, those who look at the headline and then scan the content in a zigzag pattern. Such readers are assisted by subheads, photos, and graphs, as well as by boldface, italic, and other highlighted text.

Another effective technique for diagonal readers is to provide a brief two- or three-line summary of the article that tells readers what they will learn from the article. This is another good use of your planning sheet. Look to the Twitter-like news pitch and the benefit statement.

There are several ways an organization can use a blog or a website as part of its public relations program. Here are a few elements that an effective organizational blog might include:

- *Pages* with non-changing information might include short "About" pages, lists of officers or members, contact information, mission statement, history, categories list, and so on.
- *Informational posts* offer news about the organization. This often is the heart of an organizational blog created for public relations purposes. Such posts keep readers up to date about products and programs, new activities, milestones, and events.
- *Related informational posts* about the professional environment in which the organization operates. For example, a hospital blog might include information about health care, the blog of a soccer team might feature information about fitness and coordination training, a museum blog could post updates on archeology, and so on.
- *Instructional posts* with tips or how-to guides offer a direct benefit to readers by telling readers how to do something. It's easy to see how a blog for a grocery chain would include recipes or how a religious organization might use its blog to provide tips on prayer and meditation.
- *Utilities* allow blogs and websites to provide services similar to instructional posts, but instead of merely providing information they embed programs to allow readers to do things like calculate their eligibility for a student loan or a car purchase.
- *Feature pieces* such as outlined in Chapter 11 often find a home on organizational blogs. Interviews, historical and biographical profiles, and case histories can be effective posts. These might feature a short summary or introductory post with a link to a longer feature stored on the organization's website.
- *Advocacy pieces* such as outlined in Chapter 12 offer another category of blog posts. Organizations can post position papers and petitions. These also can be linked from a short introductory blog post.
- *Surveys* can be useful in soliciting priorities from blog readers. For example, at Florida International University, the campus chapter of Amnesty International uses its blog (amnestyfau.blogspot.com) to invite readers to identify topics they would like the chapter to discuss or prioritize.
- *Quizzes and polls* also have a place in the blog inventory of possible elements. A newspaper blog might develop a daily current-events quiz, or a dress shop could have a quiz testing readers' knowledge of fashion trends.
- *Research* on topics related to the organization is appropriate material for blogs. For example, a pediatrician's blog might include short and easy-to-understand summaries of recent studies on childhood illnesses and diseases.
- *Lists* are popular items on many blogs. Top 10 reasons for this or 12 favorite thats are very popular with many blog readers.
- *Call-to-action buttons* make it easy for blog readers to do something. Public relations-oriented blogs might include learn-more, sign-up, buy-now, and make-a-contribution buttons. Blogs also can feature buttons for readers to ask to be placed on a mailing list, generate a letter to a legislator, or download a report. Keep the language and the design simple, and position call-to-action buttons for maximum visibility.
- *Links* to other blogs or websites, your own or others.

Writing Blog Posts

Social media strategist Muhammad Saleem offers several suggestions on effective text formatting for blogs. Here's a summary of his advice:

- Use caps and lower case. Writing in all-caps reduces reader speed by 13 percent.
- Use a serif font such as Times New Roman for text, and use a sans serif font such as Arial for headlines, captions, and other non-paragraph information.
- Use a type size of no smaller than 12 points for serif and 10 point for sans serif fonts.

You can find more advice at his blog: muhammadsaleem.com.

Blogs are written by different organizations for different purposes and are directed toward different audiences. There is no one-size-fits-all approach to writing blogs. Nevertheless, there are a few useful guidelines that blog writers should consider, tailoring each to their own particular writing tasks in producing effective blogs. Here are some guidelines:

- *Adopt a writing style.* Some blogs, particularly those written by individuals, feature casual or chatty writing. Others adopt more of a news style. Organizational blogs developed for public relations purposes usually fall into the latter category. Give some thought to the appropriate writing style for your blog, and try to be consistent.
- *Keep the writing tight.* Make your writing concise and brief. Revise and rewrite drafts of blog entries so that each work carries its weight. Eliminate unnecessary words that don't add to readers' understanding.
- *Adopt a tone.* Blogs can be passionate, funny, or professional. They may use a lot of jargon or reflect sober scientific thought. They may be inspirational, or they may feature rants and critiques. Perhaps any of these tones and themes can be appropriate, but try to keep your organizational blog consistent.
- *Write a strong post title.* This is the label for each post. Pick a style: headline with a verb, title without. Then be consistent in all your postings. Spend some time with this, and let your best and most creative writing shine through in the headline or label. Make the heading descriptive enough to be useful with search engines and blog archives.
- *Keep the post short.* Many blog researchers indicate that 150–200 words is a good target to aim for. Short posts also are more scannable, a characteristic addressed earlier in this chapter on writing for websites in general.
- *Write short paragraphs.* Like writing in a newspaper column, blog entries benefit from frequent indents and paragraphs of only a few lines. Don't give readers too much solid gray text. It's less about writing in essay structure and more about the visual benefit of frequent paragraphs to relieve large blocks of type, which can scare readers away.
- *Use inverted pyramid style.* The tried-and-true style for news articles is appropriate for blog posts. Put the most important information at the top, followed by material of lesser significance to readers.
- *Use bullets.* Readers find lists indicated by bullets or dashes easy to read and easy to understand. Use them freely in your blog entries.
- *Use standard spelling.* The blog is no place for spelling innovations such as "nite," "thru," or "str8." Save that for texting or tweeting.
- *Attribution.* Although the author of a post may be an expert, the reader deserves to know where the information came from. Cite the source. If relevant, provide a link to a published document or authoritative report. Make it clear to readers when you provide an opinion, and indicate whose opinion it is.

- *Use a stylebook.* Blogs are relatively informal, but they still suffer if the writing style is inconsistent. Use the organization's stylebook for internal media, such as the Common Sense Stylebook in Appendix A of this text. Or adopt a special stylebook just for the blog. Either way, make sure that all posts by all authors use the same writing style.
- *Emphasize people.* It's common in an organizational blog used for public relations purposes to highlight the name of people associated with the organization, such as officers, employees, customers, and so on. Such highlighting not only helps break up gray text, it also humanizes the post by emphasizing people.
- *Respect copyright.* Blogs are online publications of your company or nonprofit organization. Don't risk legal action by using copyrighted material without the permission of the author or publisher.
- *Edit the post.* Because blog entries can be written and published so quickly, many writers fail to edit them with the attention they warrant. Writers often find it difficult to edit their own work, especially when they have written it just seconds before. Try to separate yourself from the writing and allow some time to pass before you do the final edit and hit the publish button. Use a spell check, but never rely on this exclusively. The most important editing resource is a careful read by a good writer.

In addition to the writing tips above, here are a few formatting and technical tips for organizational blogs.

- *Focus on searchable key words.* Review the information on labels and key words in the section on optimizing online presence in Chapter 10. Apply this same approach to writing blog entries so search engines can drive traffic to your blog.
- *Highlight key elements.* Use boldface, italics, and/or color to highlight names of people and other key bits of information. Avoid underlines, because they usually signal a link; using an underline merely for emphasis may confuse readers. If you stick with the recommended length of 150–200 words, you won't need subheads, though subheads should be used to guide readers through longer documents that may be linked from the main blog post.
- *Include the publication date.* The blog software generally automatically generates this. Readers are savvy enough to be aware of the publishing date and to be wary if the information is not recent. Try to add new posts often, and make an effort to update older posts.
- *Include the author byline.* The software also automatically generates this. Include at the "About Us" page a short biography of each contributing author so readers can assess the credibility of the information being presented.
- *Use photos.* Blogs can look pretty bleak without any photos. You don't need to include images with every post, but try to have a few. Make sure not to use photos of the same person (such as the president or executive director) too often. Attribute the source of photos, especially if they are not internal to your organization.
- *Create some rules for comments.* For example, most professional blogs require a name and/or e-mail address and refuse to publish anonymous comments. Many blogs have come to this policy the hard way, having learned that anonymous postings often lead to rude and abusive comments. Other rules include requiring that writers

disclose any business connection they have to what they are posting and that overt solicitations are not allowed. A maximum word count for comments also is a reasonable rule to encourage shorter and thus more reader-friendly comments.

Blog Evaluation

Blogs have become very popular, with estimates ranging upward of 400 million active English-language blogs. Dozens of blog-producing software programs are available. With so many blogs available, they warrant careful analysis as to their relevance and usefulness. Here are some criteria on which to objectively analyze various blogs:

- Purpose
- First impression
- Length of posts
- Frequency of comments
- Source of information
- Authority of information
- Writing mechanics (language, spelling, punctuation, and so on)
- Fast download
- Graphics
- Side menu
- Frequency of new posts.

Exercise 14.2

Planning a Blog

For this exercise, select a client organization such as your academic department, a student organization, or another organization identified by your instructor. Prepare a business plan for this new blog. This plan should identify the following elements:

1. Purpose: How does this proposed blog grow from an overall public relations plan for the organization?
2. Publics: Who are the key publics to be served through this blog?
3. Objectives: How specifically do you hope to impact upon these publics? What measurable outcomes do you anticipate?
4. Theme: What topic areas will this blog discuss? Write sample headlines for 10 hypothetical posts.
5. Posting: Write a 150–200 word entry for two of the headlines in the previous "themes" step of this exercise, using facts associated with an actual current or recent activity.
6. Comments: Will you allow reader comments? Explain why you will or will not allow comments. If you do allow them, what is your editorial policy on comments?
7. Links: What side links do you identify for your blog?
8. Evaluation: How will you evaluate the effectiveness of this blog?
9. Search engine optimization: Identify key words that you will work into your blog to maximize SEO to attract visitors to your blog site.

Wiki

Another specialized type of website is the **wiki**, an online database in which readers also can serve as editors. The term itself comes from the Hawaiian term "wiki wiki," which means "fast."

A wiki serves as a forum for team writing. Wikis were designed to facilitate the shared creation of documents, often between members of a work team within a company or organization. They grew from there to become more public websites.

Most wikis feature material that is continually expanding, primarily because readers can add their own information. Such open editing allows readers to modify text, undo earlier edits, and even delete information. Some wikis have an editor who occasionally polices the information; others are password protected so that only authorized readers can edit an entry.

What's the difference between a blog and a wiki? Perhaps an analogy can help. Consider this pair of similes.

- A blog is like a call-in talk show, with one host and many callers asking questions or offering comments.
- A wiki is more like a panel show with several participants asking questions and giving comments among themselves, while the audience listens in.

Wikis also often feature internal links to related wikis and external links to outside websites. Some wikis are presented in encyclopedia-like format. An example of this is Wikipedia, the largest online encyclopedia in which users can create and modify content.

Beyond encyclopedias, wikis exist in many different formats. Some examples of popular wikis include WikiTravel (a worldwide travel guide), WikiHow (how-to manuals for all kinds of everyday topics), WikiAnswers (reader-generated questions and answers on any topic), WikiSummaries (short synopses of books), WikiCars (a collaborative auto guide), WikiAfterDark (a user-generated sex guide), and ShopWiki (an index of nearly everything that can be purchased online). The prime feature of each of these is collaboration, with readers serving also as editors or contributors to the ever-expanding wiki.

Some wiki sites are open to all viewers; others require readers to join a group. A **wiki farm** is a single website that hosts many different wikis, usually around a similar theme.

Public Relations and Wikis

The public relations world has adopted wikis, though less quickly than websites and blogs. A study published in *Public Relations Review* in 2008 reported that 18 percent of public relations practitioners used wikis (compared with 41 percent using blogs and 24 percent using social media).

Some public relations agencies and departments also are using wikis to collaborate with their publics. Some say it is better and faster than blogs. Some companies have created dedicated wikis for interacting with reporters and other journalists.

Eastwick Communications, a high-tech public relations agency based in California's Silicon Valley, is credited as being the first agency to create a wiki (launched in 2005 and dubbed "EastWiki"). This wiki is used for internal collaboration among its employees. The agency also has set up similar wikis for some of its clients, both for internal collaboration among employees and for external partnering with clients and others.

Meanwhile, public relations educators, like their colleagues in other academic disciplines, sometimes use class wikis. Students can write and edit each other on terms or on pioneers of the profession, or they can collaborate on developing projects and campaigns for various clients.

Wiki Writing

As with other venues associated with new technology, wikis offer a few specific dos and don'ts when it comes to writing. Much writing for wikis follows the same style as for blogs: short, balanced, and professional. Here are a few additional guidelines specific to writing for wikis:

- Unlike blog entries, which can be personal, wiki pages usually are more professional in nature and thus are written in the third person.
- Information should be verifiable from external sources, and the source should be documented within the wiki.
- Information should be balanced, neutral, and presented without bias.
- Editors should adopt the tone of the existing article.
- The background or credentials of the original writers and subsequent editors should be made known to readers. It is particularly important to note if an editor is connected in any way with organizations mentioned in the wiki entry or with competitors or colleagues.
- Editors should adopt user names that reflect their relationship to the organization they represent.
- Writers can use a watchlist function to be alerted if someone updates the pages that interest them.

The need for public relations practitioners to be transparent and objective is particularly important in the wiki world.

Wikipedia, for example, has guidelines calling for entries with a neutral point of view, which means citing verifiable and reliable sources from only published sources (not original information provided by the editor). It has a conflict-of-interest standard that proscribes writing about yourself, your organization, or your client. Wikipedia also has provisions for setting the record straight when a reader feels that an entry has errors or is unfairly negative.

Wiki Ethics

Because public wikis are so easily edited, they give rise to special ethical considerations. A term sometimes used about public relations is **spin**. Invariably this term has a negative context. Spin implies propaganda, information intended to manipulate public opinion. It often is applied to areas such as politics and business, though any organization can be accused (rightly or wrongly) of spinning information. While the accusation sometimes is deserved, often opponents and critics toss around the term loosely.

Spin is something that ethical and effective public relations writers try to avoid, especially when dealing with public wikis. In the wiki world, spin takes on new dimensions because it is so easy for organizations to inject themselves into public presentations about themselves and their environment. The concept has given rise to three related terms:

- **Whitewashing** (writing that deceptively glosses over failings, scandals, crimes, and other significant problem areas)

- **Greenwashing** (unwarranted touting of an organization or product as being environmentally friendly)
- **Bluewashing** (unwarranted touting of an organization as being socially responsible or having humanitarian motivations).

Each of these terms suggests verbal excesses, unwarranted exaggerations, or otherwise deliberate efforts toward miscommunication.

Accuracy, honesty, and mere common sense call for an organization that is truly working from humanitarian concerns or environmental commitments to make that known to its publics. The issue rests on an ethical basis: Is the claim accurate? Do the facts warrant the conclusion?

Full Frontal Scrutiny, a project of Consumer Reports WebWatch and the Center for Media and Democracy—no friends of the public relations profession—offers a critique of some practices involving Wikipedia that have tarnished the reputation of public relations practitioners. Often the criticism would better be lodged against people posing as public relations practitioners, for they often have few or loose ties to the profession.

The project cites, without documentation, ethical lapses that impact upon the public relations credibility of organizations: ExxonMobil employees changing their Wikipedia entry to highlight their environmental record; a pharmaceutical company editing to make false product claims; Pepsi employees deleting references to health problems linked to soft drinks. Interestingly, the Center for Media and Democracy uses wikis so environmental activists can report negative information when they suspect organizations of greenwashing.

15 Flier and Brochure

Fliers and brochures may have been the first written materials used for public relations purposes. Thirty-eight centuries ago, the Babylonians in Mesopotamia prepared fliers (carved on stone tablets) as part of a public education campaign to increase agricultural efficiency and thus shore up the foundations of the empire. The Reformation and the American Revolution, the opening of the American frontier, the abolition of slavery, women's suffrage—each owes a measure of success to the distribution of fliers.

Brochures, meanwhile, are an American contribution to the field. The first apparently was a fundraising brochure for Harvard College in 1641.

Fast-forward to the beginning of the third millennium. Every company, cause, and nonprofit organization has its own website. Most also have blogs and a presence on social-networking sites. Each of these is an excellent location for disseminating fliers and brochures. Electronic distribution of information to both internal and external audiences is a key part of every organization's communication plan, and these self-published communication vehicles affect consumer, political, and cultural choices.

This chapter will look at fliers and brochures, which are among the most direct kinds of organizational media that allow public relations writers to take their messages directly to their publics. Here are your learning objectives for this chapter:

- To write and design a flier
- To develop a brochure.

Flier

Fliers are frequently used public relations tools with several pseudonyms: **circulars**, **broadsides**, and **handbills**. Whatever you call them, fliers are among the easiest kinds of public relations writing. Gather the relevant data, present it clearly and succinctly, and you've done most of the work.

Fliers also offer great flexibility for the writer. It is not uncommon for organizations to distribute many fliers in their efforts to present information about events and activities of interest both to the organization and to its various publics. Fliers generally are used to announce specific events such as meetings, new products such as books, or new programs such as college courses.

All fliers share some common attributes that distinguish them from other forms of public relations writing. A flier can be defined as an unfolded sheet meant to be read as a single unit, providing time-specific information that increases the reader's awareness about a topic. Let's look at each of these points individually.

- *Fliers are unfolded sheets* designed to be posted on bulletin boards, delivered by mail, or distributed by hand. If they are folded, it is only for the convenience of distributing them.
- *Fliers are read as single units.* They are designed to present a single message rather than a series of separate message units. Fliers with **poster-style layout** are dominated by artwork or graphic designs. Those with **editorial-style layout** feature prominent textual information. The latter style sometimes takes the form of a letter written directly to the strategic public, often a folksy or rousing pitch for them to participate in an upcoming activity such as an open house or product demonstration.
- *Fliers are time specific.* They address a particular event, often with the objective of promoting attendance or participation. A high school band may distribute a circular among the student body to announce auditions. A manufacturing plant may post a flier about a change in employee benefits. A public utility may include a flier in its bills to announce a proposed rate increase.
- *Fliers serve awareness objectives* by presenting information. Whereas other public relations tools seek to motivate, inspire, and lead readers to action, fliers more often are informational tools that seek to create awareness about upcoming events and activities. Occasionally, however, fliers have an action component, such as when police departments post fliers with information about a missing child. Primarily, this is based on the information model, though the police are hoping that a citizenry attuned to this information will help them locate the missing child.

"Flier" is the stylebook preferred spelling for both a public relations publications and an aviator. "Flyer" is the spelling for the names of some trains and buses, and it's the root for spelling the Philadelphia hockey team. Spelling counts.

Design for Fliers

The key to effective fliers is their visual appeal. Type should be pleasingly placed on the page. Use type within the same family. For emphasis, use different type sizes, or use variations within a single family of type, such as roman, italic, boldface, lightface, condensed, extended, and so on. Times Roman is a popular font with **serifs**, short lines capping the top and bottom strokes of each letter. Arial and Helvetica are popular **sans serif** fonts, without those capping lines.

Two other type-related features are available with some printing systems: changing the **leading**, spacing between lines, and changing the **kerning**, the space between letters.

Also consider the alignment of characters. Fliers often use centered type, sometimes with boxes or text passages set for justified left and right margins, called **full justification**. Other type alignments are possible. **Flush left**, with a straight left margin and ragged right margin, looks less formal than fully justified columns. **Flush right** copy, with a ragged left column, generally is avoided because it is difficult to read. **Centered** type also is difficult to read in paragraphs, though centering often works well for one or only a few lines such as in headlines or subheads. Additionally, too much centering of type offers little or no impact.

Reverse type (light lettering on a dark background) is difficult to read for body copy, though it can be effective for display or headline type. Fliers can be visually enhanced by discrete use of lines, borders, tints and boxes, and by the use of logos, sketches, clip art, and photographs.

Most font software also includes typographic elements known as **dingbats**, decorative features that include bullets, boxes, arrows, and other icons such as these: ✣ ⌧ | ✧ ✓ ☯ ✳ ▷. Wingdings and Webdings are two common dingbat fonts copyrighted by Microsoft. One thing to keep in mind when designing a flier is to work with a visually dominant item: a headline, graphic, or piece of art. Elements should not compete for the reader's attention. Design the flier so that the most important or useful element draws the eye, with other elements gracefully flowing one to another.

Many computer software programs include a wide variety of display fonts for titles and other special uses. Additionally, some computer programs make it easy to give special design treatments to titles and headlines. Don't overdo the special typographical effects, though, because too much of a good thing is not a good thing. Remember: Give readers a single focal point with dominant visual attraction.

Exercise 15.1

Writing a Flier

Prepare a flier using one of the two following scenarios:

1. A flier promoting an upcoming activity in your academic department, such as a scheduled speaker, a new course being offered next semester, an alumni event, or a scholarship deadline. Interview your instructor, department chair, or some other well-informed member of the faculty or staff for details about the activity.
2. A flier promoting participation in the following program. (You have more information than you can possibly use in a single flier, so make some choices about what to include and what to leave out.) Use the desktop publishing capabilities of your computer to prepare a camera-ready flier.

- Your client is City-County Library, located at 1234 Main Street, Middletown. The telephone number is 123–4567. Jana O'Sullivan is executive director of the library; Paul Eric Jones is director of children's services.
- Your public is parents of children aged 2 to 6.
- The library will begin its series of children's story hours on the first Wednesday of next month; provide the specific date. The sessions are held from 4 to 5 p.m. each Wednesday for two months, with a new program each week. The sessions also are repeated each Saturday morning from 9 to 10 a.m. The story hours will be held in the Children's Suite of the library.
- The series is entitled "Yarns and Legends." Each week volunteers from throughout the community will present a different children's story. The presentation will include readings and paraphrases from children's stories.
- Some of the stories are children's classics; others are contemporary pieces.
- The stories are designed to appeal to children between the ages of 2 and 6.

continued . . .

Exercise 15.1 . . . *continued*

- Admission is free.
- The hour-long presentation will include a get-acquainted time, the story presentation, discussion about the story, and refreshments of juice and cookies. Following the story hour, librarians will be available to help children and parents select age-appropriate books to take home.
- Parents may remain with their children, or they may browse elsewhere in the library.
- The program is funded by grants from the United Way and is assisted by the Early Childhood Education Program at your college or university.

Dissemination of fliers is easy. Often they are posted on bulletin boards, handed out, or sent through organizational internal mail. Sometimes they are placed under windshield wipers in parking lots. Regardless of the physical method of disseminating fliers, they generally are posted as PDFs at an organization's website or links from a blog or social networking site.

Brochure

When a message must last longer than it can with a flier, public relations writers often turn to brochures. These publications serve many purposes and offer many opportunities for presenting an organization's message to its various publics. Some distinctions exist among the various types of publications that an organization may produce. **Leaflet** and **folder** refer to a folded single-sheeted publication. Multipage publications are called, according to their increasing size, **pamphlets**, **brochures**, or **booklets**. Other names for multipage publications are **tracts**, **bulletins**, and **packets**. All of these publications are known generically as brochures.

A **brochure** can be defined as a controlled, nonpublic medium presenting information of more than transitory interest and published as a stand-alone piece rather than as part of a series. It is a folded sheet meant to be read as a booklet and providing information meant to be relevant over an extended period of time. The key points in this definition are expanded upon below.

- *Brochures are a controlled medium.* They allow the organization to determine not only the message content but also the presentation of that message, with its timing, duration, and repetition. Brochures also allow for controlled distribution as self-mailers, envelope inserts, rack items, or as handouts or pickups.
- *Brochures are a nonpublic medium.* They fall midway between interpersonal communication channels (speeches and open houses) and the public media (newspapers, radio, and television). As such, they enjoy two advantages: They can be better directed than public media vehicles such as news releases, and they can reach wider audiences than interpersonal channels.
- *Brochures are published once* rather than as part of a series. To be most effective, brochure topics should be of long-term interest, with writing that serves the needs of various readers over several months, perhaps several years. While a brochure may

be revised and updated, it must be complete unto itself (unlike serialized publications such as newsletters, which can develop a topic over several editions).

- *Brochures are stand-alone pieces* that deal with all aspects of a topic. Some organizations publish a series of brochures on related topics, but each of these must stand on its own to provide complete information on its particular topic. For example, an environmental organization may write several brochures, each addressing a different environmental issue. A bank might produce a series of brochures about its different savings and investment options. A local chapter of the Public Relations Society of America may develop a series of brochures, each about individual programs such as accreditation, professional development, community service, and so on. In your own academic department, there may be brochures for each major.

Beyond the basics, the most effective brochures share some additional characteristics that public relations writers should consider. Effective brochures feature two-way communication. The writer may provide a tear-out or clip-out response card, perhaps as an offer for a product sample, a token gift, or an opportunity to request additional information.

The writer also may invite the reader to link to a website or visit a blog or social-networking site, or they may direct traffic to a telephone hotline.

In addition, effective brochures reflect the organization. An investment company would want a brochure that alludes to its success, and a photography studio would want a brochure that showcases its best work. Both probably would opt for a four-color publication with special paper and sophisticated printing techniques. On the other hand, a soup kitchen probably would prefer a humbler look in keeping with its limited financial resources. It might even refuse the offer of a benefactor willing to foot the bill for an elaborate brochure. Some nonprofit organizations have had to apologize to donors and clients because of extravagant promotional materials.

A useful way of categorizing brochures is according to their objectives: awareness, acceptance, and action. Here is an overview of each type:

- Information brochures present basic facts about the organization and focus on awareness objectives. These information brochures seek to affect the level of awareness about some aspect of the organization. For example, a fitness organization might prepare a brochure about its success stories, while a historical site could print a visitors' brochure with a self-guided tour and an overview of artifacts on display. Information brochures also present basic information about issues important to the organization. For example, a credit union might print a brochure about loan amortization, or a medical society might produce one outlining the various nursing specialties.
- Interest brochures seek to make an impact on the interests and attitudes of readers, dealing with acceptance objectives. These brochures carry a persuasive message that is intended to gain the interest and acceptance of readers. For example, an environmental organization might produce a brochure about the health hazards of second-hand smoke.
- Action brochures feature a direct call to action or sales pitch. Their objective is to affect the behavior of the reader. One of the environmental organization's brochures might want the reader to send a financial contribution, while another could offer how-to advice about recycling.

Planning Brochures

You've heard it before; you'll hear it again: All effective public relations writing begins with a plan. Brochures are no exception. In fact, because brochures offer so many different possibilities in both content and writing style, planning is especially important. So that you don't get off track, follow this step-by-step outline for preparing brochures.

Planning Sheet. Complete a planning sheet for the brochure, giving particular attention to identifying the specific publics. Some brochures try to do too much. That's understandable, because brochures can be expensive. But remember: It is seldom a wise decision to try to shape one brochure to accomplish the work of two or three. "What Would You Do? Writing for Different Publics" offers just such a dilemma.

Continue the planning process with the usual attention to the key publics: their wants, interests, and needs; credible sources; and benefits. Identify the tone you desire for your brochure. Clearly articulate your writing objectives. Consider the life span you envision for the brochure and the way it will be distributed.

What Would You Do? *Writing for Different Publics*

Put yourself in the shoes of a public relations writer preparing a brochure for an organization that provided temporary shelter for homeless women and children. The shelter had a very small budget for public relations materials. It needed to increase volunteers and to obtain contributions of money, food, and clothing.

The writer faced a problem: Research identified two different publics with little overlap, but she could afford only one brochure. One public consisted of Evangelical Christian churches, a minority within the community but a group that provided most of the shelter's volunteers and frequent donations of clothing and food. This public expected to hear a religious message about the shelter and its purpose. The second public included businesses and private donors who provided most of the money the shelter used to pay its staff and purchase supplies. This public was aware of the religious mission of the shelter's sponsors, but it gave support because of the shelter's reputation for providing a needed community service.

What is your ethical responsibility to each public? Can you withhold or downplay the religious aspect of the shelter for the business community without betraying the trust of your religious supporters? Are you willing to jeopardize funding for the shelter by emphasizing the religious aspect of the shelter? How can you serve the needs of each on such a limited budget, when your boss has told you categorically that you simply do not have the funds to produce two separate brochures?

(See the note at the end of this chapter for an explanation of how the writer handled this actual case.)

Topical Divisions. Before you begin writing a brochure, subdivide the topic into various categories, like chapters in a book. For example, a brochure by a county agency advocating recycling might plan the following sections: benefits of recycling, items to recycle, ways to prepare recyclables for pickup, the local law about recycling, penalties for violating the law, contacts for additional information, and other communities' experience with recycling.

Identify various facets of your topic and try to deal with each in some way. You may need to eliminate some sections or combine others.

First Draft. Gather the necessary information and write a first draft to address each section. Remember to write from the perspective of reader interests rather than organizational priorities. Only if the brochure serves the needs of your readers can it be of any use to your organization. "Tips for Better Writing: Writing Brochure Copy" lists additional guidelines.

Tips for Better Writing *Writing Brochure Copy*

The following guidelines may be helpful in writing copy for brochures:

1. *Make the cover interesting.* There's a lot of competition to the reader's time, so you've got to appear to offer something worth the effort of opening the brochure and reading it. A big question mark just won't do it. Use a headline and/or artwork that pulls the reader into the topic.
2. *Highlight the benefit to readers.* Place this on the front cover. The headline doesn't have to be clever and it shouldn't be cute. Instead, it should be an accurate indication of the advantage the reader will find inside. If you have planned well and clearly addressed a specific public, your headline will be most effective when it simply indicates a topic of interest to the reader.
3. *Make the copy easy to read.* Use short sentences and short paragraphs. Highlight important facts. Consider using lists instead of narrative paragraphs. Keep the writing clear and simple. Use language with a readability level appropriate to your intended readers.
4. *Write in personal terms.* Don't hesitate to use "you" words that help readers identify with the topic.
5. *Write on a friendly level.* Consider the appropriateness of keeping your message lighthearted. Even serious topics can be presented in ways that are not ponderous. Write as if you were discussing the topic with a friend.
6. *Write in positive terms.* Even situations with serious consequences can be presented without resort to pessimism or scare tactics.
7. *Don't make information so specific and time bound that it quickly becomes obsolete.* Brochures are meant to last for a period of time. Many have been forced into a reprinting because a price was raised or a director was replaced. Avoid writing about details that change frequently.
8. *Make sure the writing is direct.* Don't make readers guess, but lead them to the desired conclusion or behavior.
9. *Increase reader interest* by providing tips or useful advice. Give readers concrete suggestions rather than abstract ideas.
10. *Highlight headlines and subheads.* These should be more than mere labels. Question heads can be useful. When you use them, make sure the questions are logical and honest. Readers will spot loaded or leading questions and lose respect for the brochure. Readers also are unlikely to tolerate dumb or meaningless questions.

Copy Revision. After you have written the first draft, review your planning sheet. Pay particular attention to the interests of the target public, the benefits your organization can offer them, and your public relations objectives. Also review the way you have segmented the topic. Compare your plan to what you have written, and revise your draft accordingly. If your planning suggests more attention or different treatment of some aspects of the topic, now is the time for revision.

Graphic Elements. You probably will have begun thinking about the design of the brochure as you were writing the first draft. In fact, you probably should begin giving some early thought to the look. But don't let design run the show. Only after you have finished the first draft should you seriously deal with design considerations. Let the message come first, then use illustrations to reinforce that message. While a paragraph provides information to the reader, a chart can present the same data in a visual form, or a photograph may reinforce the message.

The first design decision is to determine how many panels the brochure will have and how these will be folded. The most common format is standard letter-sized paper (8½ × 11 inches), with two folds into the center. This creates six panels, as shown in Exhibit 15.1. In this format, the inside cover (Panel E) has importance second only to the front cover, because it is the first panel the reader sees upon opening the brochure. The inside cover serves as a continuation of the front cover and a bridge to the three inside message panels (B, C, and D). The back panel (F) can be used either as a message panel or as a self-mailer.

Brochures can be vertical (folded on the side like a greeting card) or horizontal (folded on the top). Most brochures use a vertical design because they are easier to read. But be consistent. Avoid designing a brochure with a horizontal-style cover and with vertical inside panels. "Tips for Better Writing: Design a Brochure" offers additional suggestions.

As you consider the design of the brochure, take into account the method of dissemination. For instance, if the piece will be a self-mailer, you need to reserve a panel for this purpose.

If it is supposed to fit into a business envelope, size will become important. Postal criteria also must be considered in design. The "Business Center/Postal Explorer" link on the U.S. Postal Service website (usps.com) has instructions on designing publications for mailing, postage rate calculators, and other useful information.

Most brochures can be posted at an organization's website as a downloadable PDF, so try to adhere to dimensions that work on standard-sized paper: 8½ × 11 inches or 8½ × 14 inches in the United States and Canada, or 8.27 × 11.69 inches for the common A4 paper for international users.

Exhibit 15.1—SIX-PANEL BROCHURE The six-panel fold is the most popular format for brochures—a front cover (Panel A), three inside message panels (B, C, and D), an inside focal panel (E), and a back panel (F).

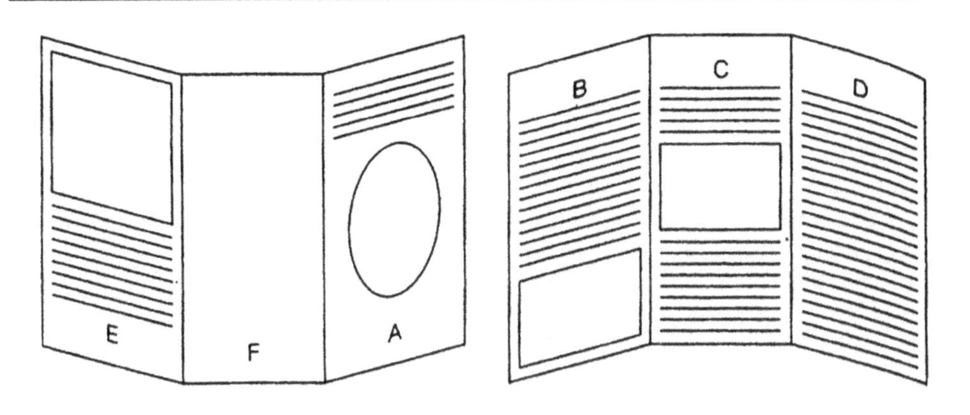

Tips for Better Writing *Design a Brochure*

Following are some guidelines related to brochure design:

1. *Emphasize the upper third of the front cover* because brochures often are used in display racks. Use a design that makes effective use of this space.
2. *Use type fonts and sizes that are reader-friendly*. Type for brochures should be at least 10 point. Serif type is easier to read in paragraphs; sans serif type may be more appropriate for bulleted information. Alternatives to paragraph form include lists, often introduced by dingbats, bullets, hyphens, squares, asterisks, and so on.
3. *Text should be set flush left*, with a solid left margin and a ragged right margin. This not only is easier to read but it also provides a relaxed feel. Use boldface and/or italic type for emphasis. Avoid using all-caps, which is the print equivalent of shouting. Use large initial capital letters sparingly.
4. *Don't be afraid of white space*. Crowded brochures give the impression of being ponderous, which signals that reading this will be a chore.
5. *Strive for short blocks of type*. Lengthy sections of text can be shortened, or they can be broken up by subheads, artwork, design elements such as lines and boxes, and white space.
6. *Spot color can be effective*. This can be accomplished graphically, using tints or colored heads. Or it can be accomplished artistically, such as with washes of color underneath the text.
7. *Colored paper can enhance a brochure inexpensively*. A low-cost way of adding color is to use paper manufactured in a light or pastel color.
8. *Photographs don't reproduce well in other-than-black ink*. If you are using a color with photos, make sure the ink is a dark shade.
9. *Balance graphic elements on the inside panels*. Spot photos or graphic devices at different locations in each panel. Avoid top-heavy or bottom-heavy layouts.
10. *Don't exaggerate the role of graphics*. Brochures are vehicles primarily for the written word. Don't fall into the trap of having a brochure that is overdesigned but underwritten.

Polished, Edited Copy. The final stages of preparing a brochure are the same as for any kind of writing: Polish your language. Aim for unity between the headlines and artwork or other graphic elements. Read the copy out loud and listen to the flow of your words. Edit your copy for style, spelling, punctuation, and other mechanics of acceptable writing.

Copy Fitting. When you are preparing copy for a brochure, you will need to **copy fit**. This involves the manipulation of type to fit within the design specifications. Complicated mathematical formulas can help writers calculate how typewritten copy will transform into typeset text of various sizes, styles, and widths.

Happily, there are two alternatives to mathematical madness. One is to ask your printer for help, if you are working with a professional printer. Many printers are convinced that public relations writers are waifs needing a guiding hand, so they often are happy to oblige requests for direction.

The second alternative is to let your computer do the work. Experiment with fonts, type sizes, column widths, and line spacing. You can write and rewrite heads and paragraphs so they fit a particular space.

Copy Testing. Pretesting messages is a vital part of effective public relations. With a brochure that will be used for a long time, it is especially important to test it before hundreds or thousands of copies are printed. This can be done informally. Show samples to people representative of your intended audience. For example, if the brochure is to encourage attendance at a senior citizen center, ask some people already attending what they think of it.

Approvals. Brochures may require the approval of one or several organizational executives. After the brochure has been pretested and found appropriate, the writer may need to obtain approval from organizational leaders to publish and distribute the brochure.

Production Schedule

Each of the steps described above takes time. The actual time needed for each step will vary depending on a lot of individual circumstances, but consider the following hypothetical case.

You have been asked to produce a brochure for use by transfer students coming into your college. The academic dean who has commissioned this project wants to distribute the brochures at the beginning of the two-week registration period for transfer students, which begins on Monday, August 13. Working backwards, such as X minus three days, you could develop the following schedule:

	X	Distribute to transfer students
3 days	X–3	Pick up from printer; distribution to admissions staff
10 days	X–13	Deliver to printer
5 days	X–18	Get final approvals from the Director of Admissions; revise as needed
5 days	X–23	Show samples of the brochure to two seven-person groups of students who transferred into the college last year; these students were contacted in May and were selected because they would be on campus during the summer months
2 days	X–25	Produce a mock-up of the finished brochure; proofread it
5 days	X–30	Vacation week
10 days	X–40	Revise the draft; polish and edit the copy; select the design and graphic elements; obtain needed illustrations
5 days	X–45	Research the subject; identify sections within the copy; write the first draft
5 days	X–50	Develop a budget; obtain budget approval
5 days	X–55	Obtain concept approval from the Director of Admissions
5 days	X–60	Begin the planning; develop strategy and concept for the project.

You have determined you will need 60 working days, nearly three months, to complete the project. This schedule is a reasonable projection of the time that could be needed to produce the brochure, though it also offers many opportunities to shorten the time span.

Exercise 15.2

Developing a Brochure

You are a public relations writer preparing a brochure for one of the following organizations:

- Your Academic Department: Brochure for alumni on maintaining a connection with the department and supporting the department's educational mission.
- Volunteerism: Brochure for students at your college or university on opportunities to volunteer on service projects both on and off campus.
- An organization in which you are interested: Brochure for one of the organization's programs or services.

Part 1: Develop a planning sheet. Sketch out two different cover designs for this brochure. Discuss your concepts with another student or a colleague, and then determine which cover design to use.

Part 2: Identify four to six possible sections that would be appropriate for a brochure. Then research the topics and write brief paragraphs for each section. Review the planning sheet and revise the copy as needed.

Part 3: Sketch out the visual elements of the brochure. Produce a final layout or mock-up of the brochure.

Part 4: Create a rough schedule for this project.

What Would You Do? *Writing for Different Publics*

The young woman who faced the problem outlined in "What Would You Do?" earlier in this chapter was an actual student in a public relations writing class, working part-time for the shelter. Her first thought was to seek additional funds to prepare two separate brochures, but no money was available. So she developed a brochure that could be used in two different ways.

First, she prepared a single two-fold brochure that featured the human service aspects of the shelter: the social problem within the community, the shelter's record of success, and the need for community support. The brochure invited contributions of food and clothing as well as money. The writer used this brochure in her appeals to the businesses and secular supporters.

Then, for the religious supporters, the writer provided an insert in the form of a prayer card that was the same dimensions as the brochure. The insert featured a religious design, Bible quotes, and a spiritual appeal in the style that the religious supporters would find appropriate. The insert was included within the brochure when the shelter presented its message to its religious supporters.

16 Direct Mail and Online Appeal

From events surrounding the Magna Carta through the American Revolution to today's political and social issues, writers often have found themselves facing the task of writing convincing letters to appeal for support for an organization or its cause.

The type of support varies. It may deal with internal relations by seeking new members or soliciting renewals. It may focus on philanthropic public relations by asking for financial contributions. It may involve fundraising for a political candidate or a charitable cause. Or it may involve advocacy, such as seeking signatures to a petition or asking people to write letters or contact legislators on behalf of your cause.

As public relations writers consider their alternatives in delivering organizational messages, they increasingly are taking those messages directly to their publics. Their increasing use of direct mail has been one of the major changes taking place within the practice of public relations. In using direct mail, regardless of the type of support needed, your writing will be successful only to the extent that it effectively engages readers and leads them to the anticipated action.

This chapter will focus on writing and packaging appeals for various purposes, both in print and online. Your learning objectives for this chapter are:

- To demonstrate an understanding of persuasive techniques for written communication
- To write an effective appeal letter
- To writer an effective online appeal letter.

Making Appeals

Americans are generous people. Annual reports that track philanthropic giving consistently show that people generously support charitable causes. The *Giving USA 2011* report tallied charitable contributions at nearly $291 billion.

Beyond financial donations, Americans also are big on volunteering. The Independent Sector, a coalition of more than 500 corporations, foundations, and charities, reported that 63 million Americans (27 percent of the adult population) gave more than 8 billion hours of volunteer service worth $169 billion in 2010. That mirrors the percentage of 3 million college students who volunteered 307 million hours of community service. See VolunteeringInAmerica.gov for details.

Nonprofit organizations frequently use direct appeal mailings for various reasons. Some direct-mail pieces such as Speaker Nancy Pelosi's letter to constituents are intended to raise

FYI *Charitable Giving*

An estimated $291 billion was contributed to American charities, according to *Giving USA 2011*, a report prepared by the Giving USA foundation and its research partner, the Center on Philanthropy at Indiana University. The report notes a 3.8 percent increase after two previous years of significant decreases. Charitable giving has increased every year since tracking began in 1954, with the exception of three years during economic recessions: 1987, 2009, and 2008.

The recent year's donations were made by more than 75 million households, more than 1 million corporations, an estimated 120,000 estates, and about 77,000 foundations.

Where do the contributions come from? The 2011 report noted the following sources (rounded here to full percentage points and the nearest billion dollars):

- Individual contributors, 73 percent ($212 billion)
- Individual bequests, 8 percent ($23 billion)
- Foundations, 14 percent ($41 billion)
- Corporations, 5 percent ($15 billion)

Where do the contributions go? The report noted that the donations (which are rounded here) went to the following causes:

- Religion and religious charities, 35 percent ($101 billion)
- Education, 14 percent ($42 billion)
- Grant-giving independent and community foundations, $11 percent ($33 billion)
- Human services, 9 percent ($26 billion)
- Public-society benefit such as United Way, Jewish Federation, etc. 8 percent ($24 billion)
- Health, 8 percent ($23 billion)
- International affairs, 5 percent ($16 billion)
- Arts, culture, and humanities, 5 percent ($13 billion)
- Environment/animals, 2 percent ($7 billion)
- Miscellaneous, 3 percent ($6 billion)

Additional information is available at the Giving USA Foundation (aafrc.org)

funds and generate continued backing from people already supportive of an organization's message. Others such as the National Museum of the American Indian seek to increase membership.

Still others are focused on advocacy, such as the letter to Senate leaders from the Parent Project for Muscular Dystrophy. Some groups appeal to members for action, such as the National Organization for the Reform of Marijuana Laws asking for letters to Congress. Amnesty USA's Urgent Action Network generates letters, e-mails, and faxes.

Following are excerpts from successful direct mail appeals from various organizations. Emphasis has been added to help readers note some of the key sections.

Fundraising. Writing for the Democratic Congressional Campaign Committee, then Speaker of the House Nancy Pelosi (D. Calif.) used a touch of "us versus them" in her appeal for contributions to support and political contributions for health insurance reform. Note the twice-repeated information about the financial match:

> If this summer proved anything, it showed how urgently we must stand together to restore civility to our politics and help President Obama seize this historic moment for health insurance reform in America.
>
> You have already taken a stand against the Republicans' attempt to shout down President Obama and restore civility in Washington. For that, I cannot thank you enough.
>
> **We have entered the make-or-break month. The media is closely watching to see which side has the momentum.** With the Republicans already claiming victory for trying to silence respectful

debate, it is up to grassroots Democrats to show the world that no amount of shouting can drown out our determination to enact health insurance reform.

Show the world that no amount of Republican shouting can drown out our determination to help President Obama reform health insurance. Contribute $5, $10 or more to our Million Dollar Match today and your gift will be matched 2-to-1, tripling its impact.

In his eloquent call for action last week before a joint session of Congress, President Obama called on us to "replace acrimony with civility." He reiterated his call to restore civility to Washington during his interview on "60 Minutes" this weekend. Yet, our opponents continue their name-calling in a cynical attempt to derail these reforms.

The Republican defenders of the status quo are shouting because they understand that this is the toughest Midterm Election that Democrats have ever faced. They also understand that this is a critical month for health insurance reform and they are trying to deal a serious blow to President Obama's agenda for moving America forward.

Show the world that no amount of Republican shouting can drown out our determination to help President Obama reform health insurance. Contribute $5, $10 or more to our Million Dollar Match today and your gift will be matched 2-to-1, tripling its impact.

It is urgent that we stand together as Democrats. With all eyes on the coming Midterm Elections, let us use this critical September deadline to show the world just how prepared we are to maintain a strong Democratic Majority for President Obama so he can keep America moving in a New Direction.

Thank you. Nancy Pelosi. Speaker of the House.

PS The Republicans recognize that September is the make-or-break month for health insurance reform. That is why they have increased their shouting and their false attacks on President Obama. It is urgent that we stand together.

Contribute to our Million Dollar Match today and House Democrats will match your generosity 2-to-1, tripling its impact.

Membership. The National Museum of the American Indian evoked a sense of commitment and appreciation of native culture with this membership letter:

At Thanksgiving, most of us look forward to a delicious meal of turkey, dressing, corn, cranberry sauce, pumpkin pie, and other traditional holiday foods. Yet how many of us know why we eat these particular foods when we give thanks each November? In fact, do most of us know what we commemorate at Thanksgiving?

As a Member of the National Museum of the American Indian, *you are committed to the first national museum* dedicated to the histories, cultures, and arts of Native Americans with a collection of more than 817,000 extraordinary Native American objects. You can visit any of our three separate facilities—the Museum on the National Mall in Washington D.C., the George Gustav Heye Center in lower Manhattan, and the Cultural Resources Center in Suitland, Maryland.

In all of our locations, we seek to *convey the vitality and adaptability* of the Native American cultures of this hemisphere.

You see, the native people throughout the Americas developed cultures uniquely suited to the environments in which they lived—*cultures that survived over time and which still thrive today*—despite every attempt to eradicate them.

As you know, the purpose of the National Museum of the American Indian goes beyond maintaining a great collection. The true goal of the Museum is to *change forever the way the native peoples of this hemisphere are viewed*—to correct the misconceptions and to demonstrate how native cultures are enriching this world . . .

I hope that you will make a special gift today—in honor of all those who participated in the First Thanksgiving—as we celebrate the history and cultures of Native Americans. *Your gift will attest to your extraordinary commitment* and will truly have an impact for many generations to come.

Government Support. The Parent Project for Muscular Dystrophy advocacy letter to Senate leaders noted progress already achieved as it urged Congress to address the organization's cause:

> On behalf of all patients and families who have been affected by Duchene and Becker Muscular Dystrophy, *we are writing to thank you* and the Committee for the strong support you have provided in recent years, and *to urge continued assistance* as you work toward preparing the FY 2007 Labor, HHS, and Education spending bill.
>
> . . . *We are making progress*, however, thanks to support from your Committee and the Congress. Just a few months ago, a clinical trial began on a treatment that could positively impact the lives of many DBMD patients. Last year, the National Institutes of Health approved three additional Muscular Dystrophy Cooperative Research Centers, further helping to target resources toward efforts aimed at developing successful and safe cures and treatments.
>
> . . . With so many exciting developments in recent years, we hope that you and your colleagues will *help spur additional advances* by continuing to fund DBMD-specific activities adequately in FY 2007. Specifically, we would like to see the following:
>
> - Increase MD funding at the CDC by $2 million, for a total of about $8.5 million in Fiscal Year 2007.
> - Increase overall funding at the National Institutes of Health to help ensure adequate funding is provided for MD research at all six MD Centers of Excellence . . .
>
> Urge CDC and the Agency for Healthcare Research and Quality to complete an ongoing initiative that would establish evidence-driven treatment guidelines for clinicians treating people with Duchene and Becker Muscular Dystrophy.

Political Action. The National Organization for the Reform of Marijuana Laws advocates legalization of marijuana for medical, personal, and industrial use. NORML asked its members and supporters to write to Congress seeking votes for a bill to protect medical marijuana patients.

> Massachusetts Democrat Barney Frank, along with a bipartisan coalition of 31 co-sponsors, is seeking to strengthen legal protections for state-authorized medical marijuana patients.
>
> House Bill 2835, The Medical Marijuana Patient Protection Act, would ensure that medical cannabis patients in states that have approved its use will no longer have to fear arrest or prosecution from federal law enforcement agencies.
>
> Fourteen states—Alaska, California, Colorado, Hawaii, Maine, Michigan, Montana, New Jersey, New Mexico, Nevada, Oregon, Rhode Island, Vermont, Washington and the District of Columbia—have enacted laws protecting medical marijuana patients from state prosecution. Yet in all of these states, patients and providers still face the risk of federal sanction—even when their actions are fully compliant with state law.
>
> It is time that we allowed our unique federalist system to work the way it was intended. Patients and their state representatives should have the authority to enact laws permitting the medical use of cannabis—free from federal interference.
>
> Previous versions of The Medical Marijuana Patient Protection Act were introduced in both the 108th and 109th Congress, but failed to receive a public hearing or a committee vote.
>
> HR 2835 is now before the House Energy and Commerce Committee. Please write your members of Congress today and tell them to stop targeting and prosecuting medical marijuana patients and providers. For your convenience, a prewritten letter will be e-mailed to your member of Congress when you enter your contact information below.
>
> Thank you for assisting NORML's federal law reform efforts.

Volunteer Action. Amnesty International USA's Urgent Action Network sent this appeal to mobilize volunteers to send letters, e-mails, and telegrams on behalf of one of its causes:

> I am writing to urge you to co-sponsor the Improvements in Global Maternal and newborn health Outcomes while Maximizing Successes Act, or the "Global MOMS Act." Hundreds of thousands of women die each year from pregnancy-related complications. The vast majority of these deaths are unnecessary and preventable, caused by a lack of access to timely, quality health care. These preventable deaths represent violations of essential human rights, including the right to the highest attainable standard of health and the right to freedom from discrimination based on such factors as gender, race, ethnicity, immigration status, Indigenous status or income level. The Global MOMS Act will support activities that help expand access to better quality maternal health services, remove barriers to such services, and ensure that they meet international human rights standards.
>
> As your constituent, I am asking you to co-sponsor the Global MOMS Act and support it once it comes to the House floor.
>
> Women dying in pregnancy and childbirth is not just a public health emergency, it is also a human rights crisis. Amnesty International has identified obstacles to lifesaving treatment faced by pregnant women around the world. In Peru, poor, rural and indigenous women face language barriers and too few accessible clinics. In Burkina Faso, women die because they cannot reach a health facility capable of treating them or because they arrive too late. In Sierra Leone, pregnant mothers are dying because they are too poor to pay for the treatment they require to save their lives. The United States has an important role to play in supporting developing countries in developing and implementing plans to reduce maternal deaths.
>
> The Global MOMS Act will make a difference. It supports:
>
> - the development of a strategy as part of the Global Health Initiative to reduce mortality and improve maternal and newborn health;
> - improved coordination among U.S. government agencies and existing programs that are currently working to reduce maternal and newborn mortality; and
> - authorization of assistance in proven interventions including family planning, access to skilled care at birth and training professionals in emergency obstetric care.
>
> Two years ago, the U.S. House of Representatives passed a resolution affirming "commitment to promoting maternal health and child survival both at home and abroad through greater international investment and participation" (H.Res.1022 in the 110th Congress). This new bill is an opportunity to match commitment with action. Please make a difference in the lives of millions of pregnant women and co-sponsor the Global MOMS Act.

Direct mail is also an effective way for public relations writers to appeal to key publics for support that goes beyond donor generosity. For example, direct mail can be useful in political campaigns and other governmental activities that rest on voter support. Members of Congress and many state legislatures have free **franking privileges**, permission for free mailing to constituents. This allows them to implement ambitious direct-mail campaigns with the voters in their home districts. What are they appealing for? Grassroots support and votes.

Direct mail also has a role in community relations situations in which an organization takes its message directly to the local residents. Corporations and other large organizations often use direct mail to promote employee morale and shareholder awareness. Meanwhile, marketing campaigns often rely on direct mail as a key selling tool, taking the message (and often a sample of the product) directly to the would-be consumer.

Are such mail appeals effective? They seem to be. Some research claims that direct mail draws 10 times as many responses as newspaper ads and 100 times as many as TV ads.

E-mail appeals are said to be even more effective. Meanwhile, the use of direct mail has increased at a higher pace than newspaper or magazine advertising; by some estimates as much as a two-to-one growth rate.

Specifics about direct mail and its effectiveness are uncertain. Much of the research associated with direct mail is proprietary, sometimes contradictory, and still emerging. What can be said with certainty is that direct mail is effective and growing. It also is expensive, so the public relations practitioners involved with direct mail will use the technique carefully.

Effective direct appeal promotions have several key ingredients. They must target the right audience and employ the appropriate mailing list. They need to include the right message, based on the self-interest of the readers and tested in pilot studies to make sure it resonates with readers. Effective promotions are packaged so that they are visually pleasing. Finally, they must involve strong writing that helps cut through the clutter of so many competing messages.

Before dealing further with appeal letters, it may be helpful to consider your personal experience with such letters.

Exercise 16.1

Freewriting on Direct Mail

Freewrite for five minutes on the following topic: *What has been your personal experience with receiving appeal letters?* Then discuss this with your classmates.

Reader Interest

You probably have found that some appeal letters are interesting while others are not. Consider the following proposition: *The only difference between effective appeal letters and junk mail is the recipient's interest in the topic.* "Mail smarter" is the axiom for direct-mail appeals.

What one person finds compelling, another may judge to be of no personal interest. If it is true that communication is a receiver phenomenon, this principle is most apparent with direct-mail appeals. The best writing will be labeled as junk mail if the topic fails to interest the reader. The real value of a direct-mail appeal is its ability to provide personalized messages of interest to particular readers.

Each year Americans generously support charitable organizations that ask for help, giving hundreds of billions of dollars. We naturally think of donations by philanthropic foundations and corporations, but more than 80 percent of the donations came from individuals—not the wealthy few, but mostly from people of average or below-average financial means. "FYI: Charitable Giving" explains further.

Effective appeal letters are based on the reader's interest, not on the need of the organization or even the need of the beneficiaries. People don't give money just because an organization asks for it. They don't even give because a child is hungry. They give because they care that the child is hungry and want to help.

People give money (as well as their time, talent, vote, or whatever else is of value to them) for self-serving reasons—noble, perhaps; compassionate and beneficial, certainly; but nonetheless reasons that satisfy their own personal wants, interests, and needs.

Some people give to fulfill a desire to help, because they think they can make a difference in someone's life or because they hope to make a contribution to their community or to humanity at large. They want to provide an education for poor students. Other people give because giving makes them feel good. They contribute because a disease has no cure and they want to be part of its cure. Perhaps they give because of a moral or religious commitment, fulfilling their accepted duty to give alms and help the needy. Still other people may give because they want to look good in the eyes of others, create a memorial in their name or that of a loved one, or simply to obtain a tax deduction.

Your task as a writer is to first identify the wants, interests, and needs of the key public and then to respond to those through your writing. Start by thinking about your own reasons for giving.

Exercise 16.2

Freewriting on Giving

Freewrite for five minutes on the following topic: *When was the last time I gave money to a nonprofit organization? What motivated me to contribute?* Then discuss this with your classmates.

To ensure reader interest, public relations practitioners give very careful attention to developing targeted mailing lists. Large organizations may have marketing teams that develop and maintain mailing lists; smaller organizations may expect the writer to oversee the lists. The writer should be able to presume that an appropriate mailing list exists for the writing project at hand. With this in mind, we can proceed to the writing task of preparing an effective appeal letter for the key public represented by the list.

Another key to direct-mail appeals is that they provide for some kind of reader response. Most media communication allows for only modest and delayed audience feedback. But direct mail has refined reader response. Through the use of response cards, stamped self-addressed envelopes, interactive websites and toll-free telephone numbers, direct mail provides opportunities that make it easy for the reader to say, "Yes, I want to help!"

Direct mail provides for continual copy testing of a message. This first happens even before the message is presented to a large-scale audience, when the public relations writer tests the message with a focus group or a small mail sample. But a valuable aspect of direct mail is that copy testing continues throughout the life of the campaign.

Some campaigns feature **split runs**, in which different versions of the same message are distributed to different segments of the key public. The versions may vary in their headlines or their photographs or other artwork. Perhaps they will have different writing strategies and persuasive techniques. Implementing a split run is an excellent way for a writer to determine which version of the message is more successful. Eventually, the most successful version is likely to be adopted for the entire key public.

Writing the Appeal

The appeal letter is the heart of the appeal package. Thus it requires top-quality writing. The letter needs a personal tone and all the persuasive effectiveness you can pull together. Following are suggestions about the standard elements found in most successful appeal letters.

- *Plan carefully.* It is most important to work from a planning sheet that guides you through the crucial planning stages of focusing your attention on the key public (in this case, the persons receiving the letter); their wants, interests, and needs; the benefits you can provide; your writing objectives, and finally the tone of your message.
- *Use a salutation.* Junk mail is defined by the recipient, and a letter that appears to have been sent to thousands of other people hardly qualifies as personal correspondence. Mail that addresses the recipient personally is likely to be read. If individual letters can be generated—and sort-merge computer functions often make this possible—address the reader by name. Be careful not to use gender-specific titles such as Mr., Ms., or Mrs. unless you know for sure that these are accurate. Imagine how many annoying letters have been misaddressed to Mr. Glenn Close or Ms. Marion Barry. Make sure you use a woman's preferred title. The Digital Printing Council reports that personalized letters draw five times the response than generic letters. But research shows that there is no particular benefit in carrying the use of the name further within the text of the letter. If a small budget, large mailing list, or limited time cause you to use form letters instead, choose an appropriate salutation: Dear Fellow Midstate Graduate, Dear Public Relations Colleague, Dear Friend of the Environment. Regardless of the salutation, effective appeal letters make frequent use of second person, "you" and "your."
- *Use simple, direct language.* Your writing should be correct, appropriate to your reader, and consistent in style. It should be simple, natural, concise, clear, and powerful. It should be full of meaning and easy for the reader to identify with.
- *Start with a powerful lead.* The beginning of the letter must create interest. Quickly. Lose the reader here, and the dance is over before it's begun. Introduce a provocative fact. Ask a pertinent question. Give a poignant example. Use a cogent anecdote. Report a paradox.
- *Ask, ask, and ask again.* You are writing an appeal letter; this is no time to be subtle or shy. If you want a contribution, request it. If you are seeking new members, invite them. If you want people to write letters to the White House, ask (and give them the address; better yet, provide an online mailing link). Ask for help early and often. The first paragraphs should request or suggest some action, at least indirectly. This is one of those situations in which repetition is a good thing.
- *Use an appropriate tone.* It is important that every appeal letter should have its own feel or attitude, appropriate to the cause and the recipient. Some direct-mail appeals are folksy, others are frenzied. Some are friendly invitations. Each letter should be consistent in its approach, and it should be suitable for the reader, the sending organization, and the person signing the letter.
- *Generate reader interest.* As with position papers and speeches, appeal letters will be successful only to the extent that they can interest the reader. The task of the writer is to explain the significance of the topic and gain the reader's interest in it.

- *Clearly state the benefit*. It is important to let the reader know how a contribution will help the cause. Even more important is to note how a contribution will help the reader who is, after all, a donor-in-waiting. You are not a beggar on a street corner. You are an agent of an organization that is of interest to this reader. You have something valuable to offer the reader. Maybe it is an opportunity to help treat an illness that has affected someone in her family. Perhaps it is a way to support a social cause close to his heart. Whatever the benefit, awaken the reader's interest. Give the reader a personal, even selfish reason for supporting your organization.
- *Tell a human story*. William Shakespeare gave Miranda good words in *The Tempest*: "Your tale, sir, would cure deafness." Our stories, if they are poignant and well told, can cure the deafness of an apathetic audience. Use a sort of poster-child approach to humanize the organization. Put a face on your message. Give a personal example. Sketch an actual or a composite portrait of a person who benefits through the organization. Present a vignette about the program. This can bring the appeal to life and make it more compelling for the reader. Even organizations not working with people can "humanize" their messages, such as the SPCA does in "Tips for Better Writing: Personalize the Message."

Tips for Better Writing *Personalize the Message*

Fundraising experts have found great success by personalizing their message, giving it a face and a name. Instead of writing about the statistical thousands or millions, they tell about one or two in ways that engage the reader. Even organizations not dealing with people can use this technique. Here is copy from an actual holiday mailing sent by an SPCA chapter:

> Although we have provided shelter and care for 14,000 animals so far this year, we never look at them as a statistic. To us, each is an individual, each has a pair of hopeful eyes and a wagging tail. Each has a unique personality and a unique set of needs. But they all have one need in common—the need for a place to call home, a family to call their own.
>
> There's Santini who spent over a month in our care at the SPCA. This great little terrier mix was turned over to us by his family because they were moving to a place with a no-pets policy. Rather than looking for pet friendly accommodations, they chose to relinquish their best friend to our shelter.
>
> Shy at first, Santini needed a little coaxing out of his shell. He waited patiently for just the right human to come along and adopt him. Now the two are inseparable. Santini's new "Dad" says it's great to have a best friend who is ALWAYS glad to see him!
>
> And little Clara, the beautiful orange tabby, was brought to the shelter because she kept having kittens. Instead of providing the simple, low-cost spay surgery needed to solve their "problem," her owners decided to leave Clara with us. We matched her up with a wonderful lady who had just lost her husband. Now, the two of them are practically joined at the hip. They share all sorts of quality time with one another. Clara is the queen of the house!

- *Keep numbers to a minimum*. Statistics don't motivate people to give. Use numbers that are compelling, and put them in human context. What does it mean to say the United States has a $1 trillion deficit? If one dollar equals one second, the deficit equals 32,000 years. Or, a trillion one-dollar bills would reach a quarter of the way to the moon.

- *Write with passion.* Write as if you were excited and enthusiastic about the cause you are writing about. If you don't seem to really care, why should the recipient of the appeal letter? Try to make the reader *want* to contribute.
- *Be positive.* Of course, you are dealing with a serious situation. You wouldn't be asking for help if it weren't serious. But don't paint the picture with too many somber tones. Recall what we know from persuasion theory about fear appeals and guilt appeals: A little bit goes a very long way. Certainly, you want to point out the seriousness and perhaps forecast the consequences of inaction. But offer your reader hope. Don't simply say, "This is an awful situation." Continue on: ". . . but you can help make it better." You need to motivate would-be donors, not demoralize them.
- *Show how to make a difference.* Donors want to know that their contribution matters. When people think they can make a difference, they are more likely to donate.
- *Understate rather than overstate.* Understatement is more effective than hyperbole. If the situation is urgent, say so. But not every appeal is a life-and-death matter or one of critical timeliness. Remember the story of the boy who cried "Wolf!" Don't risk your long-term credibility on a short-term ploy. Don't exaggerate the role your organization is playing in the situation being addressed. Any mishandling of facts is likely to come back to haunt you. Be persuasive, but keep things in honest proportion.
- *Appeal to the head and the heart.* People have different psychological make-ups. Research suggests that some people are more likely to be persuaded by factual and logical explanations while others are more influenced by emotional appeals. In the appeal letter, you have the luxury of space to provide both approaches. By all means use the facts, provide statistics, quote authoritative sources. They give credibility to the appeal, and they will be compelling for many readers. But also make the appeal personal, tell a story, humanize the cause. *Get the reader involved.* Once you have roused a passion in the reader, getting him or her to the point of wanting to help, keep things moving along. Discuss the benefits. Show how the reader can participate in this worthy cause. Don't simply ask for money; ask also for participation. Sure, money is part of it. But this reader can become an ambassador for the cause, an advocate among friends and colleagues, and a petitioner to governments and other authorities on behalf of your organization. At the very least, the donor can tell others about this cause. Ultimately, these are at least as valuable to the organization as a financial contribution.
- *Offer testimony.* Effective appeal letters often include statements of support from people who have benefited from the organization. Appeal programs often link with well-known entertainers, athletes, or community figures, both as people who will speak on behalf of the organization and as honorary directors. Often these people will lend their names as signers of appeal letters.
- *End with a postscript.* Restate your most compelling reason for supporting the organization—the need, the benefit to the would-be donor, and the potential for achieving success. Some studies indicate that the postscript receives greater attention than many parts of the body of the letter; often it is read before the letter itself. Readers may skip around the letter, but they almost always pay attention to the PS. Don't waste the PS by noting the obvious: that the contribution is tax deductible or that a brochure is enclosed. Use it effectively and strategically to restate your key benefit and repeat your request.

- *Consider the gimmick.* You gotta have a gimmick—that's the advice of many direct-appeal experts. Outrage from a political fundraiser because the other side is about to ruin the country. Weeping and wailing over an atrocity caused by reprehensible people. Irony, such as the persistence of hunger in a world spotted with grain-filled silos. Fear and despair that a cure won't be found in time. A guilty conscience for not contributing after receiving a calendar, address labels, or some other unsolicited "gift." Sometimes, the best gimmick is no gimmick at all. Heifer Project International used to send an appeal to lapsed donors, noting appreciation for the past contribution, admitting that there are many other worthy causes, and gently inviting future support for the anti-hunger organization. Oxfam America eschews emotional photos and guilt-tripping gifts and instead makes the straightforward appeal: You don't need to go to Senegal to help farmers dig a well or to Haiti to help teachers rebuild their schools. All you need to do is join Oxfam America. Pay your dues, and we'll do the work in your name.

Exercise 16.3

Writing an Appeal Letter

Select a nonprofit organization of personal interest. Prepare a planning sheet for a fundraising letter aimed at a key public of your choosing. Work with other students as an editing team for this exercise. After you have written each part of this exercise, show the other members of your team what you have written, and together discuss the strengths and limitations of each piece of writing.

Part 1: The strength of an appeal letter lies in the impact of its opening. Write three different beginnings for your letter, and discuss these with others in your editing team.

Part 2: Using the best of the three leads, write a complete letter. Make sure your letter includes each of the following elements:

- An opening section with reader impact
- A sentence or paragraph that points out the benefit to the reader
- A paragraph that puts a human face on your appeal with a story or vignette
- A paragraph that presents factual and logical information
- A conclusion to your letter that clearly asks for a contribution
- A celebrity signer, and use of this celebrity throughout the letter
- A postscript.

Putting it Together

Effective direct-mail appeals have various components: envelope, appeal letter, response devise, and acknowledgment. Each presents an opportunity for the public relations writer.

Envelope

The purpose of the envelope is to get the letter delivered and opened. An envelope with an address and a stamp is all that is needed to ensure delivery. But dissemination does not equal communication, and the envelope's job is not over when the letter carrier drops it in the mailbox. Once the letter arrives at its destination, the envelope has another function: to entice the recipient to read the contents within.

Studies indicate that half to three-quarters of unsolicited letters are thrown away unopened. A report by the Direct Mail Association indicates that 43 percent of mail recipients "read immediately" information from social, charitable, or political senders. Recipients say they plan to respond to 9 percent of such organizations.

Following are some suggestions for increasing the effectiveness of your direct mail.

Address. Hand-addressed envelopes are likely to get opened. They suggest a personal letter inside, and few people fail to open such an envelope. Nonprofit organizations sometimes find volunteers willing to write addresses on envelopes for appeal letters; some computer type fonts mimic the look of handwriting.

Individually typed addresses also are effective, whether they are prepared on a typewriter or computer generated. Least effective are address labels, which have an impersonal, one-of-thousands feel.

Envelope. Professional-looking envelopes are most effective. Most successful appeal envelopes are No. 9 (letter size, approximately 4 × 7 inches) or No.10 (legal size, roughly 4 × 9½ inches). Solid-faced envelopes are more personal than window envelopes, which may remind recipients of a bill. However, window envelopes require only a personalized letter inside the envelope without the extra task of addressing the envelope.

Teaser Copy. Direct mailers take different approaches to teaser copy on the outside of the envelope. Many avoid it because personal letters don't have teasers, and they want an appeal letter to seem as personal as possible.

Others believe that teasers can be effective if they involve a celebrity signer, powerful artwork, or some other device to entice the recipient inside. For example, envelopes sometimes appeal to a sense of urgency. A pro-choice organization uses a red banner above the address with the notice "Urgent Membership Renewal." The envelope also features a sticker "WARNING: Federal election law prohibits NARAL Pro-Choice America from sending inside political communications to inactive members" (but of course, folks who renew active membership will be able to receive the tantalizing inside information).

Mailers should be aware of the Deceptive Mailings Prevention Act of 1990, a federal provision that prohibits the use of mail solicitations that look like government notices such as IRS refund checks.

Postage. First-class postage stamps provide the most effective way to get an appeal letter opened, because they enhance the personal tone of the letter. But first-class postage is expensive for large mailings. An effective alternative is to use a bulk-rate postage stamp available to nonprofit organizations. This costs much less than first-class stamps but carries the same personal touch. Metered mail loses some of the personal tone. Least personal of all is the preprinted postage block.

Appeal Letter

The **appeal letter** is the central part of the direct-mail package. It presents the persuasive message to the reader. Thus the letter should be both attractive and easy to understand. Concerning the mechanical elements of the appeal letter, consider the following suggestions.

Letter Length. Longer letters are more effective than shorter ones. This goes against the common wisdom, which supposes that less is better. But psychological studies show that, when people care about the cause or issue, they want to know as much as possible. Optimum length varies according to the topic, the sender, the recipient, and the situation. In general, though, the longer the better. Many effective appeal letters are three or more pages long.

Make sure the letter goes to people who care about the issue (as it will if you have carefully targeted your publics). Then trust that the recipient will want to read your letter and will appreciate the information in it. Generally, people who have willingly involved themselves with organizations that focus on human rights, political issues, medical research, and so on genuinely want to receive detailed progress reports and other information about the cause.

Appeal Packet. Let the letter dominate the appeal packet. Direct-mail letters may stand alone, or they may be supplemented by brochures or other inserts. If you use more than a letter, don't allow the supplemental materials to take the focus away from the main selling letter, and don't pack the envelope so the reader sees the tangential material before the letter itself.

Letterhead. Use professional-looking paper. Put the appeal letter on organizational letterhead that is attractive. Use either white or off-white, quality-bond paper. Some studies suggest that soft-toned paper enhances response. Use standard black ink, perhaps with a subdued second color for effect.

Format. Appeal letters should look like letters. Type them with a ragged right margin and single spacing, with extra spacing between paragraphs. A more formal printed look destroys the illusion that the letter has been written for the individual reader.

Type Font. Choose a type font that is reader-friendly. Generally that means a serif font such as Times, Caslon, or a related font seen most often in books, magazines, and newspapers. Fonts with serifs are easier to read in paragraph-length passages.

Avoid sans serif text and decorative fonts such as script and gothic, because these are less easy to read. Avoid Courier fonts that have an amateurish typewriter look. In particular, resist any urge to use cute fonts best suited for birthday invitations, Halloween greetings, and cowboy theme parties.

Graphics. Use typographical devices to give your letter visual appeal and to increase legibility and readability. These are especially helpful for readers who scan the text quickly, providing them with occasional pause points in their quick trip through the letter.

Effective typographical devices include all-capital letters, bullets, boldface type, extra spacing between paragraphs, indented paragraphs, italic fonts, subheads, and underlines. Also consider using text boxes and/or color highlights for key words or phrases.

Use such graphic devices carefully. They should call attention to pertinent words, phrases, or sentences. Studies show that typographical devices can enhance readability when they call the reader's attention to a few items on each page.

But be selective, and use only one or a few of the various graphic devices available. Too much can look like a circus poster.

Photos. Photographs, charts, graphs, and other artwork enhance the written communication. Such art attracts the reader's interest, drawing the eye to an engaging selling point. The figures should enhance the story and be of high technical quality. Make sure the topic is appropriate to your appeal. Humorous photos rarely work. Effective direct-mail pieces generally include captions with each piece of art, both to explain the visual element and to take advantage of heightened reader interest to repeat the central message or appeal.

Margin Notes. Handwritten margin notations can be effective. If the subject involves apparently personal topics such as membership, children's causes, or animals, they can add a personal touch. But again, don't overuse this device.

Exercise 16.4

Designing an Appeal Letter

In addition to strong writing, the public relations person must develop a pleasing look for the appeal letter. Revise the following text of an actual fundraising letter (with only the names changed). Prepare the letter for publication, noting appropriate paragraphing, and highlight the text with graphic devices such as bullets, dashes, boldface type, italic type, underlines, and other features. Print your revised letter in its finished form.

Ezekiel Smith
15 Farnham Drive
Someplace, N.Y. 12345

Dear Mr. Smith:

One of the fondest memories of my youth is the warm, relaxed, safe feeling of visiting the public library. Merely by opening a book and turning its pages, I could raft down the Mississippi or learn that stars weren't found just in Hollywood but also in the heavens. Each trip to the library was like visiting my best friend. If you're like me, you probably still recall the title of your favorite childhood book. As an adult, you know this feeling still exists; the library is the most interesting, most inviting place in town. Whether you want to find a best-seller for poolside summer reading or sheet music for a sing-along at the family reunion, whether you're learning to "surf the Net" at "Technology Tuesdays" or bringing your children or grandchildren to summer reading programs, whether you're looking for information on recent health care issues or upcoming cultural events, the library is your best option. And that's the reason I am writing you today, to ask you, as one of the thousands of Iroquois County residents whose lives are enriched by the books, facilities and services of our outstanding Library System, to return something to the library by making a contribution toward its sustenance and growth. A tax-deductible contribution or pledge to the library is, in reality, a gift to yourself, your family, and to people of all ages in virtually every part of Iroquois County. I hope you will consider making a contribution or pledge of $75, $200 or more to keep our local libraries among the best in the nation. Of course, any amount you can afford will be appreciated. If you make a pledge, you will be billed quarterly. Our 22 branches and member libraries have always been an important source of information, education and recreation. More recently, however, the Iroquois County Public Library has become home to an international celebrity, Huckleberry Finn. Visitors can actually see the original handwritten manuscript of what has been called the greatest American

continued . . .

Exercise 16.4 . . . *continued*

novel on permanent display in the Central Library's new Mark Twain Room. And if you can't visit the Mark Twain Room in person, you can still find all of Twain's works (and all of the other authors in the library) on our new electronic catalog, Beacon. The Mark Twain Room and Beacon are two of the many projects made possible by generous donations of people like you to The Library Foundation. The days are gone when tax dollars alone can sustain all the unique and special library services our community needs, expects and deserves. That's why it is so important for people like you to take action to preserve all that our libraries offer. Help to ensure that the programs that mean so much are always there to keep our community strong. Please, act now to support the full spectrum of library resources and services that enrich so many lives and promote a brighter future for all of Western New York. Make a generous contribution or pledge to The Library Foundation. Tomorrow's library relies on the generosity you demonstrate today. (signed) Samuel R. Coltrane, President of The Library Foundation of Iroquois County, Inc.

Response Device

The **response device** is the means of making it easy for the reader to offer support. This is the card or envelope flap that the reader is expected to fill out.

Donor Intention. The most important element of the response device is the statement of support. *YES, I want to help save the whales (feed the orphans, find a cure, or get him elected or impeached)*. That YES is crucial. When the reader checks the box, the commitment has been made. All that remains is the follow-up: writing the check, filling out the membership application, signing the petition. But the reader has already taken the pledge, and follow-through is virtually assured.

Donor Information. Include space for the needed details from the reader. In addition to items such as name, postal address, e-mail contact information, perhaps a telephone number, that space also may include practical information for the reader: where to respond, tax deductibility, and so on. The reply card should not introduce any new information not previously included in the letter, but the card can restate the main benefits or summarize the appeal.

Suggested Contributions. Include suggested contributions if the appeal is for funds. Give a range of appropriate contribution levels. Studies show it makes little difference if the amounts are listed in ascending or descending order. Giving several amounts is important so that the would-be donor has an idea of what would be helpful to the organization. A give-all-you-can or a give-until-it-hurts message does not work well for an appeal letter. Instead, suggest some reasonably painless amounts.

If possible, either the letter or the response device should indicate what various levels of contribution could achieve. Studies suggest the effectiveness of highlighting the preferred contribution: listing it first, using boldface or some other typographical device such as encircling it. Always leave a space for "other." This space will be used either by people who want to be particularly generous or by those who care about the cause even if right now they cannot contribute as much as you have suggested.

Fundraising letters often include an option for recipients to defer on giving but to request information or remain connected. "I can't contribute now, but I'd like more information." This gives reason for the organization to consider the recipient as a potential future donor and to continue providing information about the organization and its cause.

For organizations operating close to home (a church building project, for example), the option of a monthly contribution is something to consider. For example, a pledge of $10 a month is a rather painless way for a donor to provide the organization with $120 for the year. This is more effective when the donor has continuing involvement with the organization soliciting the donation.

Return Envelope. The return envelope should make it easy for the donor to support the organization. It should be addressed back to the organization.

Traditional wisdom is that it should include postage so the donor does not have to scrounge for a stamp. The postal service provides the option for a pre-paid return envelope that costs the organization only for those envelopes actually returned. Studies have found that actual stamps gain a higher return rate than such postage-paid labels. Stamps are more effective than metered postage labels, because stamps are more personal. Some people simply don't want to waste a stamp on the return envelope, so they make at least a small contribution when they otherwise would not.

Sometimes nonprofit organizations note in their appeal that the recipient is helping the organization by providing his or her own stamp. There certainly is a logic to this, though to some it seems a bit cheesy to expect the donor both to make the contribution and then to pay for the contribution to be delivered.

Acknowledgment

When someone gives you a gift or helps you in some way, you should say thanks. You learned that before you went to kindergarten. The same thing is appropriate in philanthropic public relations. It also is practical. After receiving a contribution or another type of support, an organization should send an acknowledgment. This personalized letter should be as timely as possible. There is something disingenuous in a letter that thanks you for a contribution you gave 10 months ago and goes on to ask for another as part of this year's campaign.

Specifically, the acknowledgment should thank the donor. It also should reinforce the sentiment that led to the gift: for example, by pointing out how helpful the contribution is, how it will be used, or how it benefits the reader or the cause. This is an underlying purpose of the acknowledgment: to lay the groundwork for continued participation and support by the donor.

A residential treatment center for people living with AIDS found an elegant way to express appreciation to donors:

> On behalf of the residents at Benedict House, I would like to thank you for your generous and continued support of our work, especially your recent gift of $300. As you are aware, Benedict House exists almost solely through private contributions from supporters such as you. Consequently, your gift was indeed cause for celebrating.

The image of people with AIDS *celebrating* because of a donor's gift is an inspiring one indeed. It reinforces in a very positive way the original intention of the donor, and likely creates a memorable bond that underlies a long-term commitment to the organization.

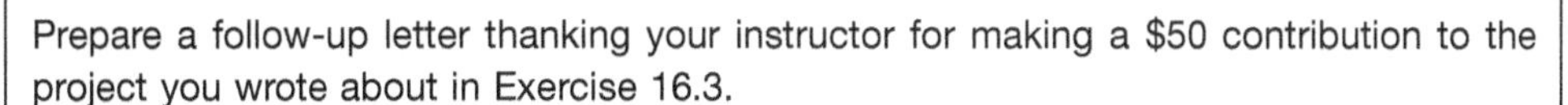

Exercise 16.5

Writing a Follow-Up Letter

Prepare a follow-up letter thanking your instructor for making a $50 contribution to the project you wrote about in Exercise 16.3.

Online Fundraising

Most organizations have turned to the Internet in fundraising. Surveys show that upward of 78 percent of people living in North America are wired into the Internet. Increasingly they are going online to send donations to charitable or other nonprofit causes. Most organizations are making it easier for would-be donors to contribute online. It's cost effective, with little overhead or promotional expenses.

Nonprofit Organizations

Americans and Canadians respond generally to disasters. Usually we send checks. But philanthropy saw a major change when Internet-based giving became a viable option.

The history of online giving follows human and natural disasters. Hurricane Mitch in 1998, one of the worst storms in 50 years, was the first occasion in which a substantial amount of money came through the Internet. After an earthquake in Turkey the following year, the American Red Cross raised $140,000 in one day online. During the humanitarian crisis in Kosovo, Catholic Relief Services raised $700,000 online, only 10 percent of the total raised through direct-mail solicitation, but a significant impact for a new tool that wasn't even active until the Kosovo crisis was easing up.

It was the September 11 attacks on New York City and Washington in 2001 that caused Internet-based giving to mushroom. More than $1.3 billion was donated within the first several weeks alone, about 20 percent of that from online donors.

Online giving surged again following Hurricane Katrina in 2005. Within a month, the American Red Cross reported that a third of the $891 million in relief donations was raised over the Internet. Groups as diverse as the American Humane Society, Paralyzed Veterans of America, Catholic Charities-USA, and the American Diabetes Association reported that as much as half of their Katrina relief was from online donors.

The American Red Cross received $5.6 million online in the first 48 hours following the 2010 earthquake in Haiti. Ultimately the ARC raised $30 million from cell phone texts and a viral campaign spurred by Twitter, Flickr, YouTube, and Facebook. The International Fund for Animal Welfare raised $1 million to rescue animals injured or left homeless by the earthquake; $400,000 of that was from online donations supported by an extensive social media network.

The Network for Good is an e-philanthropy portal site where people can donate to various causes, volunteer, or otherwise get involved in issues they care about. It was founded by Time Warner, Yahoo, AOL, Google, and dozens of other corporate sponsors representing a partnership of technology companies, media organizations, and foundations. The site (networkforgood.org) capitalizes on the instant gratification that online donors want and provides access to nonprofit organizations registered with the Internal Revenue Service, allowing donors to channel their contributions through the network to any recipient they wish.

Political Fundraising

Web-based fundraising also has been a significant tool in the political arena, and its importance is mushrooming.

Internet-based fundraising began with the 2004 presidential campaign, when more than $100 million was raised online. Online contributions averaged $111, three times the amount sent through the mail, according to a report by the George Washington Graduate School of Political Management.

In the 2008 presidential election, Barack Obama broke existing records with more than $500 million in online contributions. The average contribution was $80, coming from about 6.5 million donors.

In the 2010 mid-term election, an estimated $4 billion was raised online, according to Piryx.com, an online fundraising company.

The Institute for Politics, Democracy and the Internet at George Washington University concluded that the Internet has transformed how political campaigns communicate with their supporters and has become a tool to organize as well as raise money. The institute also developed a comprehensive profile of the online political donor:

- Most younger donors give online.
- Unsolicited contributions have increased because of the Internet.
- Internet users are more likely to be asked to contribute and are more likely to be politically active.
- Online small donors (less than $200) are no more partisan than other political donors.

Most charitable online fundraising is passive; the organization provides information at its website for would-be donors who seek it out. Some political fundraising has taken a more direct route, using e-mail to solicit donors, and political machines often have sophisticated resources to target and track contributions.

But other public relations techniques support online fundraising. One study found that nearly half of online donors said their contribution was unsolicited and not based on mail, phone, or e-mail requests. Because they don't represent potentially large gifts, most individuals are not on the mailing or call lists of most political organizations. In previous campaigns, the small giver often had to search for ways to contribute. With online fundraising mushrooming, some observers see a change in the character of American politics, shifting the base away from the wealthy few and into the hands of the average citizens of moderate financial means.

Power of the Web

Internet-based fundraising offers some real benefits for organizations seeking donor support. Overhead costs are lower. Contributions are higher. And as an added bonus, online donations make it easy for the organization to expand its donor base, yielding new names for future fundraising efforts.

More Generous. Contributions made via credit card or systems such as PayPal tend to be higher than donations made by check. They also can provide a very quick response. In late

2005 and early 2006, charitable organizations reported record donations for the tsunami relief effort in Southeastern Asia. Online donations to the Red Cross yielded twice as much in contributions than the traditional phone banks, $18 million in two days following the disaster. Catholic Relief Services was so overwhelmed by donors that its website crashed, though the organization went on to post its largest relief effort to date, $190 million.

A study by the Network for Good reported that online giving had collectively passed $2 billion. The network itself has raised $400 million online directly, which donors have channeled to 50,000 nonprofit organizations such as the American Red Cross, Catholic Charities, Human Society, Veterans of Foreign Wars, Baptist World Alliance, Doctors with Borders, Islamic Relief, and thousands more.

Within three days of the 2011 earthquake and tsunami in Japan, the American Red Cross received $81.6 million by text from cell-phone users.

Faster. For the tsunami response, most relief agencies reported that between a quarter and a half of their donors gave online: the American Red Cross received $84 million in online donations alone; UNICEF, $35 million online; World Vision, $13 million; Catholic Relief Services, $12 million; Save the Children, $11 million; Salvation Army, $8 million; CARE, $7 million; American Jewish World Services, $3.5 million; Islamic Relief USA, $1 million—all online donations within less than a month of the earthquake and tsunami.

Spontaneous. Most of the donations in the tsunami assistance efforts were unsolicited by the relief agency. Rather, they were spontaneous responses initiated by donors based on media coverage of the disaster.

But the aid organizations are not relying solely on the news media to solicit contributions. During relief efforts following the Haiti earthquake, most aid organizations maximized the media exposure with a series of requests for contributions. They used e-mail and social networking sites as well as more traditional telephone, direct-mail, and advertising techniques.

Wider Pull. Another benefit of web-based fundraising is that it is not bound by the geographic boundaries of many organizations. For example, CARE Canada receives contributions from throughout the world, though its traditional direct-mail fundraising activities are focused on the Canadian provinces. The agency said its new international donors are younger and more high-tech than the agency's usual donor base, a hopeful demographic shift introducing new potential donors that the philanthropic organization undoubtedly will pursue.

New Donor Base. The Internet also can pull in new names to expand the donor base of an organization. One study by Epsilon, a national fundraising company, found that 88 percent of online donors were new contributors to the organization. Essentially, these were people who came to the organization, waving their money and asking for the privilege of helping out. That's a real turnaround from the traditional direct-mail route of buying or renting names from database organizations.

Younger Donor Base. The George Washington University study pointed out that more than 80 percent of Americans aged 18 to 34 who contribute to political candidates or causes do so online. Such reports offer enormous hope to political and other fundraisers as the Internet solidifies its role as a major means of communication, particularly among younger and more educated people.

Cost of E-Mail Fundraising

E-mail is more cost effective than postal mail appeals. For one thing, purchasing postal mail lists often is more expensive than buying e-mail lists. While e-mail appeals cost little to disseminate, large-scale appeals using postal mail incur heavy costs because of printing and packaging, and testing with a pilot mailing, as well as the postage cost itself.

Additionally, experts who favor e-mail appeals report that they show results within seven to 10 days, compared to four to six weeks needed for response from postal appeals. Thus, e-mail provides a quicker return-on-investment for the organization making the appeal.

Another advantage is that e-mail can be "pushed" to its audience like print mail, rather than being posted as a website where readers have to "pull" it out. Plus, it is easy to track even those recipients who do not open their e-mail appeals.

Is there a downside to e-mail appeals? Sure. Like most options, there are minuses as well as pluses. Spam traps on many computers, especially business systems, filter out unsolicited bulk e-mails, so the message may not get to the reader. Older persons, often more generous in their giving habits, are less likely to be represented among e-mail users.

Meanwhile, all e-mail solicitors should be aware of the legal provisions of the CAN-SPAM Act (which stands for Controlling the Assault of Non-Solicited Pornography and Marketing Act of 2003) and the European Privacy and Electronic Communications Regulations, as well as the policies of various Internet providers.

The response rate for all fundraising efforts is low. Acquisition mailings (those intended to acquire new donors for an organization) typically generate less than 2.5 percent. Compare that to less than 1 percent for e-mail solicitations. But the lower response rate is offset by much lower distribution costs, though it can be more expensive to obtain a useful list of e-mail addresses than of postal addresses.

Writing E-Mail Appeals

Here are a few tips for writing fundraising appeals for e-mail distribution:

- *Include the appeal in the subject.* "Donate to the Earthquake Relief Effort Now." Some experts note that while the direct subject line may have a lower rate of people who open the e-mail, it generates a much higher rate of giving. The very act of opening the e-mail signals a recipient more disposed toward giving.
- *Keep the copy brief.* Unlike mailed fundraising letters, which can be long, e-mailed solicitations should be much shorter.
- *Include a link.* One way to keep the e-mail short is to offer readers a link to a website with additional information.
- *Write strategically.* Include a clear statement of the problem and acknowledge your reader's interest in the issue. Indicate what your organization is doing to address the problem, and invite your reader to assist. Give specific examples of how donations will be used. Provide examples or anecdotes that can put a human face on the issue your organization is addressing. End with a closing summary and a signature, and perhaps a PS.
- *Include a donation link.* Give the reader a link to make an online donation. Make this simple and clear: "Click here to donate."
- *Keep the transaction page simple.* When readers click on the donate button, they are taken to a **transaction page**, also called a **landing page**. This is where readers do

the business of donating, providing name and address, credit card info, or PayPal details. Keep this simple. They came here intending to donate, so there's no need for a further sell. You might provide options such as making a memorial contribution in honor of someone else and/or requesting a memorial card to be sent to a different address.

- *Includes other links for additional information.* As appropriate, direct readers to other websites where they can obtain relevant information. But be careful not to send them off to another organization's site where they might make a donation there.
- *Generate a thank-you.* After a donation has been received, send a thank-you acknowledging the gift. Follow the guidelines above for acknowledging direct-mail donations. Some organizations have found that this e-mailed thank-you itself can generate a second, smaller donation, so include a donation link.

Exercise 16.6

Writing an E-Mail Fundraising Letter

Review the direct-mail fundraising letter you wrote in Exercise 16.3. Revise this as an e-mail appeal. Include the following elements:

Part 1: Appeal letter

- Subject line
- Problem statement with reader . . .
- Statement of how your organization is addressing the problem, and invitation for the reader to join your response efforts
- Examples of how contributions are used
- Anecdotes putting a human face on the problem and response
- Closing summary
- Signature
- PS
- Donation link
- (Include other links as appropriate).

Part 2: Acknowledgment

- Thank-you follow-up.

17 Public Relations Advertising

Advertising is a clear example of persuasive communication. Its purpose is obvious: to influence the attitudes, opinions, and actions of the audience. **Consumer advertising**, also called **product advertising**, seeks to sell products or services; it is a tool of sales, merchandising, and marketing with little overlap into public relations. **Public relations advertising**, on the other hand, seeks to "sell" the organization—its ideas, its causes, and other noncommercial messages. Public relations advertising uses the tools and techniques of advertising to help an organization communicate with its publics. It can be paid placement as in advocacy advertising, or it can be unpaid as in public service advertising.

This chapter will first explore the issue of creativity, so vital to public relations advertising. It then will look at the various types of advertising, focusing in on its use for public relations purposes. The chapter then will look at various writing techniques, and finally will address the issue of public service advertising. Here are your learning objectives for this chapter:

- To identify differences between consumer advertising and public relations advertising
- To use creative techniques to develop advertising copy
- To write effective copy for a public relations advertisement.

Creativity

Let's begin by acknowledging that everyone is creative to a greater or lesser degree. Each of us holds a place on the creativity scale, somewhere between Steven Spielberg and a tree stump. The consideration is not: Am I creative? Rather the questions should be: In what ways am I creative? How can I become more creative? How can I use my creativity in presenting public relations messages?

What is **creativity**? It's the ability to develop an original solution to a problem, giving it a fresh look or a new angle. Creativity is a blend of imagination and innovation, perhaps with a touch of weirdness. Some people say that creativity is an in-born capability, a gift, a knack. Either you have it or you don't, so they say. But those people are wrong. Imagination can be nurtured, and innovative ability can be learned. As for the weirdness, most people have enough of that already, so all we have to do is acknowledge this and get comfortable with it.

Rather than being an inevitable natural trait, creativity is more like the talent of a musician or the skill of an athlete. It is a seed, present to a degree in everyone, which must be nourished for it to flower. Creativity develops through practice, patience, and perseverance. That's not simply a hope. Rather research has shown that (1) everyone has creative capacity, (2) creativity can be learned, and (3) some techniques for building creativity are more effective than others.

Actually, we should talk about creativity being relearned. Social scientists note that children are naturally creative, but as we grow up and conform to the conventions of school and society, we often lose much of that natural creativity.

Professional creativity in public relations is a product of strategic planning—the result of careful analysis of the idea or object being promoted, the public being addressed, and the organization's objectives. This creativity is the result of a person's ability to prepare an effective and imaginative response to resolve a particular problem.

Consider various traits that have been associated with creative people. Some are rooted in natural proclivities and preferences. But all are within the control of any individual, and all can be cultivated and enhanced. Creative people are:

- Able to see the big picture
- Aesthetically interested and artistically inclined
- Curious and inquisitive
- Disciplined and tenacious
- Eclectic and varied in their tastes
- Independent thinkers
- Intelligent and capable
- Intuitive and spontaneous
- Nonconformist and rebellious
- Open to new experiences
- Original and inventive
- Self-confident and resolute
- Visual thinkers
- Voracious readers.

Let's discuss two different types of creativity techniques: free association and forced association. In addition, "FYI: The Creative Environment" speaks to potential creative blocks and what they mean for public relations writers.

FYI *The Creative Environment*

At Buffalo State of the State University of New York, the Center for Studies in Creativity offers the only graduate degree program in creativity in the United States. Experts in creativity and innovation have identified several blocks to creativity that can be helpful in understanding and building a creative environment.

- *Personal blocks to creativity* include lack of self-confidence, tendency to conform, need for the familiar, emotional numbness, saturation, excessive enthusiasm, and lack of imaginative control.
- *Problem-solving blocks to creativity* include premature judgments, use of poor problem-solving approaches, lack of disciplined effort, poor language skills, and rigidity.
- *Situational blocks to creativity* include isolation, the belief that only one type of thinking is appropriate, resistance to new ideas, and reliance on experts.

What does this mean to public relations writers? The more we understand about the creative environment, the more we can try to build an environment that is likely to support our efforts to be creative.

Exercise 17.1

Freewriting on Creativity

Freewrite for five minutes on the following topic: *In what ways am I a creative person?* Then discuss this with your classmates.

Free Association

The mind, when freed of various restraints, can be prompted to generate creative ideas by using undefined connections. The methods for achieving this are called **free association techniques**. They include freewriting, brainstorming, buzz groups, and brainwriting. Each is described briefly below. In addition, "Tips for Better Writing: Limbering Up Mentally" offers some advice for pre-writing creative warm-ups.

Tips for Better Writing *Limbering Up Mentally*

Calisthenics and stretching exercises can limber up your body before you jog or work out. Similarly, creativity exercises can limber up your mind before you begin writing. One of the hallmarks of a good writer is a person who can take an ordinary item or action and look at it in a fresh new way. It's also known as thinking outside the box.

The purpose of this exercise is not necessarily to get the right answer but rather to grapple with a problem and approach it from various perspectives. Following are several exercises to limber your creative mind. Answers are listed at the end of this chapter.

1. Give at least three different answers to this question: What is half of 13?
2. What is the logical pattern for arranging these numbers in the following order: 8, 5, 4, 9, 1, 7, 6, 3, 2, 0?
3. You leave home, take three left turns, and meet two men in masks. Where are you, and who are the masked men?
4. What is the shortest day of the year?
5. A businessman preparing to travel to Tokyo asks an adult Japanese friend, who is from Tokyo, to teach him Japanese. He learns to speak just as his teacher does. When he gets to Tokyo and begins speaking, his business colleagues laugh at him. Why?
6. Look at each of the following words, arranged alphabetically, for 15 seconds. Then, within 90 seconds, arrange them in one complete and logical sentence: always an and at both calm each early emotionally exercising felt has he him hour least made morning physically that.
7. Mary goes to school every day, but seldom does homework. Of the 25 students in Mary's class, 24 are good students. Mary often is called into the principal's office, but never gets into trouble. Why?
8. What English word has six i's?
9. A window washer was cleaning the 25th-floor windows on a skyscraper. He was not protected by a harness or any other kind of safety device, yet when he slipped and fell he was not injured. Why?
10. What can be seen and has no weight, but the more that are put in an empty tin can, the lighter the can becomes?

Freewriting. You're already familiar with freewriting through the exercises in this book designed to help you develop some insight and creative approaches to your writing. **Freewriting** is a creativity technique because it helps you overcome the restrictions of grammar and style as well as the need for logic and coherence in an effort to begin writing. In freewriting, ideas should flow freely; refinements come later.

Brainstorming. You also may be familiar with **brainstorming**. A technique that can be used by one person or a small group, brainstorming calls for participants to set the goal of generating a large quantity of ideas around a particular issue, problem, or approach. One of the "rules" of brainstorming is to be open to consider far-out and seemingly unworkable ideas. Participants in a brainstorming session should not make any judgments about the quality of ideas being generated, and they are encouraged to piggyback on each other's ideas.

Buzz Group. Another method of brainstorming involves the **buzz group**, a method particularly effective with large numbers of people. This involves reorganizing into a series of small subgroups to brainstorm ideas and then reporting them back to the larger group.

Brainwriting. A related activity, **brainwriting**, has participants circulating among a series of poster sheets on various topics, writing at least one idea on each sheet. Participants write a new idea or develop one written by someone else. A variation of this is the idea card, in which the people remain in place and the cards circulate among them.

Forced Association

Another group of activities that stimulate creative ideas deal with forced relationships. Rather than wide-open connections used with free association techniques, **forced association techniques** prompt the mind to generate ideas by using defined connections, relying on some gentle coercion or stimulation to draw out innovative thinking. These forced relationship techniques for creativity include visual relationships, personification, similes, explained similes, and future statements.

Visual Relationship. The **visual relationship** technique uses photographs or other visual representations to nurture creativity. One implementation of this technique is to select a photograph and then ask a group to associate thoughts as they relate to a topic. For example, public relations writers seeking to promote community interest in a summer camp for children with physical limitations might use a photo of a clown to nurture their thoughts about the camp: fun, happy, frivolous, cheerful, light hearted, foolish, optimistic, no time for sadness. Or perhaps the picture of a tree: strong, growing, spreading, developing, hardy. Almost any kind of visual stimulus will do, if the participants let their imaginations roam uninhibited.

Personification. Using the technique of **personification**, you get personal with an object, treating it as you would a person. Using the technique of freewriting, this time in a forced association context, write about the object you are seeking to be creative with. Better yet, write *to* the object. For example, if you are seeking to be creative about perfume, write to the bottle of perfume: "When I see your shape, it reminds me of . . ." "When I smell you, I think about . . ." "When I see your color, it reminds me of . . ." "When I dab you on my arm, it makes me remember the time when . . ."

Simile. Another technique, the **simile**, is a verbal method that can accomplish much the same as the visual relationship tool. Let's go back to the example of the summer camp for children with physical limitations. Completing similes such as "Camp is like . . ." can generate a lot of mental images about the camp: paradise, a fun house, a playground, a gym floor for wheelchairs.

Explained Simile. A related forced association technique carries the simile through to explanation. An explained simile can lead to some interesting insights: "Our campers are like puppies because . . ." they are inquisitive, they love attention, they want to be part of everything, they don't know the meaning of "no," their curiosity knows no bounds.

Future Statement. Statements that focus on benefits or potential solutions also can be helpful. One commonly used **future statement** is called a WIBNI (Wouldn't it be nice if . . .?). This can be a powerful formula for freeing your imagination to think of possibilities. "WIBNI our campers could . . ." "WIBNI people in town thought our camp was . . ."

Exercise 17.2

Using the Freewriting Technique

In this exercise and the one following, you will prepare to create an advertisement using creative techniques. In so doing, you are moving beyond the traditional approach to public relations planning, a logical approach through which you have learned to develop planning sheets. Creative approaches can help you accomplish the same thing. In these exercises, you will use different ways to identify some of the wants, interests, and needs of your key public. You can focus on the benefits available to this public and gain insight into the position of your school in relation to its competition. Using creative techniques, you also will note some factual information that may become part of the eventual message.

Here's the scenario: You are a public relations writer for your school, and your task is to develop an advertisement to recruit students. But first you need to warm up your creativity muscles. Imagine yourself in the following situation: You are in a hot-air balloon floating above your campus. You can see the entire campus below.

Part 1: Use the freewriting technique to stretch your creativity. In this freewrite, look down on the campus and describe what you see.

Part 2: Go a step beyond the physical campus. Write about what you think about your school. What do the students you see walking below you think about your school? Why did they come here? Why do they remain? You spot a person walking alone across campus. It's you. What do you like about the school? What makes this a good example of higher education? What academic programs are particularly strong?

Part 3: In the balloon with you now is a younger friend who is in 11th grade at the high school you attended. Freewrite about your conversation with this friend. What does he or she think about attending college? What does your friend think about your school?

Part 4: Your hot-air balloon is beginning to drift away from its position above your campus. A strong wind takes it all the way to the campus of a neighboring college. Then the wind dies down, and you and your friend look down on that campus. What do you see? How is it different from your own campus? Go beyond the physical appearance. What do you tell your friend about how this institution compares with your school?

Exercise 17.3

Using the Personification Technique

This exercise will help you understand the technique of personification and how to use it in your own writing. Select a small candy bar. Pick one that isn't currently being heavily advertised, so you can approach this exercise with originality rather than being biased by existing ad campaigns.

Here is the scenario: You are developing an advertising campaign for a candy bar. Your key public is children between the ages of 8 and 14, but you may narrow this a bit, for example, by selecting boys or girls only.

Part 1: Freewrite a brief analysis of the wants, interests, and needs of this public.

Part 2: Unwrap the candy bar, and look at it for a short time. Then write: "When I see your shape, it reminds me of . . ."

Part 3: Look at the candy bar again, then write: "When I see your color, it makes me think about . . ."

Part 4: Now smell the candy and take a small bite. Then write: "When I smell you and taste you, I think about . . ."

Part 5: Review what you have written, then develop a magazine-type or billboard-type advertisement for this candy. Focus on three elements of the ad: a dominant picture, a headline, and a memorable tag line.

Public Relations and Advertising

Public relations and advertising often have had a love–hate relationship. They are related disciplines, but the question is: How closely related? Some colleges and universities teach public relations and advertising in the same department, sometimes even as a combined major; others separate them. In some organizations, one department may handle both disciplines; in others they are kept apart. Some agencies provide services in both areas; others specialize. This textbook isn't going to resolve the issue of the appropriate relationship between advertising and public relations, but it can look at that relationship.

First, a definition. **Advertising** is the nonpersonal paid communication through various media by an identified organization (either for-profit or nonprofit) for the purpose of informing and influencing a particular audience. Advertising can be classified into two major categories: product advertising and public relations advertising. Let's take a look at each, along with their various subcategories.

Consumer Advertising

The most common use of advertising is consumer advertising, also called product advertising, which is marketing oriented. That is, the ad is intended to sell a product or service. Product advertising types include retail, general, and business-to-business.

Retail Advertising. Most of the advertising for local companies and organizations is retail oriented. **Retail advertising** seeks to promote a sale, encourage use of a product or service, or otherwise sell something. Because it is local, retail advertising can be specific, including dates, locations, prices, and information on brands and various models.

General Advertising. The category of **general advertising**, also known as **national advertising** and **brand advertising**, does not provide specific information about sales dates, store locations, and so on (though sometimes this is possible through websites identified in general advertising). In promoting a new automobile, general advertising would tell consumers about a model of car, its quality, and its features. Or it might focus on an entire brand of car, rather than a specific model.

Business-to-Business Advertising. Most consumers never see **business-to-business advertising**, in which companies promote themselves in professional, trade, or industrial publications read by other businesspeople. For example, a public relations firm might advertise in a magazine for managers of auto dealerships, highlighting its experience and its record of generating community goodwill and support for dealerships.

Public Relations Advertising

Of more immediate interest to public relations practitioners is the category of **public relations advertising**, through which an organization promotes its nonmarketing messages related to the public image of an organization and community support. Public relations advertising includes four subcategories: institutional advertising, advocacy advertising, political advertising, and public service advertising. We'll look at each in more depth.

Institutional Advertising. When an ad promotes the merits of a new automobile, that's product advertising. When an ad promotes the name and reputation of the company that manufactures the car, that's **institutional advertising**. It sometimes is called **image advertising** or **corporate advertising**. Sometimes it is disparaged as **feel-good advertising**. During the football season, the NFL uses institutional advertising to enhance its reputation by promoting its charities. Other organizations use this type of advertising for other public relations purposes, such as an educational union's efforts to support an employee relations program by publicly congratulating teachers on the success of their students in a statewide test.

Budweiser engages in institutional advertising when it trots out the Clydesdales for its jingle bells and snowy woods holiday ads that simply say, "Season's Greetings." Polls show that viewers of Super Bowl XXXIX particularly liked a Budweiser image ad depicting soldiers heading off to war (presumably in Iraq) amid smiles and applause through the airport, with a voice-over saying "Thank you."

Sometimes institutional advertising is linked with crisis communications. BP spent $93 million on institutional advertising in the four months following the oil well blowout in the Gulf of Mexico in 2010, earning the company a doubling in public opinion on its handling of the oil cleanup.

Advocacy Advertising. A similar public relations use of advertising tools and techniques is **advocacy advertising** (sometimes called **issue advertising**), which focuses less on an organization and more on a cause or goal important to it. Advocacy advertising is advertising paid for by organizations to communicate their position on public issues related to their mission or business; usually, the issues deal with political, social, or economic topics.

Utilities use advocacy advertising to explain their position on energy sources or pending legislation. Unions use it to address issues of importance to them. Cause-related organizations use advocacy advertising to explain and justify their positions and to challenge the public to act in what they consider a responsible manner. Nonprofit organizations sometimes use advocacy advertising to speak out on issues that cannot be addressed through public service advertising.

Increasingly, companies are using some of the advertising space for article-like institutional ads that present what appear to be feature articles, often about celebrities. The boost for the company is the community relations value of being associated with a popular person and a worthwhile project.

Political Advertising. Closely related to advocacy advertising is **political advertising**, in which the focus is not so much on educating the public about important issues or presenting an organization's viewpoint on them, but rather on partisan political gain. Political advertising can deal with encouraging the support or rejection of specific candidates or particular pieces of legislation.

Political advertising has become an important weapon in the political arsenal, and many political interest groups are using it to promote causes rather than specific candidates. Sometimes the line gets blurred between addressing issues and influencing voters for or against candidates, and legal questions have been raised about the role of issue advertising in the political process, particularly the transparency associated with sponsors of the ads.

Reports indicate that spending on political advertising was $4.2 billion for the 2010 mid-term elections, up from $2.5 billion for the 2008 presidential-year elections. Most of it was for television, though Internet advertising is on the rise. Big spenders on political ads for the 2010 elections were unions, the U.S. Chamber of Commerce, NewsCorp (parent of Fox and the *Wall Street Journal*), and dozens of Republican-oriented front groups with names such as American Crossroads and Let's Go to Work.

In addition to individual candidate ads, topics for issue ads ranged from abortion, gun control, and animal rights through campaign reform, health care, education, Social Security, and the environment. The Annenberg Public Policy Center at the University of Pennsylvania identified hundreds of organizations sponsoring issue ads, not only Democratic and Republican political groups but also other organizations ranging from the American Medical Association to the National Smokers Alliance, from the United Bowhunters of Pennsylvania to the Coalition for Asbestos Resolution.

Public Service Advertising. Who says the media don't have a heart? Each year television and radio stations, magazines and newspapers give away about several billion dollars'-worth of free advertising time through **public service advertising**—promotional and advocacy advertisements for both print and broadcast media in which no placement costs are charged by the medium using the advertising.

Sometimes the line blurs between editorial and advertising, and between product advertising and public relations advertising. Cigna Insurance, for example, produced a public awareness advertising series called "The Power of Caring" that ran in magazines such as *Time*, *Fortune*, *People*, and *Sports Illustrated*. The ads presented features about celebrities and their charitable causes—Daisy Fuentes and the March of Dimes, Jimmy Smits and the National Hispanic Foundation for the Arts, Faith Hill and her Family Literacy Project, and Lance Armstrong and the Life After Cancer program. Cigna later shifted its cause advertising away from celebrities.

Corporations sometimes sponsor public service advertising for organizations and causes important to them, or that they believe are important to their customers. Benetton has produced ads focusing public attention on issues such as racism, AIDS, and war. American Express ads raised $1.7 million to restore the Statue of Liberty. Ford shows environmental concerns in some of its ad campaigns. Nike uses women's sports ads to promote positive messages for girls. Kenneth Cole addresses homelessness and AIDS in some ads, Eddie Bauer promotes the environment and recycling, and Phillip Morris uses some advertising to campaign for literacy.

Developing the Message

The late David Ogilvy, one of the pacesetters of advertising, once observed, "you cannot save souls in an empty church." To engage audiences, advertisers need to take the message to the people. We need to capture first their attention and then their imagination, and we eventually need to summon forth a commitment and action. "FYI: Cost versus Creativity" summarizes another of Ogilvy's statements and the implication for advertisers.

FYI *Cost versus Creativity*

In his seminal book *Ogilvy on Advertising*, David Ogilvy stated a suspicion, unsupported by research. He speculated that there is a "negative correlation between the money spent on producing commercials and their power to sell products."

Research Systems Corp., of Evanston, Ill., took up the challenge. It reported scientific findings that support Ogilvy's hunch. Research Systems found that the most effective advertising cost 40 percent less than less successful ads. Some of the high costs were the result of creative decisions to use expensive celebrity spokespersons or extravagant special effects that, while gaining audience attention, did little to sell the product.

What does this mean for the public relations writer? Don't let yourself be tempted by a desire for bigger promotional budgets. Some top-quality advertisements are simple visual productions, but they are based on effective and insightful messages. Develop a strategy rooted in research about your intended audience and focus on quality writing.

Society today is increasingly complex, and just keeping pace has become a chore. New countries on the map. New chemical elements on the periodic chart. A never-ending parade of newness. **Information overload** is the term social scientists give to this growing complexity. And it is a real burden, because the average person cannot even hope to keep up with new and more readily available information. More organizations are communicating, and they are communicating more.

Amid this abundance of public relations messages, we hope that one message—ours—will be heard above the din of the crowd. How can we shine brighter and sing louder? Certainly, we need effective creativity, nurtured through the planning process that you have been practicing throughout this course. We also can learn from the experience of others.

The public relations writer sometimes uses tools drawn from the field of advertising. When we enter this field, we should learn the successful recipes that have been developed by our advertising colleagues. In particular, we should learn that effective advertisers pay careful attention to each of the various parts of the advertising package. A standard method of evaluating the effectiveness of a print ad is to focus on five specific elements: visual, headline, copy, closing message, and layout. Let's look at each area.

Visual Message

The **visual message** presents the concept underlying the advertisement. Some advertisements use studio photographs or computer-enhanced imagery. Others use snapshots or news-type photos. Sketches, diagrams, blueprints, maps, graphs, and charts also figure in the visual message for print advertising. Video, actual or computer generated, is the parallel element for television and digital advertising. **Art** is the umbrella term for all of these visual design elements.

The following four guidelines may be helpful as you begin to develop the visual message for various kinds of public relations advertising. The focus here is mainly on print advertising, though the principles also hold for advertising on television and in digital media.

- *Use simple images.* The illustration is the first thing a reader looks at in an advertisement. If it seems interesting, the reader then will move on to the headline and eventually, perhaps, to the body copy. Advertising art is likely to be more effective when it is uncomplicated. A photograph of one person will attract more readers than a crowd scene. Too much background detail distracts the reader away from the main element.
- *Make instant connections.* The combination of artwork and headline provides the immediate impression for the reader. Most artwork—photos, sketches, and diagrams—carries a message that can be instantly absorbed and understood. This works for groups of people with various backgrounds, interests, and demographic traits. Therefore, select artwork that offers instant connections linking the message with the audience. Sometimes this leads to the use of stereotyped images that, while perhaps not always fully accurate, are usually effective. For example, grandmothers come in all shapes, sizes, and ages: 35-year-old dancers, 55-year-old business executives, 75-year-old globetrotting retirees. But for instant connections, you might go for the stereotype: dowdy, gray-haired, wearing an apron and baking cookies. Just be careful that, in using easy stereotypes, you don't demean the people you are portraying or depict them unfairly.
- *Show the product.* Effective advertising finds a way to display the focus of the advertising message: the service, idea, or product being promoted. Products are easy to display; people can see them. Intangibles that public relations advertisers deal with—organizations, services, ideas, attitudes, and values—are more of a challenge. When we can't show a photo or footage of something, we often display it by showing its results. Sometimes it can be "seen" through its absence, or perhaps in comparison with a competitive or alternative image. Often, we rely on symbols to give form to our message.
- *Promote benefits, not ingredients.* Grandma doesn't buy the chocolate fudge sundae because of its riboflavin content. No, she buys it to help her grandson forget his humiliation on the soccer field or to celebrate his success. An experienced advertiser isn't going to pitch the sundae with a list of nutritional traits, but perhaps rather as pick-me-up food, the soother of a wounded ego, a snack to be shared in good times or bad. The same advice holds for public relations advertising: Promote the benefit,

not the ingredients. At University A, professors have written 276 books and published 1,435 research papers. University B has professors who know their fields and who will help you get a good education and a satisfying job. Which message provides the better reason to enroll?

Exercise 17.4

Developing a Visual Strategy

You are public relations writer for your college or university, preparing an advertisement that will be used in high school newspapers in a 100-mile geographic area. Your objective is to interest students in attending your institution. Review the freewriting you did in Exercise 17.2. Then describe the *visual* strategy you might take for the advertisement.

Verbal Message

The **verbal message** includes the headlines, body copy, and closing message, which together complement and carry on where the visual message leaves off. The public relations writer is on home turf in preparing copy for advertising. This is your area of expertise, and virtually all of the work you have done in this course will come into play as you take on the role of copywriter. Consider the following additional guidelines for writing advertising copy.

- *Write headlines that focus readers.* While artwork attracts attention, headlines provide readers with needed information and strategically redirect the reader to both the message of the ad and the organization sponsoring it. Advertising guru David Ogilvy once pronounced that the headline is the most important element of an ad's effectiveness. In addition, headlines are read five to 10 times more often than body copy. The headline itself can be presented in various ways. From a strategic point of view, consider the following types and examples of headlines:

  News: "Introducing a new way to learn Spanish." (This type of headline is remembered more than any other.)

  Emotion: "Little Maria and her brothers go to bed hungry almost every night."

  How-to: "Three easy ways to get a great-paying job."

  Pun: "A waist is a terrible thing to mind."

  Question: "Ever wonder why Hudson-Wallaby employees always seem so happy?"

Beware of asking dumb questions that open themselves to sarcastic answers: "Would you like to get straight A's the easy way?" (Who wouldn't?) Avoid other types of problem headlines: the too-long head, mere labels, heads awash with hype, cute or tricky headlines that fail to reveal the topic, and headlines that don't indicate any benefit.

- *Brief is best.* Most advertising is based on concise copy, and professional copywriters pride themselves on their ability to pack a lot of meaning into a few words. This approach offers the greatest potential for the largest number of readers. But don't sacrifice understanding just to be terse. Research shows that people will read lengthy copy under two conditions: (1) if they are particularly interested in a topic, and (2) if they want more information about that topic.

- *One thought per ad.* Good ads focus on just one idea. Even advertisements of large dimensions don't have the luxury of wandering from one theme to another. For the copywriter the rules are simple: Know your point, make it, and don't stray.
- *Make it memorable.* All writers want their words to stick in the reader's mind, like a haunting melody that doesn't quite go away. Because advertising copy must be brief, we need to also make it memorable. A good copywriter will work through many drafts, seeking the precise word and creating just the right phrases and sentences. The two parts of an ad where you should strive for memorable phrasing are the headline and the **tag line** (the slogan or parting message). Often the memorable phrases are those that, in their simplicity, are brimming with potential and meaning. "Coke Is It!" isn't the most profound corporate statement ever made, but it is memorable. So is the "Just Do It!" slogan by Nike, the California Milk Processor Board's "Got Milk?" and Wonderbra's "Hello, Boys" as well as public relations slogans such as "I love New York" and "The few. The proud. The Marines." Think of some of the memorable messages of public service advertising. "Friends Don't Let Friends Drive Drunk" is wisdom packaged for a bumper sticker. "Give a hoot, don't pollute" has been helping the U.S. Forest Service for years, following a successful long-time run of "Only *you* can prevent forest fires."
- *Use strong narration.* Storytelling is an ancient and very effective form of communication. Good advertising copywriting features well-told stories. Anecdotes, metaphors and parables can be more forceful than mere definitions. Dialog that is natural and realistic can bring a narrative to life.
- *Use description.* Details and particulars also are the stuff of good advertising writing. In preparing to compose an advertisement, copywriters should know the characteristics of people and places being referred to. Study the technicalities and trivia about the subject of your writing. Picture imaginary scenes in exquisite detail. You will not use every detail, but well-chosen bits of information will flavor your writing and appeal to the audience's senses.
- *Be specific.* Any organization can make claims and assertions, especially when its writers use general terms. But provable reality and unquestioned facts are needed to "sell" the message to the reader. Consider two universities that offer professional training programs in public relations. University A claims to have "an excellent placement record." University B reports "80 percent of our graduates get jobs in the public relations field." Which is more convincing? Generalities are easy to hide behind. Facts are more demanding of the writer, requiring careful research and precise use. But facts convince readers far more effectively than vague claims.
- *Give a strong closing.* Readers should come away from the ad with a clear invitation or directive to do something. Vote for Candidate Jones. Visit our website. Ask for a free sample. Visit your pharmacist today. Come in for a test drive. Whatever the product, service, or cause being promoted, give the reader something to do. Like the PS in an appeal letter, the closing message is one of the most important and potentially most useful parts of the ad.

Exercise 17.5

Developing a Verbal Strategy

Using the information you developed in Exercises 17.3 and 17.4, develop the verbal strategy for two different approaches to the advertisement you plan to run in local high school newspapers about your college or university.

Advertising Layout

Think artwork. Think copy. Then think of them together. Most ads are a combination of both visual and verbal elements, which work together to determine the effectiveness of the advertising message. Often, the product itself will suggest the layout style. For example, an ad for a new computer may need to provide many technical details, relying heavily on copy. On the other hand, an ad for a new shampoo may be all about a strong visual that shows the happy results of using the shampoo.

Three common styles of advertising layouts that vary in their balance between visual and verbal messages are standard, poster-style, and editorial-style layouts.

- **Standard advertising layouts** feature both visual and textual messages: a prominent photo or other piece of artwork, along with a substantial written message. These are the advertising messages we see most often in magazines.
- Some ads are **poster-style advertising**, heavy on art with very little textual information. You see poster-style layouts in most billboards and often in magazine ads.
- Some ads include mainly a headline and a lot of body copy. You find this kind of **editorial-style advertising** layout in advocacy advertising in newspapers and magazines, by which an organization wants to present a detailed point of view. This style also shows up occasionally in publications in which the advertising mimics the look of an article.

Exercise 17.6

Developing an Advertisement

Using the visual and verbal messages you have put together thus far, draft two different approaches to a display advertisement 8 inches wide × 10 inches high. Both of these designs should include sketched visual elements along with headlines and copy. Working with other students in your class, compare the two approaches, select the one you consider the best, and justify your choice.

Advertising Media

Consider the different categories of media for your public relations advertising: print, poster, broadcast, and digital. Each category offers its own set of strengths and limitations.

Print Media. Print media advertising combines visual and textual messages, but there are some important differences. Newspaper advertising, for example, generally is implemented in black and white, while magazines regularly feature color advertising. Newspaper ads are sized in various dimensions, whereas magazines most often have full-page ads. Newspapers also place several ads on the same page, requiring the artwork, headlines, and text to work together to attract reader attention away from competing advertisements.

Increasingly, magazines are featuring special advertising features. This is a typical pattern for such advertising features—an ad presented in editorial layout that is strong on the textual message, and a complementary one presented in poster-style layout with emphasis on art and a simple headline.

Poster Media. Poster media such as transit, outdoor, and placard advertising highlight the visual messages because viewing time usually is brief.

- **Transit advertising** is located on buses and subways, either inside or on the outside of the vehicles.
- **Outdoor advertising** is carried on billboards that may offer the reader only a couple of seconds to grasp the message.
- **Placard advertising** may complement the outdoor and transit media, sometimes appearing in bus terminals and airports, sometimes in store windows or hanging in hallways and lunchrooms. All forms of poster media emphasize the visual message: a strong illustration, a meaningful headline.

The strategy underlying most poster communication is **reminder advertising**. It reinforces already-known images and ideas. It works best with a well-known and identifiable logo, symbol, or product that provides instant recognition. It often reinforces messages developed more fully in broadcast media.

Writers for poster media need to remember that their audiences will have very little time to see and understand the messages. For example, billboards along a highway provide the viewer with less than six seconds of viewing time. Messages on transmit media may literally be moving in the opposite direction.

Broadcast Media. Newspapers, magazines, and billboards are static media, with images that don't move and visuals that don't make a sound. But broadcast and cable television advertising features images that are active and dynamic. They offer possibilities for movement and sound that allow the writer to be creatively effective in presenting the organization's message. Following are some guidelines for writing advertising copy for broadcast media.

- *Write conversationally.* Make dialog natural. Use contractions and colloquial language.
- *Use short sentences.* Write text with active voice and simple words.
- *Be careful with pronunciation.* Avoid unintended alliteration and unanticipated rhymes.
- *Create a total package.* Make a place in your script for music and sound effects.

Digital Media. The Internet, social media, and other new technologies can enhance both the visual and the verbal message. They offer opportunities for animation, movement, color, and similar techniques that impact on the visual tone of the advertisement. Likewise, the verbal message can be accented by various types of primary and secondary sound, often in an interactive environment. For example, the advertisement can allow each viewer to select the language of the written or spoken message: English, Japanese, Arabic, Spanish, and so on.

Advertisers also can control the look of an ad in digital media. Here are two common layout styles:

- **Fixed layouts** maintain the specific size and layout created by the designer that will carry across all different sizes of monitors by various users.
- **Liquid layouts** allow text and graphic components to be positioned relative to the size of the viewer's browser and monitor.

Writing Public Relations Ads

Writing a public relations advertisement is generally a wide-open field, with few stylistic restrictions. It allows writers to be at their creative best.

Advertising copywriting observes some of the guidelines associated with broadcast writing, especially the need for natural-sounding dialog and simple words. It is rooted in conversational English, allowing the use of contractions, sentence fragments, and colloquialisms and other regional or nonstandard speech. It generally relies on active voice and strong verbs. Repetition, restatement, and reinforcement are common techniques.

Here are a few of the particular approaches that can be used for public relations ads being prepared for radio and television.

Testimonial. Straightforward, sales-type appeals called **testimonials** provide a platform for someone who has used the product or service, either an expert or an average person. This first-person endorsement can have a powerful influence over the audience; review the information on persuasive message sources in Chapter 3.

Public relations writers should be careful about ethical matters related to testimonials. The PRSA Member Code of Ethics and other codes require honesty in word and spirit. The Federal Communications Commission has standards that can affect testimonials and other types of advertising (for example, restrictions on an actor dressing like a doctor).

Celebrity Endorsement. Similar to the testimonial is the **celebrity endorsement**, testimony that comes from a well-known person. Organizations selecting celebrity spokespeople should follow two guidelines:

- Choose people who are admired by the public rather than those who simply are favorites of the organization and/or the ad writers.
- Select spokespeople whose professional and personal lives will reflect favorably on the organization and its cause.

Many organizations, commercial as well as nonprofit, have been embarrassed by off-camera antics and offenses of celebrity spokespeople. Tiger Woods lost many of his endorsements after his infidelity scandal and divorce. Don't expect to find too many companies trying to sign Charlie Sheen or Lindsay Lohan for celebrity endorsements.

Nonprofit organizations in particular cannot afford to waste production money or risk their reputations by putting their fate into the hands of the wrong spokesperson. Also remember that celebrities may be good at attracting attention for the organization but not particularly effective in creating interest in the issue or generating support for the cause.

Product Demonstration. Though they are used more often in consumer advertising, **product demonstrations** have a place in the world of public relations advertising. For example, a service agency can take the here-we-are-and-here's-what-we-do approach, providing viewers with an overview of its programs and briefly presenting the personal and community benefits it offers. Some demonstration-oriented advertising messages use parallel structure such as a before-and-after approach.

Drama. The technique of **drama** often is useful in public service advertising. Despite the brevity, accomplished writers can present a powerful message in 30 seconds. The secret of writing dramatic scripts for such short time frames is to confine the action: few characters, a single location, a simple plot that is easily set up and just as easily resolved. As with other advertising situations, these mini-dramas often rely on stereotyping and the use of clothing, setting, and other nonverbal cues to convey important information to the audience. The dramatic format itself has a variety of categories.

- **Problem-solution ads** set up an obstacle with which the audience can easily identify and then resolve it, often by a hero figure.
- The **fantasy format** may rely on make-believe characters or real (perhaps historical) persons in unreal situations.
- **Animation** sometimes finds its way into public relations advertising, especially some of the high-tech spots aimed at audiences of children, teens, and young adults.
- **Humor** is another type of advertising format that can be useful, though often public relations topics do not lend themselves to levity and comedy.

Reflective Piece. Public service advertising sometimes makes effective use of **reflective pieces**, also known as **mood pieces**. These involve an almost meditative use of music, poetry, scenery, and other nonverbal sensory elements that are designed to put the viewer or listener in a favorable frame of mind. This approach echoes the words of Martin Luther King, who observed, "Occasionally in life there are moments which cannot be explained by words. Their meaning can only be articulated by the inaudible language of the heart."

Symbol. Visual **symbols** can be very effective for public service advertising. Nonprofit organizations may have low budgets to produce broadcast spots, but high-impact visual symbols often are enough to carry the message. Think of the classic advertising spot developed by the Partnership for a Drug-Free America: a frying-pan, an egg, and a short message about your brain on drugs. That frying egg was a powerful symbol, a visual analogy. Or think of the simple visual metaphors used in the forest fire-prevention campaigns: some dry grass, a flame, and a bear cub.

Sound. **Sound** can enhance a radio or television advertisement. Sound effects can be especially useful. Background music easily sets an emotional tone. Studies also have shown that dialog or narration by on-screen characters is more effective than off-screen voice-overs.

If you plan to use music in your advertisement, make sure you do it legally. Use original music, or obtain permission to use recorded music. Copyright law protects public performances of music, even by nonprofit organizations and even for uses such as nonbroadcast and educational video and telephone music-on-hold. The American Society of Composers, Authors and Publishers (ascap.com) provides information and licensing permission.

Writers do not have the final say on how a scene is executed. That is in the domain of the art director or the video director. However, the writer often includes visual cues in the script to signal the intended impact of the visual element. For that reason, it is important for writers to understand some of the terms, such as those dealing with broadcast scripts. "FYI: Video Terms for Broadcast Scripts and Storyboards" explains the most commonly used terms.

FYI *Video Terms for Broadcast Scripts and Storyboards*

Fixed Camera Shots

(ES) Establishing Shot: Opening shot of a program, spot, or scene; often an LS; also called a cover shot

(ECU) Extreme Close-Up, (TCU) Tight Close-Up: Tight shot of character's face or other scene details

(CU) Close-Up: Shot of character to the armpits; used for showing dialog or registering emotion

(CS) Close Shot: Longer than a CU, this is a shot of the character to the mid-chest level; used most often for "talking heads"; also called a bust shot or a head-and-shoulders shot

(MS) Medium Shot: Shot of character to mid-thigh; provides for some background detail and limited movement of character within the shot

(FS) Full Shot: Shot of character head-to-feet

(LS) Long Shot, (WS) Wide Shot: Any shot longer than FS

Camera Movement

Panning: Horizontal scanning of a scene, or following a moving subject with a stationary camera

Tilt: Vertical scanning of a scene

Traveling: Horizontal or vertical movement of the camera relative to a subject

Zoom: Movement of a scene between the range of ECU and WS; accomplished optically without change in camera position

Transition Between Shots

Cut, Hard Edit: Most common edit between shots, with one shot beginning at frame following the end of a previous shot

Dissolve: Replacement of one scene with another by superimposing a fade-in of the latter over a fade-out of the former; indicates passage or time or change of scene

Fade-In: Transition into a scene from a blank screen (black or color)

Fade-Out: Transition out of a scene into a blank screen (black or color)

Wipe: Change of scenes vertically, horizontally, diagonally, or (with advancing technology) using any number of geometrical and other special shapes and effects

Cutaway: Cut, dissolve, or wipe to a transitional shot, then on to the next scene (such as a dissolve from a scene to a clock, showing passage of time, then on to the next scene)

Audio Effects

Environmental Sound: Natural sound appropriate to the scene, such as birds and animals in a wilderness scene or traffic sounds in a street scene

(SFX) Sound Effect: Enhanced special sounds beyond environmental ones, such as a telephone tone, the sizzle of frying food, or footsteps

(SOF) Sound-on-Film, (SOT) Sound-on-Tape: Natural sound that is linked with the action seen in the film/tape, such as dialog between characters

(VO) Voice-Over: Narration read over a shot

Production Procedures

(CG) Character Generator: Computer that produces lines, letters, and other graphics for onscreen use; graphics may be moved in and out of position as cuts, fades, dissolves, crawls across the screen, and roll-ups or roll-downs into the screen

Chroma-Key: Process of inserting background from video footage, slide or still photo behind a character who is shot against a solid-colored in-studio wall

Public Service Advertising

Until 1989, television stations were required by federal law to provide public service programming under the mandate to operate in the public interest. That changed with the Reagan administration's deregulation, when the Federal Communications Commission eased its requirements for stations to provide public interest programming. Most stations now provide significantly less free broadcast time to nonprofit organizations than they once did.

However, television stations still are required to operate in the public interest, and stations can cite their broadcast of public service ads to demonstrate service to the local community when they seek license renewal from the FCC.

PSAs serve another practical benefit to television stations. They generally are timeless spots that can be dropped in on short notice, such as when a scheduled advertiser withdraws a commercial at the last minute. If no other paying advertisers are available, stations often turn to public service ads as last-minute fill-ins.

Because the government does not regulate print media, they never developed a strong tradition of publishing public service advertising. However, the Advertising Council and other groups regularly provide newspapers and magazines with various sizes of public service ads. Some of these are published, especially in magazines and smaller nondaily newspapers.

Public Interest Topic

The point to remember about public service advertisements is that they are gifts, and you can't demand a gift. PSAs are given free air time by television and radio stations and free space in publications that judge the topics to be interesting and fair comments on timely topics in the public interest. This is a call that can be made only by the media. The public relations practitioner may think the topic deals with public interest and can make a case for it. But the decision on whether to provide air time or space for a particular advertising message will be made by the station.

Television programmers who make the decisions about PSAs offer four criteria for a spot to be accepted: eligible organization, local angle, appropriate topic, and creative presentation.

Eligible Organization. Only nonprofit organizations can qualify for PSA time. Television and radio do not offer free time to businesses promoting themselves, even if they are responsible and important members of the community. Broadcasters do not favor even all nonprofit organizations. Free airtime is less likely for organizations that are partisan, such as political or religious organizations, and for those that are controversial, such as many advocacy groups.

Sometimes corporations work in partnership with nonprofits, producing their public service spots that are distributed nationally and locally. This is part of the community relations program of some corporations.

For example, Ashland Oil developed a multimillion-dollar corporate advertising campaign to support education following a critical report by the National Commission on Excellence in Education. The Kentucky-based global oil company focused ads on how teachers affect individual students and society in general. It sponsored student visits to colleges and universities, and it developed an audio-visual program to encourage students to think about their future. Ashland also sponsored a stay-in-school project by the Advertising Council. Admitting that part of its motivation was to improve its image and support its sales, the company said it sponsored the ads also because "it is the right thing to do, and we are in a position to do it."

Local Angle. Many national organizations provide regional versions of their ads instead of generic national spots. Such spots have a greater chance of being accepted by local broadcasters, who naturally resent being asked for free airtime that doesn't appear to serve the interests and needs of their particular audiences. Localizing an advertising spot can be as simple as ending the spot with a three-second local tag, either provided by the national organization or added by the local station. Or it may be as sophisticated as a specially edited version of the spot with local information, images, or speakers woven into the central message.

Many stations prefer to co-sponsor a public service message with a nonprofit organization rather than simply give the organization free airtime. They may add a tag such as "This is a reminder from Channel 7 and the local Girl Scout Council." The result is a closer identification of the station with the public service message, and an ally for the organization that may have spin-off benefits such as promotions, public affairs programming, or news coverage.

Appropriate Topic. Each station and publication develops its own guidelines for what topics are appropriate materials for public service advertising, and proposed PSAs must heed these guidelines.

Acceptable themes deal with nonpolitical, noncommercial, nonsectarian, and socially acceptable themes. Contact the program director or public service manager at a television or radio station, or the advertising director of a magazine or newspaper. Acceptable topics generally include health and safety issues: seat belts, safe driving, child abuse, disease detection, alcohol and other drug abuse, handicap awareness, and medical research (unless it's a controversial aspect such as stem-cell research). Other topics that often find their way into PSA spots include education, the environment, and family life, as long as the presentation isn't partisan or controversial.

Most television and radio stations would allow for general get-out-the-vote spots, but they would not provide free airtime for partisan political advertising. Similarly, a nonpartisan group such as the League of Women Voters may receive free airtime, but the local Republican Party probably would not, even with the same get-out-the-vote message, because of its vested interest in the outcome of the voting.

Some stations allow nonprofit organizations to ask for support in PSAs but not for financial contributions. However, the station or publication may allow the nonprofit group to purchase commercial time at a discounted rate for its fundraising activities.

Likewise, stations may provide free airtime for the charitable, educational, and community service activities of religious organizations, but not for denominational religious messages. National projects such as the Advertising Council's Religion in American Life campaign and local inter-religious groups have been successful in obtaining PSA status for nondenominational messages on religious, moral, or spiritual themes.

Some of the most interesting topics of the day are the controversial ones. Issues that stir the hearts and minds of people are those that are contentious, multifaceted, and disputed. Police brutality, euthanasia, international warfare, medical use of marijuana, gay rights, human rights, pro-life/pro-choice, tax reform—these are the stuff of great and wonderful controversies. But they usually are off-limits for PSAs.

Why? Think about it. Why would a broadcaster give time to an organization presenting a message that would cause many of its audience members to complain? Forget about the myth of a liberal-leaning media. News media corporations are pretty conservative. They aren't likely to rile audiences and advertisers if they don't have to. It is difficult enough for a station to defend its own news coverage and network presentations, without also having to defend free airtime for groups with which many viewers or listeners might vehemently disagree.

So it's understandable why a broadcaster would refuse PSAs on controversial topics. This frustrates public relations practitioners working with organizations that deal with controversial issues, because in some ways it makes their successful advocacy of a point of view dependent on the charity of a broadcaster. That's one of the problems with charity: We can't demand it; we can only request it, and then be thankful when it is given.

Creative Presentation. Interesting and lively writing is essential for public service advertising. There are so many good causes, so many important messages, that a radio or television station cannot hope to provide a voice for each one. Often, a determinant is writing quality. Most television stations, for example, would refuse to accept spots that feature slides or still photographs with off-screen narration. Such an approach is a terrible waste of the impact of television.

Consider this scenario. Organization A and Organization B both have something important to say to the public. Organization A provides a bland, uninteresting script that merely repeats a timeworn message. Organization B deals with the same topic, but does so with a vigor and finesse that creates an interesting new approach. Most likely, Organization B will get the PSA time before Organization A does.

Often the best writing for public service advertising has a conversational tone. Consider the following radio spot written by the National Institute on Alcohol Abuse and Alcoholism as part of its campaign against teen drinking. The format for this spot is a simple dialog.

Radio PSA (NIAAA)—"It Never Hurts"

SFX: Telephone Ring

Parent 1: Hello?

Parent 2: (Cheery w/ phone effect) Hello, Jane? It's Julie. I just wanted to ask about the party your son Tom is having tomorrow? Our daughter, Megan, is coming and I just want to be sure there won't be any alcohol there. I hope you don't mind.

[Beat]

Parent 1: (A bit shocked) My husband and I had planned to be out of town this weekend, Julie—we didn't know anything about a party.

Parent 2: (Suddenly understands) Oh no!

ANNCR: If you're a parent, it never hurts to ask. For more information on talking with your kids about alcohol, visit niaaa.hih.gov.

Brought to you by the Department of Health and Human Services, the National Institutes of Health, and the National Institute on Alcohol Abuse and Alcoholism.

Here's a spot for the United Negro College Fund that uses the announcer monolog format to present its message.

Radio PSA (UNCF)—"Did You Know"

ANNCR: You know that the ice-cream scoop can make a child smile.
And that by slowing us down, the traffic-light can keep us going.
You know that the lawn-mower makes life easier.
That the blood bank makes life . . . possible.
But did you know all these ideas came from the minds of African Americans?

Support minority education today, so we don't miss out on the next big idea tomorrow.
The United Negro College Fund.
A mind is a terrible thing to waste.
Please visit U-N-C-F dot org, or call 1-800-332 U-N-C-F.

Brought to you by U-N-C-F and the Ad Council.

Broadcast stations have varying requirements for how organizations may submit materials for public service use. Radio stations, for example, often will accept scripts that can be read by reporters and on-air personalities. Some radio stations accept brief postcard announcements for upcoming events. Others encourage organizations to record brief announcements over the telephone. Most radio stations can use recorded announcements prepared by the organization or by professional production companies.

For television, the requirements are higher. Most stations use only professionally prepared videotaped spots. Some may provide in-studio production services to organizations that have scripted simple public service advertisements.

Most video production companies can make PSA tapes, either from an organization's script or from a script they prepare for the organization. Both of these services can be expensive. Alternatively, some nonprofit organizations help each other with scripting and production services, and others find inexpensive help from colleges or universities, public access cable television studios, and in-house corporate video facilities.

The actual presentation of a script for a television PSA also can take several forms. Exhibit 17.1 presents a United Negro College Fund ad in a traditional script format. The same PSA is presented in storyboard format in Exhibit 17.2.

Advertising Council

A mind is a terrible thing to . . .

Friends don't let friends . . .

Take a bite out of . . .

Only you can prevent . . .

You can probably fill in the blanks for each advertising message. That's a mark of the effectiveness of the Advertising Council, which developed each of these and thousands of other public service messages.

The **Advertising Council** (adcouncil.org) is a joint venture among the sponsor organizations, volunteer advertising agencies, media companies, and industry organizations such as the American Association of Advertising Agencies, the American Advertising Federation, the Advertising Research Foundation, and a variety of media organizations representing newspaper, magazine, radio, television, outdoor, direct marketing, and other types of media. It also works with the United Way.

Through such partnerships, the council brings together advertising professionals who create and deliver public service messages for various worthy causes. These ads are quite effective. Over the years, the Ad Council has introduced us to Smokey Bear, the Crash Test Dummies, and McGruff, the crime-fighting dog. To meet the council's selection criteria, a campaign must be noncommercial, nondenominational, and nonpolitical, and it must be significant to all Americans.

Exhibit 17.1—TELEVISION SCRIPT Concepts for public service advertising can be presented in storyboard format, such as in this outline format, which describes the same ad as seen on the storyboard.

"Portraits"

60-second public service advertisement for United Negro College Fund campaign
Video: Main characters are two African-American girls, depicted at various ages from 6 to 19
Audio 1: Announcer voice-over
Audio 2: Original music: "Save a place for me. Save a space for me."

		Video	*Audio 1*	*Audio 2*
:05	:05	(MS) Two African-American girls on a sliding board (age 6)	xx	Save a place for me. Save a space for me
:05	:10	(MS) Same girls on swings	xx	in your heart. In your heart.
:05	:15	(ECU) Same girls	xx	Save a place for me.
:05	:20	(ECU) Same girls (age 10)	xx	Save a space for me
:05	:25	(MS) Same girls in school cafeteria	xx	in your heart.
:05	:30	(LS) Same girls sitting and studying on apartment balcony (age 16)	xx	In your heart.
:05	:35	(MS) Same girls still on balcony, studying together	xx	xx
:05	:40	(CU) One girl sitting in college class, looking pensive (age 19)	Every year, the United Negro College Fund	xx
:05	:45	(MS) Same girl in large college class, with other black students	helps thousands of students go to college.	Save a place for me.
:05	:50	(MS) Same girl sitting in college class, looking pensive (empty seat in row behind her)	But for every-one we help	xx
:05	:55	(CU) Empty college desk	there's one we can't.	xx
:05	:60	"The United Negro College Fund. A mind is a terrible thing to waste. 1 800 322-UNCF (with logos of Ad Council and UNCF)	Please support the United Negro College Fund. A mind is a terrible thing to waste.	xx

Exhibit 17.2—UNCF STORYBOARD Young & Rubicam advertising developed three different versions (60, 30, and 15 seconds) of this spot for the United Negro College Fund, one of the offerings of the Advertising Council. This is the storyboard for the 60-second spot, the same one presented in script form in Exhibit 17.1.

Negro College Fund, one of the offerings of the Advertising Council.

THE ADVERTISING COUNCIL, INC. 

UNITED NEGRO COLLEGE FUND CAMPAIGN

Public Service Announcements

Volunteer Advertising Agency: Young & Rubicam Inc. A public service campaign Ad Council 499

The Ad Council provides public service advertising to newspapers, consumer magazines, and the business and medical press as well as to radio, broadcast, and cable television, both transit and outdoor advertising companies, and Internet and other new media. It has created adLibbing.org, a blog to help nonprofit organizations develop effective ad campaigns for traditional and social media.

The Ad Council claims to receive nearly $2 billion-worth annually of donated media each year. Eighty percent of the advertising time and space is contributed not by the networks but by local media, 22,000 different media outlets.

How successful is the Advertising Council? It has raised $2.2 billion for the United Negro College Fund in the past 40 years. It generated 40 million media impressions for the launch of a new campaign for SADD (Students Against Destructive Decisions) and 22 million impressions for a lupus campaign. The council's teen-runaway campaign resulted in more than one million telephone calls from teens wishing to return home, and its campaign to recruit new teachers generated half-a-million calls in six years.

Ad Council campaigns are credited with increasing recycling 25 percent in a five-year period, generating 18 million unique visitors after launching Homeland Security's preparedness website ready.gov, and increasing applications for Big Brother/Big Sister mentors from 90,000 to 620,000 a year after a five-month campaign run.

Meanwhile, its campaign for the Council on Alcoholism and Drug Dependence generates 3,000 phone calls each week. Smokey Bear is recognized by 95 percent of adults and 77 percent of children. A survey showed that 93 percent of children believe that McGruff, the crime dog, helps make their communities safe. In line with the message of "Friends Don't Let Friends Drive Drunk," 70 percent of Americans said they have tried to stop someone driving while drunk. And since Vince and Larry, the Crash Test Dummies, were introduced in 1985, seat-belt use has increased from 21 to 70 percent.

"FYI: Public Service Campaigns of the Advertising Council" lists several more of the Ad Council's recent projects.

FYI *Public Service Campaigns of the Advertising Council*

You've probably seen dozens of messages sponsored by the Advertising Council. Here is a listing of the 2010 campaigns provided to television and radio stations, newspapers and magazines, and billboard companies throughout the United States. See adcouncil.org.

Community

Adoption
Clinton Bush Haiti Fund
Community Engagement
Disability Awareness
Fatherhood Involvement
Foreclosure Prevention
Haiti Disaster Relief
Hunger Prevention
Mentoring
Pakistan Relief Fund
Re-Connecting Kids with Nature
Renew America Together
Shelter Pet Project
Think Before Your Speak

Education

College Access
Credit Scores Education
Early Childhood Development
Family Literacy

continued . . .

FYI Public Service Campaigns of the Advertising Council . . . *continued*

GED Achievement
High School Dropout Prevention
Hispanic Parental Engagement
Lifelong Literacy
Supporting Minority Education

Health & Safety
Anti-Steroids
Autism Awareness
Booster Seat Education
Child Passenger Safety
Childhood Asthma
Childhood Obesity Prevention
Drunk Driving Prevention
Emergency Preparedness
Fight Arthritis Pain
Flu Prevention
Hands-Only CPR
Hispanic Preventive Health
Lead Poisoning Prevention
Men's Preventive Health
Mental Health Recovery
Newborn and Child Survival
Nutrition Education
Online Sexual Exploitation
Patient Involvement
Stroke Awareness
Teen Dating Violence
Teen Suicide Prevention
Wildlife Prevention
Youth Reckless Driving Prevention

Exercise 17.7

Writing a Public Relations Ad

Alone or with a partner, prepare a series of public relations advertisements for one of the following scenarios:

1. The client is your college or university health center. Your public is students. Your objectives are to promote awareness, interest, and action regarding self-examination for breast cancer or testicular cancer.
2. The client is your campus' student life and residence life offices. Your public is students. Your objectives are to promote awareness, interest, and action in recycling on campus.
3. Select an organization of your choice as the client for this exercise and identify the publics and objectives.

Prepare a planning sheet and the script for a series of 30-second television messages for the client. Include video suggestions, shot notes, and both primary and secondary audio. Develop scripts each of the following versions:

- *Version 1*: A testimonial format (celebrity or noncelebrity) with a single voice. Script the narrative and include suggestions for sound effects and/or specific music.
- *Version 2*: A demonstration or drama format with multiple voices and a narrator. Script the dialog and narrative, and include suggestions for sound effects and/or specific music.
- *Version 3*: A reflective format or symbol format. Script the narrative, describe the visuals, and include specific suggestions for sound effects and/or specific music.

Answers to Tips for Better Writing
Limbering Up Mentally

1. Half of 13 could be 6.5 or 6½. Or it could be 1 or 3. Or "thir" and "teen." Or xi and ii.
2. They are the single-digit numbers arranged alphabetically.
3. Home plate on a baseball diamond, and the men in masks are the catcher and the umpire.
4. On the day Daylight Savings Time begins, the clock is set ahead by one hour, resulting in a 23-hour day.
5. The man's friend was a woman. He imitated the Japanese as she spoke it, which is different from that spoken by men.
6. He has always felt that exercising for at least an hour early each morning made him feel more calm, both physically and emotionally.
7. Mary is the teacher.
8. Indivisibility.
9. He was washing windows on the inside.
10. Holes.

18 Speechwriting

Grandpa said it well: "Better you should keep your mouth closed if you can't say it right." Talking isn't the same as speaking, certainly not speaking professionally. That takes skill and practice. It takes even more skill to plan and write or ghostwrite a decent speech or article, or to coach your boss or client in how to effectively handle an interview.

Classical rhetoric, the study of speechmaking, goes back about 3,000 years to the Mediterranean world of Egypt, Greece, and Rome. The formal study of rhetoric continued through the ages, particularly in medieval Europe, as well as in the classical eras in China and Japan. More recently, it is studied in universities throughout the world. Most academic work related to public speaking has centered on content, while much of the applied or professional focus has been on delivery. What hasn't been studied as much are the writing of speeches and the role of the speechwriter as a person separate from a speech giver. That is the focus of this chapter.

Here is one central thought for this chapter: Oral communication (such as making speeches or giving interviews) is more about making an impression than imparting information. Good speakers exhort. They entreat and admonish. Good interviewees use their time in front of the microphones to give audiences a feeling about an organization, such as the passion with which it pursues its ideal, the depth of its commitment to customer service, and so on. Such impressions don't deal as much with what information is presented as they do with how the speaker relates to his or her audience.

The art of **speechwriting**, in which someone crafts a speech for another person to present, lies at the heart of one of the key functions of public relations, giving advice and counsel. One of our most important jobs is to conduct research, analyze options, and make recommendations on what an organization should do and say. Part of this is associated with issues management, which was discussed in Chapter 13. The saying part is the focus of this chapter, including planning, writing, and evaluating speeches. Here are your learning objectives for this chapter:

- To prepare and write an effective speech
- To plan audio-visual presentation aids to enhance a speech
- To prepare for a question-and-answer session following a speech or as part of an interview or news conference.

Speech

Many are the benefits of a good speech. A speech is the primary example of face-to-face communication, the most effective kind of communication. Speeches before a live audience (as compared to televised speeches) provide an environment for two-way communication. Both live and televised speeches can give a human face to organizations.

There is a big difference between talking *at* an audience and communicating *with* one. Perhaps you have sat through a bad speech, a dull sermon, or a boring lecture. If so, you know that every speaker isn't necessarily a communicator. That's where the public relations writer can help. Often our behind-the-scenes roles as researcher and counselor equip us well for the task of writing speeches to be delivered by organizational leaders.

Savvy audiences realize that most speakers don't write their own speeches. Few political candidates, government officials, and corporate executives have the time needed to plan, research, and write a good speech. Even fewer have the writing ability to be particularly effective. So they often turn to public relations writers or to speechwriting specialists, people who are good at taking the would-be speaker's own ideas and weaving them into a personalized speech. Likewise, some executives ask public relations writers to research and write an article for a newspaper, magazine, or trade publication that will carry the name not of the actual writer but of the executive who has commissioned it.

Both of these are examples of the functions of a **ghostwriter**, a writer who prepares an article, speech, op-ed commentary, or some other piece of writing that will carry the name of someone else. Ghostwriting is an extension of what many public relations writers do in their news releases when they craft a quote for the company CEO or the agency director. "What Would You Do? Ghostwriting Ethics" explores this position a bit further.

What Would You Do? *Ghostwriting Ethics*

David Finn of Ruder Finn Public Relations believes business executives cheat their audiences if they rely on others to pen their words. In an article "Exorcise the Executive Ghostwriter," published in *Fortune* magazine, Finn observes that most executives simply give their name to texts prepared by ghostwriters who write what they think the executive should be saying.

Finn reports a conversation with Sir John Harvey-Jones, chairman of ICI, one of England's largest corporations, who said, "It would be incredibly rude if people came to hear what I had to say on an important subject and heard someone else's views."

What do you think is the appropriate role of a ghostwriter? Is there any difference between a speech written by a member of an executive's public relations staff and one crafted by an outside professional speechwriter? Does a speaker owe the audience an explanation of who actually wrote the speech?

Companies and nonprofit groups sometimes organize teams of presenters to spread the group's message. These **speakers' bureaus** send organizational representatives to give talks and to invite questions, and public relations officers often have a role in training the speakers, doing background research and providing them with up-to-date information, promoting their availability, scheduling their presentations, and evaluating their effectiveness.

Exercise 18.1

Freewriting on Speech

Freewrite for five minutes on the following topic: *How does persuasion fit into the activities of a public relations writer?* Then discuss this with your classmates.

Planning the Speech

For speechwriters, having a good outline or script is important. Ad-libbing is not a safe venture for the organizational executive. The more nervous or inexperienced the speaker, the greater the need for careful preparation. Following is a step-by-step plan to help you prepare a speech for someone else to deliver. For more information, you can consult speechwriting resources online at such sites as ragan.com, speechwriting.com, or executive-speaker.com.

Speaker. Unlike a document meant to be read, the text of a speech does not go directly from the writer to the audience. In theoretical terms, the speech is doubly encoded. First, the writer provides the words that encode the meaning to be shared with the receiver. The speaker, who gives a tone and temper to the text, provides a second encoding. The speaker brings to it a verbal interpretation, an attitude. The text of a speech may provide the words for a moving political rouser or an impassioned homily. But when it is presented by someone not familiar with the text or by a person unskilled in public speaking, the words may be flat and lifeless. That's because a speech has two presenters—the writer who provides the text and the speaker who gives a voice to that text.

Suppose you are asked to draft a speech for your company's president. As the president's speechwriter, you must know how she can handle various kinds of material. What words and phrases sound natural coming from her lips? How does she deliver a speech before an audience? Can she tell a joke? Use an inspiring quotation? Share a personal story?

One way to find this out is to listen. Meet with the speaker. Tape-record the conversation, so you can later review how the speaker uses language. Does she always speak in complete sentences or does she use exclamatory phrases and sentence fragments? Does she pepper conversation with anecdotes and personal stories? Does the speaker naturally use humor? Passion? Charm?

Message. Besides knowing the speaker's style of speaking, a speechwriter also needs to know what should be said. What is the topic of the speech? Is the purpose to entertain or motivate? How will the speech further organizational objectives? Public relations writers may know what needs to be said because they have been part of the strategic planning that leads to the speech. Or they can ask others within the organization to provide information "for the boss' speech."

Perhaps the best way to know what the speaker wants to say is to ask the speaker. While recording the introductory conversation, ask the speaker to talk about the topic. Even if you already know something about this topic, you need to get the speaker's thoughts on it, as well as phrasing natural to the speaker. Ask the speaker to summarize the issue and identify some key points to be made. Ask about personal experiences on the issue. Ask if there are any points on which the speaker might disagree with mainstream thought on the issue. "Tips for Better Writing: How *Not* to Write a Speech" offers an argument for getting to know your speaker and topic first-hand.

Tips for Better Writing *How Not to Write a Speech*

Consider this experience of the author, an experience shared by many other public relations people who have worked in military or other governmental agencies.

As a Navy journalist, I was assigned to write a speech for an admiral to deliver to a group of visiting dignitaries. The information came third-hand. I got directives from the public affairs officer, who had heard from the executive officer, who presumably had met with the admiral. The directions were a classic example of communication degradation: the loss of information as a message is transferred from one person to another. Logic suggested that I walk down the hall and interview the admiral. But military protocol did not facilitate such a face-to-face discussion between the admiral/speaker and the non-officer/speechwriter, so the message was watered down by the time it got to me. In the end, I was frustrated because I knew the speech was not a good one. The admiral was displeased because he had to rewrite it. And the officers in the middle were embarrassed and annoyed.

There's a lesson to be learned: Establish a relationship between the speechwriter and the speech giver.

Audience. Go back to one of the basic principles of public relations communication: As a speechwriter, you must be firmly rooted in an understanding of who will be hearing the speech. Therefore, you must identify your public. Knowing your audience also means knowing the context in which your audience finds itself. Give thought to the background and circumstances of the proposed speech. Is it part of a wider event? Does the occasion have a theme? Is it an opening keynote, a closing reflection, or something in between? How long is the audience expecting the speech to last?

Plan. Before you begin writing the speech, prepare a planning sheet. Build on what you know about the public and its wants, interests, and needs. Identify the benefits you can offer. Be clear about the objectives you have for your intended audience. Give thought to the best tone for delivering the message. Finally, consider how you will judge the success of this presentation after it has been given.

Give particular attention to how you can make an impact on the audience. Let's say, for example, that you are drafting a speech for a new county executive who ran his campaign on a platform of city–suburban cooperation. It is his first speech before a group of business leaders whom you know to be skeptical about the notion of "big government." Rather than jump right into a controversial idea of consolidation of services, you might decide first to address issues they are likely to support such as sharing resources and cost-effectiveness. Next, appealing to their experience as managers, you might note that leadership sometimes means having to make the tough and unpopular decisions. Finally, you could back into the conclusion that consolidation of services, though perhaps unpopular, is nevertheless the right approach because it will serve the long-term interests of the people and businesses of both the city and the suburban areas.

Research. Launch a more formal gathering of information related to the topic of the speech. Make sure you include recent information available from periodicals, as well as organization-based information that can be obtained from the speaker. Using the example noted above, you might find out how other metropolitan areas have handled consolidation of services. Check with government-reform organizations. Investigate information on websites of comparably sized metropolitan areas. Check out positions of organizations such as police and firefighting agencies, and compare the duplication of parallel services in the various municipalities in your region. Interview some people involved in the issue.

Writing the Speech

With your planning and research completed, you now are ready to write the speech. The best way to begin is to provide yourself with a conventional outline that includes the major elements: introduction, proposition, subordinate points and supporting information, and conclusion. Once you've got the outline, the writing itself should come fairly quickly.

Engage your audience right from the beginning of the speech. A well-crafted question that stems from what audience members really want to know is a good way to get them involved. Keep them involved with references back to the central question. Make the speech relevant to this specific audience by including references to local issues and current events.

Here is the transcript of a speech given by Robert Gates as Secretary of Defense at the National Press Club in 2010 at a meeting of the National Action Alliance for Suicide Prevention. This speech contains all of the major elements that typically are part of well-crafted speeches.

> Thank you, Secretary Sebelius, for that kind introduction, and for inviting me to speak here today. The launch of the National Action Alliance for Suicide Prevention is an important and timely effort. As Secretary of Defense, my top institutional priority is taking care of those who have borne the burden and paid the price for protecting our nation. That includes doing everything possible to prevent military suicides. It's always a horrible tragedy to see a service member safely off of the battlefield only to lose them to this scourge—we can, must, and will do better.
>
> Some context to the challenges we face: Our military has been at war for nearly a decade, the longest war in our history. The post-9/11 campaigns have demanded repeated and extended deployments and exposure to combat, placing unprecedented stresses on our troops, their families, and their support networks. Advances in protective and battlefield medicine have allowed more of our war fighters to survive their wounds. But the survivors often suffer from traumatic brain injury, post-traumatic stress, and other psychological ailments—all factors that can increase the risk of suicide. We are also confronting a historical stigma attached to these types of wounds. A lack of understanding that they, too, are an inevitable consequence of combat. That those fighting to recover deserve respect for their sacrifice. As well as the best, state-of-the-art care.
>
> The department has taken steps to alleviate the stress on the force in general, and to help all those who are struggling and at risk. Some of those steps include:
>
> - Expanding the size of the Army and Marines in order to increase the time at home among those who have been most frequently deployed;
> - Adding more than 2,000 mental health providers to military treatment facilities, part of an on-going expansion effort to increase access to these services; and
> - Improving the coordination and publicity of available services for National Guard members and their families, who often don't have access to the same support systems as active duty troops.
>
> We've also taken measures to change the culture and attitudes of our military. Troops should know that their careers and security clearances are not at risk when they seek the psychological help they need. And I'd like to honor all of those—from junior enlisted members to senior officers, such as Army General Carter Ham—who have come forward to tell their stories of survival and recovery, and thus give hope to many of their comrades.

As with almost every issue in our military, progress on this front comes down to leadership. All those in command and leadership positions—including junior officers and NCOs closest to the issue—need to aggressively encourage those under them to seek help if needed, and also set an example by doing the same.

In everything we do, we must remember that every soldier, sailor, airman, or marine is part, not just of the military, but also of a larger community. Their families, their hometowns, their civilian employers, their places of worship—all must be involved in the solution.

To that end, the Alliance's Executive Committee membership is a welcome public/private partnership, including all sectors that need to be involved for a successful nation-wide suicide prevention strategy. This is important to me personally, as many years ago my only uncle committed suicide. I want to thank Senator Smith for his being willing to take time to co-chair this effort. On behalf of the Defense Department, I'm particularly glad that Secretary McHugh will be co-chairing this committee. As Secretary, John has led the Army's suicide prevention efforts, helping to bring together the relevant actors and organizations within his department in a vigorous and comprehensive campaign. He is ideally suited to share the military's accumulated experience and knowledge on these issues, as well as to learn from other Alliance members and bring those lessons back to the DOD.

It is the ongoing duty of this department to do everything possible to care for those who protect our nation. I am confident that the insights and efforts of the Alliance will enable us to more effectively fulfill this mission.

Introduction. The **introduction** of the speech is like the lead of a feature release. It introduces the topic and sets the tone for what will follow. It establishes a rapport between the speaker and the audience, letting the audience glimpse how the speaker feels about the topic. It offers the appropriate greetings to the audience. Finally, the introduction also establishes the speaker's credibility as this relates to the subject.

Note that the Gates speech printed above has all of these elements. The speaker didn't need to recite his credentials because the audience through a prior introduction already knew them.

Proposition. The **proposition** (also called a **thesis**) is the main idea you want to leave with the audience. Speechwriters note three kinds of proposition: factual, value, and policy.

- A **factual proposition** asserts the existence of something (for example, an increase in acid rain pollution in the Eastern forests, or a plan to change your college's foreign language requirements). A factual proposition often is linked with public relations objectives focused on awareness, such as increasing attention or building greater understanding.
- A **value proposition** argues the worthiness or virtue of something (the joy of writing, the merits of welfare reform). This relates to public relations objectives dealing with acceptance, such as increasing interest or building more positive attitudes.
- A **policy proposition** identifies a course of action and encourages its adoption (advocacy for requiring a license to practice public relations, or a proposal to make parent-education classes a requirement for a high school diploma, for example). This parallels public relations objectives associated with opinion and action.

A speech might involve more than one type of proposition. Secretary Gates' testimony above involved all three types of propositions. He presented a factual proposition outlining "the challenges we face" in the second paragraph. Paragraph three provides a series of policy propositions on what the Pentagon is doing or plans to do to address the issue. Following the bullets, the fourth and fifth paragraphs offer a value proposition about giving witness and leadership on the issue of suicide.

Argument. Propositions must be supported with strong **arguments**, also called **subordinate points** or **supporting information**. Propositions are only as good as their arguments. Unsupported propositions come from poor planning or inadequate research. Not only are they weak, they also can be counterproductive because they are easy for audiences to dismiss and because they hurt your speaker's credibility. Consider one aspect of Gates' speech:

- Proposition: The Pentagon has taken steps to reduce the stress that leads some to commit suicide
- Argument: Increasing the number of troops so they are not deployed as often
- Argument: Increasing the size of the mental health staff
- Argument: Extending the program to troops not on active duty.

Conclusion. An effective **conclusion** is often a summary that pulls together the major recommendations of the entire speech. The Gates speech ends with a nod to a group dealing with the issue, a recommitment to the importance of the issue, and a statement of his resolve to address it effectively.

Effective Speechwriting

A speech can be structured in many ways. Some speechwriters use a pattern similar to that for a position statement, since the same elements should be evident in the text of any speech that seeks to persuade. In many ways, public relations practitioners use a speech to verbally present an organization's position on an issue to both the organization and its publics.

Following are some of the elements of speechwriting. "Advice from a Pro: Matt Hughes on Speechwriting" also offers additional suggestions.

Advice from a Pro *Matt Hughes on Speechwriting*

Matt Hughes is a speechwriter and novelist in British Columbia. A former newspaper editor, he has been staff speechwriter to Canada's ministers of justice, environment, and small business.

Matt is proud of the fact that he is the only speechwriter to have written convention addresses for winning candidates in leadership races in the British Columbia Social Credit, Liberal and New Democratic parties (something like writing for both the Democratic and Republican National Committees).

Here is Hughes' advice on speechwriting.

Make an Impression

Nobody remembers speeches. No one sitting through a 20-minute monologue recalls what was actually said. An audience retains no more than two or three new facts from a speech. Crowd the text with data and the listeners will remember only how boring you were. Ruthlessly pare down to the essential facts.

Get Organized

The easiest and best way to organize a speech is the "three times" approach. Announce very early in the text—the first page is good—what your speech is about and why it is important to the audience. Next, give them your message, with the basic facts or examples or anecdotes. Then close by restating the theme. Your speech will have a definite beginning, middle, and end, and the audience will not be confused.

continued . . .

Advice from a Pro *Matt Hughes on Speechwriting . . . continued*

Use Plain English

Plain Anglo-Saxon English is better than a string of jargon and 10-dollar words. It is also the language of emotion. "I'm mad as hell and I'm not going to take it any more" has way more impact than "I am extremely choleric and I encompass no intention of enduring any supplemental experience." Using Anglo-Saxon puts you in good company. From Lincoln's "government of the people, by the people and for the people," to Churchill's "we shall fight on the beaches," to Kennedy's "ask not what your country can do for you," the best speech is plain English.

Get Active

The rules of English grammar allow for an active or a passive voice. In the active, you might say "we have decided"; in the passive, it comes out as "a decision has been reached." Bureaucrats love the passive voice. Totally neutral, it lets them say without having to take responsibility for saying. But it puts audiences to sleep. To fill your speech text with life and emotion, use the active voice.

Don't Tell Them, Show Them

We all have screens inside our heads where we look at pictures that come to us as spoken or written words. Keep your audience's screens full of images. Make your points and deliver your information in word pictures. If you're warning of difficulties ahead, say something like "We're climbing a hill that's getting steeper, and there are rocks and potholes in the road." Word pictures need only a few broad strokes. Don't specify the kind of road or the species of trees in the wood. Your audience's brains will fill in the details without being asked.

Can We Talk?

When writing it, a speech is words on paper. When given, it's one human being speaking live to others. If you're more used to drafting reports or memos, don't let their usually impersonal tone creep into your text. Use "I" and "you" and "we" and "us," and strive for the comfortably informal tone of a network news anchor.

Say It Again, Sam

In reports, letters, and memos, repetition is a poor writer's vice; but in speeches, it's a virtue. Your audience can't stop the tape and press replay. They hear it live, and if they miss a key point, the rest of your speech may make no sense to them. So, if a thing is worth saying, it's worth saying again for clarity and emphasis. But don't just repeat the same words verbatim. Rephrase the point, giving two or three examples that leave your listeners in no doubt about what you're saying.

Adjust the Facts, Ma'am

What's a speech without statistics? A better speech. Figures are great in a report, but unless each member of your audience has total recall, your stats will mostly pass right through their heads. Always simplify, always round off. Replace "68.2 percent" with "over two-thirds," and "a 112 percent rise in production" with "our output more than doubled." With big numbers, look for word pictures that convey size, but avoid the hackneyed "this many football fields," or "that many times around the world." Reach for your calculator and work out that you produced enough widgets to cover Rhode Island twice. The more novel and arresting the image, the more memorable. Nobody knows how many billions of burgers McDonald's has sold, but if it were enough to make a cow five miles high, people would surely remember that cow.

Make 'Em Laugh

People also remember jokes. Find a way to make a point with humor and your message will stick.

continued . . .

Advice from a Pro *Matt Hughes on Speechwriting* . . . *continued*

If you're expecting a tax increase, you might say, "Well, Congress has finally decided how to divide up the pie; trouble is, we're the pie." Humor relaxes an audience, helping to create the human bond that is crucial to making a memorable impression. But you don't have to open with one of those hoary chestnuts cribbed from a handbook. Try to make the joke fit the substance and the circumstances of your remarks.

The Ins and Outs

The best and simplest way to open a speech is just to tell the audience that you are glad to be there. You may open with "I am pleased to have this opportunity," or "when [whoever] invited me to be your guest speaker, I was delighted," or just "I am very glad to be here tonight." Let the audience know that this is a good experience for you; nobody likes to watch a fellow human being in pain.

After you tell them how glad you are to see them, go on to tell them why: because they are good people and worth talking to. When addressing the chamber of commerce, mention the chamber's community role and good works. If you're addressing the bar association, try to find something nice to say about lawyers. Once you have shown the strange tribe that you are friendly and respect their totems, you may tell them what you're going to tell them, and get on with the job.

The end of a speech is the part most likely to be remembered by your listeners. Put your best writing here—active voice, Anglo-Saxon, word pictures and all—and lead the audience into your vision of the future, as it develops from the message in your speech. If you have hard news to announce, save it till the end. If you have a slogan or catch phrase you want remembered, use it in the wind-up and repeat it a few times. Got a joke that encapsulates your message? Make it the finale and leave them laughing.

She Sells Seashells

You've followed all the above advice, and now you have a neatly typed speech, ready for delivery. But there's still one job left: Read the thing out loud. Don't trust that silent reading voice in your head, because it won't be there to help you when you are speaking out loud. That little voice can easily read "the Leeth police dismisseth us" in black and white, but try to get it past your lips and teeth, and you've got trouble. Find the hidden verbal potholes in your text, and fill them in with a rewrite.

Additional information is available at Hughes' website: mars.ark.com/~mhughes.

Stick to the Topic. Some speeches wander from Boston to Albuquerque and back again. Bad move. Too many speeches don't seem to have a theme—and the audience is left confused and probably bored. The problem is that often you (or your speaker) will have a lot of ideas. But instead of a speech, you can end up with an inventory of thoughts or a laundry list of recommendations. Resist the urge to throw every idea at the audience. Rather, choose one idea and develop it with a series of secondary points and examples. Try to leave the audience with only one main idea. That's probably all anyone will remember anyway. Work with that central thought. State it clearly. Shape it. Repeat it. Express it with examples. Say it again in the conclusion.

Write for the Ear. A speech should not necessarily be written to look good. Rather, it should be written to *sound* good. There is a big difference. Look at "Tips for Better Writing: The Well-Tempered (Speech) Sentence." In print, this passage looks choppy and awkward.

But read it out loud, and notice how the words work when you hear them. A good speech is written in the tone of conversational English, which is less rigid than more formal styles of literary, commercial, or academic English.

People writing for oral presentations strive for a conversational tone that is rooted in the natural rhythms appropriate to the individual speaker. Generally, this involves the use of simple words, personal pronouns, active voice, and subject/predicate/object sentence structures. It also frequently involves the use of contractions and sentence fragments.

Tips for Better Writing *The Well-Tempered (Speech) Sentence*

A paragraph may look good on a page—with a minimum of punctuation marks and short sentences—but it may not really sound good.

Funny thing about speeches. They have to play on the ear . . . just so. People who write speeches—the good writers, that is—know this. They use dashes and ellipses and parentheses to provide side comments . . . just the way many people speak.

The good writers aren't hung up on the formalities of grammar and syntax, because they know that many of the formalities are more for writing than speaking. The good speechwriters know that run-on sentences can be OK—as long as they sound OK to the audience, and as long as the audience can understand them . . . and audiences can easily understand lengthy passages, when (and this is the key), when the long sentences are broken up by pauses. The same with sentence fragments.

The best advice, then, for the speechwriter is this: *Write for the ear*. Trust your ear to let you know when you've done a good job. Thank you, and have a pleasant afternoon.

Get a Good Start. As with any other type of public relations writing, the beginning of a speech is perhaps the most crucial. The introduction either will signal to the audience that this is a speech worth listening to, or it will signal the start of a boring discourse. Speechwriters have found that the lead can be written in a variety of formats: a compelling question, a shocking statement, an engaging anecdote, an appropriate quotation, a humorous observation, or simply a summary of the speaker's proposition.

Vary Structural Elements. No single structural element is required of speeches; they lend themselves to many features. Consider the role that each of the following could play in a speech you might prepare: analogies, anecdotes and stories, enumeration, examples and explanations, hypothetical situations, illustration, repetition, rhetorical questions, statistics, suspense.

Use Quotations Sparingly. Testimony from authority and attributions to experts can be persuasive features in a speech. But use them only if they are central to your message, and only if they come from people well enough known to impress your audience in the first place. Don't allow quotations to draw your audiences away from your message.

Allude to Relevant Events. The speaker may be presenting information that has been given before, but one way to keep the text relevant is to update it with references to current events. Research shows that current happenings are much more meaningful to audiences than historical allusions. As with quotations, however, make sure the allusions do not distract your audiences from the heart of your message.

Avoid Clichés. Language that is trite diminishes a speech. So do stereotypes. It doesn't matter if such language is the writer's own or if it comes from quotations from others. Avoid clichés from any source, because they make the speech predictable, thus uninteresting and unmemorable.

Use Literary Gimmicks. Games and strategies can help an audience remember a speech. Some speechwriters have used what they call the B list: Be alert. Be prepared. Be resourceful. Others have used what they call Be-attitudes to present a similar list. The object of both approaches is to give the listener an easy-to-remember listing of actions, traits, and so on. Other speechwriters rely on repetition of ideas and themes.

Avoid Common Errors in Logic. Effective speeches display a soundness of thinking. Ineffective speeches have easy-to-recognize flaws in their reasoning. Here are some of the common errors to avoid:

- **Over-generalized arguments** fail to persuade because they use limited information to make presumptions that are unsubstantiated. This is a case of leaping to an inexact conclusion.
- Drawing **unwarranted conclusions** is a similar error in logical presentation of information. This can happen when the writer begins with the conclusion and then goes searching for data to back it up.
- Building on **false facts** that present inaccurate or dishonest information is like constructing a house on sand. Neither will last. You can't make a credible case using incorrect or uncertain data.
- **Arguing in a circle** is an attempt to prove a proposition by restating it. When A equals B, we know also that B equals A. That may mean something in algebra, but in language it's called a **tautology**. It is a "proof" that relies on itself, and therefore isn't much of a proof at all. Arguing in circles is like a hamster on a treadmill—it doesn't get you very far.
- **Personal criticism** is another logical flaw. Criticize the issue being addressed rather than the person addressing it. Intelligent and fair-minded audiences are insulted when they realize they are being manipulated by irrelevant arguments, and personal insults or verbal abuse of opponents can be counterproductive. (The fact that you may be writing for something other than an "intelligent and fair-minded audience" doesn't relieve you from your own ethical commitment to avoid unfair personal criticism.)
- An **appeal to tradition** is a common persuasive technique. The we've-always-done-it-this-way argument is an invitation to trouble because it often fails to hold up under close examination. Speeches can safely appeal to tradition only if the audience unconditionally accepts the substance and source of that tradition.
- Similarly, **authority appeals** also can be unsupportive of a speaker's claims. Eventually, the argument must stand on its own strength, apart from the star quality of its supporters.

Test the Speech Out Loud. The first step after writing the draft of a speech is to read it out loud. Notice if you get tongue-tied or run out of breath. Observe if the natural cadence becomes awkward or out of rhythm. If necessary, rewrite the draft to eliminate any of these problems. The second step comes when the speaker tries out the speech. The writer should be present during the rehearsal, prepared either to coach the speaker toward a smoother presentation of the words or to rewrite the speech to accommodate the speaker's style.

Prepare a Clean Transcript. The speech text is meant to be read aloud, and speechwriters prepare their final draft in the same style they would prepare a broadcast release. This involves writing out words and providing a pronunciation guide. The text itself should be typed with margins of at least one inch and with double spacing. Use both capital and lower-case letters for easy reading, rather than all-capital letters. Underline any words that require particular emphasis by the speaker, or use boldface type or perhaps a larger font. Break pages only at the end of sentences. Use the same kinds of pronouncers that were introduced for broadcast writing in Chapter 9.

Some speechwriters suggest marking sections of the text that can be eliminated if the speaker finds there is less time than planned to deliver the speech. This allows the speaker to present a carefully crafted message. Without this assistance, the speaker might simply present only the first half of the speech, delivering an incomplete message.

Maximize Impact. The speech has been researched and written. It's been rehearsed and presented. End of speech? Not necessarily. An insightful speechwriter can suggest ways to recycle the speech, attracting additional attention to the speaker and spreading the message more widely.

There are many ways to magnify the reach of a speech, including handing out copies to interested listeners, distributing reprints to important internal and external publics, highlighting the speech in the organization's newsletter.

When a speech is particularly significant beyond the organization, the news media might be included in the dissemination program. For example, you might send out news releases or media advisories about the speech, such as Hewlett Packard did when its CEO testified about the company's ethics violations before a House subcommittee and AT&T did when its chairman testified before a Senate subcommittee. You might provide radio and television stations with audiotapes or video clips respectively, with some of the best sound bites from the speech.

Use the Internet to further disseminate the speech. Post the text of the speech at your website. Create an audio clip that can be downloaded. Post a video of the speech at your YouTube page, and link to this from your company blog.

For major speeches of public interest, you might contact a member of Congress to see about placing the speech in the Congressional Record. You can also submit the speech for possible inclusion in Vital Speeches of the Day, ERIC/Educational Resources Information Center (accesseric.org) for documents dealing with education, or other full-text document resources.

Exercise 18.2

Writing a Speech

You are a public relations writer who has been asked to prepare a speech dealing with one of the following scenarios:

- The question-and-answer piece you drafted in Exercise 11.6
- The position statement you drafted in Exercise 12.2.

continued . . .

Exercise 18.2 . . . *continued*

Part 1: Define an appropriate target public and prepare a planning sheet. Since you already know your instructor's speaking style, presume that he or she is the organizational spokesperson who will give the speech.

Part 2: Write an introduction for the speech.

Part 3: Write the proposition statement.

Part 4: Outline the subordinate points and supporting information. This section may be in bullet form rather than in complete narrative paragraphs.

Part 5: Write a conclusion for the speech.

What Would You Do? *Putting Words into Someone's Mouth*

You are public relations writer for a major bank with branches in most states and Canadian provinces and several major foreign cities. You are preparing a speech to be delivered in three days by your CEO, announcing that the bank commission in your headquarters state has just approved the merger of your bank and a small regional bank. This is part of an ongoing series of mergers that your company has undertaken in recent years. The approval was expected, and there is nothing unusual about the situation.

Your CEO is traveling on banking business and his whereabouts are not to be divulged at this time. You know that the CEO is involved in a series of high-level meetings, scheduled first in Quito, Ecuador and following in Osaka, Japan. The vice president who handled the merger negotiations wants you to write a speech for the CEO to deliver at an employee meeting of the small bank that is becoming part of your banking system. The vice president suggests a congratulatory statement to the staffs of the acquired bank and a promise to customers that service will not be disrupted and in fact will improve.

You can use information from the vice president, but you are told that the quote should be in the name of your CEO. You also have some corporate reports from recent weeks in which the CEO has enthusiastically discussed the merger.

What should you do? Are there any ethical issues in ghostwriting a speech? Does it matter that you are not able to meet with the CEO prior to submitting the final draft?

Audio-Visual Aids

Visual aids can greatly enhance speeches and other oral presentations. Some studies have found that audiences learn between two and 10 times as much when they have visual aids such as charts and photos to supplement what they hear than when they simply hear it.

The value of visual aids is backed up by research. A study from the University of California at Los Angeles reported that more than 90 percent of what an audience understands comes from a combination of visual messages (55 percent) and spoken messages (38 percent), compared with only 7 percent for written messages. A study by the University of Pennsylvania found that audiences remember 50 percent of what they see and hear in presentations, compared to only 10 percent of what they merely hear. A study by the University of Minnesota concluded that presenters who used overhead transparencies and computer-generated slides were 43 percent more persuasive than presenters who used no visuals. The Minnesota study also found that using visuals cuts the length of the speech by 28 percent.

At the beginning of this chapter, it was noted that most speeches can do more to make an impression than to impart information. Especially for workshops, classes, persuasive talks, and other information-sharing presentations, visual aids are crucial.

What are some of the other benefits of presentation aids? Besides fostering greater understanding, audio and visual aids make speeches and presentations more memorable. They also can lessen the likelihood that an audience will become bored or distracted. Finally, they save time by eliminating the need for lengthy explanations. A picture not only is worth a thousand words, it communicates a lot quicker.

There are myriad presentation aid options. Some of these include: printed handouts, chalkboards, dry-erase whiteboards, electronic whiteboards, overhead transparencies, computer presentations, YouTube and other Internet-posted videos, slides, audio- and videotapes. Each of these presentation media offers opportunities for several different types of content: graphs and charts, schematic drawings, diagrams, key words and text, maps, photos, models and objects.

Having good visual aids is one thing. Using them well in a presentation is something else. Here are a few guidelines for effective use of presentation aids, whether you are personally delivering a speech or prepping your CEO to present a speech you researched, drafted, and/or are staging.

- *Plan for the visual aids.* Include them in your planning right from the start so that they form an integral part of the presentation rather than an afterthought.
- *Keep visual aids simple.* Don't crowd too much detail into photos, charts, graphs, and other aids. Use each visual aid to make a single point. Just because your PowerPoint slides can hop, skip, jump, and do a pirouette or a moonwalk doesn't meant they should.
- *Make sure everyone can see the visual aid.* Use props and materials of appropriate size. Instead of one television monitor, consider using two or several hooked up to the same video playback system.
- *Know how to use the visual aids.* Both the speaker and the audience get annoyed when a computerized presentation won't work. Practice with the equipment and know how to use it.
- *Have a backup plan.* With any kind of equipment, be prepared for problems. Have an extra overhead presenter or laptop computer in case the one you are using fails to work. Have extra paper for a flip chart, and have handouts available in case the transparencies or computer presentation can't be used.

Exercise 18.3

Planning Presentation Aids

Select one of the following scenarios:

1. You are preparing a 10-minute presentation explaining your academic department to potential students for a college or university open house.

continued . . .

Exercise 18.3 . . . *continued*

2. You are preparing a 10-minute presentation to generate support for the position you outlined in Exercise 12.2.
3. You are preparing a 10-minute presentation on behalf of the organization for which you developed a brochure in Exercise 15.2.
4. You are assisting your CEO in developing a 10-minute presentation to company employees to explain the same information as you wrote for the newsletter article in Exercise 13.3.
5. You are making a 10-minute speech on behalf of the organization for which you wrote the fundraising appeal letter in Exercise 16.3.

Identify and roughly sketch out at least 10 different specific presentation aids that could be used during your presentation. You may use more than one of the same kind of aid, such as several overhead transparencies.

Evaluating the Speech

Speechwriting and speech giving don't often go through a formal evaluation process, but you can be creative in measuring, both objectively and subjectively, the effects and outcomes of your speeches.

Keep records of various speeches you write for use within your organization. Note the number and tone of comments the speaker receives. Note particularly the compliments and criticisms, any feedback that shows a real interest—positive or negative—in the speech. Also keep a record of the number and kinds of questions that the speech generates.

Follow the speech after its presentation. Note the instances when the speech finds its way into media use, perhaps as a sound bite or a quote. Also note the number of speaking invitations that are generated, and try to find out if these resulted because someone was impressed with previous speeches given on behalf of your organization or client.

Exercise 18.4

Analyzing a Speech

Obtain the text of a speech. You can do this by using a search engine to identify "speech transcripts" or by going to a website such as the Department of Defense (defense.gov/speeches) or the United Nations (un.org > search "speech transcript").

1. With a double underline, mark the speaker's proposition. In a margin note, indicate if this is a factual, value, or policy proposition.
2. With a single underline, mark each of the subordinate arguments that support this proposition.
3. Draw a box around the sentence(s) or paragraph(s) that comprise the conclusion.
4. Briefly analyze and evaluate the writing style of the speech.
5. Write a brief analysis and evaluation of the logic used within the speech.

Question-Answer Session

Giving a speech is just part of many face-to-face communication situations. Often, the speech is followed by a question-and-answer session, an encounter that can really test a communicator's stamina. Speakers' bureaus organize public presentations and invite questions. Some public relations vehicles change the emphasis—a brief oral presentation followed by an extended question-and-answer session. Town meetings use this approach. So do news conferences that feature a brief statement followed by a volley of questions from reporters.

Answering questions and giving interviews are among the best ways to tell your story. Through your response to the questions, you can present a message and perspective of your organization to a wide and diverse audience. Organizations vary in their ease of dealing with interview situations. In general, the more open an organization is and the more it interacts with its publics, the more successful it will be with creating a favorable public opinion.

Any person who gives an interview should be accurate, fair, and professional. Without betraying confidences, the interview giver should provide honest and complete information. If one is to err, let it be on the side of openness, honesty, and confidence in the informed opinion of your publics. Here are some guidelines to help you prepare for your question-answer situation:

- Know the source of the questioner's information. If you aren't sure, ask, and then consider the credibility of the source.
- Identify the publics most affected by the topic. Present your information with them in mind.
- Never try to play it by ear. If you can anticipate questions ahead of time, organize your thoughts around them. Write some talking points about your topic and the questions that might flow from it.
- Consider the likelihood that you may encounter some hostile questions or queries on topics that can be embarrassing for your organization. Consider how you would address such questions.

Exercise 18.5

Preparing for an Interview

You are public relations director for LakeLand Chemicals, a company that uses chemicals in the manufacturing of paint.

First thing this morning, you learned that the state Environmental Protection Agency is listing LakeLand as a "borderline violator" for discharging a toxic chemical through its smokestack. The chemical is called tri-chlorofluoromethane, CFM-3; it is in the family of chlorofluorocarbons known as CFCs, which have received considerable media attention in your area because of their negative environmental consequences. The chemical is harmless when used as a liquid, which is how it is used by LakeLand. But it can destroy ozone in the upper atmosphere when it is released as a gas, and the production process at LakeLand transforms some CFM-3 into gas, which escapes through smokestacks.

continued . . .

Exercise 18.5 . . . *continued*

LakeLand's current emissions of CFM-3 are 91 percent clean; the government requires them to be 92 percent clean. Because of the borderline levels, the EPA will give LakeLand six months to improve emissions before any penalties might be levied.

You learned the information first thing this morning. You know that the EPA will release the information to reporters by noon today.

You also know that LakeLand has been discussing the purchase of an expensive new high-tech smokestack filter that could significantly decrease the toxic emissions, but you are not yet at liberty to announce this.

Prepare for interviews with reporters with the following activities:

Part 1: Prepare a brief planning sheet indicating your company's key publics; an analysis of their wants, interests, and needs; and your main objectives in dealing with reporters.

Part 2: Anticipate questions reporters might ask. Make notes of appropriate responses to these questions.

Part 3: Summarize the main point or points you want to communicate to your key publics. Sketch out anecdotes or examples that might convey that point.

Being Interviewed

Just shortly before the interview time arrives, take a few minutes to quiet yourself. Focus, center, pray, meditate, or do whatever you do to relax and become balanced. Approach the interview as an opportunity to say something positive and be grateful to give public witness, even on controversial subjects.

Don't feel obliged to respond in depth, especially if you are questioned unexpectedly and don't have time to prepare for the interview. Say: "I just can't talk about that right now, but as soon as the contract is negotiated [or whatever the holdup is] I will be happy to answer all of your questions." Or use the occasion to announce that you will make a statement at some specific later time: "I'll be addressing that at my meeting tomorrow with the stockholders."

The setting for the interview can vary. A question-answer session following a speech may be busy, with some people leaving the auditorium and others trying to get closer to the speaker. A news conference can be bustling with cameras, microphones, and reporters moving around.

A one-on-one interview has a much different feel and often takes place on home turf, such as your office or a conference room in your building. Be careful not to relax too much; you may be in familiar surroundings, but keep a keen awareness that you are being interviewed. For a television interview, you may find that the reporter or camera operator asks you to answer questions in a livelier setting, perhaps outside your building, on the floor of your manufacturing plant, or in front of the construction site for your new office complex.

Tips for Better Writing *Effective Interview Techniques*

During an interview, you may find the following recommendations helpful.

- *Be confident*. You are not an uninformed nobody with irrelevant opinions. You are the expert the reporter has sought out. Take confidence in that fact.
- *Be honest*. Answer as fully and as sincerely as you can. The impression you make as a professional representative of your organization will last far longer than the particular facts you convey.
- *Be accurate*. There is nothing worse than an error of fact (except a deliberate error of fact). Don't guess. Say "I don't know" or "I'll find out for you," but try not to appear ill prepared or uninformed.
- *Be brief*. For radio and television, think in terms of headlines and sound bites. You'll probably have two or three sentences to tell your story, and perhaps time for a couple of quick answers to questions. For print media, you can expand on that capsule.
- *Stay on topic*. The more you talk, the more opportunity you give a reporter to use peripheral comments instead of central information. Stick to the topic. State the key message in different ways.
- *Be interesting*. Use colorful and pithy language. Use brief anecdotes. Speak directly to the audience. Imagine one individual out there (other than the reporter) and speak to him or her.
- *Be motivated*. Display your motivation and your enthusiasm. The impression you leave with your audience will linger far after they have forgotten your words.
- *Restate your key point*. If you are amid a controversy and are pressed for a comment, use the occasion to reiterate your intended message instead of responding to the detail of the controversy. Question: "Mr. Jones says you environmentalists are trying to impose your beliefs on others." Answer: "We all favor individual freedoms, but the issue here is whether one person's privilege to smoke is more important than everybody's right to clean air in a public restaurant. We believe a public right is more important than a private privilege."
- *Hold your tongue*. Don't comment if you cannot. But give a reason for your inability to answer: "Our policy is not to discuss former employees." Don't say "No comment" when you mean "I can't address that topic now" or "I don't know."
- *Help the reporter*. Insist that your opponent be heard. You can never go wrong by being an advocate of getting both sides out. It's even better if you actually help the news media get in touch with someone from the "other" side. Reporters will find the opposition anyway, and you might be able to steer them toward moderate critics (or perhaps to more extreme rivals who betray a zealotry that actually helps your position). Your insistence that there are various perspectives can only enhance your credibility and integrity.
- *Signal your message*. "The most important thing about this point is . . . " Or "Three things stand out here. One . . . Two . . . And finally . . . " This will make your message clearer, and it will decrease the likelihood that you are quoted out of context.

Exercise 18.6

Conducting an Interview/News Conference

Select two members of your class to act as the organizational spokesperson and public relations counsel for LakeLand Chemicals. The rest of the class will play the role of reporters asking questions about the industrial emissions outlined in Exercise 18.5; these reporters should be interested in the topic but not particularly hostile to the speaker. Conduct a question-and-answer session based on this scenario.

When the question-and-answer session is ended, critique the responses given by the spokesperson.

Handling Hostility

Most news interviews are civil. Reporters are professionals doing a job that requires an unbiased and objective approach. Their job, however, is not to make you look good, and sometimes they may pursue a line of questioning aggressively. But be aware that you don't control the agenda in a news interview.

Question-answer situations sometimes can become hostile. Many government officials have felt that constituents have ganged up on them during town-hall meetings. Audience questioners following a speech can use their time at the mic for blistering criticism or hostile questions.

If you need to deal with hostility, the No. 1 rule is to concentrate and listen carefully to the questions being asked. Identify any inaccurate statements, unsound conclusions, unacceptable paraphrases, or false implications.

Don't let questioners put words into your mouth. If confronted with a loaded question, call it for what it is, then restate the question and answer in terms you are comfortable with. Try not to repeat the charge in your response. "No, it's unfair to say that. What we really are doing is . . ." Refute incorrect statements or prejudiced questions. Correct the questioner who misinterprets what you have said or done: "Actually, that's not quite right. What we are doing is . . ." Keeping your answers short should prevent interruptions. And try to identify the basis of critical information.

Above all, never lose your cool! Don't aggravate the situation by sounding arrogant. Keep an even, professional tone. The words that come out of your mouth are your responsibility and must always be under your control.

News Conference

The **news conference** is a practical strategic tool of public relations. It stands at the confluence of a speech, print and broadcast news releases, multimedia presentations, an advocacy statement, and question-answer sessions.

A news conference is staged to provide an organization's message simultaneously to not only a group of reporters and other media folk (photographers, bloggers, potentially editorial writers) but also other publics such as employees, consumers, opponents, regulators, and so on.

Implicit in planning a news conference is a double litmus test: The topic must be of major significance to the organization, and it must be deemed newsworthy by the media.

A news conference can be one of the most interesting and rewarding activities a public relations practitioner can undertake. It also can be one of the most risky. The outcome depends on how prepared you are and how much you can prepare the spokesperson and control the situation. As the public relations person, you will identify the topic, but you will have little to no control over the questions reporters will ask, or how or even whether they will use the information you provide.

The decision to call a news conference should be based on a strategic decision that it would be effective in helping an organization communicate in a given situation. Keep in mind that news conferences are not favorites of most reporters, who prefer to get their information and do their interviews individually rather than in a group with their professional rivals.

When it does seem appropriate to call a news conference, give some thought to timing. Consider media deadlines. Select a time most convenient for reporters. For example, 7 p.m. may be too late for all or even most editions of a morning newspaper, and a late-afternoon paper may have a noon deadline. An evening television news show may need information before 4 p.m., while a radio station may be able to take stories up to about 10 minutes before each hourly report. Online publications obviously have no built-in deadlines. Ask reporters how much time they need to prepare a story and what they consider the best times for a news conference.

You won't be able to accommodate everyone's schedule each time, especially reporters on competing morning and evening newspapers. Just make sure you don't continually favor one deadline over another.

While a news conference requires solid news, it's also a bit of a theatrical event. If the subject can be demonstrated, do so. If a new building or bridge project can be shown in a model, use one. Stage the news conference to take advantage of every potential for visual impact.

FYI *Online Interviews and News Conferences*

Gather public relations practitioners, and they talk about dwindling interest in the traditional news conference. Reporters are busy or not particularly interested in traveling to the organization's location to obtain information, especially "talking heads" presenting good news rather than crises and emergency activities.

Is there an alternative to the traditional news conference? Decidedly, yes. It's found in the growing use of live online news conferences and interviews. Organizations can use sophisticated teleconference technology or simpler computer-based videoconferencing through Skype, iChat, and similar services that let reporters conduct one-on-one interviews or join news conferences from their own office or home. Either way, journalists can interact with news sources who may be across town or in another hemisphere.

After the news conference or interview, the content prepared for reporters can be posted online also. In today's 24-hour news cycles and fast-paced newsrooms, these Internet-based alternatives are sometimes more successful than traditional on-site news conferences.

Another advantage is that online interviews and news conferences can be accessed not only by reporters but also by other interested and credentialed people, allowing organizations to

continued . . .

FYI *Online Interviews and News Conferences* *. . . continued*

communicate directly with key publics. For example, politicians hold online news conferences to announce their legislative agendas, business leaders use them to introduce new products, charities go online with information on fundraising campaigns, and other nonprofit organizations promote new programs through online news conferences.

Live online interviews and news conferences also allow for the materials to be archived as podcasts, audio and video news feeds, Web extras, and other online services as well as printed transcripts for both journalists and other audience members. Television stations provide full coverage of news conferences on their websites, augmenting the few seconds of highlights they can broadcast during their regular broadcast programming. In another major benefit, the organizations themselves can post the news conference at their own websites and online newsrooms, as well as at their Facebook and other social media sites.

Let's look at all the writing elements associated with a news conference.

Planning Sheet

A news conference deserves careful planning. A good public relations practitioner will invest the necessary time to design an opportunity to engage the media in a way that will serve the interests of the sponsoring company or organization, as well as the needs of the media. The standard planning sheet saves time and focuses on your goals and objectives.

In addition to the planning sheet, plan the logistics of the news conference itself: appropriate room, credentials or access for reporters who will cover the event, arrangements for videotaping the conference, and so on.

Invitational Advisory

Public relations practitioners invite media representatives to news conferences. Such invitations take the form of media advisories that give information of interest to city editors and assignment editors, bloggers, and photographers. This information includes the general topic; logistical information such as date, time, and place; identification of the speaker; information on the access for photographers for both print and video photographers; and the name of the public relations contact.

Remember the difference between a news release and a media advisory. For the invitational advisory, provide only a general topic. Don't give too much advance information, or you might read an article in the morning newspaper that reports the substance of your news conference scheduled for later that day.

To get the word out, many organizations post their invitational advisory at the online media page. Others use the services of a company such as PR Newswire and Business Wire or other news-dissemination services.

Occasionally you may find yourself in the situation of knowing that a news conference will be held pending some other activity. For example, if the vote on a strike settlement is near, you may send an advisory indicating that you will call a news conference on short notice when the vote is decisive. This allows reporters to do background research and formulate questions. At other times you will be dealing with an emergency or unexpected situation. In such cases, you may need to hold a news conference fast, with little lead time.

News Conference Agenda

A news conference is a staged event. As such, it needs planning and smooth execution. A carefully prepared agenda can be an invaluable tool in staging an effective news conference.

Exhibit 18.1 features an agenda that a sports information director at a Midwestern university prepared for a news conference announcing the hiring of a new football coach. Note that the agenda and subsequent information does not identify the new coach, minimizing the likelihood of a leak before the news conference.

News Statement

A news statement is a combination of a news release, position paper, and speech. Make sure the information is of high news value. Focus on the SiLoBaTi elements of news: significant, local, balanced, and timely. As with a position paper, the statement should present your organization's opinion and reasons for it. And, like a speech, it is written for the ear, considering delivery as well as content. Exhibit 18.2 includes an example of a news statement.

News value is a particularly important ingredient for a news conference. Journalists can easily deal with non-news in releases simply by tossing them away. But lack of news in a news conference wastes reporters' time. Worse, it cheapens your reputation as a reliable ally of the media, since you betray that you don't know or care what is news.

What if your information, though interesting, is not hugely newsworthy? Consider two alternatives to a news conference: a special event and a photo op.

A **special event** is an activity created and/or sponsored by the organization in order to attract attention to something with a certain news value. Sometimes called a **staged event** or a **pseudo-event**, this might take the form of an anniversary celebration at a car dealership, tree-planting ceremony, groundbreaking event, and so on. It generally involves engaging one or more of the organization's publics and inviting the media to observe and record the interaction. Even if the media do not show up, the involvement with the public justifies the event. It also allows the organization to report on the activity through its online newsroom, website, blog, social media pages, newsletter, and elsewhere.

Be careful that a legitimate special event doesn't devolve into a mere **publicity stunt**, which is an event with little or no news value created simply to attract media attention.

A **photo op** is an occasion, likewise created or sponsored by the organization, offering something of particular interest to photographers in print or video media. Examples of photo ops are officials signing documents, donors presenting checks, politicians visiting senior centers, and so on. Nothing wrong with them, but even photo ops need to have some element of news, or at least a really strong visual dimension.

A lot of street theater associated with social activism is staged as a photo op, such as rallies or protest demonstrations.

Media Kit

The better reporters understand your organization's message, the more accurately they can present it to their audiences. Much background and detail may be given to reporters as part of a media kit.

Exhibit 18.1—NEWS CONFERENCE AGENDA

10:58 a.m.	Sports Information Director welcomes media and explains what will take place during the news conference and who will be available for one-on-one interviews following the news conference
11 a.m.	SID introduces Athletics Director
11:05 a.m.	AD introduces new coach, who gives an opening statement, and opens floor for questions
11:15 a.m.	SID concludes news conference, again explaining who will be available for one-on-one interviews and where those will take place. Also states what will be going on for the rest of the day (lunch and other photo opportunities) and upcoming football events (first day of spring practice, media day for fall practice)
11:20 a.m.	Coach commences interview with radio affiliate; AD, other members of hiring committee, and several student-athletes are made available for interviews with media
11:30 a.m.	Coach begins one-on-one interviews with area TV stations, allotting five minutes per station; SID checks with media for other interviews/requests
Noon	Coach starts interview(s) with newspapers. SID states lunch will be served starting at 12:15 p.m. and gives a rundown of the sports calendar for the week
12:15 p.m.	Lunch served. Save meals for coach and newspaper reporters
1 p.m.	Coach made available for photo opportunities walking through football facilities, campus
1:15 p.m.	Tour/interviews end.

Athletics Director Talking Points

- What the program was looking for in the new coach
- How many candidates applied, how many were interviewed
- What made new coach stand out among the candidates
- Introduce available committee members.

Coach Talking Points

- Why I applied for the position
- School's successful tradition
- What to expect in the years to come.

Strategic Planing for News Conference

Goal: Present university's new football coach.

Objectives: Hold the news conference to generate media coverage; get 100 percent of local media in attendance; get 90 percent of regional media in attendance; generate coverage of other teams.

Research: Reviewed what other institutions had done as well as previous announcements by the department; met with media to determine what format and what timeframe work best for them; met with peers to determine which methods had been successful or not and why.

Outcomes: Had 100 percent of local and regional media attendances; generated coverage in following weeks with outreach effort with morning radio shows; helped create a "push" for season ticket sales.

Evaluation: Generated media coverage above expectations; saw a 10 percent increase in season ticket sales; set a plan in place for future hiring news conferences.

News conferences generally include a variety of print materials for journalists attending. Most common among these are news releases and fact sheets. Photographs and other graphic pieces may be useful. Biographies or organizational/project histories also may be appropriate.

Plan on presenting a media kit for every news conference. The only exception may be when you are deep in a crisis situation with no time to prepare media kits, but even crisis communication generally allows time to update a fact sheet for reporters.

Questions and Answers

After the speaker has given the news statement, and after the public relations person has given reporters written information, the news conference usually turns into a question-answer session. Initially, this is time for reporters to clarify information. Even though it becomes an attempt by reporters to probe for additional information, the Q&A also offers an opportunity for the organization to present information that is significant, newsworthy, and strategic.

Sometimes the organizational spokesperson at the focus of the news conference may be able to answer reporters' questions, sometimes not. But every planned encounter with reporters requires that the spokesperson prepare for the news conference. Generally, public relations practitioners prep the spokesperson with a set of questions that reporters are likely to ask, along with appropriate responses.

Exhibit 18.2 is an example of a news conference statement, along with Q&A responses.

News Conference Follow-Up

Immediately after the news conference, all materials that were presented to reporters who attended should be posted at the organization's online newsroom. In addition, the podcast of the conference itself should be posted. Minimally, this podcast should be an audio file, though preferably video.

An e-mail should be sent to invited journalists who did not attend, indicating that the materials are available online.

Evaluation

Finally, the public relations practitioner should begin a debriefing report and evaluation of the news conference. This can be presented in three stages.

First, write a brief report and personal evaluation. Who attended? Who was invited but did not attend? Did reporters seem to understand the news statement, or did they need clarification? What was the tone and substance of questions? How well did the speaker(s) respond? What kind of coverage do you expect? Indicate any follow-up you may need to provide reporters.

Second, as the information becomes available, begin a file on the coverage. Include links or PDF files of print reports, blog reports, and other types of coverage. Write a synopsis of broadcast reports, and include a link to any online postings of the reports.

Finally, write a brief conclusive evaluation of the news conference. Go back and review your objectives, and consider how successful the conference was in meeting those objectives. Indicate any lessons you learned that can help you in the future. Such a written evaluation can help you become more effective in preparing future news conferences, because it leads you to analyze and understand each of your encounters with the media. Just as important, an evaluation report shared with your supervisor or client will position you as a manager and strategist.

Exhibit 18.2—NEWS CONFERENCE STATEMENT WITH Q&A

Organizational Spokesperson: As you know, for the last 29 months, employees of LakeLand Chemicals have been working without a pay increase. This salary freeze affected plant managers and members of the United Chemical Workers of America local 213, more than 400 employees in all.

It was a painful but necessary step to prevent layoffs while we tried to become more productive.

I am pleased to announce the following news: Beginning next month, our employees will receive a 7 percent salary increase. We expect to follow this in six months with a second-stage increase of between 3 and 5 percent.

Two factors make the increase possible. First, business is beginning to improve for us. Sales are up, and we have just signed a two-year export agreement with Guatemala worth $7.3 million. Second, an unexpected benefit of our environmental commitment is saving us substantial money. The new electronic smokestack filter that we installed six months ago reduces air pollution to below federal and state levels. It also makes it possible for us to recover a rather expensive chemical called tri-chloro-fluoro-methane. We can reuse this chemical in the production of paints. Because the filter is more efficient than we had anticipated, we find that it is saving us $32,000 a month.

These last 29 months have been difficult for both LakeLand Chemicals and all the people of Middletown. The union has been understanding of the financial problem and committed to the long-term welfare of union members. After weeks of negotiating, we have come up with an arrangement that I believe we all can live with.

Q&A Briefing

How many employees do you have?
Current personnel: 56 managers, 352 union members. Total 408

How much will the salary increases cost?
Almost $20,000 a month with the 7 percent increase.

When will you know the extent of the second increase?
Probably within the next quarter when we see exactly how strong our recovery is.

What does the chemical do?
Tri-chloro-fluoro-methane is a CFC, which is under government regulation because it can destroy ozone in the upper atmosphere. LakeLand Chemicals uses it in the manufacture of paint, where it is safe as a liquid. The environmental risk occurs when it is released as a gas. That's why we installed the smokestack filter.

How was the expert agreement reached?
With help from the U.S. Agency for International Development, as well as local and state chambers of commerce.

There are reports that the union was strong-armed to accept the wage freeze.
Talk to the union. I assure you, no coercion was made by company management. We all were being "strong-armed" by a poor economy and a very real threat that the plant might have to be closed. But we sacrificed together, and now we can share in the benefits.

Are any CFCs being released despite the filter?
This filter is the result of the best technology we know of to prevent CFGC release into the atmosphere. Government tests show that our emissions are 94 percent free of CFC, 2 percent cleaner than the government requires.

Wrap-Up for Part Three

The chapters in Part Three of this book have focused on writing in non-news style, rounding out the many venues available to public relations writers. It is unlikely that a writer working on a single project or working for a particular client will prepare material for each of these categories. As with any other menu, the idea is to pick and choose to provide the most well-rounded outcomes.

In Part Three you have learned about many different writing venues. Some of these are associated with established print and broadcast media. Others are related to emerging digital media. Here is a review of the learning objectives from these six chapters, in which you have learned how . . .

- To write an effective newsletter article
- To write an effective headline for a newsletter article
- To understand the purpose and importance of corporate reports
- To edit and proofread documents carefully and effectively
- To show an understanding of laws related to copyright and trademark
- To analyze a website for effective presentation of information
- To plan a blog to support an organization's public relations plan
- To write effective blog posts for public relations purposes
- To write and design a flier
- To develop a brochure
- To demonstrate an understanding of persuasive techniques for written communication
- To write an effective appeal letter
- To write an effective online appeal letter
- To identify differences between consumer advertising and public relations advertising
- To use creative techniques to develop advertising copy
- To write effective copy for a public relations advertisement
- To prepare and write an effective speech
- To plan audio-visual presentation aids to enhance a speech
- To prepare for a question-answer session following a speech or as part of an interview or news conference.

The common theme throughout these chapters is the wide variety of writing opportunities beyond the category of media relations. Newsletters, websites, blogs, brochures, and related internal publications allow organizations much control over the packaging and dissemination of their messages. A characteristic of this category of writing is that publics come to the organization, often with an information-on-demand approach. These information-seeking publics play a powerful role in the strategic communication program of any organization.

Meanwhile, direct mail and advertising allow organizations to push their advocacy messages toward their publics, often into their own homes. The final category of speechwriting helps the organization communicate personally with members of its publics.

Green Packaging

Environmentally conscious organizations will find a parallel in Part Three with the information previously outlined in Part Two, where it was evident that social media releases, online newsrooms, and other technologies associated with emerging media offer an opportunity for organizations to reduce paper and be more environmentally friendly in disseminating their messages to journalistic publics. A parallel opportunity exists with the venues associated with Part Three of this textbook.

Websites allow organizations to post all kinds of information that is available to visitors without the need for printing and mailing.

For example, while blogs, e-zines, and online newsletters don't eliminate the need for printed materials, they do offer a cost-effective and green supplement. Some organizations are taking this a step further, using such media not as a supplement but rather as an alternative to printed versions.

Websites post PDF files of brochures and reports, making a significant pro-environmental impact.

In the area of fundraising and advocacy, meanwhile, online methods are proving to be as effective as printed direct mail. Particularly in crisis situations or in times of breaking news, the online versions sometimes are even more effective than letters that are printed and mailed.

Organizations recycle speeches written for specific audiences by posting them at organizational websites as text, audio podcast, and/or video.

Online news conferences also offer environmental benefits, saving not only paper by posting material for journalists online, but also saving monetary and environmental costs associated with transportation, sometimes lodging, and other logical needs required for in-person news conferences. In today's 24/7 news cycles and fast-paced newsrooms, Internet-based alternatives are sometimes more successful than traditional on-site news conferences. They also can be uploaded to an organization's website or its YouTube page for reporters who were unable to participate when the conference originally took place. This also allows organizations to make such information available to publics other than journalists, increasing the opportunity for communicating with many different publics through a single event.

Public relations is an integral part of the environmental movement. As companies and nonprofit organizations become greener by developing products and adopting practices that are environmentally friendly, they are calling upon their public relations teams to communicate that to their various publics. However, public relations practitioners also can lead the way, or at least model the organization's commitment, by using the emerging new tools and technologies that cut down the use of paper, ink, plastic, and other consumable or disposable products.

Appendix A Common Sense Stylebook for Public Relations Writers

A stylebook is a manual with rules and norms for writing and editing.

A good stylebook helps writers use language in a way that is natural, smooth, and consistent. Following are guidelines for various public relations writing purposes. They deal with aspects of language that students have identified as needing clarification and order. The style suggestions here are consistent with the Associated Press Stylebook, the most widely used stylebook for journalistic writing. Thus public relations writers will find this Common Sense Stylebook useful in preparing news releases and other writing for newspapers and magazines.

Writing for organizational media—websites, blogs and social media, as well as print media such as newsletters and brochures—sometimes calls for a stylistic practice that may be different from that used for public media. Nevertheless, writers need to be consistent in style. This Common Sense Stylebook includes guidelines about stylistic options appropriate for organizational media. Though optional, they should be consistently used, according to the organization's internal stylebook.

For more complete references, consult authoritative guides such as the Associated Press Stylebook, Webster's New World Dictionary Fourth Edition, Webster's Third New International Dictionary, and National Geographic Atlas of the World.

Abbreviation

Avoid abbreviations except in situations of common usage. In general, when writing for print media, use capital letters without periods for abbreviations of organizations or terms in which the letters are pronounced separately: *CIA*, *IBM*, *CEO*, *UCLA*, *TV*, *VCR*, *ABC News* (but *Fox News*). Exception: Abbreviate *U.S.* and *U.N.* when these are used as adjectives but do not abbreviate *United States* or *United Nations* when these terms are used as nouns. For broadcast media, use a hyphen between letters to indicate that they are to be pronounced separately: *C-I-A*, *Y-M-C-A*, *U-C-L-A*.

See the following entries in this stylebook: Academic Degree, Address, Date, Dateline, Military, Organization Name, Period, State Name, Title of People (Courtesy) and Title of People (Formal).

Academic Degree

In general, avoid abbreviations for academic degrees. Write out the names of college or university degrees, using lower-case letters except for proper nouns or proper adjectives: *obtained an associate's degree in masonry, received a bachelor's from Central State, obtained a master's degree in business administration, holds a doctorate in French literature* (not *holds a doctor's degree*). Use capital letters but no apostrophe when citing the formal name of a degree: *Bachelor of Arts degree, Master of Science program.*

Do not abbreviate academic degrees for public media. Academic abbreviations are an option for organizational media if readers are likely to be familiar with the abbreviation: *M.S., Ph.D., M.F.A.* Place these after the name, set off by commas. See Professional Credential.

Address

When referring to a street without a specific address, spell out *Street, Avenue*, etc.: *Ransom Road, Madison Avenue.*

When referring to a specific address, abbreviate *Ave., Blvd.* and *St.* Write out related words: *Alley, Court, Drive, Parkway, Place, Road, Terrace*, etc.: *20 Mango Lane, 8033 Thyme Circle.*

Use numerals for an address number: *27 Anderson Blvd., 1356 Linwood Ave.* Exception: *One North St.*

Write out a compass point when it is the name of the street: *1550 South Drive.* Also write out the compass point if the street name is used without a specific address: *West Main Street.* Otherwise, abbreviate compass points within a complete address: *15 W. Main St.*

For numbered streets, spell out and capitalize *first* through *ninth*; use ordinals for *10th* and above.

Age

Use numerals for all ages: *The child, 5, was . . . At age 15, he went . . .* Use a numeral with a hyphen when the age is used as part of a compound modifier before the noun: *2-year warranty, 5-year-old girl.* Do not use hyphens when using age as a noun: *A 5 year old was rescued. . .*

Bracket the numeral with commas when the age is used parenthetically: *Johnson, 37, was appointed . . .*

Ampersand

Use the ampersand (&) only when it is part of an organization's formal name: *J & R Rentals, Inc., Johnson & Johnson.*

Apostrophe

Use an apostrophe with an *s* to designate possessives of most words (singular or plural): *women's hockey, the judge's ruling, Ohio's capital.*

Use an apostrophe without an *s* to indicate the possessive of a word (whether singular or plural) already ending in *s*: *girls' sports, the witness' response, Arkansas' capital.* Exception: Use *'s* with words ending in another letter with the sound of *s: Marx's biography, the fox's den, the prince's schedule.*

Use an apostrophe to indicate omitted numbers: *in the '60s, class of '09.* Do not use an apostrophe to designate the plural of numbers: *in her 30s, during the 1980s, size 8s.*

Use an apostrophe to indicate the plural of stand-alone letters: *A's and B's, the Oakland A's*. However, do not use an apostrophe with multiple letter designations: *RBIs, WMDs*. Also, do not use an apostrophe to designate the plural of words: *dos and don'ts*.

Brand Name

Capitalize trademarks and brand names: *Xerox*, *Toyota*, *Gucci Envy*. For public media, use lower case for generic terms: *Lee jeans*, *Corolla sedan*, *LexisNexis database*, *GarageBand music application program*. For organizational media, capitalization of generic terms is optional. Also optional for organizational media is the use of trademark indicators: *LexisNexis®*, *GarageBand™*.

Capitalize brand names and trademark with food items: *Tabasco sauce*. In general, capitalize proper adjectives when they are part of food names: *Boston baked beans, Swiss cheese, Waldorf salad, Russian dressing*. Consult the dictionary for such usage.

Capitalization

For public media, avoid unneeded use of capitalization. Use capital letters for proper nouns, full names, and formal titles. Do not capitalize planets, academic or organizational departments, or job titles. Do not capitalize seasons and their derivatives: *spring*, *wintertime*. Capitalize proper nouns, including brand names, awards, and holidays. See the following entries for specific guidelines on capitalization: Academic Degree; Geographic Region; Government; Organization Name; Politics; Race, Ethnicity, and Nationality; State Name; Title of Composition; and Title of People (Formal).

For organizational media, the writer may choose to use capital letters more freely to indicate importance or prestige within the organization.

Use capitals for adjectives derived from proper nouns: *Boston crème pie*, *German shepherd*. However, some such words have become generic and do not require capitalization: *french fry*. Use www.merriam-webster.com/dictionary as an authoritative online source.

Collective Noun

Nouns that refer to a grouping of people or things are singular: *committee*, *board*, *company*, *management*, *team*, *family*, *class*. When referring to such a grouping, use a singular pronoun and a singular verb: *The company will build its office* (not *their*). *The board of trustees wants to vote* (not *want*).

When referring to all the individuals within the grouping, use a plural noun to make this clear: *The company managers will build their office. The trustees want to vote.*

Colon

Use a colon to designate a sentence within a sentence or an enumeration: *His promise was simple: He would balance the budget. She indicated three favorite authors: Thomas Merton, Shushako Endo, and Thich Nhat Hahn.* Capitalize the first word following a colon only if it is a proper noun or the beginning of a sentence: *He has several pets: a dog, two cats, and a ferret.*

Comma

In general, place a comma between each element in a series: *The book includes an overview of European history, a discussion of the influence of religion, and an analysis of the effects of the rise of literacy*. But with a short and simple series, do not use a comma before the conjunction: *The book deals with history, religion and literacy.*

Put a comma before the conjunction when another conjunction is used within one or more elements in the series: *The book deals with European history, the influence of religion and education, and the rise of literacy*. Use a semicolon instead of a comma to separate items in a series if at least one of the items includes material with a comma: *The book deals with European history; the influence of Christianity, Judaism and Islam; and the rise of literacy.*

Place commas before and after parenthetical material and nonessential (nonrestrictive) phrases and clauses: *The president, 42, will . . . The visitor, a native of Mexico, was . . . The senator, who is left-handed, wants . . . The student, who got an F, explained that . . .* Do not use commas with essential (restrictive) phrases and clauses that provide necessary information for the meaning of the sentence: *Students who get an F must repeat the course.*

Use a comma before coordinating conjunctions (*and, or, but, for, nor, yet, so*) when they join independent clauses: *Jaleesa wanted to go to the park, but the weather was bad*. Use a comma after an introductory clause beginning with subordinating conjunctions such as *after*, *although*, *because*, *since*, *when*, etc. *Because the weather was bad, Jaleesa decided to stay home*.

Use a comma after an introductory clause or phrase: *After entering the university as a journalism major, she changed to public relations*. But do not use a comma following a short introductory phrase: *After dinner she changed her sweater*.

Use a comma to separate a quotation from its attribution: *"This is a beautiful day," he said*. Do not use a comma if the quotation ends with a question mark or an exclamation point: *"Do you think this is a beautiful day?" he asked*.

Commas, like periods, always go inside quotation marks.

Country and Political Entity

Do not abbreviate *United States* when used as a noun. Abbreviate as *U.S.* when used as an adjective. Give similar treatment to *United Nations*, *United Arab Emirates* and *United Kingdom*. Similarly, write out District of Columbia as a noun, but abbreviate as an adjective. *Visiting the District of Columbia. Using the D.C. metro system.*

Use commonly known designations for foreign nations, avoiding formal titles: *Norway* rather than *Kingdom of Norway, San Marino* rather than *Most Serene Republic of San Marino, India* rather than *Union of India, Jordan* rather than *Hashemite Kingdom of Jordan*.

Use *China* to refer to the mainland nation ruled from Beijing. Use *People's Republic of China* or *Mainland China* only if necessary to distinguish from *Taiwan*, formally called the *Republic of China*. Distinguish between *Ireland* or more formally *Republic of Ireland* (with its capital in Dublin) and *Northern Ireland* (with its capital in Belfast). Likewise, distinguish between *England* (a country in Western Europe), *Great Britain* (an island including the countries of England, Scotland and Wales), and the *United Kingdom* (a political union that includes the countries of England, Scotland, Wales and Northern Ireland).

Date

For public media, use Arabic numbers in the traditional month–day–year format: *Jan. 2, 2007*; *March 15, 1997*. Optional for organizational media or when writing in a military or international context is the construct *15 March 2007*. Do not use ordinal numbers with dates: *May 1* (not *May 1st*); *April 7* (not *April 7th*).

Abbreviate months with more than five letters (*Jan., Feb., Aug., Sept., Oct., Nov., Dec.*) when the specific date is included. Spell out each month when it is used alone or with a year only: *next September, December 2012*. Do not use a comma to separate the year from a month without a date: *January 2011*.

To indicate a span of years, use an *s* without an apostrophe: *throughout the 1990s, founded in the 1800s*. Lower-case *century* in most usages: *21st century, the last century*.

Write out days of the week when used with the date: *Monday, Dec. 16, 2002*.

Presume the reference A.D. unless the reader is likely to become confused: the *10th century*, rather than the *10th century* A.D. The abbreviation refers to the phrase *anno Domini* (Latin = in the year of the Lord) and is computed on the birth of Jesus, though in common usage it does not have a religious connotation. An alternative term is C.E., referring to the *Common Era*.

B.C. is the traditional designation for years and centuries prior to the A.D. era. The term refers to *Before Christ*. This is the common usage for public media. An alternative and more inclusive term is B.C.E., *Before the Common Era*.

A.D. or C.E. time is computed by adding from the zero point, while B.C. or B.C.E. time is computed by subtracting from the zero point.

Dateline

These designations at the beginning of a news release indicate the place of origin for the release. For U.S. datelines, use city (all-capital letters), state abbreviation (caps and lower-case), followed by a dash: *MEMPHIS, Tenn.—Police arrested . . .* For Canadian datelines, use city (all-capital letters) and province name (caps and lower-case) [but not the country name], dash: *KINGSTON, Ontario—Officials expected . . .* For other foreign datelines, use city (all-caps), country (caps and lower-case), dash: *SAN JOSE, Costa Rica—Authorities investigated . . .*

Some cities are well known regionally, nationally or internationally and may stand alone without the state/province/country designation. Consult the AP Stylebook for a listing of these cities. Let common sense prevail. For datelines in regional releases, omit the state if it is not needed for clarity.

Dimension and Size

Use figures for dimensions, but spell out terms such as *inches* and *feet*. Do not use hyphens or commas. *She is 5 feet 7 inches tall. The carpet measures 6 feet by 9 feet.* However, use hyphens when using compound adjectives before a noun: *the 5-foot-7-inch woman, the 6-by-9 carpet*.

Use technical forms (an apostrophe to indicate feet and quotation mark to indicate inches; *x* to indicate length and width) only in charts or graphs: *10′ 11½″ platform, 6 × 9 carpet*. Use figures for sizes: *a size 7 dress, 10W shoe*.

Enumeration and Sequence

Use capitals and numerals for numbers of most items for enumeration: *Room 7*, *Apartment 15B*, *Channel 7*, *Route 90*. Use capitals and numerals for parts of a whole: *Chapter 6*, *Page 17*, *Section B*. Exception: *a Page One story*. Use *Act 2* to refer to the second act. Capitalize and abbreviate *number* and use a numeral to indicate rank: *the No. 1 draft choice*.

Foreign Personal Name

Use spelling according to the individual's preference, if known, or use the nearest English phonetic equivalent: *Alexander Solzhenitsyn*, not *Aleksandr Solzhenitzyn*. If the name has no close equivalent in English, spell it phonetically to approximate the sound in the original language: *Anwar Sadat*.

Follow an individual's preference in using foreign names. Arabs often use two or three names, but on second reference use the final name in the series. *Amed Butros Yamani* on first reference; *Yamani* on subsequent references. Some Arab names include al- or el-. For example, the ruler of Qatar is *Hamad bin Khalifa bin Hamad Al-Thani*. Hamad is his personal name, he is the son of Khalifa who in turn was the son of Hamad. The family name is Al-Thani. In writing, upon second reference, call *Sheik Hamad*, *Prince Hamad* or *Emir Hamad*; in news-style writing, refer to him as *Al-Thani*.

The official Chinese spelling system known as Pinyin eliminates hyphens previously used in many names. *Mao Zedung* rather than *Mao Tse-Tung*. Keep the traditional hyphenated spelling for well-known historical names such as *Sun Yat-sen*.

Chinese and Japanese names traditionally place the family name first, followed by the personal name. Keep this format for Chinese names. However, for Western audiences, Japanese names are usually revised toward the Western style (personal name first, then family name).

Foreign Place Name

In general, use common spelling for the name of foreign locations: Moscow, Paris. Use the common English equivalent: *Florence* rather than *Firenze*, *French Riviera* rather than *Côte d'Azur*. But use the local name for less common places such as *Paciano*, Italy or for locations that are not commonly translated into English, such as *Kyoto*, Japan.

Use spelling from Webster's New World Dictionary or National Geographic Atlas of the World. Use www.merriam-webster.com/dictionary as an authoritative online source.

Foreign Word

Use sparingly. If the meaning is clear and usage is common, write foreign words without explanation in the text: *bon voyage*. If foreign words or phrases are not commonly known, use quotation marks and provide an explanation in parentheses. *"We will soon have peace, insha'Allah (God-willing)," said the ambassador.*

Geographic Region

Capitalize specific regions: *Midwest*, *Northeast*, *West Coast*, *South Atlantic*. Capitalize words derived from geographic regions: *Western decor*, *Southern politician*, *Mediterranean climate*, *an Easterner*.

Capitalize geographic adjectives that are part of a proper noun: *Northern Ireland*, *West Indies*, *North Carolina*. Use lower case to indicate geographic sections within an area: *northern France*, *central Mississippi*. (Exception: *Southern California* is a widely used designation that is capitalized.)

Use lower case to indicate direction: *She traveled south. They hiked northwest.*

Middle East is preferable to *Mideast*, though the latter is not incorrect. There is no internationally accepted definitive list, but generally the Middle East includes the countries of the Arabian peninsula (Bahrain, Kuwait, Oman, Qatar, Saudi Arabia, United Arab Emirates and Yemen); the so-called "Fertile Crescent" (Iraq, Israel, Jordan, Lebanon and Syria) and Northeastern Africa/Mediterranean area (Cyprus, Egypt, Sudan and Turkey). Sometimes Iran, Afghanistan, Pakistan, Kazakhstan and the other -stans are included, though properly these are located in *Central Asia*.

Government

Capitalize *House of Representatives*, *Senate*, *Assembly*, *Legislature*, *Parliament*, *Ministry of Justice*, *Supreme Court*, *Board of Supervisors*, *City Council*, and so on, when the term refers to a specific governmental body.

Retain capitalization when condensed forms of the term clearly refer to a particular governmental body: *the Securities and Exchange Commission* (first reference), *the Commission* (subsequent references).

For public media, use lower case when these terms stand alone generically: *Many city councils throughout the state* . . . For organizational media, use of capital letters is optional.

Capitalize *City*, *County*, *State*, *National*, *Provincial*, *Federal* and so on, when the term is used as part of a formal name: *Federal Communications Commission*, *St. Louis City Council*, *the Chamber of Deputies*, *Ontario Provincial Police*. Use lower case in other references: *the city official*, *25 counties in the state*.

Capitalize *Constitution* when it refers to the U.S. Constitution, regardless of whether the *U.S.* designation is used. For references to constitutions of states and other nations, capitalize only if it is preceded by the name of the state or nation: *the Kansas Constitution*, *Poland's Constitution* (but *the constitution of Poland*).

Capitalize sections of the U.S. Constitution: *Bill of Rights*, *Second Amendment*, *the Preamble*. Capitalize *Congress* when it refers to the U.S. Congress; use lower case for *congressional*. Capitalize *Capitol* when it refers to the building in the District of Columbia or to specific state capitols.

Historic and Geological Time

Capitalize terms of geological time, such as *Mesozoic Era*, *Jurassic Period*, *Paleocene Epoch*.

Capitalize names of commonly recognized historic time, such as *Bronze Age*, *Shang Dynasty*, *Asuka Period*, *Islamic Golden Age*, *Gupta Empire*, *Industrial Revolution*, *Victorian Era*, *the '90s*, *Information Age*.

Capitalize names of historic events such as the *Boston Tea Party*, *Great Depression*, *Prohibition*, *Holocaust*, *War of 1812*.

Do not capitalize informal designations such as *civil rights movement*. Capitalize only proper nouns or adjectives when referring to general descriptions of a period: *classical Greece*, *ancient Egypt*. See Date entry.

Holiday and Holy Day

Capitalize the name of holidays and holy days: *Groundhog Day, Christmas Eve, Kwanzaa, Passover, Ramadan, Memorial Day, Martin Luther King Jr. Day, Lantern Festival (Chinese), Green Corn Festival (Native American), Children's Day (Japan)*. Use an apostrophe for days such as *New Year's Eve, All Saints' Day, April Fool's Day*. Exceptions: *Veterans Day, Presidents Day*.

Home Town

Do not use commas when designating the home town of a person or organization when the word *of* is used: *Lee Chang of Chicago said . . .; Harder Sporting Goods of Williamsport built . . .*

Hyphen

This punctuation indicates a connection between words or parts of words. Use it to prevent confusion. Use a hyphen to connect compound modifiers before a noun: *a first-rate story, a part-time job*. But usually the same word combinations are not hyphenated when they occur after the noun: *The story is first rate. His job is only part time.*

Use a hyphen to connect phrases used as modifiers before a noun: *her don't-give-me-attitude look.*

Use a hyphen in suspended situations, with a space after the hyphen in the suspended usage: *a six- to 10-month waiting period.*

Use a hyphen with the following prefixes: *all-, anti-, ex-, out-, post-, pro-, self-*. Use a hyphen with *co-* when referring to occupation or status. Do not use a hyphen with the following prefixes: *ante, bi, extra, half, in, multi, mini, non, over, pre, re, semi, sub, super, un*. An exception to this is if the prefix creates a double letter, which would be confusing without the hyphen: *re-elect, over-rated, pre-existing.*

Do not use a hyphen with the following suffixes: *like, fold, wide, wise*. An exception to this is if the suffix causes a triple letter, which would be confusing without the hyphen: *shell-like.*

Do not use a hyphen following *very* or following an adverb ending in *ly*.

Inclusive Language

In general, avoid language that unnecessarily excludes groups or is biased about gender, race, religion, age or physical condition. Try to use inclusive words. However, avoid awkward-sounding or unconventional words that draw attention to their inclusiveness. For example, use *firefighter* rather than *fireperson*. Avoid *he or she, him or her, his or hers*. For public media, avoid *s/he* and *he/she*, although these may be appropriate for internal (especially business) media.

Internet

The *Internet* (capitalized) is a decentralized worldwide network of computers, also known as the *Net*. The *World Wide Web* (capitalized) is a global system linking documents, images and other files using the Internet. The *Web* (capitalized) is an acceptable shorter form. Derivative works such as *website, webcast, webmaster* are not capitalized.

Observe correct punctuation when using an Internet address: *www.buffalostate.edu*, *yahoo.com*. Use a period following the address when it ends a sentence. If an Internet address does not fit entirely on a line, break it at a natural point but do not add a hyphen or other punctuation mark.

Use a lower-case prefix with a hyphen for terms such as *e-mail*, *e-book*, *e-commerce* and *e-philanthropy*. Use *dot-com* as an informal adjective describing a company that does business on the Internet.

Addresses for the Internet follow a protocol of the Uniform Resource Locator (URL). Various categories of Internet addresses have specific suffices: *com* or *biz* for commercial enterprises, *org* for nonprofit organizations, *edu* or *ac* for educational institutions, *gov* for government agencies, *mil* for military sites, *net* for network operators, and *int* for international organizations. Some new suffixes are available for specific industries, including *museum*, *aero*, *travel*.

Other sites use a suffix indicating the country in which they are based. Some of the common national suffixes are *jp* for Japan, *ca* for Canada, *au* for Australia, *fr* for France, *es* for Spain, and *il* for Israel. Some less familiar national suffixes include *az* for Azerbaijan, *va* for Vatican City, *bf* for Burkina Faso, *gl* for Greenland, and *zw* for Zimbabwe.

Additionally, some American Indian sites use the suffix *nsn* (Native sovereign nation) such as *hopi-nsn.us, www.mohegan.nsn.us* or *rosebudsiouxtribe-nsn.gov*.

Military

Capitalize names of military organizations when referring to U.S. forces, regardless of whether the designation U.S. is used: *He served in the Army. She is an ensign in the U.S. Coast Guard. Congress is debating Navy policy.*

Capitalize military titles when they appear as a title before a name; do not capitalize such titles in other situations. For print media, abbreviate most military ranks when used before a name: *Gen.*, *Adm.*, *Cmdr.*, *Maj.*, *Capt.*, *Sgt.*, *Cpl.* Do not abbreviate qualifiers for such terms: *Lance Cpl.*, *Master Sgt.* Exceptions: *Ensign*, *Seaman*, *Petty Officer*, *Airman*. Also, do not abbreviate complex forms of such terms: *Senior Airman*, *Petty Officer 1st Class*. Do not abbreviate any military titles for broadcast media.

Both *Marines* and *Marine Corps* are appropriate terms. Do not use abbreviations such as *U.S.A.F.* or *U.S.M.C.*

Do not abbreviate titles standing alone without a name.

Use short titles before a name: *Lt. Jones retired . . . Adm. Marvin attended . . .* Use longer titles following the name: *Lewis, a petty officer 2nd class, was . . .*

Money

Use lower case with names of money, both American and foreign: *dollar*, *nickel*, *euro*, *yen*, *peso*, *Canadian dollar.*

In general, round off amounts of money to the nearest dollar without using a decimal: *$25*, not *$25.00.* If it is necessary to designate cents less than a dollar, use numerals and the word *cents: 5 cents*. For amounts more than a dollar, use the dollar sign and decimal: *$1.05*.

For dollar amounts less than $1 million, use the dollar sign and numbers: *$250*; *$198,750*. For dollar amounts of $1 million or more, use the dollar sign and numerals up to two decimal places with the appropriate word: *$3 million*, *$5.25 billion*.

Do not use a hyphen when using dollar amounts as nouns: *$10 million*. Do not use a hyphen with *million* or *billion* used as a compound adjective: *the $10 million surplus*.

Do not use the dollar sign for informal expressions: *I feel like a million bucks. She has a million-dollar smile. I'd like a nickel for every time . . .*

Number

Write out cardinal numbers below 10: *one, five, nine*. Use numerals for cardinal numbers of 10 or above: *15, 103, 5,372*. (For exceptions, see the following entries: Age, Date, Dimension and Size, Enumeration and Sequence, Money, Time, and Weight.)

For print media, use numerals and words without a hyphen for rounded cardinal numbers of 1 million or above: *5 million, 6.5 billion*. For specific cardinal numbers above 1 million when the exact number is important, use numerals only: *a city of 2,378,525*.

For broadcast media, use hyphenated numerals and words as the number should be pronounced for cardinal numbers above 100: *one-hundred-and-three, 86-thousand spectators, 14-thousand dollars*.

Numerals should not begin a sentence. *Fifty-seven people attended*. To prevent an awkward sentence beginning with a long number, rewrite the sentence. *More than 11,000 people attended*.

With ordinal numbers, use numerals: *1st, 115th*. (Exception: Spell out commonly used ordinal numbers: *First Amendment, second base*.)

Use Roman numerals to designate sequences for wars and for people: *World War I, Queen Elizabeth II, Pope Benedict XVI*. In using Roman numerals, I = 1, V = 5, X = 10, L = 50, C = 100, M = 1,000.

For fractions, spell out amounts less than one and use a hyphen: *one-fourth, two-thirds*. Use numerals for fractions greater than one: 1½, 4⅔. Or translate fractions greater than one into decimals.

Within text, percentages should be written as figures: *0.8 percent, 1 percent, 7.5 percent*. Write out the word *percent* within text. In statistical matter such as charts and graphs, the percent sign (%) may be used without a space following the number.

Ratios should be used with the word *to: student–teacher ratio of 25-to-1*. Odds and election or competition results are used without the word *to: 3–2 against her*; *vote of 675–346*; *a 27–23 victory*.

Do not use numerals for casual references to numbers: *I've told you a million times*.

Organization Name

On first reference, spell out the full name of an organization. Do not immediately follow the full name with an abbreviation in parentheses. On subsequent reference, use initials or organizational abbreviations with no periods: *IBM, PTA*.

In unusual situations, follow the organization's preference: *eBay, Toys Я Us*.

For public media, abbreviate common terms for business organizations (*Co., Inc., Corp., Bros., Ltd.*) when they are used with a specific name: *Robotron Inc., Boffo Corp*. When they stand alone without an organization's name, do not abbreviate such terms.

Spell out *association* in all instances: *Benjamin County Lung Association*.

For public media, use lower-case generic names when designating organizational groupings: *biology department, marketing section, sales division, board of directors*. Capitalize proper names in such a context: *English department, Japan division*. Capitalize organizational groupings if the structure is unusual or unique to the organization: *General Assembly of the United Nations, Standing Council of Canonical Orthodox Bishops*.

For organizational media, capitalization of organizational groupings is optional.

Commonly used alternatives may be used in place of lengthy formal names. *U.S. Department of Defense, Defense Department* and *the Pentagon* all refer to the same government agency.

Period

Do not use periods with the initials of well-known organizations and individuals: *CIA, PRSA, UNESCO, JFK*.

Use periods with abbreviations of states and nations: *W.Va., U.K.* Do not use a space between the letters.

Use periods with *U.S.* and *U.N.* when these are used as adjectives: *U.S. Mint, U.N. secretary-general*. Do not use a space between the letters.

Personal Name

For public print media, use the following order: first name or initial; middle initial(s) or middle name(s); surname; qualifiers such as *Jr.* or *III* with no commas: *Robert L. Marsteen Jr.*; *J. Winston McNamara*. Do not use a space between two consecutive initials: *C.J. Johnson*.

Identify a woman by her own first name rather than that of her husband: *Dawn Smith* rather than *Mrs. Ronald Smith*.

For public broadcast media, common practice is to use only the first name and surname. *Robert Marsteen* (instead of *Robert L. Marsteen Jr.*). An exception to this is when the individual is commonly known by a more complete name: *Martin Luther King, Michael J. Fox*.

For all public media, use full names unless people are well known by single names: entertainers such as *Bjork, Elvira, Madonna, Brandy, Yanni, Eminem* and *Ludacris*; athletes including *Ronaldo* and *Pele*. Avoid using nicknames unless these are used consistently and professionally by the individual: *Jimmy Carter, 50 Cent, Magic Johnson, Ice T, Meat Loaf*. For organizational media, the use of middle initials and nicknames is optional. Use quotation marks around a nickname when the full name is given: *Paul "Bear" Bryant, Eric "E-Train" Lindros*.

For foreign names, use the foreign spelling when it is familiar to the reader: *José Canseco*. Otherwise use spelling and pronunciation guides that approximate English usage. If there is no English equivalent, use an English spelling that approximates the pronunciation of the name.

Place Name

For towns and cities, write out terms in place names such as *Point, Fort, Mount*. Abbreviate *Saint* in place names: *St. Louis, Port St. Lucie, Sault Ste. Marie*. Exception: *Saint John, New Brunswick*.

Politics

Capitalize the names of political parties, whether they are used as a noun or an adjective: *that Republican, this Socialist candidate, the Democratic platform.* Capitalize the word *party* when it is used with the specific name: *the Reform Party.*

Use lower case when the term refers to a political philosophy: *conservative cause, liberal agenda, democratic ideals.*

When party affiliation is relevant, use the full party designation before or after the name: *Democratic Assemblyman Kim Chang . . . Assemblyman Kim Chang, a Democrat . . .* Or use abbreviations for the party and the state or district: *Kim Chang (D-Colo.).* (Note the lack of a period with the party affiliation.)

Professional Credential

Do not use professional credentials for public media. For organizational media, use them sparingly. If they are necessary and recognized by readers, place them after a name, set off by commas and used without periods: *Ronald D. Smith, APR.* See Academic Degree entry.

Pronoun Agreement

Indefinite pronouns use the form of the verb that agrees with their meaning. Some indefinite pronouns are singular: *each, everyone, nobody,* etc. Singular pronouns take singular verbs: *Nobody is happy about this.*

Other indefinite pronouns are plural: *both, few, many, several.* Plural pronouns take plural verbs: *Few are happy about this.*

Some indefinite pronouns can be either singular or plural: *all, any, most, none, some.* These pronouns take the verb appropriate to the meaning of the prepositional phrase following the pronoun: *Some of the candy was gone. Some of the candy canes were gone. Most of the people were happy to see her.*

Proper Noun

Capitalize any proper nouns that refer to a specific person, place or thing: *Susquehanna River, Willamette Valley, Pendleton Ballroom.*

For public media, use lower case when the noun stands alone: *river, valley, ballroom.* For organizational media, use of the lower case on subsequent reference is optional.

Capitalize the word *church* when it is used in reference to a denomination: *The doctrine of the Episcopal Church.* Capitalize the word when the proper name is used in reference to a specific congregation or building: *St. Timothy Episcopal Church.* But use lower case when it refers to a building without the proper name: *An Episcopal church on the corner.*

Quotation Mark

Place quotation marks before and after all quoted matter. Periods and commas always precede closing quotation marks. Question marks and exclamation points are placed before closing quotation marks if they apply only to the material being quoted. They follow quotation marks if they apply to the entire sentence.

Quotation marks are not needed in formats clearly identified as questions and answers, or as indented blocks of text, as in an academic or business report.

For quoted material that runs more than a single paragraph, use open quotation marks at the beginning of each paragraph but use the closing quotation mark only at the end of the final paragraph.

For news release formats, a quotation usually begins a paragraph. Generally, the attribution follows the quoted sentence or is inserted within the quoted sentence(s): *"I hear you," she said. "But I don't like what you are saying."*

Use quotation marks around the names of songs, plays, computer games, television and radio programs, poems, speeches, and works of art. Do not use quotation marks for names of magazines, newspapers or reference materials such as dictionaries, handbooks and encyclopedias. For journalism-orientated materials such as news releases, follow AP Style and use quotation marks for names of books. In more literacy publications such as books, use italics for names of books. For organizational media such as brochures, web publications, and so on, adopt a consistent style. See Title of Composition entry.

Race, Ethnicity and Nationality

Capitalize proper names (either as nouns or adjectives) of races, nationalities, tribes, peoples, etc.: *Arab, Jewish, Caucasian, Sioux history, Nordic pride.* Lower-case informal terms for race: *black, white, mulatto.* Do not mention race unless it is pertinent to the story; avoid derogatory racial and ethnic terms. When pertinent, use terms of personal heritage that are preferred by members of the group. Avoid terms that are outdated or those that may cause offense.

Both *American Indian* and *Native American* are acceptable umbrella terms, but it is better to be specific: *Navajo tribal official, Ojibwa writer, Lenape journalist.* Avoid insulting terms such as *squaw* and potentially offensive terms such as *warpath.* Capitalize the names of American Indian tribes and nations: *Arawak, Cherokee, Hopi, Seneca Nation of Indians.*

Hispanic and *Latino* are umbrella terms, encompassing specific ethnicities such as *Cuban, Dominican, Puerto Rican* and *Chilean.* Note that people from Portugal and Brazil are Latino but not Hispanic. Avoid *Chicano* as a pejorative term.

Note that *Arab* and *Muslim* are not synonymous terms. Arab is an ethnic identity; Muslim designates a person who professes the religion of Islam. Not all Arabs are Muslim (many are Catholic or Orthodox). Not all Muslims are Arab (many are Asians, Berbers, Turks, Kurds or Persians).

State Name

Do not abbreviate the name of one of the 50 states when it is used without a city name within text, either as a noun or adjective. Within text, use common abbreviations (right columns, below) when the state is used with a city or town or with a military base: *Watertown, N.Y., Patuxent River Naval Air Station, Md.* For mailing purposes, use the official two-letter postal abbreviations (left columns, below) for states and U.S. territories.

AK	Alaska	CT	Conn.
AL	Ala.	DC	District of Columbia
AR	Ark.	DE	Del.
AZ	Ariz.	FL	Fla.
CA	Calif.	GA	Ga.
CO	Colo.	GU	Guam

HI	Hawaii	NV	Nev.
IA	Iowa	NY	N.Y.
ID	Idaho	OH	Ohio
IL	Ill.	OK	Okla.
KS	Kan.	OR	Ore.
KY	Ky.	PA	Pa.
LA	La.	PR	Puerto Rico
MA	Mass.	RI	R.I.
MD	Md.	SC	S.C.
ME	Maine	SD	S.D.
MI	Mich.	TN	Tenn.
MN	Minn.	TX	Texas
MO	Mo.	UT	Utah
MS	Miss.	VA	Va.
MT	Mont.	VI	Virgin Islands
NC	N.C.	VT	Vt.
ND	N.D.	WA	Wash.
NE	Neb.	WI	Wis.
NH	N.H.	WV	W.Va.
NJ	N.J.	WY	Wyo.
NM	N.M.		

Use *New York state* to distinguish it from *New York City*, and *Washington state* to distinguish it from *Washington, D.C.* In such uses, the word *state* is not capitalized because it is not part of the formal name. However, use capitals for the names of government agencies, such as *New York State Board of Regents*.

Use the common abbreviation when it intrudes into a proper noun: *The Sacramento (Calif.) Bee, Lock Haven (Pa.) University*.

Time

For print media, use figures with lower-case designations: *7:30 p.m.* Use the simple form for hourly designations: *10 a.m.* rather than *10:00 a.m.* An exception to the use of figures is to write out *noon* rather than *12 a.m.* and *midnight* instead of *12 p.m.* There is no space between the letters a.m. and p.m.

For broadcast media, use conversational time designations: *10 o'clock this morning, 7:30 every night.*

Title of Composition

Capitalize principal words of composition titles (plays, articles, blogs, television programs, movies, songs, computer games, works of art, speeches, and public relations materials such as news releases). Place quotation marks around such composition titles. Do not underline or italicize titles of compositions.

When writing for journalism-orientated materials such as news releases, follow AP Style and use quotation marks for names of books. When writing in more literary publications such as books or in professional publications such as annual reports, use italics for names of books.

Adopt a consistent style when writing for organizational media such as brochures, web publications, and so on.

Capitalize but do not use quotation marks with reference books such as catalogs, dictionaries, almanacs, encyclopedias and handbooks or with periodicals such as newspapers and magazines. Also, capitalize but do not use quotation marks with religious scriptures such as the Bible or the Quran.

Capitalize the word *the* when it is part of the formal and preferred name of a periodical: *The Wall Street Journal*, *The Nation*. Capitalize the word *magazine* only if it is an official part of the title: *Newsweek magazine, Harper's Magazine.*

Title of People (Courtesy Title)

Courtesy titles are polite designations of personal and marital status. First names and surnames used without courtesy titles are the preferred usage for first reference. Do not indicate marital status unless it is pertinent to the piece being written.

For subsequent references for men, the surname without the courtesy title *Mr.* is standard.

For subsequent references for women, it has become common to apply this same standard when the context is professional. *Secretary of State Hillary Clinton will visit . . .* (first reference). *Clinton will visit . . .* (subsequent reference). When the woman's role is more social or when it flows from her husband's status, it is not uncommon to maintain the traditional practice of using the courtesy title—*Mrs.*, *Miss*, *Ms.*—according to the woman's preference, followed by the surname: *First Lady Michele Obama said . . .* (first reference). *Mrs. Obama added . . .* (subsequent reference).

Do not use *Mr.* (except as *Mr. and Mrs. Jones*). Do not indicate marital status unless it is pertinent to the piece being written.

For organizational media, it is common to use the courtesy title with the surname for subsequent references. Use *Mr.* for men, and *Mrs.*, *Miss* or *Ms.* according to the woman's preference. These abbreviations may be used for both print and broadcast media.

Generally, courtesy titles are not used for people under the age of 18. Instead, use the child's first name.

For print media, abbreviate *Junior* and *Senior* after a name and use without commas: *Emmanuel Lee Jr.* Do not abbreviate these titles for broadcast media.

Title of People (Formal Title)

Formal titles are governmental, professional or religious designations that are an integral part of the identity of an individual. In general, capitalize the title when they are used before the name and as part of the name, but use lower case if titles stand alone or are used after the name.

For both internal and public media, capitalize formal titles when they appear before the name, but use lower case when the title is used without the name: *President Obama said . . . The president said . . .*

Most titles of government officials are written out rather than abbreviated: *mayor*, *president*, *prime minister*, *king*. A few common governmental titles are abbreviated for print media when they are used before a full name or a surname: *Gov. Anne Crosby-Jones*, *Sen. Nathaniel Stern, Rep. Seneca*. Do not abbreviate these titles when they are used without the name or in any usages for broadcast media.

Do not abbreviate titles of religion: *bishop, rabbi, monsignor, father, sister, brother, imam, mullah*. An exception to this is *Rev.*, which is abbreviated and used as an adjective with the word *the*: *the Rev. Lee Breckenridge*.

For print media, abbreviate most military ranks when used with a name: *Gen., Adm., Cmdr., Maj., Capt., Sgt., Cpl.* Exceptions: *ensign, seaman, petty officer, airman*. Do not abbreviate any military titles for broadcast media.

Do not abbreviate academic titles such as *dean, professor* and *chancellor*: *Professor Marta Borodin*.

Do not abbreviate qualifiers: *Associate Justice Jaime Gonzalez, Assistant Professor Marc Tannenbaum*. Capitalize formal qualified titles before the name, but do not capitalize informal qualifiers: *He met with acting Mayor Jones*.

For all print media, abbreviate *Dr.* Spell out *doctor* as a title with a name when writing for broadcast media. Because readers of general publications will probably presume that the title of doctor refers to someone with a medical degree, be clear if you are referring to someone with an academic degree. Do not use the title of doctor for someone holding an honorary degree.

For organizational media, abbreviations of formal titles and their use on subsequent reference are optional.

For public media, do not repeat a personal title on subsequent reference: *Mayor Kevin O'Malley said . . .* (first reference). *O'Malley said . . .* (subsequent references). As an exception to this guideline, repeat the title of persons known only by a religious name: *Patriarch Theodosius, Mother Teresa*.

For women, use a courtesy title or a religious title with the surname on subsequent reference, unless the woman prefers not to have the title used: *Mayor Maureen A. O'Malley said . . .* (first reference). *Mrs. O'Malley said . . .* or *O'Malley said . . .* (subsequent references). For organizational media, use of titles on subsequent reference is optional.

Formal titles of honor generally are not used for public media. For organizational media, it is appropriate to use both forms of religious titles such as *Father Joseph Martin* or *Pastor Soo*, as well as more formal titles such as *the Right Rev. Joseph Martin*. It also is appropriate to use titles of nobility and prestige in organizational media: *His Honor, Her Majesty, His Eminence, Her Royal Highness*.

Formal titles sometimes are used following the name. Lengthy titles should follow rather than precede the name.

For public media, do not capitalize formal titles used after the name: *Julio Castaneda, the senator from Texas*; *Eugenie Buchanan, professor of fine arts*. For organizational media, capitalization of formal titles that follow the name is optional.

Title of People (Functional Title)

Functional titles are descriptions of an individual according to an occupation or a role within an organization. *CEO* is an acceptable title, but avoid *CFO* and *CRO* and instead spell out similar job titles such as *chief financial officer* and *chief reputation officer*.

Short functional titles may be used either before or after the name. Use no commas when they are placed before the name, but use commas when they follow the name: *Newspaper editor Pierre Mercier said . . . Pierre Mercier, the newspaper editor, said . . .*

Long functional titles should follow the name and should be set off by commas: *Evelyn Brown, senior director for public affairs, said . . . Mitsuo Ogawa, interim vice president for administration, will begin . . .*

For public media, do not capitalize functional titles preceding or following the name. For organizational media, capitalization of functional titles is optional.

Weight

Use figures for weights, but spell out terms such as *pounds* and *grams*. Do not use hyphens, but use commas to separate categories. *The baby weighs 8 pounds, 11 ounces*. However use hyphens and no comma when using a compound adjective before a noun: *the 8-pound 11-ounce baby.*

Appendix B Copy Editing

Following are common copy-editing symbols. Use them during the proofreading stage of writing in preparing copy for its final, publishable version.

Abbreviate: Draw a circle around the word to be abbreviated: Saint Paul's Church.

Add letters to a word: Write in the miss ing letters.

Apostrophe: Write in an apostrophe above the line: Editing is a writers tool.

Boldface: Draw a squiggled underline to set in boldface.

Capitalize: Draw three lines below the letter(s) or word(s) to indicate capitals: Becoming a public Relations Writer.

Center: Indicate brackets on each side:]centre[.

Colon: Draw a circle around a colon at the place where it should be inserted, such as before a listing (:) .

Comma: Write in a comma below the line at the place where it should be inserted: Within a sentence, add a comma.

Dash: Write a horizontal line with vertical marks on both sides to indicate a dash.

Delete a letter and close up the space: Draw a slash with a bridge to dellete a letter.

Delete one or more words and close up the space: Draw a horizontal line and a bridge to delete the words that may be be unnecessary.

Extensive deletions: Draw ~~horizontal lines through the text to be deleted and draw~~ guidelines from the end of the previous section to the beginning of the subsequent section.

Flush left: [Indicate a bracket with the solid side on the left.

Flush right: Indicate a bracket with the solid side on the right].

Hyphen: Use short double horizontal lines to indicate a hyphen: full service bank.

Insert: Add a mising letter or a word.

Italics: Draw a straight underline to set text in italics.

Lower case: Draw a slash through the letter to indicate lower case: Becoming a Public RElations Writer.

Numbers (Change from words to numerals): fifteen books.

Numbers (Change from numerals to words): 9 pigeons.

Paragraph indent: . . . one sentence ends. Another paragraph begins.

Paragraph run-in: . . . one sentence ends.
Another paragraph begins.

Period: Draw a circle around a period at the place where it should be inserted, such as at the end of a sentence

Question Mark: Draw in a question mark: Why he wanted to know.

Quotation marks: Insert quotation marks, I said.

Semicolon: Write in a semicolon below the line at the place where it should be inserted: . . . so ends the clause a new clause begins.

Space (add): Use a vertical line to indicate space: Add aneeded space.

Space (close up): Draw a bridge to eliminate a space: Close up an unnecess ary space.

Spell out: Draw a circle around a word to spell out an abbreviation; the First St. Station.

Transpose: Draw a backward S to transpose lettres or to words transpose.

Undo a change: stet (Latin for "let it stand").

Verification (punctuation): Place a check mark above a punctuation mark to verify unusual placement . . . in colours of red, brown, blue and green, and yellow.

Verification (spelling): Draw a circle around the word OK to verify unusual spelling: James R. Smeth.

Bibliography

Advertising and Copywriting

Blake, G., & Bly, R.W. (1998). *The elements of copywriting: The essential guide to writing copy that gets the results you want*. Macmillan.

Bly, R.W. (2006). *The copywriter's handbook: A step-by-step guide to writing copy that sells* (3rd ed.). Owl Books.

Gabbay, J.J. (2003). *Teach yourself copywriting* (3rd ed.). McGraw-Hill.

King, J.M. (2006). *Copywriting that sells high tech*. WriteSpark.

Lewis, H.G. (2003). *On the art of writing copy: The best of print, broadcast, Internet and direct mail* (3rd ed.). Racom & Direct Marketing Association.

Sheridan, S. (2000). *Writing great copy*. How To Books.

Stelzner, M.W. (2006). *Writing white papers: How to capture readers and keep them engaged*. WhitePaperSource.

Sugerman, J. (2006). *The advertising copywriting handbook: The ultimate resource on how to write powerful advertising copy from one of America's top copywriters*. Wiley.

Broadcast Writing

Attkisson, S., & Vaughan, D.R. (2002). *Writing right for broadcast and Internet news*. Allyn & Bacon.

Barnas, F., & White, T. (2010). *Broadcast news writing and reporting* (5th ed.). Focal.

Dotson, B., Lauer, M., & Block, M. (2003). *Make it memorable: Writing and packaging TV news with style*. Bonus.

Papper, R.A. (2009). *Broadcast news and writing stylebook* (4th ed.). Allyn & Bacon.

Rowe, J. (2005). *Broadcast news writing for professionals*. Marion Street.

Thompkins, A. (2002). *Aim for the heart, write for the ear, shoot for the eye: A guide for TV producers and reporters*. Bonus.

Brochures and Newsletters

Abbott, R.F. (2001). *A manager's guide to newsletters: Communicating for results*. Word Engines.

Beach, M., & Floyd, E. (1998). *Newsletter sourcebook*. F&W.

Brooks, P. (2002). *The easy step-by-step guide to writing newsletters and articles*. Rowmark.

Katz, M.J. (2003). *E-newsletters that work: The small business owner's guide to creating, writing and managing an effective electronic newsletter*. Xlibris.

Woodard, C. (2005). *Starting and running a successful newsletter or magazine* (5th ed.). NOLO.

Woodward, D. (2007). *Every nonprofit's guide to publishing: Creating newsletters, magazines & websites people will read*. NOLO.

Fundraising Writing

Ahern, T. (2005). *The mercifully brief, real world guide to . . . Raising more money with newsletters than you ever thought possible*. Emerson & Church.

Ahern, T. (2007). *How to write fundraising materials that raise more money: The art, the science, the secrets*. Emerson & Church.

Kuniholm, R. (1995). *The complete book of model fundraising letters*. Aspen.

Warsick, M. (2008). *How to write successful fundraising letters*. Wiley & Sons.

General Writing

Gordon, K.E. (1998). *The deluxe transitive vampire: A handbook of grammar for the innocent, the eager, and the doomed*. Pantheon.

Gordon, K.E. (2003). *The new well-tempered sentence: A punctuation handbook for the innocent, the eager, and the doomed*. Mariner.

Hale, C. (2001). *Sin and syntax: How to craft wickedly effective prose*. Three Rivers.

Lederer, R., & Dowis, R. (2001). *Sleeping dogs don't lay: Practical advice for the grammatically challenged*. Griffin.

O'Connor, P.T. (2000). *Words fail me: What everyone who writes should know about writing*. Harvest.

O'Connor, P.T. (2004). *Woe is I: The grammarphobe's guide to better English in plain English* (2nd ed.). Riverheat.

Strunk Jr., W., White, E.B., & Angell, R. (2008). *The elements of style* (50th anniversary ed.). Allyn & Bacon.

Walsh, B. (2000). *Lapsing into a comma: A curmudgeon's guide to the many things that can go wrong in print—and how to avoid them*. McGraw-Hill.

Walsh, B. (2004). *The elephants of style: A trunkload of tips on the big issues and gray areas of contemporary American English*. McGraw-Hill.

Zinsser, W. (2006). *On writing well, 30th anniversary edition: The classic guide to writing nonfiction*. Harper.

Journalistic Writing

Hicks, W., Adams, S., & Gilbert, H. (2008). *Writing for journalists* (2nd ed.). Routledge.

Kessler, L., & McDonald, D. (2007). *When words collide: A media writer's guide to grammar and style* (7th ed.). Wadsworth.

Knight, R.M. (2010). *Journalistic writing: Building the skills, honing the craft* (3rd ed.). Marion Street.

Mencher, M. (2010). *News reporting and writing* (12th ed.). McGraw-Hill.

Rich, C. (2009). *Writing and reporting news: A coaching method* (6th ed.). Wadsworth.

Stephens, M., & Lanson, G. (2007). *Writing and reporting the news* (3rd ed.). International Thompson.

Stovall, J.G. (2005). *Writing for the mass media* (6th ed.). Allyn & Bacon.
Whitaker, W.R., Ramsey, J.E., & Smith, R.D. (2012). *MediaWriting* (4th ed.). Routledge.

Magazine Writing

Daugherty, G. (1999). *You can write for magazines*. Writer's Digest.
Jacobi, P. (1997). *The magazine article: How to think it, plan it, write it.* Indiana University Press.
Ruberg, M., & Yagoda, B. (2004). *Writer's Digest handbook of magazine article writing* (2nd ed.). Writer's Digest.
Sloan, C. (2004). *Writing for magazines: A beginner's guide* (2nd ed.). McGraw-Hill.
Sumner, D.E., & Miller, H.G. (2009). *Feature and magazine writing: Action, angle and anecdotes* (2nd ed). Wiley.
Wray, C.S. (2004). *Writing for magazines: A beginner's guide* (2nd ed.). McGraw-Hill.

Online Writing

Bly, R. (2003). *The online copywriter's handbook: Everything you need to know to write electronic copy that sells* (2nd ed.). McGraw-Hill.
Carrol, B. (2010). *Writing for digital media*. Routledge.
Covington, C.R. (2008). *The definitive guide to making money online with your writing*. Two Harbors.
Hammerich, I., & Harrison, C. (2001). *Developing online content: The principles of writing and editing for the Web.* Wiley.
Holtz, S. (1999). *Writing for the wired world: The communicator's guide to effective online content.* IABC.
Mill, D. (2005). *Content is king: Writing and editing online*. Butterworth-Heinemann.
Nielsen, J. (2000). *Designing web usability*. New Riders.
Nielsen, J., & Loranger, H. (2006). *Prioritizing web usability*. New Riders.
Nielsen, J., & Pernice, K. (2009). *Eyetracking web usability*. New Riders.
Porter, Y., Sullivan, P., & Johnson-Eilola, J. (2003). *Professional writing online* (2nd ed.). Longman.
Quinn. S., & Filak, V. (eds.). (2005). *Convergent journalism: An introduction: Writing and producing across media.* Focal.

Persuasion

Barbato, J., & Furlich, D.W. (2000). *Writing for a good cause: The complete guide to crafting proposals and other persuasive pieces for nonprofits.* Fireside.
Carrick, N., & Finsen, L. (1997). *The persuasive pen: Reasoning and writing*. Jones & Bartlett.
Charvet, S.R. (2010). *Words that change minds: Mastering the language of influence* (2nd ed.). Kendall-Hunt.
Faigley, L., & Selzer, J. (2009). *Good reasons: Researching and writing effective arguments (MLA Update)* (4th ed.). Longman.
Graff, G., & Birkenstein, C. (2007). *"They say, I say": The moves that matter in persuasive writing*. Norton.

Howe, M. (2004). *Persuasive writing made easy*. OC Publishing.

Mills, H.A. (2000). *Artful persuasion: How to command attention, change minds and influence people.* AMACOM.

Public Relations (General)

Aronson, E.W., & Pinkleton, B.E. (2006). *Strategic public relations management: Planning and managing effective communication programs* (2nd ed.). Lawrence Erlbaum.

Burnett, J., & Moriarty, S. (1998). *Introduction to marketing communications: An integrated approach*. Prentice Hall.

Caywood, C.L. (1997). *The handbook of strategic public relations and integrated communications.* McGraw-Hill.

Cutlip, S.M., Center, A.H., & Broom, G.M. (2008). *Effective public relations* (10th ed.). Prentice Hall.

Harris, T.L., & Kotler, P. (1999). *Value added public relations: The secret weapon of integrated marketing.* McGraw-Hill.

Harris, T.L., & Whalen, P.T. (2006). *The marketer's guide to public relations in the 21st century.* South-Western.

Kendall, R. (1999). *Public relations campaign strategies: Planning for implementation* (3rd ed.). HarperCollins.

Levine, M. (2008). *Guerrilla PR 2.0: Wage an effective publicity without going broke.* Harper.

Levinson, J.C., Frishman, R., & Lublin, J. (2002). *Guerrilla publicity: Hundreds of sure-fire tactics to get maximum sales for minimum dollars*. Adams.

Newsom, D., Turk, J.V., & Kruckenberg, D. (2009). *This is PR: The realities of public relations* (10th ed.). Wadsworth.

Reis, A., & Reis, L. (2004). *The fall of advertising & the rise of PR*. Harper.

Scott, D.M. (2010). *The new rules of marketing and PR: How to use social media, blogs, news releases, online video, and viral marketing to reach buyers directly* (2nd ed.). Wiley.

Seitel, F.P. (2010). *The practice of public relations* (11th ed.). Prentice Hall.

Smith, R.D. (in press). *Strategic planning for public relations* (4th ed.). Routledge/Taylor & Francis.

Wilcox, D.L., Cameron, G.T., Ault, P.H., & Agee, W.K. (2009). *Public relations: Strategies and tactics* (9th ed.). Allyn & Bacon.

Public Relations Writing

Aronson, M., Spetner, D., & Ames, C. (2007). *The public relations writer's handbook: The digital age* (2nd ed.). Jossey-Bass.

Begovich, R. (2001). *Writing for results: Keys to success for the public relations writer.* Alta Villa.

Bivins, T.H. (2010). *Public relations writing: The essentials of style and format* (7th ed.). McGraw-Hill.

Bordon, K. (2002). *Bulletproof news releases: Help at last for the publicity deficient* (2nd ed.). Franklin Sarrett.

Foster, J.L. (2008). *Effective writing skills for public relations* (4th ed.). Kogan Page.

Marsh, C., Guth, D.W., & Short, B.P. (2008). *Strategic writing: Multimedia writing for public relations, advertising and more* (2nd ed.). Allyn & Bacon.

Newsom, D., & Haynes, J. (2010). *Public relations writing: Form and style* (9th ed.). Wadsworth.

Treadwell, D., & Treadwell, J.B. (2005). *Public relations writing: Principles in practice*. Allyn & Bacon.

Wilcox, D. (2009). *Public relations writing and media techniques* (6th ed.). Allyn & Bacon.

Yale, D., & Carothers, A.J. (2001). *The publicity handbook new edition: The inside scoop from more than 100 journalists and PR pros on how to get great publicity coverage*. McGraw-Hill.

Reference and Stylebooks

Associated Press (2010). *The Associated Press stylebook 2010: Style book and briefing on media law* (45th ed.). Associated Press.

Bass, F. (2002). *The Associated Press guide to Internet research and reporting*. Perseus.

Cappon, R.J. (2003). *The Associated Press guide to punctuation*. Perseus.

Cook, B., & Martin, H. (2004). *UPI stylebook & guide to newswriting* (4th ed.). Capitol.

Horton, B. (2000). *The Associated Press guide to photojournalism*. McGraw-Hill.

Kalbfeld, B. (2001). *Associated Press broadcast news handbook*. McGraw-Hill.

Martin, P.R. (2002). *The Wall Street Journal guide to business style and usage*. Wall Street Journal.

Schwartz, J. (2001). *The Associated Press guide to reporting*. McGraw-Hill.

Siegal, A.M., & Connolly, W.G. (2002). *The New York Times manual of style and usage: The official style guide used by writers and editors of the world's most authoritative newspaper*. Three Rivers Press.

Wilstein, S. (2001). *The Associate Press sports writing handbook*. McGraw-Hill.

Speechwriting

Carpenter, R.H., & Thompson, W.D. (1998). *Choosing powerful words: Eloquence that works*. Allyn & Bacon.

Cook, J.S. (1996). *The elements of speechwriting and public speaking*. Longman.

Detz. J. (2009). *How to write and give a speech: A practical guide for executives, PR people, the military, fund-raisers, politicians, educators, and anyone who has to make every word count* (2nd ed.). St. Martin's Griffin.

Lancaster, S. (2011). *Speechwriting: The expert guide*. Robert Hale.

Lehrman, R. (2009). *The political speechwriter's companion: A guide for writers and speakers*. CQ.

Neale, T.H., & Bowers, J.M. (2004). *Speechwriting in perspective*. Novinka.

Glossary

active voice grammatical term indicating syntax emphasizing the doer of an action; compare with **passive voice**

actuality cassette or tape recording accompanying printed release, providing quotations for radio use; see **sound bite**

adjective word that modifies a noun; see **limiting adjective** and **descriptive adjective**

adverb word that modifies a verb

advertising nonpersonal paid communication through various media by an identified organization for the purpose of informing and influencing a particular audience; fits into two categories of **product advertising** and **public relations advertising**

Advertising Council joint venture of advertising agencies, advertisers, and the media to provide persuasive messages of public interest

advertising layout approach to design of print advertisements; categories include **standard advertising layout, poster-style layout**, and **editorial-style layout**

advocacy advertising type of **public relations advertising** to promote a cause or goal

agenda-setting theory theory that public media are effective in telling people what to think about

alliteration writing construction in which words begin with the same sound

altruism a person's innate desire to help others; important to public relations writers involved with volunteers and fundraising

analogy writing technique in which an unfamiliar thing is explained by likening it to something familiar to the audience

animation type of dramatic advertising technique sometimes used, particularly in ads directed toward children, teens, and young adults

announcement release type of **news release** that announces an upcoming activity

annual report organizational progress report required of stock-issuing companies and voluntarily produced by many others

ANR see **audio news release**

apologetics systematic attempt to assert the reasonableness of an idea and to refute opposing arguments

appeal letter central part of a direct-mail package that presents the persuasive message to the reader

appeal to tradition logical error invoking the status quo

appositive word or grouping of words that defines, describes or renames the preceding noun

arguing in a circle logical error involving restating a proposition in an effort to prove it; see **tautology**

argument element of a speech presenting evidence for the proposition

art umbrella term for visual design elements such as photographs, computer-generated imagery, sketches, diagrams, maps, charts, etc.

attractiveness rhetorical aspect of **charisma**

audience group of people who use a particular medium such as newspaper, radio station or television station; of interest to public relations writers only to the extent that it includes members of an organization's **public**

audio news release public relations information packaged as a completed broadcast report for radio; **news release** written for radio use and accompanied by an **actuality**; sometimes called a **radio news release**

audit see **public relations audit**

authority rhetorical aspect of **control**

authority appeal logical error resting on a speaker's claim rather than on the strength of the argument itself

B-roll see **video B-roll**

B-roll package public relations presentation of video B-rolls without a written news release; intended for background use

background fact sheet type of fact sheet that presents information about an organization or issues it deals with; sometimes called a **factoid** or a **breaker box**

background lead type of lead for **broadcast news releases** that provides background information

backgrounder type of public relations release that provides factual information to give a context to an organization or an issue

balance element of newsworthiness stressing the fair and accurate reporting of information; see **SiLoBaTi + UnFa**

balance theory theory suggesting that people seek an attitude similar to that of their communication partners; also called **consonance theory** or **symmetry theory**

bandwagon technique associated with persuasive communication and **propaganda**

benefit statement part of **planning sheet** that articulates the benefit or advantage the organization can offer the target public; also part of a news release that articulates this benefit or advantage

biographical narrative factual, usually chronological, presentation of personal information; compare with **personal profile**

black hat SEO unethical and sometimes illegal approach to preparing material for search engine optimization; contrast with **white hat SEO**

blanket consent release written to grant general permission for information to be published or communicated

blog type of website featuring short articles and reader comments

blog page information at a blog that is not frequently updated

blog post individual article at a blog; also called **entry**

blue paper type of **position statement** with lengthy and detailed information, often accompanied by a **white paper** serving as an executive summary

bluewashing unwarranted touting of an organization as being socially responsible or having humanitarian motivations; see also **greenwashing** and **whitewashing**

brainstorming creativity technique of free association used to generate a large number of ideas

brainwriting creativity technique of free association used to generate ideas within a group

brand advertising see **product advertising**

brand name see **trademark**

branded journalism euphemism for paying stations to broadcast material provided by public relations sources; similar to **secured placement**

breaker box see **background fact sheet**

breaking news type of news dealing with events as they occur

broadcast faxing method of transmitting multiple and simultaneous fax messages; also called **bulk faxing**

broadcast media umbrella term for radio and television; cable television is popularly included within this term, though cable is not technically a broadcast medium; usually refers to public media and excludes organizational video and audio services

broadcast news release version of a **news release** prepared specifically for radio and television, usually briefer than releases for print media, more conversational in tone, and including **pronouncers**

broadside see **flier**

brochure printed form of organization media, usually folded sheets meant to be read as a booklet and providing information meant to be relevant over an extended period of time; also called **leaflet, folder, pamphlet, booklet, tract**, and **bulletin**

bulk faxing see **broadcast faxing**

bullet theory theory based on the **powerful effects model** of communication bulletin; see **brochure**

business-to-business advertising type of **product advertising** to promote companies to venders and other professional colleagues and constituents

buzz group creativity technique of free association used to generate ideas when working with a large group of people

Canadian Public Relations Society major Canadian professional organization focused on public relations

card stacking technique associated with **propaganda** but seldom with ethical persuasive communication

case study consumer-interest release that narrates how a particular organization identified and addressed a problem or issue; also called a **case history**

casual research category of informal research

celebrity endorsement advertising strategy featuring testimony from a well-known person

centered type set with ragged left and right margins; compare with **full justification**

charisma element of persuasive communication based on how well an audience likes the message source

circular see **flier**

cliché expression that is so overused that it is trite and boring

cognitive burden negative impact of promotional language, which causes readers to expend mental energy to filter out hype from facts, thus slowing down reading

cognitive dissonance theory theory focusing on confusion caused when information is out of step with a person's attitude, with the suggestion that people try to reduce the confusion, usually by ignoring the information or reinterpreting it to fit their attitude

collective noun singular word with a plural meaning; usually takes a singular pronoun

color rhetorical style of information that makes a story come alive; includes analogies, metaphors, quotes, and descriptions

column head see **standing head**

common trademark general designation of a trademarked item, not registered with the Patent and Trademark Office; compare with **registered trademark**

communication competence rhetorical aspect of **credibility**

conclusion summary of a speech

conditioned reflex theory theoretical model serving as a basis for the **bullet theory** of communication

congruity theory theory that people experience confusion when two attitudes are in conflict and that they attempt to resolve the conflict, usually by adopting the easier attitude or by trying to blend the opposing attitudes

connotation implicit suggestion or nuance of word meaning that goes beyond the explicit definition; compare with **denotation**

consonance theory see **balance theory**

consumer advertising category of advertising focusing on selling a product or service; also called **product advertising**; compare with **public relations advertising**

content analysis formal research technique that provides quantitative information about the content of texts such as letters and news reports

contingency statement type of position statement prepared in different versions to accommodate various potential situations or outcomes; also called a **stand-by statement**

control element of persuasive communication based on the power or authority the message source has over an audience

cookie stored information of personal interests and past online accessing that becomes active when a user connects to a particular website

copy editing process of marking type prior to setting it into its finished design

copy fit process of rewriting text to longer or shorter length to fit into a predetermined space

copyright legal designation of ownership for written and other artistic creations; the current U.S. Copyright Act was revised in 1976; copyright means material may not be used without permission

copyright notice symbol or words claiming copyright ownership; also **noticed copyright**

corporate advertising see **image advertising**

corporate backgrounder see **organizational profile**

corporate report required publications reporting information to company stockholders; see **annual report**

corrections column feature in many publications that offer public relations writers an opportunity to clarify or correct a misstatement

creative writing approach to writing that emphasizes imaginative, artistic and sometimes innovative style; coexists in public relations with functional writing

creativity ability to develop an original solution to a problem

credibility element of persuasive communication based on the ability of the message source to be believed

cultivation theory theory that exposure to public media cultivates a person's perceptions and expectations, with a major difference between heavy and light viewers

cybernetics field of study that deals with sensors and control mechanisms, applied to communication with the concept of feedback

cyberzine see **e-zine**

dateline designation in a news release of the name of the city or town where the release originates; the actual date is not included

deckhead line(s) of type placed below the main line of a headline; also called an **underline**

defamation communication that harms a person; see **slander** and **libel**

denotation dictionary meaning of a word; compare with **connotation**

dependency theory theory that audiences use media to the extent that the media provide information important to them

descriptive adjective type of adjective that describes a quality of the object

diagonal reader readers who look at headlines then scan the content of a blog or other website in a zigzag manner

diction literary term associated with word choice

dingbat generic term for typographic elements other than letters and numerals such as bullets, boxes, arrows and icons

direct news information of interest to publics

doublespeak language that obviously and sometimes deliberately obscures the real meaning behind the words

down style approach to writing style that uses capital letters as little as possible; compare with **up style**

drama advertising strategy featuring a scenario that is acted out

e-mail computer technology that provides opportunities for business communication, research, and dissemination of information

e-mail news release public relations communication delivered via e-mail; in format, it is briefer and more concise than a printed release

e-newsletter online electronic newsletter

e-zine online electronic magazine; also called a **cyberzine**

editorial statement type of **mission statement** indicating the purpose and philosophy of a publication

editorial-style layout design of print advertisements and fliers that emphasize written text, with a minimum of artwork; compare with **poster-style layout**

elevator pitch one-minute persuasive message to present an idea or advocate a cause

embargo designation that information provided in a news release should not be used before a given hour and day

end mark typographical device indicating the end of a news release or similar written piece; usually a series of hatch marks, or the word "end"

environmental audit type of public relations audit that identifies an organization's publics and issues important to these publics

ethos rhetorical concept focusing on source credibility; compare with **pathos** and **logos**

event listing writing format that provides basic information for use in calendars and other listings of upcoming activities

expectancy-value theory theory that people make media choices based on what they want and expect from the media

expertise rhetorical aspect of **credibility**

explicit permission written permission, such as a consent release

factoid see **background fact sheet**

factual proposition thesis within a speech or written commentary asserting the existence of something; compare with **value proposition** and **policy proposition**

fair comment and criticism legal defense against **defamation** based on the right to critique and criticize in matters of public interest

fair use freedom to use copyrighted material for purposes of education, news, commentary, satire and noncommercial research

false facts logical error involving inaccurate or dishonest information

fame element of newsworthiness stressing the prominence of personalities figuring in the report; see **SiLoBaTi + UnFa**

familiarity rhetorical aspect of **charisma**

fantasy format type of dramatic advertising technique that relies on make-believe characters or real persons in unreal situations

FAQ common Web page of frequently asked questions about an organization or issue

fear appeals rhetorical technique of shaping a message to appeal to the fear or insecurity of the audience

feature type of story that emphasizes personalities and human-interest angles rather than hard news

feature head type of headline or title for magazine or newsletter

feature reprint public relations practice of reprinting and selectively disseminating a published article that includes positive information about an organization

feedback theoretical concept referring to the ability of receivers to respond to the sender of a message

feel-good advertising see **image advertising**

fixed layout type of digital advertisement that maintains a specific size and layout that carries across all different sizes of monitors by various users; compare with **liquid layout**

Flesch–Kincaid scale readability formula that indicates grade-level equivalency

flier printed form of organization media, usually unfolded sheets meant to be read as single units and providing time-specific information; also called **circular, broadside**, and **handbill**

flush left type set with even left and ragged right margins; compare with **full justification**

flush right type set with even right and ragged left margins; compare with **full justification**

focus group research technique that provides in-depth anecdotal information from a small group representative of an organization's public

Fog Index readability formula for measuring the level of reading difficulty for any piece of writing; also called **Gunning Readability Formula**

folder see **brochure**

follow-up release type of news release in which the organization responds to prior news reporting

forced association techniques for creativity that prompt the mind to generate ideas by using defined connections; examples include **visual relationships, similes**, explained similes, and **future statements**

formal research see **primary research**

framing theory that news media create a framework for how audiences think about topics

franking privilege permission given to members of Congress for free mailing to their constituents

free association techniques for creativity that prompt the mind to generate ideas by using undefined connections; examples include **freewriting, brainstorming, buzz groups**, and **brainwriting**

freewriting technique of writing without stopping and without self-editing for a period of time to get initial thoughts on paper; creativity technique of **free association**

full justification type set with even left and right margins; compare with **flush left**

functional writing approach to writing that emphasizes purpose, format and objectives; coexists in public relations with creative writing

future statements creativity technique of forced relationships that elicits ideas through the use of benefit statements and potential solutions

gatekeeper person who controls the flow of information; usually applied to editors, news directors, webmasters, and others who make decisions about what information will be presented to media audiences

gender bias language that does not display characteristics of inclusive language because it excludes members of a target public or audience on the basis of sex; sometimes called **sexist language**

general advertising type of product advertising focused on national brands

geodemographics application of persuasive communication that segments audiences by geographic and other demographic factors

ghostwriter unidentified person who assists the signer or speaker by drafting or refining the draft of a column, letter, speech or other commentary

glittering generalities technique associated with propaganda but seldom with ethical persuasive communication

graphic organizer visual technique for outlining prior to writing

green paper type of **position statement** with background information but no proposals; see also **blue paper**

greenwashing unwarranted touting of an organization or product as being environmentally friendly; see also **bluewashing** and **whitewashing**

guest editorial opinion piece presenting the opinion of a person or organization not affiliated with the publication; presented as an editorial of the publication; similar to **op-ed commentary**

Gunning Readability Formula see **Fog Index**

handbill see **flier**

handout inappropriate term for **news release**

hard copy physical version of a written message, as compared to an electronic document

hard news type of news dealing with information about momentous events

headline approach to article identification in newspapers, magazines and newsletters that focuses on summaries rather than labels; compare with **title**

hidden persuaders motivating factors associated with Vance Packard

hierarchy of needs listing of levels of personal need that motivate and interest people, associated with Abraham Maslow

hit number of times an online file is requested from an Internet site

house organ generic term for a publication written by an organization for public relations purposes

house style type of writing style adopted by an organization for internal printed and online publications

how-to article consumer-interest release that provides step-by-step instructions in addressing a problem or issue; also called a **service article**

human interest see **unusual**

humor type of dramatic advertising technique sometimes used, though often public relations topics do not lend themselves to levity and comedy

hypodermic needle theory theory based on the **powerful effects model** of communication

identification paragraph optional concluding paragraph of a news release providing information about an organization; also called **organizational identification**

image advertising see **institutional advertising**

implicit permission legal concept based on the notion that a reasonable observer would see that a person is willingly participating in a situation, such as an interview or a posed photograph; compare to **explicit permission**

inclusive language language that is neutral in its application to all members of a target public or audience

info/action statement part of a news release that clearly presents information on how audiences can take action

information digest consumer-interest approach that presents information based on technical reports in language for nontechnical readers

information overload sociological term indicating the growing quantity and complexity of information

information subsidy term referring to the benefit provided to journalists by public relation practitioners, including news releases, interviews, and background information

information theory communication theory based on observation that an information source produces a message that is converted by a transmitter and sent via some channel to a receiver that reconstructs the message

INR see **Internet news release**

institutional advertising type of **public relations advertising** to promote the name and reputation of an organization

intellectual property body of law associated with issues of copyright and trademark

intensive interview technique of formal interviewing

internalization adoption of an attitude because it is understood to be consistent with a person's beliefs or values

International Association of Business Communicators large professional organization focused on public relations

International Public Relations Association global alliance of national public relations associations

Internet news release adaptation of video news releases that could be transmitted over the Internet

interstitial see **pop-up window**

interview (1) method of research to gather information from knowledgeable persons; (2) type of feature article based on an interview with a knowledgeable person

interview notes type of public relations release that provides reporters with an unedited transcript of an interview they can use to develop a story

introduction beginning of a speech, similar to a feature lead

intrusion legal concept associated with **privacy** referring to information gathered secretly or surreptitiously

inverted pyramid pattern of news-style writing that presents the most important information first

issue advertising see **advocacy advertising**

issue advisory type of position statement prepared for internal audiences

issues management category of public relations that predicts and tracks public issues that accept an organization and its mission

jargon technical language; words and phrases that have a particular meaning within a limited environment

journalese type of nonprofessional jargon often seen in newspaper headlines

kerning horizontal spacing between the letters in any printed material

key public specific public identified by a public relations writer or strategist as the primary focus of a public relations action; also called strategic public; compare with **target public**

kicker introductory line of type placed above the main line of a headline; also called an **overline**

landing page see **transaction page**

lead beginning paragraph of a news release, written to gain the attention of the audience

lead-in transition in a broadcast news release introducing a sound bite or actuality; also called a **throw**

lead time amount of time needed by reporters and editors between receiving or gathering information and final publication or presentation of the resulting news report

leading vertical spacing between the lines in any printed material

leaflet see **brochure**

letters to the editor column in many publications that offers public relations writers opportunities for publicity and advocacy

libel written **defamation**; compare with **slander**

likability rhetorical aspect of **charisma**

limited effects model approach to communication theory that concludes the media exert a weak influence over people

limiting adjective type of adjective that qualifies or limits meanings to a particular type or quantity

linkage concept from systems theory that helps identify an organization's publics by focusing on consumers, producers, enablers, and limiters

liquid layout type of digital advertisement that allows text and graphic components to be positioned relative to the size of the viewer's browser and monitor; compare with **fixed layout**

literature review research technique that provides current information about an issue or a topic

local element of newsworthiness stressing the proximity of the audience to events or issues being reported; see **SiLoBaTi + UnFa**

logos rhetorical concept focusing on appeals to logic or reason; compare with **ethos** and **pathos**

magapaper type of newsletter that is a hybrid with a newspaper; also called **minimag** and **maganews**

marketese writing that is overly promotional and marketing-oriented

mathematical theory of communication see **information theory**

media advisory memo notifying reporters about an upcoming activity; also called **media alert**

media directory collection of data related to newspapers and magazines, radio and television, telecommunications, advertising and other media-related areas

meta tag words and phrases imbedded in websites that help search engines identify sites with information sought by users

metaphor grammatical term indicating an indirect comparison between two dissimilar objects; compare with **simile**

misappropriation legal concept associated with **privacy** referring to the unauthorized use of a person's name, image or voice

mission statement written statement of the purpose and philosophy of an organization or a program; similar to **editorial statement;** often used in tandem with a **vision statement**

MNR see **multimedia news release**

moderate-to-powerful effects model approach to communication theory that concludes the media exert a significant, complex, and long-time influence over people

more line designation at the bottom of a news release page to indicate a continuation to a following page

multimedia news release repackaging of print, audio, and video message with Web links for a comprehensive presentation of an organization's public relations information

multistep flow of communication theory outgrowth of **two-step flow of communication theory**

name calling technique associated with propaganda but seldom with ethical persuasive communication

narrative feature written story based on interviews

national advertising see **general advertising**

network English see **operational English**

network standard version of English most appropriate for professional interaction; also called **operational English** or **standard English**

news information of interest to media and their audiences

news brief opening paragraphs of a news release including the summary lead and the benefit statement, written either to stand alone or to provide the beginning of a lengthier release

news fact sheet type of fact sheet that provides information about a newsworthy activity; compare with **background fact sheet**

news flag designation on a news release heading emphasizing the term "news" or "news release"

news peg concept linking organizational activity or issue with an active news event

news pitch element of planning sheet similar to an **elevator pitch**

news release common format used by organizations to provide information to the news media; types include **announcement releases** and **response releases**

news value element that indicated newsworthiness

newsletters printed form of organizational media, usually multipage serialized publications prepared for particular publics; categories include **member newsletters, external newsletters**

newswire service that distributes news releases to media on behalf of public relations clients

noise theoretical concept referring to anything that interferes with the clarity of a message

non sequitur conclusion or inference that does not logically follow from the arguments or premises

noticed copyright explicit use of the word "copyright" by the creator of an artistic piece

nut graf news lead that follows a feature lead

odious labels legal term referring to defamatory words that portray people in a negative light

official statement type of position statement that focuses on brief proclamation of timely issue

one-voice principle practice of designating a single organizational spokesperson or a coordinated team of spokespersons to provide a consistent message from an organization, especially in a crisis situation

op-ed commentary opinion piece presenting the opinion of a person or organization not affiliated with the publication; presented as a column; similar to **guest editorial**

operant conditioning theoretical model similar to **conditioned reflex theory**

operational English common form of English most often used in business, communication, education and other settings where geographic and cultural variations are inappropriate; also called **standard English** or **network English**

opinion letter official auditor's statement in corporate **annual report**

organizational history type of public relations release that provides a feature article based on the background of an organization

organizational identification optional part of news release presenting paragraph with standard wording about the organization

organizational profile type of public relations release that provides information about the structure and mission of an organization; often used in tandem with an **organizational history**

original work legal designation of an artistic copyright owned by the person who created it

outdoor advertising promotional messages located on billboards

over-generalized arguments logical error involving leaping to an inexact conclusion

overline see **kicker** and **legend**

oxymoron figure of speech in which contradictory terms are used together, rendering a confused meaning

packets see **brochure**

page view number of times a particular Web page is accessed

pamphlet see **brochure**

parallel structure repetition of a grammatical pattern for elements that are part of a series or compound construction

passive voice grammatical term indicating syntax emphasizing the receiver of an action; compare with **active voice**

pathos rhetorical concept focusing on appeals to emotion or sentiment; compare with **ethos** and **logos**

performance/perception audit type of public relations audit that tracks an organization's performance, visibility and reputation

personal criticism logical error involving attempts to prove an argument by disparaging critics

personal interview information-gathering technique in which a writer obtains information directly from the source

personal profile feature article presenting personal information; compare with **biographical narrative**

personification forced association technique of treating an inanimate object as a person

persuasion process of communication that intends to influence through ethical means that enhance a democratic society

persuasive communication type of communication with its main objective to persuade

petition hybrid of advocacy letter and proclamation, providing a common statement with numerous signers

pitch letter promotional letter to media gatekeepers to persuade them to report on some aspect or activity of an organization

placard advertising promotional messages on poster media and displayed in locations such as terminals, store windows, and hallways

plain folk appeal technique associated with persuasive communication and propaganda

planning sheet outline to guide a writer toward preparing effective pieces of writing; focuses attention on **target publics**, benefits, objectives, and **tone**

plural noun type of noun referring to more than one thing; takes a plural pronoun

policy proposition thesis within a speech or written commentary advocating a course of action; compare with **factual proposition** and **value proposition**

political advertising type of **public relations advertising** to promote a political party, candidate, or issue

pop-up window ability of websites to push unsought pages to users; also called **interstitials**

position statement public relations format presenting the formal and public position of an organization on a particular topic; also called **white paper**; categories include **position paper** and **position paragraph**, depending upon the length of the statement; compare with **official statement** and **contingency statement**

poster-style layout design of print advertisements and fliers that emphasize artwork and headline, with a minimum of written text; compare with **editorial-style layout**

power rhetorical aspect of **control**

powerful effects model approach to communication theory, which concludes that media exert a direct and predictable influence over people's attitudes, opinions, and behavior; associated with **bullet theory** or **hypodermic needle theory**

prepotency concept associated with **hierarchy of needs**

press advisory see **media advisory**

press release inappropriate term for **news release**

primary research category of research gathering new information

priming theory that news media remind audiences of previous information on a topic

privacy right to be left alone, including right not to be written about

private facts legal concept associated with **privacy** referring to personal information that is intrusive and not of legitimate public concern

privilege legal term referring to situations in which a writer is exempt from prosecution for defamation, such as when reporting court or legislative testimony

problem-solution type of dramatic advertising technique that sets up an obstacle with which the audience can identify and then resolves it

proclamation formal statement issues by an organizational or public authority commemorating an event; also called a **resolution**

product advertising see **consumer advertising**

product demonstration advertising strategy showing the product or service in use

pronouncers phonetic tips included in news release, scripts, and other public relations vehicles to help readers correctly pronounce unfamiliar words, usually names of people and places; also called a **pronunciation guide**

proofreading process of revising a written draft by considering and correcting errors of style, spelling, punctuation, etc.

propaganda persuasive communication that is deceptive about the source of the message or that presents misinformation to audiences; draws on some acceptable rhetoric techniques

proposition central message of a speech or written commentary; also called a **thesis**

pseudo-event newsworthy event created by public relations practitioner to attract media attention; compare with **publicity stunt**

psychographics application of **psychological type theory** to marketing aspects of persuasive communication that segments audiences by personality and lifestyle factors rather than demographic ones

psychological type theory theory that innate personality factors give each person a predisposition toward particular persuasive techniques, with some people more influenced by emotional appeals and others by logical appeals; related to **temperament theory**

public group of people sharing a common bond or relationship with an organization; see **key public**

public advisory announcement notifying media audiences about an important matter, usually one with potential harm

public communication range of communication that extends beyond personal interaction between people or small groups

public relations advertising category of commercial and noncommercial advertising focusing on advocacy and image rather than on the marketing of products and services; compare with **consumer advertising**

public relations audit systematic analysis of an organization, its communication practices and its relationship with its publics; categories include **environmental audit** and **performance/perception audit**

Public Relations Society of America largest of several professional organizations focused on public relations

public service advertising type of **public relations advertising** in which media donate time or space to nonprofit organizations to promote messages that the media consider to be in the public interest; also called **PSAs**

publicity function of public relations focused on using the news media to present an organization's message

publicity stunt gimmick used mainly to attract media attention to events with little inherent news value; compare with **pseudo-event**

pull quote highlighted excerpt from an article used as a graphic element

punch lead type of lead for broadcast news releases that presents a phrase or brief sentence to grab the attention of audiences

quarterly report type of **corporate report**

query letter see **story idea memo**

question-and-answer piece consumer-interest release that uses a format of brief questions posed directly to readers and responses to each question

question lead type of lead for broadcast news releases that poses a question for listeners

quotes statements within news releases and similar types of public relations writing that provide comments and opinions, presented with attribution to the source; more formally called **quotations**

radio news release see **audio news release**

readability concept associated with ease of reading, often based on the educational range of the key public; see **Fog Index**

receiver phenomenon theoretical concept suggesting that the ability to communicate is controlled by the receiver of a message, who has the power to choose whether to receive a message and how to interpret and act upon it

redundancy (1) use of words that repeat a meaning already existing; (2) an aspect of communication theory referring to the deliberate repetition of a message

reflective piece advertising strategy featuring music, poetry, scenery, and other nonverbal elements; also called **mood piece**

registered trademark designation of a trademarked item that is registered with the Patent and Trademark Office; compare with **common trademark**

reminder advertising strategy that reinforces already-known images and ideas

repetition technique associated with persuasive communication and propaganda

research systematic way of gathering information about a topic

resolution see **proclamation**

response device card or envelope flap within a direct mail package that the reader is expected to fill out

response release type of news release that provides comment or follow-up to an activity

retail advertising type of **product advertising** focused on promoting sales for local companies

reverse type use of white or light-colored lettering on dark background

rhetoric art of persuasive communication, with ancient origins and contemporary insights

rhyme writing construction in which words end with the same sound

RNR see **audio news release**

RSS feed online mechanism for journalists to subscribe to news releases and other information presented by an organization

rule of threes technique used by writers to create parallel structure

sans serif type font without short lines capping top and bottom strokes of letters; compare with **serif**

scannable characteristic of online writing that makes it easy for readers to move through it

scrutiny rhetorical aspect of **control**

search engine online programs that look for user-identified key words in hundreds of thousands of websites

search engine optimization techniques that enhance the likelihood that an organization's website will be identified by search engines and thus will be accessed by users seeking information available at the website

secondary research category of research uses existing information

secured placement euphemism for paying stations to broadcast material provided by public relations sources; similar to **branded journalism**

selective attention, avoidance, exposure, perception, recall, retention see **selectivity theory**

selectivity theory family of theories related to the observation that people expose themselves to messages they think they will like and avoid what they expect not to like; related concepts are **selective attention, selective avoidance, selective exposure, selective perception, selective recall** and **selective retention**

SEO see **search engine optimization**

serif type font with short lines capping top and bottom strokes of letters; compare with **sans serif**

service article see **how-to article**

service mark legal designation of ownership of a name, logo, symbol, or other identification of a service or program; compare with **trademark** significance element of newsworthiness stressing the importance of information; see **SiLoBaTi + UnFa**

setup lead type of lead for broadcast news releases intended to pull audiences into the story

sexist language see **inclusive language**

short-form Q&A type of question-answer format that has only a few questions and brief answers, presented in a non-narrative Q&A format

shovelware printed text carried into a website without adapting it for online presentation

SiLoBaTi + UnFa mnemonic device referring to ingredients of news value—significance, localness, balance, timeliness, plus unusualness and fame

similarity rhetorical aspect of **charisma**

simile creativity technique of forced relationships that elicits ideas through verbal techniques; also, grammatical term indicating a direct comparison between two dissimilar concepts; see **metaphor**

sincerity rhetorical aspect of **credibility**

singular noun common type of noun referring to one thing; takes a singular pronoun

situational theory aspect of the theory of publics associated with James Grunig

slander oral **defamation**; compare with **libel**

sleeper effect hypothesis that, over time, people forget the source of a message but remember the message itself, weakening the effect of source credibility or noncredibility

slug line designation within a news release of topic and number of pages following the first page

SMR see **social media release**

social judgment theory theory that attitude change is more a change in a person's perception than a change in belief

social learning theory communication theory that media provide a model for personal behavior

social media newsroom online site for where an organization posts social media releases with text, audio, video, photos, links, and interactive elements

social media release packaging of print, audio, and video message with Web links and interactive features for a comprehensive presentation of an organization's public relations information

soft lead type of lead for broadcast media that is an attention-getter rather than a summary; also called **throw-away lead, tune-in lead,** and **warm-up lead**

soft news type of news dealing with information about lighter activities

sound element of advertising production involving narration and dialog as well as sound effects and background music

sound bite brief, memorable quote used by a news source, especially for radio and television reports; see **actuality**

source credibility factor in message persuasiveness that deals with the believability of a message source; factors include expertise and sincerity

spamdexing see **black hat SEO**

special type of news release written especially for a particular publication or for media in a particular geographic area

specialized news type of news dealing with information about specific segments of the media and/or of interest to particular publics

speakers' bureau public relations project to prepare and send organizational representatives to give talks and invite questions

speech tag phrase such as "she said" used to attribute information in a news release and similar types of writing; used for both direct quotes and paraphrases

speechwriting process of writing a speech for another person to present

spin derogatory term for public relations messaging that implies propaganda intended to manipulate public opinion; see **white-washing, greenwashing**, and **bluewashing**

spiral of silence theory theory that public media may hinder communication by giving people a sense of isolation and reluctance if their opinions differ from the majority opinion presented through the media

split run technique in direct-mail campaigns in which different versions of the same message are distributed to different target publics

stand-by statement see **contingency statement**

standard advertising layout design of print advertisements that blend artwork, headline, and written message

standard English see **operational English**

standing head type of headline for newsletter or magazine; used for a recurring column

statement lead type of lead for broadcast news releases that begins with a compelling fact or opinion

status rhetorical aspect of **credibility**

stereotype technique associated with propaganda but seldom with ethical persuasive communication

stimulus-response theory see **conditioned reflex theory**

story idea memo memo to interest the media in reporting on a person or program, usually involving soft news or feature possibilities; similar to a **query letter**

strategic news information about an organization that is of interest to both media and publics

stylebook listing of preferences for spelling, word usage, punctuation and other elements of writing; adopted by a publication or organization to maintain writing consistency

subhead (1) secondary phrase that complements and expands on a headline; (2) phrase serving as a section divider within a text

subordinate points see **argument**

substantial truth legal defense against defamation based on the accuracy of the information published

summary news lead most common beginning for news releases, providing a succinct overview of the report

supporting information see **argument**

survey formal research technique that provides quantitative information from a sample representative of an organization's public

symbol advertising strategy featuring visual elements with emotional or evocative value

symmetry theory see **balance theory**

syntax aspect of grammar that deals with orderly arrangement of words into sentences

systems approach technique for identifying organizational information based on **systems theory**

systems theory communication theory based on the concept of **cybernetics**

tag line slogan or parting message in an advertisement

talk paper type of internal position statement used by organizations to provide common messages for spokespersons; also called **talking points**

target public alternative but less accurate term for **key public**

tautology attempt to prove a proposition simply by restating it; see **arguing in a circle**

technical language see **jargon**

temperament theory theory that innate personality factors give each person a predisposition toward particular persuasive techniques, related to **psychological type theory**

testimonial technique associated with persuasive communication and propaganda; also an advertising strategy featuring straightforward, sales-type appeal

thesis see **proposition**

throw see **lead-in**

throw-away lead see **soft lead**

timely element of newsworthiness stressing the recency of information; see **SILoBaTI + UnFa**

tip sheet see **story idea memo**

title approach to article identification in newspapers, magazines, and newsletters that focuses on labels rather than summaries; compare with **headline**

tone part of planning sheet that articulates the ambiance sought for the message

tract see **brochure**

trade dress trademark-like protection of distinctive shapes and packaging; compare with **trademark**

trademark legal designation of ownership of a name, logo, symbol or other identification of a company or product; also called **brand name**; trademark means materials may not be used without identification of the trademark holder; compare with **service mark**

transaction page online page for making donations for a nonprofit organization; also called **landing page**

transfer technique associated with persuasive communication and propaganda

transit advertising promotional messages located on buses and subways

tune-in lead see **soft lead**

turnaround statement technique used by writers to create parallel structure

Twitch news pitch packaged as a 144-character Twitter summary of a news release; also called **Twitter pitch**

two-step flow of communication theory observation that the media influence opinion leaders, who in turn influence others through interpersonal means; later extended into the **multistep flow of communication theory**

umbrella lead type of lead for broadcast news releases that presents general information on more than one focus

underline see **deckhead**

unique page views number of different users who access a particular Web page

unique visitor number of different users a particular Web page is accessed

unusual aspect of newsworthiness that focuses on unusual or touching information; see **SiLoBaTi + UnFa**

unwarranted conclusion logical error in which arguments do not support the stated conclusion

up style approach to writing style that uses capital letters as much as possible; compare with **down style**

uses-and-gratifications theory theory that people make active choices in selecting media for particular purposes

value category factor associated with Harold Lasswell's eight motivators

value proposition thesis within a speech or written commentary asserting the worthiness or virtue of something; compare with **factual proposition** and **policy proposition**

verbal message body copy within an advertisement; compare with **visual message**

video B-roll type of video news release that provides unedited videotaped pieces for reporters' use

video news release public relations information packaged as a partial or completed broadcast report for television; see **video B-roll**

vision statement written statement of what an organization hopes to achieve; often used in tandem with a **mission statement**

visual message headline and artwork within an advertisement; compare with **verbal message**

visual relationships creativity technique of **forced relationships** that elicits ideas through the use of photographs or other visual props

voice element of grammar that refers to the relationship between the subject and predicate of a sentence; see **active voice** and **passive voice**

VNR see **video news release**

warm-up lead see **soft lead**

white hat SEO ethical approach to preparing material for search engine optimization; contrast with **black hat SEO**

white paper see **position statement**

whitewashing writing that deceptively glosses over failings, scandals, crimes, and other problem areas; see also **greenwashing** and **bluewashing**

wiki type of website that serves as a forum to team writing and editing

wiki farm single website that hosts multiple wikis, usually with a common theme

work for hire legal designation of an artistic copyright owned by the organization because it paid a salary or commission to the creator; compare with **original work**

writer's block temporary situation in which a writer doesn't know where to begin writing

Index